PENNSYLVANIA

BIRTHPLACE OF A NATION

PENNSYLVANIA

BIRTHPLACE OF A NATION

by Sylvester K. Stevens

EXECUTIVE DIRECTOR
PENNSYLVANIA HISTORICAL AND
MUSEUM COMMISSION AND
FORMER STATE HISTORIAN

RANDOM HOUSE · NEW YORK

TO DANNY, ROBIN AND MIKE

Books by Sylvester K. Stevens

WILDERNESS CHRONICLES OF NORTHWESTERN
PENNSYLVANIA
(with Donald H. Kent)

AMERICAN EXPANSION IN HAWAII, 1842–1898

PENNSYLVANIA AT WAR
(with Marvin Schlegel)

PENNSYLVANIA: TITAN OF INDUSTRY
(three volumes)

PAPERS OF COLONEL HENRY BOUQUET
(with Donald H. Kent)

EXPLORING PENNSYLVANIA
(with Ralph Cordier and Florence Benjamin)

PENNSYLVANIA: THE KEYSTONE STATE
(two volumes)

PENNSYLVANIA: BIRTHPLACE OF A NATION

PREFACE

Pennsylvania is a great state, with a stature not limited to the past, but with a continuing potential for the future. It deserves a good and sound history, which it lacks; in this situation lay the incentive to write the present book. Just recently I was disturbed when a speaker at Colonial Williamsburg referred to Virginia and Massachusetts as the states whose history is more important than that of any other. In my opinion they must at least share such an accolade with Pennsylvania. I have sometimes made the statement that Pennsylvania is itself the leading state so far as history is concerned. I hope this book may help prove the validity of that statement, and show it to be based on objective historiography rather than mere local pride. The importance of Pennsylvania does not rest upon a few events, and a few landmarks in the American story, but upon a long and continuing series of events and landmarks ranging from political through the social, cultural, and economic history of the nation. What state can claim more firsts of genuine significance in American history?

Pennsylvania's importance has not been recognized as it should have been in the general writing of American history in past years because the Pennsylvania story has not been researched sufficiently, nor adequately presented in scholarly articles, brochures, and books. There was a deadly repetition in much of the early writing on Pennsylvania history. It carefully avoided for the most part the all-important realms of social, cultural, and economic history in favor of politics and wars. It avoided also the more recent history of the state, and was content to rest upon colonial and post-Revolutionary history. Even a casual scanning of the pages of the *Bibliography of Pennsylvania History* will reveal these serious gaps in the structure of Pennsylvania historiography. It is because of the lack of such studies that it is hard even today to write a general history of Pennsylvania, let alone provide the writer of any general American history sufficient sources from which to secure the basic information needed to give Pennsylvania a proper place in the total story of the nation.

This is a situation, I am happy to say, that is being corrected with some success. The University of Pennsylvania, under the inspiration and guidance of Dean Roy F. Nichols and others; the Pennsylvania State University, led by Dr. Philip S. Klein and other colleagues; and the University of Pittsburgh, guided by men like Dr. John Oliver, Dr. Alfred James, both now retired, and the late Dr. Russell Ferguson, helped direct the attention of graduate students to Pennsylvania themes for detailed study. The emphasis, however, always remained on political affairs. As State Historian for many years, I had an opportunity to aid in the publication of many of these studies by the Pennsylvania Historical and Museum Commission. This, I hasten to add, would hardly have been possible had it not been for the keen interest in and strong support of a succession of able members of that commission, and the willing financial support by successive governors and legislative leaders in terms of appropriations for the Commission. I wish it were possible without slighting many to mention a few of the names of these persons. The commission was also able to publish less scholarly but nevertheless vitally important volumes, such as Dean Stevenson Fletcher's two volumes on Pennsylvania agriculture and country farm life from 1640 to 1940, a unique contribution. The University of Pittsburgh Press has contributed in a major way to publishing worthy additions to Pennsylvania historical literature, and the number of volumes and bibliography attributed to the University of Pennsylvania Press in the last twenty years is a distinguished one. More recently the Pennsylvania State University Press has joined the academic publishers, turning out two important Pennsylvania biographies. We owe much also to the forward-looking University of North Carolina Press for its willingness to publish Pennsylvania studies.

The literature of Pennsylvania history of significance has at least doubled in the past twenty years. It is now possible with much more ease and certainty to write intelligently on the general history of Pennsylvania as a result of this parade of worthy books. Unfortunately, much of merit remains unpublished in the form of doctoral dissertations. These, however, are now generally available for use, and add to the store of material ready for the general historian. Many of these have been brought together on film or in original copies in the library of the Pennsylvania Historical and Museum Commission. It also has collected a vast volume of original source material on microfilm, including files of early newspapers on film for a majority of the counties.

This book would not have been possible had it not been for this groundwork of research and writing on the part of many others. They have added a growing stream of history and biography to the riches now available to the historian writing on almost any phase of the state's history. We remain weak, however, in cultural and economic history for all periods, except possibly the colonial and early Federal era. We are very weak in the all-important history of the period since the Civil War, especially since the turn of the century. I find bibliography skimpy in these areas, and some thoroughgoing research had to be done through the past years by myself.

If I had any advantage in writing this book it was that of having had personal contact with much of the research going forward, and with some of its publication. I also have had the advantage of working actively in Pennsylvania history and government from the vantage point of Harrisburg and the commission for over twenty years. Some of this personal experience is reflected in my chapter on Pennsylvania politics since 1900. I could hardly have written it from any other source. One of my very real opportunities has been in my becoming acquainted with the whole of Pennsylvania in the course of my work. Pennsylvania remains a state with peculiar regionalisms not yet broken down even by modern communication and transportation. I believe I understand equally Philadelphia and eastern Pennsylvania, and Pittsburgh and western Pennsylvania, but I am sure they do not yet entirely understand each other. I hope this understanding of all of the state, and my personal acquaintance with it and its people make this a better book, and one that will interpret all of Pennsylvania to the reader rather than stress any one section.

I have enjoyed writing this book. I wish to express my gratitude to Random House for seeing fit to publish it, and to Howard Price and Paul Lapolla for supporting the book and helping with many problems. I owe a great deal to my staff for suggestions as to sources, reading of parts of the manuscript, and other assistance at various times. My wife was forbearing in letting me clutter up one whole room for a year with books, pictures, and other things that enter into writing a book and getting a manuscript off to a publisher. My daughter-in-law, Pat Stevens, helped with typing, as did Miss Sybil Jane Worden. Many a librarian and historical society director has readily answered requests for help, especially in providing pictures. Danny, Robin, and Mike, my grandchildren, encouraged me by the inspiration of their devotion to their grandfather.

I might add I have chosen with deliberation a major emphasis upon the Pennsylvania story since 1865, and have also centered three chapters on the history of the state since 1900. I have emphasized the growth and even the temporary decline of the economy of Pennsylvania because I think it has been sadly neglected. Within my own limitations, and with the aid of others, I have tried to do justice to social and cultural affairs. If I have made some small addition to the information available on the heritage of a great state I shall have been repaid. Any mistakes or omissions are mine.

CONTENTS

CONTENTS

CONTENTS

CONTENTS

CONTENTS

PENNSYLVANIA

BIRTHPLACE OF A NATION

CHAPTER ONE

A LAND NOT TO BE DESPISED

"The country itself, its soil, air, water, seasons, and produce, both natural and artificial, is not to be despised," wrote William Penn in one of his many early descriptions of his magnificent land grant from King Charles II of England. Penn wrote with an exuberance no doubt increased by the fact that he had become England's largest single private landowner. He was interested in disposing of this property to prospective settlers. But Penn was also describing country he had seen and in which he had developed great confidence as to its future possibilities. Time and again Penn wrote of the prospective riches to be found in Pennsylvania. Few of these would be realized in his lifetime, or that of his immediate descendants. Did his new province actually have the qualities of a land such as Penn described? Indeed it did, and even more than he realized. The history of Pennsylvania has been shaped so greatly by its landscape, and by the basic riches and resources originally in and on the land that it is worth while to find out how this landscape came into being and how resources were placed there.

PENNSYLVANIA'S LANDSCAPE WAS SHAPED IN GEOLOGIC TIMES

Pennsylvania covers an area of over 45,000 square miles. It extends westward more than three hundred miles from the bend of the Delaware to the borders of the Ohio. It reaches 158 miles southward from its New York boundary line to Maryland. The features of this landscape were shaped from six to four hundred millions of years ago in the dim ages of the geologic formation of North America. In very early times today's eastern coast of North America was a land mass made up of a chain of islands. This broken land mass is called Appalachia by the geologists. The interior of Pennsylvania, at that stage of the earth's evolution, was almost entirely a huge inland sea. Through many millions of years the land mass of Appalachia underwent processes of erosion through which rock and sediment were washed down into this inland sea and deposited upon its bottom. Appalachia itself was rising and sinking during these countless ages of time, continually providing new rock layers exposed to erosion. The sea bottom was also rising and sinking, and sometimes left large areas of uplifted land exposed in what is now central Pennsylvania. Eventually the inland sea disappeared. The islands which formed Appalachia also vanished. The Atlantic Ocean came to cover the area Appalachia had occupied on the eastern coast.

The all-important fact is that while this titanic process of uplift and sinking of gigantic masses of land with the alternate retreat and then return of sea waters was going on, the land we know as

GEOLOGIC TIME SCALE

LIFE RECORD ROCK RECORD GEOLOGIC NAMES

MILLIONS OF YEARS AGO	Typical Fossils	Predominant Rocks	Periods	Eras
1		*Glacial deposits*	QUATERNARY	Cenozoic Era
		EROSION		
65		*Sands and Clays*	TERTIARY	
		EROSION	CRETACEOUS	Mesozoic Era
135		*Sands and Clays*		
		EROSION	JURASSIC	
180		*Shales and Sandstones*	TRIASSIC	
230		*Diabase intrusions*		
		EROSION	PERMIAN	Paleozoic Era
280		*Shales Sandstones, Coals, and Limestones*	PENNSYLVANIAN	
310			MISSISSIPPIAN	
350		*Shales, Red beds, Sandstones and Limestones*	DEVONIAN	
405			SILURIAN	
425		*Shales and Sandstones*	ORDOVICIAN	
500				
		Limestone and Dolomite	CAMBRIAN	
600		*Sandstone*		
		EROSION		Precambrian Time
	ALGAE	*Granites, Gneisses, and Schists*	PROTEROZOIC ERA	
			ARCHEOZOIC ERA	
4000+				

ORIGIN OF THE EARTH

Geologic timetable in Pennsylvania.

4

*Artist's drawing showing the nature of the vegetation growth that led
to the formation of Pennsylvania's rich coal reserves.*

Pennsylvania was being enriched in many ways. The sediment which was eroded from the land masses and washed into the bottom of the inland sea, under pressures created by the upheavals and foldings of the mountainous land masses, became the rich limestone of central Pennsylvania. This was not only to create a rich soil, but became a resource for making iron and steel. Sandstone and other building stones, cement rock, and many other materials, such as clay of various kinds useful in both early and later industry—all of these were riches being built up for Pennsylvania in the hundreds of millions of years of geologic time ranging from Precambrian and Cambrian down through the Ordovician, Silurian, Devonian, Mississippian, Pennsylvanian, Permian, and Triassic to the Quaternary eras in the history of the earth, the latter of which was about a million years ago.

The Carboniferous Age, a portion of one of the larger spans of geologic time, was aptly named for it was one in which the retreating of the inland seas exposed large areas of the sea bottom, which became swamps and were covered by heavy swamp vegetation. The extensive layer upon layer of this vegetable debris was often later covered by waters of the sea again washing inward. Then began alien deposits of sediment which covered this decayed vegetation with thick beds of shale and sandstone. This era was followed over a period of another several millions of years by extensive mountain building, and most of the eastern United States, including Pennsylvania, was now raised above the ocean to a considerable elevation. These masses of alternate shale, rock, and carbonaceous materials resulting from swamp vegetation were blended and folded by the gigantic forces of nature. From this came Pennsylvania's great beds of anthracite and bituminous coal; the hardness or the softness of the coal differs in the land today as the degrees of pressure differed in those faraway ages when this mighty rising and folding of our lands was taking place. There are various theories as to the exact way in which petroleum and gas were formed in this process. They are found in the same types of rock formations of the same general age as those with coal, but they are also found in older rock formations and almost always at much greater depths than coal. It is agreed by geologists that the

This rich farmstead in York County is typical of the southern portion of the Great Valley region with low-lying mountains in the background.

existence of both natural gas and petroleum are related in some way to the degree of pressure involved in rock folding. And they owe their origin to the same swamp vegetation from which came coal.

About 18 per cent of the total mineral wealth of the entire country rests in the soil of Pennsylvania. Before the 1890's it was the largest producer of iron ore, which became, with coal, a major source of its industrial power. No Indian or white man brought this iron ore with him. It was another gift of those tremendous forces of nature which had shaped the land in those dim ages of the past. Pennsylvania's deposits of iron ore were produced largely by processes of the weathering of certain rock formations, resulting in the concentration of the iron oxides in these rocks from the action of ground water. To provide these great deposits took, of course, a few million years of doing. The most valuable deposits collected in those areas where hot waters under the surface of the earth dissolved the limestone and left the iron oxide as iron ore. The famous Cornwall mines, more than two centuries old, are of

A country road in one of the many lovely unspoiled sections of Pennsylvania.

this nature, as well as the large Morgantown ore deposits. The same geologic forces brought together in certain parts of Pennsylvania this remarkable combination of limestone and iron deposits to form the basis for the early iron industry. Copper, zinc, nickel, chromite, and lead are other metallic minerals found in the state and have been mined at different times, but none had a decisive influence on the state's economy.

By the end of the Carboniferous Age, the relationship between the land and the sea in eastern North America, including Pennsylvania, was established, in essentially its present form. The new mass of land, however, was much higher and more rugged, possibly as rugged as the Swiss Alps. During the following Triassic time a vast erosion of this mountain mass in southeastern Pennsylvania took place. Volcanic action is evident to geologists, and sometimes lava reached the surface to add to the accumulated debris of earth and stone in the deep valleys between the mountainous land mass. In the millions of years that followed, the processes of erosion determined the shape of the landscape, which was influenced also by the vast glacial ice sheet that spread over the northern United States and deep into Pennsylvania. Recent studies conducted by the Carnegie Museum in Pittsburgh indicate that the glacier reached much farther into central and western Pennsylvania than was before believed. The land was ground down from the force of the glacial action and entirely new deposits of glacial debris were left to change its face. These are very evident in northern Pennsylvania. To the south, streams began to form and to cut their way through the softer of the rock masses which formed the basic early landscape form.

The shapes of the rivers and streams as they are today were formed long before any red or white man saw Pennsylvania fixed by this process of nature. Erosion and the streams created over millions of years form the land known to man. It produced a beautiful state with an endless variety of scenery, both broad and narrow valleys, mountains, ridges, rivers, and streams of varying utility.

It provided also the basic land areas which characterize the commonwealth and have had so much to do with shaping its history. At the extreme southeastern corner of the state was left the Atlantic coastal plain, provided by the Delaware River with a pathway to the Atlantic Ocean. Here was an accessible land, for the first settlements and the first industry. Moving inland, one reaches the Piedmont, or foot of the mountains. It runs westward from near Philadelphia to the South Mountain near Reading and south and west to Maryland. The low rolling hills and broad valleys of this region are rich in limestone. This limestone country was akin to the Rhineland of the first German settlers. It provided room for a rapid expansion of settlement from the farming fringes of the Delaware into central Pennsylvania. It also had the iron deposits and limestone which provided the basis for early iron making and wealth in the same area.

North and west of the Piedmont had been carved out the landscape of the Ridge and Valley Region, taking in about one-third of the state. A key part of the region is the famous Great Valley. It reaches from the Delaware eastward to the Susquehanna and then south and west through the Cumberland Valley toward the Shenandoah Valley of Virginia. East of the Susquehanna, the Great Valley is known locally as the Lebanon Valley and west of the Susquehanna it is the Cumberland Valley. Unlike most valleys, this one was not formed by a river. Actually, the Susquehanna River cuts right through it by way of an interfering South Mountain Ridge on its way to the Chesapeake. It is also limestone and iron-ore country. It likewise furnished a great valley pathway for people to move south and west. It was the way followed by both the Boones and the Lincolns when they left Pennsylvania for Virginia and then on into Kentucky and even farther westward.

Stretching across Pennsylvania all the way from New York to Alabama are the great Appalachian plateaus. In Pennsylvania the region more often is called the Allegheny plateau. It covers almost two-thirds of the state. The western Pennsylvania area of the plateau is most frequently called the Allegheny Mountains. But a look at a topographic map shows clearly the uniformly high-plateau nature of the landscape. It does contain Mount Davis in Somerset County, with an elevation of 3,213 feet, Pennsylvania's highest mountain. Driving west from Harrisburg through the first tunnel of the Pennsylvania Turnpike provides a clear picture of the plateau formed by these high ridges as the motorist leaves the broad Cumberland Valley driving west from Carlisle and into the mountainous plateau ahead. Reversing the trip from the west reveals the open and sweeping valley beyond. Northern Pennsylvania is a part of the same region, along with northeastern and north central Pennsylvania. Here are the stores of hard and soft coal provided by natural forces of millions of years ago. Here also are natural gas and petroleum. To the people moving west these mountains were a barrier which had to be surmounted at great cost of time and effort. How the Pennsylvania pioneers overcame these obstacles is a tale as great as that of the Oregon Trail, though not as well publicized.

The Erie Plain completes a most important part of the landscape with a narrow strip of land which provides Pennsylvania with a port on the Great Lakes. Today, with completion of the St. Lawrence

*The gorge cut by tiny Pine Creek to form the "Grand Canyon" of Pennsylvania near Wells-
boro is typical of the deep valleys and wooded hills of the region, once a rich source of timber.*

9

Seaway, its importance is greatly increased. Lake Erie was once much larger, and the total plain is really the bed of the once huge lake. The onetime lake bed has a very fertile soil, while the present Lake Erie serves to moderate the climate. These combine to make it a fine farm, orchard, and vineyard area, while the port serves as a center for

course of settlement. They were perhaps even more important as a source of power in the days when water wheels turned the machinery of the early saw and grist mills and even for generating the blast of the furnaces that made iron. As they became less important for these uses, their indispensable value to industry and urban living as a

The Susquehanna River cuts a broad and rocky path through the mountains north of Harrisburg on its way to Chesapeake Bay.

industrial and commercial development. The state's Presque Isle Park makes this a choice recreational area.

STREAMS AND WATERS

Water has had a varying importance in Pennsylvania history. In the early days of settlement and down through the years until the coming of the railroad and better land transportation, the early streams and rivers were vital as carriers of both people and goods. They helped shape the

water supply became steadily the greater. The resources shaped in those far-distant times when mountains were being cut down by the slow action of water and streams became one of Pennsylvania's richest legacies, and one without which even the wealth of its mines, farms, and factories could have hardly been exploited.

The river most important to eastern Pennsylvania is the Delaware. It rises in New York's Catskills and flows south for 375 miles before it empties into Delaware Bay and the Atlantic south of Philadelphia. For two-thirds of its length it provides the boundary between Pennsylvania and neighboring New York and New Jersey. For that reason its waters today are not the exclusive right of Pennsylvania to utilize. A Delaware River Compact was drawn in 1960 in which these three states, along with Delaware and the Federal government, participated in one of the most unusual

history of its own, but there is not the space here to tell it. It is enough to say that Indian and white settlers used all these waterways in years past. They helped float the products of farm, forest, and later the mine and furnace to market. Their valleys opened routes for canals and railroads. Today they serve as essential sources for water

The Delaware Water Gap was formed as the river, flowing more than 300 miles from its Catskill Mountains origins, cut its way through a mountain barrier on the way to the Atlantic.

efforts in the history of the United States jointly to plan and utilize the water resources of a key river. The Delaware is joined by three other Pennsylvania rivers after it reaches the state. The Lackawanna enters near Milford; the Lehigh at Easton, famous as the "Forks of the Delaware"; the Schuylkill at Philadelphia. All three not only bolster the waters of the Delaware proper but drain and serve as rivers the large area of eastern Pennsylvania in which they flow. Each has a

supply for cities and industries.

Central Pennsylvania has the Susquehanna and the Juniata. The Susquehanna often has been called a useless river. This is true, if it is compared with the mighty Hudson as a major transportation route for the great distance it flows. It is a lovely river, flows through beautiful and broad valley country on its northern way from Lake Otsego at Cooperstown, New York, to the Chesapeake in Maryland. It is really two rivers,

11

because the North Branch flows from Cooperstown 165 miles to join a West Branch at Northumberland. It has in turn flowed peacefully all the way from the Allegheny plateau near Carrolltown for some 238 miles. The twins, then united, flow to a point a few miles north of Harrisburg where the Juniata adds to their waters. From that point, the Susquehanna makes its sprawling way over masses of jagged rock to Chesapeake Bay, some degree of usability being provided at Conewago by an early canal built around the falls at that point. The Susquehanna serves nearly half the entire drainage area of the state. Never usable by steamboats, despite many historic attempts in early days, at times of the early spring freshets it was navigable by arks and rafts from even as far as its New York origins. Lumber rafts made particular use of the West Branch. Both the West and North Branch valleys provided the route for canals and later railroads. Today, hydroelectric plants on the lower Susquehanna are an important source for electric power. With its tributaries, the Susquehanna has always been an important water-supply source, and today it is being studied for further improvement and utilization in this way.

The Juniata, which joins the Susquehanna, is another hybrid river in that it has two points of origin. The Raystown and Frankstown branches join to form the main river at Huntingdon. The Raystown branch rises in Bedford County and is the larger of the two, flowing for over a hundred miles through rugged mountain country. The Frankstown branch rises in Blair County and is only fifty-six miles long. The main river then flows eighty-six miles to its Susquehanna River junction. The beautiful "blue Juniata" is famous in song and history. It was narrow but deep and afforded, with its valley leading through the rugged mountains of north-central Pennsylvania into the heart of the Alleghenies, a route of settlement, and highway for river commerce. It became the water level for the old Pennsylvania Canal and the later Pennsylvania Railroad all the way into the Pennsylvania heartland to the very foot of the Alleghenies.

The Potomac is often overlooked in any study of the streams of Pennsylvania. While it drains only some 3 per cent of the central southwestern part of the state, with its tributaries it reaches into Adams, Bedford, Cumberland, Fulton, Franklin, and Somerset counties. The waterways which linked this region in early days with Virginia and Maryland are of the utmost importance in the early history of southwestern Pennsylvania in terms of a pathway for settlement and trade as well as a source of water power.

The Gulf of Mexico receives 34.5 per cent of all the waters which flow out of Pennsylvania, a fact of unique importance in the development of the commonwealth. The rivers which provide this volume of water for the Gulf are the Allegheny and the Monongahela, which unite to form at Pittsburgh the Ohio, which the early explorers called the "*la belle rivière.*" Historically, the junction of these two rivers became known as the Point. When the forces which were shaping the landscape of western Pennsylvania provided this magnificent outlet to the vast Ohio and lower Mississippi valleys for the western regions of later Pennsylvania they waved a magic wand indeed. The Allegheny is the major of the two rivers and rises in what is hardly more than a tiny spring in Potter County over three hundred miles from Pittsburgh. Its tributaries are the Clarion and the Kiskiminetas rivers and French Creek. The latter, having its origins near Erie, became the historic pathway for the French military exploration and invasion of western Pennsylvania in 1749 and later. It has a far richer history than most streams labeled simply as "creeks." The Allegheny lazily flows into New York and then returns to Pennsylvania, gathering volume until it finally reaches Pittsburgh. It was a waterway of more than ordinary importance to the early Indians and the first white men, whether explorers, men of war, or peaceful settlers. A venturesome soul once ran a steamboat up the river as far as Olean in New York. Rafts and other river craft made use of it for many decades and it served to provide the farms, as well as early industries, of northwestern Pennsylvania with a great market by way of Pittsburgh. The key points on the Allegheny became town and industrial centers, most of which are still active today.

The Monongahela is the lesser river but only in that it is not as long nor does it serve so large a region. It has its origin near Fairmount in West Virginia. It flows from this point into the southwestern corner of Pennsylvania. The Youghiogheny River flows into the Monongahela at West Newton and together they served the earliest settlers as a means of reaching the Ohio and Pittsburgh either for markets or to move farther into the heart of the midwest. Like the Allegheny, the Monongahela and its tributary became a favored location for many towns, some of which grew into small cities and keys to the industrial development of the region. The Monongahela flows through the heart of the bituminous-coal country and so also became a means of carrying coal and coke to the great iron and steel mills of Pittsburgh. This, naturally, influenced the growth of an industrial complex along the river which continues to the present day.

The junction of these two major western Pennsylvania rivers at the Point in Pittsburgh made this one of the most historic spots in all the United States. Here were the forks of the Ohio. Here from the earliest times was a "Gateway to the West," a thought noted by no less a person than young George Washington in 1753 when he rode down to this meeting of the rivers on his mission to Fort LeBoeuf to warn the French to leave the country. All of the traffic which came from all of the rivers met here, whether explorers, military men, pioneers just passing through, or men of the river moving goods down the Ohio. Then there were the settlers, such as those who came in 1787 from New England to settle in Ohio, building their boats at West Newton on the Youghiogheny after having crossed Pennsylvania from the distant Delaware at Easton. From any way they might have come, the Ohio flowed from Pittsburgh, almost forty miles through Pennsylvania to continue its way to the great western land which lay beyond.

THE CLIMATE AND RAINFALL

Among the natural features of any land that are beyond the control of man are climate and rainfall. The history of civilization shows in facts no one may ignore that these are mighty factors in determining the life and culture of any region.

Climate determines temperature and usually the amount of snow or rainfall, or the lack of these, with consequent amount of moisture in the soil to sustain vegetation and crops. Temperature also enters into this determination.

Pennsylvania has as one of its more important natural gifts from the processes through which highlands and lowlands were formed in ages past in North America a very favorable climate and rainfall. In fact, the state is situated most advantageously just about halfway between the North and the South, where the northern and southern climates of the Middle Atlantic States meet. This is a very significant reason why Pennsylvania truly is a "keystone state"; it has been most important in shaping Pennsylvania's history. Pennsylvania's record high temperature of 111° Fahrenheit is on record for southeastern Pennsylvania in 1936. The recorded low was 42° below zero at Smethport as far back as 1904. Northern Pennsylvania's mean temperature ranges from zero or below in winter to 70° in summer, resulting in short growing seasons. The average temperature in central and southern Pennsylvania is about ten degrees higher, resulting in a longer growing season for all crops. Temperature pretty much determined the nature of farm life in different parts of the state. Pennsylvania also has an average rainfall ranging from about thirty-six inches a year in northern and western counties to forty in eastern and southern areas. Northern Pennsylvania normally has a fairly heavy snowfall.

Central Pennsylvania had an ideal climate for grain growing, which made it, until the development of the great grain-growing regions of the Middle West, the "breadbasket of America." The same climatic conditions gave northern Pennsylvania the great pine and hemlock forests which were the foundation of the lumber industry in which the state assumed towering importance until about 1890. Farther south, hardwoods mingled with the pine and hemlock and were also favored by the climate. Nature gave the state a basis for a truly key position in the farm and forest resources which played so vital a role in its history. Rainfall was abundant enough to feed many streams so important in early days as a source of power and now for recreation and basic water-supply needs of a modern day.

THE FORESTS AND THE LAND

When William Penn arrived to view his province, fully 90 per cent of Pennsylvania was covered by virgin forest. Climate and soil combined to make this heritage a varied and useful one. The southern part of the state was covered mainly with mixed hardwood trees. These included stately oaks, black walnut, chestnut, hickory, and maple. The limestone soil also was favorable to these trees. Northern Pennsylvania was thick with the common conifers, pine, and hemlock common to the more northern climes. There were great stands of white pine in much of the north-branch country of the Susquehanna. Some more or less primeval stands remain today in the Black Forest region of Potter County and the Cook Forest in northwestern Pennsylvania. These original wooded areas covered nearly thirty million acres and are estimated to have had within them nearly three hundred billion board feet of timber. In the age when wood was a more basic raw material than today, the forests were among the most important of the store of natural resources available to the people. True, the pioneer settler looked at these often almost impenetrable forests as a serious obstacle to getting enough land on which to cultivate a crop. But even in clearing the land for his first planting, he obtained logs for his first wilderness home, and rails with which to fence his land. The Pennsylvania settler was able thus to adapt to his needs for housing the log cabin of the Swedes of northern Europe. Even ashes from burned timber contained valuable potash. Bark for leather tanning, lumber for buildings, charcoal for making iron, timber from which staves and barrels could be made, wood for household utensils and early farm implements—all these were obtained in abundance from the early forest by the first farmers even before the days of commercial lumbering, which became later a major Pennsylvania industry. Wood products such as lumber, staves, and potash entered largely into early commerce. The forest even provided the first settler with food obtained by killing the deer, bears, and smaller game common to those early days of the wilderness. And skins and furs from many of these animals were a valuable part of the early economy, and also furnished the pioneer with much of his first clothing.

The soil is man's most basic resource in the early stages of developing settlement and civilization. The minerals beneath it had little value to the Pennsylvania pioneer, even if he had known about them. The forests which grew upon it were something which first must be removed to make way for crops. What happened to the tiny seedlings the pioneer so carefully planted in his first small clearing depended upon the quality of the soil in which they rested as it was warmed by the sun and wetted with the gentle rains of spring and summer. William Penn himself wrote of the "divers sorts of earth" in his province and especially of the "fast fat earth, like our best vales in England; especially by inland brooks and rivers." He wrote also of "the back lands being generally three to one richer than those that lie by navigable rivers." Here again during the millions of years of time while the Pennsylvania landscape was shaped, that large portion of rather level land in the southeastern and south central area which forms about one-sixth of the entire area of the state has been accumulating the sedimentary soil which provided about one-fourth of the farm land. These Hagerstown soils, as they are known to the geologist, are among the richest in all the United States and it is here that there still flourishes some of the richest agriculture in all the nation. It was indeed fortunate that the thousands of early Pennsylvania German people flowing into Philadelphia by ship found here in the heartland a countryside which could blossom as even their own Rhineland did. They made it a "garden spot of America." Soils had much to do with shaping the course of Pennsylvania's history.

THE MINERAL HERITAGE

The first settlers knew little and cared little about the great store of coal and petroleum underlying the land. Some may well have heard from the Indians about a "black rock" and some type of oily substance called "Seneca oil" which seeped from the ground in northwestern Pennsylvania. These were minerals which were not needed in an agricultural age. Of far more importance to early Pennsylvanians were the common rock materials such as sand, clay, and limestone. Limestone in particular could be used as a building stone, and in some places was pure enough to be burned for lime itself. As early as 1698 Gabriel Thomas was writing about mines "where there is Copper and Iron, besides other Metals and Minerals" to be found in the back country. As mentioned earlier, the processes of erosion and sedimentation in the dim and distant past provided Pennsylvania with a great variety of these metals. But of all of them the most valuable by far was iron in either the form of hematite or the magnetite deposits of iron oxide. Iron was one thing colonial America badly needed if it was to achieve any degree of economic independence. By 1750 it was common knowledge that southern and eastern Pennsylvania had the necessary iron deposits which could be combined with the limestone of the region and burned with readily available charcoal from the heavy timberlands of the same area to make pig iron. Stone was readily obtained with which to erect the first furnaces. There was the necessary clay with which to line them. No single gift of geologic times had more to do with the early rise of Pennsylvania as an important industrial state. No single spot in the entire country was ever provided with a happier combination of the basic ingredients for an important industry. When iron was finally married to coal, a titan was soon born.

Sand, gravel, and clay may be thought of as very ordinary resources, but they were another sedimentary product with real value to the growth of a commonwealth. The range of these values was such as to serve the earliest settlers down through to the needs of modern industry. Clay, for example, was available to serve the potter's wheel in fashioning utensils needed in a frontier civilization, to aid the building of the early log or stone dwelling, to line iron furnaces, and to make brick. As if through the waving of a magic wand, the flint or fire clays of central Pennsylvania were later found to be the essential base for fire brick with which to line huge modern steel furnaces. Pennsylvania's sand provided an early and most useful glass-making industry. With gravel, sand was indispensable in early building as well as in later modern highway and building construction.

THE INDIANS OF PENNSYLVANIA

Pennsylvania's first inhabitants were the American Indians. Most authorities attribute the original home of the Indian to Asia and think he came to North America by means of a northern land passage that later disappeared. The Indian then moved east and south in a period of time which may have ranged as far back as six to even thirty thousand years before the birth of Christ. The Paleo-Indian era covering this earliest period has been generally associated with archeological investigations in the western part of the United States, but a recent Indian site investigated not far from Harrisburg indicates the red man may have occupied the eastern United States at about the same time. Paleo-Indian man lived in the early and crude stages of the Stone Age in the history of mankind. These men were hunters. They may well have been the men who exterminated the prehistoric mammoth. The Indian of the Archaic Period is better known as a result of the discovery of more extensive remains. This Indian roamed the state eight thousand to three thousand years ago. His stone weapons were better, and he was combining wild fruits and vegetable products with hunting as a source for food. He did no farming, nor does he appear to have known how to make even crude pottery. The Indian of the following Woodland Period of some three thousand to four hundred years ago was the red man encountered by the first white settlers in Pennsylvania. He was living in an advanced Stone Age culture, which included settled life in villages and farming. He was making pottery vessels for his cooking and for the storage of food. He was even decorating his pottery in the later years of this era. Remains show a steady progress in making pottery over the centuries of Indian life. He was growing corn, along with tobacco. He lived in semipermanent bark houses and they were grouped into villages. His stone implements and tools uncovered by today's archeologist show steady improvement through the centuries. Indeed, the easier killing

15

of game made possible by better weapons may well have forced the primitive Indian into more reliance on farming as his improved "firepower" eliminated the wild game. The Indian still lacked knowledge of the use of metals or of power. He did not know how to make and use the wheel and had no domestic beast of burden.

The seventeenth-century Pennsylvania Indian obviously intrigued William Penn as a human being as well as a neighbor. His descriptions and comments about them are frequent and reflect a combination of his highly practical approach to problems and a certain amount of the romanticism inherent in the thinking of the European intellectual about the red man. Penn described those he saw as "generally tall, straight, well-built, and of singular proportion; they tread strong and clever, and mostly walk with a lofty chin." He also spoke of their "lofty" manner of speaking. In councils he found them very well able to conceal their true feelings in a certain impassive attitude. This was due in part, no doubt, to the language barrier, but nevertheless stood out in the minds of most observers as a dominant characteristic. He noted their "liberality" and that "nothing is too good for their friend." He felt they were the "most merry creatures that live," full of feasting and dancing. The Indians' ideas of property were highly communal, a fact Penn noted in saying that "they never have much, nor want much: wealth circulateth like the blood; all parts partake; and though none shall want what another hath, yet exact observers of property." This is a picture of Indian character as he first encountered the white man which some are inclined to write off as romantic sentimentalism about the "noble savage." Yet it has a great validity in truly estimating the basic characteristics of these native people before they met the pressures of living, or trying to live, with white neighbors who had entirely different ideas as to the property or other rights of a native people.

The Indian population when Penn arrived was a meager fifteen thousand or so, and thinly scattered through the province. The Susquehanna valley had been the home of an Indian people, first encountered by Captain John Smith of Virginia in 1608, and whom he called the "Sasque-sahanocks." Smith thus revealed a common white man's practice of naming Indians on a basis of the places where they lived. If a group of Indians lived along the path of any major river, which they usually did, they became Susquehannocks, Delawares, or such. There were few Susquehannocks about when Penn arrived, which may well have been fortunate, because they were in language and nature relatives of warlike Iroquois in New York. When John Smith met these people, their major settlement was on the lower reaches of the Susquehanna near present Lancaster. Smith described the Susquehannocks as "great and well proportioned men" who "seemed like Giants." Of course the good captain is well known for exaggerating somewhat. By the time of Penn's arrival, this once powerful group had been virtually eliminated by the Iroquois, with whom they fought over the valuable fur trade. The French knew the Susquehanna River Indians as Andastes and Gandastogues. This latter name is the origin of the later English place name Conestoga. The remnants of the Susquehannocks are known in later history as Conestogas. The French explorer Champlain wrote in his 1615 journal of an extensive settlement of the Andastes at Tioga Point, where New York's Chemung River joins the Susquehanna. It was the remaining now friendly and defenseless Susquehannocks, with a few Indians from other scattered tribes, who were massacred at Conestoga by the Paxton Boys in 1763. This was the fate of a once proud and powerful original Pennsylvania Indian people. Historically, the early end of the dominion of the Susquehannocks throughout northern and especially central Pennsylvania was a factor aiding the rapid and early expansion of white settlement into this region, which otherwise might have been sealed off by a warlike and well organized Indian people.

The link between the Susquehannocks and the Iroquois calls attention to the fact that one of the Indian groups which had most to do with Pennsylvania's early history was this New York-based tribal confederacy known as the Five and later the Six Nations of the Iroquois Confederacy. This confederacy first combined the New York Onondagas, Mohawks, Senecas, Oneidas, and Cayugas,

who were joined about 1722 by the Iroquoian tribe from the Carolinas known as the Tuscaroras. The famous Tuscarora Indian pathway across central Pennsylvania to southern New York is the route through which these Iroquois kept in touch with each other and over which the Tuscaroras finally moved north. The New York Iroquois were not greatly different in physical appearance or culture from their fellows in Pennsylvania. They were likewise a Stone Age people, but they had a particular genius, lacking among most Indian people, for political organization. Out of this union as a confederacy a group of possibly 12,000 Indians with central New York as their homeland came to occupy a dominant role in the history of early New York, Pennsylvania, and even the Ohio Valley. The first impact of the Iroquois on Pennsylvania came through the liquidation of the Susquehannocks, their real rivals for control of the entire Susquehanna Valley. By about 1640 the trade in furs with the French in Canada and the Dutch, Swedes, and English on the Hudson and Delaware river posts had become a rich prize to the Indians of present New York and Pennsylvania. In the resulting "Beaver Wars" the Iroquois Confederacy had the necessary unity and strength to defeat its rivals, among whom were their language partners in northern and central Pennsylvania, the Susquehannocks. Since the Iroquois were interested in the pelts of beavers rather than white scalps or settlement by their own people, they were willing to keep the vast lands they had conquered in northern and central Pennsylvania to be settled as pleased the Iroquois by weak and displaced tribes forced from their earlier homes by the pressures of white settlement. The Iroquois were wise enough to realize they did not have enough of their own people to colonize the region successfully. The elimination of the Susquehannocks thus not only ended any possible interference on their part with the expansion of the Pennsylvania frontier by a warlike people but also made the vacuum thus created a permanent one.

Another decisive assist given to provincial Pennsylvania entirely unwittingly by the Iroquois came about as a result of their long-established enmity toward the French. Though the French enjoyed generally a much better reputation for good relations with their Indian neighbors in North America than did the English, their one great failure was with the Iroquois, whose country and people they attacked in 1666 and again in 1687. Two years later the Iroquois raided all the way to Montreal in New France. In the words of one Frenchman, a few thousand Iroquois were "able to make a whole new world tremble." In 1701 the Iroquois drew up a treaty at Montreal with the French to keep the peace, but on their own terms. The strength of the Confederacy was such that it actually was able to maintain a certain balance of power between the French and the English from that date through the later French and Indian War. "If we lose the Iroquois, we are gone," declared Penn's Provincial Secretary James Logan in 1702 in reviewing the situation. The significance of this statement lies in the fact that in the Montreal Treaty the Iroquois had won trading rights with the French but also had agreed to remain neutral in any conflict between France and England. To the French this was a very important concession. At the same time, on this basis Pennsylvania's famous Indian negotiator Conrad Weiser and New York's Sir William Johnson were better able to preserve the peace with the Iroquois. Their neutrality during the French and Indian War was far more important to Pennsylvania and the English than to the French. Without it the entire New York–Pennsylvania frontier would have been exposed all the way to Philadelphia to Indian attack and it is doubtful whether the British could even have won control of the forks of the Ohio under General Forbes in 1758. That same year the Iroquois went so far as to sign at Easton a treaty of peace with the Province of Pennsylvania, ignoring their wards the Delawares and Shawnees who, made angry by white inroads on their lands, were already taking up the hatchet against the frontier settlements. No single development did more to stabilize the frontier. This peculiar situation relative to the Iroquois and their potential power to have literally wiped out the western movement of settlement in Pennsylvania was without doubt one of the decisive influences on the early history of Penn's commonwealth.

Equally important to the initial success of Penn's Holy Experiment was the fact that the first Indians with whom the white settlers along the Delaware came into contact were the Delawares, or Lenni-Lenape—the "original people." The Delawares were of Algonkian stock and probably the truly original Indian occupants of the region from the Delaware through most of New Jersey and even to the Hudson. They too were a Stone Age people but probably a little more advanced than most Indians of the region in terms of their devotion to farming and a village-type community life. The Delawares had no near enemies over a long period, due to the end of the Susquehannocks. Years of peace and village life led them to be a peaceful people with all of the qualities of the noble savage which Penn and others saw in them. It was not until they had been pushed from one area of settlement to another by the whites that the Delawares finally in the French and Indian War and Revolutionary War eras took up arms against the whites from their new home in western Pennsylvania. Their original location brought them into an earlier and more prolonged contact with the explorers and settlers of the Middle Atlantic region than probably any other eastern Indian people and this resulted in a more nearly complete written record of their life and culture.

Living at peace, Delaware life was organized around the open village community, which usually covered a rather wide area with good land and a water supply available and close to good hunting and fishing. When the soil would no longer grow corn, or hunting and fishing resources dwindled, the village would move to a new location. The main feature of the Delaware village was the habitation known as the "longhouse." A longhouse was made by driving poles made from saplings into the ground in a somewhat rectangular shape ranging from thirty to a hundred feet long and twenty feet wide. These poles were then bound to other poles which became the crosspieces for the roof, and the entire resulting framework was covered inside and out with sheets of bark bound together with strips of bark and thin poles. The sides were lined with beds, also made from poles and bark for sleeping. Several families of the same lineage lived in the same longhouse.

This was practical for the Delawares, since they, like most American Indians, traced family lines from the mother rather than the father. The husband of the mother, unmarried children, married daughters and their families belonged to the same family lineage. Each family had its own spot in the longhouse for a fire, cooking, and sleeping. Contrary to some popular ideas about Indian life, Delaware and other Indian women were far from being slaves of their warrior husbands. Indeed, the role of the Indian woman was on a perhaps even higher plane than that of the average white woman of those times. Indians had a great respect for family life. Under the Delaware matriarchal system, the woman was the head of the family and owned all property. She took care of household duties, which included dressing game, tanning the leather, and working the fields, which actually were hardly more than gardens in which corn and and a few vegetables were grown. The worth of a woman in the Indian social order was indicated by the fact that legally in any exchange she was worth two men.

Indian education was simple because there was no reading, writing, or arithmetic to complicate the problem. Girls and boys were taught in actual practice the simple duties associated with their part in the life of the family and the community. Government, as typified by the Delawares, was also a simple problem. The Delawares had no such peculiar genius for governmental or legal organization as the Iroquois, though the various groups which made up this people did have a very loose confederacy. The lack of a tighter confederation may well have been due to the lack of need for it because they had no strong enemies to force such a combination. There were, of course, no written law codes such as were common to the white settlers. Delaware law was based on basic ideas of right and justice as applied to their own situations. Stealing another's property or harming his person were major crimes. Punishment for such crimes might be a matter for consideration in council, depending upon their severity, or meted out by the chief. If the problem was one of an Indian slaying another without cause, a member

of that family had the right to demand justice through killing the guilty party. This was called blood revenge and the issue stopped at that point. The killing was a matter of justice, rather than revenge, and lasting feuds were thus made impossible.

In Delaware governmental organization, tribes and clans were headed by a chief elected mainly because he was recognized as a natural leader. Common consent of members appears to have been the deciding factor in selecting such a leader, the most elemental type of democracy possible in any society. Tribes and clans were themselves the result of lineage or family groups banding together in a simple consent arrangement. Despite the popular concept, the Indian chief under this system was by no means an all-powerful person. He presided over councils and was the spokesman in dealing with other tribes or the white men. The council was made up of the older and spiritual leaders of the tribe or clan, and it was a decisive influence in governing the Indian community. A more simple but effective democratic society working for the common concern and good of all is hard to imagine.

Religious life, however, was complex. The Delaware and other peoples based their religion upon worship of a Great Spirit and his agents. These peoples were children of nature and at the mercy of nature, so it was perfectly natural that they should worship the forces which appeared to shape such things as the weather, the shifting seasons, and the sun and moon. The Great Spirit demanded high standards of moral law, not because if these were violated it could bring punishment particularly on the individual, but communally in the form of bad crops or other such manifestations of displeasure. Personal morals were the problem of the family. Conrad Weiser was one colonial in close touch with the Indians who felt that their religion, in terms of its search for higher power and faith in basic moral principles to guide the conduct of men, was a powerful and moving force with dignity in its expression.

The dress of the Delaware and other Pennsylvania Indians is worth mention, if for no other reason than that it has been the victim of the promoters of the "show Indian" with his elaborate headdress and ceremonials; these may have some validity in terms of the western Indian of the Great Plains, but had no place in early Pennsylvania. The male Delaware dressed in summer in little more than a soft deerskin belt and breechclout so worn as to form a small apron front and back. Penn thought their bare upper half rubbed with animal fat was a deliberate effort to create a tanned appearance, but this is doubtful. It is hard to think of an early Delaware as seeking deliberately a sun tan. In winter added protection was afforded by a fur robe or deerskin jacket. Women wore a knee-length skirt and a jacket, also made from deerskin. Pennsylvania Indians wore their hair closely cut except for a narrow scalp lock or crown about two inches in diameter. A few feathers might be worn for ceremony or when on the warpath, but never an Indian bonnet with upstanding feathers which would catch the trees and brush through which they moved. Faces were painted at times, but again mainly for ceremonial affairs. There were many of these because the Indian loved to sing and dance. Such in brief were the simple life and customs of the Indian with whom the first white settler came into contact in Pennsylvania.

Despite the efforts of William Penn to pursue a policy of complete justice in dealing with these really simple and natural people, even to the extent of negotiating treaties for the purchase of lands which already had been granted him by the great white king in England, Charles II, there proved to be no way by which the Indians could be saved from the white invasion. Successive treaties with the Delawares moved them from the lower Delaware River farther and farther away from their early homeland. Efforts to prevent individual settlers from squatting on Indian unpurchased lands proved impossible to execute. Even Penn's sons tricked the Indians in the famous Walking Purchase in 1737 in which they secured at least three times as much land as the Indians even thought they were selling. The Delaware people were by 1750 split into groups of wanderers seeking some land they could occupy in peace. The Susquehanna Valley and finally western Pennsylvania and the Ohio country became their new home.

In the meantime, the Iroquois were welcoming into the vacant northern Pennsylvania lands of the Susquehannocks a miscellany of tribes from various quarters to create an Indian frontier to protect their own New York homeland.

Since the Indians all lacked a written language to record their troubles and their movements, little that is specific and detailed is known about the various other tribes which at one time moved in and out of present Pennsylvania. There are those who doubt there was ever a people known as the Erie living in northwestern Pennsylvania, or a Monongahela people in western Pennsylvania. The tribes known historically as the Conoy and Nanticoke came into Pennsylvania from Maryland to occupy for a time some of the North Branch Susquehanna territory once held by the Susquehannocks. The Tuscarora moved all the way across Pennsylvania over a period of several decades to join the Iroquois in New York about 1710 to 1760. The Iroquois Seneca occupied northern and northwestern Pennsylvania to a limited extent after about 1750. A Siouan people from the South known as the Tutelos came into the North Branch of the Susquehanna country after 1744 and finally moved into New York as "younger brothers" of the Iroquois. The savage Shawnees, associated so intimately with the history of the frontier as the Indians who made early Kentucky a "dark and bloody ground," were Algonkian stock and appeared rather widely in central and western Pennsylvania about 1700. Their earlier home appears to have been somewhere in the Ohio Valley. After 1750 they moved southwest and out of the state to appear on the pages of frontier history after the Revolution in Kentucky. Finally, under their great chief Tecumseh, they led a last vain attempt to drive the whites from their midwestern lands.

It is possible to moralize at length on the fate of the Pennsylvania Indian. Before contamination by the white traders' rum and the doubtful morality of the earliest traders and settlers with whom these Indian peoples came into contact, there can be little doubt they were a simple but on the whole fine and often noble people. The interpreted addresses of their greatest leaders such as Shawnee Kishacoquillas, who in 1739 signed a treaty with the whites to last as long as "the Sun, Moon, and Stars endure," Shickellamy, vice-regent of the Iroquois at Shamokin and his son Chief John Logan, Tamanend head chief, and Teedyuscung, "king of the Delawares", are a few whose eloquent defense of their people is an inspiring thing for anyone who wishes to read the accounts of the councils with the white men in which they sat and spoke.

Pennsylvania's most notable historical figure among the great Indian leaders and chiefs was Cornplanter, the half-breed son of a Seneca woman and a Dutch trader. His greatness rests upon the fact that he was the only Indian leader of his time who came to realize the futility of warfare as a means of protecting the rights of the Indian. Born about 1750, Cornplanter's uncle was the Seneca war chief Guyasuta. Cornplanter himself fought against the United States during the Revolution. Some think he fought even earlier against the whites. In the critical years after the Revolution he became the spokesman of the Iroquois for peace. His opponent favoring war was the great Red Jacket. Cornplanter was able to keep the Seneca from taking part in the campaigns in the Northwest which finally ended in General Wayne's victory at the Battle of Fallen Timbers in Ohio in 1794. This may well have decided the campaign in favor of the American forces. Cornplanter visited Philadelphia to see President Washington in 1790 and to present a plea for his people. In simple but eloquent language he called attention to their plight. Cornplanter said that his people "continually ask where is the land our children and their children after them are to lie down upon." He invited Quaker teachers to go with him so that his people might "be taught to read and write, and such things as you teach your children, especially the love of peace." In grateful recognition of his services, the Pennsylvania Assembly in 1791 granted Cornplanter and his heirs "in perpetuity" three tracts of land on the upper Allegheny. These were never "reservations" but an outright gift. Two of these he later sold. One of these was the site of present Oil City, sold in 1818. If held until forty some years later it would have brought a possible fortune in oil royalties to Cornplanter's descendants. The third tract of some 600 acres on the west bank of the Allegheny above Warren became Cornplanter's home until his death in 1836. He died on his land and was buried there. In 1869 Pennsylvania placed at his grave the first monument to an Indian ever erected in this country. In recent years few Cornplanters continued to live on the gradually eroded and increasingly worthless land of his tract, though the state continued to maintain a school there and a semblance of a road into it. It was inundated by the Kinzua Dam which forms a key part of the Federal flood-control program for upper Allegheny, despite the efforts of the Senecas and their Quaker friends in Philadelphia to prevent this disregard for one of the last of the many white man's promises to the Indians.

In the days following the Revolution the demoralization of the Indian was complete. The Quaker concept of treating the Indian as a human being with a soul and rights had long since disappeared. Robert Morris, along with others who conducted treaty negotiations with the Indians to acquire land, commonly resorted to the use of whisky, usually referred to as "rum," as a means toward securing their ends. In 1797 Morris and his associates, in projecting a treaty conference with the Senecas, purchased some 1,500 rations of whisky, along with the customary tobacco and trinkets, to woo the Indians. The Seneca chief Red Jacket, Cornplanter's chief opponent to a policy of peace with the whites, was in a drunken stupor the greater part of the gathering. Needless to say, Morris got what he wanted in the way of Indian land for the small price of rum, trinkets, and cheap gifts.

Despite this sad record of the relationships between white and red men in the later years, the Pennsylvania Indian made certain real contributions. The early trade with the Indians in the far wilderness was itself a source of real wealth for Philadelphia merchants and an important factor in the colonial economy. Indians were great travelers, and long before the coming of the white man had traced through the wilderness their pathways. These were no mere short paths but reached over great distances. There were paths, for example, from central New York all the way across Pennsylvania into the South. There were paths from the forks of the Delaware at present Easton to the forks of the Ohio at today's Pittsburgh. A great early path known as the Minqua Path reached from Philadelphia to Lancaster. It then went on to cross later the Susquehanna to the west. Virtually every early Pennsylvania road from the day of the Braddock and Forbes expeditions down through the building of the great turnpikes and the National Road followed closely a pathway created by the Indians. The same routes were often followed by the earliest railroads. These paths had their names determined by local points. Usually the same great path as it reached across the province came to have two names, determined primarily by the destination of the traveler.

For example, the path leading through central Pennsylvania from the Tulpehocken Valley to the Indian town of Shamokin, now Sunbury, and thence on to Frankstown in present Blair County and to Kittanning, the great Indian town on the Allegheny was known on its eastern section as the Tulpehocken Path; from Shamokin westward it was called sometimes the Great Shamokin Path, or the Kittanning Path. Naturally, this has been a great source of confusion to historians because exact limits of paths are hard to fix and a map of these early travelways is a confusing mass. Early settlers commonly referred to most north-south paths as the Warriors Path, partly because they were sometimes used for war and also because they ran through territory without well established place names. Anyone today who looks at a map showing major Indian paths will be struck by the extent to which all modern transportation follows closely in general direction and the utilization of convenient natural features of the landscape these earliest pathways of the red man.

The Indian helped further early settlement in other ways. The helplessness of the first European settlers in coping with the totally new wilderness and frontier environment which they encountered in the early days of the province is difficult to appreciate and is usually ignored by historians. None were equipped in backgrounds of living and experience to meet the problems of making farms and homes out of a New World wilderness. They lacked even an idea of how to clear land. Few were able to bring with them the tools they were accustomed to using in Europe, such as the plow. They lacked horses and cattle, and even wagons. Indeed, they were lacking in knowledge of the type of crops which could be grown in the New World. Penn himself warned prospective settlers they must face a year of more or less hardship before they could accommodate themselves to new conditions and provide food and other needs of their existence. Hence the aid of friendly Indians in teaching pioneer settlers the arts of their own simple farming, how to build a shelter, how to live to a large extent from hunting and fishing for a time, and even how to tan the skins of wild animals shot for food to make useful clothing was all-important. Pennsylvania's first settlers escaped a "starving time" common to many other first settlements in the New World largely because of the helping hand of the friendly Delawares. Here the first pioneers in Pennsylvania met not a warlike but a remarkably friendly, simple, hospitable people whom William Penn and the Quakers could understand and work with in starting a truly "Holy Experiment."

CHAPTER TWO

SEED OF A NATION

THOSE WHO PRECEDED WILLIAM PENN

Shortly after receiving the news that Charles II had conferred upon him the proprietorship of Pennsylvania, William Penn wrote with great feeling to a personal friend in Ireland concerning his ideas about his province. Among other things Penn fervently declared his conviction that God would not only bless "Pennsilvania" but make it "the seed of a nation." Prophetic were these words indeed, but the original exploration and settlement of Pennsylvania had been going on for several decades before 1681 and deserves attention as a part of the foundations upon which this seed bed was to be planted.

The original exploration of those who preceded William Penn to Pennsylvania, as well as the very first settlements, preceded the "Holy Experiment" of William Penn by several decades. They were a result of the era of exploration on the part of Europeans in the New World which followed the great discovery by Columbus in 1492. Most of this early exploration was fathered by great trading companies, which were organized to seek the riches of the "Indies." One of these was the Dutch East India Company. It was formed, like most companies of the type, to reach and explore the riches of the East Indies which were still the goal of Europe's new and self-seeking national states. Navigators and managers for these expeditions were not easily had in those days. Few and far between were those who knew anything of consequence about how to reach or better still to circumnavigate this strange new continent which blocked the reaching of a more important objective, the known riches of the Indies.

The Florentine explorer Verrazano sailing along the coast under French colors should have seen the mouth of the Delaware, but if so he left no record. As a result, the first authentic explorer to approach present Pennsylvania was Henry Hudson, an Englishman sailing under the orders of the Dutch East India Company. Hudson entered the Bay of the Delaware in August of 1609 on board the Dutch ship *Half Moon*. He was searching for the elusive passageway around America to the northwest and had little use for a river which was to be most important to later Pennsylvania. He called it the "south river." Hudson left the next morning to visit what he called the "north river." This is today's Hudson River. Why did this apparent misnaming of rivers take place? Why did the second of the rivers visited by Henry Hudson win his name, though he did not himself make any special distinction? There appears to be no conclusive answer. Most accounts agree that it was Captain Samuel Argall, searching for provisions for starving Jamestown, who next entered the area about 1611, and named the point of land the Cape De La Warre in honor of his patron Thomas West the Lord De La Warre, Virginia's then governor. The name was then applied to the river and even to the Lenni-Lenape Indian peoples who lived in the area.

Hudson thought well enough of the country, despite his brief visit, to lead the Dutch to send others to explore the region more thoroughly. In 1615 one of these explorers named Captain Cornelis Hendricksen reached the place where the Schuylkill River enters the Delaware at present Philadelphia and thereby gave a Dutch name to this important river into the interior. By 1623 the Dutch realized that all of the potential riches resulting from great explorations were not necessarily to be found in the fabulous East Indies, and another possibly valuable land intervened. A Dutch West India Company had been organized to search out the potential of the West Indies. The Dutch spent the next some fifteen years exploring the lower Delaware with a view to its trading potential. Since this was believed to be sound, the Dutch proceeded to build a few forts to protect their claims. The first of these was on the Jersey shore, Fort Nassau. It was not until somewhat later that the Dutch built Fort Beversreede at Passyunk on the east side of the Schuylkill.

The Dutch were concerned with trade protected by forts. Whether the Dutch would have become colonizers is doubtful, in view of the general history of Dutch expansion in that and later times.

A more active interest in the colonization of this particular part of the New World came from Sweden. This particular north European country was experiencing in the early seventeenth century a birth of vigorous national expansion and consolidation of its power in northern Europe under the youthful but great and warlike Swedish leader, King Gustavus Adolphus. Among other things, it had conquered Finland and taken part in other European wars. Sweden's territory had swelled to about twice what it is today, and it sensed the beginnings of great commercial empire. Sweden was ripe for further expansion and on no modest scale.

Despite the death of Gustavus Adolphus on the battlefield of Lützen while leading his cavalry, the surge for expansion continued. Even before his death, Gustavus had authorized formation of a Swedish trading company. When he fell in battle in 1632 his daughter Christina was but six

Gustavus Adolphus, king and mighty warrior for Sweden.

years old, and for twelve years Sweden's government was in the hands of a commission for the regency. Headed by the great Swedish statesman, Oxenstierna, the organization of the New Sweden Company went forward. As a result, the *Kalmar Nyckel* and the *Fogel Grip* or *Grippen* left Sweden in 1637 as an expedition to settle the Delaware. This term is used advisedly because Sweden had a determined desire to plant as a settlement this land which they were claiming. The expedition was headed by no less a person than Peter Minuit, the man who had bought for the Dutch, according to story, the Island of Manhattan for a song.

Those Delaware Indians who might have been gathered along the banks of the Delaware about where Wilmington is located, must have been very bewildered when in the early spring of 1638 two strange vessels flying an equally strange flag came sailing up the river, disembarked and went through the formal ceremony of claiming the land for Sweden in the name of Queen Christina, who thus may be said to have become the first woman to govern Pennsylvania. But the Swedes were doing more than some fancy flag-raising; settlers and their supplies were unloaded from the ships. Before the Dutch governor at New Amsterdam could gather his wits, the Swedes were in possession. Minuit started at once on the building of Fort Christina to protect the new settlement. He also began immediate negotiations with the Indians to purchase the land needed for the Swedish experiment in colonizing. This was a part of his instructions. It marked the beginning of a policy of dealing with the native Indians to acquire land, even though the European sovereigns could claim it anyway on a basis of discovery and exploration. Having taken care of these details, Minuit started his return voyage to Sweden for more settlers and supplies. He and his ship never returned to New Sweden, because they were lost at sea.

In the meantime, the tiny band of Swedes and Finns left behind did their best to cope with a wilderness environment quite alien to their homeland experience. Had it not been for the friendly Delaware Indians, New Sweden might well have had a "starving time" as did the pioneers at Jamestown, Virginia, or have perished. It was not until 1640 that Peter Hollender arrived with a second expedition to bolster the struggling settlement. That fall a third expedition arrived. Now

Model of the Kalmar Nyckel, one of the two ships which brought the first Swedish settlers.

there were more settlers, domestic animals, added supplies, and also a minister of the Swedish Lutheran faith. According to the custom of their homeland, the Swedes from the start began to cut down trees and to cut them into logs for building their pioneer homes. The Swedes on the Delaware thus became the first to introduce the log cabin into the history of the American frontier. In 1643 still another band of settlers arrived. With them came the rotund but vigorous Swedish soldier, Johan Printz, a man weighing some three hundred pounds. This picturesque and sometimes tempestuous soldier governed New Sweden for a decade with a firm but on the whole wise hand.

Printz is the first individual to figure prominently in the early history of Pennsylvania. One

The landing of the Swedes at Wilmington, 1638.

of his earliest decisions was to move his capital from Wilmington, now in Delaware, up the river to Tinicum Island. There he built a second fort, erected a building, principally of logs, known as the Printzhof to house himself and the government of the colony, a Lutheran church, and a storehouse. Tinicum thus became the first site of a permanent white settlement in the limits of Pennsylvania. At the same time it became the first

Johan Printz, Pennsylvania's first governor.

capital, and was the location of the first courts of law, the first church, and the first school. In 1938, in grateful recognition of the great importance of this location in the early history of Pennsylvania, the Swedish Colonial Society as a part of the observance of the tercentenary of the coming of the Swedes to America, purchased the site of Tinicum, no longer an island but now a part of the mainland alongside the Delaware, and presented it to the Commonwealth. It is preserved as Governor Printz Park, a major historical shrine.

Printz carried out faithfully his instructions from Queen Christina, though he did not entirely agree with all of them. He made further treaties with the Indians, but his soldier's temper led him to chastise them on occasion. Generally, peace prevailed. Though Lutheranism was the state church of Sweden, Queen Christina ordered that the Dutch should be allowed to worship according to their own Reformed faith. Under the combined auspices of the crown and the private Swedish West India Company, settlers continued to arrive and New Sweden became a largely self-sufficient settlement in terms of pioneer agriculture and industry. It developed also a valuable fur trade with the interior Indians.

In carrying on this colonial venture the Swedes were treading on very dangerous ground from the beginning because without question the Dutch had prior rights in terms of Hudson's voyage and the later Dutch forts. At the time the Swedes began their settlements the Dutch, whose government was centered at New Amsterdam, were in no position to do more than make verbal protests. When stern Peter Stuyvesant learned in 1654 that the new Swedish Governor Rising had seized Dutch Fort Casimir on the Delaware, his one good leg began to move him into vigorous action. Unfortunately for Rising, he had picked a very poor time to dispute with the Dutch, because his own government was having its troubles at home and unable to give him any assistance. Stuyvesant stormed about and assembled a Dutch force of some three hundred soldiers and seven ships which sailed from New Amsterdam to look after the Swedes on the Delaware. The Dutch not only recaptured Fort Casimir, but sailed on up the river and on September 16, 1655, Governor Rising was forced to haul down the Swedish flag and to surrender Fort Christina and all of New Sweden to the Dutch. Sweden was unable to retaliate and New Sweden came to an end. The Dutch flag now flew in triumph not only over the Hudson but also over the Delaware.

This triumph was short-lived, but the Dutch conditions for surrender of New Sweden were very mild and in accord with the Dutch desire to foster the best possible conditions for trade. Few Swedes returned home from New Sweden. At least four hundred kept their homes and lands and pledged their allegiance to the Dutch. The population along the Delaware when Penn arrived was made up mostly of the Swedes and Finns remaining in New Sweden.

The Swedish influence on early Pennsylvania was thus an important and a pioneer one. It deserves more recognition than it usually receives. Penn himself wrote, with his usual perception, "The first planters in these parts were the *Dutch;* and soon after them the *Swedes* and *Finns.* The *Dutch* applied themselves to *traffick;* the *Swedes* and *Finns* to husbandry." Swedish governors were instructed to promote "agriculture and the improvement of the land" as well as the early culture of "grain and other vegetables" and "to procure a good race of cattle, sheep and other animals." They were also ordered to attend to the "culling of choice woods" from the forests. All Europeans of the day were crazy for silk, and the Swedes were no exception. No doubt this carried over from the idea that silks and other such riches would pour in from the East Indies, with which this new continent seemed to interfere. Among the tasks entrusted to soldier Johan Printz was that of forwarding a silk industry. One can only imagine the expressions used by this rough soldier on reading these instructions and viewing the landscape and the conditions which confronted him. Needless to say he did not produce a silk industry. Generally, no person who seeks to know the origins of Pennsylvania can ignore the story of New Sweden and the fact it was the pioneer white settlement within the Commonwealth. It eased the way for later English settlement and development in many ways. It was fortunate that the good ship *Welcome* bearing the Quakers did not arrive upon the same land as did the Swedes. Otherwise their story might have been different. The first pioneers had paved some roads of experience. Among those of utmost importance were the friendly relationships with the Indians.

Peter Stuyvesant's triumph lasted a very short period. A new national state had been formed in England under the good Queen Elizabeth. The ships and captains of this island were roaming the whole world in search of trade and empire. Before and after the year 1500 John Cabot and others sailed their ships everywhere to seek the fabulous Northwest Passage. In the meantime they explored most of North America. English explorers established new frontiers which this hardy new nation with its power at sea proceeded to exploit. By about 1655 the English had established a large seed bed for colonization along the Atlantic seaboard. The seizure and settlement by the United Netherlands or Dutch of the lower Hudson and Delaware river valleys after 1629 changed the entire picture, and by 1650 was a real threat to English plans for a colonial empire. The basis for English questing was the desire for both trade and permanent settlement. The Netherlands and England, as two competing national states in the new fields of world trade opening with the discovery of the New World, had been at odds for some time. Troubles at home, plus a war with France, weakened the United Netherlands while England grew stronger. Under the Stuart kings, England pushed its program of expansion in the South. New England also saw foundations laid. By the mid-seventeenth century, England found itself with no less than ten colonies along the Atlantic, with a population of quite a few thousand people. New England was peopled with Puritans, perhaps better termed Congregationalists, who were basically Calvinists. Roman Catholics sought Maryland as a refuge. In England the wild political turmoil coming in the days of the Stuarts, followed by Cromwell, produced a maelstrom of religious and political conditions which led thousands to flee their mother England in search of either religious or political security. When English authorities finally woke up they realized their northern and southern colonies were separated by the Dutch holdings along the Delaware.

The total result of this situation was that in 1664 English forces under Sir Robert Carr seized the Dutch posts on the Delaware, which included former New Sweden. Except for a very brief time in 1673 when the area was briefly returned to the Dutch, through an involved treaty written without doubt by persons who had no knowledge at all of New World geography, England occupied the Delaware. The no doubt now perplexed settlers were required once more to swear out a new allegiance. But most of them were Swedes and Finns who by now must have taken this as a matter of natural risk in embarking on a pioneer venture. The all-important fact in early Pennsylvania history is that there were these amazingly orderly, peaceful transfers of people and territory without the wars and other upsets that could well have taken place.

Once the existing settlers had taken their oath, courts of law were set up under the British. Sir Robert Carr exercised the duties of both military and civil commander in a way that may well have established a part of the tradition of intelligent British rule of colonial areas for many decades in the future. Three English courts of law were created and in 1676 the Duke of York's laws were put into effect as the basic English law relative to Pennsylvania, Charles II of England having granted these lands earlier to his brother James, Duke of York. Swedish settlers were added to by a few Englishmen who came to the Delaware, now that it was England's land. Upland, renamed Chester by William Penn, was made the capital of British authority and was the center of the government under the Duke of York. This was what could be termed Pennsylvania's second capital. The settlement at Upland was almost entirely Swedish and Finnish population. About two hundred of these Swedes and Finns comprised the entire population of Pennsylvania under the Duke of York.

WILLIAM PENN, THE MAN AND THE QUAKER

No single state can claim as founder so distinguished a person in world history as does Pennsylvania in the person of William Penn. To this great figure Pennsylvania can trace its basic origins not merely in terms of originating a developing settlement but also in establishing fundamental foundations of government and policy which shaped the destiny of a commonwealth. This is a strong statement, but it is one which will hold up in the face of any challenge. Strangely enough, few Pennsylvanians today fully understand or appreciate this fact. It is equally strange that the written pages of history until rather recently bear little witness to the importance of the personality and the ideas of William Penn. It took the tercentenary of the birth of Penn in 1944 to produce at long last some considerable recogni-

tion of the man and his thinking as a force in world history and not just as a man who founded another English colony in the New World. At that time such magazines as *Fortune* and *Life* aided in bringing new dimensions to the character and influence of Penn. They have been followed by many new and penetrating studies of the man and his thinking.

William Penn's beliefs were opposed in every area of thought to the accepted and conventional ideas of his time. He put the conscience of the individual ahead of all else. In the individual man he saw, in accord with accepted Quaker belief then and today, an Inner Light of God showing through which, above all else, was the basis of men's thinking and action. "If we would amend the World, we should mend Our selves, and teach our Children to be, not what we are, but what they should be," wrote Penn. His writings include a number of homilies of this type, many of which Ben Franklin in one variation or another later made famous in his *Poor Richard's Almanac.* Here they caught on, as did not the philosophical writings of Penn.

But the career of Penn was quite different from that of Franklin. Penn was in prison for his beliefs no less than six times, despite the fact he was born the son of an admiral in the Royal Navy who was in turn the son of a naval and consular officer. William Penn senior, father of the Quaker founder, was knighted for his services in the navy. Much has been made of the differences between father and son. The younger Penn, following his birth in London on October 24, 1644, received the training proper for an English gentleman. He helped administer the family estates of his father in County Cork, Ireland. He was educated by private tutors. He then was enrolled at Oxford as a "gentleman commoner" in 1660, but it was here that he revealed for the first time the great impression made upon him at Macroom in Ireland by the English Quaker preacher Thomas Loe. Penn wrote later, "I had an opening of joy . . . in the year 1661 at Oxford twenty years since . . .", revealing his early foundations in Quaker faith.

The fact that Penn left Oxford because of his nonconformist beliefs is well known. He studied law at Lincoln's Inn in London, toured and

28

studied abroad, and then was entered in the military service in Ireland, from late 1666 until about the following December, during which time the famous portrait of Penn in armor was painted. This was done probably at the urging of his father, but certainly the youthful Penn must have agreed to it and the fact he did shows some weakening of his earlier Quaker leanings. This brief period in Penn's life is one about which he wrote or said little in later years.

It was in Ireland that Penn again met and was exposed to the teachings of Thomas Loe, and received what he termed his "convincement" in the Quaker faith. His first arrest for preaching as a Quaker soon followed. He returned to London as an open and influential advocate of the Friends. He possessed more than ordinary influence because of his substantial background as a gentleman commoner and the son of a respected member of the knighthood. This is a point not to be overlooked in understanding the leadership Penn quickly acquired in Quaker circles. In 1668 he published the first of many tracts. This one was *The Sandy Foundation Shaken* and it won him confinement in the Tower of London. This simply gave Penn more freedom and time to write, and out of it came *No Cross, No Crown*. He was still on good terms with his father, and returned in October of 1669 to Ireland to manage his affairs. But Penn now took time also to look after Quaker affairs and wrote and preached on behalf of the Friends until his father, no doubt deeply perplexed and bothered by the doings of his promising son, asked him to return to London. Here, in late August of 1670, with William Mead, he was quickly thrown into a "noisome and stinking" jail for addressing a padlocked Quaker meeting outside in the street. This resulted in the famous trial in which Penn upheld not only the idea of freedom of religious teaching, but also the basic right of all Englishmen to have a trial by a jury of their equals and free of intimidation by court officials representing the crown. A review of the record of this trial or hearing sheds light upon Penn as a man who was not a mere religious fanatic but a person with deep conviction in his particular religious beliefs who also possessed a keen and logical mind. "It is intolerable that my jury be thus menaced," exclaimed Penn as he appealed to the "fundamental laws" and the "proper judges by the great Charter of England." He went on to say; "What hope is there of ever having justice done, when juries are threatened and their verdicts rejected? I am concerned to speak and grieved to see such arbitrary proceedings." It was then that the mayor shouted, "Stop his mouth! Jailer, bring fetters and stake him to the ground." Penn replied quietly, "Do your pleasure, I matter not your fetters." Penn appeared throughout this proceeding not so much as a defender of the Quakers, but of the basic rights of Englishmen to trial by a jury of their peers. The trial thus became a landmark in the history of the long struggle for this right. The "not guilty" verdict of the jury was rejected by the court. The jury itself then appealed the verdict and was upheld by the higher court on exactly the same grounds of argument as had been presented by Penn during the trial.

Admiral Penn appears to have sensed now the depth of the thinking of his son, who must have appeared earlier as merely a disturbed young man who still could be shown the proper ways of life. In *No Cross, No Crown,* the younger Penn writes that his father gave him the basic philosophy "Let nothing in this world tempt you to wrong your conscience; whatever you design to do, lay it justly and time it reasonably. . . ." The admiral added, "Lastly be not troubled at disappointments." Admiral Penn, though his son wrote to him from his prison, "I entreat that thee not purchase my liberty," evidently arranged to pay the fine to secure his release on September 7, 1670.

The admiral was now in his last illness. He died shortly afterward, leaving young Penn considerable wealth and an expression on the part of his father to King Charles II and James, Duke of York, that they should show to the son the same favor they had shown to him. This appeal, however, was without immediate avail, for the hands of the King were tied by his strongly Cavalier and Anglican ministry. In February, 1671, Penn was once more arrested for preaching at a Quaker meeting and taken to the Tower of London where he was sentenced to six months in Newgate prison for his refusal to take the oath of allegiance and supremacy. He was tried without a jury and once more presented his arguments against the charge that he did nothing "but stir up the people to sedition"; "I would have thee and all other men to know that I scorn that religion which is not worth suffering for, and able to sustain those that are afflicted for it," declared Penn. When the court official asked that a corporal and file of soldiers should be assigned to take him to prison, Penn calmly commented that this was not necessary because "I know the way to Newgate." During his imprisonment, Penn again made good use of his time in writing numerous tracts and letters, and in revising his famous *The Great Case of Liberty of Conscience,* a marshaling of the case for religious liberty from writers of all ages in support of his thesis that "men cannot be said to have any religion, that takes it by another man's choice, not his own." In 1673 Penn was before the King's court. This time he was defending the great Quaker, George Fox.

WILLIAM PENN ACQUIRES A PROVINCE

All of these trials and tribulations point up the great leadership of William Penn as not merely a devout believer in the beliefs of the Society of Friends but in the total principle of religious freedom and the rights of free Englishmen. The natural outgrowth of this situation was a concern for the establishing of a haven of refuge for the Friends in the New World. About 1675, Penn and other Quakers became associated in the establishing of a settlement in West New Jersey. Penn took part in drafting for this colony a constitution entitled *Concessions and Agreements of the Proprietors, Freeholders, and Inhabitants of the Province of West Jersey,* which embodied many principles later evident in Penn's charters of government for Pennsylvania. His experience with the West New Jersey settlement certainly influenced his colonial venture on his own in Pennsylvania. Among other things, it gave him a considerable knowledge of that portion of the New World under English rule. This helps to explain just how Penn was able to provide so shortly after he was confirmed as proprietor of his province so much useful detail to prospective settlers and others.

In any event, in 1680 Penn petitioned Charles II that letters patent be granted him for a tract of land north of Maryland and on the east bounded by the Delaware, limited to the west as was Maryland but extending northward "as far as plantable." The tradition is that this grant was made to satisfy debts owed by the King to Admiral Penn and now to his son, but the actual record of the transaction fails to reveal any such understanding. This was first laid before Privy Council and then moved to the Committee on Trade and Plantations, where it met with some objections from both the Duke of York as regarded his Delaware counties and Lord Baltimore, proprietor of Maryland. Penn won his case and on March 4, 1681, Charles II signed the charter, officially proclaimed on April 2. William Penn was now the proprietor and governor of a vast tract of New World lands which made him the largest single landowner in the entire kingdom, with the possible exception of King Charles himself. The original of this precious document is now housed in Harrisburg as Pennsylvania's most fundamental historical treasure. The charter is a very wordy affair, and few would care to take the time to read, let alone digest it. Its major provision was a grant to Penn and "his heires and assignes, the free and undisturbed use" of "all the soyle, lands, fields, woods, underwoods, maountaines, hills, fenns, Isles, Lakes, Rivers, waters, rivulets, Bays and Inletts" within this territory as described in the charter. Perhaps even more vital to the future of the province was Section Four of the document, which made the same William Penn and his legal heirs "the true and absolute Proprietaries of all the Lands and Dominions aforesaid" with "free, full and absolute power, by virtue of these presents to him and his heirs, and to his or their Deputies, and Lieutenants, for the good and happy government of the said Countey, to ordayne, make, enact and under his and their Seales to publish any Lawes whatsoever, for the raising of money for the publick use of the said province, or for any other end apperteyning either unto the publick state peace, or safety of the said Country, or unto the private utility of perticular persons, according unto their best discretions, by and with the advice, assent, and approbation of the freemen of said

Charter for Pennsylvania granted by Charles II. Original in the State Archives.

Countrey, or the greater parte of them, or of their Delegates or Deputies, whom for the Enactment of said Lawes, when, and as often as need shall require. WEE WILL, that the said William Penn, and his heires, shall assemble in such sort and forme as to him and them shall seeme best, and the same lawes duely to execute unto, and upon all people within the said Countrey and limits thereof." Any interpretation of such a broad statement of governmental powers makes it clear that Penn and his heirs were left great freedom in determining the degree to which "freemen" might or might not participate in the forming of the laws and the government of the province.

The naming of Penn's new province was not entirely in accord with his desires. In a letter to his friend Robert Turner in Ireland, Penn wrote January 5, 1681, that "this day my country was confirmed to me under the great seal of England, with large powers and privileges, by the name of *Pennsilvania,* a name the king would give it in

honour of my father." He went on to say, "I chose *New Wales,* being as this, a pretty hilly country. . . ." But when this was proposed, the secretary, a Welshman, "refused to have it called New Wales, *Sylvania,* and they added *Penn;* and though I much opposed it and went to the king to have it struck out and altered, he said 'twas past . . . ; nor would twenty guineas move the under secretary to vary the name, for I feared least it should be lookt on as a vanity in me, and not as a respect in the king, as it truly was to my father, whom he often mentions with praise." So Penn's new colony obtained its name. Penn concluded with a few words which well indicate the depth of his thinking about his new venture. He wrote, "Tis a clear and just thing, and my God that has given it me through many difficultys, will, I believe bless and make it the seed of a nation. I shall have a tender care to the government, that it will be well laid. . . ." Penn's intention to plan wisely for the government of his province was further en-

31

larged upon in a letter to Friends in Ireland dated April 12, 1681. He wrote that "my understanding and inclinations have been much directed to observe and reprove mischiefs in governments, so it is now put into my power to settle one." In "matters of liberty and privilege, I purpose that which is extraordinary, and to leave to myself and successors no power of doeing mischief; that the will of one man may not hinder the good of a whole country," Penn declared.

and industrious people." "I shall not usurp the right of any, or oppress his person; God has furnished me with a better resolution, and has given me his grace to keep it," wrote the proprietor and governor. Penn at this time hoped to sail for his new province within five months but it was more than a year before he was able to fulfill his great desire to see the new land and its fruits. Much of the intervening time was devoted to the very practical business of attracting settlers from vari-

Penn's letter in 1681 directed to the "King or Kings of the Indians of Pennsylvania" informing them of his desire to live "justly, peaceably and friendly with you."

The machinery for colonial government was set in motion at once by sending his cousin William Markham to act as deputy governor and to organize the government. Penn sent a message of greeting and assurance to the scattered English, Swedes, Dutch, and Finns already settled along the Delaware. In it Penn writing to "My Friends" emphasized that God had given him an understanding of his duty. "I hope," he wrote, "you will not be troubled with your change and the king's choice, for you are now fixt, at the mercy of no Governor that comes to make his fortune great; you shall be governed by laws of your own making, and live a free, and if you will, a sober

ous parts of Europe. Penn wrote and published *Some Account of the Province of Pennsylvania,* a glowing account of the benefits to be found in Pennsylvania. He also wrote many letters and by July, 1681, had entered into a preliminary agreement with the first purchasers containing twenty articles on *Certain Conditions and Concessions.* Among these were provision for laying out a large town, surveying roads, regulations to protect the rights of the Indians, and regulations governing land sales. "I am like to have many from France, some from Holland, and, I hear some Scotch will go," he wrote in August. Early that autumn commissioners were sent to Pennsylvania to arrange for the reception of new settlers, as well as to lay out the promised town. This was to be a "great Towne," Penn told the commissioners and should be located where the Delaware "is most navigable, high, dry, and healthy." Penn suggested that every house be located in the middle of a town lot "so there may be ground on each side, for Gardens or Orchards or fields, that it may be a greene Country Towne, which will never be burnt, and always be wholesome." Thus Penn laid the foundations for Philadelphia, perhaps the first planned city.

Penn also gave much time and thought to the details of framing a government. Here there came into play an often overlooked facet of the true greatness of William Penn. While he had become a Quaker, and his very personal letters reveal a deep sense of belief that his mission was directed by God and was indeed a Holy Experiment, it must also be kept in mind that Penn was accustomed to the use of authority and was close to royalty in England, where the power of the crown was not yet greatly weakened. The charter did place some mild restraint upon him in terms of calling for an assembly of the freeholders in making the laws, but such a procedure was called for only "when, and as often as need shall require." In short, a regular assembly for lawmaking purposes was by no means demanded under the charter. Furthermore, the absolute ownership of the land as proprietor placed perhaps even greater power in Penn's hands. It is a great tribute, therefore, to the depth of Penn's convictions relative to placing government in the hands of the people that he proceeded steadily throughout his lifetime to give still more liberties to the people of Pennsylvania. And not infrequently his patience was tried sorely with the people and their demands for these liberties.

THE "FIRST FRAME OF GOVERNMENT"

Penn's *First Frame of Government* was adopted in England April 25, 1682, by the proprietor and some of his first purchasers of land. His friend, the great English liberal Algernon Sidney, thought Penn retained too much power, but even so it was a great step forward in the history of self-government in the world of that time. As the *First Frame* itself well stated in its preface, there was no "model in the world" for such a document. These were Penn's words as he endeavored to explain and to some extent justify his new constitution. He placed emphasis upon the "divine right of government beyond exception" but hastened to say that this did not place that power in the hands of one man or a group of self-appointed men. He pointed out that the worst form of government in good hands might do very well and that the best form of government in the hands of "ill ones can do nothing that is great or good." The *Frame* included Penn's famous statements: "Governments, like clocks, go from the motion men give them, and as governments are made and moved by men, so by them they are ruined too. Wherefore governments rather depend upon men, than men upon governments. Let men be good, and the government cannot be bad; if it be ill, they will cure it. But if men be bad, let the government be never so good, they will endeavour to warp and spoil it to their turn." He went on to say that "liberty without obedience is confusion, and obedience without liberty is slavery" in explaining the need for just laws but laws which must be enforced by the proper magistrates. The *Frame* itself consisted of twenty-four articles and forty laws. The articles placed the government in the hands of the governor or his deputy and freemen in a Council, together with a General Assembly. Through this machinery the laws were to be made and executed and all workings of government to function. The Council was made up of seventy-two persons chosen by the freemen with the governor or his deputy as perpetual president. Membership was divided in such a way that an annual succession of twenty-four members would take place each year and no member might serve more than three years. The General Assembly was to consist the first year of all the freemen; afterwards of two hundred and never to exceed five hundred. Provision for freedom of religion was included in the *Frame*. The basic laws could not be altered except by consent of the governor and six out of every seven members of the legislative body. These fundamental laws were in a very real sense in the nature of an original compact between the proprietor and the freemen of the province. In August, 1682, Penn achieved yet another important goal in persuading the Duke of York to cede to him the so-called Lower Counties, now Delaware. Another important final legal detail was cleared on August 21, 1682, when the Duke of York conveyed by deed any and all claims he had to Pennsylvania.

On September 2, 1682, the *London Gazette* reported briefly, "Two days since sailed out of the *Downs,* three ships bound for *Pensilvania,* on board of which was Mr. *Pen,* with a great many Quakers, who go to settle there." One of these ships was the *Welcome* and Mr. Penn indeed was aboard. The *Welcome* entered Delaware Bay on October 24 and three days later Penn first put foot on New World soil at New Castle, Delaware, where the following day he took formal title to the "turf, and twig, and water, and soyle of the river Delaware." On the twenty-ninth he landed at Swedish Upland, which he promptly renamed Chester. A fellow Quaker voyager, Richard Townsend, described the land as "a wilderness; the chief inhabitants were Indians, and some Swedes. . . ."

THE FIRST ASSEMBLY, THE GREAT
LAW, AND A SECOND FRAME

Penn called a meeting of the General Assembly at Chester for December 4. This first Assembly promptly passed an act of union annexing the lower counties and accepted the *First Frame of Government.* The same session saw the enactment of the famous *Great Law,* Pennsylvania's first code of laws. The notable preamble and first chapter reaffirmed freedom of conscience and worship for all those "who shall confess and acknowledge one Almighty God. . . ." In March, 1683, Penn met his second General Assembly in the newly laid out town of Philadelphia. Stirrings of democratic thought already were evident and resulted in a request to the governor that changes be made in the *First Frame of Government.* Penn asked frankly whether the people wished the old charter or a new one. They asked for a new one, and on April 2 the *Second Frame of Government* provided by Penn giving heed to criticisms was adopted by the General Assembly. The major change con-

sisted of limitations on the power of the governor, who was now made more subject to the advice and consent of the Council. Here, for the first time, Penn might have drawn a line of authority and refused to surrender to the people any restraint on his powers as governor. Thus the true depth of his greatness and of his belief in a democratic order were tested and not found wanting within six months of his arrival.

Penn was a very busy man during his first visit. He made business and social calls on neighbor colonies and became a leader in affairs of the Society of Friends throughout the region. He looked after the early development of Philadelphia. He laid plans for a large country estate of several thousand acres at Pennsbury Manor some twenty miles above Philadelphia along the banks of the Delaware. This, by the way, is another evidence of the basically aristocratic tastes of the proprietor. He continued to write long and detailed letters extolling the virtues of Pennsylvania's climate, soil, and other natural advantages for settlement. He never ceased to be something of the realtor working to sell his property to prospective settlers. By the summer of 1683 he was writing to the Earl of Sutherland, ancestor of Winston Churchill, of his labors and progress, as well as commenting upon the character of the Indians and the richness of the natural products of his beloved Pennsylvania.

PENN'S INDIAN POLICY

Pennsylvania's Indians, who were of course Delawares, intrigued Penn. This is not unexpected, because he was a man with a great curiosity as well as deeply faithful to the Quaker ideal of the equality of men on a basis of individual conscience and without regard to race or color. Penn wrote extensively about the Indian. His writings, on the whole, are one of the most sound evaluations on record of the character and the culture of the American Indian, as he first encountered the white man on the eastern seaboard. They deserve more attention than they receive on the part of the sociologist and anthropologist of today. It is sometimes charged that Penn may have mixed with his observations a bit of the "noble savage" concept of the early European liberals, but it must be kept in mind that he looked upon Indians at first hand and before there was much, if any, such thinking about the American Indian. Even before his coming to Pennsylvania, Penn had emphasized—as early as 1681—in his instructions to his commissioners, "Be

adjustment of a meager aboriginal population to European and American civilization. The Swedes, it is true, had made Indian treaties for land, but Penn met many times with the leading chiefs among the Delawares to perfect his understanding with them, and not merely to win their marks on a parchment treaty granting title to lands over

Penn's first treaty with the Delawares in 1683. Original in the State Archives.

tender of offending the Indians, and hearken by honest Spyes, if you can hear that anybody inveigles the Indians not to sell, or to stand off, and raise the value upon you." He went on to say that his representatives should "soften them to mee and the people, lett them know that you are come to sit down Lovingly among them. . . ." How Penn thus early could have so understood the importance of this approach to the Indian is not easily explained in any terms other than the suggested combination of intellectual interest with a deep Quaker faith, not necessarily shared by all of his associates then or later.

In any event, certainly one of the most positive developments of Penn's early sojourn in his province was the start of an Indian policy which, if followed in colonial and later America, might have meant less bloody and more constructive

which they had no real control under Indian law and custom, but in an effort to treat them as equals among all mankind. West's famous portrait of the Indian treaty under the elm is not very accurate in any detail, but it does somehow capture the idea that Penn was a man of understanding rather than a person who, as did most later treaty makers, rely upon cheap trinkets and rum to secure Indian assent to cession of valuable lands. Whether this treaty was ever held cannot be fixed in terms of fact, but there is every evidence that there was an early meeting and many later meetings with the Delawares relative not only to land cessions, but to peaceful relations as well. Penn's Indian policy was based on the thought that the Indians had a community and a sort of government of their own, and from that there could be established certain legal relationships by negotiation and treaty. In this he surely did not understand fully the nature of Indian society and government. In any event, his personal relationships with the Delawares were established on his very first visit as those of everlasting friendship. Not only did he develop the idea of treaties for governmental land acquisition, which was often mere paper work, but Penn's original agreement in 1681 with his first purchasers provided "That no man shall by any ways or means in word or deed affront or wrong any Indians, but he shall incur the same penalty of the law as if he had committed it against his fellow planter. . . ."

Penn's weakness was that he himself never quite understood the nature of the Indian's thinking on these matters of property because the same agreement said that if any Indian should "abuse in word or deed any planter of this Province" there might be an appeal to the white government on the part of the "planter." Differences resulting might be settled by a jury of six planters and six natives. This has been hailed by some as equal right of trial by jury, but this is a white man's legal theory and meant nothing to an Indian. The same agreement of 1681 said that the Indians should have the "liberty to do all things relating to the improvement of the ground and providing sustenance for their families, that any of the planters shall enjoy. . . ." Again, how could a white planter and an Indian understand mutual rights? Many writers on Penn and Pennsylvania have overdone the picture of Penn and the Indians. If it is put on a more realistic basis it can be granted that Penn was foremost but by no means perfect in a policy of Indian understanding. He was a "Brother Onas," as the Delawares called him.

PENN LOSES AND REGAINS HIS GOVERNORSHIP

A year later in August, 1684, the seriousness of the boundary dispute with Lord Baltimore of Maryland forced Penn to return to England to endeavor to assert his very real influence in protecting his interests. Things were going well for Penn when in February, 1685, the death of King

Charles II brought the Duke of York to the throne as James II. Penn was closer even to James than to Charles but when the "Glorious Revolution" of 1688–89 drove the Stuarts from the throne, and William and Mary became the new sovereigns Penn's close association with the two Stuarts led his loyalty to the new regime to be questioned. Factions arising in his province did not help matters for Penn, and his deputy governors were having their troubles with Pennsylvania's legislative body. In October, 1692, Penn was relieved by King William as governor, though he was not deprived of his proprietorship. This move was due largely to the desire of King William to consolidate the management of all the northern colonies for purposes of better defense in the bitter war with France which involved England's very survival. Penn's governorship was restored in August, 1694.

Penn was not able, however, to return to the province until September, 1699. His first wife having died, he was now accompanied by his second wife, Hannah Callowhill Penn, his daughter Letitia and James Logan, the man who was to become his most trusted adviser. Logan noted at once the existence in the province of a "faction that had long contended to overthrow the settled constitution of the government," but which on Penn's return now received a "universal damp." This spirit of factionalism had arisen soon after Penn's departure. He then left the government rather much in the hands of the Council, of which Thomas Lloyd was president and thus became virtually deputy governor. The very nature of their doctrine, with its intense belief in the equality of the individual man and his freedom of conscience was bound to make most Quakers critical of almost any government. Quakerism also placed strong emphasis upon the virtues of hard work and material advancement of the individual. It was not long before some class distinctions began to appear in the social order as some Quakers became more wealthy than others. Philadelphia was growing rapidly as a center for trade and commerce, and many Quaker merchants began to emerge as much better off than their fellows. The more wealthy and aristocratic element tended to be represented in the Council while the commoners were entrenched in the Assembly. The interests and the ideas of the two came into some conflict. Furthermore, when Penn was deprived of his governorship, Benjamin Fletcher from New York was made "Captain-General and Governor in Chief" of Pennsylvania. Fletcher was a military man and given the task of providing a united front in King William's War. He came down to Pennsylvania and demanded funds to meet its share of the common colonial defense, and in his drive to secure these monies ignored entirely the constitutional niceties which had flowered in Pennsylvania. Fletcher not only was demanding money for war from pacifist Quaker legislators, but at the same time stepping on the toes of both Council and Assembly in his arbitrary conduct of the affairs of government. The powers of a royal governor did not sit well when exercised in Pennsylvania. The Quaker Assembly refused to raise a militia, but under threat of dissolution it did at long last vote funds to take care of needy Indians. These monies Fletcher was able to divert to colonial defense. In fighting with Fletcher, however, the Assembly won even more protection for the rights and powers of that body, and thus whetted the appetite for more freedom from any governor or proprietor, including the right to initiate the laws.

"CIVIL GRIEFS" LEAD TO MARKHAM'S
FRAME AND THE CHARTER OF PRIVILEGES

Penn's authority was restored on the major condition that Pennsylvania should provide more cooperation in colonial defense measures. Penn's colonial venture had been far from profitable. In such financial difficulties he could not return at once to the province. Penn turned again to William Markham to continue to serve as deputy governor and to secure the necessary support of the legislative body for colonial defense. Markham promptly ran into the insurgent and independent spirit which had developed in the battles of the Assembly with Fletcher. By this time, what may loosely be termed the democratic forces in the Assembly had found a strong leader in the person of David Lloyd. Lloyd was a lawyer and had served Penn faithfully as a legal adviser and

attorney general in the earlier affairs of the province. He was not a Quaker when he came to the province but later joined the Friends. A shrewd and calculating man, Lloyd quickly accumulated considerable landed wealth as well as winning distinction as a political leader. His economic and personal interests shortly led him into questioning the power of the proprietorship, and into becoming the political spokesman of those who believed more democracy should be written into Pennsylvania's frame of government. Markham won his monies for the king, but was forced to grant, with Penn's approval, a third constitution which came to be known as *Markham's Frame.* It gave the Assembly the all important power to initiate laws and to call and to adjourn its own sessions. Further restrictions were placed on the governor to act without the consent of Council. In general, Whig doctrines of constitutional representative government were marching ahead far faster in colonial Pennsylvania toward the end of the seventeenth century than in even England itself.

Penn was conscious of these "civil griefs," as he termed them. His return late in 1699 helped quiet the factious spirit which had arisen during his absence, but it was accomplished only by making further concessions to the forces demanding more representation. In an address to the Council on April 2, 1700, Penn spoke frankly of the fact that there were now "some laws which may be accounted obsolete, others hurtfull, others imperfect, that will need improvement; and that it will be requisit to make some new ones." He went on with equal frankness to tell them, "If in the Constitution by Charter there be any thing that jarrs—alter it." At the same time he urged: "Away with all parties, and look upon yourselves, and on what is good for all, as a bodie politick; first as under the King and Crown of England, and next as under mee by Letters patent from that Crown."

Once more, however, the true greatness of William Penn comes to the surface. "Some say I come to gett money and be gone," he told the Council, and this was truly the content of some of the most vicious charges made against the proprietorship. After long discussion of all problems

Penn resolved the entire Council into one committee "to read the Charter and Frame of Government, and to adopt what is good in either, to lay aside what is inconvenient and burdensome, and to add to both what may best suit the common good of all: And if you be under any doubt or scruple, I will endeavor to solve it." What could be more startling in those days! Long debate and discussion followed, though Penn appears to have thought something concrete would be presented to him in a matter of perhaps a day. Unable to agree among themselves, the Council and Assembly agreed to deliver the old charter to Penn to prepare a new constitution, subject to the approval of the legislative body. Truly, the course of representative government was running at full speed in Pennsylvania. Penn was presented with this proposition on June 7, 1700. More than a year later in October, 1701, it was a tired and probably somewhat frustrated man who wrote to the Assembly as "Your Friend, and Proprietary, and Governor" urging that they: "Yield in Circumstantials to preserve Essentials." "Make me not sad now I am going to leave you, since it is for you," pleaded Penn. The final result was the famous *Charter of Privileges* adopted on October 28, 1701. It was the final constitution for colonial Pennsylvania. So fundamental were its provisions that it remained the major foundation for the first State Constitution adopted in 1776, while the Revolution was in progress. The original is now the proud possession of the American Philosophical Society in Philadelphia, and was on the famous Freedom Train. The document is one of those most treasured in the history of the nation in terms of its contribution to the progress of our American liberties.

Once more Penn was in such a position that he could have threatened the full use of all of his proprietary and governmental powers to halt demands for further liberties. Instead he chose to accept even the need for such a revision, and took upon himself the final responsibility for submitting the ultimate proposal. Joseph Growdon as Speaker for the Assembly accepted and signed on "Behalf, and by Order of the Assembly the document as the Whole and being distinctly read in Assembly, and every Part thereof being approved of and agreed to us, we do thankfully receive the same from our Proprietary and Governor, at Philadelphia, this Twenty-eighth Day of October, One Thousand Seven Hundred and One."

The charter itself, despite all the controversy and travail back of it, was a rather simple and forthright statement of fundamentals, and a great tribute to Penn as the person who did most to draft it. Pennsylvania may well treasure the legend (it cannot be proved in any historical document) that most of the labors involved in the drafting were centered in Penn's peaceful study at Pennsbury. Who knows how many times he may have taken time to walk down to the banks of the smoothly flowing Delaware just a few yards in front of this splendid country retreat and pondered upon the problems of a proprietor and a governor of a "Holy Experiment" which had paid him nothing in money but cost much in heartache and soul-searching for a man who believed deeply in and respected freedom and toleration, even when their ultimate virtues arose to perplex and conflict with him. There were only eight sections in the 1701 Charter but perhaps they refined more than any other document or writing the deep faith of Penn that "no People can be truly happy tho' under the greatest enjoyment of civil Liberties, if abridged of the Freedom of their Consciences, as to their religious Profession and Worship." The only limitation upon this was the fact that only those who professed to believe in Christ should "serve this Government in any Capacity, both legislatively and executively." The popular election of an Assembly was guaranteed to convene at a specified fourteenth day of October at Philadelphia with their own powers of adjournment, as well as establishing qualifications and conditions for election of their membership. The power of the Assembly to prepare bills to be enacted into laws was established. Elections for Assembly were also to include the selection of a double number of persons to be presented to the governor as selections for such local officers as "Sheriffs and Coroners." Justices for the counties were allowed to nominate three persons to serve as "Clerk of the Peace." This gave a new opening for a more democratic judicial system, for we must keep it in mind that this local "clerk of the peace" was a very important local office in colonial times, and was vitally concerned with the total scheme of the efficient administration of law and justice throughout a very scattered settlement.

In particular the charter indicated that "the Laws of this Government shall be in this Stile,

PENN'S LAST YEARS AS PROPRIETOR AND GOVERNOR

Penn's last years were not happy. Falsification of his accounts in England forced him to mortgage his province and to become involved in several lawsuits. In 1708 he even spent several

Pennsbury Manor as restored and re-created by the Pennsylvania Historical and Museum Commission.

viz. *By the Governor, with the Consent and Approbation of the Freemen in General Assembly met. . . ."* This was the final triumph of colonial democracy. It was a monument not only to William Penn but also to such men as David Lloyd, who had fought for greater democracy in the government of the province. Pennsylvania was becoming not merely a "Holy Experiment" but a true seed of a nation in terms of the flowering of processes of orderly representative government resting upon the people as a body politic. The charter has been called properly the most notable of all colonial constitutions because of these advances in truly representative government. It meant an end to proprietorship in everything but name because the rules and regulations upon which Pennsylvania was to grow in terms of land and settlement were now very much dependent upon the General Assembly. Penn was himself happy with the result, and returned to England, after having chartered the city of Philadelphia and appointed Andrew Hamilton as lieutenant governor.

months in debtors' prison, where he languished until friends were able to pay off the alleged claims of his creditors. The great concern which he held for his colonial experiment did not add to his later happiness. As a venture in landholding, Pennsylvania was a complete failure. Penn himself wrote frequently of the fact he had not received any material returns from his grant which compared with the outlay from his small personal fortune. It should be kept in mind that Penn was not a wealthy man. One of his major inheritances from his father was the debt which the crown owed to the admiral and which was paid off neatly with "Pensilvania." Like George Washington and Robert Morris, Penn was land poor. The mere fact that he could be thrown into a debtors' prison indicates his basic poverty, though he continued to move in what most persons would consider the better social circles.

Penn had hoped that there could be an end to political parties in his province, but this was a vain thought. Political differences had arisen before he returned to Pennsylvania and had been quieted only by the peculiar magic of his idealism and his willingness to give to the most demanding faction just about what they wanted. Indeed, the privileges for representative government which Penn had himself written into the 1701 constitution were themselves necessarily a basis for political controversy in terms of policies and laws which became the subject of legislative consideration. Penn might himself have benefited from actually serving in a legislative body. He was never able to understand that granting from the top any charter or frame of government could ever guarantee political calm. Again, it must be realized that William Penn was a man who worked at the problem of government in terms of the idealist with power and authority under the terms of his charter. His final greatness rests upon the fact he chose to use that power and authority with complete dedication to the ideal of a government and society in which the right of the individual man must be allowed to express itself in a representative government.

In this respect Penn was following true Quaker doctrine, but he actually out-Quakered the Quakers in his devotion to this ideal. There was on the part of Penn a peculiar type of thinking which some have termed "mysticism." An equally potent and more expressive word is "idealism." The rewards due this type of mind historically always rest with the ages, and this most surely is true of William Penn. Internal political conflict was something he could not end. Indeed, his belief in the right of the people to representation in government encouraged it. Penn's God-given conscience was never quite able to understand that the majority of even Quakers were not so driven by their faith as to accept a government in which they had every wish represented in terms of the frame, but also to agree finally as to the direction of that frame, which was another and entirely different matter.

The last few years of Penn's life were relieved from particular distress in the province. Penn reasoned that his province was on a sound basis but his peculiar idealism would prevail. However, the history of representative government shows clearly it is not a smooth path, either in the past or

today. The very principle that the people speak means a resulting conflict of opinions and ideas. Even the benign and generally remarkable new constitution did not end controversy, but rather opened the door to continuing differences of policy in the Assembly. This was not only inevitable but very proper. Both the resulting "parties" inevitably were made up mainly of Quakers, as they dominated the population. As mentioned before, Quakers were shaping up into social groups and in other ways were indicating they were not as idealistic in their approach to practical problems of government as was the proprietor. Many of the Quaker merchants actually opposed the proprietary government.

Mention has been made of David Lloyd as the leader of the "democracy." James Logan, who came with Penn from England on his second visit, was secretary to the Provincial Council and thus in a most important position. He was a keen student of the most advanced Whig political thinking of the time and thus attuned to the progressive forces at work in Penn's colony. Since he had come with Penn there is little doubt but that he knew and reflected rather intimately Penn's own ideas. James Logan, like his opponent David Lloyd, has been much overlooked in colonial history. James Logan may properly said to have been one of the most learned and cultured men in all colonial America, ranking with Benjamin Franklin. His personal library and his home, Stenton, were certainly as fine as any in the colonies. He was an amateur scientist of note who experimented and invented in both the physical and the biological sciences. His works were published and held in high regard in the best scientific circles of Europe. He was interested in economic affairs, and was an early participant in the rise of the Pennsylvania iron industry. In short, James Logan represented the best traditions of a growing Quaker aristocracy centered in Philadelphia, and based upon accumulating wealth from commerce, and later the ventures in iron. While Logan's writings are filled with expressions of fear of the "mobbish" spirit inherent in the mass of the people and he shuddered at times at the influx of such elements as the Germans and the Scotch Irish, with their threat to the political control of the Quakers, he represents the finest in the liberal aristocracy which was the backbone of Whiggism in England and in Pennsylvania.

William Penn in his later years, from a chalk portrait by Francis Place and acquired by The Historical Society of Pennsylvania in 1957.

Before Penn's death, the outlines for permanent differences of political interest were clear in Pennsylvania. The formidable power of the Quaker aristocracy, with the exception of a few persons, was in complete support of the Penn proprietorship and Penn's deputy governors. The death of Governor Hamilton in 1703 resulted in a short interim service on the part of Edward Shippen in his capacity as president of the Council. A year later, the arrival of John Evans to serve as deputy governor and accompanied by William Penn, Jr., resulted in a renewal of the conflict with the Assembly, over its rights under the Charter of Privileges. Evans also tried to force the Assembly to authorize raising armed forces. David Lloyd as leader of what may well be termed the "popular party" was the major spokesman for the Assembly in which the growing number of farmers, small tradesmen, and shopkeepers were strongly represented as opposed to the wealth and standing of the Council members. Penn himself was drawn into the controversy and impelled to write a letter chiding the people for the sharp factionalism evident in the government. As usual, Penn's word worked a certain magic and the popular party was unseated in favor of those more strongly back of the powers of the proprietor. The last few years before his death on July 30, 1718, were ones of comparative harmony in the political affairs of Pennsylvania. Penn's own affairs were by no means in as happy a state. Colonizing had proved an expensive business and Penn thought seriously of selling his province to the crown. Good Queen Anne was Penn's friend and he believed a transfer to the crown could be accomplished in such a manner as to preserve "all the Laws and privileges I have granted." Since he was a victim of paralysis for six years before his death, he could do little to implement such ideas, and they came to nothing. The effect of such a move on the fortunes of Pennsylvania is hard to estimate, but it is hard to believe that it could have enjoyed the continued growth of its liberties under a royal governor. Penn's Holy Experiment had moved so far ahead in terms of the evolution of representative institutions and ideas that a clash would have been inevitable under a crown-colony status.

THE WORLD'S GREATEST GIVER OF LAWS

The death of Penn marked the close of an era in the colonial history of Pennsylvania. The magic of his name and the wisdom of his counsel had calmed the troubled political seas on more than one occasion. He had led a continued expansion of the principles of representative government which as early as 1701 had provided Pennsylvania with what may well have been the most enlightened frame of government anywhere in the world of that time. Every Pennsylvanian has a right to be proud of the Penn heritage. William Penn was no ordinary man. His name has not shone forth on the pages of history with anything like the luster it deserves. Religion, political and governmental principles, social problems, and even international relations were subjects for his writing. And it is hard to find anything Penn wrote, other than some of his theological polemics, whether a mere letter, a pamphlet, or a book, which is not worth reading even today.

The most basic element in his thinking quite naturally was the Quaker ethic with its emphasis upon the Inner Light or conscience of the individual man which entitled him to freedom of thought and expression. Penn wrote in *Some Fruits of Solitude,* ". . . there should be a Time and Place for everything; and whatever else is done or omitted, be sure to begin and end with God." This philosophy he applied objectively to all that he did and, unlike most men, he possessed an ability to do so. Fine phases are easy to come by, but their application is not so easy. As pointed out before, the ability of Penn to apply this philosophy to the continued expansion of principles of representative government in his several charters is the key to his true greatness. It is because of this that the *Charter of Privileges* of 1701 is a landmark document in the history of free government and human liberty.

The same ethic applied to the treatment of the Indian won from them a recognition that in William Penn they had a true friend willing to treat them with the same regard for their rights as individual men as he accorded others. Penn's concern that prisons should be places to reform rather than to punish, and that the poor and the unfortunate should receive proper treatment reflected the same philosophy applied to the social conditions of his times. Thomas Jefferson once wrote that William Penn was "the greatest lawgiver the world has produced." The force of ideas is always the shaper of institutions. William Penn did indeed make Pennsylvania a "seed" for a nation.

CHAPTER THREE

THE PEACEABLE KINGDOM
COMES TO AN END

One of the best-known paintings of the Quaker folk artist Edward Hicks is titled "The Peaceable Kingdom," depicting a rural scene and peaceable country ways. This is what William Penn ardently desired for Pennsylvania. His powers were such as to grant him literally a kingdom. He built a country estate at Pennsbury along the Delaware, distant even from his "greene Country Towne" of Philadelphia. His admonitions to his colonists and to his assembly remind us of the English gentleman who thought in terms of a civilization rather narrowly confined in terms of territorial limits and made up of largely open country divided into manors or estates with a small number of scattered large and small towns located at strategic points to serve as centers for commerce and trade. One cannot escape the conclusion that this is what William Penn expected Pennsylvania to become as a colony, despite his earnest efforts to bring increasing numbers of people to his province and his continued references to its interior riches. Along with this ideal, Penn brought with him the theory that government could be established and operated without reference to "party." The word "party" in those days, and indeed as late as the time of George Washington was the type of dirty word that some persons more or less attach to the word "politics" even today. Government without "party" or "politics" literally is impossible in a democratic world. Only dictatorship can eliminate these expressions of opinion.

HANNAH PENN AND HER SONS

As has been pointed out, political differences and the semblance of parties within the Assembly had appeared even before Penn's death. Hannah Penn actually ruled Pennsylvania for fifteen years following 1712 and the time when Penn was first stricken. Her portrait in The Historical Society of Pennsylvania is not exactly that of a "Mona Lisa," but it does reveal a not unattractive matron who, as shown in her administration of affairs until her death in 1727 as Pennsylvania's first and last woman governor, was an energetic and capable woman. However, Hannah somewhat complicated Pennsylvania colonial history by leaving three sons, John, Thomas, and Richard. None were the equal of their father in the art of governing Pennsylvania. Much of this may well have been due to the fact they had never gone through the rewarding if sometimes harrowing experiences of their father in establishing a pattern for the government and in understanding of the people. Thomas and Richard Penn even deserted the Quaker faith and became Anglicans. John and Thomas Penn came to Pennsylvania shortly after the death of their mother. John Penn, the eldest son and a bachelor, inherited in accord with Eng-

John Penn, eldest son of William Penn and principal proprietor until 1746.

lish law one-half the proprietary interest of his father. After the death of John Penn in 1746, his share went to Thomas, who became the owner of a three-quarter interest in Pennsylvania and probably the largest landholder of his time. Penn's third and youngest son, Richard, had a one-quarter interest in the province which he bequeathed on his death in 1771 to his son John. When his uncle Thomas Penn died in 1775, William Penn's grandson, John Penn, became the sole proprietor and governor. It was he who faced the brunt of the revolutionary forces generated much earlier. Stronger and abler men than the later Penns might have weathered better the storms of the period and it is certain that had William Penn himself lived and exerted his influence throughout the colonial era the history of the times might well have been different. The best indication of this is that Penn's great charter of 1701 withstood the political battles of the era despite the rise of new issues and new factions or parties in colonial government. Indeed, it became the foundation for Pennsylvania's first constitution as a state in 1776. Fortunate indeed was it

that Pennsylvania had developed thus early so solid a framework for democratic government, one which could survive and adjust itself to the winds of political controversy, even when they raged most gustily.

PENNSYLVANIA GROWS

Back of the political controversy and the issues of the period were certain factors connected with the growth of Penn's commonwealth which need to be touched upon briefly as a basis for their understanding. In the first place, Pennsylvania was growing in population at a very rapid pace. Next to the last colony to be founded, it was by 1750 third largest in population, led by Virginia and Massachusetts; by 1776 it was probably second only to Virginia, though accurate figures are not available for that day. This rapid growth was in large part due to the attractive social climate offered by Penn's province for persons who sought some relief from persecutions in Europe. Certainly the idea of a government "where the Laws rule, and the people are a Party to those Laws" appealed to many, as did Quaker pacifism, which meant the absence of a compulsory military service, something to which most Europeans were then subjected.

The climate of freedom which prevailed in Pennsylvania under Penn developed at a time when England actually preferred the royal colony with greater control from London. It was a climate which attracted people seeking freedom from outright oppression, but Penn also was active in soliciting immigrants during his lifetime who were persons of means and members of the upper class in Europe. Conditions of freedom of thought and religion made it possible for the individual to develop culturally and intellectually in colonial Pennsylvania. Here there was no fear of the printing press, such as was expressed by the royal governor of Virginia, nor was there the persecution of persons of a dissenting faith so common to New England and which forced Roger Williams to found Rhode Island. All of these factors produced what for colonial times was a population explosion in Pennsylvania. The numbers of people who flowed into the port of Philadelphia and who spread out in lands then available became very large for those times.

The rapid growth of Pennsylvania was reflected in the equally rapid development of Philadelphia. As early as 1750 it could boast of its position as the largest city in all English colonies with its nearly eighteen thousand people. By the eve of the Revolution it had more than doubled its population and was not only the largest city in the colonies, but pressing all cities in England with the exception of London as the largest in the British empire. It quickly became a great center of commerce, both foreign and domestic. The Swedish missionary, the Reverend Israel Acrelius, in 1754 counted 117 large ships anchored in the Delaware in one day. They were loading or unloading cargoes coming from or going to all the seven seas. They were bringing to the colonies the manufactures and other products of Europe, especially England, and taking out the furs, foodstuffs, lumber, and wood products of the colony. Many were engaged in distributing some of these products to other colonial ports in domestic trade. At the same time, Philadelphia was building in its busy shipyards along the Delaware many of the vessels in which these goods were carried. Great mercantile houses arose as a consequence of this trade. A lucrative inland trade soon emerged. Shopkeepers and artisans flourished, meeting the needs of a growing city with growing wealth.

The social and political consequences of this activity were several. Philadelphia became overwhelmingly dominant in Pennsylvania affairs as the center of its government and its most powerful single economic influence, that of the mercantile class. Indeed, wealth from trade and commerce rather than landholdings was the source of distinction and social and political influence and power in colonial Pennsylvania. Class distinctions soon emerged between the "grandees" of Philadelphia, mostly Quaker merchants, and lower levels of artisan, shopkeeper, and ordinary workers. These were reflected not merely in social distinction as measured by wealth and scale of living but in the politics of the time where many of the "lower classes" were disenfranchised by the requirement of ownership of fifty acres of land or fifty pounds worth of other property for voting.

The speed with which Pennsylvania's population grew had another very important consequence and that was a rapid expansion of the interior frontier. It is questionable whether any other single colony experienced either so quick or so extensive an expansion of the frontiers of original settlement on the Atlantic coast and the rivers, which usually reached only a short distance inland. While this will be treated more fully later, it is important here to note that the first county created outside Penn's original three was Lancaster County in 1729. The town of Lancaster, laid out a year later in 1730, was soon a thriving interior colonial town. By 1750 settlement had reached beyond the Susquehanna on the route west and into the upper Schuylkill, Delaware, and Lehigh valley regions in sufficient numbers to demand erecting new counties. Along with the counties went such new towns as Reading, Easton, and York. By the approach of the Revolution, the latest of the recent frontier counties, Westmoreland, had its limits west of the Alleghenies. Indeed, Pennsylvania had created within its limits the first transmountain American frontier.

GROWTH CREATES PROBLEMS

The influences of this growth on colonial politics and problems of government was far reaching. One of the most immediate was that of the policy relative to distribution of the land. Penn himself favored, as might be expected, a policy of rather liberal disposal of land to individual settlers, though his instinct as a country gentleman and large holder of land in his own right led him to attempt to preserve certain large units as colonial "manors." Over seventy of these manors, each consisting of a reservation of 10,000 acres in every 100,000 and "which shall lie in one place," were created in colonial times, starting with Pennsbury Manor on the Delaware of 8,431 acres for Penn's personal country estate. This was in agreement with Penn's original charter but in actual practice became virtually meaningless in the development of the province, despite the fact that the theory of the reserved manor was extended even into the latest counties formed prior to 1776.

Penn sold land even before his arrival in the amount of over 300,000 acres, mostly to Quakers, and in properties averaging about 5,000 acres. The lands were not surveyed at the time but were to be settled within three years after a survey was made, resulting in much confusion and irritation as men of more modest means and desires sought to own land. After Penn's arrival, a land office was opened in Philadelphia and Thomas Holme began his survey of the lands in the province. Penn's price was five pounds per hundred acres for small holders, plus one shilling quitrent annually. Penn's sons were more grasping and in 1732 Thomas Penn reorganized the land office and tripled the price of land per acre to fifteen and a half pounds, and made the quitrent a halfpenny per acre. The quitrent was a survival of the feudal theory that all holders of land were leaseholders rather than freeholders and indirectly tenants of the king, or in this instance of the proprietor, for whom the rent was collected. Pennsylvania settlers paid little attention to it and from the start collection of the quitrent from individual farmers was impossible. It was, however, a source of irritation.

Speculators in western lands, mainly Philadelphians, looked with favor upon a higher price and tighter regulation of land disposal, but such was not the view of the pioneer settler. Enforcement of land law was next to impossible on a rapidly expanding frontier where settlers were inclined to pull up stakes and move from one location to another every few years. Even the most prosperous farmer on a new frontier was apt to get the urge within a decade or so to move to where the grass appeared to be greener farther westward. Taking up land without purchase and clear title by simply "squatting" on it became common on the part of land-hungry pioneers. As early as 1740 it was estimated that some 400,000 acres were occupied by "squatters" and efforts to collect payment from them were resisted with force. By 1750 "settlement rights," known on the frontier as "tomahawk rights" because of the settler's practice of laying out a claim by blazing the surrounding trees, were forced upon the pro-

prietors by the political power created by the growth of settlement, which broke down niceties of land purchase through prior purchase of titles. Under this new policy the rights of a settler created by actual occupation and clearing of land were recognized as having priority when it came to purchase. Of course, the frontiersman was supposed still to buy the land but it was a first triumph of agrarian democracy in the long history of the American frontier and won over opposing eastern interests. At no time after 1750 were the opportunities for liberal acquisition of land by individual farmer-settlers seriously threatened, though the land policy remained an underlying issue between eastern and western counties in the politics of the colonial era and a source of friction in the Revolutionary movement in Pennsylvania.

Frontier defense and Indian policy were related issues in colonial politics which can be attributed mainly to the expansion of settlement. Penn in his lifetime, with population confined to the lower Delaware, solved the Indian problem by peaceful purchase of their lands. The first real crack in this half-century-old policy of amity and friendship came in 1737 with the Walking Purchase. The story of the purchase is well known and does not bear repeating in all its details. Actually, the action confirmed an arrangement made as early as 1686 through which the proprietor had acquired by treaty additional lands along a boundary parallel to the Delaware River and running inland as far as a man could walk in a day and a half. The provincial authorities carefully laid out the route and employed walkers who actually ran rather than walked, and covered some sixty miles, about twice the normal distance. A large group of hitherto peaceful Delawares eventually were forced from their historic homes onto lands on the upper Susquehanna. Subsequent land acquisitions were made by treaty but the old confidence which had prevailed in the days of William Penn disappeared as agents of the proprietors failed to convince the Indians of the complete integrity of their proposals. It must be said in defense of the Penns that the rapidity with which the frontier was biting into large sections of the interior greatly aggravated the problem of Indian relations and land purchases. In the first place, the proprietors were pushed faster than would normally have been the case to clear interior Pennsylvania of Indian claims and occupation. A large purchase was made in 1749 clearing much of central Pennsylvania for white settlements. Others were made in 1754, 1758 and the last in 1768 with the Treaty of Fort Stanwix clearing a large area running diagonally from the northeastern to the southwestern boundary of the province and leaving only northwestern Pennsylvania in Indian hands, about one-third of the province. Within less than twenty years nearly two-thirds of the total area of Pennsylvania was wrested from its Indian inhabitants in answer to the voracious demand of white settlers for more land. The Quaker element so strongly entrenched in the Assembly had little heart for this action but it was not consulted by the governors except to provide necessary funds for Indian conferences.

A stronger basis for antagonism between eastern and western interests was provided by the problem of protection of the rapidly expanded frontier. Prior to the 1750's and actual attack upon the province by French and Indians, this was an issue involving the efforts of the British to enlist colonial support in the long series of imperial conflicts in which England became involved in building the British Empire. William Penn was held responsible for the failure of Pennsylvania to do its part in aiding the mother country, and it was a factor in his temporary loss of the control of government. He was restored to full governmental powers on the condition that this would be remedied. Strong Quaker pacifism in control of the Assembly made this a difficult condition to fulfill by either Penn or his successors. Battles over this issue were fairly common even in the royal colonies with royal governors, and so it is not surprising that it arose in Pennsylvania with its Quakers. By 1740 Deputy Governor George Thomas, backed by Thomas Penn, was battling for money and recruits to aid the English and were meeting resistance. When King George's War began in 1744, England again called for aid in its struggle with both France and Spain. The Quakers again resisted on the ground that the province itself actually had no problem of defense. It did appropriate funds for the provisioning of

an English garrison at Lewisburg, though it had earlier refused to contribute funds for the expedition. When French privateers actually appeared in the Delaware in 1747 the Quaker Assembly refused even to fit out a ship to defend Philadelphia. A group of merchants finally raised the money to protect their own shipping.

Benjamin Franklin, based on a print from the Duplessis portrait.

FRANKLIN AND WILLIAM ALLEN

This deplorable situation gave rise to the first great public service rendered by Benjamin Franklin. By this time Franklin was starting to emerge as, among other things, an extremely clever political figure. He demonstrated that astute knowledge of popular reactions which stood him in such good stead in his career as a political leader and diplomat by devising a plan for colonial defense which appealed to the moderates among the citizenry. As Richard Peters said, it was a plan which fell "fowl of the Quakers & their opposers equally" but was designed "to animate all the middling persons to undertake their own defense in opposition to the Quakers & the Gentlemen." The proposal centered on the organization of volunteer "Associations" for defense whose members became known as the "Associators." It was the direct ancestor of the National Guard idea. There were moderates even among the Quakers and Franklin won many of these to support his scheme by publishing one of his innumerable pamphlets, *Plain Truth or Serious Considerations,* which included extracts from writings of Quakers which approved of self-defense measures when attacked. A petition was directed to the Assembly for financial aid, and about one-fourth of the signers were Quakers. But the Assembly did not budge. Franklin was forced to resort to lotteries to raise the money and with it the Association bought cannon and located batteries to protect the city. The idea was successful enough to raise about ten thousand men in a year. Since it was not only a volunteer organization but all officers below the rank of colonel were elected by the associators and these officers in turn elected the colonel, it was an exercise in democracy applied to the basic problem of home defense. Indeed, it would appear that Franklin thereby set the standard of practice for the American volunteer armies of later date. While the most immediate problem was the defense of Philadelphia, the Association appealed widely to the German and Scotch-Irish population which was beginning to settle the interior and from which most of the volunteers were drawn. It became a lasting part of the Pennsylvania preparedness system through the remainder of the colonial wars and made the volunteer militia system even later an important part of Pennsylvania life.

Even as it was founded, Franklin's Association attracted the attention of political rivals who saw it as more than a device for preparedness. The Quakers who were not moderates opposed the idea because of their deep-seated pacifism. By 1750 the Scotch-Irish in particular were showing signs of political sensitivity; more so than the German farmers. The great leader of the Scotch-Irish Presbyterians, with whom the Anglicans were associated politically against the dominant Quaker element, became William Allen. Allen was born in Philadelphia in 1704 and educated in England. He returned in 1725 as a result of the death of his father, and found himself already a wealthy man in terms of mercantile and landed interests. The youthful Allen was a real entrepreneur in his own

William Allen, leader of the conservatives.

right and added rapidly to this fortune. His political enemies claimed much of this added wealth came from illegal trade with the French, but in any event he fast became a very wealthy man. He married into the famous Hamilton family and was the brother-in-law of James Hamilton, twice deputy governor. One of his daughters later married John Penn. His mansion at Mount Airy was nearly the equal of James Logan's home, Stenton, as a place of beauty and a center of culture. He loaned money to the province to erect the State House (Independence Hall) and supported almost as many institutions of learning and science as did Benjamin Franklin, though his name has never received nearly as much attention in history. Allen was elected mayor of Philadelphia in 1735. Legally trained, he was appointed chief justice of Pennsylvania in 1751 and served until 1774. His influence with the proprietors, naturally, was very great.

Franklin, though accused of playing politics in founding the Association, did not enter battle with Allen at this time. In general, Franklin by 1750 had emerged as a new leader of the democratic forces represented by the majority of the colonial population. To Thomas Penn he appeared as "a dangerous man" and an "uneasy spirit," though Penn recognized that Franklin as a "sort of tribune of the people" must be "treated with regard." The makings of strong resistance to the proprietor and to the political power of men of wealth like William Allen were well established.

In November, 1748, Pennsylvania-born James Hamilton became deputy governor. He was of Scotch extraction and an Episcopalian in religion. He had served in the Assembly, as a member of Council, and as mayor of Philadelphia. His instincts were those of fierce conservatism defending the rights of property and the proprietor. By this time another of the issues of the east against the frontier had arisen in Pennsylvania and it was one which would have a long history in American politics. Early Pennsylvania was growing so rapidly it suffered from a lack of money. Gold and silver were drained off by the unfavorable trade balance with England. In 1723 the Assembly approved issuing 45,000 pounds in paper money called bills of credit. Despite opposition from the proprietary interests, as well as the British government, the amount of paper money was gradually increased. The debtor and frontier interests in particular liked it and by 1750 it was about the most lively political issue in the colony, with Hamilton trying to keep the lid on more paper money and the growing influence of the popular party demanding a constantly increasing supply. The debtor and frontier interests won out, but Pennsylvania currency, as it became known, had a high value in relation to gold and silver among all the paper monies issued in the colonies.

THE FRENCH INVASION

All the existing normal currents of Pennsylvania affairs were upset by the reopening of the imperial wars which had been raging at intervals between England and France, with other powers involved at various times, in the world-wide struggle for balance of power. When King George's War ended in 1748 Quaker Pennsylvania hopefully looked for "peace in our time." Such was not to be the case. Seeds for a more serious conflict which would directly threaten Pennsylvania for the first time already were being planted. The province had been most successful in preserving its peace up to this time and for a variety of reasons. Quaker efforts to treat the Indians fairly and justly had combined with the fact that neighboring Delawares were a peaceful people and the warlike Susquehannocks had been annihilated by the Iroquois to prevent any Indian wars. England's wars had produced only one temporary direct threat to the province. Hence, Pennsylvania had enjoyed not only peace but an existence without armies or forts. This was another side of the peaceable kingdom which now suffered a rude shock.

By 1740 a serious conflict of interest between France and England involving western Pennsylvania was in the making. French traders began to enter that region more or less regularly before that date. They also encouraged settlement there by Shawnee Indians from eastern Pennsylvania whose lands had been lost to Pennsylvania settlement. French missionaries worked with the Indians increasingly and the French outpost at Fort Niagara became a major base for these French activities. France, it should be remembered, claimed all of this territory on a basis of explorations by La Salle. As time passed, the French also sensed more and more the importance of this earlier somewhat forgotten Ohio country as a key region in terms of connecting their existing centers of strength in Canada, the Illinois country, and Louisiana, by control of the Ohio and Mississippi rivers.

The Baron de Longueuil in 1739 traversed the area by way of Lake Chautauqua, Conewango Creek, Allegheny and Ohio rivers to join forces with French from Detroit, Illinois, and Louisiana in a campaign against the Chickasaw Indians in northern Mississippi. A young engineer named Chaussegros de Léry made the first map of the country while on this journey and the expedition itself showed how important this territory was to French expansion. In 1749 the French decided to take the step of laying actual claim to the region and sent Pierre Céloron de Blainville with about two hundred soldiers and thirty Indians over the same route covered by de Longueuil. Starting at the junction of Conewango Creek and the Allegheny at the present Warren, Céloron buried the first of several lead plates which proclaimed "the renewal of possession which were taken of the said river Ohio, and of all those which fall into it, and of all the territories on both sides as far as the source of said rivers." This was quite an order in terms of the total territory involved. A metal sign with the coat of arms of the king was put on a tree for the Indians all to see and so on this July 29, 1749, western Pennsylvania was declared the possession of King Louis XV of France. The next day Céloron met with the Indians nine miles down the Allegheny from Warren at Buckaloons, warning them against the English and their traders. Other conferences within Pennsylvania were held, the most important of which was at Logstown near present Ambridge, where three days were spent. The Indian response was more or less noncommittal and even Céloron felt they leaned toward the English because of favorable trade relations. Several English traders encountered on the journey were warned by the Indians to leave the country.

The encounters with English traders pointed up the extent to which traders from Pennsylvania, Maryland, and Virginia had penetrated the region seeking the profitable Indian trade. Along with the desire to link French possessions for military and other reasons went a new awareness on the part of the French of the importance of keeping control of the Indian trade of the vast Ohio country. Every key Indian village had its English traders by 1749 and the French were quick to realize the need for stepping up their own competitive efforts in the Indian trade. The next few years saw French trading posts multiplying in a drive to capture the political and economic advantages attached to successful trade with the Indians, whose allegiance usually followed the best deals offered by the traders.

The French realized also the need for stronger measures than sending more traders with better bargains into the Ohio country. Céloron warned that the Indians "are very badly disposed towards the French, and are entirely devoted to the English." Establishing forts at strategic control points garrisoned with armed men was the method decided upon when Marquis Duquesne arrived at Quebec and became the new governor of New France in July 1752. It was no mean undertaking,

as it involved some two thousand men who must be supplied from the meager resources of New France. The overall commander was a sixty-year veteran, Sieur de Marin. Warehouses, boats, supplies, men—all had to be gathered under the most difficult circumstances at the major base at Fort Niagara. War in a wilderness was a tough, hard business, as the English would also find out a little later. The advance party left Montreal in February and at that time it was planned to use the Chautauqua portage route. Late in March, Duquesne, on a basis of new information as to its safety and resources, decided to continue on Lake Erie to the harbor at Presque Isle, the present Erie, and to build the first fort at this point. Here, wrote Duquesne, was the place which "gives us an easy entrance to the Belle Rivière." The landing in May was made under the command of a young French officer, Charles Deschamps de Boishebert, and he began at once the construction of Fort Presque Isle without awaiting the arrival of Marin and his main force in early June. By July 12 the French, who were moving with great speed, also had started Fort Le Boeuf on Le Boeuf Creek at the present Waterford, having located a portage route of some nineteen miles overland from Presque Isle. Le Boeuf Creek flowed into French Creek a few miles distant, and it in turn emptied into the Allegheny at present Franklin, thus giving the French command of the most distant northwestern headwaters of the Ohio. Fort Le Boeuf was somewhat smaller than Fort Presque Isle. Both were square, with bastions at the corners and built with logs placed upright rather than lengthwise, as was the customary English construction.

Interestingly enough, the first protest against the French invasion did not come from the English but from the lower Allegheny Iroquois, who claimed the region and were traditional foes of the French and bound by trade and treaty with the British. Early in September the picturesque and active Seneca leader who represented the Iroquois in the region, Half King Tanacharison, with some other chiefs arrived at Presque Isle for council. The mission was prompted in part at least by warnings from Pennsylvania's Governor James Hamilton as to French intentions. The Half King in a long and rambling discourse warned the French "only to send there what we need, but not to build any forts there" and that "I shall strike at whoever does not listen to us." The French were unyielding but the end of 1753 brought threats of Iroquois interference with their lines of communication to Canada. This threat, plus illness and unrest among the troops, combined with low water in the creeks to delay French plans to continue their speed in building forts at other control points. Captain Joncaire did reach Venango late in August and captured John Fraser's trading post, turning it into a French outpost. The French at the end of 1753 were about six months behind schedule, despite their vigorous start.

WASHINGTON'S JOURNEY TO FORT LE BOEUF

The delay gave breathing time to Pennsylvania as well as to Virginia, which also claimed the forks of the Ohio and had active trading interests in the region. Governor Hamilton early gave up hope of any action by the Pennsylvania Assembly and called upon Virginia. Governor Dinwiddie was willing to cooperate and tried to arrange for a joint protest which would include New York. Failing, on October 31, 1753, Dinwiddie commissioned twenty-one-year-old George Washington "to visit and deliver a letter to the Commandant of the French forces on the Ohio." Thus began the long years of public service of George Washington of Virginia, many of which were to be spent in Pennsylvania. Washington started the same day at Williamsburg and by December 4 he had called upon Captain Joncaire at Fraser's former trading post. With him were Christopher Gist as guide, his French interpreter, an Indian interpreter, three frontiersmen and four Indians, one of whom was the Half King, who had joined him at Logstown, where Washington had spent some time in conference. He had passed the forks of the Ohio on the way and noted it was "extremely well situated for a fort." On December 7, with four Frenchmen added to the party, he set out for Fort Le Boeuf and arrived there on the eleventh. The next day Washington was presented to Legardeur de Saint-Pierre, French sol-

dier and recent explorer of the Far West. Washington presented Dinwiddie's letter of concern as to the French invasion and his polite request for "your peaceable departure." While awaiting the French reply, Washington carefully observed the fort and put down details of the construction in his carefully kept journal. On the fourteenth, de Saint-Pierre replied saying he must send the letter on to Marquis Dusquesne and deploring that the Virginian had not been authorized to do so himself. "As to the summons you sent me to retire, I do not think myself obliged to obey it," wrote the French commander, denying at the same time that anything had happened which could "be construed as an act of hostility, or as contrary to the treaties between the two Crowns; the continuation of which interests and pleases us as much as it does the English." The French made every effort to win the Indians away from Washington and the promise of liquor and presents did separate them from the party when Washington left Venango on the twenty-third. His journey back to Williamsburg was mostly on foot with Gist as his only companion. On the way he was fired upon by hostile Indians, nearly drowned crossing the Allegheny, and suffered from icy winds and snow in "as fatiguing a Journey as it is possible to conceive." He reached Williamsburg January 16, 1754 and Dinwiddie at once ordered Washington's journal printed for general use.

VIRGINIA TAKES THE INITIATIVE

In Canada Marquis Duquesne treated the Virginia claims on the Belle Rivière as "sheer imagination, for it belongs to us incontestably." He also scoffed at the idea of successful resistance. But the colonials were now willing to contest the issue. A small force of Virginians was sent at once by Dinwiddie to the Forks to build a fort. The French, however, were moving with equal speed and on April 16, 1754, Sieur de Contrecoeur, who had been with Céloron as well as commandant at Fort Niagara, forced the English to surrender. Thereupon he began at once the erection of Fort Duquesne to command the Forks, though the original location had been thought of as Logstown. With the English it was now a case of too

PENNSYLVANIA

little and too late. Washington was on his way back with forces to strengthen the English outpost from the Indians when he learned of the French success. At the same time he learned that a French detachment was on its way to scout his actions. Washington seized the initiative and aided by the Half King and his Indians attacked the French under Jumonville on the morning of May 28 at Jumonville Glen, as it became known, about six miles east of the present Uniontown. Jumonville was killed along with several of his men, and with one exception the others were captured. The cold war was now a hot, shooting war with Washington winning the first round. The French were too powerful, however, and a force from Fort Duquesne besieged Washington's small group, forcing him to surrender on July 4 at Fort Necessity, which he had hastily erected at

March, Braddock having arrived in February. Each regiment was to be recruited to about seven hundred men in the colonies. Braddock was greeted at once with word from Governor Dinwiddie that no aid had been forthcoming from Maryland or Pennsylvania. Maps requested from Governor Morris had not even been received. Provincial recruits appeared even to Virginia's governor as idle and drunken. No supplies had been gathered and no transport organized. Pennsylvania's Governor Morris was forced to write, "Such is the infatuation and obstinacy of the people I have to deal with, or at least their representatives, that even though their country is invaded, yet I could not persuade them to act with vigor at this juncture, or even grant the supply expected by the Crown." Washington was the only man Braddock met who knew anything

Fort Necessity, site of the first battle of the French and Indian War, as restored by the National Park Service in 1954.

Great Meadows in late May and early June. The French and Indian War was not yet a declared war between England and France but it certainly was a shooting affair in western Pennsylvania by the summer of 1754.

BRADDOCK MEETS DEFEAT

London was as slow as Philadelphia to take action in the face of the French invasion. However, early in 1755 British redcoats were placed on the march into the wilderness of western Pennsylvania, commanded by the somewhat pompous but, on the record thus far, able Major General Edward Braddock. A thousand men in two regiments and by no means the best in the British Army began arriving at Hampton Roads in

about the country through which they were to march. Braddock thought he confronted about fifteen miles of wilderness and was dumfounded to learn that over fifty miles of mountain terrain lay between Wills Creek and Fort Duquesne. Governor Morris again wrote of Pennsylvania's failure to aid in its defense "either by establishing a militia or furnishing men, money or provisions."

But the campaign had to get on, and in April the British regulars and the provincial recruits whom Braddock thought "very indifferent men" moved slowly through what seemed to Braddock a "drear and desolate country." The only bright spot for Pennsylvania was Franklin's promise to Braddock that he could secure plenty of wagons from Pennsylvania farmers. Franklin, true to his

52

promise, advertised for "one hundred and fifty waggons, with four horses to each waggon, and fifteen hundred saddle or pack horses" for which he would contract at Lancaster and York. William Franklin was empowered to contract in Cumberland County. Franklin cleverly implied that if these were not forthcoming voluntarily they might be seized as necessary because "the king's business must be done." On May 10 Fort Cumberland was reached. On May 20 ninety sturdy Pennsylvania wagons arrived. Eleven of these from Philadelphia were loaded with a gift of provisions, wine, and spirits for Braddock's mess, thus easing the bitterness against the province in a way that only wily Ben Franklin could have thought up. As of June 8 Braddock had at Wills Creek 2,300 men and the long painful march started into the wooded and mountainous wilderness.

The remainder of the story is well known. The French and their Indian allies watched every move from Fort Duquesne with its meager garrison of some three hundred French regulars and Canadian militia and eight hundred Indians camped outside. It could hardly stand a solid attack, much less a siege. The choice was to wait or to march out and stage what might be a suicide attack on the oncoming redcoats, who kept their solid and conservative English traditional marching patterns even in the wilderness. Washington's efforts to persuade Braddock of the need to take heed of Indian methods of warfare were thrust aside just as earlier had been those of Franklin. On July 7 Braddock reached Turtle Creek. At nearby Fort Duquesne, Captain Beaujeu was determined to advance against him, but was finding difficulty in persuading his Indian allies to go along. Braddock's army crossed and recrossed the winding Monongahela without resistance. The main body crossed with drums beating, the great union of the king's colors flying in the July breeze, and the fifers playing the "Grenadiers' March." They were within six or seven miles of the objective, and Braddock planned to pitch camp in the afternoon and start the attack in the morning. Glorious victory seemed at hand when, a quarter of a mile from the river and with more open country ahead, the advance guides came running back shouting that French and Indians were coming down the

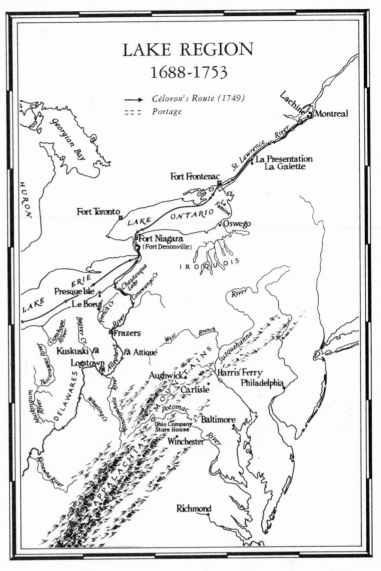

Map of the Great Lakes Region, 1688–1753, showing key points in the French and Indian War.

trail on the run. At the same moment Beaujeu, who was leading his force, saw the red coats of the British grenadiers and waved his French and Indians to scatter into the forest.

The British advance tried to meet the attack the only way they knew how, kneeling and firing blindly into the woods. Beaujeu went down, though the British did not know it, and the battle was almost won by Braddock as Canadians and Indians wavered. But the French and Indians rallied and continued to pour a crossfire into the

British from higher ground. The disorganized grenadiers fell away. Braddock ordered his main force into regular positions but retreating men backed into them and added to the confusion. Washington tried in vain to persuade Braddock to scatter his men and fight out of the exposed rigid formations. By four o'clock half of his officers and men were killed or wounded and four horses had been shot from under Braddock as he sought to rally his forces. As he was about to mount a fifth, he fell fatally wounded. The battle was soon over and the triumphant French and Indians, who had expected so little, found they had won much. The British retreated in disorder, never again even to try to rally their forces. The ill-starred general was left in a hidden grave in the western Pennsylvania wilderness. A truly gigantic effort had failed because of stubborn adherence to European military tactics in a wilderness battle.

PENNSYLVANIA DEFENDS ITS FRONTIER

The war was now brought to the Pennsylvania home front. Even before the Braddock defeat Indians had started to stage raids on the western frontier. By October the red men were raiding as far east as Snyder County at Penn's Creek, where some twenty-six settlers were killed, wounded, or captured. The raiders swept even farther to the east and Philadelphia itself began to fear attack. The frontier was entirely defenseless, thanks to the policies of the Assembly in Philadelphia. Despite the clamor from the frontier for protection, the Assembly still delayed, trusting the faithful Delawares would keep the peace. When the Delawares, led by the great Teedyuscung, so long a friend of the whites, launched the fiercest attacks of all on the settlements of the northern frontier, action was forthcoming. Governor Morris with support of council literally declared war on the Delawares and Shawnees, offering a bounty for scalps. Angry frontiersmen marched on Philadelphia demanding relief for their losses, and the Assembly finally voted £65,000 for the purpose with 50,000 of it in paper money. The Penns contributed another £5,000 to avoid a tax on their estates. Franklin revived the Associators.

In the 1756 elections feeling was strong enough to reduce Quaker representation in the Assembly from twenty-six to twelve and stronger measures were taken. Out of the crisis came the frontier forts of Pennsylvania. Between 1756 and 1763 some two hundred defense bastions, ranging from full-scale forts erected at provincial expense to armed stone and log structures—often used also for other purposes, but now fitted with openings from which guns could be fired and garrisoned by home militia—made their appearance on the frontier. Most of the forts were located at strategic points guarding gaps through which Indian paths led from the west or north into central Pennsylvania. The entire region from the Susquehanna to the Delaware was thus given protection. Conrad Weiser was commissioned late in 1755 to coordinate these defenses and was followed by military men like Colonel James Burd.

Much of the program revolved around a home- or civilian-defense plan utilizing local militia at strategic points to defend the frontier. Groups of rangers numbering from sixteen to sixty men garrisoned forts, depending upon their size, and smaller bodies of armed men scouted the surrounding region. Franklin had a hand in developing the provincial fort system. Among the major provincial forts were Fort Littleton near McConnellsburg, Fort Shirley in Huntingdon County, Fort Granville at the present Lewistown, Fort Bedford at Raystown, Fort Loudon near Chambersburg and Fort Hunter at Harris' Ferry. Forts Hamilton, Hyndshaw and Norris were built in the upper Delaware area along with Fort Allen north of the Lehigh, Fort Lebanon, Fort Henry, Fort Morris at Shippensburg and Fort Swatara in central Pennsylvania. By far the largest and most powerful of these forts was Fort Augusta, built at the present Sunbury, commanding the junction of the two branches of the Susquehanna. It had four bastions and four outlying blockhouses and was well armed with cannon.

There were other forts too numerous to mention. Along with the forts went another departure from previous practice; the province by the supply act of November, 1755, which made possible the building of the forts, also provided for enlisted and paid troops. The first such troops were militia taken into provincial service; this began in

Northampton County late in 1755. The added financial burden provoked a new political issue over taxing of the proprietary estates. An estate tax was levied in 1755 but carefully exempted the Penns in consideration of a gift of money. By 1759 taxes levied on estates included the Penns. Altogether between 1755 and 1760 the province appropriated £490,000 for military purposes, a revolutionary change in policy produced by actual war.

Besides these measures, Pennsylvania struck directly at the Indians in the west with a force of some three hundred Pennsylvania troops led by Colonel John Armstrong. Based at Fort Shirley on the upper Juniata, in August Armstrong began his march from there and on September 7, 1756, fell upon the great Indian village of Kittanning on the Allegheny. Armstrong destroyed the village and the surrounding crop lands, a crippling blow at this time of the year. These combined measures almost completely subdued the Indians and led to a series of treaty councils promoted by such Quaker leaders as Israel Pemberton, who still clung to the idea of peaceful coexistence. The most notable of these gatherings was held at Easton in 1758 and it did quiet the Delawares under Teedyuscung.

FORBES AND BOUQUET

During the period following the Braddock disaster Pennsylvania actually was without any protection from a British army and in 1756 and 1757 it indeed did a rather good job of defending itself, in view of previous laxity in this respect. For a time it appeared that Great Britain had given up any hope of dislodging the French in western Pennsylvania and indeed, in view of the lack of support the colonies had given the Braddock expedition, it might well have been justified. In 1757 the situation changed as the great William Pitt became Prime Minister and set about a vigorous and thorough overhauling of empire policy. Pitt prepared at once to send a powerful army to the colonies to contest and if possible break the power of France. Brigadier General John Forbes was placed in command of the southern district to move against Fort Duquesne. This time it was decided wisely to use Pennsylvania as the base for

operations. The point of organization early in 1758 was Carlisle, while Fort Bedford and Fort Ligonier became fortified stepping stones to the west. British regulars to the number of 1,600 arriving by way of Philadelphia were combined with some four thousand militia from Virginia and Pennsylvania. Colonel George Washington commanded the Virginians and Colonel John Armstrong the 2,700 Pennsylvanians. Both were experienced in frontier warfare. Forbes soon became ill and had to be carried on a litter much of the way, but his second in command was probably the shrewdest commander ever to serve under the British flag in the colonies—Colonel Henry Bouquet.

Colonel Henry Bouquet, hero of Bushy Run.

Forbes confronted the same problems of transport as had Braddock. Horses and wagons were scarce and expensive on the frontier yet tons of supplies must be moved for the army. The fifteen shillings a day offered for a four-horse team and driver was not considered enough. By May Bouquet was as exasperated as his predecessors, since civil authority to enforce warrants was almost nonexistent in the frontier counties. However, the army did get under way, following as

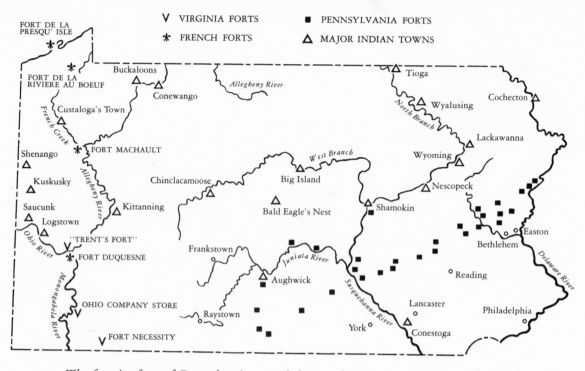

VIRGINIA FORTS   PENNSYLVANIA FORTS
FRENCH FORTS   MAJOR INDIAN TOWNS

FORT DE LA PRESQU' ISLE

FORT DE LA RIVIERE AU BOEUF

Buckaloons

Conewango

Allegheny River

Tioga

Cochecton

Wyalusing

Custaloga's Town

North Branch

Lackawanna

French Creek

Shenango

FORT MACHAULT

West Branch

Wyoming

Chinclacamoose

Big Island

Nescopeck

Kuskusky

Allegheny River

Kittanning

Bald Eagle's Nest

Shamokin

Saucunk

Logstown

"TRENT'S FORT"

FORT DUQUESNE

Ohio River

Frankstown

Juniata River

Easton

Bethlehem

Reading

OHIO COMPANY STORE

Monongahela River

Aughwick

Susquehanna River

Lancaster

Philadelphia

FORT NECESSITY

Raystown

York

Conestoga

The frontier forts of Pennsylvania erected during the French and Indian War era.

closely as possible the Raystown Indian and traders' path from Carlisle as widened by axmen under Bouquet. At Shippensburg the path forked and Forbes took the one with lightest grades leading to frontier Fort Loudon and crossing the Tuscaroras at Cowan's Gap. From this point his march led to Fort Littleton, then to Bedford and Ligonier. Forts Littleton and Bedford had been built by Pennsylvania as part of its chain of frontier defenses and with their connecting roadways through the wilderness made the passage of General Forbes much easier and faster than that of Braddock. The army's route cut from Fort Ligonier toward the present Greensburg and thence to Fort Duquesne, avoiding the difficult river crossing of Braddock.

Major Grant was sent ahead with eight hundred men to scout the French and destroy Indian camps, but was discovered, captured, and defeated within the limits of present Pittsburgh. Forbes and Bouquet were not to be denied and pressed ahead to find that the French had abandoned and burned the fort, retreating to their outposts on the upper Allegheny. On November 25, 1768, Forbes took over the smoking ruins of Fort

Duquesne and sat down to compose a letter to William Pitt from "Pittsburg" telling the Prime Minister of his success and his intention to name the place and the new English fort after the man whose vision and determination had at long last settled the issue. Out of the ruins of Fort Duquesne soon arose what was probably the most powerful fortress in colonial America—Fort Pitt. The forks of the Ohio were now a part of the British Empire beyond recall and an English-rooted civilization was determined for North America.

THE PONTIAC UPRISING

Frontier troubles were not ended, despite this triumph. The western Indians were mobilized in 1763 under the shrewd and able leadership of Pontiac, chief of the Ottawas, in a last desperate effort to dislodge the whites from their encroachments upon the Ohio country. Every English outpost was overwhelmed all the way to Fort Pitt and it was in danger when Colonel Henry Bouquet marched out from Carlisle, starting July 23, with five hundred of the finest in the British army to save the day. At Edge Hill, near the present Jeanette, on August 5 the ferocity of Pontiac's finest warriors fell upon Bouquet's force, who were outnumbered three to one. The battle raged all day; Bouquet's men fought from behind a barricade of flour bags hastily thrown up on a rise of ground. That night Bouquet wrote from his camp "26 Miles from Fort Pitt" to Sir Jeffrey Amherst, "we were attacked from every side, and the savages exerted themselves with uncommon resolution" and that "we expect to begin at daybreak," expressing fears for his success. The next morning the Indians attacked early "shouting and yelling" around the entire embattled British line. A clever flanking maneuver finally routed the Indians, and that evening from the new camp site a mile away Bouquet reported, "The behavior of the troops on this occasion, speaks for itself so strongly, that for me to attempt their eulogium would not detract from their merit." The American Indian rarely recovered from a major reverse and this proved true in 1763, for Bouquet marched forward from near defeat to relieve Fort Pitt and save the Pennsylvania frontier from complete annihilation. His expedition later continued into the Ohio region and effectively ended for the time Indian resistance to frontier expansion. The grateful province recognized him by official act of assembly as an honorary citizen of Pennsylvania.

AFTER THE FRENCH AND INDIAN WAR

The end of the French and Indian War and Bouquet's victory at Bushy Run and in the Ohio country gave the green light to the movement of pioneers into the West. As early as 1760, some settlers were moving west of the Alleghenies though Indian claims had not yet been cleared. The growth of population west of the mountains began to stir anew the cauldron of provincial politics. The western settlements began to complain they were not represented adequately in the Assembly at Philadelphia, as indeed they weren't. Most of the frontiersmen were "wild Irish," as the Scotch-Irish were sometimes called by easterners, and they had little use for any Indian whether peaceful or on the warpath. Eastern

dominated Indian policy was not viewed with favor in western Pennsylvania which had been face to face with raiding Indians. Threats to the safety of peaceful Indians Christianized by the Moravians at Bethlehem led the authorities to remove them to Philadelphia for protection. The smoke of the French and Indian War had hardly cleared when in the late autumn of 1763 frontiersmen from near Harrisburg fell upon a few Conestoga Indians, mostly women and children and remnants of the Susquehannocks living near Lancaster, and massacred all of them, even invading the Lancaster jail to do so. The Paxton Boys, as the leaders were known, decided to march on Philadelphia when the Quakers in the Assembly proposed to bring the perpetrators of the Conestoga massacre to trial. Knowledge that the Philadelphians were protecting some one hundred of the "Moravian" Indians while the frontier itself was left unprotected added to the indignation of radicals among the frontiersmen. Over five hundred settlers constituting virtually a revolutionary mob did march on Philadelphia but their ardor cooled when on approaching the city they found themselves ordered to disperse in the King's name under penalty of death and faced three companies of the Royal Americans. Ben Franklin and Colonel John Armstrong, hero of the Indian wars, met the radicals at Germantown, listened to their complaints and persuaded them to return home, the number now having dwindled to about two hundred men. High among complaints presented to Franklin and which he promised would receive the attention of the Assembly were lack of protection of the frontier and unequal representation. The existing situation was declared "oppressive, unequal, and unjust, the cause of many of our Grievances." Taxation without representation had thus become a battle cry in Pennsylvania long before 1774.

The net result of the situation was to increase opposition to the proprietors. In the resulting gyrations strange political bedfellows often slept together. The Quaker element led the fight against the proprietary form of government in favor of a royal colony. This was the age of the pamphleteer, and political pamphlets flowed freely from both conservative and liberal forces.

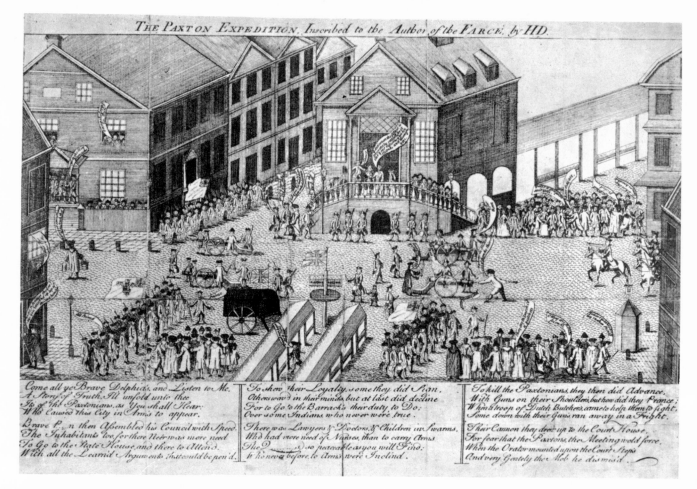

*Political cartoon based on the controversy aroused by
the march of the Paxton Boys on Philadelphia.*

Wily Ben Franklin became the acknowledged leader of the liberal or antiproprietary party. The aging William Allen remained the leader of the conservative forces and characterized Franklin as having "Republican, Anarchial Notions." Allen's party was made up mainly of Presbyterians and Anglicans and was often called the Presbyterian Party. Through the period from 1764 to 1774 Franklin emerged not only as the leader of the antiproprietary element but as one of the shrewdest political leaders in the history of Pennsylvania. In 1764 Franklin was sent to England as the Assembly's agent to seek shifting of the government to the crown. He was not long in learning that sentiment in London was against the change, and the petition he carried with him was never offi-

cially presented. The Penns had more influence with the ministry than was generally thought. The question of what form of government should prevail was soon overshadowed by the controversy over the Stamp Act and succeeding efforts of England to wring some revenues from the colonies to help pay for having saved them against the French. Feeling was strong in Pennsylvania against all these measures. The general trend of colonial politics during the decade was a mounting pressure for more representation in the Assembly from the newer counties and greater recognition of their interests as expressed in legislation. A seed ground for the revolutionary movement was being laid and even well cultivated prior to 1774.

58

CHAPTER FOUR

THE PEOPLING OF
PENNSYLVANIA

Other than the quality of the land itself and its natural resources, no other factor is more important in determining the destiny of a state or a nation than the character of the people who make up its population. Indeed, it was the people who had to make use of these resources who were the most basic factor in determining the future of Pennsylvania after its founding by William Penn. This was true in terms of not only the rapid increase in its population but also the nature of the people who came to early Pennsylvania as settlers.

Burke in his *European Settlements in America* wrote in 1761, "In some years more people have transported themselves to Pennsylvania than to all the other settlements together." Burke cited to prove his point that there were 6,208 immigrants in 1729 and over 5,000 in 1750. When Penn came, a mere handful of people were clustered along the lower Delaware but by 1740 the population was estimated as 100,000. By 1760 it had doubled; by 1776 it was at least 300,000. This great migration took place in the face of the difficulties of Atlantic crossing in those days with sadly overcrowded ships, poor food, and at the time almost inhuman treatment of the poorer classes of Europeans who took to ship to find a new way of life in Pennsylvania. In 1732 on one ship alone no less than one hundred of 150 Germans perished before reaching Philadelphia. Many Scotch-Irish suffered in the same way.

WHY DID THEY COME?

There were many factors which influenced Europeans to come to Pennsylvania, and debate still continues as to the motivating force behind certain groups. Three main forces, however, are easily detected and they influenced just about equally the different religious, ethnic, or national groups that contributed to peopling Pennsylvania. The desire for religious freedom was certainly very high on the list of those advantages sought by the early settlers. The first of these in large numbers were Quakers and it was to provide them with a haven that Penn had sought his province. Quakers in England, however, were certainly not the victims of as vicious religious persecution as were dissenters in most parts of the Continent.

The bulk of the Quaker settlers came from the English lower classes and they may well have been as interested in economic opportunity as in greater freedom of worship. Certainly Penn himself advertised his province widely in Europe more in terms of its promise as a land flowing with opportunity and productivity than as a religious refuge. In one pamphlet Penn literally guaranteed that an immigrant could buy 500 acres and for about £100 or less move his family and two servants to Pennsylvania and end up with some profit the second year. This must have looked very attractive to a poor European farmer or city dweller who at the same time may have been a member of a religious sect not tolerated by the current ruler.

As Pennsylvania grew and conditions in the province became more widely known through exchange of letters between early settlers and relatives in the Old World, as well as by accounts of contemporary observers who put their observations on paper for others to read, the decisions that were made to come to Pennsylvania may well have been influenced more largely by other factors than religion. Relief from political persecution sometimes has been cited as an important influence leading people to seek refuge in Pennsylvania. Persecution of this type, so far as it affected the individual in terms of harm to his person or even interference with personal liberty, was not usual in eastern Europe at the end of the eighteenth century. Lack of representation in any way in the government, denial of the right of trial by jury, which Penn had fought himself in England, involuntary military service for the prince or king, and a general lack of freedom of expression were, however, common in Europe. Pennsylvania under Penn's liberal charters and the added rights won gradually by the Assembly offered a genuine contrast. Here prisons were not used as places for cruel and unusual punishments. It was rather easy to accumulate enough land to become a voter and take part in a representative form of government and even to become a part of the governing machinery as an elected official. There was no compulsory military service. Basic civil liberties were guaranteed even to an Indian. All of these were freedoms enjoyed by Pennsylvanians to a degree which certainly were quite attractive to many Europeans.

The economic advantages of Pennsylvania likewise became more obvious as early propaganda was replaced by later fact. Of course not every immigrant found life as happy as expected, but in general the accounts of settlers as sent back home were such as to arouse interest in this new land. As Benjamin Franklin wrote in 1760, there were in that day in Pennsylvania "few people so miserable as the poor of Europe, there are also very few [who] in Europe would be called rich; it is rather a happy mediocrity that prevails." In Pennsylvania, wrote Franklin, if a man "has any useful art, he is welcome." Land, Franklin pointed out, was cheap and a hundred acres of fertile land could be had for a small sum and near the settled parts of the province. "Multitudes of poor people from England, Scotland, Ireland, and Germany, have by these means, in a few years become wealthy farmers, who, in their own countries where all the lands are fully occupied, and the wages of labor low, could never have emerged from the poor condition wherein they were born," wrote Franklin in as succinct an explanation of what Pennsylvania offered the average lower-class European in terms of opportunity as could be penned. In addition, Penn's province was blessed by peace on the Indian frontier for over half a century following its founding and an opportunity rapidly to expand its area available for settlement.

THE MELTING POT

The natural result of this welcoming attitude to all of Europe, this combination of a freedom and opportunity unknown in the Old World, made Pennsylvania America's first great melting pot. Varied ethnic, religious, and national groups combined to bring to Penn's province a diversity of talents and abilities with which to develop the fullest potential of a colony already blessed with rich resources. One result was a considerable variety of opinion reflected in early and later Pennsylvania politics. Most newcomers were severely critical of any policy which tended to restrict their freedom, and at the same time pushed for even more democracy in the affairs of the province. In short, those who came in search of freedom helped create a climate and a ferment of freedom. Little wonder that George Washington wrote after the Revolution that Pennsylvania "has become the general receptacle of foreigners from all countries and of all descriptions, many of whom take an active part in the politics of the state; and coming over full of prejudice against their government—some against all governments —you will be enabled without any comment of mine to draw your own inference of their conduct." Washington was commenting of course as a basic conservative and a Virginia aristocrat. Washington and many other contemporary observers overlooked the fact that by no means all of those who came to Pennsylvania in search of new freedom and opportunity were "have nots" or members of the lowest classes in European society of the times. Many, if indeed not a majority, were representatives of Europe's new middle class of free farmers, artisans and skilled workers in various crafts, or small merchants and businessmen. Despite the numbers who came to Pennsylvania as indentured servants, the colony never had as large a strictly servant class as did Virginia or Maryland. Studies of emigration of various groups reveal clearly that in few cases were those who came to Pennsylvania the dregs of Europe's population, which was not true in royal colonies such as Georgia, where forced emigration was sometimes used to increase the population.

In evaluating the character of the people who came to Pennsylvania in those early days it is well also to recognize that dissent in European countries was something which took more than ordinary courage and intelligence, whatever form that dissent might take. The dumb and driven peasant still feeling the yoke of feudalism was not apt to be a dissenter. William Penn was himself an example of a man of learning and substance who led dissent and there were many like him who found their way to Pennsylvania, either from Europe or from other colonies. Men of not only considerable substance but also of high intellect appear among those who helped shape Pennsylvania's early years before the province itself gave birth to such men. Such persons as Francis Daniel Pastorius, James Logan, Benjamin Franklin and many of the leading Quaker merchants and political leaders of the early province, including the Norris, the Shippen, Carpenter, and Richardson families, were among those who came as immigrants. Penn personally welcomed to his colony those "that have eye to the Good of Posterity,

and that both understand and delight to promote good Discipline and just Government among a plain and well intending people." The result of Penn's ideal was such that the Reverend Jacob Duché observed in the *Pennsylvania Journal* of March 25, 1756: "The people of this Province are generally of the middling sort. . . . They are industrious Farmers, Artificers, or Men of Trade; they enjoy and are fond of Freedom, and the meanest among them thinks he has a Right to Civility from the greatest."

THE QUAKERS AND THE ENGLISH

It was quite natural that the heaviest settlement following the founding of Pennsylvania should be from Quaker sources. Not all of these were English. The so-called Welsh Barony was settled by Welsh Quakers and Germantown by German Quakers, along with a scattering of Mennonites. Pastorius, founder of Germantown, was himself a Lutheran converted after his arrival to Quakerism. There were even a few Irish Quakers. Non-English Quakers, however, were soon absorbed into the predominantly English Quaker community and lost much of their identity. Many Quakers came from other colonies where they were not only for the most part not welcomed but also discriminated against in various ways. Some came from the West Indies, especially Quaker mercantile families who saw greater opportunities in Philadelphia than in possessions directly under the crown. The major non-Quaker English settlement in Pennsylvania resulted from the migration of Marylanders into southern Pennsylvania and Virginians into southwestern Pennsylvania. Virginia's claim to this western region led to this migration after 1760. Connecticut's claim to northeastern Pennsylvania and the fertile Wyoming Valley led the earliest English settlement of this area from that source about 1770.

The Quakers not only dominated the early peopling of Pennsylvania but its early trade, culture, and politics. It was not until about 1750 that their control of the Assembly was entirely broken, due mainly to the growing strength of the Scotch-Irish Presbyterians and their alliance with the small number of English Anglicans. Loss of political control did not mean an accompanying loss of other influences. Quakers continued to dominate trade and commerce and much of the pioneer development of early industry, including the iron industry. Money talked then as now, and the Quaker merchants who had accumulated wealth from early trade continued to multiply their fortunes and to spread their investments in every area where a growing economy offered an opportunity.

marriage between leading Quaker families. This, plus their shrewd business dealings, led non-Quakers frequently to charge Friends with avarice and sharp business practices. Usually these charges came from those less successful competing with Quakers.

Not all Quakers by any means sold goods. The larger merchants were few and far between among early comers, though Quaker owners of many smaller businesses soon enlarged their operations

Arch Street Friends Meeting in Philadelphia, typical of Quaker meeting houses in the city.

The distinctive nature of the Quaker religious faith created a strong unity. A Friends' meeting was not merely a religious gathering. It adjudicated many differences between Friends without recourse to courts and lawyers. It influenced standards of business conduct as a matter of religious ethics and often, on the same basis, took a stand on matters of political policy. The Quaker faith placed great emphasis upon the virtues of thrift, diligence in all pursuits, and plain living. It was suited ideally to the diligent conduct of business seen as good in the eyes of God. Friends were known throughout the world for their caution as well as their shrewdness in commerce, and also for their complete honesty. The strong community of interest in religion was accompanied by an equally tight community of interest in business and politics as well as frequent inter-

and their fortunes. Early Quaker records for Philadelphia show a large percentage of artisans and craftsmen among the Quaker population, though the small merchant predominated. A visitor to Philadelphia in 1710 noted that there was "hardly any Trade in England, but the same may be met with in Philadelphia." Few early Quaker settlers were farmers. Almost all the Friends stayed in or about Philadelphia and were the business and skilled artisan class that played so important a role in the sound economic growth of that city and its dominance in the colonial economy.

The nature of the Quaker population had many influences. The accumulation of wealth produced the "Quaker grandee" who dominated the social aristocracy of Philadelphia but also found time to dabble in colonial politics and to hold such key offices as mayor of the city and major posts in the

Assembly or on the Council. These Quaker aristocrats frowned upon ostentation and display. They wished their clothing and the furnishings of their homes to be "of the best sort but plain." Publicly at least they frowned upon having their portraits done in oil and preferred the silhouette as plainer, and also cheaper. The visages of most important Quakers of the time are indicated in this art form rather than in the fullness of formal portraits. The desires which could be satisfied by wealth sometimes strained Quaker simplicity, especially when the wealthy who belonged to other faiths were willing and able to display their wealth in fine living. In colonial times the fine carriage was as much a badge of distinction as is a fine automobile or private plane in today's society. By the eve of the Revolution the wealthier merchants were building fine, large houses on the outskirts of Philadelphia and were driven to their businesses or on pleasure in private carriages. Records indicate that in 1772 there were eighty-four such fine equipages in the city, of which thirty-three were owned by Quakers. It is questionable whether Quakers of means did not form a higher percentage of the wealthy community, and the inference is that many a Quaker aristocrat still refrained from ostentation.

Plain living was not the only Quaker characteristic which still lingers to some extent at least in southeastern Pennsylvania. The state has been noted throughout its history for its humanitarian and philanthropic advances. These derive to a great extent from early Quaker ideals of faith in the fact that every man was a vehicle of God and deserving of consideration amidst his worst misfortunes. Quakers helped their own in distress, but as early as 1713 they opened an almshouse for all. From the very first, prisons were made workhouses where men could be rehabilitated and returned to their freedom with a useful trade. The Quakers believed strongly in education but thought it should help develop the ability of those who partook to assume a useful station in life. The Quakers were pioneers in education for both sexes and in vocational education. William Penn and James Logan had possibly the largest and best-rounded libraries in the colonial America of their time. Quakers were interested in science

and James Logan ranks next to Franklin as a major figure in the world of colonial science. Only artists, actors, and lawyers may be said to have suffered from neglect on the part of the Quakers. Lawyers were not essential because the Meeting handled disputes, while artists and actors were frivolous, distracting, and wasteful of time.

The Society of Friends with its religious philosophy and its profound influence upon their personal lives had a dominant influence in shaping the character of early Pennsylvania. Quaker influence in this respect was the greater because of the fact that, though increasingly outnumbered in the colonial population, they retained virtually absolute control over the government and its policies for better than half a century, and a very real minority influence during all the colonial era. Quaker control over the economic growth of the province was even greater. Their religious beliefs, which determined their way of life, had an equally decisive influence on the cultural and social climate of the times.

THE PENNSYLVANIA GERMANS

While the Pennsylvania Germans arrived by way of Philadelphia, almost all spread quickly into the country just outside the periphery of early English and Quaker settlement and control. The first real German settlement was at Germantown, founded by Francis Daniel Pastorius on behalf of the Frankfort Land Company, which made a large purchase from Penn. These Germans started to arrive in 1683 and actually were mainly German Quakers with a scattering of Mennonites. "We named the place Germantown, which means the Brother City of the Germans," explained Pastorius. This was only the beginning. Penn advertised the wonders of his province very widely in the "Germanies," a term important to keep in mind because there was not a single German nation at that time. Germany was a collection of principalities, each with its own ruler and his personal ideas on religion and government. Each had a state religion and little sympathy for any dissenters. Furthermore, the entire country was suffering from the ravages of the Thirty Years' War, in which rival armies had fought back and forth and pillaged or destroyed everything.

The early German settlers were mainly members of various sects which suffered from religious persecution in the Rhineland. A powerful religious movement known as Pietism was sweeping Europe. It had little more in common with the established Lutheran, Reformed, or Anglican churches which had been the major product of the Reformation than with the Roman Catholic church. The German sects produced by Pietism, however, had much in common with the Quakers. They were primarily small farmers and working class people. Their faith was simple and without formality and ostentation. They believed in the basic dignity of man as a divinely oriented person capable of thinking for himself and guided by his own conscience. They frowned, therefore, upon

early location for the Amish and Mennonites.

Most German princes adopted either the German Lutheran or Reformed churches and hence members of these faiths, known as the "church people," suffered much less from religious persecution in the Germanies than did the members of the sects. While the search for religious freedom was certainly a dominating force back of the coming of the Pietists, economics probably had much more to do with the later coming of the larger numbers of Germans who belonged to the Reformed or Lutheran persuasion. Pennsylvania by 1740 was catching on in Germany as a land of opportunity. This section of Europe was at the time in poor circumstances, to say the least. Many of these Germans who came were very poor; a majority were farmers who saw great promise in

Amish man and boy, from an original painting.

ministers or priests and upon elaborate churches and church ceremonials. They lived plainly and sought to be left alone to worship as they saw fit in small informal congregations centered around their particular way of life. The Mennonites were among the first of the sects to come in some numbers. The Moravians founded Bethlehem in 1741. The Amish and the German Baptist Brethren were another large group. The Schwenkfeldians from Silesia were yet another sect. While some settled first around Philadelphia, the main body of the sectarians moved north and west into the interior counties. Lancaster County was a favorite

the ease with which rich land could be acquired at small cost. Many came as indentured servants because this was the only way they could secure passage. The Germans came in such numbers after 1740 that they soon numbered nearly half the population. The peak of the German flood, which reached such proportions that some of the English began to fear they were going to be inundated, was reached about 1754. From that time until the end of the Revolution the German population of Pennsylvania grew by only about twenty thousand and was reduced to about one-fourth of the total population.

This contemporary Lancaster County farm scene shows the farm landscape that appealed so to the early Pennsylvania German settlers, many of whose descendants have been farming this land since colonial times.

Since the Germans were mainly farm folk, naturally they sought fresh and fertile farm soils as the place to settle. This was to be found in the interior and not on the coastal plain around Philadelphia. The Germans sought lands in Berks, Lebanon, Lehigh, Lancaster, and Northampton counties. Later, many spread into other central Pennsylvania counties. Amish found their way as far as Mifflin County. The area of early German concentration remained the heart of the so-called Pennsylvania Dutch country of today. Here these immigrants from the German Rhineland found the same broad valleys and fertile limestone soil they had known in their homeland. Here it was not held by some semifeudal prince or lord but was easily bought with a modest amount of money, and a farmer could become master of all he surveyed in a very short time. The natural genius of these German people for farming was put to work on some of the most fertile soil in America and made the region for about a hundred years the "breadbasket of America." Some of the most valuable farmland in the country is still to be found in this region and in the possession of descendants of those who first settled it some two

hundred years ago. Every early visitor to Pennsylvania was struck by the fertility of these farms, the great stone barns, and often fine stone houses which came to grace the countryside in the Pennsylvania German country.

Not all Pennsylvania Germans were farmers. To think this is as bad a mistake as dismissing them as "dumb Dutch" given to superstition and hex signs. The German settlers were very German but they soon came to be known as Pennsylvania Dutch mainly, it appears, because of a common corruption of the German *Deutsch* into plain "Dutch." Their tendency to live closely together as a "foreign" element led to the continuing use of either German or the mixture of English and German which merged gradually into the language known as Pennsylvania Dutch. This in turn led outsiders who found it hard even to converse with these people to dismiss them as stupid or lacking in understanding. The Pennsylvania Germans helped little by hanging onto their close way of life, which included their own churches and schools to perpetuate their language, culture, and manner of living. Certainly they were far from stupid; as time went on the German people of Pennsylvania made varied and rich contributions to early Pennsylvania culture.

They were first in the art of printing at Germantown and Ephrata. They made their contributions in religious literature. Their music was distinctive, especially that of the Moravians at Bethlehem and of the Seventh-Day Baptists at Ephrata. It was the earliest fine music in the colony. Many Germans were expert craftsmen and the settlers at Germantown early made it a great center for manufacturing textiles and hosiery. It was Pennsylvania German craftsmen who invented the Pennsylvania Rifle and the Conestoga wagon. The poorest Pennsylvania German farm family had an instinctive love of art, quite contrary to the Quaker tradition, and the result is the vast storehouse of Pennsylvania German folk art—in almost every possible form of expression from decorating chests and household wares to barn paintings—which is one of the nation's greatest treasure troves today. Even the barn decorations, which are still seen today in the Pennsylvania Dutch country, are decorative and not hex signs, as some persistently but erroneously endeavor to interpret them. The total contribution of the Pennsylvania Germans to the economy and the culture of the colonial era was very substantial.

THE SCOTCH-IRISH

Between 1717 and 1776 about a quarter of a million people came to colonial America from Ulster in northern Ireland. By far the largest number came by way of ports on the Delaware and into Pennsylvania. On the eve of the Revolution it is estimated that some 70,000 were settled in the province. During the colonial period these immigrants were commonly referred to simply as "Irish" because they came from Ireland. An occasional use of the term "Scotch-Irish" may be found but it was not until as late as about 1840 when the great influx of Irish Catholics from the south of Ireland began that the descendants of the original Irish immigrants began to lay claim

One of the finest of the Pennsylvania rifles produced by Pennsylvania German craftsmen from the William Penn Memorial Museum collections. Note the fine workmanship and art designs.

to the title of "Scotch-Irish." Thereby hangs a tale. The colonial immigrants from northern Ireland were Scots and their descendants who had been colonized in that region from Scotland as a result of a deliberate policy on the part of the British government trying to neutralize the fierce and unconquerable Catholic Irish. Northern Ireland was a short distance from Scotland and the move resulted in the complete peopling of this part of Ireland with Scots. The Scots were hardy and they were devoted Presbyterians. This settlement of northern Ireland was accomplished in the seventeenth century but by the early 1700's the Scots in Ireland found themselves in real economic difficulty due to English restrictions on now thriving woolen manufactures as well as the higher rents now imposed by landlords. These were predominantly English landholders who had been given large grants by the crown. By 1717 the situation became acute, and it continued so for several decades. Whole areas of Ulster soon were virtually depopulated by the thousands who sought opportunity in the colonies, especially in Pennsylvania which was gaining fame as a place where land could be had cheaply. These people for the most part were farmers, though many were skilled in woolen manufactures. English and German elements had gained possession of most of the choice land in eastern Pennsylvania by the time the Scotch-Irish began to arrive in large numbers and they quickly sought the farther frontiers for settlement. By 1720 this brought them into central Pennsylvania in what are now upper Lancaster and Dauphin counties, and then across the Susquehanna into the Cumberland Valley region. After 1760 they began to push the frontier across the Alleghenies.

A hardy people accustomed from their early history in Scotland and Ireland to hardship and fighting for what they got, they were natural frontiersmen. In fact, James Logan on behalf of the provincial government first welcomed the Scotch-Irish as a bulwark on the frontier against the Indians. By 1729, however, he had changed his views and began to wonder if Ireland were not sending "all its inhabitants thither" and that "if they thus continue to come they will make themselves proprietors of the Province."

This painting is typical of the fine Pennsylvania German folk art in the collections of the Pennsylvania Farm Museum.

This example of fine Pennsylvania German hand printing is from the famous Ephrata ABC Book and is a selection of the decorative raised letters. The book was completed in 1750.

He also began to fear the effect of their contact with the Indians, for "the Irish are very rough on them." This was quite true, and hardly states their treatment strongly enough. Presbyterian Scots believed themselves divinely ordained and had none of the sympathy for native people char-

stern, unyielding people. Everywhere they went they took their Presbyterian churches. Their migrations may be traced by the dates of the founding of churches all the way from historic Derry in Dauphin County and Donegal in Lancaster County to Pittsburgh. Presbyterian ministers

Stern Scotch-Irish Presbyterian tastes are reflected in the interior of historic Rocky Spring church near Chambersburg.

acteristic of the gentle Quaker or Moravian faith. They were a rough-and-tumble people from their earliest history and it is small wonder Logan wrote on one occasion that "five Scotch-Irish families in a settlement gives me more trouble than fifty of any other people." The Scotch-Irish were the initiators, it would seem, of the frontier philosophy that the only good Indian is a dead one. Of course they had the bad fortune to reach the frontier in large numbers just at the time when the French and Indian War broke down the peaceable pattern of Indian relations so carefully built up by the Quakers. Not only were the Scotch-Irish rough on Indians, but they were also hard people for the land office and tax collectors to cope with. By far the largest number of "squatters" without purchase on frontier lands were Scotch-Irish. Again quoting Logan, the Presbyterian squatters declared that "it was against the laws of God and nature that so much land should be idle, while so many Christians wanted it to labor on, and to raise their bread."

All in all, the Scotch-Irish were a self-sufficient,

were powerful voices among their flocks and often as influential in political affairs as in those of the soul. Theirs was a stern faith which frowned upon all frivolity. Long sermons full of "fire and brimstone" emphasizing the inevitability of man's sin and his eternal damnation were common in frontier days and for a long time thereafter. This did not prevent the Scotch-Irish from turning their grain into rye whisky, which they consumed in great quantities, impressing visitors who did not understand their folkways as a wild and riotous lot—except on Sunday.

The Scotch-Irishmen took to politics like ducks to water and were the first to join with Anglicans in the 1740's in challenging the Quaker domination of the provincial government. Their rough-and-ready spirit of independence made them leaders in the early Revolutionary movement. It was Scotch-Irish who marched on Philadelphia after the French and Indian War demanding their rights in a "Declaration and Remonstrance." The Scotch-Irish were mainly responsible for forcing vigorous frontier defense measures after 1753, and were in the vanguard of the later Revolutionary movement. King George III is said to have called the Revolution "a Presbyterian war." A Hessian officer wrote in 1778 that the Revolution was not an "American rebellion" but "nothing more or less than a Scotch-Irish Presbyterian rebellion."

If the Scotch-Irish were unruly, they were at the same time great believers in education. Everywhere they went, they founded schools which were the seed for later colleges and universities. Princeton University, according to tradition, grew out of William Tennent's Log College for training Presbyterian ministers in 1736–1746 in Bucks County. No other single religious denomination founded as many colleges in the early days of the United States. Many leaders in early Scotch-Irish settlements were men of learning with surprisingly excellent libraries for the frontier. No one can dispute the great contribution of these hardy and persevering people in the early history of Pennsylvania.

OTHER GROUPS

No other single group of people approached the English, Germans, and Scotch-Irish either in numbers or breadth of influence. The fact remains, however, that virtually every ethnic and religious group in Europe was represented in the colonial population of Pennsylvania. Many French Huguenots came to the province in search of religious freedom and increased opportunities, mainly by way of Germany, where they had fled to escape persecution following revocation of the Edict of Nantes in 1685. The Huguenots were not numerous but were very influential. The Welsh have been mentioned, and while this migration ceased almost entirely after 1720, such places as Bryn Mawr and Gwynedd are reminders today of this early Welsh influence. In terms of religious faiths, the majority of the early comers were Protestants but a scattered migration of Roman Catholics came, mainly from Maryland and into southeastern Pennsylvania or Philadelphia. Jews found a haven in the province, though they were not given equal political rights with Christians. Next to the Quakers, Jews were the most important

leaders in the commercial life of Philadelphia; their numbers, however, cannot be estimated and were certainly few. In all, early Pennsylvania was a land of diverse peoples in some numbers from everywhere. And every group added something to the diversity of Pennsylvania's early life and culture.

THE SPREAD OF POPULATION

With settlers arriving in such large numbers it was inevitable that the population should spread rapidly from the narrow confines of the coastal-plains area along the lower Delaware into the interior in search of land. It is a common mistake to think of the American frontier as something which came into being only after the Revolution. Pennsylvania in particular had an expanding frontier reaching westward by 1730. By 1776 it had reached west of the Alleghenies to produce the first transmountain frontier in American history. The peopling of Pennsylvania after 1682 was basically a frontier process. Farmers followed on the heels of the first traders and carved a farming frontier from the wilderness. As settlement grew, towns were laid out and some of the towns grew into cities in the wilderness. Thus Pennsylvania in colonial times was the scene of exactly the same frontier process which ordinarily is associated with the story of Kentucky and the Northwest Territory following the Revolution.

The first county formed outside the three original counties was Lancaster, carved from Chester County in 1729. Population had grown in this region sufficiently to justify the Penns in laying out the town of Lancaster in 1730 and it rapidly became the great inland town of the colonial era. This was the more remarkable because, unlike most early towns in colonial America, it was not on a waterway but maintained contact with the sea and Philadelphia by overland travel. By another twenty years population had moved across the Susquehanna in large enough numbers to justify establishing York County (1749) and laying out the town of York (1741). A year after York County was created, Cumberland County was formed as the Scotch-Irish pushed into the broad valley of the same name. This particular outward thrust of population from the lower Delaware followed an overland route long developed by the Indians for trade and communication to the northwest, the old Minqua Path. It is significant that the movement of early population was so great in this direction rather than up the valleys of the Delaware or the Schuylkill. It was not until 1752 that Berks and Northampton counties were organized. Reading, however, was laid out by the Penns in 1748. Easton, at the historic forks of the Delaware with the Lehigh, was laid out in 1752. Moravian Bethlehem had already been in existence since 1741 as a result of the particular migration of this German sect.

The continuing frontier thrust of the province's growing population reached such proportions before the Revolution that the Juniata Valley, the upper Susquehanna beyond Harris' Ferry, and even the trans-Allegheny region were penetrated. Northumberland County was created in 1772 to govern the Juniata and Susquehanna settlements. A year later Westmoreland County was created to provide a semblance of local government for the farthest flung of the westward settlements. Sunbury on the Susquehanna was laid out in 1772. Bedford grew out of the settlement developed around Fort Bedford after 1758 and was early known as Raystown. Pittsburgh was both a fort site and a frontier village grown up in Fort Pitt's environs by 1776. By the eve of the Revolution, Philadelphia had grown to about 30,000 from a population of some 13,000 in 1750. Only Lancaster, Reading, and York had reached a population of over a thousand. Lancaster was a town of between 2,500 and 3,000 people by 1776; Reading had a little less than 2,000; York boasted about 1,500 people at that time. However, the volume of commercial activity and the work of artisans of every variety in these early towns made them major centers of colonial life.

INDIAN LAND PURCHASES

As has been pointed out earlier, the rapid movement of settlers inland soon placed a strain on provincial Indian policy as to land purchases. Penn's early slow conduct of treaty negotiations did not meet the demands of the years after 1730.

Treaties in those days were not followed by immediate surveys. In 1718 lands between the Delaware and Susquehanna had been purchased and in 1736 a treaty with the Iroquois which disregarded the peaceful Delawares added still more territory. This was followed by the Walking Purchase of 1737 in which the Penns acquired a tract running parallel to the Delaware but going some sixty miles inland rather than the thirty the Indians expected. This stratagem, which actually confirmed for survey a land purchase made in 1686, gained about twice as much territory for the Penns as the Indians had contemplated. The result was to force the peaceful Delawares entirely out of their old homeland and into the upper Susquehanna Valley. In 1749 another purchase cleared the Indian claims to land included in what are today Carbon, Dauphin, Monroe, Pike, and Schuylkill counties.

In 1754 at the Albany Congress a treaty was negotiated with the Iroquois to acquire land west and south of a boundary run from present Sunbury to Lake Erie and reaching to the extreme southern limits of the province. This was a factor in arousing the Indians to attack the Pennsylvania frontier during the French and Indian War. In an effort to keep the peace a large treaty conference was held in 1758 at Easton at which the great Delaware chief, Teedyuscung, was placated by what amounted to a repurchase of much Delaware land. The largest purchase of the colonial era was completed in 1768 with the Treaty of Fort Stanwix, which confirmed title to a strip of land running diagonally across the province from the northeastern to the southeastern boundaries. About one-third the total land area of the province still remained in Indian hands in northwestern and north central Pennsylvania. No permanent settlement penetrated this region until after the Revolution. As a result of these pressures, about two-thirds of the colony was opened to settlement by 1768 and this made possible steady expansion of population into these regions.

BOUNDARY TROUBLES

Pennsylvania was plagued by boundary disputes from the very beginning and, as has been pointed out, Penn was forced to return to England to battle Maryland claims even before 1700. The disputes grew out of two situations. In the first place, there was in London an amazing lack of any exact geographical knowledge of the English colonies. Then to add to the confusion, Pennsylvania was next to the last colony founded and so ran afoul of vague provisions of earlier charters of Connecticut, Maryland, and Virginia which were products of this lack of geographical facts. While the story of these disputes is dull reading today their outcome was vital to Pennsylvania's future. If Connecticut's claims had been honored, Pennsylvania would have lost its store of anthracite coal, to say nothing of the large land area involved with its stores of timber and its farm resources. Maryland's claims could have taken Philadelphia from Penn's province. Virginia claims would have taken the richest bituminous coal deposits of western Pennsylvania along with Pittsburgh.

Penn had hardly secured his charter before Lord Baltimore began to contest the Maryland boundary. Baltimore contended that his northern boundary included the area between the thirty-ninth and fortieth degrees of latitude, as his charter said it "lies under the fortieth degree of northern latitude." Penn's charter, however, placed his southern boundary as "on the south by a circle drawn at twelve miles distance from New Castle, northward and westward, unto the beginning of the fortieth degree of northern latitude. . . ." It was then to run by a straight line westward "to the limits of longitude above mentioned." This seemed clearly to secure the southern boundary of Pennsylvania, but Lord Baltimore's charter was dated 1632 and had legal priority. The dispute went to the Privy Council which in 1685 declared that the lower counties or Delaware belonged to Penn. Other aspects of the problem were left unsettled, but Lord Baltimore began to press again in 1731. The boundary was ordered run in 1750 but Baltimore managed to postpone action until 1760. At that time the famous New Castle circle was finally drawn by David Rittenhouse, the noted Philadelphia mathematician and surveyor. The issue was fully settled when Charles Mason and Jeremiah Dixon finished the survey of the boundary, thereby winning a place in history as the men who created the Mason and Dixon Line between the North and the South.

The dispute with Virginia was drawn out longer and more seriously because Virginia traders and settlers moved into and occupied western Pennsylvania ahead of any real Pennsylvania settlement. Possession is always nine points of the law and Virginia had this; in addition it took a major role in defending western Pennsylvania against the French during the early years of the French and Indian War. The Virginia claim dated all the way back to 1609 and to the London Company charter, which established a boundary running 200 miles north and 200 miles south from Old Point Comfort and "up into the land throughout, from sea to sea, west and northwest." This, of course, would take in Maryland if actually applied. When Virginia became a royal province in 1624 the unoccupied land reverted to the crown but Virginia continued to claim all land not assigned to another colony.

About 1747 a group of Virginians, among whom was George Washington, organized the Ohio Company to exploit some half million acres of land "on the branches of the Allagany" and to "trade with the several nations of Indians" in the region. A grant of 200,000 acres was authorized by Virginia in 1749, and settlements actually started near present Connellsville, to be protected by a Virginia fort. Virginia also started a fort at the forks of the Ohio but this was captured by the French shortly after it was begun. The French and Indian War put a stop to trade and settlement by anyone until the British could oust the French invaders. The war had the virtue of arousing more interest in the region on the part of the provincial government seated at Philadelphia and its end also opened the west to traders and pioneer settlers from eastern Pennsylvania. Some trouble occurred with Virginia settlers who refused to recognize Pennsylvania local government, and in 1773 Philadelphia officials decided to create Westmoreland County to strengthen the Penn position.

The British withdrew from Fort Pitt in 1772 and a year later Governor Dunmore of Virginia decided to visit Pittsburgh. He liked what he saw and returned to Williamsburg determined to forward Virginia claims and settlement. In January, 1774, Virginia actually occupied Fort Pitt and named it Fort Dunmore in defiance of Pennsylvania. This was Lord Dunmore's War, which was mostly a war of words. Dunmore had overextended himself because in taking over Fort Pitt he was occupying British property. The dispute remained warm despite efforts to compromise on the part of the Board of Trade, and in 1775 Virginia set up the District of West Augusta to govern southwestern Pennsylvania. In August, 1776, the first court west of the Monongahela was held by Virginia at Augusta Town, about three miles southwest of present Washington, Pennsylvania. Additional counties of Monongahela, Ohio, and Yohogania were organized by Virginia.

Franklin's admonition that the colonials had better hang together or they would hang separately quieted the dispute during the early Revolutionary turmoil. In 1779 the Continental Congress persuaded the disputants to agree to a joint commission to settle the issue. With the high-handed and usually very independent and lordly Virginia governors under the crown out of the way, the two new states agreed to extend the Mason and Dixon Line due west five degrees of longitude and hence north to Lake Erie. The boundary was surveyed by 1786 and Pennsylvania recognized land titles of Virginia settlers within the region as part of the bargain. Pennsylvania had won again.

While all this fuss was taking place in western Pennsylvania a similar and equally dangerous dispute developed with Connecticut involving northeastern Pennsylvania. Again, it was a product of faulty geography and resulting ridiculous boundary lines drawn in early charters. The Connecticut charter of 1662 blithely gave the colony a boundary running west from sea to sea, excepting only territory not held by another colony. This saved New York but to the west of the southeastern tip of Connecticut the westward line cut right across northern Pennsylvania. In 1750 Connecticut people decided to do a little exploring and "discovered" the rich Wyoming Valley

in northeastern Pennsylvania. It looked good enough to settle and was much better land than New England "rocks and rills" provided. Land speculators pricked up their ears and by 1753 the Susquehanna Company was organized as a stock company to promote settlement in the Wyoming Valley region. Once more, the French and Indian War intervened and life on this exposed frontier was not very healthy. The Connecticut folk who came down in 1762 lost some scalps in 1763 and hastily retreated. However, another company, the Delaware Company, had been organized in 1754, and it began the first permanent settlements in the Cushetunk region of the upper Delaware in present Wayne County.

The Treaty of Fort Stanwix strengthened Pennsylvania's claim so far as acquiring Indian rights was concerned and the British home government ordered Connecticut to cease its occupation. The New Englanders refused to back down and in 1769 settlers again moved into what is now Forty Fort in the upper Susquehanna Valley and built a fort of that name to protect themselves in 1770. A little earlier in April, 1769, Connecticut settlers started Fort Durkee at present Wilkes-Barre across the river. Pennsylvania retaliated by building in 1771 Fort Wyoming not far from the enemy outpost but it was soon seized by the New Englanders. This rather bloodless exchange between 1769 and 1771 is known as the First Yankee-Pennamite War. Connecticut did not officially participate in the "war" of the colony, which was an affair of the Susquehanna Company and the settlers.

In 1772 Pennsylvania created Northumberland County, seated at Sunbury, to provide a closer local administration for the region. In 1775 hostilities again broke out when Colonel William Plunkett attacked a Connecticut settlement which had daringly reached as far down as present Muncy. He was defeated by Colonel Zebulon Butler. This began the second of the Yankee-Pennamite Wars. In the meantime the New Englanders had laid out Wilkes-Barre in 1770 and in 1776 made it the county seat of the newly created County of Westmoreland under Connecticut laws. By 1776 some 2,600 Connecticut settlers had infiltrated Pennsylvania. As was the case with

Virginia, the outbreak of the Revolution quieted the local dispute and once more Continental Congress stepped in to restore order. A five-man commission met at Trenton, New Jersey, in late 1782 and after forty-one days of hearings of both sides of the question handed down the Trenton Decree in December which fully recognized Pennsylvania's claim. It was not until after 1800

however, gave a lasting New England tinge to the character of northeastern Pennsylvania. Other New Englanders came later and added to the New England-like culture of the region.

The peopling of Pennsylvania was not over by 1776 but the ethnic and religious patterns which would shape its future were set. Its boundaries, at long last, were determined and there was no

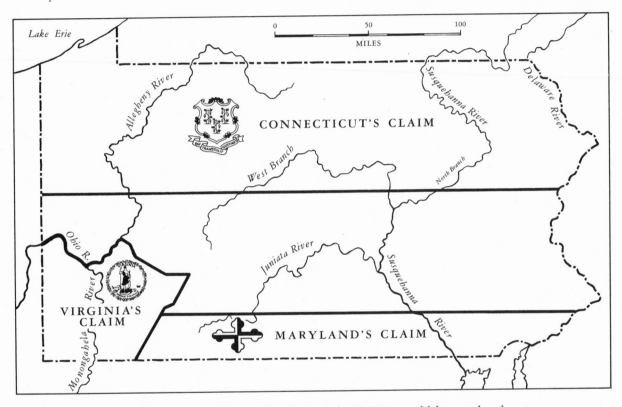

*Claims of Connecticut, Maryland, and Virginia would have reduced
Pennsylvania to a narrow belt of land running east and west and
robbed it of the location of major cities and resources.*

that all the resulting local legal disputes over land titles were solved. In 1786 Pennsylvania created Luzerne County and its government was forever established in the Wyoming region. Again, Pennsylvania had won a boundary argument which, had it gone the other way, could have had crippling consequences. The Connecticut settlement,

longer this threat to its future growth. About one-third of the area of the state was as yet unsettled. From the Revolution to around 1840 there would continue an expansion of settlement which would lead to the passing of any semblance of a frontier.

WHEN FARMER AND MERCHANT RULED THE ECONOMY

The colonial era was one in which the farmer and the merchant were the real rulers of the Pennsylvania economy. The early settlers, as has been explained, were predominantly farmers who sought land to cultivate. Pennsylvania was fortunate in having so large a part of its early colonial population made up of the Germans who loved the soil and knew how to make it richly productive. The far frontier was entirely a farming frontier. The Quakers were ideally adapted to mercantile pursuits and soon made Philadelphia the greatest of the colonial seaports. All real wealth in colonial Pennsylvania sprang from the enterprise of the farmer and the merchant. Such industry and craftsmanship as developed in colonial times was related primarily to the needs and desires of merchants and farmers.

THE BREADBASKET OF AMERICA

For over a century after the arrival of the first farmer-settlers Pennsylvania was known as the "breadbasket of America." It was not until the great Middle West was settled and developed to a point where its agriculture became a factor in the American economy about 1840 that Pennsylvania lost this position of leadership in agriculture. The combination of fruitful limestone soils in central Pennsylvania with the industry of the Pennsylvania German farmer made this area the heart of the most productive farmland east of the Mississippi. That noted gentleman farmer George Washington once commented that the portion of Pennsylvania with which he had become acquainted was as farmland "inferior in their natural state to none in America." Every early visitor who traveled in interior Pennsylvania commented upon the richness of its agriculture. The ever observant William Penn obviously was impressed by both the natural and the artificial, or transplanted, products of the land. The fine stands of timber which covered the land were themselves testimony to the fact that rich soil was underneath. Most farms had to be carved out of these forests but the rewards were great once the land was available for the plow. At the same time, the felled trees provided materials for the settler's first log cabin. Sawed into timber at the early sawmills which sprang up in every early settlement, they were of further use in building as well as providing a product which could be sold or traded in the commerce of the times.

Utilizing the riches of the soil was aided by the liberal land policy of the Penns. As already pointed out, Penn's sons raised the price of land over that set by their father but by any standard the price was still a modest one. Furthermore, probably one half or more of the some 670,000 acres occupied between 1732 and 1740 was taken boldly without grants by those whom James Logan characterized as "bold and indigent strangers" or just plain "land-grabbers." By 1776 those who were not mere wanderers on the land took up what were known as settlement rights and became a solid part of the farm population of the province. This condition, naturally, was common to the expanding frontier. It was a habit especially of the Scotch-Irish, and a substantial number of German farmers were addicted to this practice.

Whether the farmer acquired land by purchase or simply by staking out a claim, he was apt to be an independent and democratic person. William Penn looked forward to the development of a type of farming in his province similar to that in England and centering around the village, but his dream fell short of its goal in Pennsylvania. The German sects, the Moravians, Amish, and Mennonites, were the only people who tended to found settlements as communities. The typical settler-farmer was a lone wolf who sought out land by himself. As others took up land and settlement, villages and town grew to serve the needs of a community. The average early farm ranged in size from 100 to 500 acres. Large families were the rule because every child, male or female, added to the working force. Women often worked with men in the fields when the need was urgent, as in the harvest season. The yield of grain from the rich soil was miraculous as compared with the worn-out soils of Europe. Wheat, which commonly was the first crop planted on newly cleared land, ran twenty-five to thirty bushels to the acre and corn as much as sixty.

The absence of towns forced the farmer to make by himself most of his utensils for the home and many tools for the farm. The wife and children wove and spun wool or flax to provide the clothing. The typical early Pennsylvania farm was a remarkably self-contained and independent economic unit. This stimulated early the generative forces for what is termed agrarian democracy, a term usually applied to later frontier thinking, but one not to be ignored in the understanding of the ferment of freedom common to early Pennsylvania. The independent farmer came naturally by a belief in the natural rights and liberties of man. He was not even bound to the land he owned because there was plenty of other land farther to the west. It was by no means uncommon in colonial Pennsylvania to find that farmers who appeared firmly settled and attached to their land suddenly decided to sell out and move to a new location. It was this spirit which made Pennsylvania so powerful a force in the peopling of the early frontiers west of the Alleghenies, in Kentucky and Tennessee, usually by way of Virginia and in the Ohio country. The ancestors of Abraham Lincoln, Pennsylvania Quakers, were cast in this mold.

FARM LIFE ON THE PENNSYLVANIA FRONTIER

The life of the farmer on the first frontier was always hard. His house was almost sure to be at first a log cabin, copied from those of the early Swedes on the lower Delaware. He was able to bring with him, especially before the first crude roads were carved out of the wilderness, few tools. The use of wagons was not common in interior Pennsylvania until the Conestoga was "invented" about 1730. The Dutch and Swedes on the Delaware used two-wheel wood carts made entirely of wood. It was not until about 1740 that the pioneer Pennsylvania iron furnaces and forges began to turn out an abundant supply of iron which could be used by blacksmiths. Before that time iron was an imported and expensive item.

There were few horses on the early frontier. The earliest inland settlements tended to hug streams or follow Indian overland paths into the wilderness. Settlers came on foot or with belongings packed on the back of a horse. If a cart or crude wagon was used it was apt to be drawn by oxen. Even tools were made mainly from wood, including the wooden plow. Crude wooden harrows were hauled by oxen to break the soil further. Grains were broadcast by hand and corn was planted the same way. It was cultivated with a hoe. Grain was cut with a hand sickle; even the

An artist's view of life on the farm frontier. Note the
oxen and trees cut for lumber, or for more log houses.

grain cradle was not in common use in colonial
days. Once cut, the grain was bundled and
shocked by hand. The harvested wheat was
threshed either by tramping it out, by human or
animal feet, or by use of the wooden flail, which
beat it out. Ears of corn were laboriously shelled
by hand. As local iron became more available for
the use of the blacksmith, gradual improvements
were made in tools and implements utilizing iron.

The life of the farmer held few comforts in
colonial Pennsylvania. It was a life of hard manual
labor from the sun's rising until it sank in the
western skies. Only the Pennsylvania Germans
achieved much advance in the way of raising livestock. They became noted for their fine stone
barns, which the traveler often commented upon
as better than their houses. Leather from skins
provided the material to be worked into clothing
in the homes of settlers on the far frontier. In
more settled areas the flax and wool produced on
the farm provided homespun cloth and clothing.
Community life consisted of such get-togethers
as were provided by religious services, barn- or

house-raisings, harvesting, or weddings and
funerals.

THE THREE STAGES OF SETTLEMENTS

It must be kept in mind, however, there is no
such thing as a truly typical pattern for farm life
in colonial times. The pattern changed with the
passing years and the growth of settlement. Contemporary observations agree that the first stage
in the growth of a farming frontier was the true
wilderness of the typical frontiersman. He usually
merely squatted upon the land for a time and
lived in a very crude cabin or lean-to. He was the
man with the leather jacket and breeches, the fur
cap, and the long Pennsylvania rifle with which
he shot game, or Indians, if occasion made it necessary. He came on foot, or at best with a pack
horse or mule. He was not apt to own any livestock and lived from hunting, fishing, and crude
cultivation of the soil in a small clearing where
he raised some corn and vegetables. This type of
pioneer was restless and did not wish to be

crowded. When a few others penetrated his wilderness fastness he felt crowded and sought a new wilderness home.

In his footsteps came the pioneer farmer with a family. In later colonial times he came by wagon, drawn usually by oxen, and carried with him a plow, some other tools, and his household belongings. As a rule he had with him some livestock. He wanted land for a farm and cleared more of it for use. He built a substantial cabin, which he gradually improved with a wooden floor and glass windows. He grew more substantial crops but usually lacked a ready market for any surplus and so supplied only his own needs for food for his family and livestock. The pioneer farmer was easily attracted by tales of richer new land farther west. Roads to the West were always crowded with this type of pioneer moving his family and belongings to yet another frontier. His property was purchased by the more permanent settler who took up his land with the thought of making it a lasting home where he would work out his destiny. The Pennsylvania Germans especially were among those who settled themselves on lands passed over by the pioneer type of farmer.

Under such conditions the typical colonial farmer is difficult if not impossible to describe. He was sure to be young and rather poor, depending upon a barter economy and his ability to provide for himself. Pioneering was for the young and hardy. Large areas of early Pennsylvania were peopled with such rapidity that means of transportation were far behind the needs of the times. Few advances in any kind of road building were made in colonial times except between the larger towns and cities. Overland transportation to any kind of market was not only laborious but expensive. Philadelphia was not well connected with the interior in terms of natural waterways and only those farmers along the lower Delaware and Schuylkill had access to it as a market by water. Under these conditions the colonial farmer had to exist under conditions of a self-sufficient economy with a limited exchange of some farm commodities for goods imported from the great city of Philadelphia by way of town merchants in such places as Lancaster, Reading, or York. These interior towns did not come into being until the

middle of the 1700's but their appearance was a token of a slowly evolving economy reaching more mature stages of development.

An artist's conception of a pioneer settler.

PHILADELPHIA COMMERCE AND TRADE

The rapid growth of Philadelphia made it in a very short time the third most important commercial city in the British Empire, overshadowed only by London and Liverpool. This was a tribute both to Quaker sagacity in business and to the natural location of the growing city and its access to both foreign and domestic commerce. As settlement grew in the province, it also found wealth in a rich interior trade. The fringe of farm settlement close enough to Philadelphia to utilize it as a

market was large enough to provide a store of products of the farm valuable in commerce. Bread, flour, pork, beef, grain, tobacco, wheat, and a variety of wood products were valuable exports. Wheat, flour and bread accounted for more than one-half the total exports. Most of these products went to the West Indies. Some went to Europe. Some, especially foodstuffs, found their way into trade with other colonies.

The famous triangular trade was an especial source of wealth to Philadelphia. Foodstuffs and barrels and staves were in great demand in the West Indies with their concentration upon sugar plantations worked by slaves. New England profited from the slave trade that was tied in with supplying West Indian needs, but Quaker merchants disliked this practice and sent their ships from West Indian ports to England with sugar and island products. These were sold to English factors and the ships returned to Philadelphia loaded with English manufactures needed in the province. When Pennsylvania's iron industry began to be important by 1750, iron became an important commodity available to export in the form of both pig and bar iron. About the same time the fur trade with the Indians on the western frontier began to assume real importance and furs and skins became an important part of Philadelphia's export trade.

The trade of Philadelphia grew at a more rapid pace than that of either Boston or New York.

Peter Kalm, the noted Swedish economist, listed 199 ships arriving at Philadelphia in 1735 and over 300 in 1740. In 1735 he listed 221 ships as having sailed from the port and over 300 on an average in following years. Kalm commented: "Philadelphia reaps the greatest profits from its trade to the West Indies, for thither the inhabitants ship almost every day a quantity of flour, butter, flesh and other victuals; timber, plank and the like. In return they receive either sugar, molasses, rum, indigo, mahogany, and other goods, or ready money." He noted that "England supplies Philadelphia with almost all stuffs and manufactured goods which are wanted here." There is abundant evidence of the close connection between the growing commerce of Philadelphia and the raw material provided from farms and forests of southeastern Pennsylvania. A visitor in 1765 found that "Everybody in Philadelphia deals more or less in trade." Every European visitor marveled not only at the volume but also the variety of products involved in the city's trade. Philadelphia had become without question the major port in all the colonies. Tonnage ran into thousands of tons and by 1770 the value of Pennsylvania's exports was stated as well over £700,000.

PHILADELPHIA'S INTERIOR COMMERCE

Philadelphia's interior trade formed an increasingly important part of its mercantile economy

Philadelphia about 1760, showing a rather pastoral scene.

after 1750. The wilderness was the haven of beaver and other fur-bearing animals and beaver pelts especially grew in demand to supply hats and furs for European gentry. Indians rather than whites had to be depended upon to supply this all-important commodity. As has been pointed out earlier, the penetration of colonial traders into the Ohio country by about 1740 helped produce the conflict of interest with France which led to the French and Indian War. Careful studies indicate the presence of as many as two hundred or more individual Indian traders on the Pennsylvania frontier in the mid-1700's. As there were no roads and only Indian paths to follow, the traders moved their supplies purchased in Philadelphia laboriously overland by pack horse to the tiny trading posts they set up in key places in the wilderness. The traders became the first white explorers of the interior and the first to bring back information about it. Many grew to be men of wealth and importance, and they figure largely in founding settlements and developing western Pennsylvania. Among these were George Croghan, John Harris, Sr., William Trent, and George Morgan.

Several major Philadelphia mercantile firms were closely associated with the Indian trade. Shippen & Lawrence; Bayton, Wharton, & Morgan; and Levy, Franks & Simon were among them. Such firms received the furs from the traders, stored them and shipped them abroad. From these firms, traders purchased the cheap goods used in the Indian trade. Lancaster owed its earliest prosperity to its place as a commercial center. Shamokin, later Sunbury, Logstown, near the present Ambridge, and Venango at today's Franklin were major trading posts. John Harris, Sr., operated a trading post on the site of present Harrisburg, along with his famous ferry. After the English won control of the forks of the Ohio, traders flourished in the protective shadow of Fort Pitt. The story of the Indian trade is not pretty. The typical white trader lived by his wits and drove the shrewdest possible bargain with the red man for his valuable furs. Rum was used all too frequently in this process. The good Quakers of Philadelphia tried their best to abolish its use in the Indian trade, but with little success. It was the trader also who furnished the Indian with guns and the powder with which to fire them, and in later years these were turned upon the white settlers with deadly consequences.

With the build-up of British military forces under Braddock and Forbes to forward the king's business in the French and Indian War, supplying the armies became a lucrative business for Philadelphia's merchants. The correspondence of British officers in charge of supply in connection with these two major expeditions is full of the names of the leading mercantile houses of Philadelphia. The British needed many of the same trinkets used by traders for their own negotiations with friendly Indians. They needed also to be supplied with food, gunpowder, rum, and other ordinary necessities for an army on the march or garrisoned in forts. The ability of Philadelphia to supply such needs was enhanced by its position as a port and its existing trade connections with the interior. As a result, many a British pound landed in the coffers of Philadelphia merchants between 1754 and the Revolution.

THE WORLD OF COMMERCE

Commerce was organized in Pennsylvania along the same pattern as in other colonies except for that extra shrewdness and drive common to the Quakers. Of course, business was not conducted very much as it is today. With the exception of those Quaker merchants who moved to Philadelphia from the Indies, most ventures were small in their early stages, though they often grew into large-scale operations. Some persons started on their own as small merchants, but those who engaged in foreign or larger-scale domestic trade usually grouped together as a partnership of two or three. Philadelphia merchants carried much of their goods in their own ships, which increased the profit. Philadelphia with its early shipyards was well suited to this unified operation for ships were readily to be had. The typical cargo ship cost little more than the cargo and might pay for itself in a single voyage.

Starting a mercantile venture required a capital of from £3,000 to £5,000, a sizable sum in those days. The merchant was a kingpin in the economy as he bought from the iron manufacturer, the miller, and the maker of staves and barrels, as well as from those dealing in produce. In turn he furnished the retail merchants of the city and inland with goods which he imported from England and elsewhere. He might own the ship which carried the goods to a foreign or colonial market. He operated the machinery of credit involved in trade, and purchased finished goods in England to be brought back to Philadelphia. Some merchants started and remained in business as factors, selling and procuring goods on a commission. The large mercantile houses were involved in outright sale of the goods they purchased from suppliers and bought on the markets abroad, mainly in England, for resale in the colonies. They also were usually engaged in intercolonial trade and trade in the interior of Pennsylvania. Transactions in England usually were carried on with a single favorite mercantile house in London, Bristol, or Liverpool. Quaker merchants liked naturally to deal with Quaker merchants abroad.

Paying for goods in England was taken care of by bills of exchange. This convenient device originated during the commercial expansion of the Middle Ages. It involved an order on the part of the first party on a second party to pay a third party a specified amount. This, of course, was the forerunner of modern banking and the use of the check and in those times the merchant became

also a banker of sorts. Sometimes a bill of exchange was endorsed by another party as a further guarantee of payment. Bills of exchange circulated among merchants in much the same way that a bank check does today. Philadelphia merchants received bills from the West Indies drawn on English merchants. Bills of exchange were sent in quadruplicate because of the danger of loss and it was understood that the first copy received was honored and others discarded. Voyages took many months to complete, especially when ships took a cargo to the West Indies, sold it, loaded another cargo for England, sold it, and loaded again with goods for Philadelphia. The resulting lack of accurate knowledge of markets and prices made trade not only risky in terms of changing prices but also made those engaged in trade highly dependent upon the honesty and fair dealing of those with whom they were selling and buying. Sometimes the value of a cargo would change considerably during this long-drawn-out series of transactions. Not all transactions could result in an even exchange of values and hence considerable trade was conducted on a credit margin. Actually, the whole system resembled a gigantic scheme of barter because of the lack of actual money which changed hands.

When the merchant in Philadelphia received his goods from England and they were unloaded at his wharf, he might utilize different ways of disposing of them. He might sell directly to one or more retail outlets in the city. He might engage in a sale by auction to the highest bidder, though Quaker merchants frowned upon this and it was finally restricted by the Quaker-controlled Assembly. One suspects the Quakers looked upon this as breaking down the closely knit trade relationships they had established among themselves as a mercantile community. The larger mercantile houses conducted a flourishing trade as wholesalers either to Philadelphia merchants or those in interior towns such as Lancaster and Reading. The Indian trade, as mentioned, was also serviced by them. Larger houses also engaged in coastwise trading and shipped goods as re-exports to other colonies, something which Philadelphia's keystone location between New England and the South greatly favored on a profitable basis. This

A Philadelphia waterfront scene about 1700 showing Dock Street, from an old print.

was true especially in terms of trade with Southern colonies because they had a less well developed commercial system.

THE MERCANTILE GRANDEES

Philadelphia's commercial life was closely knit. A person wishing to learn the business started as an apprentice. This involved the keeping of accounts, handling business correspondence, and related routine tasks of such a type as to insure learning the business from the ground up. A tested apprentice might be allowed to make one or two trial voyages and manage the business details. The apprentice could continue as an employee of the firm at a higher level or, if ambitious, launch himself into his own business. Generally speaking, the world of large-scale business did not offer the same chance for starting independently that shopkeeping, small crafts, or farming did.

The larger firms tended to find the best places for friends or relatives of the owners. The world of the larger merchants was closely knit not only by the nature of the conduct of trade but also religion. This became true more and more in Philadelphia as a small mercantile "aristocracy" became common. The "Quaker grandees" of Philadelphia soon evolved a structure of aristocratic living comparable to that of the plantation

lords of the South, the merchant princes of Boston, or the landed aristocracy of the Hudson Valley region. Penn's ideal of a landed gentry disappeared in the face of a rising mercantile one. The real economic power in Philadelphia rested with the Quaker merchants. They were also all-powerful in the government and dominated the Council which advised the governors. Many served in the Assembly from Philadelphia, Chester, and Bucks counties. They almost entirely dominated the government of Philadelphia itself. Though restrained by the Quaker distaste for ostentatious living, the mercantile aristocracy succeeded in living well indeed. While their clothing, their homes, and their carriages were plain they were always of the finest quality money could buy. Politically, they naturally tended more and more toward favoring conservative policies in government which protected the business interests in which they were involved.

The merchant was the true king of the colonial economy. He was the one person engaged in a pursuit which promised an accumulation of wealth and capital above immediate needs. The Philadelphia merchant became, therefore, the one real source from which capital was forthcoming for any new ventures. Naturally, most of this capital was at first plowed back into enlarging the business. There came a time, however, when the wealthy merchant was apt to look for other fields to conquer. During the colonial era land, a common field for large-scale and speculative investment, did not attract much attention on the part of wealthy Pennsylvanians. This is due in part, it would appear, to the rapidity with which land was bought up by small landholders as settlers, a process which quickly exhausted the supply of land in southeastern and central Pennsylvania. Western and northern Pennsylvania, where later speculators bought large holdings, were not opened for purchase to any extent until after the Revolution. Quaker capital was also apt to be less interested in speculative investment. As a consequence, capital from Philadelphia was available for more substantial purposes.

IRON PLANTATIONS

One of the new enterprises which did attract this capital was the colonial iron industry, which began to establish its roots about 1720. This was an industry demanding larger sums for an initial venture than was true of any other type of enterprise outside commerce itself. It demanded large areas of land to supply ore, limestone, and charcoal which became known as "iron plantations." Here surplus capital garnered from trade played a very important role in the colonial economy. Iron was first made at Saugus, Massachusetts, about 1640 but New England was lacking in the raw materials for a large iron industry. Iron was very much needed in the colonies and its importation from England was a drag upon their economy.

Thomas Rutter, aided by Philadelphia mercantile capital, began Pennsylvania's iron industry about 1716–20 by building a bloomery and furnace on Manatawny Creek in Chester County. It was named Colebrookdale. The French Creek area soon became a major iron-making section. The famous Durham Iron Works was established in the lower Delaware Valley by 1728. The great Cornwall mines were discovered about 1740 and Cornwall Furnace started by Peter Grubb. Before the Revolution iron-making had spread even west of the Susquehanna as the rich magnetite ore deposits of the province were found to be widely scattered. Nature had also placed large deposits of limestone in exactly the same places, along with tremendous stands of trees. Limestone was basic in making iron and the charcoal needed in such large quantities could be obtained by chopping down the forests and converting them into this fuel. By the mid-1700's Pennsylvania was leading all colonies in making iron and was soon exporting it to other colonies and even to England.

Making iron was an industry quite unlike any other in early days. It was the first large-scale industry in America. It required more capital and more application of special technological know-how than any other early industry. It took a substantial capital—several thousand pounds—to begin to make iron, because of the natural resources required and the necessity of bringing them together in a single technical operation. Partnerships were utilized to raise such needed capital. Some of the most prominent names in Pennsylvania's colonial history figure in the rise of the iron industry. Large-scale operation produced not only the iron plantations but also the master of capital and industry, unique in the early economy, known as the "ironmaster." His mansion overlooked a village compound which housed the labor force and gave to the iron industry a character of large industrial might peculiar to making iron.

The industry's technology changed little in colonial days, or for some decades thereafter, other than the building of steadily larger furnaces. Its product was charcoal iron, so called because charcoal was the fuel used to reduce the iron ore and limestone to pig iron. Charcoal iron furnaces, some of which still stand, were built usually of limestone in the shape of a pyramid and lined with hard sandstone. The space between the inner and outer wall was filled with clay to protect against the heat. The size varied and tended to become larger as operations expanded but there was a definite limit to the practical size of a furnace. The average furnace measured about twenty-five feet square at the bottom and the height was about the equal of the square.

The furnace was filled or charged from the top, a process that consisted of placing in it alternate layers of iron ore, limestone, and charcoal. Fur-

This drawing shows a typical charcoal-furnace operation. Note the use of the water-driven bellows to create a cold blast for the furnace.

naces customarily were built against a hillside to make possible a bridge from the bank to the top of the furnace; over this these materials were transported. The furnace was put in "blast" by lighting the charcoal. A water-powered bellows then fanned the furnace with a cold blast of air. This meant that furnaces must be located close to a stream which could turn the water wheel to power the bellows. As the mass within the furnace melted under heat the limestone acted as a flux and absorbed the impurities in the ore. These impurities rose to the top of the furnace and were puddled off as slag. The molten iron dropped to the bottom of the furnace and was tapped and drawn off into sand casting beds, located within a casting house at the front of the furnace. The iron cast in these beds or molds was called "Pigs," and the main gutter or feeder from the furnace was known as the "sow." The cooled iron was known as pig iron. Not all iron from a furnace found its way into pigs; castings such as stove plates and other iron wares were sometimes made directly from the furnace.

Further refining was necessary before pig iron could be used for making tools, implements, and related iron products. Pig iron was refined at a forge where it was heated again. The pigs were then lifted from the forge with huge tongs and pounded out by a large iron forge hammer. This was an up-and-down device made of large timbers with a heavy iron hammer at the end; it operated by water power. Additional impurities were driven out of the pig iron in this process and a bar or bloom was the result. It might be heated and hammered further if a greater degree of refinement in the product was desired. A bar of iron averaged about fourteen feet in length, two inches in width and about half an inch in thickness. This was the iron utilized by the blacksmith in his forge to shape various articles for which iron was used. By the Revolution iron wire and nails were another product based upon pig iron from the furnaces. Pioneer steel-making was also begun, despite English efforts to check the secondary manufactures from iron. Pennsylvania's iron industry was firmly established by this time as a basic element in its growing prosperity among the colonies.

THE ECONOMY OF THE INTERIOR

Frontier life was dominated by farming as contrasted with the busy commercial life of Philadelphia. As mentioned before, this bred a high degree of self-sufficiency. Lacking any contact with a good market for its products, the frontier could hardly escape depending upon itself. Settlement expanded so rapidly in the colonial era that

83

it was impossible to develop road-building to keep contact with the frontier. By 1750 there were a few larger towns in central Pennsylvania and they became centers for early trade and the mercantile life common to Philadelphia, though on a much restricted scale. The merchants of Lancaster, Reading, York, or Easton imported merchandise from Philadelphia usually known as "English

and footwear in the home. Food, of necessity, was prepared for future use in the home by drying, salting, and like means. An occasional journey to a distant town sometimes provided such necessities as sugar and salt, and possibly a bit of cloth or hardware items on a barter basis with the local merchant. The first industry carried on outside the home was certain to be a local grist mill and

This sketch shows an early blacksmith working at his smithy.

goods" or "West Indies goods" depending upon the origin. Finer china, glassware, cloth, and the like were from England. Sugar, molasses, spices, and rum or fine wines were from the West Indies. The stores in these towns were also sure to carry some hardware, including items for both the farm and the home.

All of these goods were brought in from Philadelphia and the town merchant often took the produce of neighboring farmers in exchange for what he had to offer. The farther a farmer-settler lived from town the less likelihood there was of his being able to take part even in this system of barter. Because of this, the local economy varied in the province in relationship to the development of markets as provided by growing towns and their contact with Philadelphia. On the far frontier, the economy centered not only upon farming but also upon manufacture of virtually all necessary tools, household utensils, and even clothing

sawmill, usually under the same ownership. Here a farmer could bring grain to be ground or logs to be sawed into rough lumber, usually for a charge consisting of a part of this product. This form of relationship between the farmer and local industry persisted for generations in many parts of Pennsylvania. Under this system, on the frontier it was the miller rather than the farmer who became the person who sold meal, flour, or lumber as a product for money in a larger town.

The growth of towns in the interior of the province gave rise to craft industry. The blacksmith, the wheelwright, the cabinetmaker, the shoemaker, and the tailor were common in the larger towns where there was not only a local population as a market for their wares but some trade with the countryside within a day's journey or so from the town. It is a mistake to think of the early frontier as characterized by poverty over a long period of time. The transition from the

84

rigors and hardships of first settlement to a fair degree of prosperity was often amazingly rapid. Daniel Boone, for example, was born in a log cabin but some years before he left his home at the age of seventeen his father had erected the fine large stone mansion which has been restored and known as the Daniel Boone Homestead near Reading. This prosperity, however, was not based so much on wealth in terms of hard money as on the ability to exchange products to make possible a better scale of living. Within the colonial towns themselves there were people who enjoyed some wealth and in their way copied in dress and social habits the life of the "grandees" of Philadelphia. This, in turn, stimulated the finer arts of the craftsman to produce wares which could compete with the best in Philadelphia or those imported from abroad. Even on the Pennsylvania German farm, the desire for "nice" things stimulated the finest examples of folk decorative art in the home to be found in colonial America. Folk art was in its way a domestic industry because it was done in the home.

FROM PACK HORSE TO CONESTOGA WAGON AND DURHAM BOATS

Contrary to the general situation in colonial America, not all of Pennsylvania's early large towns were so located as to provide easy water transport. Easton and Reading, which were on rivers, made some early use of this form of transportation. The lower Delaware gave birth to the Durham boat, invented mainly to provide a way to get the iron from furnaces and forges to Philadelphia. In fact this unique type of river boat got its name from Durham Furnace in upper Bucks County. A Durham boat was a local invention and in its way one of Pennsylvania's several major contributions to transportation. It was about fifty feet long, eight feet wide, and two feet deep. It was shaped something like a huge canoe and could carry as much as fifteen tons of iron because of its slight draft. It could be operated with a sail but was usually poled, making use of the natural current. These boats were developed about 1740 on the Delaware and their use later spread to the Lehigh and the Schuylkill to carry grain and farm produce.

When the first counties were laid out and settlement began to move inland it was necessary to provide some roads. The King's Highway was started from New Castle in Delaware toward Chester and Philadelphia about 1687. By 1700 the county judges, who were then the major representatives of the proprietor in all matters of local government, were authorized to lay out local roads. All roads ordered opened by the provincial authorities were designed to connect Philadelphia with other towns. The Old York Road to Doylestown and Easton was projected in 1711 and by 1721 a road was ordered opened running toward Lancaster. The inhabitants of that town about 1730 petitioned that it be extended all the way to Lancaster. This was done in 1733 just after the town was laid out. When York was founded west of the Susquehanna and this part of Pennsylvania began to fill up, Baltimore made use of the Susquehanna Valley to tap the trade of this region. This led to an early agitation in Philadelphia for improved transportation into the interior settlements to counteract the Marylanders. Thus began one of the prime pressures for improved internal transportation in Pennsylvania which helped speed improvements for the next hundred years. Philadelphia never lost its fear of Baltimore's trade rivalry and kept up a constant demand for improvements to combat it. Nothing approaching an improved road existed west of York, Carlisle, or Chambersburg until after the colonial era.

The Conestoga wagon was the first practical answer to the need for a vehicle to carry heavy freight overland.

85

In eastern Pennsylvania prior to 1730 the pack horse was the major means for carrying goods to the interior settlements. The pack-horse masters followed the old Indian paths and it was these same routes which were used for the most part as the location for the later roads built to accommodate wagons. Gradual improvement of roads in eastern Pennsylvania and the growing need to get goods from Lancaster to Philadelphia led to the invention of the remarkable Conestoga wagon, which took its name from the land of its birth in the Conestoga Valley near Lancaster. It was an invention truly because nothing like it existed in Europe or anywhere else in the colonies. Pennsylvania German wheelwrights and blacksmiths began to build these wagons about 1730, and over seven thousand were said to have been in use by 1750. Lewis Evans wrote in 1753 that "Every German farmer in our Province, almost[,] has a Waggon of his own." Their first extensive use for carrying heavy loads long distances came during the Braddock expedition when Franklin engaged Conestoga wagons and horses from Lancaster, York, and Cumberland counties to carry supplies from Philadelphia and elsewhere to Braddock's army.

The Conestoga wagon was designed uniquely for its particular use. Its long, deep bed, about sixteen feet long, could hold a large quantity of freight, as much as 2,500 to 3,500 pounds, depending upon road conditions. The bed was sloped to provide a sag in the center to prevent the load from shifting from one end to the other on hills. It also helped in fording streams by giving the wagon something of the effect of a ship on water. A heavy white cover of hempen or linen cloth stretched over six to eight bows more or less closed in at the ends sheltered the freight from the weather. Early wagon builders used an artistic touch when they invariably painted the wagon body a bright blue with red for the running gear. Much artistry also went into the ironwork. Each wagon was the pride and joy of those who built it. The four-inch-wide tires on the five- to six-feet-high wheels commonly used on the heavy freight wagons were well suited for both the mud of early roads and the packed stone of later turnpikes. Along with the wagons went the breeding of the famous Conestoga horses which comprised the distinctive "Six-Horse Bell Team" of the early wagoners. The Conestoga wagon is entitled to the distinction of being looked upon as a true invention because it was a device born of the necessity to provide growing settlements with a way to move large quantities of goods to distant markets over roadways which were barely improved or were the remains of military roads carved from the wilderness by Braddock, Forbes, or Burd. Its use later on the farther western frontier and its evolution into the famous "prairie schooner" entitles it to a distinctive position among early contributions to the development of the West.

THE COLONIAL LABORER AND HIS HIRE

The attraction offered by cheap land in the country and the rewards of the craftsman in the city combined to make the problem of the supply of ordinary labor a troublesome one in colonial Pennsylvania. It was especially so because the commercial and industrial growth of the times and the increasing number of towns with their need for ordinary labor needed to be met. Negro slavery existed in the province but the number was never more than a few thousand. The Quaker faith as well as that of the German sects frowned on limiting the freedom of any man regardless of color, though William Penn and other Quakers did own slaves. The basic Quaker tenets prevailed and led to the earliest colonial protests against slavery expressed at Germantown as early as 1688 by Quakers and Mennonites. Aside from moral considerations, the varied economy of Pennsylvania did not lend itself to ready use of Negro slaves imported directly from Africa.

The principal answer to the need for a supply of labor was met by the use of indentured servants, sometimes known also as redemptioners. They won the latter name because they worked to redeem their passage money. The term "indenture" rose from the use of a legal agreement to work to secure passage. The system was ideal for Pennsylvania not only in terms of the answer to a labor shortage but also because large numbers of those who wished to come to the colony did not have money to pay for their passage and were therefore quick to seize upon this method to do so. The Scotch-Irish were in this class, along with many Germans. As a result Pennsylvania led all the northern colonies in numbers of its servant population.

There was nothing disgraceful about indentured servitude. The individual agreed with the shipowner to place his service for a term of years in the hands of the best bidder on arrival. The coming of a shipload of indentured people was advertised in the Philadelphia press. The term of service was rarely more than five years and often less. With true Quaker humanitarianism, the Pennsylvania Assembly carefully regulated the conditions of indentured servitude by law. Once the term of service was over, the servant was provided with some tools, extra clothing, and sometimes a small sum of money to make his way in the world of freedom. The province itself presented him with fifty acres of land. Some were employed on iron plantations, a few on farms near the city, and many by craftsmen and small businessmen. Thus the indentured servant was given a ready opportunity to fit himself for a better life once he had served out his contract. Many entered such a way of life and others were content to remain free laborers.

Wages in a free economy were dictated by demand for labor and hence tended to be high for the times in the colonial era. They were much higher than those in Europe of the time. Laborers received from one and a half to two pounds a month with their keep and female house servants about half that sum. Unskilled iron workers received from one to four pounds a month, depending on lodging, while a skilled founder would get as much as twelve pounds. A furnace manager naturally was paid somewhat more. While detailed figures are not available for those times, it is agreed generally that the trend of wages was steadily higher in colonial Pennsylvania because of the great demand for free labor. For the same reason, the indentured servant found it easy to better his position once he was free of his labor contract.

The pattern of Pennsylvania's economy for many decades to follow was set firmly by the end of the colonial era. It would continue for some time to become a land where the farmer and agriculture were the basic factor in the life of a majority of the people. Philadelphia's place as a great center of commerce was well established. It was also a center for the accumulation of capital which could reach out to support new ventures such as aiding industry and transportation to advance. The foundations of a powerful and permanent iron industry were well established as the first step in Pennsylvania's march to a position of industrial dominance in early America.

CHAPTER SIX

THE ATHENS OF AMERICA

It was Philadelphia which won the characterization of "The Athens of America" in colonial days, but the term may also well be applied to the entire province. To do otherwise is to divorce Philadelphia from the remainder of the colony, and this should not be done in the realm of culture and social progress any more than in the economy or the politics of Pennsylvania. Philadelphia was a part of the province, and indeed the town life and culture of the entire colony were influenced and even dominated by what went on in Philadelphia. In no other English colony can there be found cultural advances and the finer arts of living superior to those common to Pennsylvania interior towns such as Reading or Lancaster. The possessions of early Pennsylvania settlers even on the fringe of the frontier as shown in records of wills and estates, plus the observations of travelers, indicate a truly amazing degree of education and culture. The quality of the libraries which many of these pioneers took with them to the early settlements is astounding. The love of fine furniture, musical instruments, and the like, as revealed by what these people left to their descendants, is equally amazing.

Lancaster may well have been the first town in America outside of a coastal city to establish a library. Town life generally was a smaller edition of that in Philadelphia. Furthermore, Pennsylvania's religious groups everywhere generated a vigorous concern with education and founded more colleges than were set up in any other colony. They were also concerned with schools at a lower level. The Germans, other than the Amish, were lovers of music and decorative art. Thus the rough edges of pioneer life were rubbed off with remarkable rapidity. Freedom of expression and opinion encouraged writing, especially in the fields of religion and politics, to a degree not common in most of the colonies.

CHURCH AND SCHOOL

The church and the school were one in colonial Pennsylvania from the earliest time, with the minister often the first teacher. The Swedes started it when the governors were enjoined to "support at all times as many ministers and schoolmasters as the number of inhabitants shall seem to require." The first teaching in New Sweden was in the Lutheran church at Tinicum. The Quakers believed strongly in education and the Great Law provided in general that the rich and the poor both should be educated and that children should know how to write by the time they were twelve. The colonial government used the term "public schools" in reference to its plans for education, though they were slow to mature. Public education in the modern sense floundered in colonial times partly because of the desire of the church people, especially the Germans, to teach their children in their own schools. Quaker educational doctrine favored training in trades and skills, known today as vocational education. They also believed in education for girls as well as boys. Both were revolutionary ideas for the times.

The dominant influence in education in Pennsylvania for over a century was either the church school as such or schools strongly influenced by religious groups. In 1689 the Quakers opened the Friends' Public School, which was chartered in 1692. It is the fountain from which emerged today's famous William Penn Charter School. As the name indicates, it was a public school though controlled by the Quakers. Tuition was paid by those able to do so and it is doubtful whether many poor people unable to pay such a fee attended even though they had the opportunity. The first schoolmaster of this famous school was George Keith. Even before this, Enoch Flower in 1683 had become Philadelphia's first schoolmaster. Quaker schools of the colonial day attained a reputation for the quality of their work which has persisted right down until today; no finer schools could be found in colonial America. The Lutheran and Reformed churches with their predominant German membership insisted for more than a century on the maintenance of their own church schools. This was dictated in part by religious reasons but equally so by their desire to preserve their own language and culture. Since the largest number of Pennsylvania Germans were farmers they tended to look upon education as of doubtful value beyond reading, writing, and simple arithmetic. All these schools were conducted in the German language, which made Pennsylvania bi-lingual for over a century. The Scotch-Irish believed strongly in education but again of a simple variety. As settlement grew the neighborhood school, so called because it was founded by and served a new community, became more and more common in the interior. These schools provided the rudiments of an elementary education and were free from church control.

RELIGION AND THE CHURCH

The story of religion and the church is of more than usual importance in Pennsylvania's history because no other English colony had such a variety of religious faiths with so much influence in shaping its life and culture. The first church on Pennsylvania soil was the Swedish Lutheran. The origins of famous Gloria Dei or Old Swedes Church in Philadelphia go back to 1700. The Mission to the Swedes in America was maintained by the mother Swedish Lutheran Church until 1786.

Quite naturally, the meeting houses of the Society of Friends became the symbol of religion after 1683 with the coming of the Quakers. Log, stone, or brick, they numbered by 1750 at least fifty houses of worship where Quakers met without benefit of clergy or any form of music and sat in silence until the spirit moved a Friend to speak. Not all Quakers remained in Philadelphia, though it was the center of their strength. The log Quaker meeting house at Catawissa in central Pennsylvania built about 1787 is still standing. The Quakers were west of the Alleghenies by 1776. The approximately 30,000 Quakers in Pennsylvania by this date had suffered a severe schism in their ranks. Led by George Keith, a more liberal branch of the Society of Friends made its appearance. Keith himself finally became an Anglican, as did a number of other Quakers, including the sons of William Penn.

Other church groups predominantly English in origin included the Church of England, or Episcopal Church, with membership drawn predominantly from the wealthy non-Quakers. The first Episcopal church was built in Philadelphia about 1696 and ministered to by the Rev. Thomas Clayton, representing directly the Bishop of London. Historic old Christ Church was completed in 1754 and St. Peter's in 1758–61. On the eve of the Revolution there were about thirteen Episcopal churches or chapels with some three thousand communicants, of whom about one-third may well have been converted Quakers. Episcopalians were highly pro-English and the church was in bad standing during the Revolution and for some years later.

Historic Christ Church in Philadelphia.

The Baptist Church was Welsh and English in its beginnings and the first congregation dates back to 1684. The first permanent Baptist church was located in Pennypack in 1688 and the First Baptist Church of Philadelphia was founded in 1698. Great Bethel Baptist Church in the present Uniontown was founded in 1770, the first church west of the mountains. The Philadelphia Baptist Association was organized in 1707 to become one of the earliest formal religious organizations of its kind. The spread of the faith beyond the mountains led to organization of the Redstone Baptist Association in 1776. The total Baptist membership was about a thousand adults, with some twenty churches, by 1776 but it was a religion which appealed strongly to many of the common people.

Methodism got a late start in Pennsylvania. Its beginnings stem from the preaching of Thomas Webb, an English army captain converted by John Wesley in England and who came to Philadelphia in 1768. Out of early Methodism in Philadelphia grew historic old St. George's in 1769, the oldest shrine of Methodism in America. Bishop Francis Asbury preached his first sermon here in October, 1771, and here also in 1773 was held the first Methodist Conference. Methodism was in its infancy at the end of the colonial era but gaining strength with the common people.

It has been said that in colonial days anyone who scratched a Scotch-Irishman would find Presbyterian blood coming from his veins, and this was almost literally true. Nearly every immigrant from Ulster was a Presbyterian and a "hard shell" one at that. While Pittsburgh by 1776 was not yet the "capital" of Presbyterianism it later became, western Pennsylvania was the major concentration point for the Scotch-Irish and the Presbyterians. Quite naturally, however, the first congregation and church of this rugged faith was in Philadelphia in 1697–98. The first church edifice was put up in 1704 and another in 1743. The rapid spread of the Scotch-Irish into central Pennsylvania moved the Presbyterian faith into central Pennsylvania, where the Presbytery of Donegal near Lancaster was organized in 1732. Derry Church at the present Hershey was founded in 1729 and Hanover Church, not far distant, in 1736. The Paxton congregation in the present Harrisburg dates back to 1732. The Presbyterians moved on into the Cumberland Valley and then west of the mountains, though a western Presbytery was not organized until after the Revolution. The names of the Rev. Charles Beatty, Rev. George Duffield, and Rev. John McMillan are among the noted leaders of the circuit-riding Presbyterians of western Pennsylvania at the close of the colonial era.

The churches originating with the German people who flocked to Pennsylvania were the most numerous and probably the most influential in colonial times and for some time afterward. The various German sects were generated in Europe by the wave of Pietism or the desire for a "pure" religion without formalism and involved doctrine which also produced the Quakers. The Mennonites, who really differed little from the Quakers in their basic religious philosophy, were the first German sectarians to arrive at Germantown in 1683. Their next major place of settlement became Lancaster County.

Here also came the Amish, the followers of Jacob Amman, who split off from the Mennonites in the late seventeenth century. Mennonites were pacifists and believed in severity in garb and customs. The Amish went even further and gloried in their position as truly "plain people" with their broad-brimmed black hats, black bonnets for the women and plain black clothing worn without buttons and using only hooks and eyes for fastenings. This combined with their custom of the men wearing beards gave them their distinctive appearance, which is still familiar in the Amish country. The Amish, unlike the Mennonites, built no churches but worshiped in homes. Almost all were farmers then and are today. They frowned upon education in schools, preferring such schooling as was given limited to the home and family.

The Schwenkfeldians came to Pennsylvania in 1734 and settled mainly in Montgomery County, where Pennsburg is still the center of their culture. Their leader and pastor was George Weiss. A formal church organization was not perfected until 1775, headed by Christopher Schultz. The sect numbered only a few hundred and had no formal churches in the colonial era.

The most widely influential of the minor German sects was the Moravians of Bethlehem and Nazareth. They were led by Count Zinzendorf and Bishop Spannenberg and came to Pennsylvania from Georgia in 1741 to found the town which remained their religious and educational center in the historic area of old Bethlehem. Nearly a thousand Moravians were clustered at Bethlehem by 1756 and twenty years later they numbered some 2,500, settled not only at Bethlehem but also in Nazareth and Lititz. The Moravians were notable for their zeal to convert the Indians to Christianity. Christian Post, David Zeisberger, and John Heckewelder are among the great names associated with this noble effort, which met with some success. Several mission schools were organized and reached as far west as the Ohio country. The Moravians were the greatest single missionary force among the Prot-

estant denominations in colonial times. Their archives at Bethlehem are a firsthand story of early Indian and frontier life as written down by their missionary leaders; the like of this story, in comparable detail, exists nowhere else, except possibly in the records of the Roman Catholic Church. The Moravians were quick to found schools and in 1749 opened a girls' school in the Bell House in Bethlehem as well as one at Lititz. The Moravians were famous for their beautiful religious music. They also carried on the earliest industry in this part of Pennsylvania.

The minor German sects included certain religious communal groups. Johan Kelpius brought a group of "priests" to the Wissahicon in 1694. They lived as hermit monks and went their various ways after the death of Kelpius in 1708. The largest and most lasting communal settlement was that of the Seventh Day Baptists at Ephrata, under the stern and able direction of Conrad Beissel. Beissel led his followers to Ephrata in 1735 on the banks of Cocalico Creek after having deserted the German Baptist Brethren. An order of brothers pledged to celibacy and monastic living founded the *Kloster.* An "Order of Spiritual Virgins" was soon created and a Sisters' House built to complement the Brothers' House. Monks and sisters dressed in long robes and lived under conditions of the utmost severity. The buildings which housed the brothers and sisters had narrow corridors and doors, the doors so designed that it was necessary to stoop to pass through them. All of this emphasized the need for humility and the following of the straight and narrow path. Beds were boards with a wooden block for a pillow. Some three hundred followers were at Ephrata at the peak of its population. Members tilled the fields by day and tended their flocks, thus furnishing their own food and clothing, processed in the community by the brothers and sisters.

Printing became a fine art at Ephrata, some of it being done in the hand-illuminated script of the medieval times. Ephrata was famous for its early Bibles and for the *Martyr's Mirror,* printed in 1748 in German for the first time. It has been called "the greatest volume printed in Colonial times." Beissel is credited with starting the first

The restored cloisters at Ephrata showing the Saron and Saal. The "Whitehaus," Beissel's cabin, is on the right.

Sunday School in America. He also created the words and music for about a thousand hymns printed in 1747 in the *Turtel-Taube* and sung by the Ephrata choir. The medieval-like Sisters' House still stands, restored by the state as a historical shrine, along with several other smaller buildings of the Ephrata community.

The so-called "church Germans" were members of either the Lutheran or Reformed faith. German Lutherans made up the largest Protestant denomination in early Pennsylvania other than the Presbyterians. By 1776 it is estimated there were at least 60,000 Lutherans in the province. Their spiritual leader was the Rev. Henry Melchior Muhlenberg who came to Pennsylvania in 1742. Old St. Michael's Lutheran Church was then founded in Philadelphia. Lutheranism, however, was strongest in the rural German regions and New Hanover was the "mother church" of Lutheranism. Its congregation was organized in 1703 and a church erected in 1768. The second Lutheran church built was at Trappe in 1743, the oldest Lutheran church still standing. The German Reformed Church outnumbered the Lutherans until about 1740. Its great leader was

John Phillip Boehm, who organized his first church at Falckner's Swamp in 1725. Michael Schlatter after his arrival in 1746 perfected the further organization of the Reformed Church. While German in its membership, the Church was directed by the Synod of Holland until 1793. The total German Reformed Church membership in 1776 was about 30,000. Both the Lutheran and Reformed churches made use of the German language in their services and schools, thus helping to cement and retain a German culture in early Pennsylvania.

The Roman Catholics of early Pennsylvania came originally for the most part from Maryland. Since Maryland was a Catholic colony they did not come in search of religious freedom but for economic reasons. Father Joseph Greaton came to Philadelphia in 1720 to minister to local Catholics. In 1733 St. Joseph's Chapel was erected, the first in Philadelphia, with a congregation which included twenty-two Irish Catholics and fifteen Germans. Father Theodore Schneider established a Roman Catholic church at Bally in Berks County in 1743. Father William Wappeler was another frontier priest who established a Jesuit

Mission of the Sacred Heart station at Conewago in the present Adams County in 1730. This chapel is one of the oldest in continuous use in the United States and the first Sacred Heart church in Pennsylvania. Conewago Chapel is one of the major historic shrines of Roman Catholicism in America with the status of a Minor Basilica. The growth of Catholicism was steady in the colonial era, increasing from some 1,365 members in 1757 to at least five thousand by 1776.

The First Menno-nite Church, Philadelphia.

Augustus Trappe Lutheran Church, built in 1743.

Basilica of the Sacred Heart of Jesus of Conewago near Hanover. Known in colonial times as Conewago Chapel, it was built in 1741. The present church was built in 1785–87 and is the oldest stone Roman Catholic Church in America. It represents more than two centuries of Roman Catholic religious endeavor in the region.

While Pennsylvania provided complete toleration for the Jewish faith it did discriminate against Jews in terms of their right to suffrage and holding office, which were limited to Christians. The Philadelphia Jewish community, however, became a sustantial one in colonial times. Some of the larger mercantile houses in the city were owned by Jews. A Jewish congregation existed in Philadelphia before 1750.

ADVANCES IN EDUCATION

Education at the elementary level in colonial times was fairly available throughout the province except on the farthest frontier where community life had not come into being. It was confined to the church school and the scattered neighborhood schools, as has been mentioned. It was also limited to the familiar three R's. The same basic educational opportunity existed in the towns as in Philadelphia. There was, however, no such thing as schooling for everyone despite the Quaker belief in a thoroughly democratic system of education. Education primarily was for those who could afford to pay for it and the best in schooling was to be had only for those well able to pay for it. There were, however, significant steps forward in providing for secondary education and this took the form of the academy and so-called grammar school.

Franklin was a leader in promoting better educational opportunities and took the lead in founding the Philadelphia Academy in 1749. It merged in 1753 with a charity school founded nine years earlier to become the Academy and Charitable School of the Province of Pennsylvania. Two years later it gained college status as the College of Philadelphia with William Smith as its head. It finally emerged after the Revolution as the University of Pennsylvania. Dickinson College at Carlisle grew out of a grammar school started in 1773. The academy and grammar school were spreading and creating a new level of education but again for those who were able to pay for it. Quaker and Moravian belief in education for women was a Pennsylvania advance of importance. Girls were admitted to the Friends Public School for elementary subjects and in 1754 Anthony Benezet was able to persuade the overseers to admit them to grammar school. In 1767 Benezet started a morning school for poor girls and in 1753 William Dawson opened a night school for working girls. These schools, however, were hardly successful in making education for women a public affair.

Along with education for young women, the Quakers created the beginnings of vocational training in schools to prepare those who attended for a useful trade. These were, however, feeble pioneer steps which made no deep impression on education. As to higher education, the College of Philadelphia graduated some two hundred men between 1757 and 1776 and in 1765 opened the first medical school in the colonies. This was due

94

in some measure to Franklin's influence and his belief in science as having a place in education. William Smith, however, as head of the College of Philadelphia and a strong Anglican, kept it heavily in the then current classical tradition.

THE PRINTED WORD

Colonial Philadelphia has been termed the literary center of colonial America and certainly the status of the newspaper and magazine in the city had much to do with the validity of the claim. Thanks to the influence of Benjamin Franklin and Andrew Bradford, the Quaker city was a major center of publishing in the whole Empire. There were no less than eight printer's shops in the city by 1740 and in 1776 there were twenty-three. It is authoritively estimated that during these thirty-six years over 11,000 separate printed items came from these presses. They included almanacs, political pamphlets, and religious tracts. Franklin's *Poor Richard's Almanack,* launched in 1732, was by all odds the most famous publication of its times and its homely sayings remain a part of American literature today. The variety of religious faiths in Pennsylvania combined with the high degree of religious disputation characteristic of that day to make it a major center for a steady flow of religious pamphlets. A growing democracy in politics and government encouraged the political pamphleteer. About 15 per cent of the product of the presses was in German, indicating the great influence of German-speaking people on the culture.

Early journalism was a hazardous business, as is indicated by this notice of the expiration of the Pennsylvania Journal.

Andrew Bradford began issuing his *American Weekly Mercury,* the first newspaper in the Middle Colonies and the third in all the colonies, on December 22, 1719. Franklin's *Pennsylvania Gazette* started publication in October ten years later. Andrew Bradford's nephew William began the *Pennsylvania Journal* in 1742. The *Pennsylvania Chronicle* of William Goddard was born in 1767. John Dunlop began his *Pennsylvania Packet and Weekly Advertiser* as a weekly on the eve of the Revolution. It grew in 1784 into the nation's first daily newspaper and today's *Philadelphia Inquirer* traces its ancestry as the country's oldest daily newspaper back to Dunlop.

The permanent German press of America began in 1739 in Pennsylvania with Christopher Sauer's *Der Hoch-Deutscher Pennsylvanischer Geschichsschreiber.* It eventually became the *Germantauner Zeitung* (Germantown Journal), one of the most influential weekly newspapers prior to the Revolution, with a circulation of several thousand reaching as far south as Georgia. Other less lasting German press ventures date back to 1732. The first printing press in the province outside Philadelphia was installed at Ephrata in 1745. Lancaster's first newspaper, the fortnightly *Gazette,* was started in 1752 with alternate columns in German and English but lasted only three years. In 1762 William Miller founded the *Philadelphische Staatsbote,* which became a very influential newspaper among the German population. Pennsylvania was the only center for the German press and cultural influence in this era.

By the eve of the Revolution there were no less than seven newspapers in Philadelphia with editions ranging from 500 to 3,000 copies. The publication dates were such that it was only on Wednesday that a news-hungry Philadelphian found himself absolutely without a new newspaper for that day. Philadelphia papers circulated outside the colony and as far as the West Indies and enjoyed a high reputation.

Philadelphia also gave birth to the American magazine. Again it was Andrew Bradford who pioneered, with his *American Magazine,* first issued in January, 1741. Franklin was close behind with his *General Magazine* a few months later. Both were unsuccessful ventures and in 1757

William Bradford came forth with a new venture, *The American Magazine and Monthly Chronicle.* Within a year Bradford found himself in jail for political reasons and his magazine languished. Five magazines had their birth in Philadelphia by 1776, though none enjoyed more than a few months of life. Their existence does indicate, nevertheless, the lively state of literacy in the city of that time.

Philadelphia colonial printers were busily engaged in reprinting the works of the best English authors for colonial consumption. Pope's *Essay on Man,* Blackstone's *Commentaries,* and More's *Utopia* were rather typical of this output and of the literary taste of the times. Such books found a market not only in Philadelphia but also among the better-educated people in the interior. Even a frontier lawyer found need for Blackstone. There were also pamphlets, almanacs, scientific works, and even a few primers from local pens. Works on medicine, geography, mathematics and even Latin grammar were written locally. The faculty of the College of Philadelphia wrote some eighteen medical works before 1776 and all were notable contributions to printed colonial medical lore. The products of the local printers, along with imported books, found their way into the several bookstores which grew up in Philadelphia. Even book auctions were held at times. Philadelphia's Robert Bell became one of the first and the leading dealer in books of all types in the colonies; his trade ranged from disposing of entire private libraries to selling individual used books.

Philadelphia's role as the mother of the American library is not unusual in view of this situation. Although in existence as far back as 1731, the Library Company of Philadelphia established by Franklin and his discussion club, the Junto, was not chartered until 1742 to become the first of its kind in all the colonies. Its membership fees were high and in 1746 the Union Library Company was formed to serve those less able to pay. Ten years later Philadelphia artisans took the further step of organizing the Association Library and the Amicable Company, both of which later merged

The Pennsylvania Gazette *in 1737.*

THE
Pennsylvania GAZETTE.

Containing the freshest Advices Foreign and Domestick.

From November 10. to November 17, 1737.

To the AUTHOR *of the* Pennsylvania
GAZETTE.

SIR,

 FREEDOM OF SPEECH is a *principal Pillar* in a free Government: when this Support is taken away, the Constitution is dissolved, and Tyranny is erected on its ruins. Republicks and limited Monarchies derive their strength and vigour from a *Popular Examination* into the Actions of the Magistrates. This Privilege in all Ages has been and always will be abused. The best of Princes could not escape the censure and envy of the times they lived in. But the evil is not so great as it may appear at first Sight. A Magistrate, who sincerely aims at the *Good* of the society, will always have the inclinations of a great majority on his side; and impartial Posterity will not fail to render him Justice.

These abuses of the Freedom of Speech are the excrescencies of Liberty. They ought to be suppressed; but to whom dare we commit the care of doing it? An evil Magistrate, entrusted with a Power to *punish Words*, is armed with a *Weapon* the most *destructive* and *terrible*. Under pretence of pruning off the exuberant branches, he frequently destroys the Tree.

It is certain, that he, who robs another of his moral reputation, more richly merits a Gibbet, than if he had plundered him of his purse on the high-way. *Augustus Cæsar* under the specious pretext of preserving the characters of the *Romans* from defamation, introduced the Law, whereby *Libelling* was involved in the penalties of *Treason* against the State. This established his Tyranny; and for one mischief it prevented, ten thousand evils, horrible and tremendous, sprung up in the place. Thenceforward every person's life and fortune depended on the vile breath of Informers. The Construction of words being arbitrary, and left to the decision of the Judges, no man could write or open his Mouth, without being in danger of forfeiting his Head.

One was put to death, for inserting in his History the praises of *Brutus*; Another, for stiling *Cassius* the *last* of the Romans. *Caligula* valued himself for being a notable Dancer; To deny He excelled in that manly accomplishment was High-Treason. This Emperor advanced his Horse *Incitatus* to the dignity of Consul; and, tho' History is silent, I don't question but it was a capital crime to show the least contempt for that High Officer of State. Suppose then, any one had called the Prime Minister a *stupid animal.* The Emperor's Council might argue, that the malice of the Libel was aggravated by it's being true, and consequently more likely to excite the family of this illustrious Magistrate to acts of revenge. Such a prosecution would appear ridiculous: Yet, if we may rely on Tra-

dition, there have been *formerly* Proconsuls in *America*, tho' of more malice, but hardly superior in understanding to *Incitatus*, who would have thought themselves *libelled*, to be called by their *proper names.*

Nero valued himself on his fine voice and skill in musick; *a laudable ambition this!* He performed in public and carried the prize. It was afterwards Resolved by all the Judges, as good Law, that whoever should insinuate the least doubt of *Nero's* Pre-eminence in THE NOBLE ART OF FIDLING, ought to be deemed a Traitor to the State.

By the help of Inferences and Innuendo's, Treasons multiplied in a prodigious manner. GRIEF was Treason. A Lady of noble birth was put to death for bewailing the loss of her murdered Son. *Silence* was declared an overt act to prove the treasonable purposes of the heart. LOOKS were construed into Treason. *A serene open aspect* was an evidence that the Person was pleased with the calamities that befel the Emperor. *A severe thoughtful countenance* was urged against the man that wore it, as a proof of his *plotting* against the State. DREAMS were often made capital offences. A new species of Informers went about *Rome*, insinuating themselves in all companies to fish out their Dreams, Which the holy Priests, O! *nefarious wickedness!* interpreted into High-Treason. The *Romans* were so terrified by this strange method of process, that, far from discovering their Dreams, they durst not own that they slept. In this terrible situation, when every one had so much cause to fear, even FEAR itself was made a crime. *Caligula* when he put his Brother to death, gave it as a reason to the Senate, that the Youth was afraid of being murdered. To be eminent in any virtue, either civil or military, was the greatest crime a man could be guilty of. ------- *ob virtutes certissimum exitium.*

These were some of the Effects of the Roman Law against Libelling.

THOSE of the British Kings who aimed at Despotic Power, or the oppression of the Subject, constantly encouraged prosecutions for words.

Henry VII. a Prince mighty in politics, procured that Act to be passed, whereby the jurisdiction of the Star Chamber was confirmed and extended. Afterwards *Empson* and *Dudley*, two voracious Dogs of prey, under the Protection of this High Court, exercised the most merciless acts of oppression. The Subjects were terrified from uttering their griefs, while they saw the Thunder of the Star Chamber pointed at their Heads. This caution, however, could not prevent several dangerous tumults and insurrections. For when the Tongues of the People are restrained, They commonly discharge their resentments by a more *dangerous organ*, and break out into open acts of Violence.

During the Reign of *Henry* VIII. a high-spirited Monarch, every light expression which happened to displease him, was construed by his souple Judges into a Libel, and sometimes extended to High-Treason. When Queen *Mary* of Bloody Memory, ascended the Throne, the Parliament, in order to raise a Fence against the violent Prosecutions for Words, which had rendered the Lives, Liberties

97

with the original Library Company. By 1776 the Library Company with its over 8,000 titles was the largest and strongest library of its type in colonial times. It was used by all classes of people and its thriving condition was a further tribute to the literacy of Philadelphians in that day. James Logan, whose personal library was one of the largest and finest in the colonies, left his collection to the city in 1749 "for the facilitating and advancement of classical learning," and it became in 1768 the Loganian Library. The circulating-library idea was started by Lewis Nicola in 1767 with his New Circulating Library. The Carpenters' Company maintained a library at its hall. The State House was equipped with one of the best law libraries in the colonies and the American Philosophical Society was known for its library of science. The movement of culture outside Philadelphia was shown in the founding in 1759 in Lancaster of the "Juliana Library Company in Lancaster," perhaps the earliest in interior America. The library was named in honor of the wife of Thomas Penn. Libraries were organized even earlier in Darby in 1743 and in Germantown in 1745.

James Logan, statesman, scientist, and man of letters.

LITERARY STRIVINGS

Colonial Philadelphia expanded its literary production some seven times while its population was tripling, a remarkable evidence of the lively cultural growth of the times. Since the colonial aristocracy favored classical learning and traditions, the literature of the times was also classical in tone. The often overlooked James Logan was perhaps the foremost classical scholar in colonial America. His *Cato's Moral Distichs Englished in Couplets,* which appeared in 1735, has been termed the first translation of any classic which was both made and printed in the colonies. To prove this was no flash in the pan, Logan was the author of three scientific works in Latin published in Europe and at his death left other major manuscripts unpublished. He has been called the "first among colonial classicists." Scientific writing was also enhanced by four theses written in Latin by the first graduates of the College of Philadelphia's famous medical school.

Not everyone, however, wrote in classical Latin. Mention has been made of the pamphlet essay which appeared so commonly in the newspapers of the time. These were in English and designed for reading by ordinary citizens rather than scholars. The noted provost of the College of Philadelphia, William Smith, was a founder of *The American Magazine* and a literary society, one of the first in the colonies. His accounts of contemporary Pennsylvania and of Bouquet's expedition of 1763–64 were published in the colony and abroad. Among poets was Francis Hopkinson, whose pen took to both verse and the essay. Another early poet was Nathaniel Evans. Verse became a favorite form of expression, and Richard Fraeme attempted its use even in historical writing. Thomas Godfrey, Jr., was the son of a glazier who wrote poetry and also tried his hand at original drama with *The Prince of Parthia*. Godfrey went so far as to accompany the Forbes expedition to find inspiration for new themes. His drama was first performed in 1767 and was the first native product to be acted by professional talent, which has led many to term him the "father of American drama." It was, however, in the classical tradition, despite Godfrey's association with actual and stirring local events in history, and this has led some to contend that *The Disappointment, or the Force of Credulity,* written by Thomas Forrest but not actually produced professionally, deserves this title.

Pennsylvanians began to write their history even in colonial days. William Penn was Pennsylvania's first historian with his *Some Account of the Province of Pennsylvania* (1681). Thomas Budd with his *Good Order Established in Pennsylvania and New Jersey* and the notable Francis Daniel Pastorius's *Particular Geographical Description of the Lately Discovered Province of Pennsylvania* kept up the procession of historians, along with Gabriel Thomas and his often quoted *Historical and Geographical Account of the Province and Country of Pennsylvania.* Several others made efforts toward collecting and writing the early history of the state.

EXPRESSIONS IN THE ARTS

As a colonial city of great importance it is not without logical result that Philadelphia was a center for artistic expression. No less a perceptive personage than Ben Franklin wrote that "After the first cares for the necessities of life are over, we shall come to think of the embellishments." This was in 1763 and Franklin added to this comment the fact that already "some of our young geniuses begin to lisp attempts at painting, poetry, and music." Charles Willson Peale noted in 1771 that the people in Philadelphia, and indeed outside the city, had "a growing taste for the arts, and are becoming more and more fond of encouraging their progress amongst them!" Quaker wealth, as indicated earlier, did not favor the arts for religious reasons. It must be kept in mind, however, that only perhaps one half of the truly wealthy people of Philadelphia were Quakers after 1750. As Quaker influence lessened people began to desire more sparkling entertainment than that offered by reading. The history of

the theater begins with Louis Hallam's American Company which appeared in the city in 1754 after earlier performances in New York and Williamsburg. The late appearance was due mainly to earlier Quaker opposition to the theater. It was David Douglas who made the theater an accepted art in the staid Quaker city and who in 1766 built the first permanent theater building in the colonies, the famous Southwark Theatre.

Music also was frowned upon by Quakers, but not by German church people, whatever their persuasion. English expressions of music in the colony other than Quaker followed conventional patterns and lack any distinction. A visitor in 1750 found that "the cultivation of music is rather rare as yet," even though at Bethlehem the Moravians already were providing the earliest distinctive church music in the colonies. Ephrata was equally notable for its music as Conrad Beissel made it a very part of his religious faith and ceremonies with the hymns which he composed sung by the Ephrata choir. Beissel is looked upon by some as the first composer of music in the colonies. Folk music, which means literally the music of the people and consists of simple songs with or without some musical accompaniment, is one of the richest heritages in Pennsylvania culture and one of its major contributions to American music. It began in colonial days, mainly with the German and Scotch-Irish elements, who brought with them to Pennsylvania the songs and the accompanying folk tales of their essentially rural existence in the Old World.

The more formal and classical types of music were common in Philadelphia. Teachers of music were in appearance as early as 1750. Francis Hopkinson is famous for his "My Days Have Been So Wonderous Free," accepted as the first purely secular musical composition of any lasting quality in America. There were many stores in early Philadelphia which sold both music and musical instruments and their wares were advertised in the journals of the period. Musical instruments of almost every variety were both made and sold in later colonial Philadelphia. Gustavus Hesselius and others were organ builders of note. Signor Giovanni Gualdo arrived in Philadelphia in 1767 and in two years organized and presented the first concert in America utilizing the talent of native artists. He is known also as the first composer of any orchestral music of value in the colonies and the first conductor of such music.

People of means imported fine-art objects, but until the later years of the province there were few who could indulge in this happy practice. In any case, most wealthy Quakers frowned upon the idea and if they bought art, it was in secret. Early Pennsylvania expressed its sense of freedom in art in a number of different ways. There were many taverns patterned after the old English "pub" with its tavern sign. One of the first challenges presented to many a local artist was painting these signs. A good tavern-sign painter was encouraged to try his hand at a landscape or even a portrait of some local notable. It was a step ahead to undertake portrait painting. Colonial Philadelphia, according to experts, produced at least thirty-six portrait artists. Gustavus Hesselius, the builder of organs, in 1735 painted two Indian chiefs for Thomas Penn along with the famous "Cruci-

Portrait of Tish-Co-Han,
Delaware chief, by Hesselius.

fixion." The most famous artist of the times is of course Benjamin West, who became the ultimate darling of English art. The departure of West, who really contributed little to Pennsylvania art other than his Penn treaty painting of very doubtful historical authenticity, left Philadelphia without much to guide its artistic future, except for those few artists who had some touch with the West tradition.

In the field of architecture, Pennsylvania naturally kept to the pattern of European concepts which were brought to the colony by the people who came from various lands. Even the log cabin was an importation from Sweden. The colonists progressed rapidly from such crude habitations to houses built from native stone. The abundance of easily quarried limestone accounts for the predominance of this type of home in southeastern Pennsylvania. The Pennsylvania Germans in particular took to limestone for building because this was the customary fine building material of their native Rhineland. Even in this section, however, there was considerable early use of log buildings, and two-story log houses were not uncommon. Such houses were built using square-hewn logs, with sawed boards for flooring and hand-hewn shingles for roofing. Stone chimneys were the rule. These houses were quite refined dwellings. Germans were also famous for their fine large barns, also built usually from stone. Lewis Evans commented in 1753 that these barns were "as large as palaces," though the owners might live in a log house. Thomas Anbury found that by the Revolution two-story houses built from stone were common in the Pennsylvania German country. The English Quakers built smaller and narrower houses and used both stone and brick, though English settlers more usually turned to brick, which was available in the Philadelphia region at an early date. The Scotch-Irish built their better houses with brick, though as frontiersmen they relied heavily upon logs for not only homes but also early churches and school buildings. Quite naturally because of its greater wealth, Philadelphia was the center of the finer architecture of colonial times. Andrew Hamilton's design for the Pennsylvania State House which became Independence Hall resulted in one of the truly

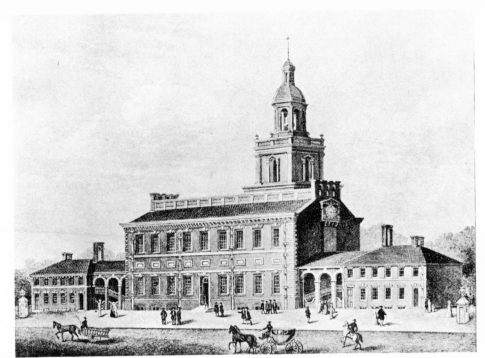

The State House of Pennsylvania (Independence Hall) in 1776, as depicted in an old print.

The Pennsylvania Hospital, from an old engraving.

distinctive buildings in the colonies. Christ Church, the Pennsylvania Hospital, the old Court House at Chester, and Old Swedes' Church (Gloria Dei) were all built in the midcolonial era and represented some of the best architecture anywhere in the British Empire of the time. At the same time, wealthy Philadelphia grandees were erecting some of the finest homes to be found outside the planter aristocracy of the southern colonies. Some of the best examples of these commonly two-story brick or stone houses are James Logan's Stenton, the Powel House, Cliveden, the John Bartram House, and the Perot-Morris House.

FROM HOMESPUN TO SILKS AND SATINS

Growing wealth was reflected also in the dress of the people and in the furnishing of homes. While homespun and even tanned leather were common materials in the dress of the frontier, a gradual improvement could be noted in the life

101

Detail of the doorway of the Bell House at Bethlehem. Fine building was not confined to Philadelphia.

of the farmer of colonial days, depending on location and degree of wealth in the area. Thus skins gave way to homespun in the years from 1700 to 1775 in a great part of interior Pennsylvania, even though the far western frontiersman would still be characterized by cruder garb. The same change could be noticed in household furnishings and utensils. As frontier living conditions eased or ended, the farm home would contain more utensils of iron and pewter rather than rely upon home-produced wooden vessels. It is surprising also how rapidly the more prosperous farmers were finding ways to buy home furnishings from the town craftsman rather than depending upon their own crudely hewn furniture. In the towns workers dressed in homespun rather than in skins and their homes were furnished better than those of the early frontier farmer. Craftsmen with special skills who had a better income lived even better. The mercantile class in the larger towns was able to live on a scale not far below that of their wealthier brethren in Philadelphia. In that city the aristocracy not given to Quaker ways

dressed in the rich silks and velvets of the time and furnished their homes in a style the equal of that of the aristocracy of England or the plantation lords of the South.

Quakers, as mentioned before, tended to find ways in which they could dress well and furnish their homes with some elegance and yet keep from ostentation. However, many a Quaker gentleman succumbed to the colorful velvet breeches and bright velvet or satin waistcoat, fine silver buttons and buckles, and silk stockings common to the "gentleman" of colonial days. The products of such excellent Philadelphia silversmiths as the Richardsons would be found in most wealthier Quaker homes. By 1776 the larger percentage of persons of wealth in Philadelphia were non-Quakers and the social life and customs of the upper class differed little from those of the aristocracy of England. However, Philadelphia Quakerism succeeded for generations, and even down to the present day, in giving Philadelphia society a certain austerity and conservatism not found elsewhere in major centers of wealth.

SCIENCE AND MEDICINE

Pennsylvania, because of Philadelphia, was the capital of advances in both science and medicine in colonial America. The advances in the world of science were especially significant because they represented the first field of intellectual endeavors in which there was a true breakthrough in emancipating the colonies from a slavish copying of English practices. While most patrons of science were from the aristocracy it is notable that the world of science, thanks in no small measure to the influence of Franklin, was open to all classes. The Junto, founded by Franklin, had among its members a glazier, surveyor, joiner, and shoemaker. Franklin was then himself a rather humble printer.

The library of James Logan has been mentioned and along with Franklin he stands as colonial America's most distinguished scientist, and was recognized as such abroad. Logan helped others and was the patron of Thomas Godfrey, who invented the mariner's quadrant nearly a year before the Englishman John Hadley developed a similar device. Logan produced a notable work on the sexuality of plants, distinctive enough to achieve European publication in 1739. Logan also aided the work of John Bartram with his studies in plant life as well as paleontology and geology. As early as 1756 Bartram, though best known for his studies in plant life, developed the scheme of boring in the earth to test mineral resources. Franklin's experiments in electricity are so well known as to need no mention other than to recognize their outstanding importance in the world of science. Thomas Hopkinson, Ebenezer Kinnersley, and Philip Syng made other notable experiments in the same field. Dr. John de Normandie laid foundations for chemistry, developed further by Dr. Benjamin Rush, whose *Syllabus of Chemistry* in 1770 was the first in America. Pennsylvanians did much to correct the woeful lack of geographical knowledge of colonial America. Lewis Evans in 1749 published the first edition of his Pennsylvania map and improved upon it in 1752. By 1755 he had produced his famous *General Map of the Middle British Colonies in America,* followed by his notable *Essays.* The mathematician and surveyor Nicholas Scull produced maps of Pennsylvania in the 1750's.

Science flourished partly because of the notable Philadelphians who surrounded Franklin but in addition was aided by marvelous scientific collections and apparatus. Logan's scientific library was probably without peer. The American Philosophical Society, America's first and oldest learned society, started in 1744 with Franklin's effort to found a society to promote useful knowledge "among the British Plantations in America." In 1766 the American Society for Promoting and Propagating Useful Knowledge grew out of the earlier Philadelphia Junto. Its leader was Charles Thomson and it represented a youthful and liberal movement in the field of science. Franklin became president in 1768 and a year later it merged with the society founded by Franklin in 1743 to become the American Philosophical Society of today. It became notable not only for its support of research but also for its library of science. The society's first volume of *Transactions* was issued in 1771. It sponsored the observations of the transit of Venus by David Rittenhouse, experiments in the improvement of agriculture, and studies of possible internal improvements in Pennsylvania. Its membership in 1776 included nearly three hundred colonials and forty-three Europeans, making it even an international institution of science.

The spirit of science was abroad throughout the province and encouraged invention. At Lancaster, William Henry was perfecting a system of interchangeable parts in the making of rifles and launching an experimental steamboat on Conestoga Creek in 1763. Franklin invented the famous Franklin stove, the first real advance in home heating, in 1742 and it was soon produced in many ironworks. Andrew Lamb was making and selling octants for taking latitude at sea by 1750. David Rittenhouse became the leading colonial maker of clocks and instruments. Thomas Gilpin, who moved to Philadelphia from Maryland, was perhaps the first professional engineer in colonial times. He designed the Schuylkill suspension bridge, and made surveys for major transportation improvements. Whitehead Humphrey made significant improvements in steelmaking and developed a screw-cutting machine to turn out iron screws. By 1771 Christopher Collins had opened a school in Philadelphia to teach hydraulics and mechanical engineering. He also tinkered with steam engines. Most of these activities were of a pioneering variety but they marked the degree to which the inventive type of mind was flourishing in colonial Pennsylvania as in no other single English colony.

When Dr. Thomas Wynne arrived with Penn and his band of Quakers on the *Welcome* there began a record of advances in medicine which made Pennsylvania a leader in this field. Along with Dr. Wynne must be listed in the early history of medicine such names as Dr. John Goodson, Dr. Thomas Cadwalader, Dr. Thomas Bond, and Dr. John Morgan. It was Dr. Bond who took the lead with Franklin in founding in 1751 the Pennsylvania Hospital, first in America. A decade later Dr. Morgan, a native-born Quaker, led in founding the first medical school in the colonies. Around it was centered the leadership of such medical men as Dr. William Shippen, Jr., and Dr.

Benjamin Rush. These men were more than physicians in the ordinary sense; they were leaders in experimentation in medicine and much of this found its way into print and became available to advance the frontiers of medicine in not just the colonies but all over the civilized world. On the eve of the Revolution Pennsylvania stood out as a major center of medical knowledge and advances in medical science in the world of that day. Dependence on England still remained because all of these leaders in medicine were of necessity trained abroad.

Looking at colonial Pennsylvania as it came to the end of that era when the clouds of revolution began to darken the land, one finds it hard to realize the wonders which had been created in the colony where many people were actually living in caves along the Delaware in 1683. In something less than a century it had become the major center of the intellectual, scientific, and cultural advances of colonial America. It was truly the "Athens of America."

CHAPTER SEVEN

A SHOT IS HEARD IN PENNSYLVANIA

The first shots of the American Revolution were fired by embattled colonial villagers and farmers and British redcoats at Lexington and Concord, on April 19, 1775. These shots lighted the fires of rebellion, but they had been fed hundreds of miles away in many colonies other than Massachusetts. No colony of Britain had been a more central point for the sparking of the first flames than Pennsylvania—land of peaceful Quakers. A year earlier the First Continental Congress had met at Philadelphia in Carpenters' Hall in September, 1774, to assert the colonists' rights to "life, liberty, and property" and indeed to all the "rights, liberties, and immunities" of Englishmen. From this gathering the colonials left to organize their local "committees of safety and inspection." These were the groups that collected the fagots with which to build the fires. The winter of 1774-75 determined whether they would be touched off. Even as the muskets sounded in New England, in April delegates from the several colonies once more were on their way to Philadelphia to meet on May 10 to discuss major and common issues developing from the unsettled dispute with the mother country. They arrived to realize that a shot had been fired which literally would be heard around the world.

SEEDS FOR REVOLUTION IN PENNSYLVANIA

The American Revolution was a social as well as a political affair, and internal as well as external. With the roots of a free and equalitarian society and economy expressing themselves in a continuing drive for more nearly complete and equal representation in government well established for nearly a century in colonial Pennsylvania, it inevitably was a seed ground for the revolutionary movement. The earlier conflicts of interest and the basic politics resulting from them were evident in a continuing drive for greater democracy from the earliest history of the province, dating back to William Penn. The rapid growth of the frontier in Pennsylvania, which had larger quantities of land open for easy settlement on its frontier than did any other single colony, kept this spirit of democracy alive and alert. Wrote Gottlieb Mittelberger in 1750, "Liberty in Pennsylvania extends so far that everyone is free from all molestation and taxation on his property, business, house and estates." Little wonder that a protest on taxation without representation in Parliament should meet with support in Pennsylvania even though many a Quaker and German opposed the use of force on religious grounds.

Certainly all was far from calm and quiet in the Quaker colony when the rifles sounded at Concord. The pattern of a strong movement for democratic action was well established. Frontier unrest against Quaker and Philadelphia policy relative to Indian relations and other matters was equally well grounded. Some of this unrest was submerged in the French and Indian War which brought the usual halt to domestic strife. Basic discontent, however, was not relieved. As pointed out earlier, one of the most potent issues which led to the rebellious march on Philadelphia by Scotch-Irish and German frontiersman in 1764 was "oppressive, unequal, and unjust" representation in the Assembly. There is abundant evidence that more peaceful frontiersmen also thought deeply about inadequate representation at Philadelphia and consequent disregard for their problems. A Cumberland County protest in 1764 listed "not being fairly represented in Assembly" as the "Bottom of all their grievances" and the "Source of all their sufferings." Contemporary politicos on the side of the frontier made medicine with this issue.

Actually, the City of Philadelphia had an equal case with the recently created western counties. Between 1752 and 1771 the Assembly was made up of thirty-six members. Of these there were twenty-six representing the three original counties, including the City of Philadelphia with only two members. The later counties had only ten members despite the fact that in 1760 the three original counties, exclusive of the City of Philadelphia, had a taxable and voting population of only 13,587, while the newer counties had a taxable population of 15,443. Robert Proud, early historian, pointed out that in 1771 the original counties with 15,365 taxables had twenty-four representatives compared with eleven for five new counties with 20,550 taxables. The later creation of three new western counties brought their Assembly representation to fifteen but there were still twenty-six members from the three original counties.

Representation in Assembly was an issue of moment in the friction between the seaboard and the frontier, but suffrage qualifications also were an issue in rural areas as well as in larger towns and cities. Colonial tax lists show that in the more settled rural areas about 50 per cent of adult males owned the fifty acres of land necessary to qualify for voting. The percentage was much less on the frontier. In the City of Philadelphia, where the personal-property qualification was more essential, in 1775 only about 10 per cent of adult males were able to qualify for voting. While estimates as to the percentage of the total adult male population of Pennsylvania which could vote vary somewhat, it is agreed that probably not much more than 25 per cent enjoyed the suffrage in colonial days. Under these conditions it was an easy matter for the merchants and larger landholders to control the government, making taxation without adequate representation a live issue in Philadelphia and much of the interior.

PENNSYLVANIA REACTS TO BRITISH TAX MEASURES

Local issues were submerged in large measure by the general protest engendered by British tax policies which followed on the heels of the end of the French and Indian War as the mother country tried to make the colonials pay some of the costs of the burden of their defense. The Stamp Act in 1765 brought united condemnation from all factions in Pennsylvania. John Dickinson became the principal author of the protest resolutions drawn up at the Stamp Act Congress of October, 1765, in New York. In the "Declaration of Rights" and "Petition to the King" it affirmed the right of British subjects to be taxed only by their own consent or that of their "legal Representatives," and taxation otherwise to be "unconstitutional and subversive of their most valuable Rights."

As a colony with an expanding frontier, Pennsylvania had been shaken even earlier by the Crown's Proclamation of 1765 which tried to close the frontier to further settlement. The Currency Act of 1764 forbidding colonial paper money and providing that taxes must be paid in gold or silver did not sit well either with Pennsylvania merchants. Pennsylvanians in 1765 took an active part in organizing nonimportation agreements along with Sons of Liberty societies.

In 1766 Parliament repealed the Stamp Act, but a year later the Townshend Acts levied new indirect taxes by attempting to collect import duties on tea, glass, lead, and paint colors. Writs of assistance authorizing arbitrary search and seizure of suspected violators possessing smuggled goods were also put in force. Philadelphia had its own Tea Party on December 27, 1773, but in the form of a protest meeting to which the captain of the British tea ship was invited. He anchored on the Delaware and saw and heard enough to lead him discreetly to withdraw his ship without an attempt to unload its cargo. In the meantime John Dickinson had unlimbered his pen once more to write in 1767–68 his famous "Letters from a Farmer in Pennsylvania" which appeared in the *Pennsylvania Chronicle* and were reprinted throughout the colonies. They presented a carefully reasoned case against the British policies and had great influence in organizing colonial resistance to them.

During this early stage of unrest against Britain the spirit of internal party difference was quieted. Conservative and liberal who were united as merchants in Philadelphia found themselves joining in spirit with frontiersmen and citizens of nearby counties. Some, like Joseph Galloway, who would later turn Tory, were vociferous in denouncing English policy because it trod heavily on mercantile toes. The normal conservatism of the mercantile seaboard began to reassert itself after 1765 as there were those who began to wonder just where all these natural rights doctrines might lead the "rabble." Quaker pacifism also reacted against any prospect of violent action. The British Intolerable Acts in 1774, which included closing the port of Boston, led to a call for help from the New Englanders. No less a person than Paul Revere arrived in Philadelphia May 19, 1774, with a "Public Letter" from the people of Boston and many private letters to prominent Philadelphians. Liberal leadership now coalesced under Charles Thomson, Thomas Mifflin, and Joseph Reed and a Committee of Correspondence was formed. The firm support of Pennsylvania for the "Cause of American Liberty" was offered in a message to Bostoners, but a couple of months later it was watered down con-

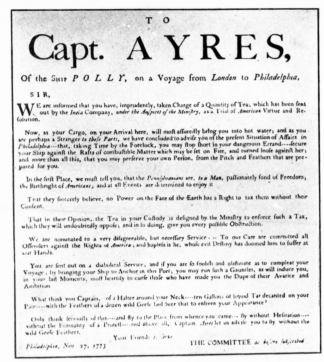

Philadelphia's tea party took the form of this warning to Captain Ayres not to land his cargo of tea on board the Polly. Dated November 27, 1773.

siderably by more conservative voices led by Galloway. Liberal groups held more meetings and "mechanics" appeared more and more to take a leading role in the protest movement in Philadelphia.

THE REVOLUTIONARY MOVEMENT GAINS IMPETUS

Petitions to Governor John Penn to call a session of the Assembly to deal with revolutionary issues were ignored in June, 1774, and led to a huge citizens' meeting in Philadelphia on June 18 attended by some eight thousand people. Out of it grew an all-important call to establish throughout the province county committees of correspondence as citizens' organizations. Representatives of these committees were called upon to gather in Philadelphia on July 15. The existing machinery of the colonial government was ignored on the grounds that it had refused to heed the petition of the people to act. The resulting

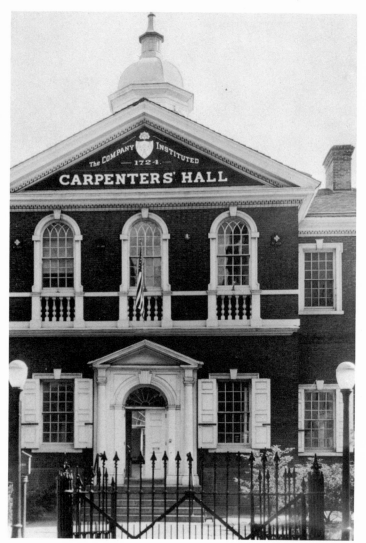

Carpenters' Hall, meeting place for the First Continental Congress.

body and it endorsed a proposal for a congress of all the colonies to consider how to cope with British threats to their rights.

The work of the First Continental Congress needs attention only in terms of Pennsylvania's role in it. It opened September 5, 1774, at Carpenters' Hall at the suggestion of the city, though the State House had been offered by the Assembly. This was itself a victory of the Pennsylvania revolutionary element, because its organization had been perfected in these same halls. Joseph Galloway typified the frightened conservatives whom he termed men of "loyal principles" with large fortunes, who now feared actual revolution on the part of those who were "congregational and presbyterians or men of bankrupt fortunes," and who were "overwhelmed in debt to British merchants." Political turmoil ensued in Pennsylvania. Pennsylvania's Assembly was the first colonial legislature to meet following the dissolving of the Congress October 26. Its action was of the greatest importance. On December 10, thanks to John Dickinson, Pennsylvania ratified despite much conservative opposition the action of the First Continental Congress in asserting colonial rights, reviving nonimportation, and approving the further organization of Committees of Correspondence. On December 15 the Assembly approved appointments of seven delegates to the Second Continental Congress already called for May 10, 1775.

Acting again outside the regular provincial governmental machinery, another revolutionary convention was called to meet at Philadelphia on January 23, 1775. Lines of action now were even more firmly drawn as the convention called for a standing committee to consider further action without regard to the regular Assembly should it attempt to subvert the patriot cause. On May 2 Governor Penn asked the existing Assembly to approve a plan for reconcilation with England, which it rejected, though at the same time refusing to approve a Philadelphia petition for colonial defense monies. The leaders of the revolutionary movement at once revived Franklin's voluntary militia, or Associators, of French and Indian War days. When John Adams arrived to attend the Second Continental Congress he found the mar-

Provincial Convention met at Carpenters' Hall with seventy-five delegates present and representing no less than eleven counties. Thomas Willing was elected chairman and Charles Thomson secretary. The Convention sat for seven days and adopted sixteen resolutions, along with some "Instructions" for the local committees. All of this activity was outside the bounds of legal governmental process and highly revolutionary in nature. The antirevolutionary group now rallied behind Governor Penn and the regularly elected Assembly, which also met in July. The revolutionary forces soon captured partial control of that

tial spirit "astonishing" and some two thousand Philadelphians marching about in daily drills. Even Quakers, he noted, were to be found in the ranks. By November, 1775, revolutionary feeling was so strong that those who refused to join this militia were made subject to a special tax. When, in 1776, the Assembly was called upon to appoint two brigadier generals to command the now recognized Associators, the volunteers themselves took the initiative in defying the Assembly on the ground that they did not have "a proportional Representation" and elected their own leaders. The provincial Assembly was now utterly without power in the face of the revolutionary forces of the last several months. The tide of revolution had become so strong that even John Dickinson now emerged as a conservative opposing actual violence.

The last colonial Assembly was elected in October of 1775. In November it selected a narrow majority of what might be termed "liberals" as representatives in the Continental Congress, though their instructions still warned against measures "that may cause, or lead to a Separation from our Mother Country or a Change of the form of this Government." As John Adams put it, many "started back" now that they saw that "independence was approaching." The conservatism of wealthy merchants and the natural pacifism of many Quakers and Pennsylvania Germans began to assert itself in resisting moves which could lead to armed revolution. Theory was now replaced by the prospect of stark reality.

Revolution against Britain was now tied inseparably with revolt against the government headed by the last of the Penns, as well as the wealthy landholders and merchants allied with the proprietor and the Church of England as the "establishment." This, of course, was not different from the general pattern of eighteenth-century revolutionary movements. It is noteworthy that throughout the period debates in the Assembly stressed on the part of the revolutionary leaders the fact that the provincial government itself was guilty of taxation and formation of policy without the adequate representation of all of the people. The colonial Assembly adjourned on June 14, 1776. Four days later the second of the Provincial

Conferences met at Carpenters' Hall to represent the revolutionary committees. Every possible effort was made by the supporters of what some persons now openly termed the "radicals" to secure full and proper representation at this meeting. Franklin, Benjamin Rush, and Thomas McKean were among the best-known members. It agreed that the existing government was incompetent.

AN INDEPENDENT COMMONWEALTH IS BORN

The resulting convention opened in the State House on July 15 and elected Franklin as its head. The crucial Declaration of Independence already had been approved on July 2 by the Continental Congress with the aid of a three-to-two vote of the Pennsylvania delegation present and voting. Franklin, James Wilson, and John Morton cast the affirmative votes, while such notables as Robert Morris and John Dickinson abstained. It was proclaimed to the public in front of the State House on July 8. The Pennsylvania Convention met in the now crowded State House along with the Congress. By September 28 the Pennsylvanians hammered out a new frame of government for an independent state. A conservative reaction even then was in process. The new document was hastily pushed through to adoption without reference to the votes of the people and by proclamation on the part of the Convention itself. Twenty-three members did not sign it, for better or for worse. Pennsylvania was first to adopt a formal constitution. It was a distinctive document which relied heavily upon Penn's liberalism as expressed in the Charter of Privileges of 1701 and the thinking behind England's revolution of 1688. It contained a Declaration of Rights, which was carried through with little change into all later Pennsylvania constitutions. The Declaration is a brilliant statement of the social compact and natural-rights theme justifying even today the "inalienable and indefeasible right" of the people "to alter, reform or abolish their government in such manner as they may think proper." Few Pennsylvanians today appreciate the fact that their state government is so subject to change. Religious liberty was extended

A Declaration of the Rights of the Inhabitants of the Common Wealth or State of Pennsylvania

First

That all Men are born equally free and Independant, and have certain Natural inherent and unalienable rights, amongst which are the enjoying and defending Life and Liberty, Acquiring, Possessing and Protecting Property and pursuing and Obtaining happiness and Safety —

Second

That all Men have a Natural and unalienable right to Worship Almighty God according to the dictates of their own Consciences and Understanding, And that no Man ought or of right can be compelled to attend any Religious Worship, or Erect or support any place of Worship, or Maintain any Ministry, contrary to, or against his own free Will and Consent Nor can any Man who acknowledges the being of a God be justly deprived or abridged of any Civil right as a Citizen, on Account of his Religious Sentiments or peculiar Mode of Religious Worship, And that no Authority can or ought to be vested in, or assumed by any power whatever that shall in any Case interfere with or in any Manner Controul the right of Conscience in the free Excercise of Religious Worship —

Third

That the People of this State have the sole exclusive and Inherent right of Governing and regulating the Internal Police of the same —

Fourth

That all power being originally Inherent in and consequently derived from the People, therefore all Officers of Government whether Legislative or Executive are their Trustees and Servants, and at all times accountable to them —

Fifth

That Government is or ought to be Instituted for the Common Benefit Protection and Security of the People, Nation or Community, and not for the particular Emolument or advantage of any Single Man, Family or set of Men, who are a part only of that Community, And that the Community hath an Indubitable, Unalienable and Indefeasible right to reform alter or Abolish Government in such Manner as shall be by that Community, Judged most conducive to the public Weal —

Sixth

That those who are Employed in the Legislative and Executive Business of the State may be Restrained from Oppression, the people have a right at such Periods as they may think proper to reduce their public Officers to a private Station and supply the Vacancies by certain and regular Elections —

Seventh

That all Elections ought to be free, and that all Free Men having a

B Franklin No 2

The Declaration of Rights in the Constitution of 1776, which has been repeated in all succeeding Constitutions. Original in the State Archives.

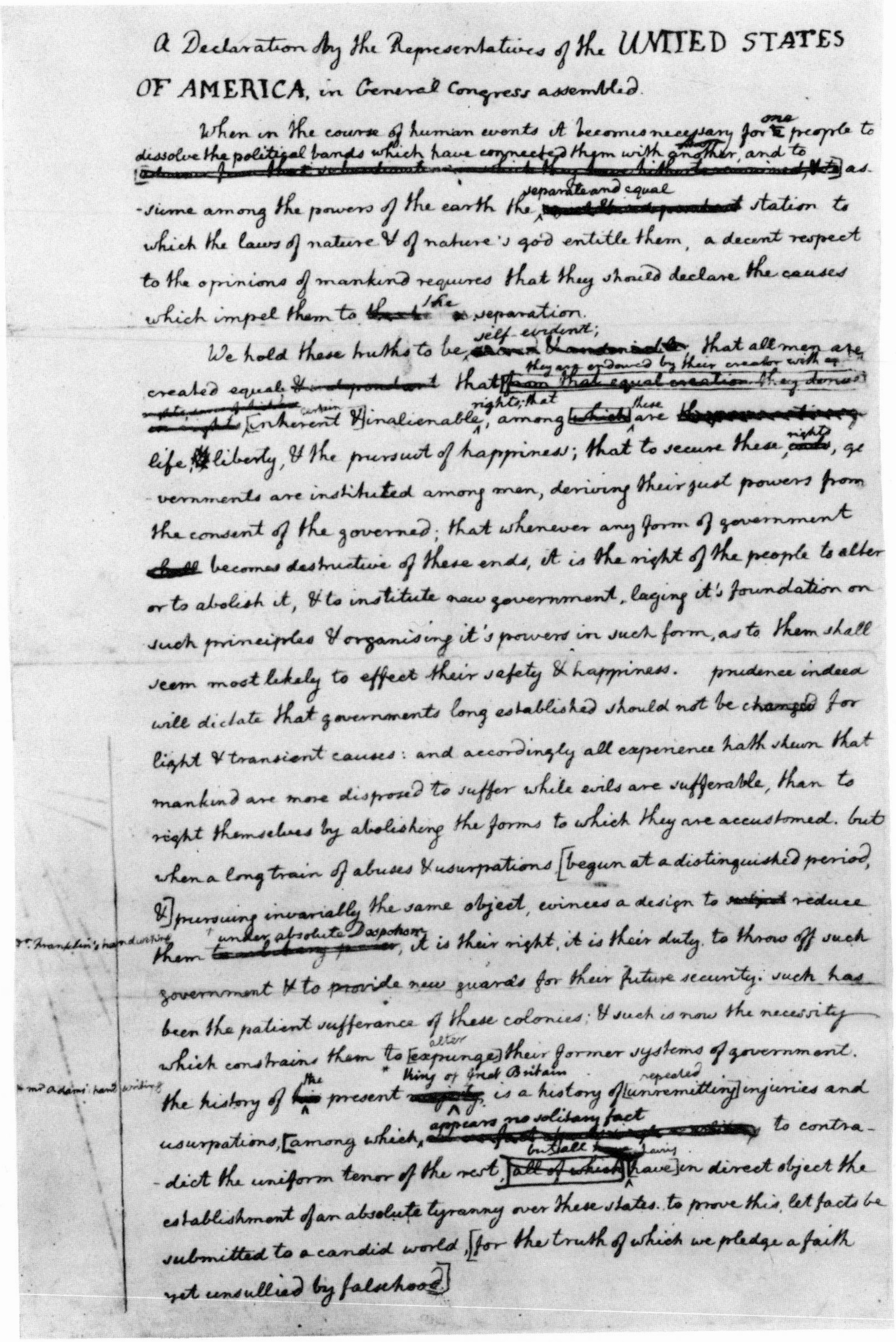
A Declaration by the Representatives of the UNITED STATES OF AMERICA, in General Congress assembled.

When in the course of human events it becomes necessary for one people to dissolve the political bands which have connected them with another, and to assume among the powers of the earth the separate and equal station to which the laws of nature & of nature's god entitle them, a decent respect to the opinions of mankind requires that they should declare the causes which impel them to the separation.

We hold these truths to be self-evident; that all men are created equal; that they are endowed by their creator with certain [inherent &] inalienable rights; that among these are life, liberty, & the pursuit of happiness; that to secure these rights, governments are instituted among men, deriving their just powers from the consent of the governed; that whenever any form of government becomes destructive of these ends, it is the right of the people to alter or to abolish it, & to institute new government, laying it's foundation on such principles & organising it's powers in such form, as to them shall seem most likely to effect their safety & happiness. prudence indeed will dictate that governments long established should not be changed for light & transient causes: and accordingly all experience hath shewn that mankind are more disposed to suffer while evils are sufferable, than to right themselves by abolishing the forms to which they are accustomed. but when a long train of abuses & usurpations [begun at a distinguished period, &] pursuing invariably the same object, evinces a design to reduce them under absolute Despotism, it is their right, it is their duty, to throw off such government & to provide new guards for their future security. such has been the patient sufferance of these colonies; & such is now the necessity which constrains them to [expunge] alter their former systems of government. the history of the present king of Great Britain is a history of [unremitting] repeated injuries and usurpations, [among which, appears no solitary fact to contradict the uniform tenor of the rest, but all have] in direct object the establishment of an absolute tyranny over these states. to prove this, let facts be submitted to a candid world [for the truth of which we pledge a faith yet unsullied by falsehood]

Dr. Franklin's handwriting

Mr. Adams' hand writing

Jefferson's rough draft of the Declaration of Independence drawn up in Philadelphia, presumably at his room at Seventh and Market Streets. Original in the Library of Congress.

by removing such oaths as prohibited Catholics from holding office.

Quaker morality called for laws encouraging "virtue" and aimed at preventing "vice and immorality," beginning the tradition of the Pennsylvania "blue laws." Property qualifications for suffrage were ended but paying a poll tax was required to vote, a feature of Pennsylvania government which lasted until the 1930's. A unicameral legislature or People's Assembly was set

genuine product of the revolutionary movement and reflected most of its distrust of authoritarian government. It did greatly increase the strength of the newer counties and was a triumph of the west over the east. Its statement of liberal natural rights and social-compact philosophy contained in the Declaration of Rights had an influence on the thinking of even French revolutionary leaders, thanks to Franklin's influence.

In general, the Pennsylvania Constitution of

Reading the Declaration of Independence on July 8, 1776. A print from the Abbey drawing.

up, which reflected long-standing distrust on the part of supporters of democratic movements against an upper house which commonly represented an aristocracy in the population. The Assembly was elected annually, with six members from each county. Distrust against "kingly" power was also evidenced by the creation of a Supreme Executive Council rather than a single governor as the executive authority. It was elected every three years, with two men from each county and one from Philadelphia. The head of the Council was known as the president, and Pennsylvania had this official rather than a governor as its ceremonial executive head until 1790. A Council of Censors was another feature of the new state government; it was made up of two representatives from each county and one from the city, elected by the people. It was to meet at least every seven years to take a look at all the other departments. The new constitution was a

1776 was one of the most liberal and truly influential to come out of the American Revolution. It divided the conservative and liberal forces sufficiently to produce the first real strength of the Tory or Loyalist movement. Perhaps one-third of the population turned Tory, and it included many who had been earlier supporters of strong protest against imperial policy, notably Joseph Galloway. Many merchants and larger landholders failed to see the necessity for revolution and looked upon it as a radical manifestation of what they termed the "rabble." Quakers and many German sects were pacifist by religious principle and opposed armed revolt, though many deserted this conviction. It is a mistake to label all the wealthy, the able and the well born as Loyalists merely because of this position in society. There were Quakers like Timothy Matlack who could write, "I have ever considered personal liberty and safety as the first object of civil government, and possession and security of property the next." There were many notable scientists, lawyers, manufacturers, merchants, and landholders who were stalwart patriots. Indeed, James Cannon, professor of mathematics at the College of Philadelphia, has been termed the "chief architect of the Pennsylvania constitution" in terms of its actual writing, though this is an honor usually associated with Franklin. Generalizations about the motivation for Loyalist sentiment are not easy and often it involves study of the individual. The same is true of most Revolutionary sentiment.

The Liberty Bell.

PENNSYLVANIA BECOMES A KEY BATTLEGROUND

Be that as it may, the issue was resolved in 1776 and Pennsylvania was not only the seat of the united colonial movement for independence and of its continued Revolutionary government but also a powerful force in winning that independence by war. The revived Associators soon reached at least seven battalions numbering some thousand men each. By the autumn of 1776, at least thirty-five thousand Pennsylvanians were enrolled in the Flying Camp of the Continental forces. These were essentially militia used only in case of emergency. Thirteen regiments under "Mad Anthony" Wayne were in the Pennsylvania Line, mostly on an annual enlistment basis. By 1776 the "Pennsylvania Navy," consisting of twenty-seven ships, had been organized to defend the Delaware. The United States Navy and the Marine Corps both had their birthplace in Philadelphia, mainly because of the urgency of defending the Delaware as an avenue of attack by the British on the "nest of rebellion" which that city so completely represented. Pennsylvania riflemen were at Bunker Hill from as far west as Carlisle. They were also in the campaigns in Canada.

In 1776 Washington with his feeble army was forced back from Long Island and across New Jersey into Pennsylvania on November 28. The British were talking now of a "total end to the war." British officers were convinced the so-called patriots were a mere rabble with "scarce a pair of breeches." Washington had perhaps three thousand men and the numbers were dwindling under the one-year enlistment policy. At the Thompson-Neely house in what is today Washington Crossing State Park, Washington planned the strategy which took him across the ice-choked Delaware on Christmas night to strike the British at Trenton and capture over a thousand Hessian prisoners. Pennsylvania riflemen and militia brought to Washington's aid gave him new strength for this maneuver and for another brilliant movement through which he surprised Cornwallis, leaving his campfires burning to deceive the enemy, and the next day badly cut to pieces three British regiments at Princeton. He then retired to the hills of Morristown, New Jersey. From this point he was able to raid British communications with New York and here Washington spent the critical winter of 1777 in a considerably better position than at the close of 1776.

The British were not dismayed but instead strengthened their plans to bring the uprising to an end with a three-pronged movement to cut the northern colonies into two parts. Lieutenant Colonel Barry St. Leger aided by his Indian allies was to move an army from Fort Oswego on Lake Ontario by way of the Mohawk Valley to the Hudson River. General John Burgoyne led a second army down the historic Richelieu River and Lake Champlain route into central New York. General Howe was supposed to move up the Hudson from New York. Thus a powerful pincers movement would consolidate to separate New England from the Middle Colonies. St. Leger was turned back by the Continentals at Fort Stanwix.

Burgoyne met disaster at Saratoga. In the meantime, Howe ignored his part of the plan.

For some perverse reason of his own, or through a failure to receive his orders, General Howe embarked his army of some eighteen thousand men on board ship and headed for an invasion route to the south. Delaware Bay may have been his original objective but it was strongly defended and Washington had his forces in readiness as he moved defensively to meet a British thrust. Howe then sailed down to the Chesapeake seeking a safer landing and disembarked his army at the Head of Elk on August 25. Howe's personal strategy was aimed at cutting off Pennsylvania from the southern colonies. If the total British campaign had been successful it could well have ended the Revolution. Washington was unable to halt the British and lost the Battle of the Brandywine on September 11 as Cornwallis executed a flanking movement he may have learned earlier that year from Washington at Trenton. Wayne's corps was nearly wiped out on September 20 in the "Battle of the Clouds" at Paoli. In Philadelphia the dread cry, "The British are coming," was heard at every street corner as both the Congress and many citizens fled the city, which Howe occupied on September 25. Attacking the British early on the foggy morning of October 4 at Germantown, Washington again failed to win victory. Howe was left free to occupy Philadelphia without hazard and settled down for a pleasant winter wining and dining with its Tory society. Washington withdrew his beaten, hungry, and tattered army to Whitemarsh and finally to Valley Forge. Washington did test the British again in November and Howe advanced to Whitemarsh in December where, though he outnumbered the Continentals by two to one, he decided not to press an attack.

TRAVAIL AT VALLEY FORGE

Valley Forge, on the west bank of the Schuylkill and twenty-one miles from Philadelphia, was an excellent protective position which placed Washington's army between the British and possible raids upon the iron furnaces and powder mills of the interior. The travail at Valley Forge has been told and retold. The lack of proper supplies and food reflected the low ebb of the patriot cause. It brought to light the resulting unwillingness of some fair-weather patriots, as well as about one-third of Pennsylvanians who had never committed themselves one way or the other, to aid the cause of liberty. Food and clothing were to be had but there were all too few who were willing to sell it for Continental money as opposed to British gold. Congress, sitting at distant York, helped little with its bungling efforts. The result was an army at times almost starving and without adequate clothing encamped at Valley Forge in the midst of plenty.

But there were some brighter lights in the darkness. Among them was the arrival at Valley Forge of the Prussian drillmaster General Baron von Steuben who brought new discipline and organization. Then there were patriots who did provide food and clothing, sometimes without any promise of money. Pennsylvania's popular General Thomas Mifflin met with some success in new recruiting. Best news of all was that of the treaties of commerce and of alliance with France signed on February 6, 1778, and in the negotiation of which Franklin had so large a role. Spain and the Netherlands also came to the support of the American cause. Baron von Steuben was joined by Baron de Kalb, the youthful Marquis de Lafayette, Casimir Pulaski, Thaddeus Kosciusko and others. The first feeble steps toward a new national government were taken by Congress at York as it endorsed the Articles of Confederation. On June 16 the British left Philadelphia, and with them went some three thousand Tories. Washington marched out of Valley Forge on June 19, now celebrated as "Evacuation Day." The major campaigns for Washington's army now moved elsewhere.

WAR ON THE FRONTIER

In Pennsylvania itself the problem of protection of the frontier against the British-incited Tories and Indians became a major concern of not only the state but also the Congress. Both Congress and the British sought Indian support, but here again Continental currency and a feeble treas-

December 30, 1777.

TEUCRO DUCE NIL DESPERANDOM.

First Battalion of PENNSYLVANIA LOYALISTS, commanded by His Excellency Sir WILLIAM HOWE, K. B.

ALL INTREPID ABLE-BODIED

HEROES,

WHO are willing to serve His MAJESTY KING GEORGE the Third, in Defence of their Country, Laws and Constitution, against the arbitrary Usurpations of a tyrannical Congress, have now not only an Opportunity of manifesting their Spirit, by assisting in reducing to Obedience their too-long deluded Countrymen, but also of acquiring the polite Accomplishments of a Soldier, by serving only two Years, or during the present Rebellion in America.

Such spirited Fellows, who are willing to engage, will be rewarded at the End of the War, besides their Laurels, with 50 Acres of Land, where every gallant Hero may retire, and enjoy his Bottle and Lass.

Each Volunteer will receive, as a Bounty, FIVE DOLLARS, besides Arms, Cloathing and Accoutrements, and every other Requisite proper to accommodate a Gentleman Soldier, by applying to Lieutenant Colonel ALLEN, or at Captain KEARNY's Rendezvous, at PATRICK TONRY's, three Doors above Market-street, in Second-street.

A Loyalist recruiting poster in 1777.

ury could not cope with British gold and liberal supplies of guns, powder, and rum. By tradition, the Iroquois in New York were friends of England. Besides, Pennsylvania frontiersmen who pressed westward after 1763 had not endeared themselves to the Indians. By 1778 the notorious Colonel John Butler emerged as a leader of Tory and Indian raids in the upper Susquehanna Valley. In June, 1778, these attacks forced settlers to flee in the "Great Runaway" from this region. In July, Butler's minions fell upon the defenseless region around Wilkes-Barre and perpetrated the infamous Wyoming Massacre on July 5. Pennsylvania fought back with an expedition led by Colonel Thomas Hartley which left Fort Muncy September 21. Hartley marched overland and destroyed the Seneca town of Queen Esther Montour just south of the present Athens. Hartley returned to Fort Muncy on October 1 after marching some 300 miles in about two weeks and upon having fought another rear-guard battle with the Indians near Wyalusing Rocks.

Hartley's raid was followed the next spring by one of the major undertakings of the entire Revolution, the Sullivan-Clinton expedition. Washington announced tersely, "It is proposed to carry the war into the heart of the country of the Six Nations, to cut off their settlements, destroy their next year's crops, and do to them every other mischief which time and circumstances will permit." General John Sullivan was ordered to organize an army at Easton at the forks of the Delaware. On June 18, 1779, Sullivan began his long march northward toward Wilkes-Barre and Tioga Point. Old Fort Wyoming at Wilkes-Barre was rebuilt as a base. Sullivan marched on and arrived at Tioga Point (Athens) on August 11. There he built Fort Sullivan. General James Clinton, in command of the northern department, had organized a second army at the headwaters of the Susquehanna at Cooperstown, New York, and joined Sullivan at Tioga Point August 22. The combined force now amounted to some four thousand men. The Indian and Tory forces were encountered and defeated just south of Elmira, New York, in the Battle of Newtown. The expedition then marched into the heart of the Seneca and Cayuga country in New York. A

third prong of this major operation had been organized under Colonel Daniel Brodhead at Fort Pitt. Brodhead marched in August from Fort Pitt with the intention of joining Sullivan and Clinton in continuing the campaign all the way to an attack on Fort Niagara, center of British control of the Indian country. The late season and Brodhead's failure to move with enough rapidity led to the abandonment of this final phase of the campaign.

At least forty major Indian villages were destroyed, along with their all-important corn fields in southern New York. Though the larger strategy was not successful, the Sullivan-Clinton expedition had a healthy influence in weakening for the remainder of the war the ability to incite Tory-Indian raids on the American frontier in the Susquehanna Valley. Western Pennsylvania, despite the American outpost at Fort Pitt, continued to be the victim of bloody raids from Indians in the Ohio country. The state and local citizenry resorted to settler forts on the frontier similar to those of French and Indian War days in an effort to protect themselves against the enemy.

PENNSYLVANIA, A KEYSTONE IN THE REVOLUTION

Pennsylvania made many contributions to American success in winning independence. Military leaders of more than average note included Thomas Mifflin, Ephraim Blaine, "Mad Anthony" Wayne, Arthur St. Clair, Edward Hand, John Armstrong, William Irvine, and Peter Muhlenberg. Pennsylvania riflemen trained on the frontier in the use of the long rifle were noted as among the most expert sharpshooters of the Revolution. The vigorous fighting abilities and the numbers of Scotch-Irish from the Pennsylvania frontier in the Continental Army led more than one Hessian and British soldier to note their presence and refer to the Revolution as an "Irish" uprising. Franklin's achievements in European diplomacy which won France and others to the patriot cause deserve his recognition as one of the truly decisive individual leaders influencing the outcome of the Revolution. James Wilson, Benjamin Rush, Joseph Reed, George

Charles Willson Peale's portrait of Robert Morris.

can Navy. There were at least sixty power mills in the state at the end of the Revolution. Lead mines in central Pennsylvania not far from today's Altoona provided so important a lead supply as to necessitate building Fort Roberdeau to insure their protection. Riflemakers of the Lancaster and York county region provided their vital wares in abundance while Pennsylvania furnaces cast cannon and balls. Their product was important enough to justify the use of Hessian prisoners to bolster the labor supply on the iron plantations. Armies move on their stomachs, and Pennsylvania wheat provided much of the needed flour. Philadelphia was a major port from which many supplies moved to other states for wartime use. Its financial resources made it possible for Robert Morris and Haym Salomon to become the financiers of the Revolution. All in all, Pennsylvania not only gave birth to the Revolution in terms of providing the locale for the Declaration of Independence and the seat for the work of the Continental Congress but also in a variety of other ways which reflected its position of influence at the end of America's colonial era.

Bryan, Thomas McKean, Robert Morris, and Haym Salomon all played distinctive roles in trying areas of government and finance in those crisis years from the start of the Revolution until its end.

Pennsylvania's resources always have been important in wartime, and the tradition goes back to the Revolution. The fact that Pennsylvania as early as 1750 had won leadership in the iron industry in itself was a prime factor in determining the outcome of the Revolution. Philadelphia was a center of wealth and enterprise in colonial America, and while many of its more wealthy merchants turned Tory there was never any doubt that the major influence of Pennsylvania's economy and its leadership was thrown behind the patriot cause. Few ironmasters, for example, were ever counted as Loyalists. Samuel Wetherill was a "fighting Quaker" merchant and manufacturer who supplied clothing for the Continental Army without too much regard to payment. Delaware shipyards provided the vessels for the first Ameri-

A SECOND STATE CONSTITUTION IS ADOPTED IN 1790

Since the Revolution was a social as well as a political movement, its aftermath represented a continuation of the basic struggle between certain conflicting forces which had motivated its beginning. The removal of large numbers of the more conservative population as a result of the Tory exodus did not change essentially the nature of the movement. While the transition from colony to commonwealth had been achieved in 1776 by a new Constitution, along with the end of the Penn proprietary and governmental interest, this did not mean an end to political differences within the new state. The political interests associated with the proprietorship were merely pushed aside by the new revolutionary government; without any use of force, in the autumn of 1776 it simply ignored the dying Assembly of the John Penn era. The land interests of the Penns were seized by the state, but not without compensation. The very fact that the Constitution of 1776 was not sub-

117

mitted to the people was bound to give rise to unrest. Immediate criticism of it led to the informal grouping of its supporters as Constitutionalists, led by Franklin, George Bryan, William Findley, and John Smilie; men like James Wilson, Robert Morris, and Thomas Mifflin were the Anti-Constitutionalist leaders. The great power of the unicameral legislature, the lack of any real executive branch, and the Council of Censors with its general authority to pass on the validity of all phases of the operation of the government were points of question.

Since the Council was elected by popular suffrage, with two members from each county and two from the City of Philadelphia, it provided the fulcrum for a contest. Early in 1784 the Anti-Constitutionalists captured a majority of the Council and moved for a study of possible amendments to the Constitution. The resulting report proposed abolition of the Council of Censors, advocated a single executive authority and a bicameral Assembly. Representation, said the report, should be based on the number of taxables and should not be equal in terms of political units. The Anti-Constitutionalists further showed their conservative and anti-frontier bent by suggesting that the five western counties should be represented by four members in a proposed upper house in the legislature as contrasted with twenty-five for the older eastern counties. The Constitutionalists later in 1784 regained control and the Council finally rejected the need to call a convention "to alter, explain or amend the Constitution." The Constitutionalists were not able to hold their position and by 1789 the more conservative forces in the state had won a dominant control of the Assembly. The Council of Censors was now ignored and the Assembly itself issued a call for a convention to revise the Constitution, which it upheld despite an effort of the Executive Council to defeat what it termed an extralegal action. The forces of counterrevolution now were in the saddle and had gained their point in much the same unconstitutional manner as had the original revolutionary leaders in 1776.

The Constitutional Convention which met at Philadelphia on November 24, 1789, has been termed "probably the most capable and talented body of Pennsylvanians that ever gathered together to perform a public function." This was true of both the conservative and the liberal leadership. The great minds of the entire Revolutionary era were at this conclave. The names of James Wilson and Thomas McKean stand out among the conservatives; those of Albert Gallatin, William Findley, and James Smilie are less well known as national figures. The latter were from western Pennsylvania and all had emerged as leaders of a western and agrarian democracy and their names bore weight in the politics of Pennsylvania of that day. Thomas Mifflin was elected to preside. Constructive suggestions were made by both sides to improve the old constitution, which admittedly was hastily drawn. Only five members of the convention in 1790, for example, opposed a bicameral legislative body and there was unanimity also on the need for a single chief executive authority. The issue of representation in the Assembly furnished the greatest divergence of opinion and liberal versus conservative opinions clashed frequently as western agrarian interests viewed with suspicion eastern commercial concerns. There were a few ultra-conservatives sincerely suspicious of any popular democracy. James Wilson emerged as the man who was best able to establish a judicial balance between the rival groups. The convention adjourned in February, 1790, for a breathing spell, during which the people were given an opportunity to express their views on a suggested draft. It assembled again in August and adjourned on September 2 with its labors completed. There was little reaction one way or the other from the people.

Major changes were made in the structure of the state government. A bicameral Assembly was created with an elective State Senate representing districts on a basis of four-year election periods. The House of Representatives was elected annually by the people. A governor elected by popular vote and serving a three-year term, but subject to re-election for nine out of any twelve years, replaced the plural Executive Council. His veto power and appointive privileges made him a powerful figure, and in later years these gave rise to a basic criticism of the Constitution of 1790.

James Wilson's rough draft of the Constitution in 1787.
Original in The Historical Society of Pennsylvania.

The Declaration of Rights was retained with very slight changes. Suffrage was vested in all adult white freemen with two years' residence in the state prior to an election and who had paid state or county taxes assessed at least six months before an election. This was a liberal provision for the times. The resulting Constitution of 1790, mainly because it was a result of some reaction against enthusiasms of the early days of the Revolution, is sometimes referred to as representing a conservative reaction. In a sense it did show signs of more conservative thinking on matters of government. On the other hand, the Constitution of 1776 had features which virtually everyone agreed by 1789 were inadequate or unsuited to good practice in government. These were corrected and the resulting Constitution of 1790 remained one of the most advanced in the new nation. Kentucky in 1792 took a large part of its constitution from Pennsylvania. This action of the first new state west of the mountains hardly bears out any thinking that Pennsylvania had drafted a reactionary document.

All in all, the era of the Revolution represented a steady progress of Pennsylvania toward greater democracy in its own government and society. The Loyalists who left the state did not deplete its resources of talent in either government or business. Indeed, they were hardly missed. The sound foundations of constitutional government laid by William Penn as early as 1701 proved their solid worth. Pennsylvania through its contributions and leadership during the Revolutionary era demonstrated its place as a keystone state in a new nation.

BIRTHPLACE OF THE FEDERAL CONSTITUTION

The battle over the Constitution of 1790 took place in the midst of the events connected with the Constitutional Convention of 1787 in Philadelphia. Once again some of the wisest minds in America turned to Philadelphia and the Pennsylvania State House in the midst of crisis. The Articles of Confederation, approved by Congress while sitting at York and ratified by the states during the Revolution, had not provided the strong bonds of union needed to meet the problems of the new nation. Commissioners of Maryland and Virginia meeting at Mount Vernon with General Washington to decide a boundary dispute decided to call a meeting of delegates from several states, including Pennsylvania, New York, Delaware, and New Jersey, at Annapolis, Maryland, in September, 1786. The poorly attended meeting concerned itself mainly with interstate trade problems. It decided to attempt a more national convention in Philadelphia in May, 1787. Pennsylvania was very much of a key state in the calling of such a convention. Virginia feared New England as supporting even more disunity and wanted Pennsylvania on its side. Some Pennsylvanians leaned toward New England's idea of continuing a decentralized government. On the other hand, Philadelphians were desirous of securing the national capital for that city and willing to cooperate with southern states on certain issues in order to get it. This paid off when in the first session of Congress a compromise was arranged to center the capital at Philadelphia until 1800 when it would be moved to Washington.

Called to meet on May 14, the Convention did not get under way until May 25, 1787, because travel difficulties slowed several arrivals. Though seventy-four delegates were appointed, there were nineteen who for various reasons did not attend. Much to the dismay of those with democratic views, the meetings were held in secrecy behind doors closed and guarded by sentries. The basic issue was just how far the members would go in perfecting a central union in the face of the still strong revolutionary thinking against any strong central government. The labors and the compromises which resulted in a final decision in the Constitution of 1787 as drafted are a part of the history of the nation rather than of Pennsylvania.

The delegation sent by Pennsylvania to the convention was among the most distinguished of any single state. Its dean was the eighty-one-year-old Benjamin Franklin, who did not take an active part in debates but whose sound wisdom and kindly humor at times held the meetings together in the face of possible disruption. James Wilson was one of the great legal minds influencing the new Constitution and was second only to Virginia's James Madison as its major architect.

Adoption of the Constitution in 1787, from the Froelich painting in the State Museum.

Gouverneur Morris was one of the stylists who helped to write the document in proper form. Also present were Robert Morris, Thomas Mifflin, George Clymer, Thomas Fitz-Simons. Admittedly, it was a delegation which favored conservative thinking.

Ratification of the completed Constitution was a major issue in the politics of the state in 1787. Public meetings were held, and the newspapers and pamphleteers entered into the battle. All in all it became the most spirited political issue since 1776. It was understood generally that Philadelphia and the eastern counties were for the new Constitution and the western counties against it. When the Assembly resolved to call a convention elected to debate the ratification of the Federal Constitution by Pennsylvania the issue was joined. Gouverneur Morris and others feared "the cold and sower temper of the back Counties." When it was all over the Federalists, or supporters of the Constitution, had won. The ratifying convention met in Philadelphia on November 21 and lasted until December 15, 1787. The basic issue debated remained that of rights of the states as opposed to stronger central government. Dr.

Benjamin Rush and James Wilson were chief supporters of ratification. On December 12 by a vote of forty-six to twenty-three the Constitution was ratified and the following day members of the Convention marched in colorful procession with officials of the state, city, and university to the courthouse to announce the decision to the people. Pennsylvania was the second state to ratify, led by only a few days by Delaware. It was the first large state to ratify and thus boosted greatly the final triumph of the Constitution.

The decision was not received with jollification in the western counties, where the frontier democracy continued to uphold what George Bryan called "the Standard of Liberty." These leaders, who now included Albert Gallatin, got in touch with opponents of the Constitution in other states to encourage at least support of early amendments. Credit must be given to the vigorous opponents of the Federal Constitution as drawn up at Philadelphia for securing the early adoption of the Bill of Rights, the first ten amendments to the Constitution, which clarified several disputed points regarding the cherished rights of citizens and smoothed the remaining opposition to it.

CHAPTER EIGHT

SOCIAL AND CULTURAL PATTERNS FROM THE REVOLUTION TO THE CIVIL WAR

The years between the Revolution and the Civil War were vital ones in the development of the social and cultural patterns of the new nation. Those were the years during which the United States began to establish foundations for truly national institutions. Pennsylvania played a key role in forming these foundations. It was a state with an already strongly developed tradition of democracy, and was an influential force in support of the growing social democracy of the period. Pennsylvania down to about 1840 continued to have a frontier, with its varied influences upon social and cultural institutions. It was a state with strong elements in its population dedicated to humanitarian reforms, notably the Quakers. Pennsylvania was a state with a growing economy based upon the utilization of such resources as coal and iron ore, and a maturing industrial revolution with accompanying major improvements and advances in transportation. Out of this newly flourishing economy came the wealth to support cultural and social progress. Continued growth in

population and wealth meant the further growth of towns and cities with their favorable civilizing force. Throughout history, urbanization and growing wealth, along with improvements in transportation and communication, have been major forces determining social and cultural changes. Pennsylvania's favorable geographical position and the continued importance of Philadelphia as a major center of the nation's commercial, industrial, and financial affairs further aided Pennsylvania to become very much a keystone state in the pattern of national cultural and social change which followed the Revolution.

THE FRONTIER ENDS AS TOWNS AND CITIES THRIVE

The growth of Pennsylvania's population after 1790 was at a rate of about 30 per cent in every decade down to 1860. Between 1820 and 1860 it more than doubled from 1,049,458 to 2,906,215. Even more important, in terms of its bearing upon social and cultural change, was the marked increase in the density of the population. As late as 1840 there were only 38.3 persons living within each square mile; by 1860 it had reached 64.6 persons. The land was being filled with people. In 1820, 87 per cent of the people of the state were living in rural areas. In 1790 it had been almost 90 per cent. By 1860 it was a ratio of 69 per cent in rural areas, as compared with 31 per cent in urban areas. The farm slowly was giving way to town and city.

It is hard to realize that large areas in Pennsylvania remained largely unsettled at the end of the Revolution and that northwestern Pennsylvania in particular was not yet free of the menace of Indian marauders. Pennsylvania grew so rapidly that by 1840 the frontier, in terms of that thin line of settlement moving into previously unsettled and undeveloped land, came to an end. This was a process which had been going on for over a century and a half. True, there remained many parts of the commonwealth which were but sparsely settled and developed, but the frontier had vanished.

Everywhere new towns were appearing on the map, many of which would emerge later as key cities. In western Pennsylvania there were now included in census returns for the first time Erie, Franklin, Greensburg, Washington, and Meadville. In the center of the state such important places as Lewistown, Lock Haven, Bellefonte, and Williamsport were founded and growing with every decade. Pittsburgh was becoming a major city of the West. As late as 1800 it really was only a large frontier town with hardly over 1,500 people. By 1860 it had grown to a small city with 77,923 people. In central Pennsylvania the larger cities of today were hardly more than moderate-sized towns. By 1830 Bethlehem, Allentown, and Easton were growing into small cities. Reading had 23,162 people in 1860; Lancaster was a smaller city with only 17,603 people. The new state capital at Harrisburg was hardly more than a large town in 1860 with a modest 13,405 residents. Altoona, Johnstown, Scranton, and Pottsville were among the new towns showing signs of activity by 1860. Their founding and growth were related to coal, iron, and railroads. In 1800 there were only five places, all in the east, with a population which entitled them to an urban classification. By 1860 the number had grown to forty-six, fairly well distributed between Philadelphia and Pittsburgh. Large areas of Pennsylvania even as late as the Civil War awaited any substantial de-

North Queen Street in Lancaster about 1836, from an old print.

velopment of urban centers of population. But small or large, the town and city was the center for the slow advance of a new social, cultural, and intellectual life. Here were to be found the finer homes, the better schools, the largest churches. Here also were the library, the lyceum, and the traveling theater, all of which offered something new in the social and cultural life of the community.

LIFE IN RURAL PENNSYLVANIA

Under the conditions of rapid growth and change which prevailed between the Revolution and the Civil War it is hard to generalize about the life of the typical Pennsylvania farmer in this era. It varied much as it had in colonial times and in direct relation to proximity of markets and the resulting chance to dispose of some of the product of the farm for actual money, which in turn could be used to purchase the things the farmer might wish to have to improve his farm and his home. The life of those times is not documented for the historian with the elaborate statistical surveys, studies, and reports which provide today minute detail on contemporary social conditions. The diaries, the letters, and especially the country newspapers of the time are the only grist for the historian's mill for this early era. In northern Pennsylvania along the New York border contemporary accounts as late as the 1830's tell of a rugged existence which, except for freedom from the peril of possible Indian attack, was not much different from the hard days of an earlier frontier in western Pennsylvania. Even a grist mill was miles away from a pioneer settler, and wild game shot in the forest was a staple source of food while the farmer strove to clear some land in the forest to raise his first crops. Potter County settlers as late as 1840 were building log houses and barns. Towns of any type were few and far between. Roads in this region remained uniformly bad. Under such conditions, manufacture of most tools and implements and even some clothing in the home was not uncommon as late as 1850. Such industry as existed resembled the era of craft industry with the town shoemaker, wheelwright, blacksmith, and tailor.

In contrast, in those sections of the state which prospered from the growth of industry and were reached by the new turnpikes, the canals, and later by the first railroads the life of farm people was greatly improved as they shared in a new prosperity. Charles Joseph Latrobe, visiting the Pennsylvania German country in the 1830's, was carried away by the "verdant farms" and their "substantial houses, most of which are both handsome and commodious, painted in foreign style." Even the barns were "spacious and solidly constructed." There was in the mid-1800's a substantial prosperity and a good life common to farming in the entire eastern section of Pennsylvania. Products of the farm found a ready market for cash. As late as 1840 this region was widely known as "the breadbasket of America."

Towns and cities of any size remained, however, far from the reach of many rural Pennsylvanians in western and northern counties before the Civil War. The county seat was about as far from home as many a Pennsylvania farmer of that day commonly reached. In the more developed areas, the county fair by 1850 became an event of great importance in the life of rural Pennsylvania. The annual fair, as one observer in 1854 put it, "presented a lively and animated appearance." Fair or no fair, the craze for turnpike road building by 1850 brought some type of improved highway into almost all but the farthest removed portions of the state, thus providing new means of communicating with the outside world and reaching a market for goods which could be sold without the resort to a barter system. Rural hamlets sprang up at many a crossroad where at least a country store, a blacksmith shop, and other convenient services such as a grist mill and a sawmill were available to meet the needs of the countryside. The first reports which flowed into Harrisburg as the Free School Act of 1834 began to find substantial root throughout the state by the 1850's show the importance of these villages. They were centers for growth of the public school system. They were also the place where the first community churches were erected. Even the smallest village thus became a center for the cultural and social improvement of a surrounding and often rather large community.

Philadelphia in 1787, showing the new market from Spring and Second.

PHILADELPHIA AND PITTSBURGH

Philadelphia continued as the metropolis of Pennsylvania, though it was outgrown in population by New York in 1830 and demoted to the role of the nation's second city. However, Philadelphia remained a large city with well over half a million people in 1860. New York drew ahead of Philadelphia mainly because of the great immigrant influx. Philadelphia continued to be, in the almost unanimous opinion of European visitors, the most refined and the most beautiful city in America. Alexander Farkas de Bolon, visitor from Hungary to the United States, summed it up when he wrote in 1834: "Many travellers write and say that Philadelphia is the most beautiful city in the world, I heard this exclusive praise about so many towns that, although I expected Philadelphia to be beautiful, I did not imagine that after ten days' residence there, I should admit that the city is really one of the most lovely. . . ." He went on to compliment the city upon its support of "the sciences and philanthropic institutions" rather than falling into the common American habit of allowing itself to be "monopolized by trade and politics." Philadelphia, he wrote, "is the center of academic erudition and the cradle of science." "Perhaps nowhere else are books sought as much as here," wrote Farkas, pointing to sixty-four public libraries with 64,000 volumes, thirty-two print shops and fifty newspapers and periodicals in publication as proof of his statement.

The continuing position of Philadelphia as

something of the Athens of America rested in part upon its still vigorous commercial empire. This was supplemented after 1830 by a remarkable expansion of its industries, new connections with the rich coal and iron business of interior Pennsylvania by canal and railroad, and a strong reservoir of surplus capital for investment in enterprise all over the country which made it the true financial capital of the nation. This wealth continued to support the philanthropy and the cultural climate which had become so distinctive a part of the Philadelphia heritage in colonial days. Despite its cultural advance, Philadelphia remained a city dominated in no small measure by the Quaker tradition of austerity and highly moral behavior. Farkas, for example, noted that "Philadelphia certainly is not a city of pleasure. But he who pursues intellectual delights, will find inexhaustible sources of that here."

No other Pennsylvania city could match Philadelphia, in size, distinction of its buildings and design as a city, or general culture. A visitor to Pittsburgh in 1831 noted that the center of the city was not "pleasant, joyful, and original." It looked like Manchester or Birmingham and "there is an eternal smoke over the city; the houses and the tremendous factories are wrapped in smoke; in streets and on the wharves a tumult of . . . carts; everywhere scenes of loading and unloading; iron foundries and the humming of factories." There was little time for cultural pursuits in the Pittsburgh of that day.

Despite all handicaps, cultural strivings were evident in even the smallest towns. A music teacher was advertising his services in the tiny Central Pennsylvania village of Lewisburg as early as 1832 and twenty years later a hardy artist announced he was ready "to give lessons in Drawing, and Water-Color Painting" as well as to "execute portraits in Water-Colors." There were numerous more or less itinerant artists and musicians floating from community to community offering their services to those interested and able to pay the fees.

THE TRIUMPH OF FREE PUBLIC SCHOOLING

The greatest single triumph of an onward marching democracy in the new United States was the establishing of a system of free public schools. Pennsylvania was not first in this movement, due largely to the conservatism inherent in the great influence of the church in Pennsylvania education. The idea of education for everyone, however, was by no means a new one in the Quaker commonwealth. It was an integral part of Quaker philosophy on the rights of the individual. Penn's first Frames of Government stressed education, though it was omitted strangely in the Charter of Privileges of 1701. The first state Constitution of 1776 provided that a "school or schools" should be set up in every county and that public funds should be used to aid in payment of their expenses. Public responsibility for education was reaffirmed in the Constitution of 1790 but free education was limited to the children of the poor. In 1809 a statewide census of children between the ages of five and twelve whose parents could not afford schooling was ordered by the Assembly with the aim of providing for their education at public expense. This was free education only for those who declared themselves paupers. Further laws designed to encourage public education found their way into the statutes from time to time, but none were truly effective.

In the meantime, education was not entirely neglected. Elementary education before 1834 became the task of the church or the community itself, except for those wealthy enough to enter private schools. The growth of church schools in which the church assumed full responsibility

George Wolf, whose determined support of the free-school law as governor cost him re-election.

was encouraged especially by the Pennsylvania Germans desirous of thus preserving their language, religious faith, and culture. With the growth of population there were many who did not want this religious control of their children's education. Neighborhood schools based upon a voluntary association of the families in a community became very common. The neighborhood provided the school building. The teachers were either traveling pedagogues charging tuition or hired teachers, often paid in part by boarding around with the families of the children. The usual tuition was $1.25 to $2.50 per pupil, depending upon whether it was a three- or six-month term. The one-room log, stone, or brick neighborhood school was to be found by 1830 in every part of the state. It was not an answer to the need for a truly democratic school system, because only those who were able to pay received the advantages of education.

The movement for a school system really based on democracy was gradually gaining in strength. Among its major leaders in the state were Timothy Pickering and Samuel Breck, both New Englanders by birth. Thomas Burrowes was another heroic figure in the battle. Strength was given to the demand for free schools by the growing number of wage earners in the cities who wanted education for their children. In 1833 Samuel Breck was elected to the State Senate. He was a well educated man of means but, like many men in his class, believed strongly in public education as necessary foundation for democratic government. In his diary for December 11, 1833, Breck set down his determination that his "chief occupation" in the Assembly would be "the formation of a system of general education." He secured a resolution to create a legislative committee to study the problem and became its chairman.

Governor George Wolf already had given support to public education in his message to the

The Free School Act of 1834. Original in the State Archives.

127

General Assembly. Breck's committee reported out and secured passage of a "general education" bill which was signed into law on April 1, 1834, by Governor Wolf. It provided that each county should constitute a school division and each city ward, township, or borough a school district. School directors were to be elected by the people. The counties were authorized to levy a school tax which had to produce revenue equal to twice the amount of any state subsidy for education in that county. No county refusing to adopt a school tax could receive any state aid. In September, 1834, more than half of the potential districts accepted the provisions of the law, though nearly three hundred rejected it. Some of the more wealthy people opposed the idea of paying for the education of the children of those less well off. Many church people opposed it, especially the Pennsylvania German element, because they feared the influences of a public school upon their particular culture, rooted as it was so strongly in religious teaching and doctrine.

By December the new legislature was confronted with bills either to cripple or repeal the law. Thousands of voters signed petitions importuning their legislators to destroy this monster. The Senate by a vote of nineteen to eleven virtually repealed the law. The less conservative House brought out a more favorable bill; a compromise was necessary. The tide was turned by a famous and stirring speech by Thaddeus Stevens of Adams County. Elected on a pledge to repeal the act, Stevens reversed himself and in a lofty

expression of democratic feeling stated ably and effectively the need for free education in order that "the blessing of education shall be carried home to the poorest child of the poorest inhabitant of the meanest hut of your mountains so that even he may be prepared to act well his part in this land of freedom, and lay on earth a broad and solid foundation for that enduring knowledge which goes on increasingly through increasing eternity." The feeling against the law defeated Governor Wolf for a third term, but it was never again challenged. The number of free public elementary schools increased from three thousand in 1836 to ten thousand by 1852. The number of pupils increased four times, all in the same period. By 1865 some 645,519 children were enrolled. The Pennsylvania State Education Association was founded in 1852, beginning a sound organization of the state's public school teachers. The normal-school system for training teachers was established by the state in 1857. The same year the state school system, formerly administered by the secretary of the commonwealth, achieved the dignity of a separate office of a Superintendent of Common Schools.

THE ACADEMY AND THE COLLEGE

In 1860 public schools beyond the elementary level were unknown outside a few cities. The first high school was chartered in 1836 in Philadelphia as the Central High School. As late as 1860 there were not more than possibly a dozen high schools in other cities. Secondary education was primarily the task of the academy. Academies were so much an answer to the educational needs of the state that they were not only chartered by it but many were also assisted and encouraged by financial support from the state. Virtually every town of any size came to have its academy. Here, for a modest tuition fee, a sound classical education might be obtained which emphasized philosophy, classical literature, and Latin and Greek. It was a grounding for studying law, entering the ministry,

Statue of Benjamin Franklin in the Franklin Memorial and Institute in Philadelphia, founded 1824.

128

"Old West" at Dickinson College, designed by Benjamin Latrobe.

teaching, or college. Frequently the faculty was made up of ministers. Not a few early academies were founded primarily to train persons for the ministry. The academy served a highly useful purpose in its day and more than one grew later into a college.

Higher education made great strides forward in this era, and it was not long before Pennsylvania enjoyed the distinction of having the largest number of colleges. There were only three collegiate-level institutions in the state in 1791, of which the most distinguished was the newly named and nondenominational University of Pennsylvania, famous for opening the first medical school in America. A rapid growth of colleges followed the Revolution. Dickinson at Carlisle was chartered in 1783 under early Presbyterian and later Methodist influence. In 1834 its famous law school was opened. Franklin College opened its doors in 1787 and in 1853 united with Marshall College, founded in 1836 at Mercersburg, to become Franklin and Marshall. The Pittsburgh Academy of 1787 became in 1819 the Western University of Pittsburgh. In northwestern Pennsylvania, Allegheny College was chartered in 1817 at Meadville. It is the oldest college in continuous existence under the same name west of the Alleghenies.

Canonsburg Academy at Canonsburg and Washington Academy at nearby Washington

grew into separate colleges under Presbyterian auspices and later merged into Washington and Jefferson. The Quakers founded Haverford in 1833. The Baptists established the University of Lewisburg in 1846, later named Bucknell for its benefactor, William Bucknell. Lutherans had a great zeal for higher education and present Gettysburg College dates back to 1832. Lutherans also founded Muhlenberg College in 1864 and Susquehanna University in 1858. Lafayette College was chartered in 1826 with Presbyterian support; it endeavored to present work in science, engineering, and the "useful arts." The Presbyterians were also back of the founding of Waynesburg College in 1850 and Westminister College in 1852, both of which admitted women. The two colleges were the first to graduate women students. Moravian College had its beginnings at Nazareth in 1807 and moved to Bethlehem in 1858 as the Moravian College and Theological Seminary. The oldest institution in the world for the higher education of Negroes is Lincoln University, founded in 1854 and opened in 1857 for the "scientific, classical and theological education of colored youth of the male sex."

Education in advanced science, engineering, and the science of agriculture was sadly lacking in this period. Experiments in chemistry were an integral part of the program only at the University of Pennsylvania and Dickinson College. After

1830 the charters of other institutions often called for some instruction in science but rarely was it put into practice. This was due in part to the lack of instructors for such courses. America remained largely dependent upon European and especially the German universities for any real education in science, engineering, or agriculture. West Point offered the only sound training in engineering in the United States prior to 1860. The technological advance of the country was such in the decades just before the Civil War as to demand that something be done. The first attempt at an answer was the founding, in 1855, as a result of agitation on the part of the Pennsylvania Agricultural Society, of the Farmer's High School. It grew into the Agricultural College of Pennsylvania and shortly was named the Pennsylvania State College. It was designated as the state's land-grant college by act of Assembly on April 1, 1863, implementing the Morrill Act. The beginnings of Girard College in 1848 as a school for white orphan boys where a trade could be learned was a step toward more utilitarian education. The Franklin Institute for the Promotion of Mechanical Arts was established in 1824. The general program at the college and university level remained for the most part severely classical with emphasis upon classical literature, Latin, Greek, philosophy, and even theology.

HUMANITARIAN REFORM

By 1840 America was in the midst of a great wave of humanitarian reform reflecting a growing demand for social democracy. Pennsylvania's influence in this movement was very strong. It had strong traditions of freedom and justice in terms of its settlement. It was steeped in the Quaker and German sectarian philosophy of the essential equality of all men and their right to equal justice. There were many injustices in supposedly democratic America of the time which denied this philosophy. One of them was Negro slavery. Another was unequal rights for women. Imprisonment for debt persisted and such notables as Robert Morris and James Wilson were victims. Prisons were stinking holes where no attempt at all was made to aid the inmates to regain their place in society. The poor and unfortunate not only were sadly neglected but often actually abused.

Pennsylvania had a distinguished record in the crusade against slavery. Quaker influences were dominant in opposing slavery, but Pennsylvania also had a large free Negro population; some 15,000 in Philadelphia alone in 1830. There were sixteen Negro churches in Philadelphia in 1838 and it was the home of the oldest Negro church in the country, Mother Bethel African Methodist, with roots going back to 1780. The free Negroes quite naturally hated slavery. Pennsylvania was the home of the Pennsylvania Abolition Society, organized by Philadelphia Quakers in 1775. On March 1, 1780, the state passed the first effective law for gradual abolition of slavery by providing that any Negro born after that date must be freed when twenty-eight years of age. Those in bondage were not made free. The state was a major center for the abolitionist press, centered in both Philadelphia and Pittsburgh. James Miller McKion, a Carlisle Scotch-Irishman, was a founder and leading agent of the American Anti-Slavery Society after 1833.

The cause of abolition frequently was tied to that of women's rights, especially by the women abolitionists. Jane Swisshelm of Pittsburgh is a notable example. Born in Pittsburgh in 1815, she taught school, married, and then moved to Kentucky. There she developed her aversion to slavery. The death of her mother led to her return to Pittsburgh in 1838 only to find that her husband under the law claimed and demanded exclusive use of all the property she inherited from her mother. Pittsburgh already had a strong abolitionist newspaper, *The Spirit,* and Jane Swisshelm wrote for it. She also began to write on behalf of legal rights for her sex. In 1847, aided by the Pittsburgh philanthropist Charles Avery, she founded the *Pittsburgh Saturday Visitor* and made it for a decade one of the leading social-reform organs in the entire country. In Philadelphia the Quakers James Mott and his wife Lucretia became antislavery leaders. Mott left a prosperous mercantile business to work for the cause. Lucretia is the better known because in 1848 she joined Elizabeth Cady Stanton in the crusade for equal

The Gradual Abolition Act of 1780. Original in the State Archives.

rights for women as a result of having been denied a seat at the world antislavery conference in London because she was a woman.

Slaves were property and a majority of people became increasingly frightened by the thought of outright abolition. In Philadelphia the Irish workers were afraid of the Negro as a free laborer. Philadelphia was itself the scene of riots against abolitionist activity and strong anti-Negro manifestations. A majority of Pennsylvanians opposed the further extension of slavery in the United States, but abolition was something else again.

131

Nor did the feminists make any real progress in securing greater equality for women. Imprisonment for debt was abolished in Pennsylvania in 1833 as a result of continued pressure from the wage earners and this battle against one form of involuntary servitude was brought to a victorious end.

EXPERIMENTS IN UTOPIA

Pennsylvania was a major center for utopian experiments which prevailed in the nation in the early nineteenth century. Some were motivated mainly by religious communalism and others by the wave of utopian socialist thinking which flourished in Europe at the time. The frontier was a good place to try out such ideas. One of the utopian settlements of some importance was that founded with the aid of Horace Greeley in Pike County early in the 1840's and known as the Sylvania Colony. It was patterned after more famous Brook Farm in New England and a product of ideas of the French socialist, Charles Fourier. It ended unexpectedly in July, 1845, when premature frosts destroyed the crops and forced the members to disband. In 1852 the colorful Norwegian violinist Ole Bull began a community settlement for his Norwegian nationalists in Potter County. Ole Bull's colony was motivated by nationalism rather than socialism. He sought a new home for Norwegians whose national feelings had been disregarded in the enforced merger with Sweden by the Congress of Vienna in 1815. Sites for four villages were surveyed and a log castle started for Ole Bull who declared that "We will here establish a new Norway, consecrated to liberty, baptized in freedom, and protected by the glorious flag of America. . . ." Some four hundred Norwegians arrived and started the settlement but Ole Bull was a better violinist than business man. Late in 1853 he found the lands he had purchased actually belonged to another party and must be rebought at a price he could not afford. Ole Bull lost his land and some $70,000 and most of the settlers drifted farther west.

Communal utopian experiments with a religious inspiration were stronger and more lasting.

The tradition of the religious communal settlement had been established by Conrad Beissel and his followers at Ephrata in 1732. The Ephrata community was on the decline by the end of the Revolution. Peter Miller, who followed Beissel as its spiritual leader, died in 1796. New followers were few and far between and celibacy prevented growth from within. A Society of the Seventh Day Baptists was formed in 1814 but the slow decline of the community continued. Ephrata lasted as a community until 1934 and five years later it forfeited its charter to the state, which acquired and restored the remaining buildings as a historical monument.

In western Pennsylvania a later communal community influenced also by German Pietism was founded in Butler County by George Rapp and his followers from Wurtemberg. By 1805 some five hundred members of the Harmony Society, as it was known, had located at the settlement they called "Harmonie." "Father" Rapp, as the dominating spiritual leader of the group came to be known, was made head of an association and all rights to individual property were surrendered by the individual members. Celibacy was practiced. The lure of new and richer lands farther west drew the Harmonists to Indiana in 1814-15. They sold their Pennsylvania holdings and founded New Harmony there. Dreams based on the second location did not bear fruit and in 1825 "Father" Rapp and his associates came back to western Pennsylvania, having sold their Indiana home to the English socialist, Robert Owen. On the site of the later mill town of Ambridge on the banks of the Ohio, about eighteen miles down the river, they laid out their third and last home. This time they chose the name "Economie" for their settlement, after the German "*Oekonomie*"; here they hoped to create a truly "divine economy." Old Economy, as it is known today, was a success for many decades. The Economite property included 3,000 acres of land with many fine buildings. It became a center of the finest arts and crafts of the time, especially the silk industry.

The society accumulated enough capital to become a potent factor in backing railroads, speculating in oil lands, and otherwise contributing to the economy of capitalism in western Pennsyl-

A view of the Feast Hall at Old Economy, one of some fifteen buildings restored by the commonwealth with their gardens and grounds at Old Economy.

vania and with resulting profit to the communal society. Communal Economy finally came to its legal end in 1916 when the state took over the remaining buildings and land in escheat proceedings. Like Ephrata, it has been restored as a historical monument to this unique social experiment.

IMPROVING THE LOT OF THE UNFORTUNATE

Improving the lot of the unfortunate was a major concern of American society in the early 1800's. There were many abuses prevalent in the supposedly democratic order of the times. Despite Quaker efforts toward reform, prisons generally were filthy holes where more crime was bred. The plight of the poor and those who suffered physical or mental disabilities was harsh and often actually cruel. Pennsylvania Quakers were far ahead of the majority of Americans in their thinking on these questions and it was natural that Pennsylvanians should be among the leaders in the movements which sought to improve conditions. No state has a more distinguished record in the efforts for relief of man's inhumanity to man in this era. Dr. Benjamin Rush wrote in 1812 the first book in America, and probably the world, on the nature and treatment of mental illness. His work at the Pennsylvania Hospital won him the title "the father of American psychiatry." Philadelphia was ahead of other cities in caring for the poor and

unfortunate, thanks in large part to Quaker philanthropy; Pennsylvania led in prison reforms. The Society for Alleviating the Miseries of Public Prisons was organized in 1787. A year later Roberts Vaux wrote his famous report revealing the abuses common to the nation's prisons. Vaux prior to his death in 1836 was the stalwart of the prison reform drive. He also led Philadelphia to develop a program to aid juvenile delinquents. The Walnut Street Prison in Philadelphia in the meantime was building a reputation as the best example of a model prison in the United States. It served both as a city and a state prison. Many experiments in prison reform were worked out here. Among them were improved sanitary facilities, separation of habitual criminals from other prisoners, prison industries, and general encouragement of rehabilitation and reform on the part of all inmates. In 1818 the Western State Penitentiary was authorized at Pittsburgh and a new Eastern State Penitentiary at Philadelphia was provided for in 1821. The "Pennsylvania System" for prison reform was studied and copied throughout the nation.

The temperance movement which swept the country in the same period was in its way another effort to relieve humanity of one of its abuses. Reports on poverty and crime in cities showed that the evil of strong drink was a major cause. Anthony Benezet, Philadelphia Quaker, was a pioneer in this crusade with his famous temperance book *The Mighty Destroyer Displayed,* which pictured graphically the sad results of the "Mistaken Use as Well as Abuse of Distilled Spirituous Liquors." The United Temperance Union was formed at a Philadelphia gathering in 1833 representing twenty states. Several states, Pennsylvania among them, adopted some type of temperance laws.

RELIGIOUS TRENDS AND FERMENTS

The era of the midnineteenth century was one of intense religious ferment in America. Pennsylvania had long enjoyed a major degree of religious liberty and was the home of varied religious faiths. This encouraged diversity in religion, and even such groups as the Mennonites and Quakers and others which were a product of division in Europe were further split. The frontier produced a rugged way of life which demanded a religion which served all its people and not just a few. A further problem of major concern to the churches after the Revolution was that of creating an American organization. All of these factors influenced religion and the church, and Pennsylvania in its experience was typical.

Presbyterianism was entrenched strongly in western Pennsylvania by the end of the Revolution. In 1781 the Redstone Presbytery was formed, the first west of the Alleghenies, with each of the four ministers taking care of the needs of two churches from eight to twelve miles apart. At least half a hundred other places were calling for ministers to preach. Early Presbyterian "preachers" rode the circuit on horseback hundreds of miles in the course of a year, often over mere trails through the wilderness, and preached in homes, schools and even in forest clearings on the frontier settlement. The Rev. John McMillan without doubt was the greatest leader of the Redstone Presbyterians in those early years. Along with organizing churches and preaching, he founded the famous "log college," Canonsburg Academy, in 1794 which in 1803 became Jefferson College. The Pittsburgh Presbytery was organized in 1802 and that city rapidly became entrenched as the capital of Presbyterianism in the West.

The Methodists and Baptists did not gain as

Peace Church near Harrisburg, built by the Presbyterians in 1794 and still standing.

134

much strength relatively in Pennsylvania as in other frontier regions despite their general appeal to the mass of the people. This was due in part to the early end of a Pennsylvania frontier and also to the already strong position of the Presbyterians. Both the Methodist and Baptist churches appealed to the people of newly settled areas because of their democratic church organization, their acceptance of a less highly educated clergy and even untrained ministers who were "called by faith" to preach, and their ardent evangelism. The American Methodist Church was organized at Baltimore in 1784 but three years earlier the first circuit outside Philadelphia was established at York. Methodism's great early leader was the famous Bishop Francis Asbury, who himself averaged 5,000 miles a year on horseback. The Redstone circuit was created in 1784 to spread the gospel in western Pennsylvania and western Virginia. By 1860 Methodism had become the strongest of what may be termed the English churches. The *Pittsburgh Advocate* was its leading journal. The Baptists moved early into western Pennsylvania and on the eve of the Revolution established Great Bethel Church at Uniontown. About one-half of all the nearly thirty Baptist congregations in the state in 1790 were west of the mountains. Soon after 1800 the Redstone Association itself had thirty churches. A Baptist General Association was organized in 1827 as the strength of the Baptists increased gradually in rural areas.

The German Reformed and Lutheran churches were the major denominations in eastern Pennsylvania, especially in the Pennsylvania German country. Neither had much strength west of the Susquehanna, though a Western Pennsylvania Synod was established by the Lutherans in 1824. The Lutherans failed to attract a Pittsburgh following until 1837 but a Pittsburgh Synod was created in 1845. The Reformed Church was rather weak and failed to develop a seminary to train ministers until 1824. Its basically Calvinist doctrines of faith led many Reformed Church followers to associate in western Pennsylvania with the Presbyterians. The Lutheran Church continued to grow and in 1796 provided for representation of laymen in the affairs of the synod,

recognizing democracy in the church. At the same time the official use of the title of "German Lutheran Church" upheld the basic German character of this leading Protestant denomination in Pennsylvania. The Episcopal denomination suffered heavily because so large a part of its membership proved to be Tory in the Revolution. It was a church which appealed more largely to the aristocracy and conservatives than to the masses. Its post-Revolutionary leadership remained mainly in Philadelphia with Bishop William White, rector of Christ Church in Philadelphia, and Dr. William Smith, former provost of the College of Philadelphia, as stalwarts in its early history. The Protestant Episcopal Church in the United States of America first achieved national organization at its General Convention in Philadelphia in 1785. The Society of Friends continued as a strongly influential religious group in the original counties of the southeast. It also spread into other parts of the state but outside Philadelphia its meeting houses were few and far apart. Its influence was far greater than its limited numbers.

Increased immigration from Catholic countries and especially from Ireland led to some expansion of the Roman Catholics. Between 1790 and 1830 membership in Catholic churches is estimated as having grown tenfold to some hundred thousand communicants. In 1808 the Diocese of Philadelphia was created by Rome to give Pennsylvania its first independent administration outside Baltimore. In 1852 the Diocese numbered about 300,000 members and it was the main center of Roman Catholicism in the state. A Diocese of Pittsburgh was created in 1842 and in 1853 the Diocese of Erie was authorized. The Seminary of St. Charles Borromeo was founded in Philadelphia in 1832. The first convent of the Sisters of Mercy in the United States was established as St. Xavier's, near Greensburg, in 1843. The Benedictines founded St. Vincent's, their first institution, also near Greensburg in 1846.

Pennsylvania's Jewish community grew slowly. Prior to 1800 very few lived west of the mountains and Philadelphia was the major center of Jewish population. In 1846 a hundred Jewish families in Pittsburgh united to form its first congregation.

They erected in 1854 Rodef Shalom Temple in the Iron City. Though their numbers are small, the Jewish population held a high place in the financial and mercantile affairs of the state.

The spirit of diversity in Pennsylvania's religious tradition was not weakened in the years following the Revolution. It was a seed ground for several new religious groupings. The "second awakening," the revival experience from about 1797 into the early 1800's which swept the entire western frontier, had as its most outstanding pioneer leader James McGready, a Presbyterian minister born in Pennsylvania, and student of the Rev. John McMillan at his Canonsburg academy and first licensed to preach by the Redstone Presbytery. Though described as a rough-hewn and even ugly person, McGready preached with such fervor that he was accused by his enemies of "running people distracted." The zeal of the revivalist could hardly be described in better terms as many Presbyterian and Methodist preachers began to exhort and shout a religion which produced nothing short of hysteria at camp meetings in western Pennsylvania and elsewhere on the frontier. The resulting ferment created shortly a New Light schism in the ranks of Presbyterians, which began in the west but appeared in western Pennsylvania after 1807 under the inspiration of Thomas Campbell and his son Alexander, both recently arrived Scotch-Irish Presbyterians. A dispute over the ritual of baptism led to an open split with the regular Presbyterian presbytery in Pittsburgh and organization in 1811 of the Brush Run Church of the "Christian Association." Until about 1830 the Campbellites, as they became known, associated with the Baptists. Alexander Campbell then led another separatist movement within the Baptist Church and from it grew the new denomination, Disciples in Christ.

Though not strictly a schism, still another new denomination, the United Brethren in Christ, developed in the same period. Philip Otterbein, one of the founders, began his work as a German Reformed missionary and later a Methodist. The other founder, Martin Boehm, was first a Mennonite. The two men, along with others associated in frontier missionary work, in 1800 decided to form a totally new church, basically Methodist in doctrine, which they called United Brethren in Christ. It spread rapidly in western Pennsylvania. In central Pennsylvania the Rev. Jacob Albright led in the formal founding of the Evangelical Church at a meeting held in a barn in Union County in 1816. It was another separatist movement from the Methodists. The first church of the denomination was started at nearby New Berlin in Snyder County the same year, along with their printing press.

Pennsylvania even had a part in the early founding and growth of the Church of Latter Day Saints. Joseph Smith, founder of Mormonism, lived near Great Bend in Susquehanna County for some years before 1830 and here translated at least a portion of the Golden Plates discovered by him in New York and which provided the foundations for the doctrines and faith of the Latter Day Saints. Sidney Rigdon, one-time Baptist and Campbellite preacher in western Pennsylvania, was an early associate of Joseph Smith and contributed considerably to Mormon theology. Rigdon later quarreled at Salt Lake City with Brigham Young and returned to western Pennsylvania, where he attempted without success to set up an eastern schism in the Mormon Church. Mormonism had a strong following in western counties in this period.

THE WAGE EARNER

By 1860 a new group or class had emerged in the nation's society. This group was made up of those persons who worked for wages in the growing number of mills and factories which sprang up like mushrooms during the expanding industrial revolution. Wage earners were totally unlike the tailors, shoemakers, blacksmiths, and other artisans or craft workers common to an earlier day who were at one and the same time workers and owners of their own tools and shops. The wage earner was employed only for his services as a laborer in a mine, mill, or factory.

Such a worker had no capital or other interest in the building in which he worked or even in the tools or machinery he used. He might or might not have any special skills. This new type of worker often was a woman or even a young child, rather than a man, especially in early textile mills and clothing factories. The wage earner as part of a new class which came to be known simply as "labor" became a noticeable influence in the affairs of the nation by 1830. Pennsylvania as a leading industrial state figured prominently in the growth of the wage-earning class and in their problems as well as their solutions.

Labor in those days was the victim of much exploitation. An investigation by a Pennsylvania legislative committee reported in 1837 widespread abuses of labor in the form of long hours, low wages, unsatisfactory working conditions, and extensive exploitation of children and women as factory workers. Children were found working at ages as low as ten to twelve and at wages averaging about one cent an hour. Eleven and even fourteen hours a day were not uncommon in the early cotton mills. It is little wonder that labor tried to organize to protect itself through trade unions or that workers through their own or existing political parties tried to secure protective legislation. Labor also favored free public education, along with more liberal requirements for voting and holding office. In eastern Pennsylvania the new class of wage earners became a major force back of liberal reforms common to the era of Jacksonian democracy. Early efforts to organize labor centered in Pennsylvania among craft laborers.

Philadelphia shoemakers organized as a craft as early as 1792. The cordwainers were organized in 1794. In 1827 the Union of Trade Associations was formed in Philadelphia to unite more elements in labor. Philadelphia workers helped organize the National Trade Union. The shoemakers of the city tried to organize a national union for their craft. Public opinion of the times was totally opposed to any acceptance of labor unions. They were viewed as a conspiracy against both management and the general public. The strike was without the pale of the law. When collective bargaining was tried the workers were simply locked out and others hired, even though the early unions were made up almost entirely of skilled workers.

Labor did make progress despite the handicaps

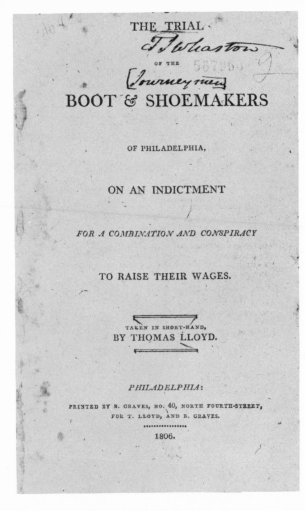

The right of labor to organize was disputed and brought into court in this 1806 trial.

it faced. By 1828 the first labor newspaper, the *Mechanic's Free Press* appeared in Philadelphia. It was associated with the newly formed Working Men's Party of Philadelphia. Neither lasted but the ground had been broken for means through which labor could express its opinions and voice its needs. A sense of organization began to permeate labor in Pennsylvania, which became the fountainhead of American trade unionism. Labor helped secure the Free School Act of 1834. It helped win abolition of imprisonment for debt and aided most of the basic reform movements of the era. In general, the cause of the wage earner was advanced before 1860 though his battles were by no means won.

PENNSYLVANIA FORWARDS A NATIONAL CULTURE

Pennsylvania contributed greatly to forwarding the nation's cultural advance in the years following 1800. A new American culture must of necessity become a product of the merging of the cultures of those ethnic and national groups which came to America from the Old World. Pennsylvania was a melting pot of peoples in colonial times and continued to be so in the years after the Revolution. It was also influenced by the growing nationalism of the times and the spirit of the frontier with its mixtures of people of all classes.

Francis Hopkinson of Philadelphia expressed this nationalism in music when he wrote in 1798 his ever famous "Hail Columbia." Youthful Stephen Foster caught on the Pittsburgh waterfront something of the spirit of the new America of the 1840's. His "Oh Susannah" literally went west with the pioneer wagon trains and voiced the optimism and spirit of the new frontier. Foster's gentle and sympathetic treatment of the life of the time with which he was associated led him before his untimely death at thirty-seven to produce some of America's greatest folk ballads. General interest in music was evident in the organization of a Musical Fund Society in Philadelphia in 1820, the Pittsburgh Musical Society at about the same time, and the Philadelphia Germania Orchestra in 1856. The Academy of Music built in Philadelphia in 1855-57 is America's oldest original musical hall. Moravian Bethlehem continued to be one of the great centers of religious music in America. Church music and folk music were means through which the common people expressed a love of music, for Pennsylvanians were a singing people.

Pennsylvania made contributions toward the creation of an American literature, though it saw no such flowering of literature as did New England. Philadelphia's Charles Brockden Brown is accepted today as author of the first truly American novel, *Wieland,* in 1798. He wrote several other less important books and all were based on American themes. Edgar Allan Poe lived in Philadelphia from 1842 to 1844, two of his most fruitful years. Pittsburgh lawyer Hugh Henry Brackenridge wrote in 1793 a three-volume work, *Modern Chivalry,* in which he poked fun at the crudities of frontier society. It was the first major new literary effort published west of the Alleghenies. Brackenridge also wrote a book on the Whisky Rebellion but his son, Henry M. Brackenridge, did a more thorough study on this topic in 1859 with his *History of the Western Insurrection.* Bayard Taylor of Kennett Square is not highly regarded today, but nevertheless was the author in this period of several books and poems which find a place in any history of American literature. His major novel was *The Story of Kennett* and *The Bedouin Song* and *Poems of the Orient* his best poetry. The newspapers of the time were an outlet for publications of everything from poetry to literary essays. Local contributions were mixed with reprints from American and even European sources, which brought some type of literature into the homes of many who otherwise were without an opportunity to read such writings.

Philadelphia led in the successful publication of the American literary magazine. The *Port Folio, Graham's Magazine, Sartain's Magazine,* and finally *Godey's Lady's Book* led this field of literary achievement. *Godey's* was the first in the nation to achieve a truly large magazine circulation but between about 1840 and 1850 *Graham's* was the most notable American magazine. These magazines published the work of such figures as Poe, Hawthorne, and Washington Irving and were major outlets for the writings of the most distinguished literary figures of the time.

Pennsylvania remained a leader in the growth of the newspaper in the United States. On July 29, 1786, Scull and Hall began the printing of the *Pittsburgh Gazette,* the first newspaper west of the mountains. The *Bedford Gazette* began in 1808 and in 1812 the *Crawford Weekly Messenger* was founded in Meadville, as newspapers moved westward. In Philadelphia, Adam Ramage developed the improved Ramage press in 1818, probably the most widely used printing press in early days. George

Clymer's Columbia Press was another much used press. In Lancaster, Hugh Maxwell about 1820 came up with the roller process for inking type. Pennsylvania was a leading state in making paper. The state was the birthplace in 1784 of the *Pennsylvania Packet and Daily Advertiser,* generally accepted as the nation's first daily. The penny newspaper was born during the antebellum period, further aiding the spread of information among the mass of the people. By 1840 Pennsylvania was the home of more newspapers than any other state. The number had reached nearly two hundred by 1860, as contrasted with the nine newspapers publishing in 1790.

THE ARTS ADVANCE

Philadelphia with some validity may be said to have kept its position as the "Athens of America" long after the colonial era. Certainly no other single city had so leading a role in the heritage of American art which grew into maturity in the years between the Revolution and the Civil War.

If New England had its leading share of great writers, Pennsylvania had the artists. Charles Willson Peale painted the best portraits of the great men of that time before his death in 1827. In 1805 the Pennsylvania Academy of Fine Arts, the pioneer art institution in America, was organized with Peale's help. It began its famous exhibitions in 1811. The city after 1808 was the home of Thomas Sully, who probably was among the greatest of the American portrait painters, as was his contemporary, Rembrandt Peale, son of Charles Willson Peale. Another son, Raphael, devoted his talents to still life and miniatures. John Peale, brother of Charles Willson, was also a portrait painter of some note and dabbled in other forms of painting. Gilbert Stuart lived and worked in Philadelphia after 1794. Thomas Birch before his death in 1851 completed some of the truly outstanding landscapes and seascapes of that time. Thomas Doughty was a self-taught pioneer in the landscape painting of the period. John Sartain was famous for his miniatures. John Neagle was another leading artist of the time. One of the most

Charles Willson Peale's "Self Portrait."

139

Edward Hicks's "Residence of David Twining, 1787." Original in the
Abby Aldrich Rockefeller Folk Art Collection, Williamsburg.

noted folk artists painting primitives, homely scenes of the countryside, was the Quaker Edward Hicks, famous forever for his "The Peaceable Kingdom."

Increasing wealth encouraged art not only in Philadelphia but also in the hinterland as persons of means sought to have their portraits done or to adorn their home with fine landscapes. Stirrings in the art world can be observed in Pittsburgh soon after 1800. Pittsburgh's David Blythe painted life as he saw it and has been called the "dean of American *genre* painters."

As cities grew so did the desire for fine public buildings and from this was generated the work of some notable Pennsylvania architects. Even in colonial times Philadelphia was noted for its fine buildings. Thomas U. Walter, William Strick-land, and John Haviland were among the architects who contributed to a remarkable tradition for fine architecture in the buildings of Philadelphia and elsewhere in the mid-1800's. Walter designed several of the Federal buildings in Washington such as the Treasury and the Post Office, as well as the dome of the Capitol. Tennessee's Capitol was designed by Strickland. Benjamin Latrobe was the architect for many fine buildings, including the Capitol at Washington. Latrobe was responsible also for "Old West" on the campus of Dickinson College and the original design of the Second Bank, now the Old Custom House in Philadelphia, though the latter was completed by his pupil William Strickland. Founder's Hall at Girard College was done by Walter. Haviland did the Eastern Penitentiary.

140

Edward Hicks's "Peaceable Kingdom."

Much of the work of these men was influenced strongly by the classical revival after the Revolution which abandoned Georgian colonial. It was followed by the Greek revival. The United States Bank Branch in Erie, now the Old Custom House, is a fine Greek revival building. The Tioga County Courthouse at Wellsboro is in the Greek Ionic tradition. Gothic revival also is evident in the work of Latrobe as well as Haviland. In the smaller towns where great architects were not available, or were too expensive, the design of buildings was in the hands of men who were both architects and builders. Anyone traveling through Pennsylvania with an eye open to good architecture will be rewarded with literally hundreds of examples of fine public buildings and private homes erected before the Civil War; and these occur in almost every major town, such as the older county seats, which reveal a fine taste in the architecture of the era. The public buildings erected in this period were places where the work of the sculptor found its expression at a time when the general public found little use for statues. William Rush and Joseph Bailey were leading sculptors of the day. Rush started his career carving wood figureheads for ships and later did full-scale statues in wood. Bailey did the Washington statue at Independence Hall. The work of many early sculptors was done in wood rather than bronze or stone.

The growth of the city encouraged the theater. The Chestnut Street Theatre in Philadelphia was built in 1796. The later 1809 Walnut Street Theatre is one of the truly historic buildings in American theatrical history, and the oldest theater in America in continuous use. The Acad-

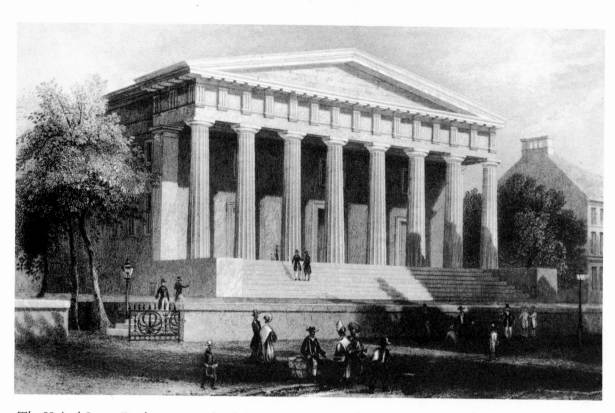

The United States Bank, an example of the fine Philadelphia architecture of the period.

The Tioga County courthouse at Wellsboro, an example of fine architecture in rural towns.

142

emy of Music was opened in 1857. William Henry Fry of that city wrote what was probably the first American opera, *Lenora,* though it found little acceptance. Reading and Lancaster had early theaters; in Lancaster the Fulton Theatre was opened in this period. In the smaller cities "opera houses" were increasingly common by 1860. Quaker Philadelphia conservatism still rather frowned upon the theater and as a result the city enjoyed less distinction in this area of cultural activity than most others. Despite this, many great names in the early American theater came from Pennsylvania. Among them were Edwin Forrest, James E. Murdock, Joseph Jefferson, and the Drew family. Forrest and Murdock were the outstanding Shakespearean actors of the time. Jefferson made himself nationally famous in the role of Rip Van Winkle. Mrs. John Drew was accepted by one and all as one of the greatest actresses of her day.

THE FLOWERING OF SCIENCE

No realm of intellectual activity provides a more nearly perfect example of the full flowering of the human mind than the world of science. The history of science in this era has been neglected. This is unfortunate not only because it was a vital aspect of the growth of our nation in terms of increasing freedom from dependence upon the science of Europe, but also because the scientific spirit and the advances it produced were the very roots of the American revolution in industry and transportation. James Cutbush, Philadelphia scientist, in a series of essays in 1808 aptly summarized the great value of science in the early nineteenth century. "Science," he wrote, "is useful to man not only because it dignifies the mind and fills it with exalted sentiments, but on account of its importance in all the affairs of life." He argued properly that the increase in scientific knowledge was vital to the national prosperity.

Devoted as it was to plantation agriculture, there was little hope for science in the South. Yale and Harvard in New England had their scientists but their contribution is feeble indeed when compared with that of Pennsylvania men and institutions. Pennsylvania, of course, had

already the great tradition of Franklin, Rush, and Rittenhouse back of it.

Science in those days was more largely an individual effort and achievement than it is today with the predominance of highly organized institutional research. However, institutions and organizations also were contributing to the advance of science in Pennsylvania. First among these was the American Philosophical Society, which continued after the Revolution to foster inquiry in virtually every field of science as well as encourage all manner of practical applications of research in transportation, industry, and agriculture. Its brilliant papers covered wide ranges of scientific research. The Academy of Natural Sciences of Philadelphia was organized in 1812 and soon began publication of its important *Journal.* The Philadelphia Academy of Arts and Sciences was organized in 1782. The Chemical Society of Philadelphia, first in the world, was founded in 1792. The Philadelphia College of Pharmacy, the College of Physicians of Philadelphia, and the University of Pennsylvania Medical School all encouraged research in medical science. A Columbia Chemical Society of Philadelphia was organized in 1811. Jefferson Medical College was founded in 1825 and Hahnemann Hospital and Medical College in 1848. The Medical Society of the State of Pennsylvania was organized in 1848. The Franklin Institute, founded in 1824 to honor Franklin, became one of the great centers of science with its library, publications, and experiments of a varied and practical nature. All of these organizations and institutions through encouragement of research, library facilities, publications, and the opportunity for scientists to exchange ideas gave a powerful impetus to all branches of science in Philadelphia. Philadelphia was wealthy and much of this wealth was poured into support of science, because, as one observer put it, "it was the fashion to be scientific."

The names of the scientists flourishing in this environment and their contributions are so numerous as to defy more than the briefest mention. In the field of natural science, remarkable achievements were a matter of record. By 1820 Charles Willson Peale's famous museum had the most significant natural history and mineralogy collections in the nation. The Harmonists at Old Economy had almost equally notable collections in these fields. Lewis David von Schweinitz, Moravian, and Henry Muhlenberg, Lutheran, were major figures in botanical study. Philadelphia by 1820 had at least three important botanical gardens, more than any other city, as centers where all manner of plants were available for study. The first professorship of natural history in the country was established at the University of Pennsylvania and held by Dr. Benjamin Smith in 1789. Dr. Gerard Troost turned from chemistry to mineralogy and geology and did important work in both. William Maclure, cultured Scotsman of means, settled in Philadelphia in 1796 to become not only a patron of science, but also the "father of American geology." His *Observations on the Geology of the United States,* published in 1817, was the first geological survey of the country ever attempted. It was Maclure who persuaded the French artist and zoologist Leseur to come to the United States in 1816. Maclure sponsored many scientific expeditions and greatly aided the Philadelphia Academy. Probably the greatest entomologist of the times, who is looked upon as the father of this science in America, was the Philadelphia Quaker, Thomas Say. Say accompanied Major Stephen Long on his two famous exploratory expeditions into the Far West in 1819 and 1823 and developed the most important entomological collections in the nation. His *American Entomology,* published in 1824-25 in two volumes, was monumental.

The remarkable world of chemistry had been only feebly explored in the eighteenth century, even in Europe. Dr. Benjamin Rush occupied the chair of chemistry at the College of Philadelphia and was a pioneer in lecturing and in research in this field in this country. One of his notable students was Dr. James Woodhouse, who succeeded Rush. Among other contributions, Woodhouse in 1797 wrote the first laboratory manual in chemistry, *The Young Chemists' Pocket Companion,* and was an authority on plant chemistry. He isolated the metal potassium, among many other contributions. Among the students of Woodhouse were Benjamin Silliman, later famous as professor of chemistry at Yale,

and Robert Hare. Hare also taught at the University of Pennsylvania. Among his important achievements was the invention of the oxyhydrogen blowpipe. Producing intense heat for melting materials, it served as the pioneer electric furnace for chemical research and study of metals. Hare also invented the electric plunger battery for use in blasting rock in quarries or mines. All of these had practical applications of importance to the future of industry. Hare also wrote the *Compendium of Chemistry,* usually called the first American chemistry text. He wrote at least two hundred papers on chemistry and electricity. Hare was a pioneer in developing practical applications for theoretical science. The scientist of the time was apt to dabble in more than one field and in western Pennsylvania David Alter, while practicing medicine, experimented with electricity and also contributed to the understanding of the laws of spectrum analysis, thereby making possible determination of the chemical nature of gases. In Philadelphia Adam Seybert was a pioneer in the manufacture of mercurials. His son Henry was a contributor to both medicine and mineralogy.

Pennsylvania became the home for two distinguished chemists who fled here from England because their views on religion did not meet with favor there. One of these was Joseph Priestley, philosopher and scientist who discovered oxygen. Priestley arrived at Philadelphia in 1793 and quickly moved to Northumberland, where he built a home and laboratory. It was here that he discovered carbon monoxide. Thomas Cooper arrived a year later. He lectured at Dickinson College and at the University of Pennsylvania on chemistry. He was also interested in geology. He was a noteworthy popularizer of science as well as a researcher. His *Introductory Lectures on Chemistry* did much to make the general public realize the importance of chemistry. "It enters every workshop, every factory, every home . . .," he declared, " and we must look to chemistry for future improvements in agriculture, in manufactures, and in all that tends to render human existence more desireable."

In no area was the relationship of the various sciences shown as clearly as in medicine. Dr. Benjamin Rush, for example, lectured and wrote on medicine and mental illness while lecturing and experimenting with chemistry. Pennsylvania's contributions to medical science were both substantial and important. Philadelphia with its several superior hospitals and medical schools was the major training ground for the leading physicians of the time. In 1820 Dr. Nathaniel Chapman of Philadelphia, one of the leading professors of medicine at the university, founded the *Philadelphia Journal of Medical and Physical Sciences*. It later became the *American Journal of the Medical Sciences* under the editorship of Issac Hays, often called the "father of American ophthalmology." The *Journal* is still published and through the years it has become the leading publication for those who have been advancing the cause of medical science. A real tribute was paid Philadelphia medicine when in 1847 it was selected as the host city for the organization of the American Medical Association, and Dr. Chapman was chosen its first president.

Medicine and botany were tied together in the career of Robert Bridges at the Philadelphia College of Pharmacy; he helped prepare the *United States Dispensary*. Joseph Carson of the same institution combined botany and medicine and edited the *American Journal of Pharmacy*. Medicine and chemistry also overlapped in the work of Thomas D. Mitchell and his *Medical Chemistry* in 1819, a pioneer work. Franklin Bache, Franklin's great-grandson, the same year produced his *System of Chemistry for the Use of Students in Medicine*. Bache was also editor of the *Dictionary of Chemistry* as well as the author of the *Dispensary of the United States of America*. He also edited Turner's *Elements of Chemistry* while a professor at Jefferson.

Pennsylvania was also a center for the improvement of American surgical practice, something of very great importance in the Civil War. Philip Syng Physick before his death in 1837 had become the "father of American surgery." Even earlier Dr. Caspar Wistar had written the first American textbook on anatomy. He was also America's first vertebrate paleontologist. Harrison Allen of Philadelphia started his career before 1860 as a pioneer laryngologist. David Hayes Agnew revived the Philadelphia School of Anatomy and in 1852 began his work on *Anatomy in Its Relation to*

Joseph Priestley's home at Northumberland, preserved as a state historical landmark.

Medicine and Surgery. John Light and Washington Atlee, Lancaster brothers, were leading surgeons of the period.

Pennsylvania provided men of importance in other fields of the budding scientific advance of the time. Alexander Dallas Bache of Philadelphia was an outstanding physicist. He was chief of research at the new Franklin Institute and superintended from 1843 to 1867 the United States Coastal Survey. Bache was the first president of the National Academy of Science. Spencer F. Baird of Reading by 1860 was known for his *Catalogue of North American Mammals,* followed a year later by a similar work on American birds. Lancaster-born Benjamin Barton published in 1803 his *Elements of Botany,* the first basic work of its type. William P. C. Barton wrote in 1819 *Vegetable Materia Medica* and a few years later *Flora of North America.* John Bartram's son William made further contributions to natural history. In Pennsylvania, with its hitherto unde-

veloped mineral riches, advances in geology and mineralogy were all-important. Samuel S. Haldeman at the University of Pennsylvania was a pioneer geologist. Henry Rogers was a notable chemist, geologist, and mineralogist. The Pennsylvania Geological Society was organized in 1832 by these men and others to promote a geological and topographic survey of the state. The society also began publication of pioneer geological survey work undertaken in the coal fields of Tioga County. In 1836 it inspired the creation by the legislature of the Pennsylvania Geological Survey program, the first of its kind.

Pennsylvania in 1860 was quite a different state from that of 1790. It had filled out its boundaries with people. It had developed a more advanced and refined condition of living on the part of the greater portion of the population. It had made contributions of immeasurable value to the cultural and intellectual progress of the new nation.

CHAPTER NINE

A REVOLUTION IN PENNSYLVANIA'S ECONOMY

When the famous English traveler, Harriet Martineau, visited the United States in 1834-35 she recorded her observations in some detail. She saw a much different America from that existing only a few decades earlier at the close of the Revolution. Large towns with factories and mills springing up around them were everywhere. These were evidences of the already rapid growth of an industrial revolution. Harriet Martineau traveled on the new turnpikes, on the Pennsylvania Canal, and the new eighty-one-mile-long railroad from Columbia to Philadelphia. She noted that a part of the Pennsylvania canal system ran through regions which only five years earlier had been "an untrodden wilderness." More was going on than even Harriet Martineau could observe. America was in the midst of an economic revolution. In no state was this revolution more marked than in Pennsylvania. It rapidly filled its unoccupied lands with people after 1790, aided by liberal land laws with special considerations to veterans of the Revolution. New towns were laid out by the score and started to grow, while those already founded as towns quickly became small cities. More counties were formed, especially after 1800. A new wave of migration from Ireland and

Germany helped swell an already growing population. Pennsylvania was on the move.

PHILADELPHIA'S NEED FOR IMPROVED TRANSPORTATION

The state was on the move even before 1800, for a series of revolutions and developments in American transportation were centered in it. Pennsylvania pioneered in the building of the first turnpike road, the invention of the steamboat, extensive canal building, and the first railroads. There is an old saying that "necessity is the mother of invention." In the case of Pennsylvania the constant necessity for improvements in transportation came from the vital need for Philadelphia to keep its lines of communication into interior and western Pennsylvania well in order. Otherwise the Philadelphia economy after 1800 gradually would have ground to a halt. Foreign trade, the lifeblood of the colonial economy of the port, suffered severely in the days of nonintercourse, the embargo and finally, the War of 1812. Though American foreign commerce later recovered, Philadelphia did not regain its former leadership in the commerce of the clipper ship

147

era and was surpassed by New York. Philadelphia needed to maintain good lines of contact with the interior of the state to supply such goods as it did ship as well as material for its newly developing manufactures. Geography created some awkwardness for Philadelphia. The westward movement in Pennsylvania was associated closely with the general growth of the new West by way of the forks of the Ohio where Pittsburgh by 1790 had become the "Gateway to the West." Philadelphia mercantile interests since colonial days had profited from the lucrative Indian and frontier trade and had a more than ordinary awareness of the importance of doing business with the growing settlements. Pittsburgh, however, was at the head of river systems which led to New Orleans. It was well over three hundred miles away from Philadelphia, with the Allegheny Mountains a barrier thrust high between the two cities.

Philadelphia's contacts with the Susquehanna Valley region were threatened by the keen rivalry of Baltimore for the business of this heartland of Pennsylvania. The Susquehanna, unfortunately for Philadelphia, flowed through Maryland to the Chesapeake Bay. Baltimore was better situated geographically than was Philadelphia to tap the commerce of this rich area. The Marylanders had access to interior Pennsylvania all the way up to the New York State border along the far reaches of the North Branch of the Susquehanna. Even Virginia, with the Potomac Company, organized in 1785, was reaching for the trade of the upper Ohio and southwestern Pennsylvania. The growth of the iron industry, which after the Revolution centered farther and farther from Philadelphia, and in which its citizens had considerable capital invested, offered yet another reason why the Quaker city was anxious to forward internal improvements. By 1840 the growing use of the rich coal deposits of the anthracite region gave further impetus to the need for canals and railroads. When all of these pressures are taken into account it is little wonder that Philadelphians in 1791 saw fit to organize a Society for the Improvement of Inland Navigation. Its formation was sparked by news of Virginia's Potomac Company. The American Philosophical Society already was offering varied encouragement to internal improvements, especially the design of canals.

THE TURNPIKE BOOM

Philadelphia's concern for better communication with the interior led in 1792 to the chartering of the Lancaster Turnpike Company to build a revolutionary new turnpike highway between these two points. It was built in 1792–94 at a cost of $465,000, the first road built with a hard stone base or foundation in America, following the design of the Scotch engineer, MacAdam. The Lancaster Turnpike Company was a stock company and tolls were charged at nine different toll gates to cover costs of building and maintenance and return a profit to the stockholders. The new road quickly was thronged with stages and heavy freight wagons. It reduced the cost of overland freighting by two-thirds. Its success inspired a wave of turnpike building throughout the country. Pennsylvania alone by 1820 had chartered some two hundred turnpike companies which reached by 1830 into the most remote corners of the state with 3,000 miles of road over which moved thousands of wagons. Heavy "Pitt teams" were moving goods all the way from Pittsburgh to Philadelphia and in both directions. The two distant cities were connected by stage in 1804. The Cumberland or National Road was projected across western Pennsylvania from Cumberland, Maryland, to Wheeling in 1806 and opened in 1818. Albert Gallatin from western Pennsylvania, and a member of Jefferson's cabinet, was its greatest supporter. All of the state's major towns and cities by 1840 were connected by improved roads. Grain from Juniata and Susquehanna valley farms could be carried now to Philadelphia by wagon with a return load of merchandise for the country stores of the region. The turnpike's greatest service, however, was to the more rural and remote areas which were not served later by waterways or canals. Roads demanded bridges and Pennsylvania soon became known as the state of bridges.

Travel on the turnpikes was a colorful affair, especially on the major roads east and west. Heavy Conestoga-type wagons were drawn by six-horse teams with their colorful tinkling bells which dangled from the harness of the horses, and heavily loaded with freight. Wagoners were a rough, tough lot but took the greatest pride in the appearance of both teams and wagons. Taverns along the route patronized by wagoners both for their personal lodging and the care of their teams were boisterous places where heavy drinking, tall stories of experiences on the pike, and sometimes songs of the wagon road were common entertainments; this was followed by sleeping on the floor or anywhere a tired wagoner might find a spot to lay his head. Travel by stage was hardly less colorful and not much more comfortable, if contemporary accounts can be believed. Patrons of the stage coach were frequently crowded together at taverns for sleeping, fed uniformly poor food at most inns, and wakened at daybreak or earlier to resume their crowded and often entirely uncomfortable journey. It was nevertheless better than travel by pack horse over a wilderness trail.

THE OVERLAND LIVESTOCK DRIVE

The turnpike era also saw the rise of the cattle drive in Pennsylvania. This is a story in American history usually associated with the picturesque era of the cowboy and the overland cattle drives over the Chisholm and other trails from Texas to railheads in Kansas at Abilene, Dodge City and other "cow towns" after the Civil War. Cattle driving actually was born in the upper Ohio valley and western Pennsylvania after 1800. By 1820 Ohio and Indiana were raising more cattle and swine than they had markets to consume. At the same time, a market did exist in the East in such cities as Philadelphia and Baltimore. The easiest way to get livestock to market, whether cattle, swine, or sheep, was to drive them under their own power. Cattle were fattened on the rich grass of the Ohio country and the drive overland started with the end of the rigors of winter. The herds numbered from a hundred to three hundred or more cattle and often were accompanied by swine. Since the herds were driven, those who directed the herds were known as "drovers." In the later West they were called "trail drivers." Rather than ride horses, as did the

Stagecoach in the State Museum. Built in Harrisburg in 1812, it was used before the Civil War on the run to Pittsburgh and later on a stage line to Lewistown. Note that later Wells Fargo stagecoaches used in the West were just about exact duplicates.

western cowboy, drovers simply walked most of the time, though two or more horses were at hand when riding was needed to keep the herds in line. The owner or "boss" alone was mounted the entire trip.

There were several overland cattle trails in Pennsylvania, but the most important, running from the Ohio border to the Susquehanna, was the famous Three Mountain Trail. It was opened about 1828 and for some thirty years was the most important cattle trail in the United States. It entered the state at or near Pittsburgh and proceeded eastward along very much the same route as today's Pennsylvania Turnpike. The trail crossed the Tuscarora, Kittochtinny, and Blue Mountain ranges, from which it derived its name of Three Mountain Trail. The livestock was then moved, with an accompanying cloud of dust and shouts of the drovers, to Shippensburg and the Cumberland Valley road on to the Susquehanna at Harrisburg. Here the drives were often met by buyers and speculators who sought to purchase the herds at the best negotiable price. As high as 175,000 cattle moved over this single trail in one season and in the period of its operation it is believed to have been walked by well over five million. Harrisburg was the usual terminal because from here cattle were either moved in smaller droves due to the more settled nature of the country or slaughtered and the resulting beef and hides shipped to market by canal or later railroad.

Moving cattle on a turnpike in large numbers was costly, and because of this the droves of livestock were moved over their own country trails as much as possible, though close to or over established highways. The trails were lined with the usual taverns, often places designed more to relieve drivers of their money than to provide rest. An overnight stop required a field in which the stock could be herded as well as fed. The west shore of the Susquehanna opposite Harrisburg was a major center for herding cattle. Each herd of cattle was headed by a boss drover leading a huge ox on which was tied the drover's extra clothing and bedding. A good drover must of necessity be a man with powerful lungs. His colorful "Caw, bawss" (Come, boss) together with the clouds of dust which accompanied the moving of several hundred cattle were an ever-present reminder to any town that a cattle drive was passing. It took the coming of the railroad to seal the doom of the cattle and livestock trail in the East just as it did in the later West. The

railroad cattle car was the first device to be found which could move cattle more cheaply than on the hoof.

THE RISE OF THE STEAMBOAT

A further revolution was at hand in the use of rivers. Arks, flatboats, keelboats, and rafts continued in use in great numbers on the Susquehanna, the Juniata, the Delaware and its tributaries, and the western waters. The raft was useful especially in getting lumber and logs to the mill, and sometimes was also loaded with heavy freight. Lumber, flour, and spirits were the principal cargo on these various river craft. An ark or keelboat could move fifty or more tons of freight and they were common on the Ohio. The steamboat changed radically this slow and costly river trade. John Fitch launched his steamboat on the Delaware for the benefit of observers in 1787, and a year later was operating a regular steamboat service to Burlington, New Jersey. William Henry at Lancaster had launched an experimental craft on Conestoga Creek even earlier, in 1763. Oliver Evans, one of the truly great engineering minds of the era, also experimented with steamboats.

It remained for Lancaster County's Robert Ful-

An artist's drawing showing a flatboat and steamboats on the Ohio.

John Fitch's steamboat.

The Steam-Boat

IS now ready to take Paffengers, and is intended to fet off from Arch ftreet Ferry in Philadelphia every Monday, Wednefday and Friday, for Burlington, Briftol, Bordentown and Trenton, to return on Tuefdays, Thurfdays and Saturdays—Price for Paffengers, 2/6 to Burlington and Briftol, 3/9 to Bordentown, 5f. to Trenton. June 14. tu.th ftf

Fitch advertises his steamboat line.

ton to unite with Robert Livingston in launching the first successful steamboat on western waters at Pittsburgh with the *New Orleans* in 1811. Fulton's *Clermont* had been launched on the Hudson four years before. The steamboat was tried elsewhere but without continuing success, due to shallow waters. But it revolutionized transportation for western Pennsylvania and opened further the markets of the entire Ohio and lower Mississippi valleys to the products of its farms, mines, and industries. River shipping was measured in hundreds of tons and Pittsburgh soon became the third-ranking city in the nation in shipping tonnage. Its wharves on the river front were stacked with goods of all kinds coming or going by river, and as many as twenty steamboats were docked in a single day. Pittsburgh not only used the steamboat for its commerce but built them for use on the local rivers and in many parts of the world. John Stevens and Robert Fulton were also pioneers in developing the use of the steamboat for ocean use. Delaware river shipyards launched

many ocean-going steamers, including the first. In 1825 a small iron steamboat, the *Codorus,* the first in America, was launched on the Susquehanna near York by John Elgar, a portent of a further revolution in steamboating.

CANALS AND MORE CANALS

Waterways are always cheaper than travel by wagon or stage. Pennsylvania with its shallow rivers challenged from the first the supporters of the artificial waterway, the canal. Even William Penn envisioned the possibility of a union of the Susquehanna with the Schuylkill and Delaware by canal. Surveys for a union canal were made as early as 1770, but it was not until 1811 that the Union Canal Company at long last was chartered to build from Middletown on the Susquehanna below Harrisburg to Reading and the Schuylkill. It was completed in 1827. Even before this, the impulse to give Philadelphia direct connection by water with the newly opening anthracite coal

151

fields in the Pottsville region inspired the organization in 1815 of the Schuylkill Navigation Company. This canal has been overshadowed in the history of American canal building by the Erie Canal in New York. The Schuylkill was opened to Pottstown in July, 1824, and on May 20, 1825, all the way to Port Carbon, a distance of 108 miles. The Erie Canal was not completed until November. In June, 1829, the Lehigh Canal was opened for use by the Lehigh Coal and Navigation Company. The Delaware and Hudson Canal by 1828 had connected the Wyoming coal fields around Carbondale with the Delaware and Hudson rivers, which provided a direct outlet for Pennsylvania anthracite to New York City. A gravity railroad from Honesdale over Moosic Mountain to Carbondale formed a part of the system. The canals into the anthracite coal fields made it possible to move millions of tons of coal to Philadelphia and New York. Indeed, the Schuylkill Canal alone by 1860 carried 1,600,000 tons a year. This sudden opening of a new market resulted in a veritable "coal rush" into the region, with new boom towns springing up almost overnight. Pottsville, described in 1825 as "hardly more than one shabby log hut," by 1831 had become a town of four thousand, with hundreds of canal boats clearing from its wharves.

The success of the canal induced such canal fever that in 1827 the British consul at Philadelphia reported, "Canals are opening everywhere." Philadelphia began pressing for a state system of public works reaching all the way to Pittsburgh. On April 11, 1825, the General Assembly answered by setting up a Board of Canal Commissioners to project such a system and by 1826 construction was under way at several points. Over 700 miles of canals and railroads were included in the State Works within the next fourteen years, and another 200 projected. The main line of the State Works utilized the eighty-two-mile-long Columbia Railroad from Philadelphia to the Canal proper at Columbia on the Susquehanna. The Eastern Division of the canal was built from this point to the junction of the Susquehanna with the Juniata. The first lock was dedicated near Harrisburg in 1827. The Eastern, the Susquehanna, and the Juniata divisions joined at Amity Hall. The Susquehanna Division was built along the North Branch from this point to the New York border. A West Branch Canal reached from Sunbury to Lock Haven with an extension along Bald Eagle Creek to near Bellefonte. The Juniata Division reached to Hollidaysburg and the foot of the Alleghenies. At this point one of the greatest engineering feats of that day was accomplished by the building of the thirty-seven-mile-long Portage Railroad over the mountains to Johnstown. From Johnstown, the Western Division of the main line continued to Pittsburgh, a distance of over 100 miles. The Portage Railroad was a series of inclined planes using five planes on the eastern and five on the western side of the Alleghenies, by means of which canal boats were raised or lowered on flat cars, using first horsepower and later stationary steam engines and cable. A 900-foot tunnel, probably the first railroad tunnel in America, was built through the peak of the Alleghenies prior to the descent to

Chester shipyards about 1800.

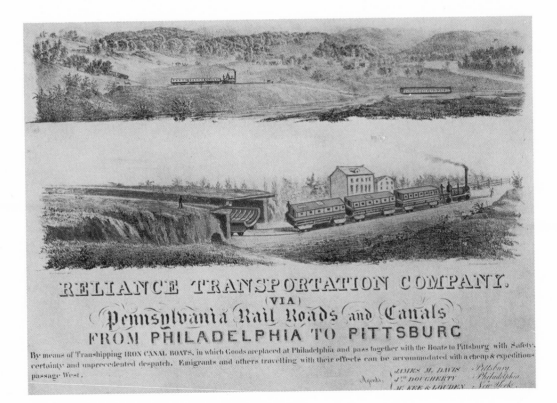

RELIANCE TRANSPORTATION COMPANY.
(VIA)
Pennsylvania Rail Roads and Canals
FROM PHILADELPHIA TO PITTSBURG

By means of Transhipping IRON CANAL BOATS, in which Goods are placed at Philadelphia and pass together with the Boats to Pittsburg with Safety, certainty and unprecedented despatch. Emigrants and others travelling with their effects can be accommodated with a cheap & expeditious passage West.

Agents, { JAMES M. DAVIS — Pittsburg
{ J.no DOUGHERTY — Philadelphia
{ McKEE & LOUDEN — New York.

The new railroad and canal route to Pittsburgh prompted advertisements of rival lines offering their service.

153

Johnstown. Building and operating the Portage stimulated the type of engineering genius which led John Roebling to invent and manufacture wire rope for use as cable. The State Works reached Pittsburgh by 1834. A canal system was built to connect Pittsburgh with Erie and another extension reached Meadville and Franklin. Bristol and Easton were united by the Delaware Canal. The rage to build canals ground to a halt about 1840, though the use of canals as a practical means of transportation continued long after the Civil War. Pennsylvania was almost bankrupted by its canal endeavors and sold the major part of its holdings in 1857 to the Pennsylvania Railroad. Canals gave a much greater lift to the economic growth of Pennsylvania than was possible with wagon and turnpike. Despite the handicaps of slow-moving horse- or mule-drawn boats, freezing, leakage, and other problems, the canal provided a quicker and cheaper way to move heavier goods. The cost of moving a ton of freight between Pittsburgh and Philadelphia was cut from $120 to $30 a ton. Grain and lumber and iron and coal were the principal freight carried by canal.

Canal travel had its own folk history and lore. Few canals, other than the main line of the Pennsylvania Canal, attracted many passengers. They were too slow and uncomfortable for other than freight service. Canal boats rarely moved at night, and at dusk the captain steered his craft to a fixed stopping place, tied up for the night, had the mules fed and stabled, and with the crew and/or passengers went to a nearby canaler's inn in town. The crew, including the youthful mule "skinner" or driver, was wakened at three or four in the morning and the journey resumed. Like wagoners, canalers were a tough and ready crew much given to drinking, singing, telling tall stories, and general revelry in the towns at which they stopped. Pirates operated at times on the early canals, especially on the Schuylkill. Unexpected storms, floods, breaking of tow ropes, or of the connections between several boats (which were often towed as a single unit) were normal hazards which made canal boating an exciting experience.

THE COMING OF THE IRON HORSE

The canal fever was still at a peak when far-sighted persons began to look to the railroad as a more satisfactory answer to the need for better facilities for carrying goods and people. The basic weaknesses of the canal were that it depended upon water, it was slow, and it was not an all-year carrier. Railroads could be built just about anywhere, they did not freeze, and they ran on schedules. As with the canals, the major pressure for building railroads in Pennsylvania grew out of the need to transport heavy freight. Thomas Leiper built one of the very first railroads in 1800 to carry stone from his quarry near Swarthmore. It did not amount to much as a railroad, being less than a mile in length. The discovery of the value of anthracite coal really gave birth to the railroad and the anthracite region in Pennsylvania properly may be called the "birthplace of American railroading." By the 1830's the region was sprinkled with numerous short-line gravity railroads using inclined planes. Iron or wooden cars which held about a ton of coal apiece rolled down the tracks by gravity and were hauled back to the mines by mule power or stationary engines. These pioneer railroads ran from a point on a canal or river to the mine. The first steam locomotive run on rails in the United States was the "Stourbridge

This drawing shows boats placed on the inclined plane to ascend the Alleghenies, using the Portage Railroad.

An artist's view of Huntingdon about 1858, showing competing means of travel then available. Note the canal boat being towed alongside the Juniata, as well as the railroad train.

Lion," imported from England and used on a trial run in August, 1829, on the railroad for hauling coal from Carbondale to Honesdale. Probably the earliest gravity railroad was at Mauch Chunk in 1828. In 1828 an "Iron Rail Road" was projected from Philadelphia to Columbia on the Susquehanna near Lancaster to connect Philadelphia with the trade of that area, and it later became the first railroad link in the State Works, Pennsylvania's state canal system. It was completed in 1834, the first railroad in the world built by a government.

The railroad fever soon was burning no less brightly than had the turnpike and canal enthusiasm. The thirties was a great decade for projecting future railroads in almost every part of the state. It took time to get the necessary capital together to undertake a railroad by arousing enough interest to sell the required stock. Philadelphia kept alive a steady agitation for railroad connections to the Susquehanna and beyond, stimulated by its continuing rivalry with Baltimore. As early as 1829 a drive started for a railroad connecting the Schuylkill at Pottsville with the Susquehanna at Sunbury. It was opened by 1838. Back of it was the twofold idea of carrying anthracite and iron for shipment to Baltimore utilizing the canal along the Susquehanna and in turn diverting products of the upper Susquehanna Valley to Pottsville and then to Philadelphia by way of the Schuylkill Canal. What the local newspapers often referred to as "gentlemen from Philadelphia" had a leading hand in almost every railroad venture. The financier Stephen Girard was one of these "gentlemen." As early as 1832 Williamsport began agitating for a rail connection to Elmira, New York. A few years later a movement started to build a railroad connecting Sunbury with Erie and surveys were completed in 1839. A statewide convention to promote such a rail connection was held at Philadelphia in 1852. It was argued that Philadelphia was eighty-one miles closer to Erie by rail than was New York and this made Philadelphia the logical outlet for the farm and industrial products of northwestern Pennsylvania.

In the meantime Philadelphia interests fought vigorously in the legislature against any extension of railroad lines from Baltimore into the Susquehanna Valley, though many leading citizens of the Harrisburg area, including Simon Cameron, looked with favor upon better trade connections with the Maryland port. In 1835 a railroad was completed from Philadelphia to Norristown with the trains drawn by "Old Ironsides," the first locomotive built by Matthias Baldwin. There were some 300 miles of railroad in operation in the state as early as 1836, but all were short lines. By 1838 Baltimore interests had extended a railroad to York. The Philadelphia and Reading, chartered in 1833, was opened all the way to Reading on December 5, 1839, when the "Gowan and Marx," another Pennsylvania-built locomotive, chugged into Philadelphia carrying barrels of flour, pig iron, coal and whisky as freight, and sixty passengers. The Reading also built the first iron railroad bridge in America at Pottstown in 1844. A railroad for the Lehigh Valley region was projected in 1846 and reached Easton and Wilkes-Barre by 1855. The Pennsylvania Railroad was chartered April 13, 1846, and was built to Pittsburgh by 1852, thanks to another great engineering feat in carrying a railroad over the Alleghenies, using the famous Horseshoe Curve just west of Altoona to climb the mountains. The Delaware, Lackawanna and Western was in operation by 1851. The Susquehanna was first bridged in 1837. The fifties saw the railroad fever burning even more strongly in just about every part of the state. Short lines were projected in every direction, usually to provide a route to another railroad or to a canal as a means of stimulating business. Cities and even entire counties pledged their resources to buy railroad-company stock and citizens everywhere who had any interest in a business or industry were also subscribing to the support of railroad companies.

Pennsylvania was not only the birthplace of railroad building, but of building and engineering railroads which helped the country and even the world to develop its nationwide railroad system. Youthful Frederick List, who became the "father of German railroads," wrote: "In the midst of the wilderness of the blue mountains of Pennsylvania, I dreamed of German railroad systems." William Milnor Roberts, who began his career engineering canals, pioneered in developing the use of a

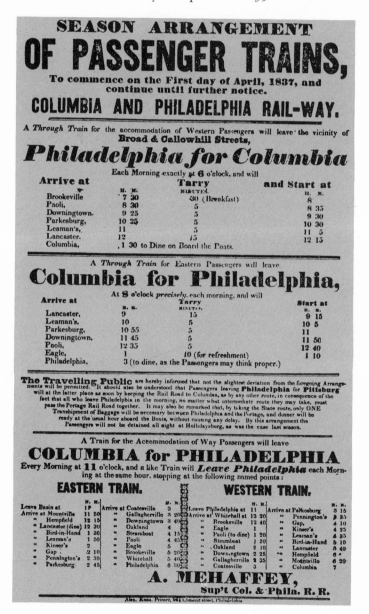

The first Pennsylvania Railroad schedule, issued in 1837.

standard-gauge track of four feet, eight and a half inches' width to replace the uneven gauges common even down to the Civil War. The first iron T-rails were rolled at the Danville Montour Iron Company works by Welsh workers brought here for that purpose and the same mills produced the first thirty-foot-long rails made in this country. Scranton's Lackawanna Iron Company made the Erie Railroad's first rails. Virginia-born Moncure Robinson was a youthful engineer who in his twenties studied early railroads and canals in Europe. He started his career in this country on the Pennsylvania Canal and turned to railroads, after having surveyed the Portage Railroad before he was thirty. He directed the building of the Philadelphia and Reading, developed the idea of the use of stone ballast and correct engineering as to railroad grades and curves. He contributed to railroad building in both Russia and Germany and was without a doubt the greatest genius of his time in the field of engineering and managing railroads. Pennsylvania pioneered also in the use of coal to fire steam locomotives. Many Pennsylvania railroaders helped lead the engineering and management of post-Civil War railroads in the West. Matthias Baldwin, Frankford goldsmith, turned his attention to steam engines and in 1829 built a model locomotive. "Old Ironsides" was built by Baldwin in 1832 for use on the Philadelphia & Germantown. The Baldwin Locomotive works by 1860 had turned out No. 1,500. Moncure Robinson also designed engines for the Reading. In York another jeweler named Phineas Davis built the first successful locomotive used on the Baltimore and Ohio.

The railroad by 1860 was playing a steadily more important role in carrying freight. Between 1853 and 1860 the Pennsylvania moved over 800,000 tons of freight to Philadelphia. The Philadelphia and Reading was carrying anthracite to the seaboard in increasing tonnage. Indicative of the freight moved by railroad, the Cumberland Valley line in 1853 moved iron, pig iron, blooms and casting, grain, and cattle and horses eastward to Harrisburg and Philadelphia, thus serving both industry and agriculture. Pennsylvania on the eve of the Civil War led all other states in railroad mileage as well as capital invested in railroads.

An anti-railroad poster of the 1830's resisting Philadelphia railroad connections with New York.

The state's railroad system had grown to 2,598 miles.

THE ECONOMY OF THE FARM

The transportation revolution had a major influence on the farm and forest economy. Turnpike roads were built by 1840 into many previously inaccessible areas and were especially useful to the farmer in enabling him to get his grain and other produce to a market by wagon. Entire towns developed as "ports" along the canals where goods were brought for shipment to Philadelphia and Baltimore. Records of canal traffic show clearly the importance of canals to agriculture through moving farm produce to market. The early railroads also freighted a large volume of flour and other products of a farm economy. Pennsylvania agriculture prospered even though by 1840 it had lost its leadership in wheat-growing to the rich new lands of the Middle West. Interest in the application of science to farming was on the increase after the Revolution and Pennsylvania was its center. The American Philosophical Society offered prizes for new ideas for the improvement of farming, and published papers on the subject. The Philadelphia Society for Promoting Agriculture was formed in 1785, the first permanent group of its kind in the new nation. In 1820 the society persuaded the legislature to authorize the organization of county agricultural societies. These caught on rapidly, encouraging also the rise of the county agricultural fair with its impetus to better farming. A growing interest in education specializing in agriculture led to the founding of the Farmer's High School in 1855 which was soon named the Pennsylvania State College. In 1851 a State Agricultural Society was chartered with some state financial aid.

Rotation of crops was a serious concern in the period. Judge John Bordley, a "gentleman farmer," in 1792 published his *Sketches on the Rotation of Crops.* Judge Richard Peters was a pioneer advocate of the use of gypsum to improve the soil and the growing of clovers and using of manures for the same purpose. After 1840 Pennsylvania farmers turned to winter wheat, rye, barley, and corn as major grain crops. Frederick Watts of Carlisle was another leading figure in agricultural improvements of the period just before 1860. Watts was the first president of the State Agricultural Society. By 1840 attention was being turned to the improvement of livestock. The first livestock association in the nation was the Pennsylvania Society for Improving the Breeds of Cattle organized at Philadelphia in 1809. The county fair gave, with its exhibits and prizes, encouragement to breeding better livestock. Sheep husbandry to provide wool was on the increase for a time but by 1860 was centered mainly in southwestern Pennsylvania in Washington and Greene counties. The birth of the dairy industry in southeastern Pennsylvania concentrating on the production of milk, butter, and cheese for a commercial market was a reality by 1860 with the growth of larger towns and cities, where a market arose for such products. The Pennsylvania Horticultural Society, founded in 1827, was the first of its kind and marked growing attention to the improvement of this field of farming.

Spurred by the growth in the market for farm products, the country by 1840 was very concerned with improvements in farm machinery. The plow, the most basic piece of farm equipment, was the first to receive attention. While Jethro Wood of New York usually is credited with inventing the iron plow, nearly twenty years earlier Robert and Joseph Smith in Bucks County patented, in 1800, the first practical design for a cast iron plow using the improved design for the moldboard perfected by Thomas Jefferson. Charles Newbold of Philadelphia was granted a patent on a cast iron plow even earlier, in 1797, but the Smith brothers' plow was actually manufactured and licensed for manufacture by others. Development of one of the first grain drills to replace hand sowing of grain is attributed to Moses and Samuel Pennock in Chester County in 1841. It was used widely in southeastern counties and enabled one man to seed as many as fifteen acres in one day. By 1850 Pennsylvanians had invented usable mechanical corn planters as well as machinery for harrowing and weeding. The grain cradle by 1840 had largely replaced the ancient sickle, which had prevailed since Biblical times in harvesting grain. The McCormick reaper was first demonstrated in Pennsylvania in 1840 near Carlisle, but it found use on only a few larger farms before 1860. The skill of the grain cradler remained at a premium on most farms.

Experiments with machinery to find a way other than flailing or treading to thresh grain are on record as far back as 1782, and in 1827 Moses Pennock took out a patent on a "vibrating threshing machine." Another early threshing machine developed in Pennsylvania became known as the "Pitt thresher." Early threshers were operated by horse power or even cattle walking on a treadmill. The patenting of a corn sheller was announced in the Philadelphia press in 1807. A horse-drawn mowing machine was patented by Jeremiah Bailey of Chester County in 1825 as "the cheapest and most expeditious mode of cutting grain and grasses." That inventive genius Moses Pennock patented a revolving wooden hay rake in 1822. A Lancaster County mechanic, Joseph W. Fawkes, in 1853 invented the first "steam plow" which was awarded the gold medal at the United States Agricultural Society fair in 1859. The *Ohio Farmer* reported, "When Fawkes gives a couple of toots of his whistle and the great steam horse speeds over the ground dragging a gang of plows, almost every man, woman and child leave horses and sulkies to their fate." Fawkes thus anticipated the modern tractor. The rich farmlands of southeastern Pennsylvania were a major trial ground for the invention and utilization of many of the pioneer devices associated with this mechanical revolution.

The typical Pennsylvania farmer, however, was not as yet using such machinery; he was content with improvements in basic farm tools, such as the ax, the cradle, the spade, and the fork. The average farmer's investment in tools and machinery in this period amounted at most to only a few hundred dollars. Hand rather than mechanical devices remained the rule on the typical farm. Pittsburgh was the largest single center in the United States for their production. As early as 1836 two Pittsburgh factories alone were turning out steel hoes, shovels and spades, and hay and manure forks by the thousands of dozens at half the price such tools cost a few years earlier.

Better means of transportation and the opening of new markets for farm produce revolutionized all phases of farm life. The log cabin had disappeared as the common habitation for Pennsylvania farmers long before 1860, though many a farmer in remote sections still found it a necessary form of home. The cart long since had been replaced by the substantial farm wagon developed by adapting the basic famous Conestoga to lighter transportation needs of the farm. Blacksmiths in small towns became inventors in their own right, designing and building wagons. By 1860 the factory production of essential wagons and carriages was an important industry in Philadelphia

and Pittsburgh. More and more tools were bought which were made in a factory, and the same was true of household furnishings. The age of homespun and home manufactures was on the way out by 1860. The value of home manufactures in Pennsylvania fell from seventy-six cents per capita in 1840 to nineteen cents in 1860. Making boots and shoes and similar craft enterprises carried on in small shops persisted in many towns in northern and western Pennsylvania, but even here little was now made actually in the home. Better and more substantial houses and barns became everywhere characteristic of the Pennsylvania farm. Barter-type economy persisted, however, in rural areas despite increased wealth as the town merchant remained in many sections the importer of factory-made goods which he exchanged for the farmer's grain or other produce.

INDUSTRY DEPENDS ON THE PRODUCTS
OF FARM AND FOREST

Despite the advance of the industrial revolution and the great importance of the iron industry, those industries which also utilized the basic products of Pennsylvania's forests and farms were a major foundation of the state's industrial economy before 1860. A case in point is the milling industry. Philadelphia in this period was the greatest single center for flour milling in the entire nation. In 1820 the milling of flour and meal in dollar value of the product was the largest single manufacture in the state. The importance of milling was so great that Oliver Evans of Philadelphia tackled the problem of improved gristmill operation and as early as 1785 perfected the first entirely mechanically operated and power-driven grist mill complete with elevators, hoppers, and all the processes of milling flour. The Evans mill was probably the earliest example in the country of the complete mechanization of an industrial process. He also published ten years later a guide to the operation of mills which influenced milling all over the country. Steam flour milling began in Pittsburgh as early as 1809 and it became an important milling center for the West. Lancaster was another important mill center. The milling industry in a large part of the state was a small-scale operation, but it helped maintain milling as a major industry based on agriculture. Quantities of Pennsylvania flour reached markets outside the state by way of Philadelphia, Baltimore, and New Orleans.

Distilling grain into whisky became common on the frontier because it was easier to get the whisky to market. Pennsylvania became one of the leading centers of distilling, especially in the western counties. Leather tanning and manufacturing made up yet another important industry based on the farm. Philadelphia was one of the leading centers of leather manufactures. It was especially noted for its shoes and other fine leather products. Tanning was mechanized by 1860 in the larger centers but it was a type of crude industrial operation in its earlier stages, and easily established anywhere. Tanning and leather manufactures ranked third in any census of early Pennsylvania manufactures. Pennsylvania had more woolen mills in 1860 than any other state and the industry was second in capital invested and the value of the product. Small woolen mills were common in earlier days but the industry was soon mechanized.

The textile industry, including the production of both woolen and cotton goods, flourished in Pennsylvania and was second only to the iron industry in 1860 in the value of its products. Philadelphia and vicinity was one of the great textile manufacturing centers of the entire nation, using thousands of women and children in the increasingly larger and more mechanized "factories," as textile mills were usually called. Philadelphia textile manufactures included carpeting and it had the first carpet mill in the nation. Philadelphia in 1860 was second only to New York in the new ready-made-clothing industry. It was famous for the production of hats, including the tall silk hat favored by the gentleman of that day. Another product of southeastern Pennsylvania farms was tobacco, and Philadelphia became well known for its cigars and for Garrett's snuff.

The forests of Pennsylvania were one of its truly rich natural resources and contributed substantial wealth in this era. The United States in the first half of the nineteenth century remained in what can be termed the "age of wood." Wood was the basic material in just about all types of buildings. The early railroads used wood for fuel, ties, cars, and even the first rails. The forest provided the charcoal for the early iron industry. Wood was the material used in making all kinds of kegs, barrels, and boxes, used to pack or package a great variety of products. It went into ships and their rigging. Every form of tool or implement, including even the latest new machinery, made heavy use of wood. The first use of the forests in industry was in shipyards on the Delaware in colonial times, and this continued right down to 1860. Philadelphia shipyards furnished a heavy percentage of the nation's shipping and naval vessels. The sawmill was one of the first industries in every new community. With better transportation a large part of the surplus could be shipped to a market. By 1860 southeastern Pennsylvania had lost much of its timber and Williamsport was assuming importance as the "lumber city" in central Pennsylvania. The great Williamsport Boom was completed in 1850 to become the largest single center anywhere in the country at that time for marshaling the logs of the lumber days. Pennsylvania was then and for some years later the nation's principal center for the lumbering industry. The lumber turned out by some three thousand or more mills large and small was valued in millions of dollars and was a prime resource in the growing economy of the state. Lumber camps with their rough-and-ready lumbermen, as ready to fight as to cut down trees, sprang up in central and western Pennsylvania by the hundreds. Entire new towns grew up to serve the needs of the industry.

IRON AND COAL BECOME KINGS

Pennsylvania by the end of the Revolution had already enjoyed a half century as the leading maker of iron in America. The iron plantations of the era before the Revolution continued to spread in the next several decades as charcoal iron retained its dominance. The technology of iron-making did not change much before about 1840 other than that furnaces, forges, and the rolling mills grew steadily larger. The valley of the Juniata and the surrounding region became after

1790 a center for the making of an especially high-quality iron which came to be known as "Juniata iron." Eli Whitney in distant New England found it superior for making his guns. The iron plantation spread west of the Susquehanna and all the way into western Pennsylvania. The industry suffered from European competition and Pennsylvania led the fight for a protective

castings demanded increasingly for heavy mill and factory machinery. Stoves, machinery and machine parts, tools and implements—all of these were needs met by the foundries and mills of Pittsburgh. By 1850 it had thirty large foundries and many smaller ones. Pittsburgh made everything from steam engines down to tacks.

The growth of the railroad age made yet further

The Morris Iron Works in Philadelphia in 1840, typical of the advance of iron manufacture in the era.

tariff on iron, which was won in 1828 with a consequent boost to the industry. The revolution in machinery and the coming of the railroad made new demands upon the iron industry with their greatly enlarged use of iron. This pressure began to motivate technological advances in the industry. A mill of a new type was put into operation by Issac Meason near Uniontown shortly after the end of the War of 1812; this reduced pig iron to slabs or blooms, and finally to bar iron, using puddling furnaces and grooved rolls rather than the water-powered hammer. Pittsburgh's first iron foundry was started in 1804 and its first rolling mill in 1818. This foundry made cannon and cannon balls for use in the war of 1812, and in 1835 built the first steam locomotive west of the Alleghenies. The blast furnace arrived some ten years later but Pittsburgh became known well before the Civil War as the "Iron City" because of its extensive facilities for making bar iron, sheet iron, and boiler iron, along with the huge iron

demands on Pennsylvania iron. Increased production of pig iron beyond existing limits was impossible so long as it depended upon charcoal to fire the furnaces. The forests to make charcoal were fast disappearing in the iron-making regions. The pressure for another practical iron-furnace fuel turned attention to coal. The first iron furnace to use only anthracite coal as a fuel was Valley Furnace, built near Pottsville in 1836. Dr. Frederick Geissenhainer, a Lutheran clergyman, in 1833 patented the idea of a hot-blast furnace using anthracite and it was put to use at Valley Furnace. David Thomas, known as the "father of the anthracite industry," and George Crane, two of the many Welshmen who came to Pennsylvania with knowledge of the use of coal in making iron, helped to develop further the use of anthracite. The anthracite furnace spread rapidly; by 1860 the production of anthracite iron amounted to half a million tons, of which more than half was poured from Pennsylvania furnaces. It quickly surpassed by a wide margin the production of charcoal iron. Many technological improvements were made prior to 1860 in the manufacture of iron. One who made many contributions was John Fritz of Chester County who later became a pioneer in the founding of the Bethlehem Steel Company. Steam engines were growing in use after 1840 to operate the furnaces and provide a hot blast with a resulting improvement in all kinds of products made from iron.

Success in using anthracite challenged western Pennsylvania ironmasters to find a new fuel and they turned to coke, made from soft coal. The Connellsville region in Fayette County became the center for experimentation with the beehive-type coke oven between 1830 and 1840. The most extensive use made of coke in a large-scale iron-making operation was at the great Brady's Bend Iron Company works in Armstrong County. This long since forgotten enterprise was the ancestor of Henry Ford's later idea of consolidating under one company and in one operation the production of raw material and its use in the finished product from coal mine and iron ore through to rolled iron rail. The Brady's Bend Iron Company owned 6,000 acres of land with contained coal and iron ore. A village built on company land housed over five hundred families of the workers. This was large-scale and integrated industrial production of a type previously unknown anywhere in America. It typifies the beginnings of a technological revolution in the iron industry which led the way just

before the Civil War to new experiments with making steel.

One of the truly major contributions of the Pennsylvania iron industry as it expanded after 1840 was the production of the first iron T-rails needed to anchor the new railway transportation systems on a sound foundation. Brady's Bend rolled large quantities of iron rails. As mentioned earlier, one of the first iron works to turn out iron T-rails in a mill built for the purpose and in quantities large enough to justify considering it a "first" was the Montour Iron Company works at Danville. It began making iron rails in 1845. The iron works of 1860 was a far cry from the iron plantation of fifty years earlier. It now made use of steam engines for power rather than the ancient water wheel. It had not one but several heating and puddling furnaces, employed usually at least two hundred men, and turned out thousands of tons of iron products. Pennsylvania long before the Civil War became the colossus of the nation's iron industry. It mined over one-half of the nation's iron ore. It turned out more than one-half the nation's pig iron, and better than one-half the total capital invested in making iron was in Pennsylvania. Making iron and its products in Pennsylvania had become one of the nation's first truly large-scale industrial enterprises. The state's capacity to make pig iron made possible the turning of this raw product of the furnace into the steam engines, the railroads and railroad equipment, and the new heavy machinery which were

An early coal mine opened near Wilkes-Barre about 1822, showing the infant beginnings of the anthracite industry.

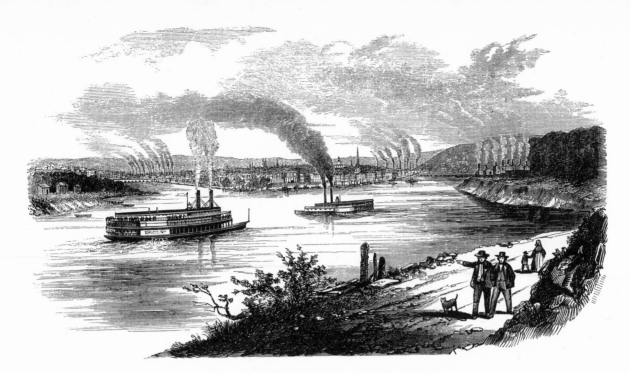

*Pittsburgh in 1850 at the confluence of the Allegheny and the Monongahela,
showing the rapidly growing city and its smoking mills.*

so vital to the progress of the industrial age in America. As a portent of things to come the Pittsburgh-born William Kelly was already experimenting with ways to make steel. Walt Whitman, looking at the American scene in 1856, wrote of the "Colossal foundry, flaming fires, melted metal, pounding trip hammers, surging crowds of workmen, shifting from point to point . . . mighty castings, such is the symbol of America." Pennsylvania was right in the middle of it.

Coal and iron went together as coordinates in the forward surge of Pennsylvania's economy. The existence of coal was known for a long time before any extensive practical use was made of it. Pennsylvania was blessed with billions of tons of bituminous and anthracite coal in the bowels of its earth. The first real use of this vast reservoir of potential energy was made in the Pittsburgh region. Here by 1820 bituminous coal was being used sufficiently by the infant industries of that time to win the city the dubious distinction of becoming known as the "Smoky City," a title it only recently has been able to outlive. The availability of this coal is very probably the reason why Pittsburgh industry began to make very early use

of the steam engine. A small but very rich bituminous field was opened in Tioga County after 1840 where "Bloss coal," as it became known, was widely exported by rail to New York as a smithing coal. The Broadtop bituminous field in central Pennsylvania was opened by railroad in 1856.

Many legends have grown up as to who was the first person to discover anthracite. One story gives credit to a man named Necho Allen. The most likely person to deserve this distinction was the Pennsylvania German farmer and later miller, Philip Ginder. Ginder one day in 1791 while digging in the mountains for good rock for millstones brought back a sample of "stone coal." A blacksmith was able to burn it and Ginder's neighbor, Colonel Jacob Weiss, had it tested in Philadelphia. The tests were good enough to convince Colonel Weiss he had something worthwhile at hand. With some Philadelphia partners he organized in 1792 the first coal mining company in the United States, the Lehigh Coal Mine Company. The romantic tale of how Judge Jesse Fell burned anthracite in his grate at Wilkes-Barre in 1808 is another landmark in anthracite history. There are of course many tales of how Phila-

163

delphia householders in early days thought they had been swindled into buying black rock when it would not burn in their stoves. The tide began to turn in 1818 when the Lehigh Navigation Company joined with the Lehigh Coal Company both to mine and to deliver coal by canal. A few thousand tons began to find a market but it took the discovery of how these "black diamonds" could be used to fire iron furnaces and steam engines to make anthracite a significant resource. Even then in 1860, only a meagre 10,983,000 tons were mined. Coal, despite its still limited utilization, was on the way to become a revolutionary source of energy in American industry.

A SYSTEM OF NATIONAL ECONOMICS AND BANKING IS ROOTED IN PENNSYLVANIA

A nation moves ahead very largely on the strength of the ideas which motivate its progress. The ideology of a national and self-sufficient economy took root in the United States after the Revolution as an integral part of the gospel of developing nationalism. Pennsylvanians made outstanding contributions to formulating the ideas on which a national system of economic growth was based. The earliest of these philosophers was Tench Coxe. Coxe in 1787 wrote his essay "An Enquiry into the Principles on Which a Commercial System for the United States of America Should be Founded." His *A View of the United States of America* appeared in 1794. Both were among the earliest positive statements of the need for a national system of manufactures. Coxe was no mere theorist, for he was active in the Pennsylvania Society for the Encouragement of Manufactures and the Useful Arts, which succeeded the United Company of Philadelphia for Promoting American Manufactures.

The United Company and the Pennsylvania Society actually were joint stock companies to forward textile manufactures and pioneered in the factory production of cloth. The Company was in business as early as 1778 and eventually had four jennies with over two hundred spindles, a carding machine, and twenty-six power looms. The Society itself advertised prizes for improved production methods and new machinery. It was

this advertising which led Samuel Slater to America. He came to New York intending to go to Philadelphia but instead was attracted to Rhode Island by news of the new factory of Moses Brown. Actually, Tench Coxe and his partner Samuel Wetherill were the first, rather than Brown and Slater, to begin factory manufacture of textiles in the United States. Coxe advocated a rapid development of American manufactures to relieve it from dependence upon England. He commented with great satisfaction upon the extent to which Pennsylvania was assuming leadership in manufactures effort, writing ". . . it must afford the most comfortable reflection to every patriotic mind to observe their progress in the United States, and particularly in Pennsylvania."

The heirs to this philosophy of economic nationalism were Mathew Carey and his son Henry. Mathew Carey was an Irish nationalist who was forced to come to Philadelphia in 1784 because of his strong views on Irish independence. A year later he started the *Pennsylvania Herald* and soon became a noted publisher, writer, and bookseller. Carey was active in organizing the Philadelphia Society for the Promotion of National Industry and wrote literally thousands of books and pamphlets urging expansion of manufacturing, internal improvements, and a protective tariff. No stronger advocate of protectionism emerged prior to his death in 1839. His son Henry Carey already had started his important three-volume *Principles of Political Economy,* published in 1837-40. His *Harmony of Interests: Manufacturing and Commercial* followed eleven years later. It is questionable whether any other two men contributed so much to the doctrine of laissez-faire nationalism and protectionism upon which the national economy became based after the War of 1812. On the side of action, in 1827 a hundred delegates from thirteen states projected at a Convention of Friends of Domestic Industry held at Harrisburg a campaign for protective duties on woolen goods, iron, and many other products. The convention's proposals formed the basis for the protective tariff demands of the Northeast.

Larger-scale industrial enterprise, mining, and steadily expanding internal improvements placed a heavy strain on existing machinery for financing capital improvements during this era of national growth. The partnership could hardly suffice for the larger new industrial undertakings or the building of turnpikes, canals, and railroads. The joint stock company of European origin began to appear increasingly because it was only through a widespread sale of stock that essential capital could be raised. This was a device widely used in early mining, textile, and iron-industry operations. It was used also to raise the money to build turnpikes, canals, and railroads. In these instances the public-utility aspect of the enterprises usually led to aid from the state government or even, in the case of the railroads, stock subscription by local governments. The age of bank credit and loans from large financial institutions to underwrite capital improvements in business and industry was merely in its infancy on the eve of the Civil War. Stephen Girard's Banking House opened in 1812 was perhaps the first example in the United States of a large banking establishment capable of investing in major improvements, but it rested on the fortune of one great financier. The foundations of several more broadly based Philadelphia banking empires, including the house of Drexel, were laid before the Civil War and made Philadelphia a center of the private banking world. This type of banking was the major source from which any large amount of credit could be secured.

Banks chartered as national or state institutions were created mainly as a means of governing the issuance of currency. The first bank in America was the subscription bank known as the Pennsylvania Bank in Philadelphia, formed in 1780 to help finance the patriot cause. It was followed by the Bank of North America, chartered by the state in 1782. Alexander Hamilton's plan for a national banking system was put into operation in 1791 with the First Bank of the United States. It was headed by Thomas Willing, who had also headed the Bank of North America. The Jeffersonian Democrats refused to continue Hamilton's scheme but the financial difficulties which followed the War of 1812 led Alexander Dallas, Secretary of the Treasury from Pennsylvania, to create in 1816 the Second Bank of the United States. Philadelphia's Nicholas Biddle became the head of this bank. The Jacksonian forces in turn destroyed the bank, leaving the country without a national system of banking until the Civil War. The Bank of Pennsylvania was chartered in 1793, with the state subscribing to one-third of its $3,000,000 capital. It set up branches in Lancaster, Reading, Easton, and Pittsburgh, but was a victim of the Panic of 1857. The Philadelphia Bank was chartered in 1804 and the Bank of Pittsburgh in 1814. A State Banking Act in 1814 divided the state into bank districts in a move to encourage an expansion of state banking facilities. Several banks were started but few survived the two panics in 1837 and 1857. In Philadelphia, Biddle and his associates, following the demise of the Second Bank of the United States in 1835, organized the United States Bank of Philadelphia but it also failed in 1841.

The nation's first savings bank was established in 1819, the Philadelphia Savings Fund Society. A similar savings bank was founded in Pittsburgh in 1833. The first trust company was also a Philadelphia concern, the Pennsylvania Company for Insurance on Lives and Granting Annuities, founded in 1812. This also was a pioneer step in the field of life insurance. Still another financial first was registered in Frankford in 1839 with the creation of the first building and loan association. Bank clearing houses were established in Philadelphia and Pittsburgh on the eve of the Civil War, an indication of the marked increase in the use of banks. But much remained to be done in developing anything similar to modern instrumentalities in credit and banking.

THE ECONOMY OF 1860

Remarkable changes had been made in the economic life of Pennsylvania between 1790 and 1860. The pattern for its later growth and the nature of that growth were well established. Of particular note was the extent to which manufacturing had spread throughout the state. Though Philadelphia's manufactures were valued at $135,979,677 in 1860 and represented about 46 per cent of the state's total, the entire commonwealth shared in the industrial revolution. The Pittsburgh region in particular had become one of the important manufacturing centers west of the Alleghenies and in some ways technologically was ahead of even Philadelphia. The iron industry was widespread. Mining coal was becoming an important part of the economy in both western and eastern Pennsylvania. The larger towns which were to become the industrial centers of the future already were well outlined by 1860. Another significant feature of the industrial change was the diversity of Pennsylvania industry. Iron and textile manufactures were dominant in 1860 and those manufactures based primarily on the farm and forest were beginning to show signs of decline. But Pennsylvania was making some of almost every type of industrial product. It had probably the most extensive chemical manufacturing facilities in the country. It was noted for its leather products, including boots and shoes. Philadelphia was the center for sugar refining. Western Pennsylvania was a large producer of salt. The first oil well was drilled at Titusville by "Colonel" Edwin Drake in 1859 marking the birth of the petroleum industry. Pittsburgh and Philadelphia were meat packing centers of note. Pittsburgh was a leading center of the glass industry and the state ranked third in the production of glass.

The state was well known not only for the manufacture of heavy machinery but also for making scientific apparatus and instruments. Pittsburgh was "toolmaker of the West." Philadelphia developed a reputation for its hardware. The Keystone Works of Henry Disston was the largest tool and saw factory in the country. Sharps and Company in the same city was a famous manufacturer of firearms, especially the Sharps rifle of Civil War days. Philadelphia was known also for its cordage and rope manufactures. Any direc-

tory of the manufacturing establishments of Pittsburgh and Philadelphia, or indeed of smaller cities, reveals that somewhere in the state there was being made by 1860 just about everything made in a mill or factory anywhere in the world. An analysis made in 1858 showed Philadelphia alone manufacturing no less than eight hundred different products. Inventive genius was very much alive in the state as a result of this diversity. Charles Goodyear's first experiments with vulcanizing rubber were started in Philadelphia. Joseph Saxton, Philadelphia engraver and watch and clock maker, is believed by many to have been the father of photography. Saxton also developed and built the system of standard weights and balances adopted by the United States government. William Metcalf of Pittsburgh was a guiding genius behind the Fort Pitt Foundry in Pittsburgh which built some of the heaviest machinery and rifled cannon developed by the Civil War. These were but a few of the men who were contributing to the continued revolution of the American economy on the eve of the Civil War.

By 1860 Pennsylvania had been remarkably transformed from the state that existed in 1790. An economy based on agriculture had shifted toward manufacturing and mining as its foundations. Population growth and spread had not only ended the frontier but had started a sharp trend toward an urban economy as opposed to that of the rural community. Remarkable new ways of transportation and communication were provided by turnpike, canal, and railroad. None of these developments had reached the stage of totally influencing a complete change in the economy but they were rooted strongly enough to grow and flower fully in the second half of the century.

CHAPTER TEN

AFFAIRS
OF GOVERNMENT
AND POLITICS,
1790 - 1860

The years between the end of the Revolution and the start of the Civil War were ones of great moment in the political history of the United States. The intense liberalism of the Revolution was followed by a Federalist conservative reaction. Then came in turn the era of Jeffersonian democracy after 1800, in which the concept of Federalism lost ground and finally failed. There was the interlude of the War of 1812 and, after a so-called "era of good feeling" in which all political differences were supposed to have vanished, the vigorous Jacksonian democratic era. Manifest destiny expressed itself in the 1840's and ended in the War with Mexico. It was followed by a sharp intensification of sectional feeling over the extension of slavery. The new Republican Party emerged out of this and other growing differences of opinion between the North and West on the one hand and the South on the other. Pennsylvania during the period was something of a mirror of national trends and had no little influence on many developments of the times.

THE ERA OF THE WHISKY REBELLION

Pennsylvania's first elected governor under the Constitution of 1790 was Thomas Mifflin. Mifflin was one of the state's Revolutionary War heroes. His leading opponent was another soldier, General Arthur St. Clair, at the time the first governor of the new Northwest Territory. Mifflin was not committed to either of the two political factions which were to develop into the Federalist Party and the Anti-Federalist, or Democratic-Republican Party. Mifflin carried every county and was re-elected to two successive terms of three years each. Mifflin tended to be a balance wheel during these years when both the Federalists and the followers of Jefferson became more and more vocal and better organized as political parties. The Federalists controlled the General Assembly though Thomas Jefferson carried Pennsylvania for the Presidency by a narrow margin in 1796. Since Philadelphia was not only the state but the national capital the issues created by Washington's policy of neutrality between France and

*John S. Copley's portrait of Thomas
Mifflin and his wife.*

tion of the tax was evident in western Pennsylvania. Mifflin refused despite pleas from the President to use Pennsylvania militia against the whisky "rebels." Chief Justice McKean of the State Supreme Court denied the power of the Federal government to use force within Pennsylvania. This was a nice question of state's rights. On August 7, 1794, Washington issued a proclamation ordering the "insurgents" to disperse by September 1. Pennsylvania was requested to provide state militia to aid in enforcing the tax. Mifflin now called a special session of the legislature and announced to the people that he must support the President. A final effort by representatives of both the state and Federal governments to mediate the issue failed and Governor Mifflin was ordered to call out state militia. The militia refused to obey the call and the Assembly authorized raising other troops.

Though more moderate leaders had asserted themselves in western Pennsylvania and any real resistance had ended, Washington was prevailed upon by Hamilton to make a show of Federal armed power and troops from Pennsylvania, Virginia, and New Jersey were gathered at Carlisle. Washington himself reviewed the troops, appointed the three state governors as commanders, and marched with them as far as Bedford. The force of some 15,000 men then marched into western Pennsylvania to Parkinson's Ferry on the Monongahela, encountering not even a semblance of resistance. Though the opposition had melted, twenty leaders of the "rebellion" were arrested and arbitrarily marched off to Philadelphia. Two of these men were condemned to death for treason but later pardoned, along with the others. One of the most active leaders, David Bradford, who had been elected major general of the "rebels," fled from his home in Washington to Louisiana.

Four years later southeastern Pennsylvania housewives provoked another major show of resistance to Federal tax authority by liberally dousing with hot water assessors who were attempting to count and measure the size of windows in houses to determine the basis for another excise tax. This uprising became known variously as Fries's Rebellion, because of the leadership of John Fries, or the "Hot Water Rebellion."

England during the era of the French Revolution had a strong impact on political opinion of the time. Mifflin, like Washington, avoided the pitfalls of direct party affiliation and remained a governor "without party," difficult though it was.

When Alexander Hamilton pushed through Congress the seven-cents-a-gallon excise tax on whisky it fell heavily upon the farmers in western Pennsylvania who were converting their grain to this more easily marketed product. By the fall of 1791 resistance to the tax was very strong and was led by men of the stature of Albert Gallatin. Washington in his September 15, 1792, proclamation warned Pennsylvania and other states where resistance was evident to comply with the law. Opposition grew rapidly and to a point where in July and August 1794, armed resistance to collec-

On the more positive side, Mifflin's administration led the way in acquiring the Erie Triangle and providing thereby for Pennsylvania a Great Lakes port. This tract of some 200,000 acres had been claimed by both New York and Massachusetts but had been surrendered by the two states to the new national government. Pennsylvania bought it from the United States in March, 1792, for $151,640.25. Mifflin's administration was also responsible for pushing the survey of newly acquired Indian lands in northwestern Pennsylvania and for laying out Erie and other towns.

In the 1780's special legislation had been passed enabling Revolutionary soldiers who had been paid in depreciated currency to purchase land at the average price of twenty-eight cents an acre in sufficient amount to cover the depreciation of the currency. The legislature later authorized setting aside in northwestern Pennsylvania what became known as the Donation Lands. On a basis of lots drawn from a lottery wheel, amounts of land ranging from 200 acres for a private to 2,000 acres for a major general were offered tax exempt to veterans. The state land policy was generally liberalized under Governor Mifflin, encouraging the rapid settlement of the remaining frontier. The population of western Pennsylvania, thus aided, grew no less than 85 per cent between 1790 and 1800.

Federal excise taxes were not liked by the rank and file of Pennsylvanians and this played a major role in the ultimate downfall of the Federalists. The arbitrary Alien and Sedition Acts added fuel to the flame and in 1799 aging but venerable Judge Thomas McKean captured the governorship against the Federalists. The Democratic-Republican Party of Jefferson also won control of the legislature for the first time. McKean was a onetime Federalist and essentially conservative by nature and training. While re-elected for another two terms, he faced a growing revolt of liberal members of his own Democratic-Republican group after 1800. The liberals made their main issue reform of the state constitution, annual rather than four-year terms for members of the State Senate, curbing the veto and appointive power of the governor, and reform of the judicial system. McKean survived the split in his own

party in the election of 1805 mainly because the remnants of the Federalist Party rallied to his support. Though labeled a Democratic-Republican, McKean actually belonged to the Federalist era.

THE ERA OF JEFFERSONIAN DEMOCRACY

In 1808 the forces of Jeffersonian democracy elected Simon Snyder to the governorship over Federalist James Ross. This marked the beginning of the end for the Federalists in Pennsylvania. In the critical presidential election four years later Pennsylvania voted for James Madison, who otherwise would have been defeated by the anti-war Federalist DeWitt Clinton from New York. This keystone position of Pennsylvania in the nation's politics which continued for many decades has provided one theory as to the origin of the nickname "keystone state." Federalism never regained any real strength in Pennsylvania. The state became a powerful bulwark of the Democratic-Republican Party both before and after the War of 1812.

Simon Snyder was the first "commoner" elected

Simon Snyder, leader of the new Jeffersonian democracy.

to the governorship and a true Jeffersonian Democrat. The son of a German immigrant, his early life was that of a tanner, storekeeper, country miller and farmer who entered politics and rose to the speakership of the House. He refused to permit any formal inauguration ceremonies, declaring, "I hate and despise all ostentation, pomp and parade as anti-democratic," and that he "would feel extremely awkward, nay in pain, during such a cavalcade." During the campaign he was pictured as "the friend of the people; the friend of equal rights" and "a republican; a foe to lordly aristocrats, who wish to live on the spoils wrenched from the industrious." His opponent, James Ross, was described as one of that class of men endeavoring "to subvert our republican institutions; who are striving to overturn our liberties; that they may establish an odious aristocracy on their ruins." Oddly enough, the Federalist Ross was also portrayed as the candidate who would drag Pennsylvania into "war, horrid war" through abetting an alliance with England while Snyder was touted as the "friend of peace and mankind."

The reverse was true because it was Snyder's party that led the United States into war with England despite Federalist opposition to "Mr. Madison's War." Snyder was re-elected in 1811 by an almost unanimous vote. In a stirring appeal to the state in 1813 he asked and received support for the War of 1812. In 1815 he was able to declare: "During the late war the soil of this commonwealth was never trodden by an hostile foot, yet it had at one time the greater number of militia and volunteers in the service of the United States than were at any other time in the field from any other state in the union. Our militia and volunteers were actually engaged with the enemy in Canada, on Lake Erie, at Baltimore and elsewhere, and stood ready to repel him from the states of New York and New Jersey." If to this record there is added the heroic story of how Daniel Dobbins built from timber hewn from giant oaks felled on the shores of the Lake Erie peninsula a fleet commanded by Captain Oliver Hazard Perry which defeated the British at Put in Bay on September 10, 1813, a truly great saga becomes a part of Pennsylvania's role in the War

of 1812—a war that no one really wanted and that neither country really won.

Perry's historic "we have met the enemy" message. Original in National Archives.

JACKSONIAN DEMOCRACY AND ITS DECLINE

The drive in the 1800's from the frontier and the mass of the common people for more recognition in government throughout the nation was implemented in the Jacksonian era by the growing numbers and influence of the wage earners. Before 1830 the pressure for greater democracy in Pennsylvania originated for the most part with the farmers on the near frontier. By 1840 the influence of the wage earners in the new mills and factories of Philadelphia, Pittsburgh, and larger towns became increasingly evident on the side of social and political reforms. Labor was interested in liberalizing the right to vote. It also advocated strongly a system of free public education. One way in which labor expressed its political interest was in the organization of third parties. The Workingmen's Party was a device for local political organization and used with some success in Philadelphia, Pittsburgh, and in some other larger cities. Petitions to the Assembly from wage earners on behalf of particular reforms such as a free school system and abolition of imprisonment for debt had a major effect on securing such reforms. Workers also cast their votes for major party candidates who supported their objective. Pennsylvania workingmen were among the first in the entire country to secure manhood suffrage and this increased their political influence. The vote of the working man was not by any means

The Battle of Lake Erie, from an early engraving.

always in the majority for candidates of the Democratic Party. The articulate working man of that day was apt to be a skilled worker who fancied himself a notch or so higher on the social scale than the unskilled factory operative and was somewhat conservative. Unskilled workers usually did not qualify to vote.

The end of the War of 1812 marked the end of the Federalist Party as a force in Pennsylvania politics. By 1817 there was nothing left for the Democratic-Republican Party members but to fight among themselves. In Pennsylvania, at least, it was far from being the "era of good feeling" which is commonly associated with national affairs of the time. William Findlay was the candidate for governor of the liberal or "organization Democrat" faction and opposed by Joseph Hiester as candidate of the conservative Democrats and the remnants of the Federalists. One important innovation in democratic government was marked by the use in 1817 of the nominating convention made up of delegates from the several counties to select Findlay. It was a device which gave the people in a party throughout the state a greater voice in picking the candidate. It replaced the old and undemocratic legislative common-caucus method. The "Pennsylvania plan," as it became known, spread widely. Andrew Jackson was the first presidential candidate selected by the convention system. Findlay was also the first governor to be inaugurated in the new capital city of Harrisburg. Removal of the state capital from Philadelphia to Lancaster in 1799 and Harrisburg in 1812 was itself a triumph of the western democracy which sought to get the government out of aristocratic, monied Philadelphia and closer to the people in the interior.

The next several years in Pennsylvania political affairs was a period in which the political game was played viciously and with few rules. Lacking an opposition party of strength, leaders of the Democratic-Republican Party battled like cats and dogs among themselves. The powerful though short-lived Anti-Masonic Party added to the confusion and bitterness. The governors of the era, with the exception of Findlay, who was

171

Scotch-Irish, were Pennsylvania Germans. Oddly enough, a majority of members of the Assembly and other elected officials were Scotch-Irish, reflecting something of an alliance between eastern Pennsylvania German farmers and their Scotch-Irish counterparts in western Pennsylvania.

The membership of the General Assembly was elected predominantly from the farms and small towns and well over half listed their occupation as farming. Lawyers were next in numbers. When Benjamin Latrobe visited the legislative chambers while the capital was at Lancaster he wrote to his wife, "I counted only twelve combed heads and two woolen nightcaps." It was truly a full flowering of an agrarian democracy in Pennsylvania.

Pennsylvania Democrats were among the very strong early supporters of "Andy" Jackson for the Presidency. The *Crawford Weekly Messenger* of Meadville declared for Jackson in late 1822, one of the first newspapers to do so. The state's key influence in the national political picture was such that Pennsylvania support could just about make or break any candidate for the Presidency at this time. Pennsylvania voted for Jackson in 1824 and in 1828 the Jackson vote was about two to one over Adams. Sentiment then waned steadily for Jacksonian democracy down to the 1840 election. Pennsylvania then by a narrow margin cast its ballot for William Henry Harrison, the candidate of the Whig Party, nominated at the Whigs' first national convention, held in Harrisburg. Within the state itself, Findlay's administration was a stormy one during which at one time he was threatened with impeachment. Findlay was defeated for re-election in 1820 by Joseph Hiester, a farmer and store clerk with a very rudimentary education but typical of the "commoner" who appealed to the voter of that day and had risen steadily in state politics. He had even served fourteen years in Congress. Hiester in his inaugural declared he would serve but a single term and that he wished to "avoid the disgraceful appelation of Governor of a party."

In 1823 the two factions in the so-called Democratic-Republican Party continued at loggerheads and John Andrew Shulze, onetime Lutheran minister and later businessman, was elected to the governorship by virtue of a heavy vote in western counties. Shulze was a reform Democrat and advocated electoral and judicial reforms pleasing to the progressives. He also launched the state system of internal improvements. Shulze was returned to office in 1826 by the regular organization which professed the utmost confidence in "the talents and inflexible patriotism of General Andrew Jackson." The extent to which the Democratic Party, as the former Democratic-Republican or Republican Party had now become generally known, was in virtually absolute control of the state is indicated by the fact that only a thousand votes were cast in 1826 against Shulze. The factionalism which reigned within the Democratic Party, however, is indescribable. Shulze was soon accused of favoring the anti-Jackson faction and ended his term with the supporters of Jackson denouncing him as that "stupid Dutch Governor." The extent of this factionalism showed clearly in the Democratic state nominating convention in 1829, in which no less than three groups tried to capture the prized governorship nomination. One faction was led by Samuel D. Ingham, Jackson cabinet member; another was led by young James Buchanan, a newcomer to state Democratic politics but a man who would emerge rapidly as a powerful figure; and yet a third by Pittsburgh Democrats. George Wolf of Northampton County emerged the victor in a compromise but not without continued opposition from the Buchanan men.

ANTI-MASONRY

The Pennsylvania political situation had become further complicated by this date by the growth of the Anti-Masonic movement. The birth of Anti-Masonry was a product of the furore aroused by the disappearance and alleged murder of William Morgan in New York in 1826 to prevent his disclosure of secrets of the Masonic order. Anti-Masonic feeling caught on rapidly in Pennsylvania among Pennsylvania German and Scotch-Irish farmers, as well as many city workers. Masonry was a secret order to which a large number of persons of wealth and influence belonged. It became associated in the minds of the poorly educated people with their hatred of anything which represented special privilege for a few as opposed to the democracy sought by the common man. Anti-Masonic leaders included also many educated persons with strongly liberal and democratic views. In a peculiar way Anti-Masonry became associated with the cause of greater social and political democracy. Its Pennsylvania leaders included men of the caliber of Thaddeus Stevens and Thomas Burrowes.

Though the Anti-Masonic Party did not achieve national organization until 1831, it emerged as a political party in Pennsylvania with the nomination in June, 1829, of Joseph Ritner as candidate for the governorship. Ritner was a Pennsylvania German farmer now living in Washington County who had risen in Harrisburg to the post of Speaker of the House. His favorite pose was that of the dirt farmer behind the plow. He was a person of limited education, and fitted nicely into the log-cabin and hard-cider school of politics which was now appealing so strongly to the masses of the people. He also offered the remarkable combination of a Pennsylvania German living in Scotch-Irish western Pennsylvania. One of his closest political mentors was that great commoner Thaddeus Stevens. Ritner's candidacy was not viewed at first with much alarm by the organization Democrats, but a faction of liberal Democrats, who had become known as the Amalgamators, threatened to hold a separate convention and nominate their own candidate. Failing in this, they went to the polls in large numbers and voted for Ritner. As a result, Wolf was not elected by any landslide. James Buchanan wrote that in Lancaster County "Anti-Masonry has overwhelmed us like a tornado."

Wolf's place in state history was firmly established by his vigorous support of a system of free public education which produced the Free School Act of 1834. At the same time, it and his efforts to stabilize the state's finances with new taxes cost him re-election in 1835. The factional bitterness in the Democratic Party was now deep enough to split it wide open, and Wolf was opposed in the election by the liberal Democrat Henry A. Muhlenberg. Joseph Ritner was again the candidate of the Anti-Masons, having been nominated in Harrisburg by "the Democratic

Joseph Ritner in his famous at-the-plow pose, a sure vote-getter in this era of Pennsylvania politics. Portrait by John F. Francis, itinerant Pennsylvania artist of the time.

Convention opposed to secret societies and political intrigue." In the meantime, the Whig Party was undergoing its birth pains. A product of the reaction against Jackson and what was termed "executive usurpation and abuse," the Whigs promised "the deliverance of the people from the usurpations of Royal and Federal power." Jackson's arbitrary striking down of the Second Bank of the United States was a major source of anti-Jackson feeling in Pennsylvania. Ritner, with Whig and Anti-Masonic Party votes, was elected to the governorship and the Whigs and Anti-Masons also gained control of the House by seventy-six out of a hundred members.

Perhaps the most significant fact about the

Political cartoon used by Ritner forces in 1835 against Governor Wolf. Note the emphasis on Jackson and the bank issue, the effort to attribute the state debt to British influence.

The same cartoon in German for the benefit of the Pennsylvania German voter. Pennsylvania was then actually a bilingual state.

election of 1835 is the extent to which the once progressive party of Jefferson and Jackson had grown tired and conservative to a point where it had broken into irreconcilable factions. This opened the door for new party organizations to take over with new slogans of reform. Ritner's administration under the prod of Thaddeus Stevens undertook at once to appoint a legislative committee "to investigate the evils of Free Masonry." Ritner also came forward with an amazing something-for-everyone proposal to repeal taxes enacted by Wolf's administration to finance internal improvements and at the same time to extend these improvements. This was accomplished by pushing through a bill to issue a state charter for the Bank of the United States, for which privilege the bank would pay the state $9,000,000 to be used to balance the internal-improvements budget. Charges of bribery or at least heavy pressure by bank supporters on legislators to secure passage of this measure were raised. On the highly creditable side was Ritner's firm support of the public school system, though many of his votes had come certainly from its opponents among the Pennsylvania German farmers.

A NEW STATE CONSTITUTION AND NEW POLITICS

The demand for a revision of the constitutional structure of the state was one of long standing and back of it was the continuing demand for more popular control of the government. The great power of the executive and judicial branches of the government had long been under attack. Suspicion of extreme executive power was, of course, a constant element in democratic thinking. Oddly enough, that great favorite of the common people, Andrew Jackson, strengthened this distrust by the way in which he exercised the powers of the Presidency. Though his inauguration in 1829 was looked upon by conservatives as the triumph of "King Mob," Jackson was denounced by 1836 as trying to make himself "King Andrew the First."

The culmination of the movement for a constitutional convention voted upon in the 1835 election came at an unfortunate time in the midst of some of the most bitter political infighting of the entire era. The people at the same election were voting for or against Martin Van Buren. Not only was there a nasty three-way gubernatorial campaign in progress but also a vicious presidential campaign in which Van Buren was pictured by his enemies as "the Federal Dandy of New York" in an appeal to growing feeling in Pennsylvania against New York as its major economic rival. The leading Democrats not only opposed the convention but painted the most fantastic picture of the excesses which it might produce, even charging it might "restore the institution of slavery amongst us." The proposal for a convention carried by only about 13,000 votes. The elected delegates included sixty-six Democrats, fifty-two Anti-Masons, and fifteen Whigs, giving the Anti-Mason and Whig coalition a bare majority control. Fifty-six of the 133 delegates were farmers and only forty were lawyers. The larger number were what one delegate called "levelers" and "agrarians." John Sergeant, venerable former Federalist, later National Republican and Whig Henry Clay's running mate in the 1832 presidential election, was elected chairman.

There were sharp tongues at the Convention. Thaddeus Stevens on one occasion denounced Philadelphia as "a great and growing ulcer on the body politic." Stevens was himself lashed by a Whig delegate as a "sneaking catamount" who was greatest in "littlest things" and "sprayed poison" on every hand. Despite this unhealthy atmosphere, the convention completed its work in February, 1838, with some major changes accomplished. The governor's appointive power was curbed by greatly increasing the number of elective local offices in the state previously appointive; the governor was now limited to two three-year terms in any nine-year period. The previous life tenure of Supreme Court justices was reduced to fifteen years. Those of other judges were cut to ten. A move to remove the taxpaying requirement for voting failed. A step proposed by Thaddeus Stevens to prohibit oath-bound societies was defeated. Suffrage was limited to white males, despite many objections. The Constitution as drafted was approved by a narrow margin of three thousand votes with the eastern counties generally against it and the western counties for it.

One thing a new constitution could not provide for was greater harmony and less abuse and invective in state politics. In 1838 the Democrats, as the result of the strenuous labors of men like James Buchanan, were again a united party and supported David Rittenhouse Porter. Porter came from a distinguished Scotch-Irish family, resided at Huntingdon and was experienced in business and as a state legislator. The coalition of Anti-Masons and Whigs backing Ritner for another term was defeated, but by a narrow margin of some five thousand votes. The Ritner forces at once raised cries of fraud and Thomas Burrowes, secretary of the commonwealth as well as state leader of the Anti-Masonic Party, declared the election returns invalid. Partisans of both sides marched on Harrisburg and created enough disorder to lead Ritner to call on the state militia armed with buckshot to restore order. No blood was shed, at least by the militia, and the disgraceful "Buckshot War" came to an end, to be remembered always as a monument to the bitter and senseless partisanship in the politics of that time. The turbulent events of these few months served to alarm all those with any conservative instincts and led to the decline of the Anti-Masons as an organized party.

Porter proved to be a strong governor when confronted with the financial crisis that resulted from the growing burden of state debt created by continued expansion of the internal-improvements program. He refused to add Pennsylvania to the list of states which were repudiating their debt, and supported taxes and loans to balance the budget. The state banks were required in 1841 to lend the state over three million dollars secured by relief notes guaranteed by the commonwealth. It was a measure of questionable soundness in terms of financial practice but it preserved at least a semblance of solvency. Porter did not favor the action but it was pushed through over his veto. Re-elected in 1841, Porter faced a nasty situation when the "native American" agitation against foreigners and Catholics by the Know-

Nothings resulted in 1844 in riots and actual burning of Catholic churches in, of all places, Philadelphia. Governor Porter in person led state militia into the city to end the disorders.

The memory of the excesses of Anti-Masonry was not slow to die and helped keep the Democratic Party united and bring it again to power in 1844 with the election of Francis Rawn Shunk as governor. At the same time the Whig Party was gaining strength and able to stand on its own. In fact, Pennsylvania became a center of strength in the growth of the Whigs. Harrisburg was the scene of the Whig nominating convention in December, 1839, which nominated General William Henry Harrison and John Tyler—"Tippecanoe and Tyler too." Harrison carried the state by 350 votes. In 1844, as an indication of the keystone position of Pennsylvania, George Mifflin Dallas was James K. Polk's successful running mate on the national Democratic ticket. The Democrats carried the state for both the Presidency and the governorship. James Buchanan was rewarded with the appointment as Secretary of State by President Polk, resigning his seat in the United States Senate. Buchanan's resignation left an opening for a new appointment to the Senate by the Pennsylvania legislature. It was filled by another figure of growing influence, whose name would figure prominently in state and national politics for more than two decades. The man was Simon Cameron, who, with his usual shrewdness in political intrigues, though then a Democrat courted both the Whigs and the Know-Nothings to win the post.

Governor Shunk was typical of the self-made men who were commonly selected as gubernatorial candidates during this period. Nothing of moment took place during his governorship. It was a time when national politics actually were of more concern than state affairs to influential political leaders of the caliber of Buchanan and Cameron. Pennsylvania was becoming an industrial state rather than agricultural. It was engaged in a tight rivalry with New York in commerce and industry. With the growth of its economy Pennsylvania became greatly concerned over policies on banking and the tariff in Washington. Even the Democrats were forced to look with favor upon measures to strengthen the nation's financial position and to secure some protection through tariffs for the new and growing industries of the state. James Buchanan, who had emerged as Pennsylvania's leader in national Democratic politics, was forced to steer carefully between his state's concern for protection and the national Democratic Party's position of tariff for revenue only and down with a national bank. Within the state the Democrats were confronted by increased strength on the part of the Whigs. Shunk was re-elected in 1847 but forced to resign due to ill health, inducing a special election which resulted in the triumph of William F. Johnston on the Whig ticket. The Whigs also carried the state for General Zachary Taylor in the presidential election. In the meantime, the outbreak of war with Mexico provoked by the aggressive manifest destiny of Polk and the national Democratic Party became a diversion. The War with Mexico was not especially popular in Pennsylvania because of the undertones of conquest of territory which would permit the expansion of slavery. Governor Shunk, in accord with the request of President Polk for six regiments of volunteer infantry made on May 19, 1846, called for the necessary volunteers on the twenty-third. On July 15 the governor was able to offer the War Department enough soldiers for nine regiments. These regiments were never mustered into service but in December two regiments were assembled at Pittsburgh to be transported to the war theater and fought under General Scott in the campaign before Mexico City. Such military figures as George B. McClellan, George Gordon Meade, John W. Geary, and Winfield S. Hancock, who would later serve with distinction during the Civil War, won their spurs in Mexico.

THE EXTENSION OF SLAVERY
AND OTHER ISSUES

New issues and new faces began to appear on the political scene in the years after the Mexican War. Hottest of the new issues was the question of the extension of slavery beyond existing limits in the slave states; with it was associated a new face—that of David Wilmot. This man's name

David Wilmot, author of the famed Wilmot Proviso and leader in the organization of the state and national Republican Party.

appears in every American history as author of the Wilmot Proviso, a proposed amendment to an appropriation bill sponsored by President Polk to provide funds to negotiate peace with Mexico, which came before Congress on August 3, 1846. Wilmot's Proviso provided simply that "neither slavery nor involuntary servitude shall ever exist in any part of the territory acquired from Mexico." The Wilmot amendment passed the House but was defeated in the Senate. It came up many more times attached to other bills and always met the same fate, due to the entrenched power of the slave-holding South in the Senate. Lincoln once said he must have voted for it in Congress a hundred times.

David Wilmot is often dismissed as a mere pawn in this move to strike at slavery's extension but he was far more than a willing agent for others. He was an influential member of Congress from northeastern Pennsylvania. His birthplace is still standing at Bethany in Wayne County, along with his later home in Towanda. The story of Wilmot is the story of how the Democratic Party gradually fell apart because it could not reconcile the diverse opinions of its followers on the issue of slavery. It was a sad fate for the party of Jeffersonian and Jacksonian democratic crusades of earlier years. Wilmot began his political career as a young lawyer in a rural region as a staunch Democrat. He ended up a leader in organizing the new Republican Party, not only in Pennsylvania but as a national party.

The General Assembly of Pennsylvania endorsed the Wilmot Proviso in 1846 with only three dissenting votes, indicating the power of this issue even this early. A vote on the question of the abolition of slavery would not have come even close to mustering a majority support because it would attack a vested property interest. As late as 1835 a citizens' meeting in Philadelphia condemned "indiscreet and improper interference" by the North with "the domestic relations of the slave-holding States of the South." But opposition to further extending this institution was bound to be at any time after 1846 just about unanimous in Pennsylvania. Resistance to the efforts of Congress under urging from the South to enforce the Fugitive Slave Law also became evident when in 1847 the Assembly voted to prohibit the use of Pennsylvania jails to detain fugitive slaves. The famous Underground Railroad was in high gear by 1851, assisting slaves to cross the state to Canada. In 1851 the efforts of a United States marshal to arrest three fugitives spotted at Christiana, near Lancaster, provoked the Christiana Riots in which the slave owner was killed. The Christiana affair created a widespread reaction against the opponents of slavery and probably helped defeat Governor Johnston for re-election. The Whigs were tagged with supporting the more radical views on the slavery question, and William Bigler, lumberman and newspaper publisher from Clearfield, returned the Democrats to power in Harrisburg. Bigler secured repeal of the 1847 law forbidding the use of jails to hold escaped slaves and asked for a cessation of Pennsylvania's open defiance of the Fugitive Slave Law. Moderation became the key to the policy of Pennsylvania Democrats on slavery. The state's next Democratic governor elected in 1857 was William F. Packer, a Buchanan man and another newspaper publisher and editor. Packer continued to follow the line of moderation in his attitude toward the slavery controversy.

Packer was the last of the long line of Democratic governors who had marked the party's supremacy in Pennsylvania. In its later years the party had grown conservative and tried to ignore entirely or skirt around many of the new issues of the times such as slavery, a sound banking system, and protective tariff. Its two major achievements in its several administrations were the establishing of the free public schools and the statewide internal improvements which centered primarily on the building of the Pennsylvania canal system. Though this latter achievement involved such heavy expenditures as nearly to bankrupt the state, the tremendous value of the system of improvements in advancing the economy of Pennsylvania was a result which justified the means.

The Democratic Party also gave the state a major role in national affairs between 1800 and 1860 and provided the national government with more leaders of distinction than has been true in any other sixty years. George M. Dallas served as a Vice-President with Polk. Albert Gallatin, Alexander J. Dallas, Samuel D. Ingham, and William J. Dunane were Secretaries of the Treasury. Gallatin, who served under Jefferson, is looked upon by many as the greatest Secretary of the Treasury in the nation's history. Gallatin was also one of the peace commissioners who negotiated the Treaty of Ghent to end the War of 1812 and served also in diplomatic posts at Paris and London. Henry Baldwin was appointed to the United States Supreme Court by Jackson. Judge James Campbell served as Postmaster General under President Pierce.

The career of James Buchanan, Pennsylvania's only President, was part and parcel of the story of national influence on the part of Pennsylvania Democrats. Buchanan served in diplomatic posts, the first of which was minister to Russia from 1831 to 1833, as Secretary of State under Polk in 1845, and as minister to Great Britain in 1853. Buchanan was one of the more able Secretaries of State, handling delicate negotiations involving the acquisition of Oregon, the annexation of Texas, and the Mexican War. Jeremiah Sullivan

Black from Somerset served Buchanan during his Presidency, both as Secretary of State and as Attorney General, and was one of the great legal minds of his time. These men were indicative of the national leadership afforded by Pennsylvania Democrats in high places.

THE KNOW-NOTHINGS

One of the peculiarities of American democracy has been its ability to spawn on occasion violently undemocratic movements contrary to every basic element in democratic thought. Such a movement exploded on the American scene in 1845 when a national organization of "native born" Americans was founded. It was spawned by growing feeling against the new flood of immigration from Germany and Ireland. The Irish in particular were victims of antagonism because they clustered mainly in such cities as Philadelphia and they were Roman Catholics. To some older stock Pennsylvanians the new Germans and Irish were totally unlike those of the same name who had arrived in colonial times. This agitation against the new foreign elements centered in Philadelphia and was known as Nativism. It led to the Philadelphia riots which forced Governor Porter in May, 1844, to call out the militia to restore order. In 1846 the national organization made up of these "native" Americans went into hiding as a secret order calling itself the Supreme Order of the Star Spangled Banner, or Sons of the Sires of '76. Members were solemnly pledged to oppose all foreign influences and to support only American-born Protestants for public offices. Because of the pledge of secrecy when members were asked about the order, the common reply was simply, "I know nothing." Thus the resulting political organization was widely called the Know-Nothing Party. Its more formal title in the 1850's became the American Party.

Within less than a year the American Party had triumphed in half the states in the union. By 1854 it was believed to have polled one-fourth the total vote in New York and two-fifths of Pennsylvania's vote. With the possible exception of Boston, the Know-Nothings had their greatest strength in any single city concentrated in Phila-delphia. Still in a minority, the Know-Nothing Party sought an alliance with the Whigs. The Whigs represented probably a higher percentage of old-stock Pennsylvanians than did the Democrats, whose ranks included most of the Irish. In the campaign of 1854 the Know-Nothings combined with the Whigs and a group of "Independent Democrats" led by David Wilmot to defeat Governor Bigler for re-election and place James Pollock in the governorship.

The election of Pollock, who proved to be an able governor during the difficult times created by the Panic of 1857, was a symptom of the extent to which the politics of the state were becoming entangled with the bitter battle over the extension of slavery. The efforts of Stephen A. Douglas to apply his doctrine of popular sovereignty as the magic wand which would wipe away the slavery-extension problem satisfied partisans of neither the North nor the South. An "Appeal of the Independent Democrats in Congress to the People of the United States" was signed by no less a person than David Wilmot. Such Pennsylvania Democratic leaders as Galusha Grow, William Duane and Samuel Ingham deserted the party. Simon Cameron, still undecided as to his best position, was struggling with Buchanan to capture control in Pennsylvania, and when he failed he also deserted the Democratic Party. Cameron also bid for the Know-Nothing's support. Such a confused situation played into the hands of the Know-Nothings and gave them a temporary balance of power until in their national convention in 1855 they too fell victims to the bitterness engendered by the slavery issue and could not unite on slavery extension.

THE RISE OF THE REPUBLICAN PARTY

So great had become the confusion and disorganization within the Whig and Democratic party organizations which strove to maintain an even national balance in the midst of the growing sectionalism of the fifties that a new party with new leadership and espousing some new issues was in order in the United States. Certainly no state mirrored this problem more clearly than did Pennsylvania with its confused and angry politics.

The new Republican Party which sprang into being so widely and so spontaneously in 1854 that few can agree on just where it was born proved to be the answer. There were several meetings in northern and western Pennsylvania in 1854 in which David Wilmot played a dominant role in organizing this new party. The first semistate convention of the party was held in Pittsburgh in 1855 and Passmore Williamson was put forward as Canal Commissioner only to be soundly trounced.

Nicholas Biddle, Pennsylvania banker and financier, and supporter of the national bank against Jackson.

In this early period the growth of the new organization centered on support from the more radical antislavery elements. The political potpourri that was Pennsylvania politics in 1856 is shown by the calling of a convention at Harrisburg on March 4 of the "regular" Democrats who got back of Buchanan for President while a "union" convention of Nebraska Democrats and Whigs held another convention in Harrisburg also on March 26. The Know-Nothings held their national convention at Philadelphia only to split wide open over the slavery issue. On February 22, an informal convention of Republican Party delegates from twenty-three states met in Pittsburgh to perfect a national organization. David Wilmot was very much present and became a member of the new national executive committee. A call was issued for a presidential nominating convention at Philadelphia on June 17, 1856, the anniversary of Bunker Hill. The resulting convention nominated the picturesque soldier and explorer of the West, John C. Fremont. The slogan of the new party became "Free soil, Free speech, Free labor, Free Man and Fremont," most appropriate for a political movement launched at the "birthplace of freedom." These events so closely associated with its national organization entitle Pennsylvania to the claim of having been the real birthplace of the national Republican Party. Pennsylvanians took a keen interest in the Republican platform, drafted at Philadelphia in 1856, which held out such interesting ideas as a government-supported railroad all the way to the Pacific and other internal improvements.

BUCHANAN, 1856 AND SECESSION

One of the ironies of history in such a turbulent time was that Pennsylvania's first and only President, though he carried his native state by a good margin, was elected only by virtue of the votes of fourteen southern states. Buchanan lost eleven of the so-called free states but Pennsylvania business interests, especially the commercial and mercantile concerns of Philadelphia, predominantly conservative and shuddering at the consequences of a break with the South, helped carry the state for "Old Buc." Fremont and the Republicans of 1856 represented the more radical element in this still not fully jelled political organism. Many Whigs shared with the Democrats the fear that Fremont's election would antagonize the South beyond amends, as it very probably would have done. Former President Filmore warned that "we are treading on the

180

brink of a volcano." Buchanan set forth as his campaign theme, "The Union is in danger and the people everywhere begin to know it." He firmly believed, as did those who voted for him, that his opponents were "Black Republicans" who must be "boldly assailed as disunionists, and this charge must be reiterated again and again." "This race," declared Buchanan from his country retreat at Wheatland, "ought to be run on the question of Union or disunion." Statements of Republican leaders like New York Governor

the states. Whether he might have stayed secession by any action he could have taken prior to the election of Lincoln is very questionable. A stronger policy probably would have speeded rather than curbed secession. After November's triumph of the Republican Party in 1860 Buchanan was a pitiful "lame duck" without real authority for policy or action. His efforts to secure some cooperation from the incoming Republican administration to arrive at reasonably firm conclusions on policy and action appear to have been

Log cabin birthplace of James Buchanan, moved from Stony Batter to Mercersburg and restored.

William Seward that "there is a higher power than the Constitution" and that "an aggressive war upon slavery" was to be hoped for helped fan the fears of all conservatives.

Another irony of fate is that Pennsylvania's only successful candidate for the Presidency should assume the office in a time of such great crisis. Buchanan's reputation was tarnished beyond repair and most unjustly by the circumstances which confronted him from his inauguration until he left the Presidency in the hands of Abraham Lincoln on March 4, 1861. No one can challenge Buchanan's devotion to the union of

side-stepped. Those not yet in office were fearful of making any committments in such a time of crisis. The nation drifted and Buchanan was blamed for not having steered a firm course under utterly impossible conditions. Buchanan, unlike Lincoln, did not have a firing by the southern radicals upon Fort Sumter to firm up a necessary decision.

REPUBLICAN TRIUMPH

That war horse of traditional Pennsylvania democracy, James Buchanan, was able to win the

181

highest office in the land in 1856 but he could not stay the onward march of Republicanism. Despite their growing strength, the Republicans found themselves very much a minority party in 1856. They were tagged by most persons of conservative tendencies, including former Whigs, as "radicals" because of their national platform and leadership. Pennsylvania Republicans in 1857 sought, as had the Whigs before them, the votes of the Know-Nothings or American Party. In order to do this a "Union convention" was called to unite the parties. As one Republican leader put it later the objective "was how to make the ticket as distinctively Republican as possible without slapping the Americans squarely in the face." The American Party was extended the sop of two nominations on the statewide ticket while the Republicans slated David Wilmot for governor. The American Party refused to accept this and rallied back of an old warhorse of Know-Nothing days, Isaac Hazlehurst. The Democrats nominated and elected William E. Packer, a sound Buchanan Democrat.

After 1856 the emotion-arousing story of "bleeding Kansas" overshadowed everything else in the newspaper headlines and it helped solidify in Pennsylvania the Republican stand of complete opposition to the extension of slavery. The Kansas situation itself had strong Pennsylvania connections. Andrew Reeder, Pennsylvania native, was first territorial governor of Kansas. John W. Geary, later Pennsylvania's governor, was appointed territorial governor of Kansas in 1856 and served eight months. He was replaced by President Buchanan with Pennsylvania-born Robert J. Walker. The bitter and bloody battle between settlers from North and South to determine whether Kansas should be slave or free was a portent of civil war. Feeling on the slavery-extension issue was fanned further when on March 6, 1857, two days following Buchanan's inauguration, the Supreme Court handed down the explosive Dred Scott decision which ruled the great Missouri Compromise unconstitutional and declared Congress had absolutely no power under the Fifth Amendment to exclude slavery from any territory as depriving a person of ". . . property without due process of law."

Pennsylvania reacted strongly against this decision, though many conservatives believed this was the only sound way to view slavery as a property institution. The last fagot heaped on the fires of sectionalism was John Brown's raid. John Brown had lived in Pennsylvania for a time and owned a tannery in Crawford County. His expedition to free the slaves by force of arms was organized at Chambersburg. On October 16, 1859, his "troops," eighteen men in all, seized the United States Arsenal at Harper's Ferry. The Baltimore *Sun* headlined it as the "Negro Insurrection at Harper's Ferry, Headed by 250 Abolitionists." The conspiracy was quickly put down by United States troops under Colonel Robert E. Lee, and John Brown was hanged after a trial which aroused intense feeling in the North and South. Ralph Waldo Emerson hailed Brown as a "new saint," a sentiment wildly applauded by many Pennsylvanians. Others denounced him as a fanatic and murderer who would have set black against white in a bath of blood. These voices were in the minority north of the Mason and Dixon Line.

Without question, the series of events which followed 1856 aroused the feelings of Pennsylvanians to a degree where they were now willing to support a new party which promised to take a fresh and stronger stand on the extension of slavery and other issues. In 1858 the Republican Party elected a majority of the members of Congress from the state. The party was successful increasingly in attracting to its ranks those who, for a variety of reasons, differed with the Democrats. Realizing the need for uniting all these divergent interests, the party continued to avoid direct use of the Republican label and posed as the "People's Party." Andrew Gregg Curtin, Bellefonte ironmaster with a distinguished family and political background, was selected as a candidate for governor. Pennsylvania was a pilot state in the national election of 1860 in terms of the success or failure of Lincoln. James Buchanan himself wrote in August, "All may perhaps depend upon Pennsylvania." Curtin carried the state in the October elections and thereby gave a decisive boost to the Republicans and Lincoln nationally. Pennsylvania was again very much a

Scenes at the Republican convention in Philadelphia in 1856.

keystone state in the nation's politics. In November Lincoln was elected. On receiving the news, James Buchanan retired to his library to thumb his Bible and meditate as to the ultimate consequences. An old era had come to an end in Pennsylvania and the nation. A new era dawned but with storm clouds obscuring the sun.

POLITICAL MACHINERY AND MORES OF THE ERA

The politics and the conduct of government in this era can hardly be appreciated without an understanding of the nature of the political machinery and mores of the times. To put it mildly, they were quite different from those of today. The decline of aristocracy in the politics of Pennsylvania was accompanied by a democratic revolution in political machinery and practices. More people were able to take part actively in politics as a result of more liberal suffrage requirements. One of the truly important reforms of the era was the appearance of the party convention, which replaced the former narrowly controlled caucus of party leaders in office as the method for selecting candidates. Expansion of the suffrage and the party convention created a great new popular democracy totally unknown before 1800

but very vocal by 1840. The convention system generated a great enthusiasm in politics as all the voters in a particular party now had a chance to express themselves by selecting delegates or taking part in local, county, or state meetings of the party. The old-fashioned convention may well have aroused more actual participation in party affairs than today's primary elections. Political conventions were akin to a New England town meeting of party members. The county convention of any particular party was a great affair as delegates selected by vote or by party committees at the local level gathered in considerable numbers, usually at the county seat. A county party convention was an occasion for a good bit of festivity and was frequently accompanied by a barbecue, or similar social occasion for not only delegates but also those party faithful who took time to come and see the proceedings. The county convention was the organization which approved by vote the delegates to the state convention of the party and adopted official resolutions. The resolutions instructed the delegates as to what the county expected them to do in the way of voting for particular candidates supported by the county organization and also voiced local opinion on state and national affairs. Disputes as to the right of particular delegates to represent their party were frequent in an era when political feelings ran high and intense party factionalism was common. These disputes enlivened many a party convention.

The keen popular interest in politics at all levels of government was fanned by alert newspaper coverage of politics and strong expressions of editorial opinion on the part of the press. County weeklies in particular were always open to the pens of those who wished to attack or to defend individuals and issues. Pennsylvania during the era had many newspapers with statewide and even national political influence. Philip Freneau's *National Gazette* and Benjamin Franklin Bache's *Aurora* were powerful early Philadelphia papers supporting the Jeffersonian cause while John Freno's *Gazette of the United States* was the Federalist organ. William Duane as editor of the *Aurora* was a great power behind Governor McKean and Thomas Jefferson. The Jacksonian forces were aided immeasurably by the great editor John Binns. Binns published in Northumberland from 1802 to 1807 the *Republican Argus* and after 1807 in Philadelphia the *Democratic Press.* Binns is credited with having changed the name of the Democratic-Republican Party to Democratic Party. The *Antimasonic Herald* of Lancaster and Theodore Finn's *Telegraph* in Harrisburg were powerful voices for the Anti-Masonic movement. The later governor, William Bigler, published the *Centre Democrat* at Bellefonte and the *Clearfield Democrat,* both influential in central Pennsylvania. William Packer before becoming governor published the *Williamsport Gazette* and later the Harrisburg *Keystone,* leading Democratic organs. The Philadelphia *Press* was a very influential newspaper in the later period. Lancaster had no less than eight newspapers in the 1850's, more even than Philadelphia. Every newspaper in the state was alive with political news and opinion. Newspapers were especially important because there was no radio or television to reach the populace.

Nor was travel by stage coach, canal boat, or even early railroads a quick and easy way for a candidate to reach many people in a political campaign in a day when a small percentage of the people were centered in a few towns or cities.

The miracle is that so much ground could be covered when the situation demanded it. Howell Cobb of Georgia came to Pennsylvania in October to campaign for Buchanan in the critical 1856 election and accomplished the incredible feat of delivering ten speeches in ten days all the way from Philadelphia to Erie. This included a talk for an hour and a half at Meadville before a crowd estimated at three thousand which endured a driving snow storm to come and listen. Such a crowd certainly could not be rallied for such a purpose in today's Meadville nor would it listen to political harangue of such length. Cobb reached Erie from Meadville by good old-fashioned horse and buggy. Such was the nature of the political enthusiasm of the forefathers.

Politics in the 1800's was far from a genteel affair. The masses understood far better the rough-and-tumble language which called a spade a spade than flowing oratory employing Latin and the classic phrase. Campaign oratory and propaganda in the party press often appealed more to passion and prejudice than to pure reason. Even a person of the high station of James Buchanan could use such terms as "Black Republican" in trying to create an image of all Republicans as abolitionists. Campaigners and their partisan newspapers did not hesitate to use pungent words such as "scoundrel," "poltroon," and even "liar" in characterizing an opponent. "Duplicity and falsehood" is a phrase commonly found in political resolutions describing the position of opponents individually or as a party. Election to office under "false pretenses," "corrupt" use of office and patronage, "arrogant and insulting behavior" in office were charges commonly leveled against candidates or officials in the highest places. Even the office of governor was treated with shocking lack of respect. Simon Snyder was called the "King of Ignorance" by the opposition. Governor Hiester was known as "Old Sauerkraut" because of his German background, and Governor Shulze was reviled as the "stupid Dutch Governor." Any weakness in the personal life of a candidate, whether true or false, was spread before the people in all its unsavory detail. Many of the attacks were so violent and provocative that they were frequently expressed in letters and broadsides signed with fictitious names such as "Conrad Weiser," "Stophel Funk," or simply "One of the People."

All in all, the story of Pennsylvania politics and government between the Revolution and the Civil War is one of growing democracy with all of the crudities connected with the breakdown of the aristocratic era of politics as the concern of "gentlemen." It is a period also in which the affairs of the state were greatly entangled with national politics and influenced by national controversy and crisis. While politics had become a much more democratic process in terms of the way in which candidates were selected and elected, the actual structure of Pennsylvania government changed very little. True, the Constitution of 1838 changed the number of terms a governor might serve and made several important offices elective rather than appointive; but these were procedural changes which had no effect upon the basic activities or operation of the government. The only major change in the structure of local government was the Philadelphia Consolidation Act of 1854 which enlarged the city to include all of the previously independent districts, boroughs and townships in the county into a unified city government. This was the single action in Pennsylvania government of the era which reflected the growth of cities. State and local government in 1860 varied little in structure or practice from that of 1790.

The theory that the government was best which governed the least, the old Jeffersonian ideal, prevailed. Very little legislation which reflected a concern for new social conditions created by the rise of cities, the new factory and mill economy, and the emerging working class was passed by the Pennsylvania Assembly during the period. A few legislative investigations into working conditions were forthcoming but such feeble legislation as resulted was entirely ignored. Under small-town and rural conditions, the township continued to be the most important single unit of local government and had most to do with the people through building and maintaining roads and schools. At Harrisburg, no new administrative departments or commissions were found necessary. A chart showing the organization of either state or local

government as of 1800 would suffice with little if any change for 1860. The failure to begin to adjust government to the problems created by an industrial revolution and the rise of cities paved the way for serious problems in later years. The formula that little government was needed kept expenses down and taxes at a minimum. The receipts of the state government in 1802 amounted to $250,969.11; with expenditures of $286,091.05. By 1835 the amounts were $3,273,563.21 in income and $3,131,860.31 in expenses. The cost of internal improvements raised expenses by 1850 to about $4,000,000. Despite this increase, Pennsylvania government was not a very costly operation. Income from land sales, bank stock, and like sources meant few taxes paid by any of the people.

One of the dictates of the popular democracy which followed the decline of the aristocracy in government in the 1800's was the right and the ability of every voter to occupy any office to which he might aspire either by election or appointment. This gave rise to the spoils system. This idea is popularly supposed to have first gained acceptance in Washington under Jackson. Pennsylvania, because it was ahead of most if not all the states in liberalizing suffrage and officeholding requirements, was likewise ahead of the country in adopting the spoils system. Thomas McKean had hardly been inaugurated before he began to fire Federalist officeholders right and left, despite the fact that his election was by a coalition of the two parties. From that time on, Pennsylvania governors wielded the patronage ax with such vigor that it became one of the major complaints about undue power in the hands of the chief executive. Some governors themselves recognized the evil.

Another concept of the popular democracy was the right of every citizen to visit in person and without notice the highest officials and to discuss with them grievances of the moment. Governors were not excepted. Governors in that day were not secluded in plush offices and surrounded by secretaries who kept undesirables carefully away. The new Capitol building in Harrisburg provided little privacy for the state's chief executive. Governor Wolf was described in his office by Samuel Ingham: "He sits in an open room from morn till night, surrounded by crowds of persons waiting to see him alone and for that purpose try to sit each other out. . . ." Some improvement was made in this situation in later years but the happy custom of making the governor available readily to the personal importunity of office seekers as well as those who sought to register personal complaints or present unsolicited advice on affairs of the state was never seriously interfered with and indeed could not have been in those days without an uproar among the public and in the press.

Political morality in terms of bribery or corruption in government is a very relative thing and evidences of it are hard to pin down in the welter of charges and countercharges common to partisan politics. The years following the Civil War were characterized by very evident graft, corruption, and bribery in Pennsylvania government at both the city and state levels. The motivation for any attempt to manipulate governmental policy in a corrupt way invariably is a desire for gain of undue privilege for the parties seeking this end. The prizes to be gained by attempted manipulation were few before 1860 as compared with those of a later date with the rise of large-scale industry, public utilities, and other large enterprises which could benefit hugely from special favors from local or state government. The small scale of enterprise and the type of government which engaged very little in the people's affairs common to the early 1800's were not conducive to any large-scale graft or corruption, simply because there were lacking substantial incentives to try it. Graft and some corrupt officials there were without doubt, but on so small a scale and involving such limited affairs as to attract little notice.

The close relationship between corruption and the power of government to influence major economic developments is shown by the fact that the canal system and the banking system were the two major areas in which charges of widespread corruption of government and its officials appear before 1860. Building and operating the state public works program involved larger sums of money and affected more deeply the development of large areas of the commonwealth than any other single enterprise of the times. Widespread

charges of manipulation were made by political opponents in the building and operating of the canal, though no manipulations of major proportions were ever revealed as a public scandal. The renewal of the charter of the United States Bank of Pennsylvania in 1836 represented so complete a reversal in the attitude of many political and legislative leaders in Harrisburg as to give rise to the strong suspicion that bank agents had crossed the palms of more than one legislator in order to produce so marked and sudden a change of heart.

In 1819 a House petition for the impeachment of Governor Findlay included charges that the governor had "corruptly exercised his official duties for the purpose of advancing his own private interests"; that he had demanded favors in return for certain appointments, and had committed other misdemeanors. The charges were dismissed but it was generally accepted that Governor Findlay had been at least indiscreet in relation to use of his patronage powers. Opponents of Thaddeus Stevens freely charged manipulation of canal affairs for his advantage. Simon Cameron was accused of more than one piece of political chicanery, including undue influence in securing railroad charters. The railroads were the first major public utility to become a prime source of great profit to their promoters, and the circumstances connected with the securing of their early charters was not without suspicion on more than one occasion. Since such charters and many other special privileges were then secured by special act of Assembly the incentive to use questionable influence was ever present and without doubt was utilized by more than one group which sought such a valuable franchise. In short, some of the seeds of the more spectacular varieties of corruption which emerged following the Civil War were being cast before that time and finding a root in the structure of a government ill suited without some major changes to deal with an era of large-scale economic enterprise with all its prizes for individual gain. In general, the political morality of Pennsylvanians was probably no better nor was it any worse than the average in the democracy of the times.

A TIME
OF DECISION

The Federal Union was born in Pennsylvania in 1787 and it nearly died there in 1863 on the battlefield at Gettysburg. Had the gray-clad fighting men led by General Robert E. Lee triumphed there when Pickett led the Confederacy's finest in that last desperate charge up Cemetery Ridge against the Union defenders on that hot afternoon of July 3, 1863, the Union hardly could have withstood the blow despite Grant's tremendous victory at Vicksburg the following day. Sad indeed that one of the finest hours in the history of American arms found northerner fighting against southerner in this bloody battle in Pennsylvania. But that is only a part of the American tragedy that was the Civil War.

LINCOLN AND CURTIN

In a way Pennsylvania helped make war between the states inevitable through its influence on the nomination and election of Abraham Lincoln. Lincoln had a Pennsylvania Quaker ancestry going back to Mordecai Lincoln, who came to Berks County in 1720. The small stone Lincoln homestead typical of the Pennsylvania frontier in that day still stands. Like the Boones, the Lincolns left Pennsylvania for the West by way of the Cumberland and Shenandoah valleys. When Lincoln's name was first put forward as a Repub-

lican candidate about 1858 he was an unknown figure in the East. Joseph J. Lewis, publisher of the *Chester County Times* at West Chester by 1860, was curious about Lincoln and wrote Jesse W. Fell in Illinois, Lincoln's campaign manager, for information. The sketch was very brief; as Lincoln put it, "There is not much of it, for the reason, I suppose, that there is not much of me." Lincoln did reveal his Pennsylvania background. Lewis dressed up the sketch and published it on February 11, 1860. It was reprinted widely, even finding its way into a Chicago paper. It is credited with giving Lincoln a major assist in his presidential aspirations.

At the Republican convention in Chicago's Wigwam, Lincoln's nomination was clinched by the withdrawal of Simon Cameron, who threw the Pennsylvania vote to Lincoln. One story is that this came about as a result of a promise made by Lincoln's supporters to provide Cameron a cabinet post. This ignores the very real political hostility between New York and Pennsylvania which had festered for several years. This made it doubtful from the first whether any Pennsylvania politician would have aided New York's Seward to secure the nomination. It is unlikely that any Pennsylvania favorite son would have taken Seward over Lincoln. The decisive influence of Andrew Gregg Curtin's election on a

Governor Curtin, from the official portrait.

Republican platform, though as People's Party candidate, in October was a genuine boost to the election of Lincoln in November, 1860. It gave the Republican campaign a needed lift throughout the North. Curtin had supported Lincoln from the first at Chicago, influenced in part by his antagonism toward Cameron. He was known as a friend of Lincoln and this aided Curtin's election. A vote for Curtin was a vote for Lincoln.

Lincoln visited Pennsylvania twice after leaving Springfield on the way to Washington and his inauguration. He was in Pittsburgh on February 15, 1861, and in Philadelphia on Washington's Birthday. At Philadelphia very early on the morning of February 22 he took part in ceremonies at Independence Hall, raising the new American flag with its star for newly admitted Kansas. His impromptu remarks on this occasion were a prelude for the famous Gettysburg Address. Lincoln reminded his scanty audience on this cold February morning that his personal political philosophy had been rooted always on the Declaration of Independence with its clarion call for freedom for all men all over the world.

From Philadelphia he proceeded by train to Harrisburg, to which he had been invited by the leaders of the General Assembly. In an appearance before the Assembly he received assurances of Pennsylvania's support and left the city for Washington in secrecy from a dinner tendered by Governor Curtin because of reports of an attempt upon his life while shifting from one railroad line to another through the streets of Baltimore. Lincoln took a secret train to Philadelphia and then to Baltimore, passing through that city during the night en route to Washington.

Governor Curtin's inaugural even before this had done much to establish a sound foundation for Lincoln's future policy. Curtin had written Lincoln after his own election suggesting that since Curtin's inauguration as governor in January, 1861, would precede that of Lincoln he would be pleased to serve as a sounding board for any sentiments Lincoln might care to express as to the explosive situation which confronted the nation. Lincoln made some suggestions and Curtin adopted them. A careful reading of Curtin's inaugural will reveal how closely he followed the sentiments later developed by Lincoln on March 4, 1861. Curtin emphasized that Pennsylvania bore no hostility toward "our brethren of other states" who rather were "friends and fellow countrymen in whose welfare we feel a kindly interest. . . ." He placed emphasis upon Pennsylvania's desire to cooperate even in enforcement of the Fugitive Slave Laws. At the same time, Curtin denied any right of secession from the Union, as South Carolina already had done. Curtin declared with all the power of his striking personal presence and oratory that it must be the "duty of the national authorities to stay the progress of anarchy and enforce the laws, and Pennsylvania, with a united people, will give them an honest, faithful, and active support." Resolutions of the Assembly followed stating strongly the necessity of preserving a united nation and pledging the "faith and power of Pennsylvania" to support "such measures in any manner and to any extent that may be required of her by the constituted authorities of the United States."

Curtin sent his own secret agents into the southern states to determine the extent of the rebellion and as a result resolved early in 1861 that the fair-weather northerners who thought that secession was a bluff were one hundred per cent wrong.

WAR BEGUN; CURTIN LEADS

At 4:30 on the morning of April 12 General Beauregard opened fire on Fort Sumter in Charleston harbor. Governor Curtin on April 9 had already called for a complete reorganization of Pennsylvania's militia system to prepare for war. The Assembly passed an act to implement Curtin's farsighted recommendations on the very day Fort Sumter was attacked. No other state was as ready to meet the challenge when Lincoln called on April 15 for 75,000 volunteers to suppress a rebellion. This was due in large part to the close cooperation of Governor Curtin with Lincoln, who relied upon Curtin as he did upon no other single war governor for advice and support. Curtin brought the Assembly back to Harrisburg in special emergency session to support this call. Lincoln's call was for a three-month period of service, partly because of easy optimism as to the end of the "rebellion" and also to ease the shock of war. The fourteen regiments requested were filled by volunteers for twenty-five within a matter of weeks. Five companies of Pennsylvania volunteers numbering 530 men were the first of a mighty flood answering to the call of "Father Abraham." They were the famed "First Defenders." Their ranks included the Ringgold Light Artillery of Reading, the Logan Guards of Lewistown, the Washington Artillerists and the National Light Infantry from Pottsville, along with the Allen Infantry of Allentown. These were the cream of the Pennsylvania organized militia. The First Defenders entrained at Harrisburg on April 18, after being reviewed by the governor, and passed through Baltimore despite threats of mob violence to reach Washington that evening to become the first truly Union troops to defend the capital and Lincoln.

Pennsylvania was alive with excitement. Flags and bunting rippled in the breeze in every town and city. Bands blared and patriotism flowed freely everywhere. Volunteers continued to flock to the colors and Curtin urged the creation of a Pennsylvania Reserve Corps of thirteen regiments of infantry, one of cavalry, and one of artillery enlisted for three years, as contrasted with three months of service. Again Curtin had shown courage and foresight. This request was acted upon favorably by the Assembly on May 15. Among the next regiments were the colorful Bucktails from northern Pennsylvania, made up to a large extent of rugged lumbermen and hardy farmers distinguished by their use of the buck deer tail on their caps. The Assembly also authorized a $3,000,000 loan to finance this operation.

Union defeat at Bull Run erased the early optimism in Washington as to a three-month war and in July the Pennsylvania Reserves were mustered into Federal service. The original three-month volunteers were now nearing the end of their term and a majority re-enlisted for the three years. By early January, 1862, Governor Curtin reported that 109,615 Pennsylvanians were in the Federal service or preparing to enter, exclusive of the over twenty thousand original three-month volunteers who had been discharged. The Reserve Corps was under the command of Major General George A. McCall. The three brigades were commanded by Brigadier Generals George Gordon Meade, E. O. C. Ord, and John F. Reynolds. When mustered into Federal service the Pennsylvania Reserves were assigned to the defense of Washington. This Pennsylvania army corps became the only such unit made up of troops from a single state to serve throughout the war. Curtin was everywhere and alert to every problem. In June, 1861, he summoned representatives of the then twenty-one railroad companies chartered by the state to a meeting in Harrisburg to consider the vital role of transporting of men and supplies.

THE CITIZEN ARMY

Preparing for what became the first "all out" war in 1861 produced real problems and entirely new demands on Pennsylvania's volunteer militia system which began with Franklin's Associators in French and Indian War days. Serving in the militia was the duty of every able-bodied male between the ages of eighteen and forty-five. The militia was organized by counties and a short drill period known as "Battalion Days" was indulged in once or twice a year by the assembled civilian militia. Battalion Days usually were more noted for fun and frolic than for serious military drill and the greater part of the citizen army was without either a uniform or guns. A Reading newspaper of the 1830's commented upon the "farcical parade of broomstick frying pans" which characterized militia days. Officers up to the rank of major general were elected by vote in a thoroughly democratic fashion. "If anything is to be learned in the ranks, it is insubordination," wrote one contemporary.

Early recruiting in 1861 was entirely local and usually volunteers were swept into patriotic fervor sufficient to sign up as a result of local patriotic mass meetings with prayers, patriotic orations, and much singing. When enough volunteers were gathered to form a company, some eighty men, these elected their officers, who in turn became responsible for drill. Once organized, the company informed Governor Curtin of its existence and when accepted marched away amidst much celebration and patriotic fervor to Camp Curtin at Harrisburg, or a camp at West Chester, Easton, Chambersburg, Philadelphia, or Pittsburgh. Camp Curtin, because of its location on the railroad line to Washington, was the largest training and mobilization center of them all. The state now assumed responsibility for paying the troops as well as supplying and equipping them. No one had either faced before this time or even dreamed of the problems connected with raising, organizing, feeding, and equipping such a large number of men. Lines of responsibility between Harrisburg and Washington were not quite clear-cut for the first two years of the war. It took time for the nation really to gird itself for such a gigantic task. Pennsylvania's Simon Cameron was Lincoln's first Secretary of War and was accused of not merely inefficiency but of manipulation of contracts and other favors. More recent judgment is milder and merely convicts Cameron of lacking

the know-how, as did most others, to deal with the new and monumental problems created by an entirely new type of war.

"THE WAR CANNOT BE LONG"

Fever rises and falls and so did the fervor of Pennsylvanians for war. By 1862 the high temperatures of 1861 were falling. The first defeat at Bull Run cooled the thinking that the war was a mere frolic. When Pennsylvania's General George B. McClellan was placed in command of the Army of the Potomac in July, 1861, something of his exuberance rubbed off on the people of the state. McClellan announced publicly, "The war cannot be long, though it may be desperate." He wrote to his wife in private, "I shall take my own time to make an army that will be sure of success." He took the time, despite prodding from Lincoln and elsewhere; he did not win success. McClellan's generalship and his personality will long remain a subject of controversy. The fact remains that after creating and evidently establishing a powerful army in a long and well prepared campaign against Richmond utilizing the peninsular approach he was defeated by Lee in June, 1862, in the Seven Days' Battles. After reaching a point within a few miles of Richmond with vastly superior forces, McClellan was forced to withdraw. Two months later, on August 29–30, the same combination of Lee and Stonewall Jackson caught General John Pope at Manassas and in the Second Battle of Bull Run inflicted a defeat so severe that the fires of his burning supplies could be seen in Washington. McClellan was a failure in terms of performance and was relieved of command of the Army of the Potomac. In Washington the irascible Pittsburgh attorney Edwin Stanton replaced Simon Cameron as Secretary of War and Cameron was given the sop of becoming minister to Russia, a sentence as it were to Siberia.

CONFERENCE AT ALTOONA

Opposition to Lincoln and his administration was on the increase, not only due to lack of military success but also in no small measure to the failure to define the objectives of the war. Was it a war to free the slaves or to save the Union? Or was it both? Early in the autumn of 1862 Governor Curtin, sensitive to the situation and in close touch with Lincoln, called the loyal governors to gather at Altoona on September 24 to deliberate on common problems. The meeting lasted two days and little is known about what went on in the secret sessions held in Altoona's celebrated railroad hotel, the Logan House. Varying interpretations have been placed upon its purposes and results. The best evidence is that it was an attempt on the part of Curtin to rally support behind Lincoln's administration at this critical time and that it did strengthen Lincoln.

CHAMBERSBURG AND ANTIETAM

Pennsylvania's patriotism was given something of a special test even before war governors assembled. Governor Curtin, moved by fear of invasion as news was received of the movement of Lee's army into northern Maryland and, according to report, actually into Pennsylvania, had issued a call on September 11 for 50,000 volunteer militia. These were mustered in and stationed near Hagerstown, Maryland, or Chambersburg. A genuine invasion scare had been thrown at the North and particularly at Pennsylvania. Even Curtin thought Harrisburg was Lee's objective. By September 24, the very day the Altoona Conference opened, these militia had been allowed to return to their homes.

The bloodiest battle of the war at Sharpsburg, Maryland, near Antietam Creek, between the armies of Lee and McClellan, ended in something of a stalemate; nevertheless, it thwarted a northern invasion by the Army of Northern Virginia. Lincoln, accepting the result as a victory, issued the famous Emancipation Proclamation. Less than three weeks later eighteen hundred of Lee's crack cavalry, led by the dashing, swashbuckling J. E. B. Stuart, on October 10 really threw a scare into Pennsylvanians by occupying Chambersburg. This city was a major supply center for Union forces, and the Confederates destroyed many army stores and took with them horses and such other supplies as they could carry, including such cloth-

General McClellan's letter of appreciation to Governor Curtin in 1862 thanking him for calling out the militia in defense of the state. It was used as a campaign document by the Curtin forces in the following gubernatorial election.

ing as could be worn by the cavalry. Stuart's raiders were gone before either Harrisburg or Washington could act. Stuart had covered 112 miles in a three-day raid which circled at least 100,000 enemy troops, and without the loss of a single man in action.

PRELUDE TO GETTYSBURG

A far more serious story was written eight months later in 1863 when the daring General Robert E. Lee determined upon a full-scale in-

A contemporary sketch of Camp Curtin in Harrisburg, major troop concentration and assignment center.

vasion of Pennsylvania to strike at the very heart of the northern industrial and transportation system centered in the keystone state. Invasion rumors began to sweep the state in May and Pittsburgh was indicated as a possible objective of the Confederates. Union forces had suffered severe reverses at Fredericksburg and Chancellorsville, while the legions of Lee were both confident and aggressive. Lee's total objective in the campaign was not so much a specific target such as Philadelphia or Pittsburgh but to throw the enemy so far off balance as to be able to maneuver his own forces rather freely to attack and to destroy as occasion shaped the battlegrounds. The heartland of central Pennsylvania was certainly a choice target with Harrisburg as the railroad center of the North, the Susquehanna River bridges, lifeline for moving troops and supplies south, and the concentrations of northern industry within the area.

To prepare for every eventuality those portions of the state west of the mountains were erected early in June by the War Department into the Department of the Monongahela under Major General W. T. H. Brooks, with the command

center at Pittsburgh, and the remainder into the Department of the Susquehanna under Major General D. N. Couch at Chambersburg. Business-as-usual ground to a sudden halt in such cities as Pittsburgh and Harrisburg as every able-bodied citizen hastened to prepare for the defense of these two cities. Temporary fortifications were hastily thrown up as far away as Pittsburgh because of the persistent rumors that Lee intended to cross the Alleghenies. Governor Curtin on June 12 and again on June 15 also called for "Emergency" militia on a ninety-day basis. Over 36,000 men were enrolled. Units of New York and New Jersey militia also were called upon for aid. Excitement reigned in every part of the state but there was very little panic. Some places, notably Philadelphia, were slow to respond to Curtin's passionate plea for volunteers. The threat of invasion sobered, however, many of those who had opposed the war and in many places something of the patriotic ardor of the days following the firing on Fort Sumter swept the populace as the "Minute Men of '63" rallied to the colors to the inspiration of parades, bands playing patriotic airs, and patriotic exhortations from the best orators of

192

every community. None of the enrolled militia saw action or smelled any smoke of cannon or gunfire as the movement toward decision by the professionals in both armies hurried inexorably and quickly to a climax.

The story of the campaign and the final battle at Gettysburg is full of controversy as to overall strategy, leadership of various commanders, and the wisdom of many decisions which had to be made on the spur of the moment. Lee's reorganized Army of Northern Virginia was made up of three corps, headed by Generals A. P. Hill, Richard S. Ewell, who had replaced Stonewall Jackson, killed at Chancellorsville, and James Longstreet. Ewell was provided with a brigade of cavalry commanded by Brigadier General Jenkins. As usual, the colorful J. E. B. Stuart's cavalry was assigned to provide the eyes and ears for Lee, scouting and harassing the Union Army. Each unit in the Confederate force had its own specific objective and Ewell, with Jenkins' cavalry sweeping ahead of his infantry, was immediately concerned with reaching Pennsylvania strong points as quickly as possible. Lee's movement northward from Fredericksburg began on June 3 and the full-scale Confederate campaign began to unfold by June 15. The Potomac was crossed at Williamsport and Jenkins sent his cavalry racing toward Chambersburg to pave the way for Ewell. On June 19 three brigades from Ewell's corps reached Hagerstown, Maryland.

As early as June 10 Washington was aware of unusual activity on the part of the Confederates. Lee's cavalry units already had had several brushes with Federal cavalry. A possible raid on Pittsburgh by Stuart's cavalry was rumored. The entire Cumberland Valley began to react to possible invasion, lining the roads with wagons and refugees fleeing with their livestock and other possessions from the invaders. Rumors, flying faster than the wind, always placed the Confederates miles ahead of their actual advance. Washington remained unsure as to whether Lee might actually send his legions into Pennsylvania or employ this threat as a diversion and turn upon the capital itself. Lincoln then placed Pennsylvania's General George Gordon Meade in command of the Army of the Potomac with orders to follow

Lee but to keep his army between the Virginian and Washington. In the meantime, Jenkins' cavalry reached and occupied Chambersburg on June 16, only to withdraw as a result of the rumored approach of Union forces from Harrisburg, and after having rounded up quantities of horses and cattle and supplies. The rebels were careful to pay for most of what they seized, but in their own Confederate scrip.

Unable to secure any assurances as to what aid might be expected from Federal forces, Governor Curtin and General Couch were thrown upon their own resources for protection against the invasion. By June 15 it looked to General Couch as if all were lost "south of the Susquehanna." Governor Seymour provided New York National Guard units numbering some 1,200 men. A New Jersey company refused to be mustered in, and other than the New Yorkers there were only a few hundred men under arms available at this time in the entire Department of the Susquehanna. Refugees and their belongings now jammed the roads as far as Harrisburg, a city which was now reported as paralyzed with fear and crowded by excited people rushing here and there. Official state papers were being packed for evacuation. The Susquehanna was a natural line of defense for Harrisburg and on the high lands of the West Shore men toiled day and night to erect Fort Washington. When news was received of the Confederate evacuation from Chambersburg some of the Harrisburg defenders moved cautiously forward to Shippensburg and Chambersburg with instructions to retreat but to slow down the enemy's advance as much as possible to allow time to complete Harrisburg's defenses.

By June 21 volunteer militia was pouring into the capital. Even central Pennsylvania north of Harrisburg now was strongly mobilized against any Confederate raids on the industries of that area. Outside observers reported that Harrisburg was a bedlam but this was explainable when nineteen regiments of volunteers poured into the city within six days. Fort Washington was now supplemented by Fort Couch and other breastworks were thrown up below the city and at mountain passes north of Carlisle. Even the area near Altoona with its railroad shops was reported as

This contemporary drawing shows the feverish effort to fortify the Susquehanna's west shore to protect Harrisburg against the Confederate invasion.

under fortification. By June 28 the Confederate cavalry under General Jenkins had occupied Mechanicsburg. On the twenty-ninth a skirmish took place at Oyster Point, present Camp Hill. Another skirmish took place June 30 just west of Camp Hill. The by now rather formidable defenses which had been so hastily thrown together on the West Shore may well have saved the Susquehanna River bridges if not Harrisburg from destruction. The Confederates had little more time to test any possibilities of further advance and were called back to join Lee's regrouping of his scattered forces.

DECISION AT GETTYSBURG

In the meantime, two great armies were moving to an ultimate showdown. Meade was moving cautiously into Pennsylvania on the heels of Lee. General Ewell, following Lee's original plan of campaign, reached Carlisle on June 27. General Jubal Early was sent to York and Wrightsville by way of Hanover to destroy railroad connections at Hanover and to cross the Susquehanna River bridge at Wrightsville to establish a position east of the river threatening the railroad to Philadelphia. Pennsylvania militia fired the bridge and thus very fortunately broke up this latter scheme. All of Lee's plans had worked to perfection up to this time. It was at Chambersburg, which Lee himself reached on June 28, that the Confederate commander learned of the close pursuit of the Army of the Potomac, now ordered by Lincoln to follow him into Maryland and Pennsylvania. Lee now had a threat to his rear which could not be ignored. He quickly decided to abandon the grand move on Harrisburg and to consolidate his forces at Cashtown, eight miles west of Gettysburg and offering a possible escape route through the mountains. These orders went out June 29 and they changed the course of the entire campaign. At this point Lee suffered from the fact that his favorite cavalry leader J. E. B. Stuart, having taken off on his own, had left him for some days

194

Thomas Nast sketched the Confederate shelling of Carlisle.

without his usual careful intelligence as to Union troop movements.

Gettysburg was a decisive battleground of the Civil War entirely by accident. General Meade, newly in command, as he neared Gettysburg from the South lacked intelligence as to Lee's exact location or the size of his forces and sent Buford's cavalry, followed by the infantry corps of Reynolds and Howard to make a reconnaissance in force on June 30. On July 1 Buford's advance ran into A. P. Hill's Confederates, who were approaching from the west in search of supplies in Gettysburg as well as to sound out Union strength in the rear of Lee's army. The initial brush between advance units developed quickly into a full-scale engagement in which the Confederates were at first forced back and then recovered with the aid of Jubal Early's division moving down the Harrisburg road to rejoin the main army. The battle which had begun just beyond Gettysburg raged through the village and ended with the Union forces pushed back to the south at Cemetery Hill, Culp's Hill, and Little Round Top. Lee, having heard the firing, rode into Gettysburg late that day but early enough to observe the disorganized Union retreat. General Ewell was given discretion as to pressing the attack and decided not to do so. This proved another key decision because the delay enabled General Winfield S. Hancock to strengthen these naturally advantageous positions on higher ground into which the Union forces had stumbled more or less by accident. Had Ewell had the dash and verve of Stonewall Jackson and pressed his advantage late on July 1 he might have achieved a decisive victory. Night fell upon troubled Gettysburg without the Confederates following up their initial success.

By the morning of July 2 the situation was vastly different. The Union forces now commanded firmly the small hills south of Gettysburg while Lee's force was concentrated on Seminary Ridge and in the town. The Union lines now assumed the nature of a huge hook connecting the higher elevations. Lee on the morning of July 2 determined to attack, though he now could have rested his forces in position and forced a Union attack. Lee's hope was that by an attack early in the morning he could buckle the Union line before Meade had moved all of his forces into place. Long delays, which plagued Lee throughout the battle, held back Longstreet's attack on the Union left on Cemetery Ridge until late afternoon. By sundown Longstreet shattered a dangerous Union salient pushed forward without orders by General Daniel Sickles, but on the north Ewell's attack on Cemetery and Culp's hills failed to break the main Union line. Lee had now lost his desperate gamble to win a decisive victory with superior numbers before Meade's army was fully anchored. Fresh troops were falling into line and new batteries wheeling into place in Union positions all through the night, so that by July 3 the Confederates had massed before them the full strength of the mighty Army of the Potomac. In fact, Meade took the initiative on the morning of July 3 with a spirited and successful attack to erase the threat to his right flank. Again Lee made a fateful decision. Instead of continuing his effort to turn Meade's army on its flanks, he decided to mass a frontal assault on the very center of the Union line. Pointing to Cemetery Ridge, Robert E. Lee told his generals, "The enemy is there, and I am going to strike him."

And strike he did, despite Longstreet's plea that he should avoid an offensive and force the Union men to move from their prepared positions. The Confederates under Lee had won most of their great battles in basic defensive actions turned into offensives when the Union forces had been forced to make mistakes. J. E. B. Stuart was delegated the task of harassing the rear of the Federal forces as a diversion but failed in his attempt. Stuart's cavalry was no longer the devastating force of earlier days. Out of the silence at one o'clock on that hot July 3 afternoon the roar of 138 Confederate cannons shook the earth in a terrific bombardment of the Union lines on Cemetery Ridge. The Federal guns replied. For two hours the greatest duel of massed artillery in history up to that time went on while the infantry of both sides rested on their arms.

The men in gray knew that at the end of the fire of the cannon they would march forward to take the Union positions just covered by this terrible rain of shot and shell. They could only hope the cannon had silenced the enemy. The men in blue understood all too well that it would be their task to repel this advance. With Pickett's division of Virginians on the right and those of Pettigrew and Trimble on the left, some 15,000 Confederate infantry moved as their cannon were silent in a mile-wide column in dressed ranks toward Cemetery Ridge. Temporarily slowed by the rail fences along Emmitsburg Road, they moved up the slope toward the stone wall which still belched blasts of double canister shot from the Union cannon and rifle fire from the Union infantry. The Confederate lines crumbled and fell apart, formed and reformed, but always to press forward, though hardly more than 150 men crossed the deadly stone wall. Federal forces on both the right and left wheeled into place to deliver a withering fire on the already devastated Confederate ranks. A counterattack swept the last remnants of the badly beaten foe from Cemetery Ridge, leaving literally thousands of dead and wounded behind on the bloody slope. Lee met those who staggered back to the shelter of the Confederate batteries in deep sorrow, taking full blame for the failure. The tide of the Confederacy "swept to its crest, paused, and receded," on that hot afternoon. All the fighting now ended. Lee had lost 28,000 men killed, wounded, or captured from his original force of 75,000. Meade had lost 23,000 from the 97,000 men he had at the start of the campaign.

MORNING OF JULY 4

The following morning was strangely quiet. Neither side was quite sure as to future action. That afternoon Lee began his retreat over the Hagerstown Road and through the mountain pass to the Potomac. After having been delayed by rains swelling the river, he crossed the night of July 13 to escape safely back into Virginia. Meade followed cautiously but did not attack, creating one of the further great mysteries in the Gettysburg story. Many believed, including Lincoln, that Meade could and should have attacked and annihilated Lee's remaining force.

Lincoln penned a bitter letter to Meade, which was never sent, revealing his distress at the failure to attack the defeated Lee and thus possibly end the war. It must be kept in mind that Meade also suffered great losses and that his men were exhausted by the furious campaign; also, his limited command of the army had given him little time to assess its offensive powers.

MEMORIAL AT GETTYSBURG

Soon after the battle Governor Curtin ordered attorney David Wills of Gettysburg to purchase land for a permanent burial ground for the Union dead. The Confederate dead hastily buried on the battlefield were returned home. While reinterment from temporary graves into the new cemetery was still in progress Abraham Lincoln came to Gettysburg, invited as an afterthought, to deliver what became in history the immortal Gettysburg Address on November 19, dedicated to the ideal that "government of the people, by the people, and for the people, shall not perish from the earth." Other northern states cooperated in creating the cemetery which became in 1895 a part of Gettysburg National Military Park. Today only ghostly memories and monuments recall those three bloody days at Gettysburg when the fate of a nation hung in the balance.

CHAMBERSBURG AGAIN

War returned briefly to Pennsylvania soil again in 1864 with another and more serious raid on Chambersburg. Washington early in July was upset by a threatened attack and Governor Curtin called for twelve thousand volunteer militia to protect the nation's capital. Pennsylvania was also, according to rumor, to be invaded. On July 30, 1864, General Early ordered McCausland's mounted brigade to raid the town the Confederates had visited hardly a year before. Vandalism on the part of Federal forces under General Hunter operating in western Virginia was given as an excuse for retaliation. Three thousand mounted Confederates swept into Chambersburg demanding a ransom of $100,000 in gold or $500,000 in currency as the ransom which would

The second or Hay draft of Lincoln's Gettysburg Address.

Ruins of Chambersburg after Confederate invasion.

keep the town from being burned down. Rumors spread that this was the prelude to another full-scale invasion involving an attack on Harrisburg. Chambersburg's bank vaults were empty and the money was not forthcoming. The Confederates promptly burned the town, leaving two-thirds of its inhabitants homeless. The state later paid Chambersburg citizens $1,628,431 as compensation for their losses. The raiders retreated by way of McConnellsburg, giving the townspeople some anxious moments, but continued their retreat after considerable looting and plundering. Another raid was threatened in August, leading to warnings from General Couch, but it was not forthcoming.

RESISTANCE TO THE WAR

Not every Pennsylvanian's heart beat with fervor for the Union during these times of tumult and crisis. The heady wartime enthusiasm of 1861 began to cool in 1862 with the failure of the Union armies to produce the expected speedy and easy conquest of the South. Casualty lists and the return of the severely wounded and disabled began to show the ugly face of war to the people back home. The demands of war were expanding business and some became more interested in the fruits of enterprise than serving in the army.

The army was temporarily stabilized early in 1862 at half a million men while Washington tried to cope with the problem of organizing supply. Heavy losses soon led to a call for another three hundred thousand and then yet another similar number. Volunteers were not forthcoming to meet such demands and by late 1862 the state was drafting men where volunteers did not fill quotas. The first draft was administered by the state under Federal regulations and used only to fill quota requirements not met by volunteering. The pernicious bounty system now came into use.

The drain on manpower was so great that on March 3, 1863, Congress passed the National Conscription Act, making all able-bodied male citizens between the ages of twenty and forty-five eligible for service. The hiring of substitutes was authorized for those who could pay for a recruit to serve in his stead. An exemption from any service could also be purchased for the modest sum of $300. Out of more than two million men who served in the Union forces during the Civil War a small fraction were raised by the draft. The bounty system started under the state draft in 1862; this sometimes provided a sum up to a thousand dollars as an inducement for service, and it proved very effective. At the same time it gave rise to the practice of "bounty jumping." A man would enlist in one place, collect his bounty, desert, and enlist again somewhere else.

Pennsylvania shared with all the loyal states serious opposition to the draft. Resistance was especially pronounced in the anthracite region where the secret order among miners known as the Molly Maguires actively opposed the draft. As the war dragged on, the opposition to the draft on the part of the Democratic press became increasingly virulent. The draft was derided as a call for "old Abe's three hundred thousand." Those who applied the draft were "Lincoln bloodhounds." Both Pittsburgh and Philadelphia were centers for opposition to conscription as laboring men objected to the ability of those with means to buy their way out of military service. Organized resistance to the draft was reported to Washington in Schuylkill, Luzerne, and Lackawanna counties in 1863. Not a little of the feeling about conscription came from those who objected to a war to free the Negro. Radical Democrats in strongly Democratic counties vigorously opposed the war and came close to if not actually encouraging draft opposition. Early resort of the Lincoln administration to arbitrary arrest and imprisonment by the military and denial of the writ of habeas corpus was a very serious complaint against the "Lincoln dynasty." Chief Justice Taney of the United States Supreme Court denounced late in 1861 the "policy of arbitrary arrests by the military while the civil courts are still functioning." He went on to say that the people "are no longer under a government of laws—but every citizen holds life, liberty and property at the will and pleasure of the army officer in whose military district he may happen to be found."

One of the truly regrettable examples of drastic measures taken against civilians by the military on a basis of what appears to have been irrespon-

sible rumor involves the tale of the Fishing Creek "Confederacy." The back country of Columbia County was strongly Democratic. Later in August, 1864, a strong force of Federal troops arrived at Bloomsburg, camped, and the next day prepared to move into the upper part of the county against an alleged conspiracy against the government said to involve forts and guns in the hands

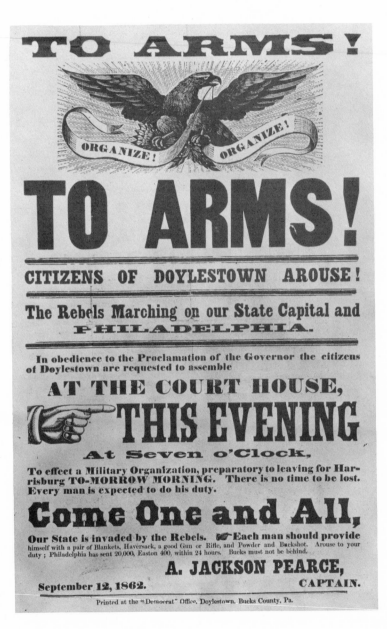

Another call to arms, a typical recruiting poster.

of a "confederacy." Over forty were arrested and hauled off to Fort Mifflin in Philadelphia. Some had a military "trial" at Harrisburg. At least one of the men, all of whom were respected citizens of their communities, died in prison before the long delay in securing their release. Tales of violent treatment of civilians during the period of arbitrary investigation were prevalent in the local press. "It is without Justice or Mercy," declared the *Columbia Democrat* at Bloomsburg. Probably no more glaring example of the miscarriage of justice under wartime conditions took place anywhere in the North.

WARTIME POLITICS

The course of Pennsylvania political affairs was far from smooth during the war years and little semblance of unity in supporting the war was evident. Wartime policies were bound to provide fodder for politicians, and especially so when the war did not go very well in 1861 and 1862. The Democratic Party was a powerful force in Pennsylvania up to 1860, and the Republicans had gained power in 1860 partly by the subterfuge of using the name People's Party. In 1861 the Democrats regained control of the lower house in the Assembly and a year later captured thirteen of twenty-four seats in Congress. Their slogan became "The Restoration of the Union as it was and the Preservation of the Constitution as it is." The Democrats also sent Charles Buckalew to the United States Senate. Democratic success was aided by Republican disunity, natural in a new party. Both David Wilmot and Governor Curtin detested Simon Cameron. Cameron resigned as minister to Russia to come back and take part in the Pennsylvania election in 1863.

Curtin was in poor health and reluctant to run for a second term but was drafted by a convention, which revealed persistent Republican Party weakness by calling itself the National Union Party. The Democrats on June 17, even as Lee was invading the North, nominated the notable lawyer and jurist George Woodward for governor. The National Union or Republican platform supported Lincoln and urged allowing an absentee ballot for those in the service, a measure more apt

to benefit their party than the Democrats. The Democrats asserted their support of the Union and their opposition to secession but criticized the arbitrary disregard of basic civil rights by the Lincoln administration. The resulting campaign was vicious and hardly constructive, in view of the critical situation which faced the Federal government. Lincoln was called by the Democratic press everything from a buffoon to a tyrant and scoundrel. The virulence of the attacks upon Lincoln is almost unbelievable. In fact, the tirades of the extreme elements in the Democratic Party boomeranged against it by putting the party into a position of downright opposition to the successful conduct of the war. The more radical Republicans tried to outdo the radical Democrats by calling their opponents "traitors" or "Copperheads," an allusion to the organized and acknowledged Confederate sympathizers in the loyal states. The Republicans charged their foes with secret alliances with southern Democrats, while Democrats said the Republicans did not want to end the war at all and were keeping it alive as a political device. Lack of success on the battlefield and the undoubted subversion of many basic and fundamental civil rights on the part of the Lincoln administration helped the Democrats.

When the shouting and exchange of ridiculous charges and countercharges was over, Curtin was the winner by over 15,000 votes, but this was less than half his margin in 1860. Curtin may well have won re-election on the strength of the vote of the soldiers in the field, whose camps and hospitals he had visited constantly, winning for himself the sobriquet of "Soldier's Friend." Without Curtin as his opponent it is questionable whether Woodward would not have been elected. Curtin's party also recaptured the House.

The 1864 presidential election was hardly less crucial to the Union cause. The Republican Party was in real trouble everywhere and even Lincoln ran as a National Union candidate and had with him on the ticket the war Democrat Andrew Johnson from Tennessee. Lincoln himself was doubtful of success. Grant had been made supreme commander of all the Union armies on March 9, 1864. He began the frontal assault en masse on Richmond which resulted in the Battle of the Wilderness and other bloody engagements with heavy Union casualties but without breaking through Lee's defenses. Grant then began a new approach by way of the James River, in a series of movements that continually outflanked the Confederates. Grant's losses were terrific and again aroused opposition to what seemed to many to be a senseless waste of manpower without results.

General Sherman, however, had begun his famous "march to the sea" and by September 2 had taken Atlanta. The Democratic candidacy of General McClellan naturally strengthened the Democrats in Pennsylvania. Lincoln remained in trouble in Pennsylvania and carried the state by a little over 19,000 votes, of which 14,000 were from men in the service. Despite this narrow margin of victory, a solid front for the Union had been gained.

Nothing succeeds like success, and the Republican Party in Pennsylvania from this point on gained in power. With the end of the war, the battle within the party between Curtin and Cameron was intensified, but Cameron won his place as the real "boss" of the Republican organization. Curtin at the end of his governorship in 1867 was "exiled" to Russia as the United States minister. The Democratic Party, which had maintained considerable strength up to 1864, now became the party which had opposed what proved to be a successful war. It was derided by the opposition as the party of disunion in the post Civil War era of waving the "bloody shirt." It took more than a decade for the Democrats to overcome this stigma.

FACTORY AND MILL UNDER WAR PRESSURES

The Civil War, with the huge numbers of men placed under arms and the resulting demand for equipment and supplies, ranging from underwear and outer clothing to rifles and heavy armament, was like no other war up to that time. It consumed vast quantities not only of men but also of material and this consumption strained the capacity of existing facilities and resources. Few northern states were in a better position to respond to the challenge than Pennsylvania, with its well developed iron and textile industries, along with its experience and leadership in the development of the new railroads. It was superiority in industrial output in terms of armament and supplies as well as transportation that spelled the doom of the Confederacy as much as did the manpower of the Union armies.

Pennsylvania became the Union's arsenal throughout the war. Coal and iron were basic sinews of war. Pennsylvania was the source for more than one-half the nation's iron ore. Anthracite coal production increased about 50 per cent, and the same was true for bituminous coal. The coal and iron ore went into the production of all iron products during the Civil War. Pennsylvania furnaces produced 580,000 of the North's 859,000-ton pig-iron output in 1860, and this compared with 26,000 tons for all the South. Pennsylvania produced also over 9,000 tons of the 11,800 tons of steel made in the North in 1860. Accurate production figures are not available. The Pittsburgh region increased its output ten times and Hussey, Wells & Co. in Pittsburgh expanded crucible steel output over ten times. Total production of pig iron more than doubled in Pennsylvania. Of the three cannon foundries in 1861, one was in Pittsburgh, where the great Fort Pitt Foundry did yeoman service. It produced the huge Rodman smooth-bores, largest of their kind. The foundry also made both land and naval guns and between 1861 and 1864 supplied over two thousand cannon and mortars and ten million pounds of shot and shell. The Allegheny Arsenal produced small arms.

In Philadelphia, C. Sharps & Co. had developed the improved Sharps breech-loading rifle before 1860 and an improved carbine. It could turn out a thousand rifles a month even in 1860, and further stepped up production to arm the Union infantry eventually with what was probably the best rifle used in the war. There were other gun factories in Philadelphia, Reading and elsewhere that also ranked high. The Frankford Arsenal was one of the leading suppliers of arms. The Philadelphia Navy Yard was busy developing the northern navy. It built the gunboats used by Farragut and Pennsylvania's David A. Porter in opening the Mississippi. Tremendous demands

Pittsburgh's Fort Pitt Foundry produced the heaviest ordnance of the Civil War.

were made on the northern navy by the necessity to blockade thousands of miles of Confederate coastline, and the demand for ships was great. The great Cramp Company shipyards on the Delaware also bolstered the shipbuilding capacity of the area. It was at Cramp's that the famous ironclad *Ironsides* was launched in 1862. Pittsburgh mills produced armor and other material to rebuild and rearm what had been peacetime river craft for wartime service on the inland rivers, as well as for the regular navy.

Philadelphia as a center of the nation's new ready-made-clothing industry and of its large cotton and woolen textile mills provided large quantities of the clothing and blankets needed by men at war. About one-half of such mills in the state were in Philadelphia but other cities too had a part in this type of war production. Mills were considerably expanded and improved to meet the demands of the armies. Philadelphia was also a center for the building of locomotives and essential railroad equipment. The war made demands on the infant railroad system of the North undreamed of in 1860. Matthias Baldwin was building some forty locomotives a year in 1860; he built 456 during the war. The Pennsylvania Railroad alone ordered 150 locomotives and 3,000 freight cars during the conflict; the Erie bought nearly as many; other railroads pressed for equipment.

The overall influence of the war upon Pennsylvania industry was considerable. Industry had gone through revolutionary stages of improvement and growth in the peaceful years of the 1850's but the new pressures to produce made even these changes seem inadequate. The number of mills and factories in Philadelphia grew from 6,414 in 1860 to 8,377 by 1866. Capitalization increased from $73,087,852 to $112,000,000 in the same period. The number of wage earners expanded from 98,397 to 160,000. Inevitably, the methods of producing goods were being altered in the same period and the technological revolution moved ahead. New and larger plants were built in the effort to expand production. The war served also to spread the state's industrial production in factories and mills. Pittsburgh and Philadelphia were not the only centers for wartime production; other cities such as Reading took a new lease on life and began to spurt ahead. The war spelled the end of any system of manufacturing in the home. Machines and the mill and factory became dominant throughout Pennsylvania. The Civil War completed the transformation of Pennsylvania into an industrial titan.

THE WAR AND THE HOME FRONT

Not least among the innovations resulting from the Civil War was a new kind of wartime activity on the home front. Thousands of volunteers began to move through major cities after April, 1861. Later, many came back again as wounded. The problem of clothing and blankets for troops in the field other than the barest necessities or even decent food challenged the people back home, especially in the early years of the war as both Harrisburg and Washington wrestled with the problems of total supply of troops. The northern defeat at Bull Run and other later battles quickly pointed up the great need for surgical dressings and even hospital clothing. Here again there was an almost total lack of any preparation by the War Department.

202

Pennsylvanians more than the citizens of other northern states found themselves especially close to these problems; many troops passed through the state on its railroads on the way to the front and it was the state nearest the major battlefields in Virginia. The women in particular were called upon to knit, sew, and make bandages in huge quantities not just for their own men in arms but for all the armies in the field. One of the earliest women's volunteer organizations was aroused to action in 1861 in Reading. Here a Ladies Aid Society and a Ladies Volunteer Society undertook heroic home front services. A Reading newspaper exhorted, "Come, girls, get out your knitting needles . . . and make knitting stockings your employment when you attend tea parties . . . instead of working upon some fancy lace work." In Pittsburgh, B. F. Jones of Jones & Laughlin iron works personally bought and gave to soldiers passing through on the trains crackers, apples, and cheese. As early as the fall of 1861 the Pittsburgh Subsistence Committee, helped by women volunteers, supplied items of food and other comforts to soldiers. Other cities were soon doing the same thing in an effort to serve as best they could. Relief committees were formed to help the needy families of volunteers away at the front. When the United States Sanitary Commission later in the war gave some intelligent central direction to home-front aid, Pennsylvanians already had responded with their own organizations, which now cooperated actively with the central relief efforts. Two great Sanitary Fairs were held in the state in 1864, one in Philadelphia and one in Pittsburgh, as part of the national war relief effort.

The reactions of the people to war in a democracy are varied and often peculiar, and the Civil War was no exception. The enthusiasm of volunteers on the home front rose and fell with the fortunes of war in the same degree as did that of volunteers for army duty. In those areas where the war was unpopular, home-front services were few and feeble. As the number of men in the armies increased, so did the number of civilians back home with a personal concern for the welfare of the men in arms, especially the wounded in the hospitals. The story is told of the wife of a very prominent Philadelphian, herself an in-tensely loyal Virginian, who visited all the hospitals caring for men in and near Philadelphia but consoling only those she found to be Confederates. The war produced also the usual manifestations of profiteering and easy living on the part of a few far from the fighting who, callous to the terrible trial and suffering of war, were busy making fortunes and spending them with that careless abandon common to the newly rich. Workers in mills and factories forgot their obligations to their country in frequent strikes for higher wages. Inflation was especially vicious in the early years of the war and profiteering by unduly raising prices was a common complaint. Human nature was no different in Pennsylvania from what it was elsewhere and the Civil War brought to the surface not only the great and the good in a majority of the people but along with it the evil and selfishness in the characters of a few.

PENNSYLVANIA'S CONTRIBUTION

The total contribution made by Pennsylvania to the North's victory is so considerable and so varied as entirely to justify its reputation as a keystone state in the Civil War. On the armed-services front it is hard to determine with precision just how many and what troops Pennsylvania furnished. This is due to faulty bookkeeping and lack of uniform records in both Harrisburg and Washington. The best estimate is that somewhat over 385,000 Pennsylvanians were recorded for service in the war. This does not count the numerous militia units formed on a very temporary and emergency basis. The contribution in manpower in the army, navy, and marines was by no means the total of what the state offered the Union cause. Pennsylvanians bought liberal quantities of the bond issues offered through Jay Cooke and paid, somewhat less cheerfully, large sums in the new taxes induced by the war. As a large and wealthy state these were, of course, Pennsylvania's due and no particular emblem of achievement.

Moving men and supplies and establishing and maintaining communications with the vast field armies of the Union was a major factor in defeating the South. Thomas A. Scott, Herman Haupt, and Frank Thomson were Pennsylvania railway engineers who played a leading part in organizing the railroad and telegraph services of the war years. Harrisburg, the connection from the West through which railway service to Baltimore and Washington was routed, occupied an unusual position of importance in the national transportation picture. The state actually increased and improved its own railroad mileage during the war.

Pennsylvania provided some of the more outstanding military and naval commanders of the war. General George Gordon Meade won at Gettysburg what most agree was the key battle of the war, despite its somewhat controversial conclusion. Meade served well during the entire war. General Winfield S. Hancock served brilliantly at Gettysburg and was among the leading generals of the entire conflict. General John Reynolds, who died on the first day at Gettysburg, was a forceful leader. General George B. McClellan was a strutting egotist who combined with this fault a tendency usually to estimate the strength of the enemy as twice what it was. McClellan nevertheless was a great organizer of military legions and did much to whip the previously disorganized Army of the Potomac into a real military force. He had a place in winning the war. Pennsylvania provided a legion of officers of lesser rank, several of whom became later governors. On the naval front, Admiral David Porter was a hero in opening the Mississippi with his gunboat fleet; without his help Grant could hardly have taken beseiged Vicksburg in 1863.

The war also had to be fought on the all-important governmental front in Harrisburg and Washington. The heroic role of Governor Andrew Gregg Curtin stands head and shoulders above all others among the governors of loyal states as a tremendous wartime leader. His unheralded and overlooked Secretary of the Commonwealth was Eli Slifer. Slifer deserves a tribute, as this was an especially key post because of Curtin's many absences from Harrisburg in the field with Pennsylvania troops and in Washington. The role of Thaddeus Stevens, the "Great Commoner," was important in the Civil War and early reconstruction years, though a subject of bitter contention. Stevens fought throughout his public career with

vigor and without compromise for the rights of the downtrodden and against any special privilege for the few. This was what made him the leader of Pennsylvania's Anti-Masons. It was why he fought for free schools and why he hated slavery. As chairman of the all-important Ways and Means Committee of the House he grappled with major wartime problems. He was a dominant force on the Joint Committee on Reconstruction set up in 1865 and leader of the Radical Republicans in Congress until his death. Another Pennsylvania Congressman of far above average stature was Galusha Grow. Grow, like Stevens, was a native of New England who adopted Pennsylvania as his home. He succeeded his law partner David Wilmot as congressman from this northeastern Pennsylvania district and rose to the post of Speaker of the House in July, 1861. He served as Speaker until 1863. Grow from the first day of his service in Congress took a keen interest in the issue of free public lands in the West, which the South had fought steadily as threatening to develop nonslave territory. Grow was so vigorous an advocate of this legislation that when it was finally pushed through in 1862 he became justly known as the "Father of the Homestead Act." This bill was one of the most important legislative acts in American history, opening the West to rapid and final settlement.

Lincoln's two cabinet appointees as Secretary of War were Pennsylvanians Simon Cameron and Edwin M. Stanton. Cameron left the post under pressure. Stanton had been for a short time a member of Buchanan's cabinet as Attorney General and was a unionist Democrat who freely denounced the "Black Republicans." Able but highly temperamental, Stanton had a fine legal mind and made a successful War Department head under the most difficult conditions. He disputed with Lincoln and feuded bitterly and vindictively with Johnson but he did establish a record which cannot be ignored in engineering the triumph of the North.

Taken all in all, the contribution of Pennsylvania to preserving the Union in the trying and critical days of the Civil War was both a major and a decisive one in terms of manpower, industrial and financial might, and leadership on both military and civilian fronts.

CHAPTER TWELVE

A GOLDEN AGE
FOR A TITAN OF
INDUSTRY

Pennsylvania before the Civil War had hardly scratched the surface of its potential as a great industrial state. It was in the midst of a very real revolution of its industrial possibilities; it started to make use of latent mineral power. It was still a state with industrial foundations resting upon the farm and forest and the industries which their resources nourished. The single exception of note was the iron industry, which for some hundred years had held leadership among the states because of Pennsylvania iron ore and limestone. Coal was little tapped as a resource. In late August, 1859, on the outskirts of the country village of Titusville the self-styled "Colonel" Edwin Drake after several exploratory attempts, had succeeded in drilling a well which produced crude oil. It was called a "discovery," but knowledge of the existence of petroleum in western Pennsylvania had been a fact for many years. An Irishman from Pittsburgh named William Kelly had experimented with a new way to make steel. Pennsylvania had been the birthplace of the American railroad; it was ready for the demands on industry and transportation made by a great civil war. Pennsylvania not only met these wartime demands but was stimulated to further exertions. The stage was set for Pennsylvania to

become a true titan of industry in the last decades of the nineteenth century.

STEEL AND COKE BECOME SUPREME
IN THE PITTSBURGH REGION

After the Civil War it was coal and steel that were king in Pennsylvania. Their fortunes were inseparable. The steel industry grew out of the tremendous demand for a better iron product. In turn, it was this demand that was inherent in the growth of railroads and the explosion of industry that began before the Civil War; it was sorely tried under wartime demands, and was given impetus by the war. Pittsburgh's William Kelly started his experiments with a Bessemer-type method of making steel on a successful basis with a tilt-type converter at the Cambria Iron Works in Johnstown in 1861–62. The first entirely new Bessemer works in Pennsylvania was blown in at Steelton, near Harrisburg, in 1867. This plant turned out the ingots from which the first steel rails were rolled on a successful commercial basis at Johnstown. Steel did not become king overnight. It was not until 1870 that it won a place as an industry, separate from iron, in the national manufactures census. Eighteen of the thirty steel

The East Broad Top Railroad made its last run in 1956. The second oldest
narrow-gauge railroad in the United States, it was built in 1871–74 to
tap the famed East Broad Top bituminous mines and offered both freight
and passenger service. Now operated as an historical attraction
and designated a National Historical Landmark.

William Kelly's original steel
converter, now in the offices of the
Bethlehem Steel Company at
Johnstown.

206

Major improvements were made in the production of coke by 1890 to meet the new needs of the steel industry.

mills in the country were then in Pennsylvania; they were making some two-thirds of all the nation's steel. Between 1880 and 1890 the production of steel ingots and castings in Pennsylvania mills grew by over 300 per cent; it reached over 61 per cent of the nation's total. Along with the increased production went rapid advances in the technology of steelmaking. The first steel made using the Clapp-Griffith process from England was at Pittsburgh in 1884; in 1888 the open-hearth process was used at Carnegie's newest works. William Metcalf of Pittsburgh was the "father" of the crucible steel industry. The Pittsburgh region quickly became the capital of the new empire of steel. In 1865 Pittsburgh was turning out about two-fifths of the nation's iron; five times more iron than steel. The huge Jones & Laughlin American Iron Works, sprawled across twenty acres on the bank of the Monongahela,

was the largest iron works in the entire country in 1870. It was not long before it turned to steel, using ore from Lake Superior.

Three factors changed Pittsburgh and its environs from the "Iron City" to the "Steel City." One was its proximity to the great new iron ore deposits which were opening in the Lake Superior region. Pittsburgh's Henry Oliver and Philadelphia's Charlemagne Tower were leaders in developing this great store of iron ore, which by 1890 put Pennsylvania ore reserves in the background. A second factor was the vast store of bituminous coal in the Pittsburgh region, easily turned into coke to fire Pittsburgh furnaces; it was readily transported from the source of supply to the furnaces by river. The last and possibly the most important of all the ingredients which turned Pittsburgh into a "city of crucible, forge and mill" was shrewd business leadership.

Carnegie's new Edgar Thomson works opened in 1875. The smoke pouring from the mill helps explain why Pittsburgh became known as the "Smoky City" in the days before smoke control.

The "folk hero" of steel is Andrew Carnegie. This industrialist was first and foremost an opportunist, but with an uncanny sense as to the direction of future developments. These could be in only one direction: ahead to fortune. Carnegie is said to have rushed home about 1870 from a trip to England, where he had seen a demonstration of the Bessemer process, declaring, "The day of iron is past! Steel is king." The fact remains that Carnegie was one person to realize that the age of the railroad would change everything. Railroads needed better and stronger rails. Bridges had to be built for them and they must have new equipment. Carnegie was closely associated with railroading and knew that iron would not meet the railroads' needs. In 1875 he and his associates opened the Edgar Thomson Steel Works mainly to serve railroad needs; it was named aptly for the then head of the great Pennsylvania Railroad. Carnegie teamed up with Henry Clay Frick. By 1885 Frick had about four-fifths of the coke-plant production in his grasp. Men like Henry Oliver, Henry Phipps, and Benjamin F. Jones were other titans in the steel business of the era. Jones kept his position as a leader of an independent steel company. The amounts of steel produced grew beyond belief. At the Carnegie works alone a production of 600,000 tons in 1888 reached some 2,000,000 tons nine years later. Instead of 5,000 coke ovens there were 15,000 at this point, with an output expanded from 6,000 to 18,000 tons in a single day. Production records were broken every week and reported to Carnegie, who always asked why this was a limit on what the plant could produce. Not all the steel was made in the Pittsburgh region. The Bethlehem Steel Company was in operation and steel mills at Bethlehem, Steelton, and Johnstown figured prominently in the steel making capacity of the state.

The early revolutionary growth in steelmaking was based upon the tremendous demand of the railroads; up to 1880 about three-quarters of the production was turned into steel rails. The nation's railroads were growing, and the great transcontinental lines such as the Union Pacific were tearing up their old iron rails and laying their tracks anew with steel rails. By 1890 the story had changed; less than half the steel ingots were rolled into rails; other railroad equipment was now being made from steel. The new metal was going into building; in Pittsburgh the new Carnegie office building constructed in 1894–95 was a pioneer steel skyscraper. By this time the National Tube Works of John and Harvey Flagler was making steel tubing. A way to plate steel with tin had been discovered and was first made at Pittsburgh in 1872, using skilled Welsh workers. The McKinley tariff gave it protection to spurt forward. The age of the tin can was at hand. Steel could now be used to make wire and cable for telegraph and telephone lines, and suspension bridges. All kinds of machinery and tools were now made from steel rather than iron. American machinery began for the first time to attract attention when displayed in the numerous international expositions of the time. Rather than

importing, America now began to export machinery and skilled workmen. By 1900 the age of iron was an age of steel, with Pennsylvania leading the way.

This revolution has a certain fascination as an example of the way in which a new American industry was born in those fabulous years of the eighties and nineties. Visitors to the steel mills—especially the specialists who knew and understood steelmaking in Europe, where it had started—were astounded by the Pittsburgh mills and their capacity to produce steel. Huge blast furnaces reared themselves a hundred feet toward the sky and their demands for ore and coke seemed insatiable. One visitor wrote: "Bessemer converters dazzle the eye with their leaping flames. Steel ingots at white heat, weighing thousands of pounds are carried from place to place and tossed about like toys. Electric cranes pick up steel rails or fifty foot girders as jauntily as if their tons were ounces."

Profits were no less fabulous than production. Investments of a few hundred thousand dollars were turned in a decade or two into millions. The Carnegie companies are said to have paid out profits of $133,000,000 between 1875 and 1900; in 1900 alone profits were $40,000,000, of which Carnegie personally collected $25,000,000. This was accomplished in an age when there were no significant controls or restraints from government and no taxation of these profits. It was an era when might was right. Labor tried desperately to organize into the Amalgamated Association of Iron and Steel Workers, and by 1891 had about one-half the workers organized, mainly the skilled employes. The power of the union was broken in the bloody and disastrous Homestead strike in 1892 by stern, brusque, autocratic Henry Clay Frick.

The mushrooming steel and coal industry fixed the pattern of mill-town life in western Pennsylvania before 1900, the residual effects of which are still clearly observable. Making steel became more than an industry; it established a way of life. One of its features was a heavy influx of unskilled European labor to undertake the hard, dirty, and dangerous tasks. Contract labor was not abolished by Congress until 1885 and this type of labor flooded the steel towns and company-controlled towns. As of 1880, Pittsburgh's Austrian, Hungarian, Italian, and Slavic population numbered about 1 per cent; by 1900 it was 6 per cent. The Pittsburgh region's foreign-born population nearly doubled in these twenty years. Increased use of machinery and larger mills in steel encouraged use of unskilled labor directed by a few skilled steel men. This was true also in the bituminous mines. By 1900 it was estimated that some 60 per cent of steel and coal workers were unskilled; the percentage was also about 60 per cent greater than in 1880, when native-born skilled labor predominated in steelmaking.

No system of labor outside Negro slavery offered a greater opportunity for exploitation of labor or for massing it together in towns and cities under conditions the average American

Typical coal miners of the times. Mining was a hazardous occupation.

workingman would not have accepted. Wages were low, averaging about $1.50 to $2.00 per day. The twelve-hour day was common in the mills; a ten-hour day was the union leaders' dream. Steel towns were literally built from the ground up around the huge mill concentrations and ranged from Braddock's some twenty thousand people to towns of perhaps eight thousand. Though the term "company town" has been applied more generally to mining towns, it is no less aptly used in describing steel towns; even Pittsburgh of the time may well be called a steel-company town grown larger because it was likewise a business, commercial, and financial center.

PITTSBURGH, A STEEL-MILL TOWN

Pittsburgh by 1900 had grown into a city of 451,512 people as compared with its 77,923 in 1860, but the larger part of Pittsburgh was a nest of wooden tenements and shanties without decent sanitary facilities, heavily populated by the foreign-born steel workers. These were situated not far from today's "Golden Triangle." The saloon and bawdy house were ever present, as they were in the smaller mill towns, and every conceivable evil that could be found in a mill-dominated city flourished in full flower, winked at by the law and the respectable citizens.

On Sunday, true to its Presbyterian conscience, all that was evil was kept behind closed doors and off the streets while Pittsburghers patronized their churches, of which there were a greater number than there were banks, and aroused visitors to comment that Pittsburgh was as dour on any given Sunday as any city in Scotland. On weekdays the mills were running full blast, usually around the clock with two shifts, day and night. One visitor in the later 1880's wrote of the scene: "Around the city's edge, and on the sides of the hills which encircle it like a gloomy amphitheatre their outlines rising darkly against the sky,

210

through numberless apertures fiery streams of light streak forth, looking angrily and fiercely toward the heavens while over these settles a heavy pall of smoke. It is as though one had reached the outer edge of the infernal regions, and saw before him the great furnace of pandemonium with all its lids lifted."

COAL

The explosion in steelmaking is associated inseparably with the large-scale utilization of the bituminous coal reserves of the state. Though it had been mined commercially since at least 1820, bituminous coal output was only about 6,000,000 tons in 1865. Anthracite had made possible a revolution in making iron, and had as well a large export market. Anthracite production was about twice that of bituminous in 1865, and was in the same relative position as late as 1890. Anthracite then slowed down in comparison, as it had a limited production area, as well as a more limited

use in the expanding industrial revolution. Bituminous output almost doubled between 1890 and 1900 and was now about 50 per cent greater than that of "hard coal." Bituminous had an advantage in its widespread location in central and western Pennsylvania in more than twenty counties. It was easily carried to the steel mills by river, as either coal or coke. It was the almost insatiable demand of the steel furnaces for coke that boomed bituminous mining; about 90 per cent of the product of Fayette County mines went into making coke by 1890. Pennsylvania's coke tonnage grew more than three times between 1880 and 1890 and to three-fourths the nation's entire output. The Connellsville region, birthplace of coke-making, alone turned out over half the country's coke. At least 90 per cent of Pennsylvania coke was used directly in Pennsylvania steel mills. Coal and coke were an unbeatable and indeed almost unbelievable combination in accounting for the spectacular growth of Pennsylvania as the steel center of the world. The peak of the power of

Typical first-generation immigrant workers in the steel mills of the Pittsburgh district about 1900.

211

this alliance had been reached by 1900, never to be attained again. No one realized it at the turn of the century, but the steel boom had reached its height.

STEEL AND COAL BEGET BIG BUSINESS

The story of the emerging concept of "big business," including the trust and large combinations of capital in the nation's business enterprise of the era before 1900, is usually told in terms of John D. Rockefeller, petroleum, and Standard Oil. This ignores the somewhat less spectacular but extensive and solid growth of big business fathered by the tycoons of coal and steel, notably Andrew Carnegie and his associates. Steel was the real father of the whole business of creating large-scale industrial consolidation under corporate enterprise. In 1836 Pennsylvania passed a special act favoring the incorporation of iron companies using coal or coke with a minimum capital of $100,000 and a maximum of $500,000. In 1874 Pennsylvania adopted another more liberal law to incorporate steel companies, and a year later a general incorporation statute. The first steel firms were puny affairs limited by the legal restraints prevalent before 1874. In 1881 Carnegie and his six partners took advantage of the new legislation to organize Carnegie Brothers and Company at the then huge capitalization of $5,000,000. This was itself the successor to a combination known as Union Iron Mills.

Carnegie was not without rivals and by no means dominated the iron or steel industry at this time. In 1881 the new Pittsburgh Bessemer Steel Company opened the Homestead Steel Works. As mentioned earlier, Henry Clay Frick made himself the kingpin of the coke business. He became a Carnegie partner in 1889. The independent Duquesne Steel Company also had been organized. In 1892 Carnegie's now truly sprawling concerns were brought together into the Carnegie Steel Company, Limited. It included all the formerly scattered iron, steel, coal, coke, and bridge-building interests in whose structure Carnegie had a part. It even included Lake Superior ore holdings. This company was a limited partnership but the capital was now boosted to

$25,000,000. In 1900 a further reorganization was accomplished into a holding company which Carnegie controlled, the Carnegie Company. Affable Charles M. Schwab, Carnegie's right-hand man as manager of this concern, and eventually head of the Bethlehem Steel Company, later explained the need for this move to the investigating United States Industrial Commission: "It was then found that this partnership had grown so large and the business of such a varied character, there were so many companies to control and so many partnerships holding varied interests, that for the sake of harmony among our partners it was decided to put all in the control of one corporation to be known as the Carnegie Company."

The greatest merger of all, one which was founded on the Carnegie enterprises, from which he now wished to retire, created the United States Steel Corporation in February, 1901. The financing was arranged by J. Pierpont Morgan, the first of his giant moves to integrate big finance with big business. By this date the era of consolidated big business was attracting national attention. More than 358 individual Pennsylvania plants and mills were involved in such combinations by 1900 and most of them were in steel, coal, and allied industry. The new United States Steel Corporation now owned 149 steel plants, a number of railroads, Great Lakes shipping interests, and thousands of acres of reserve coal, iron-ore, and limestone lands. Its authorized capital was $1,404,000,000, though the actual assets were considerably less. Such was the saga of increasing some $5,000,000 worth of capitalization in 1881 to over a billion dollars. Multimillionaires were made by the stroke of a pen in 1901 and the greater part of the productive capacity in steel on which it was founded was in the Pittsburgh region. Nothing quite like it had been known before; nor since.

BLACK GOLD AT TITUSVILLE

The wonders of the machine and automotive age made possible by the use of steel would hardly have been possible had it not been for the magic of new fuels and lubricants derived from petroleum. Knowledge of the existence of

Both coal and coke were moved by barges towed or pushed by steamboat on the Monongahela.

petroleum in northwestern Pennsylvania goes back many years before its "discovery" in 1859 by Edwin Drake. As a matter of fact, petroleum derived from seepage into salt wells near Pittsburgh, which were in themselves a highly valuable mineral resource, was refined by Samuel Kier as early as 1850. Four years later Kier had a five-barrel still in operation on the outskirts of Pittsburgh and was promoting its product as an illuminant. Pittsburgh already was a center for the "coal oil" refineries which extracted an oil from coals. When Drake drilled his well in the bright autumn of 1859, some two thousand barrels of "Tarentum crude" had already been refined in the Pittsburgh area. What Edwin Drake was searching for was a more practical method of getting at

a better source for crude petroleum, the worth of which already was known.

Drake's enterprise was a result of the aroused interest of Dr. Francis Brewer, who had moved to Titusville from Massachusetts to join his father in the lumber business. Brewer had some crude oil analyzed by chemists at Dartmouth College. The evident worth of the product attracted the attention of George Bissell, another native of New England. Bissell was joined by Jonathan Eveleth and in 1854 the Pennsylvania Rock Oil Company was formed, the world's first petroleum company. A year later the noted Yale University chemist Dr. Benjamin Silliman, Jr., reported on the value of this "rock oil." New England capital then organized the Seneca Oil Company, which

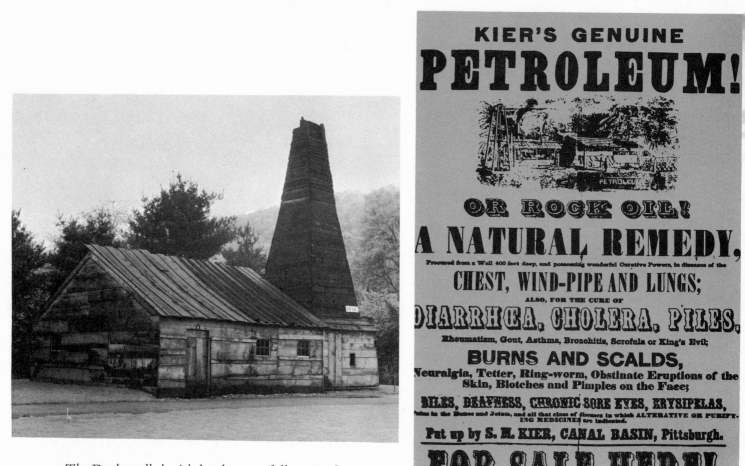

The Drake well derrick has been carefully restored at Drake Well Park, state historical monument and museum devoted to the birth of the oil industry.

An early advertisement for Kier's Rock Oil extolling its medicinal properties.

Fabulous Pithole, wild and wicked boom town of the oil regions, which quickly became a ghost town. Now preserved as a state historical monument.

Scene in the Pennsylvania oil regions in the oil boom days, with derricks everywhere.

sent Drake, a former store clerk and railroad conductor, to head the search for a way to get at this rich resource. Drake's title of "Colonel" was adopted to make an impression upon the sleepy natives of the country town of Titusville, which he made his headquarters. After early failures to get at any oil, Drake persuaded "Uncle Billy" Smith, Tarentum blacksmith and salt well driller, to come to Titusville with his fifteen-year-old son and try drilling for oil. Cast iron pipe and a steam engine were wagoned over from Erie. Using a primitive white-oak battering ram lifted by a steam engine driven windlass, Drake and Smith began the slow process of driving a well into the ground a few miles outside the town. Late on the afternoon of August 27, as the hopes of Drake for success and his capital were fast vanishing, the drill dropped into a crevice after having reached a depth of sixty-nine feet. The next morning "Uncle Billy" and his son drove out to check the site and were astounded to discover a quantity of oil oozing from the bottom of the well. The boy rushed back to Titusville crying out the exciting news to the doubting Thomases of the village that oil had been discovered.

The oil boom that followed was as fantastic as the California gold rush of a decade earlier. Companies to drill for oil were organized by the hundreds and speculators roamed the countryside trying to persuade farmers to lease or sell their land for drilling. The entire region was filled quickly with the good and the bad men and women who sought in one way or another, legitimate or illegitimate, to capitalize upon the wealth

In the early days most petroleum was put into barrels and much of it shipped on rafts or flatboats to refineries as far away as Pittsburgh.

which the "black gold" of northwestern Pennsylvania held forth to those lucky enough to tap the source. Boom towns sprang up overnight and in a few short months were sizable cities. Pithole was the largest and lustiest of them all. For sheer wickedness it could boast Ben Hogan, who advertised himself as the "Wickedest Man in the World" and operated his famous saloon with the help of "French" Kate and her "soiled doves." Life in Pithole was as lusty, lawless, and evil as that in any cattle-drive town in the West. Pithole grew into a town of fifteen thousand in a few months and within a year was on its way to becoming a ghost town.

The production of this slimy liquid with so great a potential reached over 500,000 barrels by 1860 and over 3,000,000 by 1862. It proved a substitute for southern turpentine, which made it the

sixth most valuable export product of the North during the Civil War. The export of refined petroleum reached 140,000,000 gallons by 1870. In the early eighties, production was over 30,000,000 barrels a year and then declined, to be reached again in the nineties as new wells were drilled in the McKean County region. Peak production was reached shortly after 1890. After 1900 and spectacular Spindletop in Texas, the center for drilling oil moved westward, and with it went many of the technicians and the promoters who helped create the industry anew in Texas and Oklahoma. The golden age of the Pennsylvania oil industry was showing signs of eclipse by the turn of the century.

The greatest use of Pennsylvania crude oil during this era was as a refined burning oil used for lighting and called kerosene. Almost overlooked

216

in the revolution in the daily life of the United States and all the world is the change in home lighting made possible by Drake's discovery. Tallow candles and whale-oil lamps of an earlier day were expensive and used only in homes of the well-to-do. Refined petroleum revolutionized lighting all over the world as much as Edison and Westinghouse did later with the electric light.

Rockefeller's Standard Oil Company was the first to consider fuller use of petroleum by-products. Some refiners actually drained off gasoline into the nearest stream as undesirable, leading to river fires. Standard Oil began manufacture and sales of naphtha, benzine, paraffin, and other petroleum by-products. The use of petroleum refined to make lubricants also appeared.

John D. Rockefeller was the Carnegie of the oil industry in terms of his humble beginnings and a rise to dominant control and resulting riches. By 1870 Pittsburgh was losing its early leadership in refining oil to Cleveland, thanks to John D. The trust agreement through which Rockefeller attempted to achieve control of the entire industry was the product of the legal mind of Samuel C. T. Dodd, son of a Franklin carpenter, who in 1879 became the chief legal counsel for Standard Oil. One of his able assistants was Mortimer Elliot of Wellsboro. Many battles between the Rockefeller and rival interests had to be decided by laws enacted in the Pennsylvania legislature and courts. Standard Oil entered into these battles with great vigor. There is evidence that a liberal use of money was made in buying legislative favors for the trust.

THE MAGIC POWDER AND OTHER MINERAL RESOURCES

Cement has been called the "magic powder." Natural cement was used in canal building in Pennsylvania. The stone construction demanded by canal building was the first to need a strong and new adhesive or binder. What is known as Portland cement was known in England and got its name from there, but before 1870 it was not manufactured in the United States. At the village of Coplay, not far from Allentown in the Lehigh Valley, the inventive mind of David Saylor toyed

The oldest producing oil well in the world, at Rouseville, is shown in the lower right foreground of this picture. A Pennzoil refinery is in the background.

217

with the thought that the particular kind of rock common to that region already used for natural cement might be turned into Portland cement. His first successful experiments were in 1871 and in 1889 came the use of a rotary-type kiln to heat the ground rock, and this led to commercial production of Portland cement. For the next few decades the center of the industry remained in the Lehigh region where it had been born. Portland cement came at the time when the expansion of industry and the growth of the city were making new demands on ways to erect buildings. Cement united with steel to produce a literal revolution in industrial and commercial building construction before 1900.

The thrust of the steel industry increased the need for limestone, with which Pennsylvania was well supplied. It also created a need for new heat-resistant materials with which to line the giant new Bessemer and open-hearth furnaces of the Pittsburgh region. This was met by the discovery and use of the fire clays of central Pennsylvania to make strongly heat-resistant brick. Other Pennsylvania clays were in growing demand for production of such vital building materials as brick and tile. Only Pennsylvania iron ore lost its place as a valuable mineral resource. Ore for the Carnegie mills came to a great extent before 1890 from Pennsylvania ore banks, especially those in central Pennsylvania. Indeed, Carnegie had ridiculed those who believed in the future of the Lake Superior ore deposits. By 1900 the pendulum had swung almost entirely to the Great Lakes ore reserves with their rich and easily tapped abundance, and use of Pennsylvania iron ore was largely abandoned. Natural gas emerged as a new resource in western Pennsylvania after the Civil War. It was discovered about 1874, and the largest and most productive well was drilled in 1878 near Murrysville, not far from Pittsburgh. George Westinghouse was the first to discover the potential of this new fuel and light source; he organized the Philadelphia Company to bring it into Pittsburgh. The Steel City soon had some 300 miles of gas lines, which served not only streets but also industry; there were those who thought natural gas would make Pittsburgh the "cleanest manufacturing city in the world." Westinghouse

soon invented himself out of the natural-gas business by developing a way to use electricity for light and power.

THE ALUMINUM INDUSTRY IS BORN

The steel industry was matured by 1900 but barking at its heels was the new and magic metal called aluminum. Aluminum's existence had been known for many years but it took the spirit of enterprise which had become a part of the Pittsburgh story after 1870 to bring to fruition a way to make aluminum a commercial reality. A young student at Oberlin College in Ohio named Charles M. Hall found a way to extract aluminum from its source. He was attracted to Pittsburgh and there he secured financial support. It was Captain Alfred Hunt of Pittsburgh who furnished the capital to provide a pilot experimental plant and assigned Arthur Vining Davis to help Hall. The Pittsburgh Reduction Company was founded in 1888 with $20,000 capital and it established a small experimental laboratory on Smallman Street in Pittsburgh. Here on Thanksgiving Day of that year after working just about around the clock, Hall and Davis turned out the first ingot of aluminum, and a new industry was born. Aluminum before 1900 was by no means a success as a commercial product. For a decade most persons thought of it as an interesting metal usable for jewelry. Its manufacturers were promoting its use to make household pots and pans, which gave it its first real lift as a commercial metal. Not even its founders dreamed of its value to the coming age of the automobile and airplane or in building construction.

FARM AND FOREST INDUSTRY
IN THE STEEL AGE

The farm and forest continued to provide an important foundation for the industrial economy of Pennsylvania before the turn of the century. Agriculture itself was in a process of a considerable revolution marked by a growing increase of the use of machinery. Farm technology based on machines was in its pioneer stages in Pennsylvania before 1860 but was on the increase after

1870. Farm progress came primarily from three developments: the scientific study of farming, as stimulated by the facilities for education and agricultural research at the Pennsylvania State College; the growth of agricultural societies, with their county fairs; and the organization of state associations for the improvement of farming in specialized occupations such as dairying (1874). A State Board of Agriculture was set up in 1876 and twenty years later it was organized into a Department of Agriculture at Harrisburg, the first step toward a larger recognition at the state level of the need for study and help in advancing the needs of the farmer.

The production of farm products such as grains for flour and hides for leather was important in the state's total industry in the period. The Civil War increased and highlighted the meat-packing industry as well as commercial production of foodstuffs. A human-interest story in the latter field is that of Henry J. Heinz in Pittsburgh. Heinz was a brickmaker's son and, as was common in that day, sought a way to earn a few extra pennies. He found a way by grating horseradish roots and selling the product in glass jars. Following the Horatio Alger pattern, Heinz kept on adding to the variety of his products and to his capacity to produce them. The famous Heinz "57 Varieties" slogan grew out of a visit to New York in which Heinz saw a streetcar advertising card on which a shoe store emphasized its great variety of shoes. Before 1900 the era of the tin can made possible a further change in packaging certain food products for the growing city population, which was not able to provide its own food through the traditional family garden and home-cured or home-preserved foods.

Another Pittsburgher who pioneered in providing the public with new food ideas was John Arbuckle. Born in Pittsburgh in 1839, he was associated with his brother Charles in pioneering the business of the uniform packaging of coffee to preserve freshness and flavor. Arbuckle's coffee became famous on American breakfast tables. John Arbuckle moved to New York in 1871 and there developed the innovation of packaged sugars for the housewife. He was a pioneer also in importing raw sugar for refining for his prod-

H. J. Heinz, pioneer in the food industry.

uct. The commercial production of dairy products such as packaged milk, cheese, butter, and ice cream grew enormously after the Civil War. Milton Hershey of Hershey-bar fame learned the candy business before 1900 as Pennsylvania became a center for much of this new industry.

Tanning leather, flour milling, and lumbering, with allied wood-product industries, had their golden age before 1900 in a large part of the state. Northern Pennsylvania remained the last refuge for the lumbering and tanning business. Philadelphia lost to Minneapolis its position as a capital of the milling industry, which moved westward closer to the sources of grain supply. Oddly, it was a Philadelphian, James Stroud Bell, who helped build the Minneapolis milling industry. The tanning business made an alliance about 1890 with the lumber people. The Pennsylvania tanneries needed hemlock bark to tan hides, and for some time bark speelers, as they were known, actually stripped standing hemlock trees of their bark. Pennsylvania held first place in the leather business and, like the early iron industry, needed the forests' basic resource—in this case the bark. Thousands of acres of land were bought to provide this. Soon it was realized that the trees themselves were a source of income as lumber. Tanning leather and lumbering merged about 1890 and out of the merger came the largest-scale industrial development of the forest resources of northern Pennsylvania. The Central Pennsylvania Lumber Company, organized in the nineties, became the largest lumbering concern east of the Mississippi, cutting mainly hemlocks and taking the bark for tannery use and using the timber for lumber. Pennsylvania became second in lumbering about 1870 but it was still a big business, worth, with related products, some $35,000,000 in 1900. Related wood-using industries sprang up close to the lumber area. Entire new boom towns sprang up in northern Pennsylvania, centering on lumbering. Huge tanneries with their foul-smelling red-painted wood plants, and surrounding tannery towns were found in many parts of northern Pennsylvania even after 1900. Philadelphia held onto its place as a leader in making the finer types of leather products.

A NEW ERA OF BANKING AND FINANCE

The growth of big business was associated intimately with the rise of larger-scale banking and finance. The antagonism of the frontier and debtor interests had killed all efforts to establish a sound national banking system until the exigencies of war made it imperative by 1863 that such a system be established. As mentioned earlier, the first national bank established under the new act was in Philadelphia. A rapid expansion of national banks took place in Pennsylvania after the war and by 1900 every city of any size was provided with one or more banks. The larger cities, of course, had several. In Pittsburgh, bank clearings increased from some $700,000,000 in 1890 to more than $1,500,000,000 in 1900, a clear evidence of the great growth of banking. Pittsburgh by 1900 had become one of the financial capitals of interior America.

Before 1863 the private bank was the major foundation of the banking structure. There were some twenty private banking houses in Phila-

delphia, more than in any other large city, and it was very much a financial capital of the nation. E. W. Clark and Company before 1860 was probably the nation's leading private banking house. Drexel and Company, Drexel and Morgan, and Jay Cooke and Company were leading banking houses of the 1870's. Jay Cooke failed in the Panic of 1873 due to overextended financing of the Northern Pacific Railroad. By 1900 the private banking firm of T. Mellon and Sons in Pittsburgh was emerging as a powerful financial institution, starting to underwrite such new industries as aluminum. Much would be heard of the Mellon dynasty in later years.

THE IRON HORSE COMES OF AGE

The infant railroads matured during the Civil War and demonstrated their ability to move people and goods. Railroading was further revolutionized after the war, largely as a result of technological changes centered in Pennsylvania. Within the state the main-line railroad mileage connecting towns and cities grew from some 4,000 miles about 1870 to over 10,000 miles at the turn of the century. Further construction had about reached its limits in terms of new lines; virtually every city and larger town in the state was made accessible by rail. The extent of railroad service in 1900 is hard to realize today when thousands of miles of rail lines have been abandoned and both passenger and freight service severely cut. Pennsylvania steel ingots by 1870 were rolled into rails which provided the nation's railroads with completely new high-speed steel tracks. The Pennsylvania Railroad system, headed by some of the real tycoons of American railroading such as "Tom" Scott, was the largest carrier of freight in the world and the nation's greatest single railroad system. It was also one of the nation's largest and most powerful corporations. The Pennsylvania Company, pushed through the state legislature by Scott, was the country's first holding company. It held all the many subsidiary companies which made up the Pennsylvania system. The Reading Company, which made possible the consolidation of railroad and coal-mining operations in the anthracite region, was another example of the combined interests that were brought together in this era under a single management. Railroad corporations based in Pennsylvania were among the "firsts" as large corporations in the age of big business in the United States.

Pennsylvanians also had dominant roles in the national railroad expansion of the times. Moncure Robinson built and managed much of the post-Civil War railroad system of the South. General William Palmer was among the men who helped develop the railroad systems of the West. With Philadelphia capital, he became the builder and manager of the Denver and Rio Grande, which had so large a role in developing the mineral wealth of the Colorado Rockies. W. Milnor Roberts, whose engineering career started with the Pennsylvania Canal, was a leader in setting up and operating the Northern Pacific. Tom Scott left the Pennsylvania Railroad to become head of the Union Pacific and later the Texas and Pacific. Robert Sayre and Asa Packer of the Lehigh Railroad system were nationally influential in the history of railroading in this era. Franklin B. Gowen was "ruler of the Reading" in the post-Civil War period of lusty and brawling enterprise which combined railroading with anthracite coal mining.

Pennsylvania furnished more than managerial genius to the railroads of the nation. George Westinghouse stands out as a genius in engineering the basic technical improvements that made the railroad the answer to the transportation needs of a nation that sprawled its bulk from the Mississippi River to the Pacific within a few short years after 1860. Westinghouse came from Schenectady, New York, to Pittsburgh because it was a place where things seemed to be on the move. This was in 1868. The same year a successful test of his revolutionary air brake was made on a Pennsylvania Railroad train out of Pittsburgh, using the steam from the locomotive to operate the braking system. A year later the Westinghouse Air Brake Company was in operation and the entire railroad system of the nation now for the first time was provided with a practical system of automatic brakes. Westinghouse quickly followed with his invention of a uniform control system for operation of switches and signals, which led to the

George Westinghouse, genius of railways and electricity.

creation of the Union Switch and Signal Company for manufacturing this equally important equipment. Westinghouse had made the modern railroad a reality. Standard-gauge track, standard time, steel freight and passenger cars, and coal-burning locomotives were other advances in railroading. Iron and steel bridges, built mostly in Pennsylvania mills, helped speed the newer and heavier trains on their way. The first sleeping car was operated out of Harrisburg and gave George Pullman ideas on de luxe passenger cars. The railroad was reaching just about the peak of its usefulness and service by 1900, aided by Pennsylvania invention and production.

OTHER ADVANCES IN TRANSPORTATION
AND COMMUNICATION

Though the new railroads revolutionized transportation, the old ways survived and remained useful in moving goods and people. The canal systems that had been built at such great cost and labor before 1860 remained useful in moving freight for several decades. The coal-carrying canals in particular were used well into the twentieth century. Portions of the main line of the old Pennsylvania Canal were used for some years after the Civil War, and this canal was doomed only in the 1890's when floods with their damage meant costly repairs. Freight wagons and passenger and mail coaches still moved along old Pennsylvania turnpikes and local dirt roads well after the coming of the modern railroad. Railroads could not be built everywhere; there remained, even after the turn of the century, many small towns and rural areas where the wagon and the stage were the only way to get goods or people from one place to another. Horse-and-buggy and wagon transportation, supplemented by sleds and sleighs in winter, was not by any stretch of the imagination put out of business by railroads before 1900.

Western Pennsylvania waterways became, if anything, more important in the new era of industrial growth. Coal and coke were moved on barges towed in long lines on the network of rivers about Pittsburgh. New locks were built to improve navigation on the western waters. Crude oil between 1860 and 1870 moved down the Allegheny and its tributaries to Pittsburgh refineries. Rivers and streams were the lifeblood of the lumbering industry. Huge rafts of logs and lumber jammed the narrow and turbulent waterways of western, northern, and central Pennsylvania in the days of the great lumber boom. Williamsport with its great Susquehanna River boom by 1880 was the great central Pennsylvania port of lumber days.

The shipyards along the Delaware were in the forefront of the revolution in American shipping and played an important part in the story of a new American navy after the Civil War. The war had doomed the wooden ship. The great Cramp Ship-building Company was reorganized in 1872 as the William Cramp & Sons Ship and Engine Company to build not only iron and steel ships but also new and vastly more powerful ship engines and propeller systems. Horace See and William Cramp were leading figures in the design of the new steel merchant marine and navy. John Roach built in his yards at Chester some of the largest of the new iron and steel steamships and naval vessels of the time. In 1900 Pennsylvania was first among all states in shipbuilding. Philadelphia's importance as a center for building ships helped it to keep a leading position as one of the nation's major seaports for export and import.

WESTINGHOUSE AND THE ELECTRICAL AGE

George Westinghouse was without question a greatest among the great inventive minds of his time. Besides developing the air brake, the uniform switch and signal system, and other inventions, he was the one man who made possible the practical use of electricity for lighting and power. Edison invented a serviceable light bulb in 1879 and four years later at Sunbury successfully used a three-wire electrical circuit to light a building. The great drawback to Edison's use of electricity was his insistence upon the use of direct current, which could not be transmitted long distances. Westinghouse put his inventive genius at work and developed the modern alternating-current method. His experiments in Pittsburgh were successful by 1886 and in 1890 he was able to demonstrate, also in Pittsburgh, practical street lighting with electricity. The role of the lamplighter in the American city was doomed. Westinghouse lighted the Chicago World's Fair with electricity in a convincing demonstration of its use. Before 1900 he also harnessed the power of Niagara Falls to generate electricity which could be transmitted long distances to the point of use. Westinghouse not only did all of this but in addition created his own company to manufacture the machinery and equipment needed in the new electrical age.

Electricity not only revolutionized street lighting in the nation's cities and in homes and public buildings, but also contributed to a revolution in

Rafting logs down to the lumber mills in the heyday of lumbering.

urban transportation, dooming the old-fashioned horse car. The electric trolley car was in common use by 1900 in cities and was rapidly becoming a major interurban transport facility. The first street railway system making exclusive use of electricity was in Scranton on November 30, 1886. By 1901 well over 2,000 miles of electric street railway and interurban lines were busily engaged in carrying nearly 600,000 passengers in Pennsylvania, more than the steam railroads. A new dimension had been added to the possible future growth of the American city.

LABOR FACES INDUSTRIAL CONSOLIDATION

The continued revolutionary growth of manufacturing and mining in terms not only of the volume and value of their gross product and dominance in the Pennsylvania economy but also the manifestations of large-scale business enter-prise posed new problems of the relationship of workers to capital, much more serious and de-manding than any which had appeared before 1860. The era of the small mill, factory, or mine controlled by one owner or at most by a few men organized as a partnership was rapidly being re-placed by larger business enterprises by 1880. The *Annual Report* of the Secretary of Internal Affairs for Pennsylvania in 1880–81, commented: "The massing of capital into the hands of an individual, or a limited number of individuals, to an excess above average possession, and used in the produc-tion of manufactured commodities, implies the collection of men in large bodies, whose condition is likely to be that of comparative poverty, as well as absolute dependence upon them for employ-ment." A narrow line was being drawn increas-ingly by 1870 between the few who employed and the many who were employed. Many of the con-ditions under which labor worked in the earlier days of the developing industrial revolution had been far from satisfactory—in particular the widespread exploitation of the labor of women and children in textile mills.

Much of this persisted after the Civil War. The mines made considerable use of teen-age boys in picking slate from coal, and similar operations in mines. Larger-scale mining and more use of machinery soon outmoded such labor. The steel mills employed as unskilled immigrant workers large numbers of boys in their teens who under later labor regulations would not have been allowed to work. In this sense child labor persisted. The grievances as to wages, hours, and general working conditions became increasingly serious. The railroads were guilty of serious abuses of labor in terms of wages and hours as well as lack of regard for proper safety conditions. Abundant contract immigrant labor so readily available in the steel mills meant a twelve-hour day and a seven-day week for most unskilled labor. From

seven in the morning until six at night for two weeks was followed by the "long turn," which meant from seven on Sunday morning through twenty-four hours up to Monday morning for a particular crew. True, this was followed by twenty-four hours off when the next two-week shift of crews took place. Only immigrant labor could be depended upon to accept such conditions. Skilled mill labor enjoyed an eight-hour day and better pay.

As late as 1900 thousands of unskilled steel mill workers received an average of fourteen cents an hour. Skilled labor was paid for the most part on a scale related to tonnage production, which in itself produced a drive to increase production steadily. A furnace foreman might earn as much as $9.00 a day. At the age of thirty-five even the best of steel workers were beginning to be "burned out" by the hours and strain. The dust in mills, the heat, and the strain of production under pressure took a heavy toll of workers'

Mining in the 1880's remained largely unmechanized. Horses or mules hauled the carts loaded with coal to the surface.

Child labor also prevailed in factories such as this glass factory in Philadelphia in 1880.

health. Accident averages in Pittsburgh steel mills were high; safety regulations in early days were nonexistent, or little observed. The record of English steel mills on all these fronts was incomparably better for the same period. The managers of the new steel industry could not have escaped the charge of excessive exploitation of labor in building their early empires.

The record for coal mining, whether bituminous or anthracite, was much the same. Indeed, much of the coal came from mines owned by either the steel companies or the railroads. In western Pennsylvania it was the steel or coke company that had its "captive" mines; in the anthracite region it was the railroads, through their holding-company operations such as the Reading Company. The all-powerful railroad interests pushed through the state legislature between 1868 and 1872 a series of laws which permitted creating corporations to hold the stock of other transportation and mining companies. Less well known and enjoying remarkable ano-

nymity during the days when poor John D. Rockefeller was being lambasted unmercifully for his petroleum trust, these Pennsylvania holding companies were probably the first real monopolies in the country, and they had the advantage of full legal sanction by state laws. Hours of labor in the mines varied along with wages. In the anthracite fields John Siney's Workingmen's Benevolent Association, perfected in 1868, was able to establish an average $2.50-per-day wage scale.

Led by the Reading Company's Franklin B. Gowen, the mine operators took advantage of the depressed conditions resulting from the Panic of 1873 to force wages to a lower level, at the same time breaking the union. In the course of this the power of newly consolidated capital was clearly shown. Under Gowen the Philadelphia and Reading Coal and Iron Company, which emerged in 1871, became the owner of some 100,000 acres of coal land and was in virtual control of the mining and transportation of coal so far as dictating wages, prices, and allocations of coal production and transportation was concerned. In the bituminous fields of western Pennsylvania Henry Clay Frick had built a similar monopoly of coal and coke production and was equally successful in beating down efforts at unionization. Frick also made extensive use of immigrant labor and cut wages to an average of about $1.60 a day while extracting the longest hours of work physically possible. Most mines of the time were without anything resembling modern safety applicances or practices, and serious accidents were common.

Still another abuse was the company town with its company store. The coal companies owned the houses, shoddy wooden shacks without any sanitary facilities, which they rented at a high rate to workers. The company store was a monopoly where the worker bought his food and supplies on credit charged against his wages. At the end of any given pay period little was left after the company had been paid the rent and store bill. This reduced cash wages for more than one coal miner to as low as $100 for an entire year of work. On top of this feudal economy there was organized by act of legislature in 1866 the infamous coal and iron police, a privately paid company police system which ruled not only on mine and mill property but in the company towns as well. Here they were the only law and order. Tales of their brutalities and invasion of personal rights and liberties of the workers in these towns rival those of the Cossacks of Russia or Hitler's Gestapo. Some five thousand coal and iron police were employed by mining and steel corporations by 1900.

Labor had two weapons with which to fight the newly powerful corporations. One of these was creating and strengthening the organization of labor in strong unions. The second was the strike; union organization usually led directly to use of the strike. All too often before 1900 the strike led to the downfall of the union. Corporate wealth was very powerful and well supported by the law; further, the dominant public opinion of the time considered it a vested property interest almost inviolate.

The effort of American labor to organize after the Civil War is very much a Pennsylvania story, just as it had been before 1860, due to the domi-

nance of mining, steelmaking, and transportation in the state's economy. William Sylvis, before an untimely death in 1869, was the leading figure in organizing the iron molders, who formed a national union in Philadelphia in 1859. In 1861 a secret organization of iron workers known as Sons of Vulcan was headed by Pittsburgh's Miles Humphrey. It abandoned secrecy in 1862 and emerged as the National Forge, still headed by Humphrey, and by 1876 was one of the stronger national unions. Its membership was made up of iron puddlers. Several craft unions of iron and steel workers grew up in this period and in 1876 they achieved unity in the Amalgamated Association of Iron and Steel Workers, better known as "the Amalgamated." Heads of the union were mainly Pennsylvanians. It won the support of a large percentage of skilled workers in iron and steel but never enrolled more than perhaps half the total number of workers. Unskilled immigrant labor was outside the union fold. Amalgamated's power was broken by the fateful Homestead strike. By 1900 not a single western Pennsylvania steel mill any longer had a union worker, though careful observers found the spirit of unionism still very much alive.

The story of coal is similar. John Siney, a native of Ireland who came to the Pennsylvania anthracite mines during the Civil War, succeeded in organizing the Workingmen's Benevolent Association. The Panic of 1873 and a glutted coal market enabled Franklin B. Gowen, the ruthless "ruler of the Reading" to destroy the W.B.A. Miners' wages collapsed from an average of $2.50 a day in 1872, won by the union, to $1.63 in 1881. Once more strikes ended in the death of the union. Closely associated with the miners' unions in spirit, and at times in attempted cooperation, was the Brotherhood of Locomotive Engineers which in 1863 grew out of the earlier Brotherhood of the Footboard. Three other railroad brotherhoods were organized in the next few years. The reliance on hard coal for freight by Pennsylvania railroads gave their workers considerable sympathy with mine labor.

Efforts to perfect some national organization of all labor which would bind the crafts together in a uniform fight for a better break for labor also centered largely in Pennsylvania. Between 1866 and 1872 efforts were made to establish the National Labor Union or Congress. William Sylvis was a force behind this movement in its formative stages. Uriah Stephens was another of its leaders. Stephens was also an organizer of the secret order which became the Knights of Labor. The Knights sought the union of all crafts and all types and classes of workers. In 1879 Terence Powderly became the Grand Master and in 1881 the Knights abandoned secrecy and came into the open as a strong, militant national union supporting the eight-hour day and other social reforms. It achieved at its peak a membership of possibly 700,000 workers. John M. Davis, editor of the *National Labor Tribune* in Pittsburgh, was another leader of the Knights. It too failed partly because of the Panic of 1893; also because such unfortunate incidents as the Chicago Haymarket riots in 1886 and the 1892 Homestead strike threw a fear of "anarchism" into the minds of conservatives, giving leaders of labor the label of dangerous radicals undermining the property system of the country. In the meantime, a new organization was being formed in a labor convention held in Pittsburgh in 1881—the Federation of Organized Trades and Labor Unions of the United States and Canada. This group reorganized in 1886 as the American Federation of Labor and adopted with success the tactic of federating independent unions, which retained their cherished craft independence.

The advance of labor before 1900 had been strong, but in every instance other than railroad labor it went down later to defeat. The use of the strike proved the undoing of labor. Strikes were numerous in those days but only a few made headlines. One of these was the great railroad strike in 1877. It started over the question of wages and the practice of combining two trains under one crew. The use of the "double header," as it was known, was especially common in moving trains from Altoona over the mountains by way of the Horseshoe Curve and was a particular grievance against the Pennsylvania. Pittsburgh in those days nursed a sense of injury from the company because it was widely believed, with some truth, that the Pennsylvania discriminated

An artist's sketch of the meeting headquarters of the Amalgamated Iron Workers in 1882.

in rates and in other ways against the Steel City. Many of the citizens supported the striking railroaders, with resulting rioting and destruction of property; this forced Governor Hartranft to call out troops to restore order. Soldiers also had to be used at Reading to protect the Reading Company in that city.

In the anthracite fields a sympathy strike by miners was also attempted without success. A year earlier President Gowen of the Reading had used a Pinkerton detective and the Reading's coal and iron police to ferret out the leaders of a secret order in the anthracite region known as the Molly Maguires. Since it was made up mainly of Irish coal miners, the Molly organization almost inevitably became tied into the labor unrest of that region. Several leaders were rounded up and tried for murder as a result of attacks made on mine foremen and other management representatives. Ten Mollys were hanged at Pottsville June 21, 1877; others followed, while some were jailed. This added to the public damnation of labor in the anthracite region as dangerous and even murderous. This attitude had been building up since 1875 when rioting and destruction of coal company property on the part of striking miners at Hazleton had forced Governor Hartranft into his first use of troops against striking workers.

Equally unfortunate and even more damning to labor was the Homestead strike in 1892. Like railroad tycoon Franklin B. Gowen, the coke and steel king Henry Clay Frick seems to have dedicated himself to a determined effort to destroy union labor. Frick had broken the backs of labor in his mines and coke plants before joining Carnegie's growing empire of steel. Carnegie himself was known for restraint in labor relations and even toyed with such advanced ideas as a cooperative store in which workers could hold stock and learn that "business had its difficulties." Tough steel man though he was, Carnegie's right-hand man in management, Captain "Bill" Jones, was close to his men and even believed in an eventual eight-hour day. Amalgamated's favorable contract with the Carnegie Company was subject to review in 1892. Frick, in the absence of Carnegie in Scotland, proposed to reduce the sliding-scale tonnage basis for determining the wages of skilled steel workers. The actual difference between the company's and the union's demands ended up as a dollar a ton but Frick arbitrarily closed the plant on June 29 and barricaded it, also hiring armed guards. Frick's effort on July 5 to bring in armed Pinkerton "watchmen" by river barge to break up the strike led to an inevitable battle in which twenty-five persons were killed. The Allegheny County sheriff attempted to bring in armed deputies on July 12 and also met resistance. Continuing disorder forced Governor Pattison to send in the National Guard to patrol Homestead for six months. When the New York anarchist Alexander Berkman attempted to kill Frick in his office later in July the incident further blackened the reputation of labor, though neither the strikers nor their leaders had anything whatsoever to do with Berkman's crazy attack.

At a later Congressional investigation Frick stated openly that his purpose from the start had been breaking the union. He declared without reservation: ". . . we wanted men with whom we could deal individually. We did not propose to deal with the Amalgamated Association . . . as we

A drawing portraying the trial of the Molly Maguires at Pottsville.

Western Pennsylvania mining areas were notorious for company towns like this one at Throop, ruled by coal and iron police.

had plainly told them." An impartial later student of the strike from the Russell Sage Foundation stated: "The strike, for the most part, seems to have been well managed and the conduct of the strikers orderly." That was before the arrival of the Pinkerton men. Whatever the rights or wrongs of the strike, it effectively destroyed the unions in the steel mills of Pittsburgh for some time to come.

The picture of the growth of industry in the state is one of revolutionary progress before the turn of the century. It was the heyday of the iron, steel, and coal regimes that contributed so much to making the state an industrial leader. It was also the era in which the petroleum reserves of the state were exploited to their fullest potential. A new industry had been born with the "discovery"

of aluminum. The railroad had tied the state together with rails of steel which reached far beyond its own borders to link the state with the expanding growth of the nation. It was an era in which capital thrived with virtually no limitations upon its power to do as it pleased. Neither corporations nor individuals were burdened with more than a modicum of taxation by the state or national government, and even the income tax had been struck down by the courts. Labor could be dealt with just about as management pleased, and while strikes were unpleasant they ended uniformly by strengthening capital rather than labor. Viewing it from almost any angle, one finds it hard to think of the years from 1865 to 1900 as anything other than a golden age for the titan of industry which Pennsylvania had spawned.

CHAPTER THIRTEEN

SOCIAL AND CULTURAL CHANGE IN THE POST-BELLUM YEARS

The impact of the economic revolution taking place in Pennsylvania in the three decades from 1870 to 1900, the development of the great new steel industry, a remarkable increase in utilization of basic natural resources, the spread of railroads, and a tremendous concentration of new wealth and power in the hands of the business class could hardly help making itself felt in terms of cultural and social changes. Greater wealth was placed in the hands of more people; a lot more in the hands of some entrepreneurs who became millionaires almost overnight. There was a marked growth of cities and urban living, while rural life declined with the reduction of population on farms or in small towns. As a result, the social and cultural development of Pennsylvania in this era was just about as remarkable as was its economic advance. Certainly it was also just as significant in the state's total history.

THE CHANGING POPULATION

Pennsylvania was still a growing state after 1870. Its population at that date of 3,521,951 grew by the turn of the century to 6,302,115. This was an average growth of 21 per cent per decade. This rate of growth was, however, about 10 per cent less than that of the decades between 1800 and 1860 and indicated a gradual change in the population-growth pattern of the state. More important as an influence on the pattern of the life of Pennsylvanians was the marked urban growth evident during the era. City populations increased about 40 per cent. There were in 1870 only seventy-five communities in Pennsylvania classified as urban by the United States Census; the number in 1900 was 190. In 1870 Pennsylvania still held its position as a predominantly rural state, with 62.7 per cent of the total population living on farms or in communities of less than 2,500 people. By the census of 1900 Pennsylvania for the first time showed a preponderant number of persons living in urban centers—54.7 per cent as compared with 45.3 per cent living in rural areas. The larger towns and the cities had won in the long race to determine the lives and fortunes of a majority of the people.

The pattern of urban growth is worth notice.

Philadelphia held its place easily as Pennsylvania's first city and the nation's second largest. It grew from 674,022 in 1870 to 1,293,697 dwellers within its limits in 1900. Pittsburgh in 1900 still had less than half the population of Philadelphia, despite a more rapid rate of growth. Pittsburgh in 1870 was a city of 139,256 persons and reached 451,512 in 1900. Pittsburgh's remarkable industrial growth was accompanied by increases in population in the decades of the seventies and eighties; these ran to 60 and 70 per cent while Philadelphia was averaging about 20 per cent. This in turn was a reflection of the fact that Philadelphia was more mature industrially and characterized by a much less spectacular industrial expansion after the Civil War. The typical Pennsylvania city which followed a normal pattern of growth between 1870 and 1900 just about doubled its population. Some cities tripled their growth, or a little better; this invariably was a reflection of economic factors. Allentown, Chester, Erie, Altoona, Johnstown, Reading, Oil City, Wilkes-Barre, Scranton, and York were among the Pennsylvania cities that experienced an above normal growth in the era.

In each instance the cause of this is readily observable. Pennsylvania down to 1880 did not owe its population expansion to immigration. As a matter of fact, the foreign-born population was less in 1880 than in 1870—13.7 per cent in the later year as compared with 15.5 per cent in 1870. The larger part of the immigrant population down to 1880 was concentrated in Philadelphia and the anthracite region. It was largely of German, Irish, and Welsh stock. By 1900 the greatly increased use of immigrant contract labor in the mills and mines of western Pennsylvania pushed upward the levels of the foreign-born in the total population. Pittsburgh's foreign-born population very nearly doubled between 1880 and 1900; in terms of proportion of total population, it did double from 3 per cent to 6 per cent. The new immigration was mainly from Slavic and from southern Europe, bringing in large numbers of Austrians, Hungarians, Russians, and Italians. These new immigrants provided a large percentage of the unskilled labor force for the mills and mines of the Pittsburgh region, but very few settled in other parts of the state, where openings for this type of labor no longer existed. The new immigrants gave a clearly different pattern of life to western Pennsylvania steel and mining towns.

CHANGES ON THE FARM

The life of the typical Pennsylvania farmer changed considerably after the Civil War under the impact of an expanding economy and steadily improving transportation and communication. More small towns serving the needs of a surrounding farm area sprang up. The average farmer by 1900 lived within ten miles or less from a town where there was a variety of stores, often a bank, and possibly a small "opera house." The country general store, usually at some crossroad, which sold everything from groceries to clothing and tools, still existed in the smallest towns. But the larger towns had rather specialized stores for hardware, clothing, food, feed and grain, and the like. The products sold in the stores were manufactured elsewhere rather than in the shop of some town artisan or craftsman, as had been common in the earlier day of the local tailor, blacksmith, or boot and shoe maker. At the level of the smaller farm-community towns there did persist, however, the need for the special services of carpenters, blacksmiths, wagon makers, millers, cheese makers, and the like. These were commonly known after the Civil War as the "hand trades" and were apt to be one-man operations. The census of manufactures in 1900 showed that some 50 per cent of Pennsylvania's total industrial establishments were in this category, though the value of their product in relation to the total value of the state's manufactures was insignificant.

While farmers were able increasingly to sell their products for ready cash which they could use to pay for goods and services, a surprising amount of more or less barter economy persisted even after 1870 in the more remote rural areas of Pennsylvania. A farmer might still take his grain to the miller to be ground, the miller keeping a part of the product as "toll" to pay for the grinding. Or the farmer in northern counties might be a partner in a small community cheese factory. He accepted cheese and curd for the family and whey for his hogs as part payment for his milk.

231

This farmhouse, built about 1880, is on its original site and is typical of its day. It is the Victorian-exhibit house at the Pennsylvania Farm Museum.

In this horse-and-buggy era it was still an all-day trip to most larger towns and back home again for many a farmer. Farm families therefore remained amazingly self-sufficient as to food. The farm garden produced vegetables to be canned in glass jars or stored in bins in the cellar for winter use. The farm orchard supplied the family with its apples or other fruit while some wild berries might find their way into glass jars either whole or as jam or jelly. Bread and pastries were sure to be a product of the farm wife's own oven. Pork and beef were also provided in most farm communities from animals raised and slaughtered on the farm. Only "fancy" groceries were bought in town. These included such necessities as tea, coffee, sugar, salt, and spices. On occasion a few oranges, some store candy, or bananas might find their way into the farm home from a visit to town, much to the delight of the children. Farm homes were better furnished and more comfortable in this era as a natural result of having a little more

money at hand. The farmer was now buying "store clothes"; the age of homespun came to an end with the appearance of ready-made factory clothing. The era after 1870 was one in which, in many more recently settled parts of the state, farmers were building new houses and barns to replace older log or other more crude farm buildings. This was true especially in northern and western counties. Fireplaces went out entirely and kitchen ranges of cast iron and parlor-type heating stoves came in. The kerosene lamp replaced the candle in lighting the farm home. Factory-made furniture was common in farm homes by 1890, including the plush sofas and chairs for the "Sunday parlor."

A larger community life was opened to the Pennsylvania farmer in several ways in this era. One of the most important was the founding of the National Patrons of Husbandry, or Grange. This more or less fraternal order for farmers, possessing all of the attractions fraternalism holds for

*The parlor was the "Sunday room" in most farm homes of the period. This is
the parlor in the Victorian House at the Pennsylvania Farm Museum.*

the average person—secret rituals, fanciful titles for officials, and a special secret initiation ceremony for new members—was conceived in the mind of a clerk in the new Department of Agriculture in Washington. His name was Oliver H. Kelley.

This rather unexciting individual in 1867 decided to develop his idea, which he had now formalized by visiting farm communities throughout the nation and setting up subordinate Granges. His route west was through Harrisburg; it was here that Kelley granted his first "dispensation" to organize a subordinate Grange. It was not used, and it was not until 1871 that the first successful Grange in Pennsylvania was set up in Lycoming County. Two years later the idea had caught on to the extent that the Pennsylvania State Grange was established at a meeting in Reading. By 1876 there were over four hundred Granges in the state with some eighteen thousand members, and the movement caught fire to a

point where Pennsylvania became by 1900 one of the leading centers of The National Grange. Farmers now were gathering in Grange halls throughout the state.

Here their meeting was opened with simple but impressive fraternal ceremonies led by officials elected by the group who bore special titles and carried with the office special fraternal-order duties. New members were inducted in a formal ritual. All of this was followed by a lecture by some person selected by the Grange "Lecturer." This was an undoubted carry-over from the lyceum idea in town life and was an effort to bring to farm people new and outside ideas. A social hour followed. The Grange also sponsored country dances and suppers at the hall which were an important part of farm life.

The *Farm Journal* was started in Philadelphia in 1877; the same year the *National Stockman and Farmer* was founded in Pittsburgh. The farmer profited from increased circulation of these maga-

*A typical farm
kitchen of the 1890's.*

zines. About the same time the nationwide weekly newspaper *Grit,* published at Williamsport and still appearing, began its career and soon reached into every part of the nation with its weekly edition. At the end of the nineties, the Philadelphia merchant prince, John Wanamaker, and now Postmaster General under President Benjamin Harrison, began the experiments in the Rural Free Delivery service through which mail was brought from the nearest town post office to the farmer at his farm mail box. The towns of New Stanton and Ruffsdale in western Pennsylvania and the city of Lancaster were among the places selected to start this experiment. It was in the nineties that the Pennsylvania State College began the scheme of agricultural extension courses through a system of correspondence-school instruction by mail for the benefit of the Pennsylvania farmer.

It took the automobile truly to revolutionize the social life of the farmer, but lacking it, farm folk managed to get around quite a bit even in the horse-and-buggy days. Roads were better and the horse and buggy or carriage could carry people in summer to places some distance away for an evening of dancing or singing. Community

schoolhouses and the Grange hall were favorite places for community gatherings. Of course weddings and funerals were still places for people to get together for at least a "visit." The community church was a gathering place on Sunday and perhaps attracted people quite as much for a chance to see each other as to listen to the sermons and take part in the service. The haying and harvesting season often continued to furnish a need for farmers to group together in a cooperative attack on the major problem of getting in the hay or the grain, lacking much farm machinery to ease and speed the labor. The fall threshing season was another occasion for a cooperative effort, as in many regions the only mechanical thresher was owned by some enterprising person who went from farm to farm hiring his steam engine and threshing machine at a price. This meant that threshing was a major undertaking and several farmers usually grouped together for the needed help. The women also might cooperate in feeding the threshers, as this was a task the average farm housewife could hardly cope with by herself. All in all, farm life was not as unpleasant or without social diversion in those days as sometimes is assumed. It had undergone something of a revo-

234

lution since log cabin days but was far from that of today. As of 1900, Pennsylvania farm life was simple and more or less Victorian. It would take the automobile, the improved road, with radio and television to work a further revolution.

THE CHANGING PATTERN OF TOWN LIFE

The census defined everything from a small town to a large city as "urban," but life in the smaller town was different, certainly, from that in the larger centers of population. The smaller towns were country-store and blacksmith-shop towns, and they served a more or less crossroads rural region. The larger towns were the centers which met the needs of a surrounding area radiating outward perhaps ten miles in all directions by road. If they were well located, they were apt after 1870 to be served by a railroad line with both freight and some passenger service. In a day when railroads have nearly or entirely vanished as a local transportation service in the face of the automobile, bus, and truck it is difficult to appreciate the great importance of the railroads of an earlier

day. Railroads were built everywhere there seemed a prospect for traffic and this took them into even the most remote communities of Pennsylvania in search of business provided by the local industries. Railroads brought goods and people to the towns; they also took them away. Hence, even the smallest town on a railroad line had a link with the larger and more cosmopolitan world of the outside which lifted it above the sleepy villages of an older time. The railroad brought to towns business and businessmen, including the "drummers" selling goods to the stores, from an outside and larger world.

Some small villages, such as Titusville, in the heart of the new oil regions, after 1859 grew larger almost overnight as business centers. Oil City, which got its start and its name from the oil boom, grew from a town of 2,000 to one of 13,000 in three decades. Northern Pennsylvania's lumber industry led many established towns such as county seats to grow considerably and also encouraged new boom towns devoted to lumbering and allied industries. As was the case with the oil-boom towns, most of these truly boom towns

The country store at the Pennsylvania Farm Museum, a re-creation of the country store common before and after 1900.

disappeared when the lumbermen left; but in 1900 lumbering was still a big business in the northern lumber woods and many towns were flourishing with their tanneries and woodworking industries. In older parts of the state the towns that served rural regions did not change very much, except possibly to grow a little larger with the growth of the general economy and possibly to develop some small-town industries such as milling. The pattern of life in the smaller Pennsylvania town varied with different parts of the state: along with their architecture Pennsylvania German country towns were compact with their brick or stone buildings built close to the street, while a northern Pennsylvania town was spread out and often followed the New England pattern of building out from a town square, which, if a county seat, was dominated by the county courthouse. By 1900 larger brick store buildings arranged in a continuous row on Main Street were common in most Pennsylvania towns. Side streets were residential. Small-town people actually lived in this era much the same as farm people and the town was an enlarged farm community. The stores and small industries served farmers primarily. The town was the place for the larger churches and the high school, which by 1900 was becoming more common all over the state. It was almost certain to have one or more hotels to accommodate the needs of the traveler for rest and refreshment. It was a busy place on Saturday nights when the surrounding farm families came to town for shopping and banking and perhaps to attend some diversion such as a band concert. In some larger towns this might include even a traveling theatrical performance in the local "opera house" or theater. The town was the place where the doctors were, and the lawyers. Here also were funeral directors, the photographer's studio, and such other special services as catered to the people's special needs. Towns were where political campaigns and elections were centered; if of larger size the town was apt to have a weekly-newspaper office and printery. Even the small town might well have a community band and other more or less organized social and cultural activities such as were common to that day. These could include music, discussion or debate, politics, or just plain fun. After all, the town was the center for such organized social and cultural activity as was common outside the larger city; without diversions of a modern day there appears to have been more such activity at the local community level in that era than is common today.

The town of that time had few community problems and made few demands upon the taxpayer for community services. Streets were not paved and presented few problems of maintenance other than sometimes wetting down the summer dust on the main street with a wagon-type sprinkler, or filling in ruts and the worst mud holes on occasion. Crossroad small towns did not worry about streets or other services. Volunteer fire companies with hand-drawn equipment took care of fires. Brick, gravel or flat-stone sidewalks were maintained as a rule only on the main street. Street lights, using gas or coal oil, were hardly a problem, except in the largest towns, and there they were limited to a main street. Sewage and garbage disposal were problems for the individual householder and not the community; the same was usually true of water supply. The town constable, an elected official, handled law and order under ordinary circumstances. The justice of the peace in his home or office was the court for a majority of offenders against the law. Major violations of the law were carried to a county court.

THE PENNSYLVANIA CITY AFTER 1870

All Pennsylvania cities other than Philadelphia were in a growing-up stage before 1900; only Philadelphia could by the greatest stretch of the imagination be looked upon as genuinely a city in the post-bellum years. After all, the average Pennsylvania "city" as late as 1870 ranged in population from as little as 10,000 to a maximum of about 30,000. As pointed out earlier, they doubled or tripled in size in the next thirty years. This was the product of the revolutionary growth of manufacturing, mining, or transportation, as it influenced the particular city. The typical Pennsylvania city by the turn of the century was peopled by considerably less than 50,000 persons; the distinguishing difference between the city of 1900 and that of earlier vintage was the growth of the economy. Every single Pennsylvania city which experienced notable expansion after the Civil War owed its growth to this factor. Johnstown grew as a result of the new steel industry. Altoona grew because of the Pennsylvania Railroad; Wilkes-Barre and Scranton were anthracite coal towns, though Scranton had an iron industry as well. Reading and Allentown were textile centers, though Allentown shared in the birth of the Portland cement industry. The creation of the Pennsylvania industrial centers, which as a group had become fairly well outlined even before the Civil War, was a part of the growth pattern of American cities as hubs of industrial and business activity. Industry and mining, rather than commerce, now determined the future of the Pennsylvania city and governed its character.

The growing city quickly lost all the basic characteristics of the large town, which many of them actually were about 1860. The new city blossomed forth with large brick, iron, and steel buildings in the central area, site of the new department-type of store, the larger bank, office buildings to house the new and multiplying functions of an age of larger-scale industry and business, and the specialty shops and services common to a modern city. It began by 1900 to pave its major streets as well as light and police them. The residential sections of the city changed, and often the older and more central areas which had provided housing for the upper-income families were taken over by those in lower-income brackets as the former owners moved toward suburban residential areas which now could be reached by trolleys. Thus began the problems of the so-called city slums, which would increasingly perplex the larger cities.

The outskirts of the city began to be filled with mills and factories as larger-scale industry sought more room than could be found in the more central area. Often earlier and more central industrial buildings were abandoned and the city began to be characterized by a greater separation into residential, business, and industrial districts. The problem of regulating these zones would soon become a major problem of municipal government. As cities grew larger, problems of water supply, sanitation, sewage and housing began to assume serious proportions. Not much was done about them

before 1900, and even as large a city as Pittsburgh was plagued by epidemics of typhoid before it realized something must be done. By 1890 almost every city had a board of health and was giving serious thought to public health problems.

Lighting major streets in the central areas was solved by the use of artificial or natural gas or oil until George Westinghouse by the turn of the century made electricity a factor in improving city lighting. His inventive genius also gave a boost to urban transportation with the electric trolley as an answer to growing transportation problems. Electric light, power, and traction companies were organized in most cities by the end of the eighties. By 1900 the electric utility company was becoming of real service in lighting Pennsylvania cities as well as furnishing power for electric trolley lines. The average Pennsylvania city, however, by 1900 was still in its infancy in grappling with the problems of sanitation, public health, housing, police, lighting, and transportation. These were problems thrust upon the people without much warning or opportunity for preparation. They were the penalty paid for rapid growth.

The Pennsylvania city was changing slowly on other fronts and gradually adopting the ways of a new era. People brought together in larger numbers made demands, for example, upon medicine. Medical societies began to appear at the level of the county and city. The dispensary and the hospital came to the smaller cities. Reading opened a dispensary in 1868 and it grew into the Reading Hospital, a building for which was opened in 1886. Three years later the Reading Hospital started a school of nursing and graduated its first nurses in 1891. Another institution, Community General Hospital, was opened in the same year, and the Catholic St. Joseph's Hospital was established in the same period. Reading began also to do something about a city park; Bethlehem and Harrisburg were thinking along the same lines by 1900. New public buildings began to demand some attention with the growth of local government. Reading began a new city hall in 1870, about the same time as Philadelphia and Pittsburgh. Organized sports made their appearance with baseball and basketball by 1900. Additional buildings to house stage productions were built.

Reading built a Grand Opera House in 1873; Lancaster already had its famous Fulton Theatre, built in the 1850's. Some of the greatest names in music and the stage appeared in these theaters. The literary society, the musical association, the lyceum, the choir or singing society, and the art club or society were other expressions of culture evident in almost all Pennsylvania cities of the post-bellum era.

PITTSBURGH REACHES TOWARD A BETTER LIFE

Perhaps in no single American city of the time were more millionaires created in the space of not more than a couple of decades than in Pittsburgh between 1880 and 1900. Steel did it; and at the same time, steel was turning Pittsburgh and its suburbs into a glorified mill-town region housing the thousands of immigrant contract laborers under some of the worst living conditions to be found in the entire nation. Amidst the smoke which hung over lower Pittsburgh and within short walking distance of the Duquesne Club, the "millionaire's club" of Pittsburgh, was a nest of wooden shantylike tenements into which were crowded without a thought to sanitary or other facilities thousands of immigrant steel workers. Though these housing conditions and the accompanying social evils were a black blot on the Pittsburgh of the eighties and nineties it nevertheless was a city in which strivings toward social and cultural progress were very evident.

Andrew Carnegie, wealthiest of all the multi-millionaires made by steel, began to preach his doctrine of the social responsibility of great wealth just before 1890. He tried once without success to give Pittsburgh a fine library and cultural center, which the city fathers rejected. Fortunately for Pittsburgh, Carnegie renewed his offer and in 1895 the Carnegie Museum and Library, an imposing Italian Renaissance style building in Oakland, was opened to the public. Over half a million people visited it in 1897. The first Carnegie International Art Show was held there in 1896. Henry Phipps, a Carnegie partner, built the noted Phipps Conservatory nearby. Pittsburgh already had the Allegheny Observatory, founded in 1860 with the aid of William Thaw.

Pittsburgh's absentee landlord, Mrs. Mary Schenley, late in 1889 presented the city with magnificent Schenley Park, opened to the public in 1893.

An interest in the arts was evident among Pittsburgh millionaires by the nineties. "Many valuable paintings and works of art are treasured in the homes of some of our wealthiest citizens," noted Kelly's *Handbook* in 1895. Pittsburgh began really to appear on the country's musical map in 1896 when the Pittsburgh Orchestra developed from the Symphony Society presented its first concert. Two years later the great Victor Herbert became conductor for some six years. Pittsburgh boasted in the nineties that it was "one of the best theatrical towns in America." Its Academy of Music and New Grand Opera House did attract the best in musical and theatrical entertainment and Pittsburgh enjoyed an above average position as a center for the theater. It had organized an Art Society and an Academy of Sciences and Arts. In 1894 Mrs. Schenley presented the local Daughters of the American Revolution with the historic Fort Pitt Blockhouse at the Point as a lasting landmark of the city's beginnings. A historical society was launched to preserve and memorialize the city's history.

Pittsburgh was not without a social conscience; and such it might properly have had in view of the social problems the city presented. The Reverend George Hodges of Pittsburgh's "millionaire" church, Calvary Episcopal, was joined by Father Sheedy of St. Mary's Catholic Church at the Point, in major social projects. Kingsley House social settlement was started in 1894. A day school for the care of children, children's playgrounds, and free Sunday afternoon concerts were other social experiments. Pittsburgh women were the first in the state to organize a Women's Club, and a Civic Club was founded in 1895 to fight for parks and playgrounds and other civic improvements. Concern for care of the unfortunate was increasingly evident. A Pittsburgh Association for the Improvement of the Poor was organized in 1875 and was followed ten years later by a Children's Aid Society. Catholic charities appeared with the House of the Good Shepherd in 1872 and the Home for Working Girls in 1888. The Allegheny Association for Improvement of

The Pittsburgh Exposition, from an 1878 drawing.

the Poor was founded in 1895 with county funds and a year earlier the new Pittsburgh City Home, Hospital, and Insane Asylum was opened.

During the severe unemployment and suffering in the winter of 1893–94 induced by the Panic of 1893, over $250,000 was raised by citizens' committees for relief of Pittsburgh's unemployed; of this Carnegie himself gave $125,000. Some sixty thousand persons were given aid, mostly on needed work projects such as new city parks. The city itself spent over $133,000 in the same period on poor relief. Pittsburgh at the turn of the century could well be proud of the extent to which it had rallied to challenges of a steel-city environment and problems.

PHILADELPHIA, THE CENTENNIAL CITY

Philadelphia became known throughout the world in 1876 as the "Centennial City." This well characterized its position in the post-bellum era.

Philadelphia grew in its manufactures, commerce, business and financial strength as well as in population but by no means in as spectacular a way as Pittsburgh or Scranton. Despite a slowing down of its growth, it was still Pennsylvania's oldest and most distinguished city; indeed, it kept its prestige as one of the nation's most distinguished. Its older society looked with calm, if not amusement, upon the efforts of newly rich Pittsburgh to achieve some cultural standing; Philadelphia already had it. If there had existed any doubt as to Philadelphia's place in the nation it was settled when people from all over the nation and indeed the world trekked to Penn's once green country town to celebrate the great centennial of American independence in 1876. Here was the nation's greatest single historical landmark, the birthplace of its independence in the old Pennsylvania State House, now becoming known as Independence Hall. Philadelphia itself hardly fifty years earlier had been aroused to prevent the shortsighted state

Independence Hall as it looked in 1876, when it was visited by thousands during the great Centennial.

government from allowing this great monument to freedom in the modern world to be razed.

Philadelphia in 1876 was one of the world's largest and finest cities. It was spread over more than 129 square miles, making it the largest city in land area in the world. Its size was the greater as a result of the consolidation in 1854 which made the city and county one. Its population in 1876 was estimated at 817,000, of whom some 200,000 were foreign born. The immigrant stock was mostly German, Irish, and Italian. Philadelphia prided itself upon being the "city of homes" for 130,000 out of a total of 140,000 buildings in the city were homes. The city already was noted for its substantial brick "row" houses attached one to the other and lining entire streets. Newspapers boasted that Philadelphia workers were housed better than those of any other city but the more critical were able to point to sections which were rapidly becoming slum areas. Downtown Philadelphia was still notable for residences of the upper class though an exodus to the "Main Line"

and the suburbs, aided by excellent suburban railroad transportation provided by the Reading and the Pennsylvania, was under way. The Quaker City was quite advanced in its improvements, compared with the city of that day. It had a large mileage of paved streets, mostly brick or cobblestone. It had a paid fire department and a professional police department. It had a central city water supply, though people complained even then that the water was not as pure and tasty as it might be. The Philadelphia *Press* boasted in 1876 that "there are more bathrooms in this city, in proportion to its population, than in any other city in the world." Free baths for the poor were provided in summer by charitable missions. Despite all of these advances, the city had a very high death rate among American cities and was troubled with epidemics of typhoid.

Philadelphia society and culture continued at a high level. The coming of the Centennial itself had taken some doing on the part of Philadelphians. The city and state contributed about one-

240

half of the ten millions the Centennial cost. The Centennial buildings were located in a portion of beautiful Fairmount Park, by far the largest park enjoyed by any American city. Approaches to it by bridge and roadways were greatly improved. The new city hall had been started in 1871 and became a showplace. The new building of the Academy of Natural Sciences was partially opened early in 1876. The Academy of Music was another showplace. The new home of the Pennsylvania Academy of the Fine Arts was opened also in 1876 and some buildings of the University of Pennsylvania, recently moved to its new and present location, were completed. These, with numerous other distinguished examples of fine American architecture which were of earlier date, gave the visitor to Philadelphia in 1876 a good idea of the city's greatness in many fields of American cultural, scientific and educational endeavors. Philadelphia was noted for its conservative but nevertheless extensive and lively society. Balls, receptions, and assemblies were a feature of the city's social life and especially lively in 1876 when so many national and international dignitaries were visiting. Quaker tradition still frowned upon the theater and a performance of the French operetta *La Jolie Parfumeuse* at the Arch Street Theater was looked upon as rather naughty. Several notable theaters played to the visiting public despite this viewpoint and on their boards appeared such great Philadelphians as Mrs. Drew and Edwin Booth. The Centennial itself attracted a more cosmopolitan society to Philadelphia and helped break down some of its earlier Quakerish conservatism.

Philadelphia was slowing down considerably in new and remarkable developments in science and medicine in the years after the Civil War. The city, however, was secure in its position as probably the greatest single center of modern medicine and surgery, and possessed of some of the truly outstanding hospitals in the nation. Its medical schools, such as Jefferson, Hahnemann, the Women's Medical College, and the Philadelphia College of Pharmacy and Science, upheld Philadelphia's reputation in this field. The Franklin Institute, the American Philosophical Society, the Wistar Institute of Anatomy and Biology,

founded in 1892, and other centers for scientific study, research, and invention upheld Philadelphia's reputation as a major force in the scientific growth of the nation. To the University of Pennsylvania as a leading center for higher education there was added in 1891 the Drexel Institute of Technology and in 1888 Temple University. At nearby Bryn Mawr was located in 1880 one of the nation's outstanding women's colleges. Viewed from any standpoint, Philadelphia was one of the nation's truly distinguished cities.

Entrance to Jefferson Medical College, Philadelphia.

Central High School in Philadelphia, a far cry from the old log schools.

GROWTH IN EDUCATION

Pennsylvania had moved ahead in public education before the Civil War and at its end more than 600,000 pupils taught by some 12,000 teachers were enrolled in the public school system created in 1834. James P. Wickersham as Superintendent of Common Schools in the post-bellum years deserves great credit for further advancing the state public school program over a period of some fourteen years. Cities and towns with 10,000 or more population were allowed to organize their schools under local superintendents who were required to be college or normal school graduates. In 1873 the new state Constitution provided for a "thorough and efficient system of public schools" which were to be open to all children at six years of age. The Department of Public Instruction was created; this gave more stature to the state system of public education, and the legislature was obligated to support it financially, aided by local school funds.

Advances followed closely. In 1887 a minimum-six-month term was reached; free textbooks came in 1893, and two years later compulsory attendance for children from eight to thirteen was required. Shortly after this the state adopted its first minimum-salary scales for teachers, a major step toward better teaching. In 1865 there were only a few high schools in the state, mostly in Philadelpia. The academy continued to serve most of the state at this level of education. In 1887 high schools were authorized in the larger districts and in 1895 they were approved as a part of the public school system in all districts. Soon after this the state began to aid rural high school development with direct appropriations. By 1900 there were some four hundred high schools in Pennsylvania. Attention was turned also to general kindergarten education, in which Philadelphia pioneered in 1887 when the city school system assumed responsibility for some thirty public kindergartens. The state authorized public kindergartens in 1897. Concern for industrial education in the schools was spurred by the opening in the 1870's of the Public Industrial Arts School by Philadelphia. Advances were made in training teachers as the state's normal-school system was expanded by providing some state aid in 1874. All in all, the state's public school system had assumed a modern aspect by 1900.

Higher education likewise moved forward with several major new institutions founded, which kept Pennsylvania foremost among all the states in the number of its colleges and universities. Even more important than numbers were the modern trends in higher education evident in these institutions. Among the new colleges that emerged were Albright College, 1866; Duquesne University, 1878; Elizabethtown College, 1900; Grove City College, 1876; Juniata College, 1876; La Salle College, 1863; Lebanon Valley College, 1866; Muhlenberg College, 1868; Temple University, 1888; Thiel College, 1866; University of Scranton, 1888; Ursinus College, 1869. Several of these were small denominational colleges still primarily designed for training in the ministry.

Education for women moved forward with rapid strides with the founding of Bryn Mawr, in 1880; Wilson College, 1869; Cedar Crest, 1868; Pennsylvania College for Women, 1869; Mercyhurst College for Women, 1871. Lehigh University, founded in 1866, Drexel Institute, founded in 1891, and Carnegie Institute of Technology, founded in 1900, resulted from the need for more technical training. The University of Pennsylvania, the Western University of Pennsylvania, and the Pennsylvania State College reacted to the same demand by developing more fully their work in the sciences and engineering. Penn State became a center for advances in scientific agriculture and studies in animal nutrition. New Catholic influences in education were represented by La Salle University, Duquesne University, and Mercyhurst College. The outlines of the modern college and university with broadened liberal-arts education and increased emphasis upon the sciences were clearly established by 1900. Along with it went a gradual increase in enrollment as the doors of a college and university education were slowly opening to a much larger segment of the population.

THE MAGAZINE AND THE NEWSPAPER

In the ante-bellum era Philadelphia had become known as the "Magazine City" and it lost little of this reputation after 1870. This was due in large measure to the new giant of the world of magazine publishing, Cyrus H. K. Curtis. The publisher started his magazine career in 1879 with the weekly *Tribune & Farmer*. Curtis pioneered in introducing into this essentially farm magazine a column of news and comment designed especially for women and appearing under the name of his wife, Louisa Kapp. Out of this grew the idea for the famous *Ladies' Home Journal*, which by 1889 had achieved a circulation of over half a million copies. Edward Bok became famous as its editor; its strong tone of social idealism and betterment made it a very influential magazine in the American home, where it registered these ideas with women, who were assuming gradually a greater and greater influence in American affairs.

It became the *Godey's Lady's Book* of a new generation. When Curtis brought the *Saturday Evening Post*, published in the 1840's, into his group, and later the *Country Gentleman*, one of the nation's oldest rural journals, he made Philadelphia truly a "magazine city." After 1865 Philadelphia continued to be the home of *Peterson's Magazine*, with 150,000 circulation in 1876. *Lippincott's* was established in 1868.

The newspaper as an institution upon which almost everyone depended for information was given a tremendous boost by the reporting of the Civil War. The cheap daily newspaper already had become common in larger cities and the story of postwar journalism is mainly one of the growth of important daily newspapers in the major cities. Pittsburgh by 1880 had no less than ten daily newspapers, which included the new *Evening Telegraph*, the *Press*, and the *Chronicle Telegraph*. Harrisburg emerged with three daily newspapers, the *Telegraph*, the *Patriot*, and the *Evening News*. Scranton's *Morning Republican* in 1867 was the first new daily outside Philadelphia, and Wilkes-Barre soon followed. The famous Philadelphia *North American* was established in 1876 and became one of truly important progressive newspapers of the eastern United States. The *Evening Bulletin* emerged under that name in 1870 and became one of the largest evening newspapers in the country. The *Philadelphia Times* of Colonel A. K. McClure was another great Philadelphia daily, along with the *Public Record*, founded in 1871.

Because of its increasingly cosmopolitan population probably no other state had a larger number of foreign-language newspapers. At least sixty were being published in 1900. What became without much question the nation's most widely distributed country and small-town weekly, reaching far beyond the limits of Pennsylvania, the famous Williamsport *Grit*, was started in 1882 with both state and national editions. The *Pittsburgh Courier* and *Philadelphia Independent* were among the oldest and most influential Negro newspapers in the country. The large city daily attained a wider circulation and greater influence with improved mail service through the railroads, which brought it into more homes over a larger area. Nevertheless, the small-town weekly was the newspaper read by the larger part of the town and country population. Its content did not vary very much from that of an earlier day; community news, mingled with state and national affairs and varied literary effusions, were the stock in trade of the weekly.

MUSIC AND MUSICIANS

Three of Pennsylvania's more noted composers were born in the post-bellum period and started their productive careers, though some of their major works were written after 1900. Charles Wakefield Cadman was born at Johnstown in 1881 but soon moved with his family to Pittsburgh. He worked as a youth in the steel mills but became interested in music at an early age and wrote the "Carnegie Library March" used to dedicate one of Andrew Carnegie's gift libraries at Homestead. This was in 1897 and from that time on young Cadman was dedicated to music. Reading in the Homestead Library led to his first interest in the legends and stories of the Indians, from which grew later his memorable "Land of the Sky Blue Water" and "At Dawning." Much later Cadman wrote an opera based on an Indian theme, *Shanewis*. His *Witch of Salem* was another opera. Both were among the first successful operas based on American themes and composed by an American.

Ethelbert Nevin was born in Sewickley, near Pittsburgh, in 1862 and studied piano and music at home and abroad. His first piano recital was in Pittsburgh in 1886. Before his premature death in 1901 he had composed such lasting music as "The Rosary," "Narcissus," and "Mighty Lak' a Rose."

Harry T. Burleigh, beloved Negro arranger and composer ever famous for "Deep River," "Steal Away to Jesus," "Sometimes I Feel Like A Motherless Child," "Nobody Knows," and "Little Mother of Mine," was born in Erie in 1866. His grandfather had been a slave who, blinded from a beating, made his way north. As a boy Burleigh sold newspapers and with his brother lighted the gas street lamps of Erie. At the age of sixteen he was singing in an Erie church choir and ten years later attended the National Conservatory of Music in New York. His great music grew out of songs that were sung to him as a boy by his blind grandfather. Before his death he had won national and even international fame for his Negro spirituals.

Music of a somewhat different type came from several other Pennsylvania composers and musicians. No Christmas goes by without "O Little Town of Bethlehem" being heard the length and breadth of the land. It was composed by the Rev. Phillips Brooks in 1868. "Listen to the Mocking Bird," a great favorite of days gone by and still remembered, was composed by Septimus Winner of Williamsport about the same time. Philip P. Bliss, born near Clearfield, was a great singing evangelist who left behind him "Let the Lower Lights Be Burning" and "Pull for the Shore." Another great evangelist who outlived Bliss was New Castle's Ira Sankey. Bliss and Sankey wrote a whole book of famous revival hymns still sung in churches and at revivals everywhere. Victor Herbert started his musical career in Pittsburgh as conductor of its symphony.

Though some religious groups, notably the extreme conservatives among Presbyterians, continued to frown upon music in the church, most Protestant sects held to the tradition of fine music. As larger churches patronized by greater wealth were built in the cities, paid professional choirs became common, along with larger and finer organs. Religious music became an increasing outlet for those musicians starting careers as singers, and its quality steadily improved. The Moravians at Bethlehem never lost their great love of music, and their vocal and instrumental groups held high their reputation for some of the finest religious music in America. A glance through the files of any country weekly newspaper reveals an amazing love of music and its expression in the local bands, small orchestral groups, or singing societies in virtually every town of any size. Grange halls and country schoolhouses were the setting for old-fashioned square dances with their country "fiddle" music. Singing on Sunday at the country church was another way in which farm folk had an outlet for musical expression, and just about every country home had an organ in the parlor.

This still life by Severin Roesen in the State Museum collection is typical of his artistry.

THE WORLD OF ART AND ARCHITECTURE

It is a tradition that the advance of art depends mainly upon the support of wealth. Many newly created millionaires in both Philadelphia and Pittsburgh began to try their hands at collecting art and also supporting the new museums in which fine art could be housed and shown to the people. The Philadelphia Museum of Art was started in the 1870's; the Drexel Institute Art Gallery, and Pittsburgh's Carnegie Museum with its International Exhibition were among the finest of the nation's art institutions. These fine display centers soon took the place of the smaller and more commercial museums and art shop displays of an earlier day.

In the colonial and later Federal era the portrait was the major form of art. Even before the Civil War, attention was turning to landscapes and life as the artist's principal theme. The growth of the nation was accompanied by more appreciation for the greatness of its natural features, and Americans became more aware of the West and the Indian of the Great Plains. George Catlin of Wilkes-Barre, who died in 1872, pushed into the Upper Missouri country and recorded the life and ways of the Indians. Thomas Moran, Philadelphia artist, was commissioned by the government as the official artist of the great Yellowstone country which had been set aside in the 1870's as the nation's first national park. Caleb Bingham, a contemporary of Catlin, was another artist who portrayed life on the far western frontiers. This new school of genre, or painters of the local scene, was appearing in just about every part of the state. These artists were comparable to the earlier generation of untutored folk artists who wandered from place to place painting what they saw and what the people wanted, but had considerably greater talent. Some painted portraits when some local person of wealth wanted himself done in oil. John F. Francis, who painted from about 1830 until 1886, was an artist of this sort and his wanderings brought him into central Pennsylvania as far as Bellefonte. He is especially known for his famous portrait of Governor Joseph Ritner at the plow. An artist who signed his paintings as "S. Roesen" was probably a German-born painter named Severin Roesen who ended up in Williamsport before his death in 1871, and whose work is now highly regarded. Another more or less folk or primitive painter was Linton Park, who painted country life in central Pennsylvania after the Civil War. Joseph Pickett, who lived from 1848 to 1918, was an obscure carpenter, builder of canal boats, and finally a country storekeeper on the banks of the Delaware Canal at New Hope, who represented the untaught folk artist and his work which persisted even after the Civil War. "Carvell's Ferry, 1776" is a famous work of Pickett now in the Whitney Museum. Lewis Miller, whose work has been preserved at

"View of the Susquehanna" by Lloyd Mifflin is a good example of his fine landscapes.

the Historical Society of York County, is another noted folk artist who painted local scenes almost without number before 1882. The creative forces of both painting and poetry were merged in the work of Lloyd Mifflin, whose work achieved attention before 1900 and grew in stature in later years.

The more formal world of art was encouraged immensely by the growing influence of the Pennsylvania Academy in Philadelphia and the coterie of artists who found in Philadelphia an association with a world of art which in the late nineteenth century did not exist anywhere else in America. The Centennial celebration in 1876 touched off something of a renaissance with its first international exhibition, and it was at this time that the Academy moved into its new Victorian Gothic home on Broad Street. The overpowering figure in the later history of the Academy was Thomas Cowperthwait Eakins, born in 1844. Except for a few brief years of study in Paris following the Civil War, he rooted his life and career in the Quaker City. Eakins painted people, notably Walt Whitman, in a most objec-

tive style, ignoring the posed portrait style of an earlier generation. Eakins had a great influence upon art beyond his own life as a teacher at the Academy. Walt Whitman once said, "Eakins is not a painter, he is a force." His greatest pupil and follower was Thomas P. Anshutz, native of Kentucky who came to Philadelphia in 1871 and soon became an influential member of the Academy staff. Cecilia Beaux, born in 1855, was another Academy student as well as a later member of its faculty, who first attracted attention at the institution's exhibits in 1885. Eakins and Anshutz as teachers at the Academy had a profound influence on the work of many other artists who began their careers in the post-bellum years but whose best work belongs to the twentieth century.

Pittsburgh was not very far behind Philadelphia in the number and distinction of its artists of the period. David Blythe died in 1865 but left behind him a treasury of paintings depicting the life of the common man in and around Pittsburgh, as well as some Civil War paintings. John White Alexander, born in 1856 in Allegheny, had established himself by the turn of the century as a noted portrait painter, muralist, and illustrator. His "Crowning of Labor" at the Carnegie Institute is a famous work. James Reid Lambdin was a Pittsburgh-born student of Thomas Sully. He set up a museum and art gallery in his native city in 1828 when he was only twenty-one years old. Finding art not very remunerative in Pittsburgh, he moved to Philadelphia. Lambdin became a leading portrait painter of the presidents, including all of them from John Quincy Adams to James A. Garfield. One of Lambdin's pupils was W. T. Russel Smith, who till his death in 1896 lived in both western and eastern Pennsylvania. His paintings of Pittsburgh and western Pennsylvania qualify him as a Pittsburgh artist, and it was here that he did his first work. William C. Wall was the first in a family of Pittsburgh artists which included his son and grandson, who till his death in 1887 painted notable scenes of the region's rivers. Jasper Lawman, a native of Ohio, came to Pittsburgh about 1840 and from 1850 until his death in 1906 took an active part in the artistic life of the city both as a genre and a portrait painter.

The Civil War attracted artists without end, but few of them have survived as having any distinction. From the Pennsylvania viewpoint, though artists may debate the great merit of his work, Peter Rothermell cannot be ignored. Rothermell was born at Nescopeck in 1817 and was commissioned by the state after the Civil War to do a series of paintings of the Battle of Gettysburg. His huge mural centering on the climactic struggle of Pickett's charge is hung in the William Penn Memorial Museum in Harrisburg, along with several smaller battle scenes.

New public buildings and other enterprises encouraged the work of the sculptor. The Centennial exhibited the work of Philadelphia's Howard Roberts, whose "La Première Pose," provided an American example of this ancient art. Joseph Bailly, native of France who moved to Philadelphia, did the Washington figure in the new Philadelphia City Hall and another at Independence Hall. His bronze busts of Meade and Grant are also distinctive. Alexander Milne Calder did the huge statue of Penn which tops Phila-

delphia's city hall. John Quincy Ward Adams before his death in 1910 did notable work, including his General John Hancock in Fairmount Park. Other Pennsylvania sculptors of note, among whom was Bellefonte's George Grey Barnard, were achieving attention by 1900 but with later work of more distinction.

Public buildings, along with the great new churches made possible by wealthy city congregations, challenged the talents of the finest architects of the time. The Greek-revival tradition which was popular before the Civil War was abandoned under the influences of the post-bellum era. The newly rich disliked the Georgian or Greek revival as far too simple to suit their taste, which ran to the more ornate grand-manner architecture of the Gothic, Byzantine, or French Renaissance styles. The homes of the wealthy were inclined to be castle-type versions of architecture which aped the worst in Europe. Everyone tried to outdo everyone else. Public buildings showed more restraint, though some were rather gaudy. Pittsburgh's new city hall by J. W. Kerr was in French Renaissance style, as was that of Philadelphia, created by architect John L. McArthur, Jr. Henry Hobson Richardson helped to make Pittsburgh a center of a Romanesque revival which avoided some of the lavishly ornate style of the era. The Allegheny County Court House and Jail survive as his monumental building. The University of Pennsylvania provided an opportunity for Walter Cope and John Stewardson to found a College Gothic style that found its way to other campuses. Furness and Evans of Philadelphia designed several major railroad stations. Churches of the era were commonly done in the grand and more or less Gothic-cathedral style. Pennsylvania in this era shared with the nation a considerable bad taste in buildings, whether private or public, but a taste to be understood in terms of a nation growing rich somewhat too rapidly to adjust itself to some of the finer things in life.

The total progress of the arts during the era was substantial and rewarding. The paintings of Roesen and Park, looked upon as folk art in their time, are viewed today as vital contributions to the history of art.

247

PENNSYLVANIA IN THE NEW AMERICAN LITERATURE

The term "American literature" was greeted with derision by Europeans and even most Americans until Fred Lewis Pattee at the Pennsylvania State College began in 1895 a course in "American Literature" and published a *History of American Literature.* These pioneer efforts met with much ridicule. Pennsylvania's colonial literary tradition was strong and rich but weakened in the early 1800's when it was overshadowed by New England writers. The post-bellum years saw a marked revival and new achievements. Pattee himself attributed the advance of American literature in this era to the new spirit of nationalism. Dr. S. Weir Mitchell, distinguished Philadelphia surgeon, doubled in literature with his *Westways, The Red City,* and *Hugh Wynne, Free Quaker.* Bayard Taylor continued to be a productive writer until his death in 1878 with such works as *Views Afoot.* Frank Stockton, who died in 1902, though noted mainly for his short story "The Lady or the Tiger," was the author of many novels highly regarded in his period, such as *The Casting Away of Mrs. Lecks and Mrs. Aleshine* and *Rudder Grange.* The war correspondent Richard Harding Davis was also a novelist and short story writer as well as an editor of *Harper's Weekly.* His sister, Rebecca Blaine Harding Davis, was a leading contributor to the *Atlantic Monthly* and also a novelist of some note.

Philadelphia may well be rated one of the nation's major literary centers after the Civil War on the strength of the work of Dr. S. Weir Mitchell, Henry Charles Lea, historian most famous for his treatise *A History of the Inquisition of the Middle Ages,* Horace Howard Furness, called "the most famous Shakespeare scholar of his time," George Henry Boker, poet and dramatist as well as diplomat, and Charles Godfrey Leland, poet, editor, and a first biographer of Lincoln. The literary output of Philadelphians was encouraged by the policy of the leading newspapers in publishing in their columns verse, essays, and even more extended literary work.

A GREAT ADVANCE IN SCIENCE AND TECHNOLOGY

The *Scientific American* in 1896 conducted a prize essay contest on the topic, "Progress of Invention During the Past Fifty Years." Edward M. Byrn, who won the contest, called the preceding fifty years "an epoch unique in the world's history" and commented that in this half century "nine-tenths of all America's riches and physical comforts" had come into existence. It was, as Byrn put it, an era in which there was a "gigantic wave of human ingenuity" applied to solving the needs of the nation in science and technology. Fifty years before 1896 there had been no telephone, no tin cans, no steel railroad cars moving swiftly on steel rails and made safe with air brakes and uniform switch and signal systems, no electric power or light, no products of petroleum such as

Bell demonstrates the new telephone to Emperor Dom Pedro of Brazil and the Empress at the Centennial.

kerosene or lubricating oils, no commercial production of steel, no Portland cement, no aluminum, no typewriters, no phonograph or motion pictures. Indeed, there was little in 1846 to indicate the future of modern business and industry as of 1896, or the revolution in communication and transportation which was accomplished by the turn of the century.

The details of this revolution consume pages of history. Pennsylvania had a more than ordinary share in the story. Attention already has been given to George Westinghouse as an inventive genius of the era. He developed alternating current and applied it to both power and lighting. The air brake and uniform signal systems devised by Westinghouse made possible safely the high speed of trains; they moved over rails of steel which Pennsylvania mills provided more largely by far than any other single steel-producing state. The same mills made possible barbed wire to fence the West and a host of other products which were revolutionizing the life of the nation. It provided the tin-plate industry for the canning of food in tin cans and other uses. The commercial production of petroleum was started at Titusville in 1859. Aluminum was produced in Pittsburgh by Hall and Davis in 1888 as a commercial product; just about the same time Saylor found a way to make Portland cement near Allentown. Steel used for railroad rails, barbed wire, and frames for the windmills that pumped water made possible the conquest of the Great Plains country.

A Pennsylvanian named Daniel Drawbaugh, who lived just across the river from Harrisburg, nearly had the honor of being known as the inventor of the telephone rather than Alexander Graham Bell. Drawbaugh was typical of the self-taught experimenters and tinkerers of the time. He specialized in electrical gadgets. Drawbaugh without doubt developed a telephone at just about the same time as Bell and possibly a little earlier; but he neglected to take out a patent—which Bell did in 1876. The dispute went all the way to the United States Supreme Court before Bell's patent priority was upheld. Christopher Sholes, a printer born near Danville, was a pioneer in developing the typewriter and had a patent for one as early as 1868. James Densmore of Meadville was another pioneer in making a "writing machine." By 1900 the typewriter and telephone were on the road to revolutionizing business and office methods.

Pennsylvanians helped perfect the phonograph and the motion picture before 1900. Edison patented his cylinder record in 1877. Emile Berliner in Philadelphia developed the flat-disk gramophone, first assembled and marketed in that city in 1895, and it made the phonograph popular. Motors for the Berliner machine were made across the river in Camden by Eldridge Johnson; the two united to form the famous Victor Talking Machine Company. The first stereographic photographs were produced by William F. Langenheim of Philadelphia, who also developed a "magic lantern" and lantern slides to use with it. In 1861 Coleman Sellers, grandson of the artist Charles Willson Peale, perfected the kinematoscope and achieved motion in presenting photographic slides. Casper Briggs of Philadelphia also helped along the same idea. In 1870 an Ohioan named Henry R. Heyl who had moved to Philadelphia in 1863 presented what he called "Motion Pictures" on a screen at the Academy of Music. Heyl's phasmatrope, according to a contemporary description, was able "to give various objects and figures upon the screen the most graceful and life-like movements." His picture included an address and an acrobatic performance, as well as a waltz duo actually synchronized with music. A decade later Eadweard Muybridge, an English immigrant doing research work at the University of Pennsylvania, came up with a zoopraxiscope which made pictures in motion and projected them on a screen. His work was known to Edison. Thomas A. Edison was not the inventor but a contributor to perfecting the motion picture. Another Englishman living in Philadelphia named John Corbett developed a flexible celluloid film coated with a photographic emulsion. In 1893–94 Rudolph Hunter of the same city was probably the first to build a motion picture projector. It was used at the Franklin Institute.

A Silesian immigrant to Philadelphia in 1851 named Sigmund Lubin was probably the first person to grasp a commercial potential in the motion picture and established the first successful motion picture production studios in this country in a building on Arch Street. He built a motion picture theater at the National Export Exposition in Philadelphia in 1899. The famous actor Joseph Jefferson was the first legitimate actor to perform in a motion picture. By 1900 this entertainment form was well on its way to success.

The age of aviation did not emerge until the twentieth century but Pittsburgh before that time was the site for two developments which helped make it possible. One was the discovery of a commercial process through which aluminum could be made. Before 1900 its use was confined to jewelry and pots and pans but it was the magic metal which would make an airplane practical. In the Allegheny Observatory in Pittsburgh a man named Samuel Pierpont Langley was experimenting with aerodynamics. Langley was made head of the observatory in 1867 when he was already a well-known young scientist. In the early eighties he began to investigate the problem of flight, starting with studying the flight practices of birds. He built a special whirling table to test the lifting power of wings, which he made from paper and wood. Langley left Pittsburgh in 1887 to become secretary of the famed Smithsonian and four years later published *Experiments in Aerodynamics*. Five years later he attempted unsuccessfully to launch a steam-powered small flying machine from a Potomac River houseboat. He made another attempt in October, 1903, but it too failed and his machine became known as "Langley's folly," the usual penalty of the pioneer who fails in his first efforts. But he had paved the way for the work of the Wrights at Kitty Hawk and their flight in December was successful. Time alone ran out on Samuel P. Langley as the man who might have been hailed as inventor of the airplane.

THE WORLD OF THE SPIRIT

Few out-of-the-ordinary currents were evident in the religious world after the Civil War. Churches grew larger and more ornate with the increased wealth of city congregations. Quite naturally, all churches considerably increased in membership with the growth in population. The number of Presbyterians and of Presbyterian churches, for example, nearly doubled. Lutheranism remained the strongest Protestant denomination but Methodism had become by 1870 a major Protestant denomination in the state. The most noteworthy advance of any single religious faith was that of the Roman Catholics, influenced largely by the growing immigration from Catholic countries. In 1868 a diocese was created for Harrisburg, and also one for Scranton. The Diocese of Altoona was created in 1901. The Russian Orthodox Church began to emerge as an important denomination in the steel and mining areas with the growth of immigration from Slavic Europe.

Pennsylvania kept alive its tradition of unorthodoxy in religion in the person of Charles Taze Russell. Born in 1852 in Pittsburgh, Russell was a businessman who was exposed to the Adventist teachings of Jonas Wentworth about 1870 and became a fervent evangelist for a new set of religious doctrines out of which grew Jehovah's Witnesses. In 1879 Russell began publication of two religious journals which later merged as *Zion's Watch Tower*. He wrote books and tracts by the hundreds and they were read by millions. His personal preaching reached many thousands with a new gospel that scorned the formal churches.

Old-fashioned evangelism continued to have a strong hold on the masses of the people. Ira D. Sankey and Philip P. Bliss were Pennsylvanians associated with the most famous evangelist of the times, Dwight Moody. Sankey and Bliss were "singing evangelists," though Sankey had power also as a preacher. The two of them composed and published some of the great gospel hymns of the time; they are still widely used in Protestant churches. Late in 1875 and early 1876 Moody and Sankey came to Philadelphia and conducted revivals at John Wanamaker's huge Grand Depot auditorium, which seated some ten thousand persons. It was estimated that more than a million Philadelphians were exposed to salvation in the course of the revival.

The Protestant and Roman Catholic churches to some extent began to feel the urge of the social gospel before 1900 as some church leaders could hardly ignore the fact that certain social conditions were hardly consistent with Christian teachings. The Rev. George Hodges arrived in Pittsburgh in 1881 to become pastor of the Calvary Ascension Church attended by Henry Clay Frick and more Pittsburgh tycoons than any other single Pittsburgh church. Unshaken by this array

unhappy conditions which accompanied greatly increased wealth, comfort, and power for a few while thousands suffered began to challenge the thinking of several philosophers. The Pennsylvania theorists in economics Mathew and Henry Carey helped root the theories of laissez faire and national tariff protection which came into full flower after 1870. Henry George in the seventies

Country schoolhouses such as this dotted the state in this era. The few that remain are landmarks in the history of education.

of wealth in his church, not all of which had been amassed in exact accord with what many regarded as Christian principles and practices, Mr. Hodges preached and acted as an apostle of social reform. "New Quests for New Knights" was one of his sermons. He told his parishioners: "The task of the knight of the 19th century is as of old, the rescue of a city. Jerusalem is the city in which we live." Politicians resented the reforms proposed by Mr. Hodges and in anger referred to his cohorts as that "damned Calvary crowd." Catholic and Protestant influences were behind many missions and social service movements in the cities as a gospel of social justice gathered momentum.

Social justice, however, was coming to the attention of thinking people in this era. The

emerged as a leader among those who voiced a new concept of social progress. George was less a Pennsylvanian than the Careys because though born in Philadelphia he spent the greater part of his life in California and New York. His *Progress and Poverty* in 1877 was an outgrowth of earlier articles and pamphlets in which he pointed to the fact that monopolistic use of land and its resources by a few was creating poverty for the many. His advocacy of a single tax based on land made him a national and international figure. His weekly newspaper, the *Standard,* became a leading voice for social-reform ideas. His influence was such that he once ran ahead of young Theodore Roosevelt in a three-man contest for the mayoralty of New York City. George was ahead of

A typical decorated Pennsylvania German barn.

that other great theorist of a new social democracy, Thorstein Veblen of Wisconsin, who published his famous *Theory of the Leisure Class* in 1899. Indeed, Andrew Carnegie with his new "gospel of wealth" was turning the thinking of at least some wealthy Americans in new directions which pioneered the progressive movement of the early twentieth century.

Looking backward on the years from the Civil War to 1900, one finds it easy to see just how the economic revolution of that era influenced currents of social, cultural, and intellectual change. More wealth encouraged many advances in the arts and culture as those of means began to develop at least veneers of culture. Major changes in that more people lived in town and city than on the farm were quite evident. Pennsylvania was growing up.

CHAPTER FOURTEEN

POLITICS AND GOVERNMENT IN THE NEW INDUSTRIAL AGE, 1865 - 1900

The major force behind a new type of politics and government that quickly became evident following the Civil War was the rapid growth of industry, which in Pennsylvania was mainly coal, iron, and steel. The new industrial age meant not only larger mills and mining operations but also large-scale business controlled by new and powerful corporations. The Carnegie steel interests, for example, were combined with Frick's coke empire to provide the foundation at the turn of the century for the world's first billion-dollar corporation. The Pennsylvania Railroad, along with the Reading and the Lehigh railroads, were powerful corporations in transportation; indeed the Pennsylvania Railroad in the seventies and eighties was probably the most powerful single corporation in the country. These new corporate enterprises had much at stake in terms of government policies. They also had new power with which to influence government to get what they might want from it or to check what they did not want. Industrialism also led to a spectacular growth of cities and shifted the state from a rural and small-town life to urban life. This put great new strains

on city government, which was really then a type of government framed for large towns rather than large cities. Just as local governments today in many areas find it hard to cope with problems of mushrooming populations in suburbia, so did the Pennsylvania city in the postwar era. Government also had to start coping with some new social problems created by the city itself. Pennsylvania suffered the pangs of adjusting to new problems and pressures of an industrial age, and the adjustment took time. Graft and corruption plagued government at Harrisburg and in Philadelphia and Pittsburgh.

PARTIES AND POLITICS AFTER 1865

The Civil War revolutionized Pennsylvania politics by replacing the once predominant influence of the Democratic Party with that of the Republican Party. As has been pointed out earlier, the Republican Party hardly dared present itself under that name in the sixties but it quickly overcame this situation after the Civil War. The Democratic Party suffered from its general obstructionist record during the war years and even more from the Copperhead tactics of many of its open southern sympathizers, some of whom were key statewide leaders in the party. On the other hand, the Republican Party now had the advantage of having been the party which with Lincoln's leadership had won the war despite this obstruction. The situation was the worse in Pennsylvania because in 1864 General George B. McClellan had been the Democratic white hope opposing Lincoln. The Democratic national and state platforms in 1864 condemned the war and Lincoln's leadership as failures, though to his credit McClellan repudiated the platform.

It was quite easy for the Republicans to capitalize upon this situation. They derided the state Democratic convention in 1866 as the "rebel Copperhead Convention." The Democrats did not help themselves by continuing to refuse to recognize the fact that the Civil War ended slavery. Pennsylvania Democrats opposed even the Thirteenth Amendment and accused the Republicans of "miserable niggerism" that went back to the mistaken policies of "Old Abe." The tone of some of the Democratic press of the state was so bitter that one tends to doubt that the editors knew the war had ended in the way it did. Little wonder that the northern war veteran organization G.A.R. (Grand Army of the Republic), became a right wing of the Republican Party or that it was bulwarked also by the powerful Union League. War veterans were an indispensable part of any Republican political parade. Republican candidates for almost every important office were veterans, and for more than two decades the chief qualification of a Republican gubernatorial candidate was that he be a Civil War veteran with a general's rank.

THE RISE OF THE BOSS AND THE MACHINE

There were powerful political leaders and political organizations in abundance in the earlier history of Pennsylvania politics but the postbellum era saw the rise of what came to be known generally in the history of the nation's politics as the "boss and the machine." The use of the word "machine" as applied to a political organization was truly an apt one for the new industrial age when the smoothly working machine turned out a uniform product. The new political machines worked much the same way with uniform political products. It might also be noted that the new type of political machine was better lubricated financially than the old-style political organization. The lubrication now came largely from an industrial community willing to pay for political favors. Politicians long had shaken down plums for their supporters in the form of advance information on the location of turnpikes or canals, charters for various favored business enterprises, and even the creation of new counties or towns. The prizes offered in the new era of large-scale business enterprise were much greater and worth much more than those in earlier days. Much larger sums of money were now "invested" in influencing political behavior and policies of government. The favors that were at stake in the years after the Civil War were worth so much more that they brought a higher price. The pressure on those in office or in positions of political influence to grant these favors was correspondingly greater and the rewards the more tempting. This was true especially in the case of the boss and machine organization in politics. Powerful business interests wanted many favors from the state government and these included special legislation or charters for the benefit of corporations, along with the defeat of legislation contrary to the interests of business and possibly hampering to a free economy.

In 1868–72 alone, just before the new constitution in 1874 outlawed the practice, the General Assembly pushed through over forty acts creating corporations with broad powers to do almost anything in the field of transportation, mining, or industrial development. The South Improvement Company, chartered in such a way as to aid a monopolistic control over the transportation of oil, was one of these which won national attention. Another was the famous Crédit Mobilier, chartered to build railroads, and builder of the Union Pacific. The directors of the Union Pacific and the Crédit Mobilier were the same persons and thus able to manipulate the use of government bonds and land grants to help the railroad get profits for themselves. Members of Congress were presented with stock in the Crédit Mobilier and profited from it. It was the exposure of this situation that compromised so great a national political leader and native Pennsylvanian as James G. Blaine in the 1870's. The South Improvement Company was so desirable a prize to the Standard Oil interests that they were willing to pay a high price for securing its charter. One wag remarked that the Standard Oil Company did everything to the Pennsylvania legislature to get this favor except to refine it.

Since railroads and other corporations sought protection from state regulatory measures and were willing to pay for it, this led to the suspicion that on more than one occasion certain legislators threatened to introduce or actually did submit regulatory bills in order to hold up the corporations and get a price for withdrawing or side-tracking the bills. The papers of one railroad and mining enterprise of the time that have been preserved reveal how a railroad representative reported such affairs to his company, with names of legislators and the amounts used to influence their votes. "How to put a stop to legislative corruption is now the question of the day," declared the *Titusville Herald* in 1867, going on to say that ". . . few bills are passed on their intrinsic merits, but men expect an equivalent in dollars and cents for their votes." Lord Bryce called the Pennsylvania legislature "a Witche's Sabbath of jobbing, bribing, thieving, and prostitution of legislative power to promote interests." Such a situation was one which led naturally to the effort of shrewd politicians to organize the relationship between business and government in some systematic way. Business could contribute to the support of the political party which helped insure its success at the polls and in return would be protected against "unwise" legislation as well as secure certain special favors such as a franchise or charter. Business liked this machine organization as opposed to dealing with individuals as members of a state or local legislative body. The party members in these bodies took their orders from the boss of the machine of which they were the agents as elected officials. In this way, political affairs were systematized by 1870 and in Pennsyl-

This political cartoon shows the use made by Democrats of the issue of the freed Negro against Republican Geary.

vania and other industrial states the era of the "boss and the machine" was well outlined. Something of the same centralization was achieved in politics as was done in business.

Pennsylvania probably had a better organized system of machine politics from the local to the state and then the national level than did any other single industrial state in the post-bellum era. Not only was it better organized but it held up better and longer in the face of many determined assaults from reform elements. Several factors were responsible for the solidarity and strength of the Republican political machine in Pennsylvania; and in Pennsylvania the boss and machine were of Republican vintage because it was the dominant party. Some of the most powerful corporate enterprises of the era were centered in the state and included railroads, mining, and iron and steel, all of which had interests which the Republican machine could safeguard and advance, thus establishing a framework for a powerful alliance of business and political forces. As a further factor, the Democratic Party disintegrated almost completely in the immediate post-Civil War years, while under Simon Cameron, Republican leadership was consolidated and made supreme. In contrast, leadership in the Democratic Party was fragmented among three persons rather than centered on any single strong figure. Charles R. Buckalew from Columbia County, one-time United States Senator elected in 1863 as a War Democrat and later returned to the State Senate, was one warhorse of the party. Another was William A. Wallace from the Clearfield area, who dominated the State Senate as his party's leader. Philadelphia's Samuel Randall, who had become the leader of the Democrats in Congress by 1865 and remained so until his death in 1890 after having served as a Speaker of the House, was another leading Democrat of the era. No one of the three ever won a real leadership, and Wallace and Randall in particular fought each other at the expense of any party unity. For the greater part of the period before 1900 the Democrats were ineffectual and unable to win an election except by virtue of an occasional independent revolt within the Republican organization. It was thus inevitable that the boss-made machine organization in Pennsylvania was found within the Republican Party, not because it was less moral, but simply because it was more powerful.

THE CAMERON MACHINE AT WORK

By far the most important factor in the success of the Republican machine, as the state machine in Pennsylvania, was able leadership and ability to rely upon not one but two major city organiza-

tions for a foundation. The political machine put together by Simon Cameron was more than a state organization; it had firm local foundations in the two great metropolitan centers. These were tied together by brilliant political leadership. At the state level, Simon Cameron, now in his seventies, had weathered all the political storms of the time and by 1867 had defeated the Curtin forces, made himself the dominant leader of the Republican Party, and despite opposition had secured his election to the United States Senate. A veteran of Pennsylvania's political wars who had fought and vanquished on occasion such foes as James Buchanan and Governor Curtin, Cameron was a powerful man. Not least among his current triumphs was the nomination and election of John W. Geary as governor in 1866. Geary was re-elected in 1869, the first of a long line of Civil War generals who led the state Republican ticket. Geary's personal letters reveal that he did not at all times take kindly to the orders of the machine, as was true of more than one Republican governor of the era. In 1869 Cameron selected his own colleague to serve with him in the Senate, and the legislature dutifully elected him. Cameron became a powerful figure among those members of the Senate who actually took control of the nation's government during the Grant era. Tall and spare, with an austere Scotch-Irish Presbyterian manner, Cameron was a venerable figure in the Senate; a man who would "never forgive an injury, real or fancied, and never forget a favor." His son Donald, groomed as his successor, served as Secretary of War under Grant and in 1877 took his father's place in the United States Senate and as head of the Cameron machine. The long-time progressive Republican, Colonel Alexander K. McClure, summed up the situation by saying that "all who hoped for political power or preference in Pennsylvania could command it only by cooperation with the Cameron power of the State."

Much of the permanence of the Republican machine was due to the foresight of the Cameron dynasty, which always looked to supporting leadership developed from the ranks. Robert W. Mackey and Matthew S. Quay were two of these men; the latter was the better known because of his prominence in national politics, but the former was perhaps the abler of the two. Robert Mackey was born in Pittsburgh in 1837 and entered the banking business. In 1869 he was abruptly elected State Treasurer by the legislature at the behest of the Camerons because the incumbent had refused to deposit state funds in Cameron-controlled banks. Mackey was defeated in 1870 in a reform uprising but soon returned to the post. Until his death in 1879, this small, slight man, ill from what was then called "consumption," was Cameron's chief lieutenant in manipulating the legislature as well as in the all-important task of assigning state revenues to organization banks. A. K. McClure, the astute contemporary liberal Republican, judged him "the ablest all-round leader the Republicans of Pennsylvania ever created." Mackey "never was defeated in a Republican State convention and never lost control of a single legislature," wrote McClure. Robert Mackey's magic was wrought not merely by control of the Republican organization but also by exerting a strong influence over the Democrats and splinter groups. On more than one occasion Mackey was able to manipulate the Democrats in their selection of candidates. His strategy paid dividends in Republican victories.

In the seventies, when the Greenback Party became a real power in Pennsylvania, it actually held a balance of power in the elections and under ordinary conditions would have tended to support the Democrats. Mackey, however, won the Greenbackers to the Republican side in 1875 and 1878. The astute Pittsburgh politician is also credited with having had much to do with securing the vote of Florida for Hayes in the disputed Hayes-Tilden contest, through contacts with a former Pittsburgher named Brigham, a publisher whose newspaper had been bought by the Republican machine and who later became influential in Republican politics in Florida. Another major success was scored by Mackey in arranging with the corporate interests that supported the party to accept a state corporation tax which made possible the repeal of state taxes on real estate. The real estate tax repeal was popular with farmers and small-home owners in towns and

Simon Cameron.

strengthened the Republicans in rural and small-town areas. The modest corporation tax did not bear heavily on big business when compared with the favorable climate it produced in Harrisburg for their legislative concerns.

Matthew S. Quay was born in Dillsburg in 1833, the son of a Presbyterian minister. The family later moved to western Pennsylvania, where Quay graduated from Jefferson College and began the practice of law. He was a slight, modest man with genuine learning and culture in later life, but an astute and unscrupulous politician. Quay's political career began as an associate of Governor Curtin, whom he served as military secretary and also as political leader in the House, in the Civil War years. Quay then was opposed to the Cameron organization and indeed was forced out of political life by it. He returned to Beaver County, where he edited and published for four years the noted Beaver *Radical*. With the switch of Curtin to the Liberal Republican cause in the 1870's and the power of Cameron solidified,

Quay returned to Harrisburg and politics as a Cameron lieutenant, serving not only as Republican state chairman but also in the politically potent post of Secretary of the Commonwealth under Hartranft and Hoyt. With the death of Mackey, Quay became the supreme representative of the organization in Pennsylvania, working closely with J. Donald Cameron, who retained his post as United States Senator until his retirement in 1897.

Donald Cameron was a rather unaggressive person and to most observers Quay appeared to be the dominant figure in the Republican organization even before 1897. Quay was elected himself to the United States Senate in 1887 by an obedient legislature which voted for him 166 to 80. In 1888 Quay's power as a national Republican leader was demonstrated by his successful management of the campaign of Benjamin Harrison for president when Quay carried even Grover Cleveland's home state of New York for Harrison. This was done by a very liberal use of money raised by a literal assessing of business interests which stood to benefit. Quay, despite this heroic effort, was given the cold shoulder by the austere Harrison, who appointed Quay's later bitter political foe John Wanamaker, Philadelphia merchant prince and political reformer, as Postmaster General. When Quay protested to the deeply religious Harrison and asked him just how he won the election and the Presidency, Harrison is reputed to have replied that he won by virtue of the disposition of Divine Providence and the votes of the people. Thoroughly angry and disgusted, Quay declared bluntly that Providence had nothing to do with it. Harrison's defeat in 1892 may well have proved Quay's point.

THE MACHINE IN PHILADELPHIA
AND PITTSBURGH

A powerful local organization of its forces in Philadelphia and Pittsburgh sustained the Cameron-Quay machine considerably. Philadelphia led the way and taught Pittsburgh how to develop a political machine. The antics of "Boss" Tweed and the Tammany machine in New York City led by Democrats overshadowed the affairs of Phila-

delphia, thanks largely to Thomas Nast, master cartoonist, but there is little to choose between the two cities as victims of ruthless political machines. Like all American cities, Philadelphia after the Civil War was without a government modernized to suit new conditions. It had a large foreign population, the votes of which could be manipulated, and a large number of factory and mill workers whose votes could be controlled. It also had a substantial wealthy upper class more interested in private and business affairs than in politics and entirely devoted to the Republican Party as the party of all respectable citizens and members of the Union League. The city government controlled valuable public utility operations necessary to a growing city and ripe for exploitation by a corrupt political organization. Indeed, an envious local Democrat is reputed to have said that Philadelphia was "a sort of Garden of Eden, from a political point of view."

Philadelphia's machine was led by a coterie of officeholders or former officeholders of whom William K. Kemble, William B. Mann, William S. Stokley, and James McManes were the most powerful. Kemble was a bank president and had served three terms as State Treasurer in Harrisburg, where he had become adept in the art of manipulating deposits of state funds in favored banks. Mann was the city's District Attorney, a vital post in either protecting or prosecuting certain interests. Stokley had worked his way up from lower rounds of city government to election as mayor in a bloody and riotous election in 1871. As mayor, he used police to control elections for the party. "King James" McManes was the real boss, as well as ruler of the "Gas Trust." He had risen from an Irish immigrant laborer to a position of political leadership and a trustee of the Philadelphia Gas Works. Created as a private company, this key utility was acquired in 1841 by the city and managed by a twelve-man board selected by the city council. The trustees served without salary but had a share of appointments and contracts which involved nearly two thousand jobs and several million dollars in annual contracts, along with a $4,000,000 payroll. It was made to order for use in politics; the arrangement persisted until 1887, despite efforts of reformers to do away with it. The "row offices" of Recorder of Deeds, Prothonotary, Receiver of Taxes, and Clerk of Quarter-Sessions Court operated as part of the machine and their fees went into the pockets of politicians and the coffers of the machine.

In 1869 the Cameron-bossed legislature passed

was often charged, and no doubt with truth, that in a close state election the Philadelphia machine could be depended upon to count in the proper state machine candidate. The peak of affrontery on the part of the state and city Republican machines was reached in 1878 when Quay secured his appointment to the post of City Recorder,

A Philadelphia street scene at the Republican convention in 1868, which nominated General U. S. Grant.

a law governing registration and voting in Philadelphia which gave the city Republican organization complete control of registration of voters. Slip-ticket voting made it possible to control the vote, and no unregistered person could vote without going through machine procedures. Floaters and repeaters were everywhere, sometimes under police protection. If these methods did not avail, a properly supervised count of the ballot might be used in a close election; it was by little short of a miracle that other than an organization-endorsed candidate could win in Philadelphia. It

newly created by an act of the controlled Assembly to install Quay in a well-paying office where he could closely supervise the Philadelphia organization. The public outcry was loud and clear and Quay returned to Harrisburg after a year.

In the nineties other names emerged as Philadelphia bosses, and for a time the task was shared by Charles Porter and David Martin. Boise Penrose began his career as a politician representing Quay in Philadelphia about 1895. Porter and Martin showed signs of independence after 1890 and the Quay-Penrose forces made "Iz" Durham

The Democrats tried to counter the Republican waving of the "bloody shirt" by nominating Pennsylvania Civil War hero General Winfield S. Scott for the Presidency in 1876.

newspaper, the *Gazette,* one time City Controller, state senator, and chairman of the Republican State Committee, was the first boss of Pittsburgh. The real machine was built by Christopher Magee, scion of a family which went back to the Revolution. Magee was made a clerk in the city offices and in 1872 became City Treasurer. Magee made up his mind early to make a study of how to organize a city for political purposes. He visited and studied both New York and Philadelphia machines as models. He returned to Pittsburgh with the reputed belief that "a political ring can be made as safe as a bank." Magee soon became associated with William Flinn, a contractor who decided that working with the organization was the best way to get city contracts. An early alliance was established with the Republican organization at Harrisburg and later Flinn was elected to the State Senate. The Magee-Flinn combination held Pittsburgh firmly in its grasp despite reform agitation; it was not until 1902 that anything approaching a reform administration gained control in the Steel City. Pittsburgh-dominated Allegheny County and the mill and mine barons saw to it that the controlled vote in their employ was delivered as expected. There were rifts with Quay in the nineties but generally the Magee-Flinn machine played its assigned role in the state Republican organization.

PENNSYLVANIA AND THE LIBERAL REPUBLICAN DRIVE

Dominated though it was by the Cameron-Quay machine, its power backed up by the organizations perfected in Philadelphia and Pittsburgh, there were occasional breaks in the black cloud of political domination by a one-party rule. The sad situation in the nation as a whole during the Grant era with its many examples of political misdemeanors provoked the nationwide Liberal Republican movement. Some of the outstanding figures in the founding and early growth of the Republican Party in the state turned against it as either supporters of the Liberal Republican movement or even Democrats. Former Governor Curtin and Galusha Grow were among these men. Alexander K. McClure supported the reform

the boss. At the close of the decade the same political powers elected "Stars and Stripes Sam" Ashbridge as mayor; the turn of the century saw Philadelphia in the grip of boss and machine rule of such a nature as to lead the Philadelphia Municipal League to call the Ashbridge regime "a scar on the fame and reputation of our city which will be a long time healing." It went on to state that never before had there been "such brazen defiance of public opinion, such flagrant disregard of public interest, such abuse of powers and responsibilities for private ends." This was the Philadelphia Lincoln Steffens a few years later condemned as "corrupt and contented."

At the western end of the state a similar tale was enacted of boss and machine rule under Republican auspices, and tied into the Cameron-Quay state machine. Russell Errett, for a time editor of Cameron's Pittsburgh organization movements, but did not desert the Republican Party. Colonel John W. Forney turned his powerful Philadelphia *Press* against the organization in 1872. A fusion of the Liberal Republicans with the Democrats of the state was attempted in 1872 but John F. Hartranft, another Civil War general, triumphed over the opposition by a sizable margin. Hartranft was a former Curtin lieutenant and a man of integrity against whom it was hard to campaign. As a machine-controlled candidate Hartranft was not the first nor the last of Republican candidates for the governorship in this era who represented a picture of complete integrity and love of the old Union proved in battle. These were the men who fronted for the machine and they were hard to beat in any election. More often than not after 1874 with the one-term governorship they were unhappy with their role in state affairs and unable to exert any continuing influence because of this crippling constitutional provision. Any candid view leads to the conclusion that Pennsylvania governors of the era represented a great waste of talent.

A NEW STATE CONSTITUTION

A new state Constitution was a direct result of the liberal and reform movement. The old Constitution had been under attack for a long time because of the lack of direct election of officials. It was amended before the Civil War to provide for popular election of many judicial officials and in 1871 the office of State Treasurer was made elective. The growing realization that the old forms of government were being corrupted by powerful new industrial and transportation interests added urgency in the seventies to the reform movement. The ugly word "monopoly" began to appear in public condemnation of influences brought to bear upon the Assembly. In the West the "Granger laws" had been inspired by undue influence of railroads in government and Pennsylvania was not immune to this. The railroads were the earliest large corporate influences to press for special favors. Correction of these conditions was certainly a major influence back of the call for a constitutional convention, which was supported by Governor Geary, and

was carried five to one in a popular vote in 1871.

The delegates met in November, 1872, and completed their work after an adjournment in 1873. The delegates represented an interesting and important variation from the convention which produced the 1838 Constitution and which was dominated by farmers; now lawyers and businessmen were in the majority. The convention was itself a true reflection of the new Pennsylvania produced in less than half a century. The proceedings were full of denunciations of the evil influences of lobbyists "with their pockets full of money" and what the great and aging jurist and lawyer Jeremiah Sullivan Black characterized as the "conclusive, irresistible, and overwhelming" evidence of an "utterly corrupt" legislature. Floating or elastic charters, it was charged, could be bought for $5,000, to enable a corporation to be formed which could do almost anything.

The new Constitution reflected these charges. Granting charters and special legislation on franchises for business or other purposes were ended. Heavy penalties for bribery were established; the Assembly was enlarged in the illusionary hope that a larger body would be less subject to special interests. The term of the governor was reduced to a single consecutive four-year term as opposed to a possible two terms, each three years in length. The governor was empowered to veto special items in appropriation bills rather than accept or decline the total bill. The office of lieutenant governor was created; a Department of Public Instruction was created to supervise the state's school system. Terms of county officers were fixed at three years and the tenure of judges was reduced. The general trend of the entire document was governed by the growing disgust of the people with the widespread political manipulation and corruption of the postwar years. An entire section was devoted to control of the abuses of monopoly, especially railroads, but was left very much up to the Assembly to make it effective. The Constitution was ratified in December, 1873, by a vote of 253,560 to 109,198 and became operative January 1, 1874. While it contained new checks on the influence of special interests on state government, especially railroads, it certainly did not bring them to an end.

FURTHER EVIDENCES OF A
DEMAND FOR REFORM

The Republican organization received a severe jolt in 1874 when it lost control of the Assembly and had to submit to the election of William Wallace, state Democratic leader, as United States senator. Not a little of the Republican weakness came as a result of the rise of the Greenback Labor Party. Though usually thought of as a part of western agrarian discontent, Greenback-ism appealed also to Pennsylvania farmers, as well as to labor. Its influence grew with the distressed economic conditions that followed the Panic of 1873. Victor Piolett of Bradford County, a leader of the Grange in Pennsylvania, was among several outstanding Greenback leaders and the soft-money advocates had a considerable newspaper press in the state during the seventies. In the election of 1878 the shrewd manipulations of Robert Mackey and Matthew S. Quay swayed the Greenbackers away from a potential coalition with the Democrats; as a result, Luzerne County's Henry M. Hoyt was elected governor by over 22,000 votes. Hoyt promptly made Quay Secretary of the Commonwealth. Hoyt continued the "Civil War general" tradition and was formerly chairman of the Republican state committee. Despite this fact, it was not long before he was at odds with the organization.

Early in the Hoyt administration the Republican leadership sponsored the "riot bill," which would have appropriated $4,000,000 to compensate the Pennsylvania Railroad for damages during the Pittsburgh railroad strike riots. Allegheny County legally was liable but the Magee-Flinn machine decided to let the state pick up the bill. Before it was finally passed, a public outcry induced a legislative investigation which proved that eight persons, including three members of the House, had been involved in corrupt solicitation on behalf of the bill. The bill was killed and the guilty legislators tried and sentenced to the penitentiary, only to be pardoned by the Attorney General. Still another scandal rocked the Hoyt administration when the Quay candidate elected as State Treasurer turned out to be a very high-minded individual, and demanded a strict accounting of the handling of state funds. This proved embarrassing to Quay and the former State Treasurer, who had followed the practice of making loans for speculative purposes from banks with state deposits, assuring the banks that state funds deposited in them would remain to cover the loans. Governor Hoyt was the innocent victim of such scandals and ended up by joining the forces of the Independent Republicans. The Independents refused to go along with the efforts of Donald Cameron and Quay to endorse a third term for President Grant and also rebelled against Cameron's efforts to control the election of his hand-picked United States senator. Efforts failed on the part of the Quay-Cameron machine to reach a compromise in 1882 with the Independents by nominating General James A. Beaver of Bellefonte, Civil War hero who had lost a leg in battle, for governor and conceding them the lieutenant governorship along with some pious platform promises of reform.

The Independents met in a separate convention in Philadelphia in May, 1882. While accepting the fact that General Beaver was "one of the purest and cleanest men," the Independents adopted a new platform and presented an entirely new slate. "We demand, instead of the insolence, the proscription and the tyranny of the bosses and machine rulers, the free and conscientious exercise of private judgment in political affairs, and the faithful discharge by those who assume trust of the express will of the people," declared the Independent platform. Efforts made to achieve Republican harmony failed. The Democrats came forward with youthful Robert E. Pattison, native of Maryland who had moved to Philadelphia and achieved a reputation for reform as City Controller, as their candidate. The Republican Independents united with Pattison in making the basic issue of the entire campaign repudiation of the rule of the boss and the machine. The Independent Republican candidate, State Senator John Stewart, indicted his own party as "in a state of vassalage, of bondage, and the voice of the honest people of Pennsylvania has not been represented in a Republican convention in a decade." Pattison campaigned without support of William Singerly and his powerful Philadelphia *Record,* which represented the reform Cleveland Democrats. The *Record* charged that Pattison was the tool of Philadelphia's Democratic boss, Lewis C. Cassidy and called him "Cassidy's boy." Such were the vagaries of machine politics of the day in both parties. Pattison won by virtue of the Republican split, though the Democrats showed growing strength generally by sweeping other state offices and the House.

"PENNSYLVANIA'S GROVER CLEVELAND"

Pattison may well be termed "Pennsylvania's Grover Cleveland" in view of his crusade to realize the ideal that "public office is a public trust." He suffered, however, from inexperience in that he was only thirty-two when elected and had no background in public office other than his fiscal post in Philadelphia city government. His inaugural demanded "abolition of useless offices . . . ; rigid accountability in the expenditure of public moneys; a public performance of public trusts; and the raising of the efficiency of the civil service by making fitness and integrity alone the tests of appointment." Pattison was the first Pennsylvania chief executive to call serious attention to the growing power of corporations, which he pointed out should be prevented from coming "too vast and irresponsible." "The existence of such power in any combination of men is to be deplored, and, if possible, prevented; or, at least, regulated and controlled," warned Pattison. He was also one of the first to call attention to the growing conflict between labor and capital and to warn of its dangers. Pattison indicted the Assembly for its failure to implement those provisions of the Constitution of 1873 specifically designed to curb the power of the railroads to limit competition, indulge in rate discrimination practices, engage in mining or manufacturing enterprises, or to permit their officials to be interested in supplying material or supplies to their own companies. The new Democratic governor also bore down heavily on the need to reapportion the legislative, judicial, and congressional districts in accord with population changes.

Pattison, like many a crusader for better government, had his problems. One was of his own making; the appointment of Lewis Cassidy, Democratic boss of Philadelphia, as Attorney General despite public statements prior to election that this absolutely would not be done. Pattison apparently felt the need of Cassidy's political know-how at his elbow. Pattison failed to get his legislative reapportionment legislation and called a special session which labored also without avail. He did secure judicial reapportionment. Pattison was noted for the free use of his veto powers. Most of these were entirely justified. The Constitution had been changed, but not necessarily the legislators who sought under political pressures to slip through various bills which had a devious intent to protect or facilitate certain interests. Pattison watched these bills with care. He improved the moral tone of government, but was ineligible for re-election and the Democrats had to find a new leader. Quay by now had patched up the rifts in Republican ranks and General Beaver was elected in 1886 by a wide margin. In 1887 Quay was able to dictate his election to the United States Senate and thus assume a greater national stature in Republican affairs. In the meantime, Governor Beaver was able to achieve passage of a reapportionment bill and settle this issue. Beaver proved to be an able occupant of the governor's chair in a period when new major problems challenged the state.

The general thinking of most Pennsylvania Republicans was that Daniel Hastings, another resident of Bellefonte, and Beaver's adjutant-general, who did fine work in supervising relief measures following the Johnstown Flood, would be the Republican gubernatorial candidate in 1890, but Quay ruled otherwise. Quay's man was George W. Delamater, wealthy banker and known friend of the Standard Oil interests. Hastings wanted the nomination; when it was denied him many Republicans either did not vote or deserted the Republican ticket to vote for Robert Pattison, who had returned to the political wars. Pattison was elected and his second-term inaugural again stressed political reform, including "purification of elections, involving ballot reform, personal registration, and the prevention of the

Samuel Randall was not only a major force in the Democratic politics of the state, he also exerted national influence in Congress.

misuses of money in politics; the equalization of the burdens of taxation; and the correction of abuses prevailing in the government of municipalities." Out of this drive came the adoption on June 19, 1891, of the Australian or secret ballot. Pattison was perplexed by the Homestead strike with its disorders and was forced to call out the state guard to keep order. Again the Democrats were unable to repeat their success; leaders like Wallace and Randall had grown old. Pattison himself did not emerge as a strong political leader. Thus, despite persistent scandals in state and local government, the Quay machine continued to ride high. Hastings won Quay's support and was elected to the governorship in 1894 by a margin of 241,000 votes, the largest accorded any candidate to this time. Hastings was Pennsylvania's Spanish-American War leader and the state contributed its usual quota of men, supplies, and leaders to this brief little war with such pro-

found results on the nation's position as a world power.

QUAY RIDES THE REFORM WAVE

The nineties came to an end with a resurgence of reform against the Quay machine within Republican ranks. Quay was closely allied with the forces of Mark Hanna and carried the state for McKinley by nearly 300,000 votes in 1896. This was made possible in no little measure by the revolt of conservative "gold" Democrats against William Jennings Bryan and free silver. Bryan's candidacy cost the Democratic Party in Pennsylvania what little chance it had to restore something of a more even balance of party power in the state by scaring the business interests, which had not been without connections in the state Democratic organization, half out of their wits with the threat of cheap money. Quay elected his State Treasurer, trounced soundly Independent Republicans, rallied back of Governor Hastings and made himself not only United States Senator but also chairman of the Republican state committee. He also directed the election of Boise Penrose to the United States Senate in 1896. His usually hand-groomed candidate for the governorship in 1898 was William A. Stone, native of Tioga County and a Pittsburgh attorney. Quay's simmering feud with the Philadelphia merchant, John Wanamaker, and the Philadelphia *North American* now came to a boil. Quay had defeated Wanamaker for the Senate with Penrose, but in February, 1898, some four hundred Republican leaders from fifty-five counties announced support of Wanamaker as their candidate for the gubernatorial nomination. Wanamaker later withdrew in favor of Charles W. Stone but Quay secured the nomination of William A. Stone in the convention by a margin of some thirty-four votes. The insurgents now really revolted and called their own convention, nominating Charles Stone for governor along with candidates for the Assembly with the hope of thus blocking Quay's return to the Senate. Wanamaker used money and the *North American* to aid the insurgent ticket and give Quay the battle of his entire career. Wanamaker called for a legislature free of machine control with its "corrupt and sinister spirit." "In Pennsylvania the laws are made by one man and largely administered by the same individual," declared Wanamaker in one of his slashing attacks upon Quay. He charged Quay with having "so directed legislation that the privileges of corporations are well nigh absolute, while their interests have been so well protected that an unjust proportion of taxation falls upon the people." The Republican organization was further threatened by the strength of the growing Prohibition Party, which also presented a candidate for the governorship. The combined vote of Dr. Silas Swallow, Prohibition candidate, and that of Charles Stone was greater than that of the Democratic candidate, George A. Jenks. The Republican organization candidate, William A. Stone, triumphed by 117,000 votes over Jenks amidst charges of wholesale corruption of the election in Philadelphia. "Divide and conquer" had proved again a successful machine strategy.

Reform movements at the local level in Philadelphia and Pittsburgh were continuous in the same years but without lasting success. When the Assembly met in January, 1899, Quay was under indictment in Philadelphia courts for misappropriation of state funds, a charge which grew out of the custom of depositing these funds in favored banks for political purposes. The independent Republicans and Democrats deadlocked the Assembly on electing Quay as United States Senator; but Governor Stone appointed him anyway. This was too much for even Mark Hanna to swallow, because there was grave doubt as to Governor Stone's power to make the appointment under such circumstances. Quay's appointment was rejected in Washington but he showed his real power by securing the endorsement of the Republican state convention for the post with a declaration that "We express our confidence in Senator Quay's leadership, and we believe in his political and personal integrity." On the strength of this, Quay's name again came before the Assembly in 1900 for election to the United States Senate. It was contested vigorously by the independents in his party and by organized Democrats; two Democrats absented themselves while one in the House and one in the State Senate voted for him,

thus breaking the tie and sending Quay back to the Senate. It is difficult not to agree with independent Republican leader Colonel A. K. McClure that these Democrats were gentlemen of "easy virtue."

Such was the course of political reform through the years following the Civil War. Battles had been won, scars had been made, and some progress achieved but Pennsylvania was far from being a cleanly progressive commonwealth politically by 1900.

POLITICAL METHODS AND ISSUES,
STATE AND NATIONAL

The methods of politics and government changed little between 1865 and 1900. The direct-

Matthew Stanley Quay hardly looked the part of a powerful and ruthless political leader but was a scholarly and somewhat shy person.

Robert Mackey, ablest of all the state Republican leaders of the era.

parties in their campaigns continued to be centered on the use of old-fashioned methods as no radically different means of transportation for inhabitants or communication of ideas appeared before 1900. True, the movement of people was made easier by the railroad, and the telephone began a revolution in communication, but neither can be said to have had a noticeable influence on the conduct of politics in this era. The metropolitan newspaper increased its influence as the railroad made it possible to bring it into more towns, but the mainstay of rural and small-town political news and/or propaganda remained the country weekly. Charges and countercharges on the political front were as virulent and vicious as in earlier days. The opposition was always painted in the blackest colors and the favorable candidate and party made lily white. Only a few independent dailies such as the *North American,* and the *Press* in Philadelphia achieved stature as being more objective in their political reporting and editorials.

The dominant allegiance of a large majority of Pennsylvanians was given to either the Republican or the Democratic parties. The Prohibition Party gained some influence in the seventies, as did the Greenback Labor Party, but drys, farmers, and laborers were not long wooed from allegiance to one or the other of the two major parties. Republicans had their own political gospel. Throughout the era it stressed the protective tariff as the solution to all problems. It guaranteed the stability and continued growth of manufactures and in so doing also guaranteed full employment —the "full dinner pail." This prosperity in turn washed off on the farmer and the small businessman. Everyone was better off under a protective tariff; the Democrats were the party of "free trade" continuously threatening "prosperity" in the Republican story, though Pennsylvania Democrats actually supported the protective tariff. The tariff assumed increased importance in Republican strategy as the waving of the bloody shirt weakened, since Civil War issues were becoming only a memory. Pennsylvania Republicans offered the tariff as a panacea for all the problems of the state economy.

Republicans liked also to boast of their keeping

primary system of selecting party candidates, as opposed to the nominating convention to which delegates were elected, began with the Republicans of Crawford County but it spread slowly and the nominating convention dominated the process of selecting candidates for office. Organization men, whether Republicans or Democrats, were not anxious to surrender their influence to popular-primary contests. Candidates for state offices were selected at the state party conventions and the platforms were drawn up and presented at the same time. The practice of the open ballot persisted until 1891 and printing and distributing ballots was the work of the party organizations. A better way to corrupt elections in cities could hardly have been devised. It is a prize example of older country and small-town election procedure now adopted by the large city. The success of debt and taxes down, their championing of expanding public education, attention to the interests of Civil War veterans and their widows and children, and government which encouraged sound business enterprise. Republican platforms hinted or declared openly that the Democrats were the enemies of all these policies and if they gained control would endanger them. Sound versus cheap money, or gold versus greenbacks or silver, was a national issue of great moment during the entire period, but in Pennsylvania both parties jockeyed back and forth in their stand. The Republican Party, as the party of business, naturally leaned toward a hard-money policy but on occasion, when courting the Greenbackers and Grangers, wrote platforms which could be interpreted as leaning the other way. Many of the dominant leaders in the Democratic Party were businessmen and financiers, and the Democratic platforms, while tinged more commonly with greenback or silver sentiment, hardly advocated cheap money. Indeed, in 1896 the Democratic Party split down the middle over the issue and left the Republicans in the position of compromising on the issue while the "gold Democrats" were ten-carat gold all down the line.

Quite understandably, the conduct of the government itself became a major political issue. The growth of the Cameron-Quay machine dominating the state with the aid of the powerful Philadelphia and Pittsburgh city machines laid the Republican Party wide open to the charge of not merely machine politics but frequently corrupt politics. Frequent scandals kept the issue alive and virtually every key state election, as well as those in the two cities, hinged on charges of misgovernment if not downright graft or corruption. It was this issue which put Pattison in the governor's chair and then returned him after a four-year absence. It was the issue behind Independent Republicanism and it motivated the reform movements in the state's two great cities. Democrats pointed to these conditions and promised major reforms in the way of laws which would control the abuses and outlaw conditions and practices which made them possible, as well as needed reforms of the civil service itself. Oddly enough, despite its powerful machine, the Republican

Party never cast a large percentage of the popular vote, usually skirting the margin of about 51 per cent. Had the Democrats developed an equally effective statewide organization and unified leadership they might well have put an early end to the political dominance of the Republicans by utilizing this single but powerful issue of political reform. It was a more tangible issue than the tariff, which the Democrats actually accepted anyway, but the Democrats lacked organization and their leadership was constantly divided and feuding. This weakness made it impossible for the Democratic Party to use the political-reform issue with any success.

Certainly one of the most significant developments of the time was the slow recognition of certain new problems of the public welfare as a proper concern of state government. While the administrative structure of state government and action on public-welfare problems remained stabilized on a Jeffersonian and laissez faire basis before the Civil War, the beginnings of a change are observable after 1865. For example, in 1869 legislation was passed that recognized the right of labor to form unions; by 1872 the use of the strike as a weapon on the part of labor was recognized by law, even though severely circumscribed in application to preserve the open shop. This was only a faint step and the disorders associated with the railroad strikes in the seventies and the later Homestead strike hurt the cause of labor, though the state's intervention in these labor disorders was well handled. The right to organize and to strike was in contrast to legislation about the same time legalizing the coal- and iron-police system used so effectively against labor by private companies. Governor Pattison recognized, as has been mentioned, the dangers of the growing power of the corporation and sought to strengthen regulation of business, though without success. He also noticed the problem of labor versus capital, as did Hastings and Beaver. Hastings in his inaugural declared, "Labor has the right to organize for mutual protection and advantage, the same as capital."

Governor Hastings advocated and secured creation of the State Department of Agriculture, which replaced an earlier State Board of Agriculture. Party platforms of the seventies began to contain vague statements about recognizing the interests and concerns of the farmer. A State Board of Health was created in 1885 and a State Medical Council in 1893. In 1897 the State Forestry Commission was created and Pennsylvania began its long and distinguished conservation program. State regulation of certain railroad practices dangerous to the public was provided for in the Constitution of 1873, though not well implemented by law or court action. State regulation of insurance companies was written into law in 1871 and supervision of state banks in 1891. Some attention was directed toward regulating safety and other conditions in mills and mines and both mine and factory inspection were established as state functions. But again it was only a faint start and was not well enforced. Pure-food-and-drug laws were enacted. A system of state hospitals in mining areas especially to serve injured workers was started in 1883. Laissez faire still reigned but faint cracks in the wall of conservatism could be noticed by the turn of the century, not only in law but also in the recommendations of governors.

Government remained simple and inexpensive. The salary of a legislator was $1,500 plus some expenses of a modest nature. The governor himself drew a $10,000 salary, while the Lieutenant Governor cost the taxpayers only $5,000. Most cabinet posts paid $4,000 and some only $3,500. Receipts of the state government reported by Governor Curtin for the fiscal year ending November 30, 1865, were $6,219,989.67 and, despite the war, expenses were only $5,788,525.16 with a state debt of $39,379,603.94. Governor Hastings reported for the fiscal year ending November 30, 1898, revenues amounting to $13,325,120.97, with expenditures of $13,973,803.46. The state appropriations for education accounted for nearly one-half the total cost of state government, amounting to over five millions. The operating costs of the state government itself in 1898 were less than $2,000,000. Appropriations for "charitable institutions" amounted to $1,191,000. The debt had been reduced to slightly over $1,000,000. Corporation taxes in 1898 provided almost $7,000,000; just

about one-half the total income of the state. Personal-property taxes levied by the state, of which half were returned to the counties, amounted to $2,722,000, while licenses of various types accounted for $2,051,000. Here was little evidence of expensive government or burdensome taxes. Indeed, the old state tax on real estate had been repealed and replaced by corporation taxes by the shrewd Republican leadership.

The structure of government also changed little. A few new state offices and officials appeared as a result of factory and mine inspection, concern for agriculture, and regulation of banks and insurance companies. A start was made toward conservation with a Fish Commission in 1873 and a Game Commission in 1895. A State Livestock Sanitary Board was set up also in 1895 and the State Library was created in 1889, with a Free Library Commission set up ten years later. Extensive regulation of business or of individuals by government legislation was not the order of the day. The state election laws were rather thoroughly overhauled after 1880 in an effort to curb serious evils in voting. In 1889 the cities of the state were reclassified into three classes based on population. Fees were curbed for county officials, who were placed on fixed salaries to end general abuse of the old-fashioned fee system.

At the local level, the larger Pennsylvania cities were becoming concerned about such matters as public parks and playgrounds for children, official boards of health, public aid for the unemployed rather than reliance on charity, more public money and better care for the insane and other unfortunates, along with similar social problems. Awareness of such problems was also giving rise to organizations of citizens devoted to their consideration and solution. In general, Pennsylvania differed little from other industrial states with growing cities. The seeds for the later Progressive movement were planted in the nation, though Pennsylvania would still be slow to respond. It was also a victim of the worst evils of domination by the political machine and boss. These evils persisted longer in Pennsylvania than in any other single state because of the brilliance of the machine leadership and the willingness of favored interests to continue to pay the price.

Pennsylvania during this period did not produce a President, though it had many favorite-son candidates in conventions. On the Democratic side, the distinguished Civil War general, Winfield S. Hancock, was Garfield's opponent in 1880, and under ordinary circumstances would have been expected to win; the Republicans could hardly wave the bloody shirt in the face of Hancock. Hancock lost, however, by a close vote and Pennsylvania's Republican machine rather spelled the difference, even though the Quay-Cameron forces were by no means enthusiastic over Garfield. In 1884 Pennsylvania's Samuel Randall, mentioned earlier, was a leading candidate for the nomination as the candidate of the Democratic Party for the Presidency. Governor Pattison was a dark horse in Democratic conventions after his term at Harrisburg. Despite the strength of the Republican organization, Pennsylvania was recognized as a keystone state in contests for the presidential nomination in both parties and as a somewhat doubtful state in most elections after 1876. Cameron and Quay were more influential in national affairs as political bosses than were most Presidents. In the Democratic camp William F. Harrity and William Singerly were powerful national leaders of the Cleveland era. Donald Cameron was Secretary of War for a time under Grant but was out of favor with Hayes. John Wanamaker was Benjamin Harrison's Postmaster General. All in all, Pennsylvania produced a respectable number of national leaders during the era.

Campaign poster used in the election of 1888. Note the emphasis on tariff reform as a major issue of the Democrats.

MAKE PENNSYLVANIA DEMOCRATIC

GRAND STATE RALLY FOR TARIFF REDUCTION
—— AND FOR ——

CLEVELAND & THURMAN,
THE CHAMPIONS OF REFORM.

VICTORY

DEMOCRATS and all others interested in Tariff Reform are Requested to meet at

CORNWALL HOUSE,

At 7 O'CLOCK, P. M.

SATURDAY, SEP. 29, '88.

For the purpose of listening to a discussion of the great Political Issues of the day and for a general interchange of ideas. Able Speakers will be in attendance or the issues of the day will be presented in some other interesting and intelligent manner.

By Order of the Democratic State Committee,

DANIEL MUSSER,
County Chairman.

CHAPTER FIFTEEN

A MORE PROGRESSIVE ERA IN POLITICS AND GOVERNMENT

If there is a single word which would describe the change in the government and politics of Pennsylvania since 1900 it is "progressive." The politics and government of the entire nation were due for broad changes and reforms after 1900. These included continuing political reforms such as restoring government to the rank and file of the people and striving to prevent political machines, regardless of party, from primary control of the actions and policies of government; along with a further utilization of the power of government to concern itself with the welfare of the people in terms of social and/or economic problems. Pennsylvania was slow in adjusting itself to the total program, which in the nation as a whole was known as the Progressive Movement. The pressure to change the government in ways of administration as well as policy was less successful in a state where big business flourished and forces pressing for political or other reforms remained weaker than in some other states. Pennsylvania's continued failure to modernize its 1873 constitution shows how slow has been progressivism in Pennsylvania. However, if "progres-

sive" is a word which indicates change and for the better, it is well applied to Pennsylvania. The years since 1900 have at least been progressive as contrasted with earlier decades.

TWENTY YEARS UNDER THE REPUBLICAN MACHINE

For over two decades after 1900 Pennsylvania literally was ruled by the Republican political organization without successful dispute of its power. This took place in an era when throughout the country forces of political revolt were on the march. Why were they without success in the Keystone State? Certainly a major reason was the weakness of the state Democratic Party. After recovery from the stigma of having opposed the war under Lincoln, the party by 1896 had risen with the election of Robert Pattison to two separate terms as governor and considerable success in electing other state officials and legislators, to a position of at least a respectable opposition. The revived Democratic Party had influential and conservative business interests in its ranks but

270

the candidacy of William Jennings Bryan in 1896, as pointed out earlier, drove the "Gold Democrats" into the Republican Party. This was a severe blow to the Democrats, from which it took them long years to recover. Democratic weakness was aided and abetted by shrewd Republican leadership. In much of the state the Democrats became a kept party with its leaders and organization receiving certain favors in return for a quiescent position. This situation was so well concealed that Joseph F. Guffey, veteran western Pennsylvania Democratic leader, reveals in his autobiography that it was not until 1930 that he learned that the Philadelphia Democratic organization was paid with money and a few local offices to behave. He did not know, it appears, that at one time the Vare organization even paid the rent for Democratic headquarters. At the same time, Guffey apparently found no inconsistency in his serving for nearly twenty years as secretary and general manager for the Republican-controlled Philadelphia Company, dominant utility in Pittsburgh. In most smaller counties the business and banking interests contributed to both parties to be on the safe side but the Democrats received only crumbs. The happy practice of controlling at times even the highest nominations to office in the Democratic Party which had been fostered by Mackey and Quay was continued with success by Boise Penrose and his organization.

The 1900's opened with a triumph of the Quay organization in 1902 when Robert Pattison, who had become the hope of the Democrats in adversity, was defeated in a try for a third term as governor. Samuel W. Pennypacker was Quay's selection. He was a lawyer, a judge of distinction, and a man of great culture and learning. Just how a person of this caliber could become the candidate of the Quay machine is hard to understand, but it had happened before and would happen later. The explanation is that in an era of dominant party control under the Constitution of 1873 the governorship for a single term was an office from which the machine could profit in the person of candidates of great luster in an election but with a realization he could not build an organization about his own policies in four years without promise of re-election and thus was actually with-

out any real political power. Within this limit, he could work for many constructive ideas that were his own but that did not upset the organization arrangements between business and government. Some governors revolted, but they were helpless to accomplish their ends. The Pittsburgh machine was running a little wild as a result of the illness and death of "Chris" Magee and a reform movement that won some success under a Citizens Party organization that was threatening its power in the early 1900's, but the end result was control by the regular Republicans.

In Philadelphia a new name was emerging in Republican politics as the brothers Vare came to the fore—George, Edwin, and William. The

Republican leaders gather to discuss problems at the national Republican convention in Philadelphia in 1900, as sketched by an artist.

Vares found their opportunity when the eldest brother, George, was elected to the House in Harrisburg and became a pal of "Iz" Durham, who was becoming a potent force in Philadelphia as well as in Harrisburg. Young Boise Penrose, son of a distinguished Philadelphia family and one time scholarly student of government, had been elected to the United States Senate in 1897 and, following the death of Mathew Quay in 1904, assumed his mantle of leadership of the Pennsylvania Republican organization. Penrose ruled the party with an iron hand, though not without serious revolutionary uprisings that challenged that rule, until his death in 1921, and steered the state along paths of organization control that were probably the strongest to remain alive in any single state. The rewards of organization power were much richer than even in Quay's time. Now the corporations willing to buy favors from government through the machine were incorporated in the hundreds of millions and even a billion dollars, as compared with the puny million of the earlier decades. Penrose represented an alliance between increasingly powerful government and increasingly large corporate enterprise, which was the more solid in Pennsylvania because of its powerful industrial and financial empire. Theodore Roosevelt denounced Penrose in these terms: "Penrose stands in public life for all those forces of evil against which every clean and decent citizen should unflinchingly stand." More unkind and often unprintable things were said about this giant of a man, a bachelor who made politics his major concern in life. Roosevelt's remarks were made when Penrose stood like the Rock of Gibraltar against the Progressive Party which Roosevelt had hurled in 1912 as a challenge at the massive power of the nation's conservative Republicanism. The story is told that in a visit to Harrisburg at a meeting of the state Republican leadership, Penrose was informed that Pennsylvania was for "Teddy" and that any other course would wreck the Republican Party. Penrose pounded his massive fist on the table and roared, "I know that damn well, but I will be in charge of the wreck." Penrose had a complete contempt for any and all political reforms and reformers.

A PROGRESSIVE MOVEMENT IN PENNSYLVANIA

The miracle is that Penrose and machine rule did prevail, because the wave of reform during the Progressive era before World War I was strong and insistent. Even Governor Pennypacker, though forced on the party by the Quay-Penrose forces, was something of a progressive governor. When the controlled Assembly refused to act, Pennypacker in 1906 called a special session to consider political-reform measures. Out of it came a personal registration-of-voters act and heavier penalties for election abuses. Civil service was authorized in Philadelphia for a few offices, and this was a real revolution. The Pennsylvania State Police was established, and this finally led to the end of many abuses connected with the coal and iron private or company police system. In Philadelphia the Penrose machine, led locally by "Iz" Durham, elected John Weaver as mayor in 1905; he was considered a safe member of the machine as former District Attorney. The famous "gas works gang" put through a city ordinance to renew the city lease on this important utility on a long-term rather than a short-term basis, and this aroused a strong public outcry as a "steal." This was one of a long series of such abuses. Mayor Weaver broke with the organization on the issue, fired some of the city officials involved, and thus killed the deal. The Democrats also elected a few city officials. The weakness of reform in the face of so powerful a political organization was shown when about two years later a slightly changed gas-works proposal was pushed through city council without more than murmur of public protest.

Unrest did lead to the election in 1905 of William H. Berry as State Treasurer, and this in turn exposed the infamous scandals connected with the building of the new State Capitol. On February 2, 1897, the original building was burned in a fire of undetermined origin and the new and present Capitol was not completed until 1906, at a cost of some $13,000,000. It was dedicated by no less a personage than President Theodore Roosevelt, then on better terms with Senator Penrose than a few years later. The newly elected Democratic State Treasurer discovered that the commonwealth had been bilked through a system of inflated billings that charged much more than actual cost for furnishings, and other unjustified charges. An investigation resulted that all Pennsylvanians would like to forget; several key state officials naturally were involved and the unsavory situation won nationwide attention from which the state was long in recovering in terms of its political reputation. Pennsylvania's truly distinguished Capitol with its fine art work by Pennsylvania artists Edwin Abbey and Violet Oakley, along with George Grey Barnard, were not noticed, and it has taken long years to recover this lost luster. To his credit, the Philadelphia dealer in books, Edwin S. Stuart, was the Penrose organization governor and he cooperated in aiding the investigation of the scandals. Stuart is another governor whose record was without blemish and also without particular accomplishment.

Such a scandal would have rocketed into oblivion any political organization but that of Penrose, who now placed in nomination for the office of governorship John K. Tener, native of Ireland, one-time professional baseball player, banker, and congressman. Tener was not a well-known person in the state, but what reputation he had was favorable, which made him the "untouchable" type of candidate so close to the organization pattern. Penrose was successful in wheeling and dealing with the weak Democratic state organization, and its candidate was a nonentity named D. Webster Grim. Not even Penrose could stem the tide of disgust among reform Independent leaders in both parties, and a third party, the Keystone Party, presented the hero of the Capitol graft scandals, William H. Berry, as a candidate. Indeed, Penrose may well have favored this Independent movement as a favorite machine tactic to fragment the voter. Tener won over Berry by some 33,000 votes, while Grim as Democrat was a poor third. Tener's margin was accounted for by the Vare wards alone in Philadelphia. The "divide and conquer" practice of the Republican machine once more had proved effective.

Tener proved to be an able and resourceful governor. A new State School Code was adopted,

The State Capitol, a building of beauty, was the subject of scandal connected with its erection. It is noted for its magnificent dome, shown here.

the Sproul Act began the Pennsylvania statewide highway system, and for the first time the regulation of public utilities by the state was recognized by creating a State Public Service Commission, as well as a new agency to exercise greater supervision by state government over labor and industrial affairs. A Pennsylvania Historical Commission was set up, marking a start toward official recognition of the value of preserving the state's history. A plan for expanding the capital area was also enacted into law, which began a program of future expansion which led to the present Capital Park area. It was during the Tener administration that Pennsylvania officially adopted the direct primary, which had actually been born in Pennsylvania on a county basis several years earlier.

volted against the conservatism of the past. Governor Tener was such a man and his administration may be regarded properly as at least a reflex expression of the nationwide Progressive

Roads like this were common in Pennsylvania before the modern system of state highways was established. This is a section of the present Lincoln Highway, U. S. 30, about 1920.

The terms that Boise Penrose and his associates applied to "Teddy" Roosevelt and the leaders of the Progressive movement in 1912 are hardly fit to print, and the same sentiments were echoed for the most part by the tycoons of finance and industry. When Roosevelt declared in expounding his New Nationalism that there must be a "triumph of a real democracy; the triumph of popular government, and in the long run, of an economic system under which each man shall be guaranteed the opportunity to show the best that there is in him" he was merely raising the blood pressure of the politicians and their conservative allies in business and finance. Be that as it may, it cannot be denied that even as hard-fisted and staunch a believer in controlled politics as the ponderous and heavy-handed Penrose could see the necessity to bend a little bit. Even when he did not, some of his hand-picked candidates re-

movement. Indeed, in Pennsylvania the weakness of the Democrats was such that the only hope for any progressivism must rest with some revolt within the Republican organization.

Signs of some revolt at the local level became evident in Pittsburgh when the death of "Chris" Magee in the nineties left Senator William Flinn head of the Pittsburgh organization. Flinn turned toward a more progressive and reform policy. In 1906 George W. Guthrie was elected as Pittsburgh's first reform mayor and as a Democrat. Three years later the nephew of the late "Chris" Magee, William Magee, was elected on a reform platform as the mayor of the "greater Pittsburgh" made possible by a legislative act consolidating several previously independent municipalities as Pittsburgh. Electing reform mayors never means an immediate purification of the government of any city and this became evident in Pittsburgh, but the forces of reform were on the march in the Steel City and starting to convert it from its earlier reputation as "Hell with the lid off."

The cause of reform had a harder row to hoe in Philadelphia and this may well have saved the Penrose organization. Here the Vare organization steadily strengthened its control despite waves of reform which beat upon its ramparts. The Vares became the citadel of Republican power in the state and are reported to have boasted, "We can send anybody we want to the United States Senate—anybody." The Vare power was great enough to challenge Penrose because the controlled vote could dictate the result of a state and national election, especially after the break between Penrose and Senator Flinn in Allegheny County. William Vare in 1911 decided he would make himself mayor but Penrose interposed with George H. Earle, Jr., as his candidate. Penrose still ruled the legislature through the Republican organization's power in the rural counties and prompted the Catlin Commission's investigation of Philadelphia city government, thinly disguised as a general study of city government in the state. The commission found evidence of illegal contracts in which Edwin Vare was involved, and Earle won the Republican primary. Earle in turn was defeated in the election by Rudolph Blankenburg, known as "Old Dutch Cleanser," and a warhorse of reform. Observers noted that Earle lost by a small margin of votes, most of which would have been forthcoming in Vare wards. It could have been a way in which the Vares showed their power to Penrose.

All the chips were down in 1912 when Theodore Roosevelt, after much wavering and indecision, decided to challenge the regular Republican organization of the nation as candidate for the Presidency in protest against the return to conservatism on the part of President William Howard Taft, his personal choice for his successor in 1908. In the months which preceded the final decision, Roosevelt was influenced in great measure by Pennsylvania forces. His great friend Gifford Pinchot, later Pennsylvania's two-term governor, who had been fired by Taft in a nationally debated controversy over conservation policies, was a strong force constantly urging Roosevelt after 1910 to challenge Taft and the Republican national organization—so much so that the hero of San Juan Hill came to view Pinchot at one time as a pest and a "radical." Despite the cold shoulder, Pinchot looked upon conservation of natural resources and their protection against exploitation by selfish interests as an overwhelming national issue and worked constantly to push Roosevelt into a battle with Taft. In Pittsburgh, the Magee and Flinn forces were in open conflict with Penrose and since he was a bulwark of Taft support became open advocates of Roosevelt's nomination. In Philadelphia the crusading *North American* under the editorship of E. A. Van Valkenburg joined Pinchot in backing "T.R." When Roosevelt was led to run on the "Bull Moose" ticket in 1912, he carried Pennsylvania over Taft by a wide margin. Woodrow Wilson ran ahead of Taft. The Vares were the only Republican local organization to support Penrose and Taft and gave Taft the largest majority of any single congressional district in the nation, evidence of the power of the local organization.

WORLD WAR I AND A RETURN TO NORMALCY

The prophetic words of Penrose that while failure to support Roosevelt in 1912 might well wreck the Republican Party he would be in charge of that wreck were indeed true. A common weakness of reform movements is lack of permanent organization and continuing purpose. Gifford Pinchot was backed by Roosevelt strongly in 1914 in the battle against Penrose for the United States Senate, but like virtually every other Progressive in the country went down to defeat, running only slightly better than A. Mitchell Palmer on the Democratic ticket. When in 1916 Roosevelt refused to accept the Progressive nomination, Pinchot was overcome by a "horrible sense of defeat and futility," for Penrose was back in the saddle. The Vares joined Penrose in supporting Martin G. Brumbaugh, prominent educator and former college president, for the governorship in 1914 and he was elected by some 130,000 votes. Brumbaugh was a far cry from John Tener. His political philosophy as set forth in his inaugural harked back to the nineteenth

Governor Pinchot reviews the Pennsylvania National Guard. The colorful and dynamic personality of Pinchot is evident in this photograph.

fashioned war, with youthful volunteers thrilling pretty girls and marching away to battle with bands and parades. It was old-fashioned enough to permit a person like Colonel Theodore Boal in Centre County, wealthy landowner and a gentleman soldier of the old school, to organize and equip a machine-gun troop first used to hunt Villa in Mexico, but later incorporated in the forces that went overseas to fight the Kaiser. Governor Brumbaugh organized a Committee of Public Safety, which later became the Council of Defense, following a national pattern. It forwarded and coordinated the state's war effort.

A total of 324,114 Pennsylvanians served in the military arm and the total in all armed forces reached 370,961; this was 7.79 per cent of the total United States armed forces and was in keeping with Pennsylvania's traditional manpower contribution. Over ten thousand Pennsylvanians lost their lives in World War I, and twice as many were wounded. Pennsylvania's divisions served with particular heroism in the Battle of the Marne, the Argonne offensive, and at St. Mihiel. Pennsylvania's own 28th Division was one of the more famous fighting units of the entire American Expeditionary Forces. Colonel Edward Martin, who later became governor, was one of its outstanding officers. General Tasker H. Bliss, General Peyton C. March, and Admiral S. Sims were top war leaders who had a Pennsylvania origin. Millions were raised for war relief purposes in the state. About 10 per cent of the taxes and war loans needed to finance the war effort came from the Keystone State. The mines, mills, and factories of the state responded to the utmost in filling orders for war materials and brought the state to the highest peaks of production yet reached. Heavy industry such as steel and ordnance were especially important. Governor Sproul fairly summed up the Pennsylvania effort when in his 1918 inaugural he said, "Pennsylvania's share in the greatest of our national undertakings has been a large one and, as has always been the case, our duty to the Union was well and fully discharged."

The war waged with such fervor to "make the world safe for democracy" left the nation exhausted. Too often it is overlooked that World War I, which Woodrow Wilson made an Ameri-

century; he told his hearers, "We have gone too far on the theory that legislation is the cure of our social, economic, and political ills." Laws, said Brumbaugh should "not only be regulators but educators of the public conscience. Our great assets are not material but spiritual." He used the veto power right and left, killing over four hundred bills in the two sessions of the Assembly. Child-labor legislation, advances in conservation, and a first workmen's compensation act did find their way into the law books under Brumbaugh.

When the United States entered World War I this became the major concern of the Brumbaugh administration. World War I is sometimes called the first modern war, but it was hardly so for a nation that had been through the experiences of the great Civil War. This new war, while world-wide, was far from American shores and it still retained some of the romanticism of old-can crusade to extend to the world the blessings of democracy, used up all the enthusiasm of the Progressive Era for reform. It was left an easy task for men like Boise Penrose to dictate in 1920 the nomination of a man who "looked like a President" but was a feeble excuse for a chief executive of a great nation—Warren G. Harding. Penrose was too ill to attend the Republican convention but literally from his bedside exerted a major influence in defeating the two leading candidates and creating the deadlock that made possible Harding and "normalcy." In Pennsylvania the last man elected to the governorship under the Penrose banner was William C. Sproul. Sproul was a man with a distinguished background as a successful businessman and with much experience in government as a state senator since 1896. His experience in business included newspaper publishing, industry, mining, and railroads. He had been a friend of education in the Senate and was author of the legislation creating a state highway system. He had served as chairman of the Pennsylvania Historical Commission, indicating an interest in the heritage of the commonwealth. Sproul gave the organization itself a questionable degree of normalcy. A man of stature, he evidently determined that the only way a one-term governor could achieve anything was to act with vigor and direction and let the chips fall where they might.

Penrose was ill and died in 1921 but another potential ruler of the Republican organization was already standing in the wings to play the leading role should the billed performer not be able to appear. The stand-in was Joseph R. Grundy, a Bristol Quaker and a textile manufacturer, who realized the importance of a close influence of business in government. Grundy was a small, gentle-looking man who spoke softly and frequently used the Quaker "thee" and "thou" but in business and political action his quiet manner changed to a determined, implacable, and even at times ruthless pursuit of his goals. He never forgot a friend nor forgave an opponent. Penrose viewed him as an excellent fund raiser but a poor politician. Grundy took the lead in 1909 in organizing the Pennsylvania Manufacturers' Association, with offices in Philadelphia. It quickly became the largest and most influential

such association in the country. Grundy was its president until 1947. It gradually created regional and local associations throughout the state. "Manufacturing is the Keystone of the Keystone State" was its apt motto, which meant literally in the minds of Grundy and his cohorts that "what is good for the manufacturer is good for Pennsylvania." The P.M.A., as it became known, derived great strength financially and politically from the subsidiary casualty and fire insurance companies it organized, the principal one of which was the Pennsylvania Manufacturers' Casualty Insurance Company. Grundy was the first industrialist to organize genuinely the political interests of all manufacturers, pressures for which previously had been exerted mainly by individual companies. Since the Republicans controlled the state and were the party of the tariff and generally conservative policies in finance, taxation, and welfare measures, the P.M.A. quite naturally became a right arm of the Republican Party. The annual meetings of the association in Philadelphia became a gathering place for Republican political leaders throughout the state and was looked upon as a place where governors were made or unmade, along with judges and state legislators of key importance. A powerful lobby was constantly maintained in the state capital

Pennsylvania troops in camp in World War I, last of the old-style wars.

to implement the policies of the association.

During the same period the Pennsylvania State Grange, representing the farmers, became increasingly conservative and veered strongly away from the Populism which dominated its leadership in the nineties. It became the left arm of the Republican Party in Pennsylvania, and there developed between it and the P.M.A. a virtual alliance in opposition to just about any piece of legislation which could be labeled as progressive in character, and especially against any laws that threatened to interfere with the prevailing trend of laissez faire in relation to social or economic legislation. This was despite the fact that John McSparran, long-time Master of the Grange, was a Democrat in his politics and onetime candidate for the governorship. Farm and industrial leaders were sleeping in the same political bed, but any resemblance to an alliance for progress was incidental.

Sproul was not a man to take dictation from Grundy or anyone and early encountered opposition when he sought at the start of his administration new taxes to meet the burdens on the state budget created by wartime inflation, along with several other progressive measures. Grundy controlled the speakership of the House, and that gentleman declared the body adjourned and the session ended before Sproul's bills were approved, but Sproul supporters called the body to order again and elected a new presiding officer. The hastily reassembled House was not only reorganized, but pushed through all of Sproul's program, which included a department of welfare, improvements in education, expansion of the state highway system, and other measures. It was quite evident that Sproul's long experience in state politics and government gave him a real advantage in dealing with the opposition.

THE PINCHOT ERA

Gifford Pinchot without a doubt must be accepted as one of the most colorful, progressive, and capable figures to occupy the governorship. Born in Connecticut, he was of Huguenot ancestry and spent his active political career as a resident of Pennsylvania at Milford in Pike County. He was a man who confounded his enemies as well as often alienated his friends. People either loved him or hated him; there was no middle position. He was a great progressive and democratic in his philosophy but a personal dictator whose "GP" scrawled in heavy black pencil on any state paper was a demand that this request be taken care of without question as to proper procedures. Pinchot's great hero was Theodore Roosevelt, and there can be little doubt but that he tried to imitate the doctrine of the vigorous life and other aspects of the Roosevelt tradition. Pinchot loved to ride on horseback to review the National Guard, and in campaigns and traveling throughout the state as governor he chose to ride even in the most rugged weather in an open automobile, his flowing mustache that gave him the nickname of "Old Handlebars" flying in the wind. His lasting claim to fame surely is his strenuous pursuit of conservation both as a pioneer in the movement under President Roosevelt and as Pennsylvania's governor, though this was by no means a pioneer effort of Pinchot in the Keystone State. Here conservation in the form of a state forestry program had been started even before 1900 with a Game Commission, a Fish Commission, and a Forestry Commission. Dr. Joseph T. Rothrock, Henry W. Shoemaker, and many others had taken the lead in developing for the state the sound foundations of a conservation plan that included establishing a state forest program, along with efforts to restore to the streams, forest, and fields the game and fish of an earlier day. In this area Pennsylvania was very much a leader among all the older states, even before Pinchot's governorship.

The first success of the often irascible but dedicated Pinchot, who was termed by his Republican organization opponents as "socialistic" and even "communistic," was made possible with the aid of "Uncle Joe" Grundy. Grundy had succeeded in uniting the manufacturing interests but had never quite convinced William Atterbury, doughty president of the Pennsylvania Railroad, which was long accustomed to a great influence in state affairs, that he should join the combination. Atterbury was in a position after the death of Penrose to play ball with the Vare organization in Philadelphia. In the spring primary in 1922 the

Atterbury and Vare forces supported George E. Alter, who had been Governor Sproul's Attorney General, for the governorship, and most people bet on Alter in view of this support. The Grundy-Pinchot combination won the Republican primary. Pinchot then ran against Democrat John McSparran, leader of the State Grange, in the fall and won by some 9,000 votes. The Republican organization could hardly let him down, though it may well not have relished the result. Pinchot's doctrines as put forward in his 1922 campaign were not ones which would necessarily displease the higher powers in his party. He was an ardent dry, and this appealed to rural Pennsylvania, where most farmers had a barrel or more of hard cider in the basement and worried little about prohibition. He spoke about too much centralization of government and the need for "home rule," along with the need for economy and improved service on the part of the state government. Pinchot's inaugural mentioned the same objectives and emphasized his belief that the people had voted for a "new order" in state government. There were later varied interpretations placed upon this declaration.

One of Pinchot's first steps was to call on the services of Dr. Clyde King, a brain-truster from the University of Pennsylvania, who took the entire structure of the state government and shook it up from one end to the other. The result was an Administrative Code that covered more areas of government than had any previous legislative act in the entire history of the state, and repealed more acts than had any other law. The repeal portions of the new Code took some thirty-eight pages of the Laws for 1923, and the total Code took almost two hundred pages. It provided a new administrative foundation for the state government, which has been amended from time to time, but remains the basic administrative organization and procedure for the state. Pinchot set up a budget office under the governor to establish some reasonable control and relationship between projected expenses and income, as contrasted with the former haphazard system of appropriations without regard to budget. Employment of state personnel was placed under a classification system involving basic qualifica-

tions, standards of employment, and salary; a retirement system for state workers was started, and in general for the first time certain spoils-system practices a century old were thrown into the wastebasket, and civil servants of the state were recognized as requiring necessary qualifications and worthy of being treated as professional workers in government service.

Conservation received attention by bringing together scattered functions into a Department of Forests and Waters. State forestry conservation was greatly expanded and the first steps taken toward using the forests for public recreation. A Giant Power Survey Board was created under Pinchot to study the water and other power resources of the state in terms of their use in industry, transportation, utilities, and other needs. Attention was directed toward the use of coal to generate power. The board recommendations were broad and provoked powerful dissent because the scheme was based upon stronger regulation of the public utilities. The implementing legislation met with defeat and Pinchot never achieved his desired goal. He did secure strengthening of laws relative to stream pollution and health. Pinchot had campaigned as a dry and his efforts at making prohibition a success deserve recording as a major achievement under difficulties. When what Pinchot desired is compared with what he got, the strength of organization opposition in the Assembly combining manufacturing and other interests was a lesson in practical politics for any progressive.

The ingenious arrangement through which a governor could not succeed himself worked to perfection for organization purposes in 1926, because it is hard to believe that Gifford Pinchot could not have carried his message to the people and won a second term. As it was, he was without any future other than to try for the United States Senate, where he had to contend in the primary with that most distinguished Philadelphian, more or less of an independent, George Wharton Pepper. William S. Vare, leader of the Philadelphia organization, was another candidate on a beer-and-light-wines platform, as opposed to Pinchot's dry stand. Pepper was never quite clear on the prohibition issue, but his Senate candidacy was linked with that of John S. Fisher for the governorship, and with Grundy aid. The Mellon empire in western Pennsylvania, which involved powerful financial and industrial interests, had by now replaced the old Magee-Flinn political organization in Pittsburgh and Allegheny County. It had long "suggested" the members of the United States Senate from western Pennsylvania, including Philander Knox and David A. Reed, both of whom were noted corporation attorneys. A peculiar combination of interests resulted in a Mellon alliance with Grundy to support Fisher for governor and Pepper for the Senate. The Vares supported Edward Beidelman for governor and William S. Vare for senator. Vare won in the race for the Senate while Fisher won the nomination for the governorship. Pinchot characterized Vare as "a wet gangster who represents everything that is bad in Pennsylvania." Pinchot refused to support Vare for the Senate. He was forced to certify officially as governor that on the "face of the returns . . . Vare appears to have been chosen by the qualified electors" but Pinchot added in a note to the Senate his conviction that Vare's "nomination was partly bought and partly stolen" and that the returns did not "in fact represent the will of the sovereign voters of Pennsylvania." Vare eventually was denied his seat by the United States Senate because of excessive expenditures, and certainly Pinchot's comment influenced the decision. Governor Fisher promptly appointed Joseph Grundy to the Senate vacancy, where he became famous as author of the Grundy tariff. Grundy's hour of glory was short; when in 1930 he ran for a full term he was defeated in the Republican primary by James J. Davis, amiable labor leader and well known as "Puddler Jim."

Fisher was a man with considerable experience in both business and government and proved a sound if not spectacular governor. Pinchot's reorganization of state finances and budget left a sizable surplus in the State Treasury and Fisher used it to finance a program of improvements at several state institutions and in highway building. Over 4,000 miles of new highway were built and other thousands improved. Fisher further developed the financial organization of the state by setting up a Department of Revenue and making the budget function more tightly under a Budget Secretary in the governor's office. Fisher added some 450,000 acres to the state forests, and his building program aided welfare and educational institutions. He supported also the use of voting machines on a voluntary basis by local election districts. When Fisher left office he was known as "the builder."

PINCHOT'S RETURN

Standing in the wings ready for a comeback was Gifford Pinchot. He had left office with a January, 1927, farewell address to the Assembly in which he stated frankly and at length some of his views. In it he expressed "the most hearty contempt not only for the morals and the intentions, but also for the minds of the gang politicians of Pennsylvania." The Vares, the Mellon influence in Pittsburgh, and the Mitten utility organization in Philadelphia were mentioned by name in terms of their "black, hawk-like shadows over the community." The "monied interests" had debauched the commonwealth and the average citizen got only the "crumbs which fell from the rich man's table," thundered Pinchot. To his sister he wrote that he had "a great time writing it, and even more fun delivering it." He enjoyed watching the "opposition squirm" and "rubbing it into the gangsters in the Legislature." It is not hard to understand that there were not lacking many and influential persons who not only shed no tears when Pinchot ended his first term, but had absolutely no enthusiasm for a return engagement. A man of means and with an established national reputation that could not be denied, Pinchot was good newspaper copy almost any time he wanted to get attention and was able to keep his name before the public. In Harrisburgh, close lieutenants advised him of the potency of the issues of conservation and control of utilities. A tour of the South Seas on the *Mary Pinchot* secured widespread attention through a motion picture, along with his book *To the South Seas*. The very frankness and energy of Pinchot defied the ability of traditional politicians to try to control him; to attempt it was like trying to put a lid on a volcano that might erupt at any minute. Furthermore, he was wealthy enough in his own right to be uncontrolled. He returned from the South Seas determined to become governor again.

The Grundy battle with Vare again aided Pinchot. The Vares were backing Francis Shunk Brown, respected Philadelphia lawyer; Grundy was back of Samuel S. Lewis, York County Republican power. The Vares supported "Puddler Jim," now Hoover's Secretary of Labor, for the Senate. Lewis withdrew when Grundy recognized that two candidates in the primary would probably mean a victory for the Vares. The Pittsburgh Mellon group backed Brown for governor and Grundy for the Senate. Pinchot's big primary issues were the need for stronger regulation of utilities, and the improvement and enlargement of farm life through better rural roads—"getting the farmer out of the mud," as he put it. He and Mrs. Pinchot reached every nook and cranny of the state in their usual hammer-and-tongs style, mainly at their own expense. Organized labor was lukewarm if not opposed to Pinchot. His main strength came from the powerful Grundy opposition to the Vare machine. Wet Republicans also entered the race to divide the vote further. Grundy was defeated but Pinchot pulled through by some 20,000 votes over Brown, carrying sixty counties; the party split had given him victory. Pinchot's opponent in the fall election was John M. Hemphill, a young Philadelphia attorney. Hemphill had support from the antiprohibitionists. The Vares led in creating a third organization, the Liberal Party, in an effort to divide the vote and defeat Pinchot. Pennsylvania Railroad shops even featured signs asking for votes for Hemphill. Edward Martin as state Republican chairman, along with Grundy, worked hard and long to convince the utilities and other conservatives that Pinchot was not a dangerous candidate. The Mellons remained loyal to the party slate. Pinchot was helped by the revolt of several dry Democratic leaders against Hemphill. His prom-

As late as 1925 scenes like this were not uncommon in rural Pennsylvania as farm boys and girls trudged to one-room schools before the day of the school bus and the consolidated school.

ise of improved farm-to-town highways, plus his dry views, helped Pinchot greatly in rural Pennsylvania. The campaign was vigorous enough to turn out the largest number of voters in history up to that time and Pinchot won by a plurality of 59,000, his largest by far in any race he had made.

Pinchot's twenty-minute inaugural, following example of the same simple and inexpensive ceremonies he had demanded for his first term, was carried over a nationwide radio hookup, another modern innovation. He renewed his pledge to build rural roads, took about a third of his time to attack "government by utility magnates," and pledged a further attack on waste and inefficiency in Harrisburg. He made history by appointing his 1922 Democratic opponent, John McSparran, as Secretary of Agriculture, and two women to cabinet posts. Pinchot at once launched his attack on the utility companies. He had the support of the House, which made an investigation of the utilities, while the organization-controlled Senate acted on its own. His legislative bills were killed in the Assembly and for two years the utility companies and the governor waged a knock-down-and-drag-out battle, during which through death and resignations the governor eventually won control of the State Public Service Commission which regulated the utilities. It was too late to get any action by the commission on any new fronts.

By 1930 the specter of unemployment was raising its head, and Pennsylvania began to face the evils of the nation's first major depression with an antiquated structure for dealing with large-scale distress. With fully one-fourth of the state's labor forces out of jobs, Pinchot called a special session of the Assembly in November, 1931, and asked for new taxes or a bond issue, for relief funds, since Federal aid had been denied. The organization Republican leadership refused to do either by substituting for Pinchot's request for over $100,000,000 a meagre appropriation of $10,000,000 to be paid directly to the local poor districts. By May, 1932, the unemployed in the state totaled 1,132,000. Despite Pinchot's demands, which were put forward in no less than three special sessions of the Assembly from 1932 to 1934, the conservative forces refused to face up to the facts. Many were not willing to admit that a time had arrived when large-scale state aid administered by the state was the only answer to the welfare and relief problem. A bitter wrangle went on as the conservatives continued to try to cut government expenditures enough to secure the needed relief monies. At long last, a State Emergency Relief Board was authorized to supplant direct appropriation to local poor boards.

The greatest lasting accomplishment of Pinchot's second term most certainly was his program of improved rural roads. Some 20,000 miles of second-class township dirt roads were taken over and paved with inexpensive macadam. The roads were narrow and built with few engineering improvements over existing roadbeds, but they did take the farmer out of the mud, and the "Pinchot roads," as they came to be known for a generation or more, were a great benefit to rural Pennsylvania. Pinchot in 1933 urged old-age pensions, compulsory unemployment insurance, minimum wages for women and children, maximum working hours, and stronger child labor laws. Little of this legislation got out of organization-controlled Senate committees. Despite many defeats in achieving his goals, Governor Pinchot left office recognized generally as one of the major progressive statesmen of his time and an advocate of views many of which were translated into political reality during the hectic years of the New Deal. It was not without reason that the Philadelphia *Public Ledger* in July, 1932, called attention to the strikingly similar views of Gifford Pinchot and Franklin D. Roosevelt. Indeed, in a campaign speech in 1930 Pinchot had asked prophetically, "Is it not time for a new deal?"

PENNSYLVANIA'S LITTLE NEW DEAL

Doomed for decades to the position of a political minority not unlike that of Republicans in the South Pennsylvania Democrats continued, as one political columnist put it, "hardly more than the morganatic wife" of the Republicans. In Philadelphia the Democratic organization under John D. O'Donnel was content for years with crumbs from the Vare table. Only in Pittsburgh, under the leadership of younger and more vigorous leadership centered in the persons of Joseph F. Guffey and David L. Lawrence, was there any strong urban Democratic organization. When Guffey deserted Al Smith to climb on the Roosevelt bandwagon, his political future was assured after 1932. In Philadelphia, J. David Stern, publisher of the *Record,* took the lead with John B. Kelly, bricklayer risen to wealthy contractor and sportsman, and another rising contractor, Matthew H. McCloskey, Jr., in erasing O'Donnel in favor of more progressive Democratic leadership against the Republicans. Robert L. Vann, Pittsburgh Negro newspaper editor, helped swing the Negro vote to the Democrats, while the Catholic vote, historically strong in urban areas, was attracted by the evident leadership of members of that faith in the Democratic Party. Organized labor, which had been lukewarm or even opposed to Pinchot despite his liberalism, was brought more into the Democratic fold, and when Thomas Kennedy, secretary-treasurer of the United Mine Workers, was slated by the Democrats in 1934 for Lieutenant Governor, an alliance was made sure. In 1934, putting all these forces together under the shrewd leadership of Guffey, Lawrence, Kelly, Stern, and McCloskey, the Democrats came up with wealthy George H. Earle, III, as candidate for governor. Earle was a scion of earlier sturdy Republican stock who had supported Roosevelt in 1932 and had been appointed minister to Austria as his reward. He was an early leader in warning Washington against the dangers of Nazism. His opponent was the able William S. Schnader, Pinchot's Attorney General and a distinguished Philadelphia lawyer. Earle defeated Schnader, while Guffey won the United States Senate post over incumbent David Reed. The Democrats also won control of the House by a wide margin, but there remained only nineteen Democrats to thirty-one Republicans in the State Senate. The Republican Senate promptly revised its rules to require twenty-six votes to release a bill from committee rather than a simple majority, thus throttling the nineteen Democrats.

The urgent need for state aid to relieve the

Senator Joseph Guffey, long-time leader in state Democratic affairs and an architect of the "little New Deal."

thousands out of work and the exhaustion of state funds for this purpose was the most immediate problem facing the Earle administration. Earle asked for new taxes to raise over $200,000,000 and met with the same opposition as had Pinchot. The taxes would affect business, and the Republican Senate resisted, though a compromise was reached out of necessity. Earle introduced new welfare and labor measures which passed the Democratic House only to be hamstrung in the Republican Senate. The governor did succeed early in outlawing the infamous coal and iron police for which Pinchot had steadfastly refused to sign commissions in his second administration. A more stringent child-labor bill became law, written in accord with new Federal controls. Few other progressive measures were passed, but Republican conservatism proved politically unwise when in 1936 the Democrats swept the General Assembly on Roosevelt's

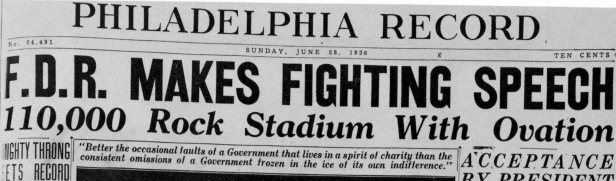

PHILADELPHIA RECORD

No. 24,491 SUNDAY, JUNE 28, 1936 TEN CENTS

F.D.R. MAKES FIGHTING SPEECH
110,000 Rock Stadium With Ovation

MIGHTY THRONG SETS RECORD IN ITS TRIBUTE

Multitude Like One Great Being Roaring Acclaim; Women Weep

BIG HAND TO GARNER

President's Mother Gets Great Cheer; His Son Praises Speech.

By DAVID G. WITTELS

"Better the occasional faults of a Government that lives in a spirit of charity than the consistent omissions of a Government frozen in the ice of its own indifference."

ACCEPTANCE BY PRESIDENT DEFIES TORIES

Ringing Challenge Given 'Economic Royalists' in Message Promising to Preserve Freedom for All in United States.

GARNER MAKES FIRST ADDRESS BEFORE FRANKLIN FIELD CROWD

Attack on Fascist Menace in Financial Despotism Seen as Rap at Smith, Hoover and Hearst.

Texts of Vice President Garner's speech and other addresses at Franklin Field are on Pages 10 and 11.

By ROBERT S. ALLEN

President Roosevelt last night threw down the gauntlet to the forces and mouthpieces of economic despotism.

JACK GARNER NAMED FOR VICE PRESIDENT AS CONVENTION ENDS

Texan Given Ovation as Marching Delegates Cheer Action.

By ROBERT H. WILSON

PRESIDENT FRANKLIN D. ROOSEVELT DELIVERING HIS SPEECH OF ACCEPTANCE

President Roosevelt's Speech of Acceptance

Following is the text of President Roosevelt's address at Franklin Field, accepting the Democratic Presidential nomination:

Senator Robinson, members of the Democratic Convention, my friends:

We meet, at a time of great moment to the future of the nation. It is an occasion to be dedicated to the simple and solemn expression of an attitude toward problems, the determination of which will profoundly affect America.

The Weather

The Philadelphia Record, *Democratic organ, hails the renomination of F. D. R. in 1936.*

coattails and for once had complete control of the legislature. Said Earle, "Liberal forces control both Executive and Legislative branches of our state government for the first time in ninety-one years. It is now our duty to translate that liberalism into positive effective action." The response was what one observer termed "the most sweeping reform program in Pennsylvania's history." A permanent Department of Public Assistance was the state's new answer to local relief as well as its "emergency" state relief program. The need for state public assistance was now formally recognized and never revoked. Improvements were made in workmen's compensation legislation, along with many other acts designed to recognize needs of labor. Pinchot's long crusade against the utilities was answered by ripping out the old Public Service Commission, which some had joked was better termed "Service to the Utilities Commission" in favor of a Public Utility Commission with much enlarged powers. A Milk Control Commission designed to protect consumers was set in motion. A Labor Relations Board, a statutory State Planning Board, a Division of Unemployment Compensation and Employment Service, a State Housing Board—all were new state agencies that marked the end of an era in which state government had had little concern with welfare problems.

The Democrats, balked by the outmoded constitutional limitations on state borrowing, created a General State Authority as a borrow-and-build agency acting as the agent of the state and subject to its control in financing large-scale capital improvements and public works through public bond issues. The State Supreme Court at first declared it unconstitutional, but later reversed its decision, and early in 1937 it was in operation. It started major public and capital improvements for the commonwealth which not only provided badly needed welfare and educational facilities but also aided employment. In the same year the imaginative Earle administration created the Pennsylvania Turnpike Commission by an act of May 21, 1937, which was also empowered to issue bonds to be paid off through turnpike tolls. The turnpike was started October 27, 1938, and opened from near Carlisle to near Pittsburgh two

years later as a truly pioneer project of its kind. The Earle administration continued and expanded the state highway network to the extent of several thousand miles. Steps were taken to make applicable in Pennsylvania, either as new measures or an expansion of earlier plans which had been started in the state, Federal funds for flood control, soil conservation, forest conservation, and related resources programs. The governor advanced earlier programs of conservation by securing liberal Federal aid. Earle also was able to make liberal use of Federal funds for unemployment relief. The WPA and PWA programs spent millions in Pennsylvania, and much of it on highly constructive projects. In the cultural and historical field surveys were made of county records, guides were written to the historical attractions of the state and some of its cities, and interest stimulated in music, the arts, and in museums.

AN ERA OF MILD REACTION

The Democrats' "Little New Deal" was a marked success in that it moved Pennsylvania government great steps ahead in recognizing that government had a responsibility long neglected for coping with many social and economic conditions produced by a new era. Only a few true diehards who wanted to turn the clock back to the time of McKinley could differ. Like many a liberal, Earle himself later turned conservative and became a rather bitter man, but the change in state affairs moved ahead with an inexorable pressure. Success is supposed to produce success, but this is not a reliable axiom in politics. Everything was moving toward the probability that Pennsylvania Democrats could elect another Democrat to succeed Earle, but internal feuding broke out and defeated these bright hopes. Earle was slated for the Senate to oppose Republican incumbent Davis. A nomination that a few years earlier was undesirable to the extent that more than one leading Democrat actually avoided it was now a plum that was blushingly or unblushingly sought by many. Guffey was rumored to want to return to the state as governor. The most logical candidate for that post was Warren Van

The Republicans came to Philadelphia in 1940 in an effort to better their luck.

Dyke, Earle's Secretary of Highways, who earlier in 1934 had stepped aside for Earle as a candidate for governor. His illness and ultimate death removed him from the picture. Charles J. Margiotti, one-time Pittsburgh Republican and noted criminal lawyer, was another active prospect. After his Republican gubernatorial aspirations were defeated in 1934, he had come out for Earle and was made his Attorney General. David Lawrence, Secretary of the Commonwealth and stalwart in making a Democratic success possible, was also mentioned. Charles Alvin Jones, a noted lawyer, was also advanced as a compromise, and it was Jones who was selected by the Democratic voters after a disastrous primary-election battle that saw organized labor and Senator Guffey backing Lieutenant Governor Kennedy, while Earle supported Jones. Margiotti, failing to win Democratic support, made vicious charges against the Earle administration involving alleged graft and

corruption that led to his dismissal from the cabinet by Earle. The Republicans were quick to take advantage by demanding an investigation utilizing the Dauphin County courts and grand jury. The investigation dragged on, and revealed little if any glaring misconduct or corruption, but it did much harm to the Democrats. As compared with earlier revelations, the charges of graft and corruption in state government produced little of consequence.

In any event, as is so often the case, the warm ardor for reform had been satisfied for many Pennsylvanians, who now were quite content to accept Arthur H. James, self-made former breaker boy and mule driver in the anthracite mines, who had risen to the office of Lieutenant Governor under John S. Fisher and a later Superior Court judgeship, as the man who assured the people he would "throw the rascals and the grafters" out of Harrisburg. The Republican over-

286

turn was complete with control of the Assembly and the defeat of Earle for the United States Senate. James waged a campaign that was imaginative and exploited his "breaker boy" background by appearing often in a miner's cap, with a group of singers presenting ballads of the mining days. James pledged an administration that would "help industry" and "a more sane and helpful relationship between industry and labor," along with resisting "rule by the overlords of labor," who he claimed with some justice had dominated the Earle regime.

The Republican desire, real or otherwise, to turn back the clock was not put into action with any thoroughness. Governor James was followed by Edward Martin, James Duff, and John Fine as successive Republican governors and none of them gave any backward motion to state government. Governor James himself emphasized that government was now "becoming the impartial

friend of both employer and employee." In 1939 he created the Department of Commerce to "forward the development and expansion of Pennsylvania's business, industry, and commerce, and to attract new industries to the state." The role of the Department of Commerce grew with passing years to include industrial and community development projects with state aid, help with community planning, and matching funds for tourist promotion. In actual practice Governor James turned back the clock very little. The Pennsylvania Turnpike was extended and Earle's taxes kept. Basically, the era of "big government," with expanding responsibilities in education and public assistance and more costly in its operations, bigger state budgets and more taxes, had become a fixed pattern of Pennsylvania state government.

Governor James was followed in office by Edward Martin, a distinguished figure in Pennsyl-

Newly elected Governor James and retiring Governor Earle ride together in the traditional horse-drawn coach in inaugural ceremonies in 1938. James is on the right and Earle on the left.

287

vania military and governmental affairs over a long period of years. Republican control of the Assembly gave Governor Martin control of his program despite the fact that the Democrats continued to carry the state for F. D. R. and also elected the State Treasurer, the Auditor General,

steps in this mobilization of the war effort by setting up the State Council of Defense, and the Selective Service Board. When the National Guard was federalized, a Pennsylvania Reserve Defense Corps of five thousand men was created for home-defense use. The Citizens' Defense

Governor Edward Martin made history as a soldier, state official, United States Senator. Greatly interested in history, he is looking here at the original Pennsylvania charter from Charles II on display at the State Museum.

and a United States senator, Francis J. Myers. Governor Martin had served his state in the National Guard continuously since 1898, rising in 1939 to the rank of major general commanding the famed 28th Division until his retirement in 1942. He had served as an elected State Treasurer, and Auditor General, and as an appointed adjutant general, and was state chairman of the Republican Party from 1928 to 1934. Upon leaving the governorship, he was twice elected to the United States Senate.

PENNSYLVANIA IN WORLD WAR II

The major task that confronted the latter part of the James administration, and the first half of that of Governor Martin, was mobilizing the state for participation in World War II, the demands of which were broader and greater than in any earlier conflict. Governor James took the first

Corps organized the state for protection against possible air raids. A Civil Air Patrol and a Coast Guard Reserve were other defense measures at home. Governor Martin had at hand a well organized civilian defense administration when he assumed office. It continued to function with efficiency for the duration of the war and at its 1943 peak, 1,661,000 Pennsylvanians were contributing in one way or another their time and devoted effort.

Pennsylvania may well be termed an "arsenal of democracy" in World War II. Pennsylvanians in the armed services totaled nearly 1,250,000 men and women. On June 30, 1945, when the armed services were at peak strength, there were 667,000 men and 12,913 women in the army; the navy claimed 249,926 men and 7,444 women; the Marine Corps, 39,466 men and 1,530 women; the Coast Guard, 11,669 men and 843 women. It is estimated that one out of every eight adults in

Pennsylvania served in some branch of the armed forces. Over 33,000 Pennsylvanians paid the supreme sacrifice in World War II and thirty-five were awarded Congressional Medals of Honor, the largest number for any single state. Men must be organized and led in war, and it was here Pennsylvania made a truly great contribution. The greatest of these leaders was General of the Army George C. Marshall of whom President Truman said, "He takes his place at the head of the great commanders of history." His later services as diplomat, Secretary of State, and Secretary of Defense make Uniontown's George Marshall, who grew up around the battlegrounds of the French and Indian War in western Pennsylvania, one of the most notable Pennsylvanians of the century. General Henry "Hap" Arnold built the might Army Air Force which General Carl Spaatz helped direct in World War II. General Joseph T. McNarney planned the reorganization of the army in 1942, was Deputy Chief of Staff for two years, commanded in the Mediterranean theater, and followed General Eisenhower as head of the Army of Occupation. General Eisenhower himself had a Pennsylvania German ancestral background. Three out of twelve full-rank World War II generals were from Pennsylvania, four lieutenant generals, eighteen major generals, and seventy-four brigadier generals. Admiral Harold R. Stark, chief of naval operations, was from Wilkes-Barre, and the state could claim to be the birthplace of five full admirals, seven vice-admirals, and seventeen rear admirals in the navy.

An amazing concentration of camps and depots sprouted all over the state, some of which became permanent. Pennsylvania's National Guard Indiantown Gap Military Reservation, acquired in 1929-31, was leased by the Federal government in 1940 as a training camp where some five major units were trained during the war. It was also used to muster out nearly half a million men in 1945-46. New Cumberland Reception Center, across the river from Harrisburg, was used for inductees from 1941 through 1945 and is still retained as a depot. New Cumberland Armed Services Depot, one of twelve in the nation, was also here. Below Harrisburg, the Middletown Air Service Command Depot in wartime later became Olmstead

Air Force Base and a major air supply center. The Air Force Intelligence School in Harrisburg was another major wartime service installation. At Carlisle, the historic military post became until 1946 the center of the Army Medical Service School and is now a unit of the Army War College. Mechanicsburg, near Harrisburg, was chosen as the location for a huge naval supply depot, which remained in use and was expanded after the war. Letterkenny Ordnance Depot near Chambersburg occupied 21,000 acres and is still used for this purpose. Two huge army hospitals were placed in Pennsylvania, one near Butler and the other at Phoenixville. Philadelphia had the Navy Yard, the Naval Hospital, the Navy Air Materiel Center and Naval Aviation Supply Depot, the Philadelphia Quartermaster Depot, the Marine Supply Depot, the Signal Corps Procurement Depot, along with famous old Frankford Arsenal and major centers of supply and service. The port of Philadelphia handled tons of war cargo. Thirty-eight of the state's colleges and universities were wartime training centers of one type or another for thousands of special-service personnel.

Modern wars are won with men, leaders, and materiel. Pennsylvania helped supply the materials of war in abundance with its varied heavy and light industry. While it held only 6.5 per cent of government contracts, Pennsylvania industry won 9.5 per cent of all army-navy "E" Awards and 12.6 per cent of the "M" Awards. The state ranked seventh in war contracts among all the states and up to May 31, 1945, had completed finished contracts, not including subcontracts or raw materials, amounting to $12,917,797,000. It provided some 30 per cent of the coal, 31 per cent of the steel, and built 25 per cent of the ships used in World War II. It was a leader in refining petroleum products, first in producing cement, and ranked third in total ordnance production. Some eight thousand plants were engaged in some type of war production, which included just about every product the government was contracting for. Total industrial production grew over two and one-half times during the war years and many a record was set which may never be reached again.

Federal taxes paid out of Pennsylvania rose to nearly $4,000,000,000 in 1945; it contributed over $9,000,000,000 in the purchase of bonds during the various bond drives, along with many millions for a variety of war relief services.

THE POSTWAR ERA

It was World War II rather than Franklin Roosevelt's New Deal that really launched big government in the United States, for the war gave a tremendous impetus to the established trend. The war hiked taxes and debt to meet new obligations. Government was thrust into the lives and concerns of people in hundreds of ways; things were never to be quite the same again despite nostalgic longing on the part of some. This was clearly the case in Pennsylvania, where Governor Martin as an enlightened conservative faced the problems of the immediate postwar period. Thousands of veterans were returned from the armed services and needed time to adjust to civilian life. A vastly expanded war production effort faced a severe and quick cutting back that threw thousands out of work. By the fall of 1945, over $4,000,000 in unemployment compensation benefits had been paid to returned veterans under liberalized laws, while a model program for veterans' aid was organized by 1945 legislation creating a Veterans Commission.

A whole host of special measures designed to aid the veteran came at the same time that Governor Martin was practicing rigid economy. Martin sponsored legislation to create a commission for postwar planning and it allocated some $200,000,000 for public works, improvements for correctional and penal institutions, and state parks and historical shrines. Martin secured a consolidation of the Pennsylvania Historical Commission, the State Archives, and the State Museum into a Pennsylvania Historical and Museum Commission in 1945, and projected a William Penn Memorial building to house a new museum and archival center. He also instigated a new program to erect roadside historical markers pointing out the historic sites and buildings so richly scattered throughout the commonwealth. The Penn-Lincoln Parkway highway improvement for Pitts-

burgh was started, along with plans for development of Independence Hall Park in Philadelphia, and Point Park in Pittsburgh.

The Martin administration also saw the passage of the Brunner Act, which began a strong program to clean up the streams of the state, which were heavily polluted by industry, mines, and the dumping of city sewage without proper treatment. Desilting the Schuylkill River was started. A State Soil Conservation Commission was created. A Pennsylvania Aeronautics Commission evidenced concern for the new air age and its proper growth. The so-called Troutman bills revised and modernized penal and correctional programs and institutional approaches to them. Attention to problems of the blind, the mentally ill, slum clearance and housing, public health, and improvements in the public assistance program was evident in the Martin administration. For a man who rather prided himself upon being conservative, Governor Martin set the pace in a number of fields of state welfare and improvement programs to be expanded in the future.

Even before Martin's term ended there was concern in Republican circles as to his successor. Martin's long experience in state government and politics had combined with his outstanding integrity and sincerity to win him the support of all factions in the party. By 1946 there were some rumblings of discontent. Joseph N. Pew, Jr., Sun Oil Company magnate, had entered the picture as a Republican power demanding consideration. The Grundy and Mellon interests were reported as not entirely in agreement on several policy matters. The Pennsylvania Railroad had never stepped out of the Pennsylvania political picture, and maintained its representative or lobbyist in Harrisburg. Sun Oil and Pew also had similar representation at the state capital. The lobbyists of these two powerful corporations were so influential as to be known commonly as the two additional members of the State Senate. The Senate had become the real seat of power in legislation. Here was the citadel of resistance to any measure that conservatives might not like, because rarely could its control be captured by any overturning from the reform movement. When the very vital problem arose of selecting a

James H. Duff was a colorful and able governor interested in conservation. Here he is assisting in planting tree seedlings.

successor to Martin, the Republican machine, even though fragmented as compared with the days of Cameron, Quay, or Penrose, still existed in terms of a council of the leaders of the factional or group leaderships. Harrisburg's long-time state senator and Dauphin County leader, M. Harvey Taylor, emerged as the leader of the Senate whenever it was under Republican control. The conflicts of interest were such that a "dark horse" candidate was the only solution, and Governor Martin presented James H. Duff of Carnegie, his Attorney General, who had been a strong advocate of clean streams and other conservation measures, as the compromise. Duff was a forceful character, who had first attracted notice in politics as a Bull Moose supporter of Teddy Roosevelt. A Pittsburgh lawyer with a Scotch-Irish ancestry, he had been a figure in the oil business, and his six-foot-plus stature and bristling crew-cut red hair had won him the title of "Big Red." Duff was not only nominated in the primary, but easily elected over John S. Rice, wealthy Democrat and fruit grower from Adams County. Governor Martin was elected to his first term in the United States Senate, and resigned as governor in time to be seated at its opening ses-

sion, leaving Lieutenant Governor John C. Bell to hold the post of governor from January 2 to 21, 1947. Thus Pennsylvania had three governors within a matter of weeks in early 1947.

Duff was a vigorous, highly intelligent, and truly independent personality, and, judged by any standard, was an able and distinguished governor. All accounts agree that Duff at once ran head on into the desire of G. Mason Owlett, who had succeeded Joseph Grundy as head of the P.M.A. (Pennsylvania Manufacturers Association), to call most of the shots for the new administration. Owlett, according to good evidence, came to Harrisburg early to outline at least to some extent the course Duff should follow, and was told in no uncertain terms that Duff was his own boss. Duff's inaugural address presented a brief, pithy, and forward-looking program, with emphasis upon clean streams and properly protected forests, a better break for the mentally ill, and for education. At the February 25, 1947, annual meeting of the P.M.A. in Philadelphia, Duff boldly declared himself as opposed to the normalcy of the Harding era, and startled his listeners by saying that "whether we realize it or not, we are definitely in a revolutionary period." That which once was a "rural and agrarian economy," he pointed out, had now become "in the main both urban and industrial." Labor and management, said Duff, "must join and play on the same team if we are to preserve the American way of life." After all, this was good Pinchot doctrine, and the facts were new only to those who, like many a Pennsylvania conservative, refused to read the signs of the times. Duff gave Pennsylvania a highly aggressive and forward-looking administration featuring highway improvements (which included extending the Pennsylvania Turnpike), education, and a new clean-streams programs (including the cleaning up of the Schuylkill), a vigorous mental-health program, and a generally higher tone of progressive government. Duff as early as 1947 was an announced supporter of General Eisenhower as the Republican candidate for the Presidency, which added nothing to his popularity rating with Pennsylvania conservatives, with whom he already ranked about zero. Duff opposed Thomas E. Dewey in the national Republican convention. Duff decided to run for the United States Senate but his election was not easy, and "Big Red" laid his prestige and ability on the line in campaigning for the post against the ill-concealed opposition of many more conservative Republicans.

Not only did Duff win the election to the Senate, but he hand picked John S. Fine, former Pinchot lieutenant in Luzerne County, lawyer and Superior Court justice, as his successor. Fine was nominated and elected over a youthful newcomer to the Democratic Party of whom more would be heard later, Richardson Dilworth of Philadelphia. What happened to the relationship between Duff and Fine after the election in 1950 remains to be explained, but an early separation of the two minds is clear. Fine was very political minded, and rumors developed at an early date that he wanted to make his own way on a basis of his personal political contacts and pledges. In so doing, he won few friends, nor did he influence many people. His was the first administration to face a financial crisis with state income failing to meet increasing needs. Fine needed over $1,000,000,000 to meet state budget needs for the first two years of his term. He proposed a flat 1

per cent income tax, since the Constitution did not permit a graduated income tax. The Republican leadership repudiated any form of income tax, and forced Fine to accept a 1 per cent selective sales and use tax. This situation, naturally, did little to ease the discomforts of the Fine administration.

Governor Fine also faced the problem of further governmental reorganization, long delayed following the first Pinchot administration some three decades earlier. The growing pressures on state government led all experts to demand a restudy, and under Fine the Chesterman Committee made such a study. As usual, the task was undertaken by a committee studded mainly with names in business and finance. It was headed by Francis J. Chesterman, retired Bell Telephone executive, and assisted in its actual work by professionals from the state's university and college departments of government and political science. The recommendations of the Chesterman Committee were made under Fine and implemented later. The final evaluation of the Fine administration awaits the longer view of history, but it was by no means a failure. The Department of Health was reorganized. A study of penal and correctional institutions resulted in the administrative transfer of this problem from the Department of Welfare to the Department of Justice. Additional progress was made on the clean-streams and mental-health programs to which Governor Duff had given so much attention. Highway and educational programs also continued to move forward under Governor Fine.

THE DEMOCRATS RETURN TO HARRISBURG

The Fine administration drew to a close in the midst of developing bitterness and factionalism in Republican ranks. Fine appeared at times to be endeavoring to build his own personal organization as well as to establish some alliance with the Grundy-Owlett forces. Duff, from his post in Washington, was in a belligerent mood and without a doubt desired to promote a progressive Republican candidate. As usual when conflicting factions were involved, a compromise candidate was agreed upon in the person of Lieutenant

Governor Lloyd Wood. Wood was an experienced legislator and political leader, a big, genial man who had few if any enemies in either camp; and this could be said of few prominent Republicans in 1954. Despite the Republican perplexities, the Democratic nomination literally went begging as Richardson Dilworth backed away from what he thought to be another futile contest with the Republicans. A young York County chicken farmer named George Leader, who had served one term in the State Senate following in the footsteps of his father, was given the nod by the Democratic leadership. Leader was a young, intelligent, and vigorous personality who waged a fighting campaign which for the first time made considerable use of television. Leader's youth and personable appearance were in sharp contrast with that of the pudgy, heavy-jowled and inarticulate Wood. Vain efforts to use the golden tongue of William S. Livingood, Republican Secretary of Internal Affairs and a possibility for the gubernatorial nomination himself, and the hard-hitting personality of James Duff were not enough to convince the voters that Wood was other than an ordinary politician. By October it was evident that Leader was bound to win, but his final margin of 279,196 votes was still a surprise. Miss Genevieve Blatt was elected Secretary of Internal Affairs on the Democratic ticket, the first woman to be elected to a constitutional post in state government. The Democrats also won control of the House by a slim margin, but the Senate remained in Republican hands.

Leader had campaigned against the sales tax as resting most heavily upon the poorer classes, and those least able to pay a new state tax. The thirty-seven-year-old Leader, second youngest governor in the state's history and the first farmer to occupy the office since Governor Ritner, drove a classified income tax scheme through the Democratic House after a long and hard fight, but was forced to bow to Republican opposition in the Senate, and not only to accept a sales tax, but to increase it to 3 per cent. Leader's 1955 budget demanded expenditures totaling $1,273,164,930 for the 1955–57 biennium, or about $218,000,000 above Fine's last budget. Education and public assistance were responsible for some 80 per cent of this

Governor George Leader, second Democrat elected after 1900. Leader was a young and vigorous champion of good government and is sometimes called the "Democrat's Pinchot." Served from 1955 to 1959. He is shown here announcing his support of Adlai Stevenson for the 1956 Presidential elections.

amount. New and increased taxes raised some $500,000,000 in new revenues. Leader began a program of state aid for industrial redevelopment and was also a vigorous supporter of the mental-health and clean-streams programs.

Leader became responsible for implementing several recommendations of the Chesterman Committee and established the Office of Administration as a new and important division of the Governor's Office. The Secretary of Administration became a member of the cabinet. Dr. James

Governor David L. Lawrence. A long-time leader in state and national Democratic politics, Lawrence was an "old pro" who continued the Leader policies and most of his cabinet, and prided himself on trying to give the state less partisan government and a balanced budget. Served from 1959 to 1963.

Charlesworth, a noted political scientist from the University of Pennsylvania, was its first secretary, and was followed by another leading political scientist, Dr. John Ferguson, from Pennsylvania State University. The major task of this office became the centralizing of management in the state government, including budgeting and control of financial operations, personnel classification and standards, new management methods in departments of state government, and records control and management. In general, the Office of Administration became a central office for directing a better coordinated and more efficient operation of state government along the lines of the administration of modern business enterprise. It was the most far-reaching move forward in state government since Pinchot's Administrative Code.

Governor Leader also placed several thousand key professional employees of the state under executive civil service, making a huge dent in the traditional Pennsylvania spoils system by his own action when the Assembly refused to establish a sound civil service system for the state. The return of a party to control after long years in the "wilderness" often is fraught with trouble resulting from the pressure of office seekers and others looking for favors denied by the opposition. Governor Earle suffered severely as a result of the misdeeds of spoils politicians among the Democrats who found their way to Harrisburg. Governor Leader met this challenge with a firmness that did little to endear him to Democratic spoilsmen. He not only developed a civil service system, but upheld high standards for all major state appointments. Those who did not live up to these standards sometimes found themselves summarily dismissed, county chairmen or not. As a result, Leader did much to raise the standards of state government in terms of qualified public servants doing their jobs with honesty and efficiency. It was not without reason that he was sometimes referred to as the Democrats' Gifford Pinchot because of his liberalism and his strong support of good government.

The approach of the 1958 election found both parties again plagued by internal jockeying for position. The Republicans agreed upon the support of Arthur McGonigle, Reading pretzel manufacturer, who lacked any experience in government and proved to be a not especially successful campaigner. Richardson Dilworth was willing to lead the Democrats again, but ran into opposition from Congressman William Green, who had become the dominant power in the Philadelphia Democratic organization. David Leo Lawrence, stalwart and leader in the Democratic Party over a long period of years and bringing with him an outstanding reputation for progressivism and redevelopment, as Pittsburgh's mayor, was selected by the party leaders despite some doubts as to whether a Catholic could be elected. Lawrence won by a margin provided by virtue of the Democratic strength in Philadelphia and Pittsburgh.

Lawrence, despite his record as an "old pro" in partisan politics, preached a policy of bipartisanship in meeting the growing economic problems of Pennsylvania. He inherited a sizable deficit from Governor Leader and was forced to increase the sales tax to 4 per cent to achieve the first balanced budget in many a year. Lawrence retained virtually all of Leader's strong cabinet, as well as his executive civil service plan. He also supported the improved management programs of Leader's Office of Administration and appointed Dr. David Kurtzman, Pennsylvania Economy League expert, as its head. Continued expansion of the state highway system, the mental-health program, and support of a strong highway safety program were strong points of the Lawrence program. The administration also worked very hard to improve the business climate in Pennsylvania and gave hearty support to the program of industrial redevelopment with state aid started in 1955. The State Chamber of Commerce paid tribute to the achievements of the Lawrence administration in making the state more attractive to business and industry. Governor Lawrence energized the project to build the $9,000,000 William Penn Memorial Museum and Archives Building in Harrisburg, and supported liberal allocations from the G.S.A. (General State Authority) for other historical restoration and improvement projects, including a new museum in Drake Well Park at Titusville, devoted to the early history of the oil industry. The press of the state generally praised Governor Lawrence as he ended his administration in 1963 and voted him a "good" governor.

The election of Lawrence in 1958 was the first time the Democrats had been able to put two governors back to back since before the Civil War. This had been due in part to the strong alliance between labor and the Democratic Party and the winning of Negro support. Governor Leader was the first to appoint a Negro to a high state post when he selected Harrisburg Negro leader Andrew Bradley as his Budget Secretary, and later Secretary of Property and Supplies. Bradley continued in this post, and he also served as the treasurer of the State Democratic Committee, from which position he exercised an important influence on party decisions. During Lawrence's term, for the first time the number of voters in Pennsylvania registered as Democrats exceeded the Republicans, who for years since the Civil War had enjoyed a registration margin of several hundred thousand. This may have been misleading, because more than one Democratic leader was led to believe that the Democratic star was shining so brightly that "we will be around a long, long time."

THE DEMOCRATS BRING REFORMS TO
PITTSBURGH AND PHILADELPHIA

Certainly a major factor in the rather sudden and remarkable rise of the Democrats to a new power in Pennsylvania was the success of the party in capturing control of its two great cities, Philadelphia and Pittsburgh. As has been made clear earlier, the strength of the powerful Republican machine had rested for decades upon its absolute control of both cities and their powerful organizations. All that had changed by the 1950's. Pittsburgh went Democratic for the first time in twenty years when in 1935 Cornelius Scully was elected mayor. Pittsburgh had struggled for years to secure a reform of its city and county government with a new charter, but reform was continuously blocked in Harrisburg by the coalition between Republicans in the Assembly and those in the city Republican organization. When legislation failed, an Allegheny County Community Development plan, better known later as the Allegheny Conference, was worked out through which private citizens were able to cooperate with the city and county officials in securing badly needed improvements.

When David Leo Lawrence, noted city, state, and national Democratic leader, was elected mayor in 1945 for the first of four terms it became apparent that the old Republican organization had breathed its last in Pittsburgh. Viewing the situation with great realism, the Mellon and related business and financial interests in Pittsburgh, which represented one of the most powerful consolidations of economic power in any city or even any single state, threw their weight into a cooperative effort with the Democratic organization in the city and county through the Allegheny Conference, in a program to renew and rebuild Pittsburgh. A "Pittsburgh package" of bills was presented to the Assembly with the support of Governor Duff and approved by it; Pittsburgh was off and running. County-wide smoke control ended the "smoky city" era for Pittsburgh, and parking authorities, new highway and parkway plans, and other measures combined state and local initiative in revolutionary improvements. Pittsburgh capital sought and secured cooperation in the private development of the famous Gateway Center in downtown Pittsburgh, where a blighted and entirely rundown area was replaced with giant attractive new office buildings adjoined by a new hotel. This was adjacent to the new Point Park, built by the state as part of the complex of highways, tunnels, and bridges that were remaking Pittsburgh's famous and historic Point where the Monongahela and Allegheny met to form the Ohio. The strength of the resulting Democratic political organization meant much to Democratic hopes in state elections, and without it neither Leader nor Lawrence could have hoped for success.

In Philadelphia, the long rule of corrupt Republican machines was too much to bear. On January 12, 1954, Bernard "Barney" Samuel died, having occupied the office of mayor of Philadelphia longer than any other man. A genial man with a ready smile and handshake, Samuel was the perfect picture of the city politician who had entered politics under the wing of the Vares as a member and finally president of the city council. When Mayor Lamberton died in 1941, he became acting mayor, and by virtue of a special decision of the then Republican-controlled State Supreme Court was kept in this post until he could be elected in the regular 1943 election. He then defeated William C. Bullitt, wealthy socialite and onetime ambassador to France. In 1947 Samuel faced trouble as a group of young crusaders, who had become Democratic leaders more by virtue of an interest in better government than by social background, were really starting to stir up staid and conservative Philadelphia. Richardson Dilworth was a Marine veteran. Joseph S. Clark, Jr., and Colonel James A. Finnegan were other war veterans in the group. Dilworth was selected to be the forlorn hope against Samuel and was

defeated, though, in the words of the *Evening Bulletin,* he "set up the Republican machine for the knockout."

The Samuel administration began to run into financial difficulties and a Committee of Fifteen created to study the situation uncovered evidence of a serious and scandalous situation. The gang wanted Samuel for another term, but Clark, who had been elected City Controller, and his associates were working with the Committee of Fifteen, the newly organized Greater Philadelphia movement created in 1951, and other groups concerned with the future of a city that was literally in a state of decline as a result of political mismanagement and consequent deterioration in city government and services, and he blocked an effort to amend the city charter to make possible another term for Samuel. The machine then resorted to its favorite trick when in trouble. Daniel A. Poling, noted Baptist clergyman, editor, and publicist, was prevailed upon to take the Republican nomination for mayor. In a truly pitiful effort Poling tried to convince Philadelphians that in some peculiar way, which even he could probably not fathom, the election of Clark as mayor would mean the end of all that was good in old Philadelphia. Joseph S. Clark, Jr., was elected, and swept into office with him Dilworth as District Attorney, and Finnegan, who became head of the city council. As the *Bulletin* put it, ". . . they pledged to make Philadelphia and the surrounding area a better place in which to live and work." Even the conservative *Inquirer* had endorsed the new ticket. A new city charter further consolidating and reforming the city-county government in 1951 had been secured, which promised much, and the Clark-Dilworth combination worked hard to put it into operation. Opposition actually was strongest among many Democratic politicians who now looked to the spoils of office to build their own organization. As mayor, Clark worked hammer and tongs to bring what he termed "good liberal government" to the city. "Decades of spoils system government, dominated by men of little vision, less ability and dubious integrity," declared Clark, had brought the city to "an all-time low" in its government.

Clark was followed in the office of mayor by

Richardson Dilworth, who continued the battle. The Clark and Dilworth combination produced not only better government in Philadelphia in the narrow sense of the term, but programs of vast improvement in housing, police, water supply, sewerage and sanitation, and indeed in every single area of urban improvement. Renewal and planning for constructive improvement of every phase of the life of a great city were watchwords for the new Philadelphia and won it national recognition—and relief from the vaudeville jokes of the twenties and thirties that capitalized upon the nationally known decline of Philadelphia into the status of a second-rate city. By 1960 Philadelphia could not only lift its head, but lift it proudly as no longer "corrupt and contented" but proud and forward-looking.

The rebirth of Pittsburgh and Philadelphia had been accomplished under Democratic auspices and had won both cities to that party because it had stood out as the party of good government. This, associated with improved organization and organized support of labor and the Negro, helped build a new balance of political power between Democrats and Republicans in the state. It should not be overlooked, however, that a decline in the Republican leadership helped the Democrats. As has been pointed out earlier, shrewd Republican leadership continually restrained the growth of the Democratic Party in Pennsylvania not only after the Civil War, but well into the present century. Republican leadership in recent years was a fragmented rather than a unified one, and this became increasingly so in the 1950's. The Republican Party found itself in the position of appearing to obstruct new ideas in government and to wish to hold the government of the state within the tight confines of an outmoded constitution.

THE REPUBLICANS STAGE A COMEBACK

The need for a more progressive leadership and point of view on the part of Pennsylvania Republicans was accented in 1962 as the Lawrence administration drew to a close. Richardson Dilworth, mayor of Philadelphia, was again ready to be the standard bearer for the Democrats. By 1962

Governor William W. Scranton proved to be the new young face the Republican Party needed to regain the governorship, and he pledged a revitalized and more forward-looking administration.

the direct primary, in which the people had something to say as members of a political party as to who should be their candidate for governor, had long since been almost totally ignored. This was due in part to the increasingly high cost of conducting campaigns and also to the growing power of a few political leaders in both parties. Congressman Green continued to be opposed to Dilworth and insisted, backed by his own public-opinion polls, that Dilworth could not be elected. Despite this opposition, and due in no small measure to his threat to run in a primary and thus split the party, Dilworth finally won the nod as the Democratic candidate, and resigned as mayor of Philadelphia. As usual, the Republicans were also in travail, but out of the scramble came the candidacy of first-term millionaire Congressman William Scranton, scion of the founder of the city of that name, whose mother had been a founder of the Council of Republican Women.

"Bill" Scranton with his wife Mary campaigned

the length and breadth of the state shaking hands and meeting people. Scranton emphasized the need to get Pennsylvania "moving again" and charged the Democrats with inability to solve unemployment and the economic decline of Pennsylvania. Dilworth challenged Scranton to a television debate, two of which were held, and in which the supposedly seasoned Dilworth came off second best. While Dilworth was one of the most knowledgeable men on public affairs in the state, he was unable to project a favorable image as opposed to the more youthful Scranton. When the tumult came to an end on election day, Scranton emerged the victor by a decided majority, though the Democrats elected Genevieve Blatt by a narrow margin to a third term as Secretary of Internal Affairs, and Joseph S. Clark to his second term in the United States Senate. Scranton made clear, both during the campaign and in the early months of his administration, his sincere belief that the Republican Party must develop a new and more progressive image in Pennsylvania. Though forced by the continued financial crisis, which had become a common feature of the Harrisburg scene, to raise the sales tax to 5 per cent, the new Republican Administration got off to a good start in 1963. It was evident, however, that Pennsylvania had at least achieved a more nearly normal balance of power between the two major parties. The organization of Congressman

Green in Philadelphia promised to become as strong and perhaps as venal as the older Republican machines. Signs of revolt were evident on the part of independent Philadelphia Democrats in 1963. In Pittsburgh the once all-powerful Democratic organization of the city and county appeared to be losing some of its momentum and signs of Republican revival were evident.

Pennsylvania politics and government of the sixties were a far cry from the days of the turn of the century. The age of big government, with extensive programs devoted to the public welfare and reaching the long hand of government into many areas which earlier had been without any contact with state government, had arrived in Pennsylvania. The era of political control by a single powerful political organization of machine proportions had been replaced by consolidations of power in the hands of several men and factions within both parties. Certainly the era of a close and dominant alliance of business and politics had been weakened as the interests of other groups, such as labor, began to demand attention on the part of the politicians in both parties. And finally, the long years of a dominant one-party control of Pennsylvania appeared to have come to an end.

1960 Presidential campaign: candidate John F. Kennedy at Market Square, Harrisburg.

CHAPTER SIXTEEN

THE CHANGING PATTERN OF LIFE IN THE TWENTIETH CENTURY

When Frederick Lewis Allen decided to write a history of the United States covering the era from 1900 to 1950 he called it *The Big Change,* and his subtitle was *America Transforms Itself.* An incredible expansion of industry and business and an even more incredible further revolution in transportation and communication produced changing times and changing ways of life. Indeed, the changes came with such revolutionary rapidity that our ways of thinking and conducting our affairs even now lag somewhat behind; few people actually think through the nature of the revolution that has taken place. This era of change was as marked in Pennsylvania as in any other single state. It created for Pennsylvania the life and culture that became part of its being as Pennsylvanians entered the second half of this truly remarkable century. It was an era that made the changes of earlier decades seem mild and insignificant in extent, and very slow in evolving. Change came after 1900 not only very extensively, but also with revolutionary speed that challenged the imagination of everyone. Sometimes the change was not progress and left shadows and problems for the present generation.

NEW INVENTIONS AND NEW IDEAS

In 1900 Pennsylvania, along with the rest of the nation, was still very much in the horse-and-buggy era, but this age did not last much longer. The automobile, then known commonly as the "horseless carriage" and driven by a wild and daring individual most people thought was actually half crazy, was just coming into use. It was then very much of a luxury and a toy for the daredevil rich, which scared horses, as well as pedestrians, and made a lot of unnecessary noise and confusion on streets and roads.

The horseless carriage expanded the limits of towns and cities as well as brought people from the country into closer contact with them, but a more immediate force in enlarging the urban community was the growth of street railway systems using the "streetcar." Though it was in use considerably before 1900, the major influence

299

of this new mode of transportation was felt after that date. Over two thousand miles of trolley track were reported in the state by 1901, and the number of passengers was nearly double the number using the railroads. The street railway served not only the city proper, but reached far beyond its established limits and connected related urban communities. It made possible for the first time a practical growth of population into outer areas on the part of people who earned a living in the city itself. Suburbia was born with the streetcar.

While advances in the mobility of inhabitants influenced significant changes in the pattern of life of a majority of people, radio and television did more to wave a magic wand before hundreds of thousands. Pennsylvania's pioneer role in the development of the phonograph and the motion picture has been mentioned. All of these means for bringing information and enlightenment to people in scattered areas were more fully developed in the decades after 1900. The best in music could be brought to the most humble home by recordings, as well as pure entertainment without regard to any special cultural values. The movie theater blossomed in even the smallest town by 1920 and was within reach of most farm people as well as the villagers who sought views of a larger world. Then came radio. Marconi developed wireless telegraphy; in Wilkes-Barre a Catholic priest, the Reverend Joseph Murgas, hit upon a method of wireless communication through use of a rotary spark gap for transmission, which he patented in 1905. Dr. R. A. Fessenden may well have developed a radiotelephone by 1906; at least a Pittsburgh company was formed to exploit it. The vacuum tube already had been invented by De Forest and in 1906 this led to a radio-type tube.

In East Pittsburgh a youthful Westinghouse technician named Frank Conrad was broadcasting on his wireless telephone the government time signals from Arlington, Virginia, and while waiting for the signal decided to play his phonograph for his own amusement. Acting on an impulse, he decided to move it to his microphone and to broadcast his records. It was not long before he was getting requests not only for more music but even special recording requests. Conrad may well

have become the very first "disk jockey." Westinghouse sensed the possibilities in this idea and took the trouble to erect a broadcasting studio and station. On November 2, 1920, those listening on the tiny crystal receivers of the time heard the historic message, "This is the Westinghouse Radio Station KDKA, Pittsburgh," and listened to the election returns in the Harding-Cox presidential contest. A year later KDKA began its first broadcast of Pittsburgh baseball, though the announcer was not allowed in the park and had to report using field glasses from a nearby high building. The age of radio was at hand and in the next few years thousands of farm and village homes, as well as those in smaller cities, were given a new dimension in the reporting of the events and personalities of the outside world, along with entertainment and music of great variety formerly known only to those fortunate enough to be able to buy tickets to theaters in a larger city. Radio was followed by the talking movie and television. Pittsburgh's WQED began broadcasting non-commercial educational television programs on April 1, 1954, to become the pioneer community-sponsored educational television station in the country.

COUNTRY LIFE IN THE NEW ERA

Only a person who lived on a farm or in a country town before about 1920 is able to appreciate fully the complete revolution in country and small-town life that took place in the next few decades. The life of the rural community changed little between about 1820 and 1920; it changed in a revolutionary way in the next few decades, thanks to the automobile and the improved roads reaching from farm to town, and to radio, the motion picture, and television. It is hardly possible to overemphasize the role of the automobile and the accompanying hard-surfaced highway in really revolutionizing life on the farm and in the neighboring town or small city. Until after World War I the horseless carriage remained something of a curiosity outside the larger centers of population, where the more wealthy toyed with it as a luxury. Henry Ford changed all this with the "tin lizzie," produced at a low cost and available to the

Farm families gather in their "tin lizzies" to attend an agricultural extension demonstration on better farming.

person with average income. By 1920 the automobile was no longer a curiosity, but a practical method of transportation, and ten years later Gifford Pinchot started building the hard-top roads that lifted the farmer's automobile out of the dust and mud. By 1940, roughly, the average farmer in just about any part of Pennsylvania was reasonably sure of all-weather use of his car. Trips to even a distant town could now be made in hours rather than as an all-day jaunt.

The new motion picture "palace," with its vigorous piano accompaniment of the silent pictures that flickered across a screen showing the perilous adventures or the comic actions of the favorite stars of the films, could now be seen by any farm family. Such occasions, naturally, were special events of the week, but almost any time the farmer needed something from the village he could now drive the few miles in a few minutes to get it. Life was never the same in the farm community after the coming of the automobile. It was a new and mobile life upon which some oldsters looked askance, especially when the automobile hearse replaced the slow horse-drawn vehicle in taking the deceased to their graves. Contact with towns and in turn their contact by

motor truck transportation with larger cities meant many changes. New sources of supply for a variety of foodstuffs such as fresh vegetables, fruits, and meats such as were common in city markets even earlier began to appear in country stores by the thirties. The home garden in town or country lost some of its appeal as the new supplies of canned or fresh vegetables and fruits appeared. Patterns of life were all changed by ease of access to town. Most clothing was now purchased in town or city stores and the best in fashions were as available to the farmer and his family as to any city dweller.

Electricity followed upon the heels of the automobile as a major force revolutionizing life on the farm. By the 1940's surveys indicated that well over 100,000 out of 170,000 farm homes had the advantages of electricity. This meant the coming of refrigeration and the home freezer, replacing home canning and the cold cellar. It meant the lighting of farm homes with electricity and soon brought, as they were developed, all the appliances of an electrical age into the farm as well as the town and city home. It meant in many homes an electric water supply system rather than pumping by hand the ton of water a day it is estimated most farm housewives used. The farm kitchen of 1960 was a far cry from that of 1920, thanks to electricity, and likely to be thoroughly modern. The man of the house also made use of the new source of power in lighting and equipping the barn with labor-saving devices.

Farm life changed also in the area of communication. The telephone came to rural Pennsylvania after 1900 mainly through the growth of community cooperatives, which built the lines and organized the central switchboard. It was not much before 1930 that the United and Bell commercial telephone companies adequately served the hinterland. But the greatest revolution of all in terms of enriching the farm home and its cultural and entertainment outlook was radio. By 1945 nearly 90 per cent of all farm homes in Pennsylvania had radio. It could be operated with batteries, which enlarged its use by the thousands. Radio caught on quickly because even earlier the ordinary phonograph with its wax disks had brought into remote homes the best as well as the ordinary in music, comedy, and general entertainment. When television brought the picture along with the sound the revolution in a farm environment, once largely isolated from the outer world, was complete.

The automobile enlarged and changed the farm community by making it possible for people to come together more easily and readily for a variety of purposes. The strictly country school began to be replaced by the consolidated and larger school in town or in some central location to which children could be transported from a wide area by school bus. The one-room school has all but disappeared in Pennsylvania. The country church also became a victim of the ability of people to attend a larger church in town. In 1947 a study of a typical northern Pennsylvania rural county showed that less than 18 per cent of the remaining churches could be called country churches, and less than 16 per cent of the schools were of the country type. Out of over four hundred farm organizations not more than 10 per cent were holding meetings in the country. Even the Grange Hall was apt to be in town; here also were located the veterans' organizations and just about every other social and civic group. Only the

Amish country held any longer to "old ways" of farm life.

The educational horizons of the farm folk of Pennsylvania were deepened and broadened by the new era of communication and transportation. The Grange, which had lagged at one time, began to increase its membership, and the *Pennsylvania Grange News* was founded in 1903. By 1940 Grange membership was well over sixty thousand in Pennsylvania, with some seven hundred active granges. A variety of other state farm organizations developed after 1900 as those concerned with special aspects of farming such as potato growing, keeping bees, or breeding certain types of livestock perfected their associations. A Pennsylvania Country Life Association was founded in 1936 and the Society of Farm Women in 1910. By 1916 a Pennsylvania Federation of Farm Organizations was in operation which finally became the State Council of Farm Organizations. Today, it takes a sizable manual to list all of the statewide farm organizations and their local chapters.

The county fair with some aid from the state continued to grow and to exert some educational influence as well as provide entertainment. "Going to the fair" became a great annual event in the life of most farm families even in the days of dirt roads and the horse and buggy, or the surrey with fringe on the top. The entire family packed food for lunch and dinner and often drove several miles to attend the fair. There products of the farm were exhibited for prizes, and the latest in farm machinery and equipment displayed by their manufacturers, while horse racing of the sulky type, acrobatic and other grandstand shows, and a midway carnival gave a bit of fun and excitement for everyone. Going to the fair was usually a dawn-to-dusk day of fun and frolic. Oddly enough, the automobile finally weakened the smaller country fairs because people were able to travel farther to see finer attractions at the larger fairs. Radio and television also helped break down the strictly country fairs and larger and better financed fair associations in such cities as Reading, Allentown, and York began to present as their grand attraction elaborate stage shows featuring stars of radio and television. The old Pennsylvania State Fair expired before 1900 and was not revived until

1921. Eight years later a State Farm Show building was authorized at Harrisburg to be operated by the State Farm Products Show Commission. It grew quickly into the nation's largest farm exposition, held annually in January and attended by thousands of persons each year. Here the showing of farm products for prizes and the sale of the prize livestock to the highest bidder was combined with

home in Philadelphia in 1877 and became a favorite farm magazine. The *Country Gentleman,* as a member of the Curtis family of Philadelphia magazines and a more literary product, was also widely read in Pennsylvania. The *National Stockman and Farmer,* founded in Pittsburgh in 1877, was another favorite and in 1928 was merged with the *Pennsylvania Farmer,* founded in 1912; the

The Livestock Cavalcade at the annual State Farm Show in the fourteen-acre Farm Show building in Harrisburg.

a fabulous display of farm equipment and machinery without rival anywhere else in the country, but without the side show and midway common to the typical state fair. The annual Farm Show also provides a meeting time and sounding board for all of the statewide farm organizations and associations. Hundreds of farm youth take an active part in Farm Show exhibits and activities.

Expansion of the R.F.D., started in 1896, was another aid to broadening farm life. Parcel post was added in 1913, bringing mail-order service to the farm home. The R.F.D. brought newspapers and magazines to the farmer's doorstep almost as quickly as to the town or city dweller. By 1912 a survey indicated that hardly a farm home was without a daily newspaper and one or more magazines. The famous monthly *Farm Journal* made its

combined magazine soon became the most distinctively Pennsylvania farm journal. The *Rural New Yorker* was another farm periodical with a large circulation. The weekly Williamsport *Grit* and the old fashioned country weekly, published usually at the county seat, were staples in any farm mail box, along with a daily newspaper of the region.

NEW EDUCATIONAL OPPORTUNITIES FOR FARM FOLK

Libraries are a luxury generally enjoyed by the people of larger towns and cities. While the state was something of a leader in developing traveling libraries, as late as 1938 it was estimated that fully 85 per cent of rural Pennsylvanians were without any library service. Five counties had no public library at all, and nine had a single library at the county seat. Attention to improving this situation was evident after 1920 and increased state aid to county libraries made possible the mobile library unit. Books could also be borrowed by mail from the State Library. State aid for libraries was increased greatly in 1961-62 and a system of regional libraries created in cooperation with the State Library's services. Today, few families are without access to library service.

The Agricultural Extension Service was placed in operation in 1892. It was expanded in 1907, headed by Alva Agee in the School of Agriculture at Penn State, and given Federal support by the Smith-Lever Act in 1914. It opened another new era in the education of the farmer. John Hamilton, Pennsylvania farm leader and onetime Secretary of Agriculture, worked hard to secure this legislation. By 1922 a system of County Agricultural Extension Associations was organized, each headed by an expert in agriculture trained at Penn State and known as the County Agent. Home economics was quickly made a part of the system of extension services, and specialists from the university traveled the length and breadth of the state lecturing and instructing as well as demonstrating improved farm and home practices. The Extension Services in 1914 began to organize rural youth into the famous Four-H Clubs (Head, Hands, Heart, and Health) which carried on various special projects of their own selection. By 1940 there were over fifteen hundred Four-H Clubs with a membership of over twenty-one thousand, and they have continued to grow.

Organized instruction in agriculture in the schools was first in the form of nature study and dates back to 1889, when a Pittsburgh teacher started taking classes out into the fields. Penn State offered nature study by correspondence by 1900 and in 1904 at Waterford the first rural high school course in agriculture was started. By 1911 the state was requiring it to be taught in all township schools and two years later a vocational agriculture department was created in the Department of Public Instruction. In 1917 federal aid was forthcoming through the Smith-Hughes Vocational Education Act, which included home

economics and industrial trades and skills. By 1940 rural high schools were commonly presenting courses in improved farming and home economics with state and federal aid. Students in these classes in 1928 founded the Future Farmers of America, which two years later achieved statewide organization. Such advances in farm training as well as in the general liberal education of farm youth were forwarded by the growth of the consolidated schools, of which there were only eight in all of Pennsylvania in 1900. By 1940 there were some seven hundred, and a full four thousand one-room schools had disappeared in the short span of forty years. The number continued to decrease in the next twenty years as larger and finer consolidated schools appeared, many of which represented jointures, bringing together several neighboring rural or small-town districts, which pooled resources with the encouragement of increased state aid for teacher salaries, transportation of pupils, and modern buildings.

FARM POVERTY

Despite the truly revolutionary and profitable changes in the life of the Pennsylvania farmer, it was not a land of milk and honey for every one of them. There was such a thing as actual farm poverty in certain areas of Pennsylvania by 1930, and there were other farmers who were not doing very well. In the first place, the average per capita income of all Pennsylvania farmers in 1929 was less than one-half that of nonfarmers. This meant that large numbers of farmers were failing entirely to reap any major benefits from the economic growth of the whole of Pennsylvania. The years from 1900 through World War I were rather prosperous ones for the Pennsylvania farmer, and all estimates agree that the average farm family enjoyed a surplus in income as matched against outlay for improving the farm home or investing in more land or machinery. The postwar depression brought down the price of farm products sharply and many a farmer who had bought more land or machinery, or possibly an automobile, on credit found it hard to make ends meet. Basically, as the years passed the cost of operating a success-

A lonely log cabin on a country road is home for this poverty-ridden family.

ful farm mounted by thousands of dollars, mainly because of increased use of expensive machinery. As early as 1933 Governor Pinchot noted, "Farmers are daily losing homes in large numbers by reason of foreclosure of mortgages." A year later, 12 per cent of the state's farm families were on relief rolls. New Deal measures in Washington helped farmers in debt through loans from the Farm Security Administration.

Many farmers could hardly be helped by such measures because the land they had farmed for years was now incapable of profitably producing crops. Fully 6 per cent of all of the farms in the state in 1934 were judged to be submarginal in terms of the ability of the farmer to make a living. In some areas in northern and western Pennsylvania the percentage was as high as forty. Later studies in 1941 and 1950 continued to point to a permanent farm poverty in many of these regions with inadequate housing, inability to wrest a living from the land, and dependence on public assistance. The same studies revealed that a higher percentage of people were on relief and getting public assistance in certain rural counties than even in the slums of Pennsylvania cities. Time led to the recognition of the fact that while Pennsylvania agriculture as a whole prospers and has provided the average farmer with a rather abundant life, there is also a persistent farm poverty that denies many the benefits of better life.

THE CHANGING TOWN AND CITY

The total population of Pennsylvania grew from 6,302,111 in 1900 to 11,319,366 in 1960, an average increase per decade of hardly 6 per cent and a definite slowing down of the growth of the state. The increase in the rural population was very slight, from 2,853,505 to 3,217,315, while urban population increased from 3,448,610 to 8,102,051. The ratio of urban population shifted from 54.7 per cent in 1900 to 71.6 per cent in 1960. There were by 1960, 442 towns and cities listed as such by the census as compared with 190 in 1900. A comparison of population statistics reveals that the growth of most of the areas that had by 1900 become marked as the centers of the industrial development of the state was not spectacular. Allentown, Bethlehem, and Erie were among the larger population centers that exhibited considerably more than average growth between 1900 and 1960. The vast expansion of suburbia is indicated by the large number of townships in eastern and western Pennsylvania that by 1960 had become large urban centers. Philadelphia grew from 1,293,697 people to 2,002,512, while Pittsburgh in the same sixty years slowed down, increasing from 451,512 to only 604,332. One marked change in population was the decrease in the percentage of whites as compared with nonwhites. Between 1930 and 1960 the percentage of white population of the state decreased exactly 3 per cent and nonwhites increased their total population by the same percentage. The nonwhite and mainly Negro population of the state grew from 160,451 in 1900 to 865,362 by 1960, and the larger part of the growing Negro population was to be found in the cities. The percentage of foreign born and those born from foreign stock in the population was on the decline; almost 10 per cent between 1940 and 1960. Those of Italian extraction continued to make up by far the larger percentage of the foreign born and first-generation descendants, followed in order by Poles, those from the United Kingdom, and French. The day of any large infiltration of immigrant stock came to an end soon after 1900 as the steel mills and mines ceased to be available for the employment of masses of foreign workers, and immigration laws became more restrictive.

The demands of an enlarged city population produced a sharp quickening of the emergence of the modern city, which had its faint outlines only established before the turn of the century. Now improved paved streets and walks, street lighting, better police protection, a good water supply, adequate sewerage and sanitation, and even city parks became a must and every city moved rapidly toward securing such improvements. Slowly but surely the modern town and city of today began to emerge after 1900 and by the end of World War I had rather fully taken shape. Some of the problems of the central city now moved to the suburbs, where townships flooded with residents from the cities grappled with problems that by 1950 had assumed major proportions. Government in townships and towns now labored and creaked under the pressures of adjusting outmoded and rurally oriented procedures in government to new needs that went far beyond merely improving a few dirt roads once a year and keeping the schools open a few months a year. A town of any size now must have paved streets along with at least some street lighting, some policing, a central water supply, better and more costly schools, and some attention to sanitation and sewerage. Growing pains came to have a very literal meaning to the majority of Pennsylvania towns and even once rural townships.

The pressures created by the growth of urbanization began to reach peaks that demanded drastic new approaches to their solution as early as 1930. One of the first problems that caught up with the urban centers was that of sanitation and sewerage and their relation to water supply. For generations the smaller towns and even the smaller cities had little or no sewage system at all and depended upon individual solution of the problem. A surprising percentage of houses in larger cities were without running water or indoor sanitary facilities as late as the thirties. By 1900 the need for community action on health and sanitation was evident as Pittsburgh, Philadelphia, and other large cities were afflicted with epidemics of typhoid. The next few decades saw notable development in public health and sanitation in the larger cities. The solution found by most smaller cities was simply that of installing the necessary sewer lines in the streets, properly connected with dwellings and business places, and then dumping the sewage into the nearest stream, where it was supposed to be purified by the running waters. This was satisfactory only so long as the volume of sewage was small and only a few places were doing it. As cities grew in size and number, however, the water supply of all communities was now threatened by stream impurities. Supplies of clean and abundant water were more and more necessary to an urban and industrial civilization, and control of the purity of this supply became an ever-present problem as over six hundred municipalities were dependent on rivers and streams for their water supply. Purity of the streams was also closely related to developing concepts of public recreational facilities for the growing millions living in cities. The state began to step into the picture in 1923 with the first activity on the part of the newly created State Sanitary Water Board. By 1937 a Pennsylvania clean-streams program was under way and towns and cities gradually were forced to develop plans for treatment of sewage in properly designed sewage-disposal plants. By the end of the fifties the era of dumping city or industrial waste into streams was drawing to an end.

URBAN PLANNING AND RENEWAL

This was but one of many new problems confronting the developing urban centers. New words and phrases began to appear in the vocabularies of those involved in local government, such as "zoning," "urban renewal," and "community planning." These were not only new words but "planning" had been earlier something of a dirty word that to conservatives implied some sort of "socialism" in government. The impulse for this new concept came in part from the decay of the older and central portions of many cities. It was given impetus also by the need to take into account the growth of suburbia, which had thrown large numbers of people into an urban environment but in a semirural setting on the outskirts of larger cities or towns. It was realized that there were problems common to large areas that overlapped and needed an organized and planned approach. Transportation and water and sanitary facilities were among these problems. It was Gifford Pinchot who set up a State Planning Board in Pennsylvania in 1934 to "prepare plans or programs for the physical and economic development of the State, by the State, its agencies, and political sub-divisions." The board never fully lived up to such an ideal, but its early and continuing director for some thirty years became Francis A. Pitkin, an able and dedicated leader in the planning movement, with state and national influence as an individual working in this pioneer field. When in 1939 the legislature created the Department of Commerce under what was known as the "Commerce Law" during the James administration, it gave further tacit recog-

nition to the need for economic planning. Under Governor Leader a Bureau of Community Planning emerged in this department. Even earlier, the Duff administration had extended state aid to housing projects in the state. The trend toward an organized approach with the use of local, state, and Federal initiative applied to problems of urban renewal and redevelopment and funds was well established by 1960. Pennsylvania urban areas began to take advantage of both state and Federal money and services, and by the sixties the watchword of local government was "planning." Urban renewal activity now involves every major Pennsylvania city.

Renewal takes varied forms as adapted to conditions, but its most basic ingredient is the elimination of downtown blighted and slum areas and their replacement with modern facilities that will improve the city. Along with this has gone zoning, and today every local unit of government is empowered to divide its areas into zones for private residential use, apartment-type residence use, commercial (store and business) use, and for light industry. A community may even decide that an area has great historical importance and set it aside for preservation. Cities such as Bethlehem, Philadelphia, and York have acted to preserve such historic areas as a part of their development plans. Pennsylvania in the sixties was on the move to overcome the decay and waste becoming common to the American city and to meet the challenge presented to the mayors of American cities at their 1963 Honolulu conference to "transform our cities into centers of vitality, progress, and beauty. . . ."

Pittsburgh and Philadelphia were among the earliest leaders in this movement, though smaller cities such as Allentown, Chambersburg, Chester, Erie, Scranton, and others were actively moving forward and some winning national recognition for their efforts to remedy conditions associated with what had become a national concern, the blight of the city. Pittsburgh was plagued with serious problems that led in 1943 to the organization of the now famous Allegheny Conference on Community Development, which included not only Pittsburgh proper but the entire county of Allegheny, along with communities in neighbor-

*Gateway Center in Pittsburgh replaced an ugly and run-down area at
the historic junction of the Allegheny and the Monongahela.*

ing Beaver, Westmoreland, and Washington counties. It was realized that Pittsburgh as a city could not separate itself from the surrounding areas within a radius of many miles in solving problems of a metropolitan area tied together by related economic interests. The conference set up fact-finding committees to study basic problems of population growth and its relation to housing, public health, smoke control, traffic, and parking. The united efforts of the conference produced smoke-control and traffic-control measures on a regional basis, along with advances in a Pittsburgh parking authority, creation of the Point Park project, and a new office development to revitalize this historic and key area at the apex of the Golden Triangle adjacent to Point Park. This is known as Gateway Center and in beauty and appointments is a rival of Rockefeller Center in New York. The conference also brought into being an ultra-modern Civic Auditorium, the Penn-Lincoln Expressway tunnel and river bridge complex to move traffic from, into, and through Pittsburgh, and a complete face-lifting operation that won Pittsburgh national attention as a progressive city meeting modern problems. Improvements in housing, sanitation, lighting, and other clean-up operations also helped make Pittsburgh a brighter and cleaner community that could no longer be joked about as the "Smoky City."

Pittsburgh's experience was reflected in an equal revolution in Philadelphia, where the Greater Philadelphia Movement was organized in 1948. Even earlier, in 1943, the city inaugurated its first City Planning Commission. Its Executive Director, Edmund N. Bacon, became one of the nation's leaders in the field of city planning. In the three centuries since Penn had laid out his "towne," Philadelphia had developed the worst symptoms of city decay and blight. Legislation in 1949 that allowed cities to take advantage of Federal monies to raze buildings and develop improved housing was utilized as Philadelphia began a $2,000,000,000 program of restoring, rebuilding, and reviving the city. Mayor Richardson Dilworth became known as one of the most imaginative city mayors in leading city planning in the entire nation, and a most vocal supporter of the idea that the American city must be reborn out of the decay with which it had become afflicted in the twentieth century. A Colorado newspaper editor was so impressed that he went home to write, "A beautiful new American city of two million people is being born on the Delaware River in Pennsylvania. Its name is Philadelphia. . . . The old and the new Philadelphia should not be confused. They're as different as night and day."

CONCERN FOR CONSERVATION
OF NATURAL RESOURCES

Before 1900 any advocate of what was then a very new idea, namely conservation of natural resources, was a prophet crying in the wilderness. The idea of a national park system had been born when Congress in 1872 made the Yellowstone country a national preserve as a natural wonder. Cleveland talked a little bit about conservation and McKinley rather forgot it. Theodore Roosevelt made conservation a national issue in 1901, and Pennsylvania's Gifford Pinchot, as head of the nation's Forest Service, began to restrict on Federal lands the exploitation on an unlimited basis of not only timber but coal, mineral, and water-power sites. Even earlier, in Pennsylvania, Dr. Joseph T. Rothrock, native of McVeytown

and physician and surgeon by profession, in 1877 had addressed with great eloquence the American Philosophical Society in Philadelphia on the importance of conservation, and in 1886 founded the Pennsylvania Forestry Association. In 1887 the state established a Forestry Commission and ten years later the Assembly voted funds to start the first 40,000 acres of state forest. By 1904 Pennsylvania, though it still was a leading lumbering state and cutting timber without much regard to conservation on the part of the lumber industry, had over 400,000 acres of state forest, which would later grow to over two million acres. Gifford Pinchot returned to head the state-forest program, taking over where Rothrock had left off. Together, Rothrock, Pinchot, George Wirt, and many others moved the forest-conservation program ahead. At the start of the Leader administration in 1955, the head of the forestry department at Penn State, Maurice Goddard, was brought to Harrisburg to head this work, and revolutionary advances were soon made in the expansion of the forestry program, as well as in the administration of the state forests and state parks, and the development of an enlarged program for recreation. Goddard early dedicated the state to developing a major state park with accompanying recreational facilities within fifty miles of every major urban area in the state, and this goal has been largely achieved. He also played a leading role in advancing study and conservation of the state's water resources.

Conservation of water resources was an area in which Pennsylvania developed leadership when in 1905 it created a commission to study the problem; out of this grew a progression of laws that brought the basic control of this vital resource under state controls. Governor Martin and in particular Governor Duff took a leading part in clean-streams and water-conservation programs, and their course of action was followed and amplified by Governors Leader and Lawrence. Pennsylvania entered into a cooperative agreement with Delaware in 1922, and later with other neighboring states and the Federal government, to regulate and control the water supply represented by the Delaware River. This was formalized in a Delaware River Basin Commission in

The Western Pennsylvania Conservancy, using private funds and initiative, has made possible the preservation of such natural resources as this beautiful waterfall on Sugar Run near Ohiopyle in Western Pennsylvania.

October, 1961. Studies of the Susquehanna River basin are now a part of this cooperative approach to the control of both the purity and the supply of water from such great reservoirs. The Potomac watershed is also under consideration.

Conservation has broader meanings today than earlier; Pennsylvania was in front in developing many of these ideas. By 1896 the once lush game lands of the state had disappeared and conser-

vationists began to be aware of this, with the result that in that year a start toward state game conservation was established. Naturally, many people resented this as an interference with private rights, but in 1903 a license to hunt game was required for nonresident hunters. The first game refuge was set up in 1905, and since that time an active State Game Commission has developed conservation of Pennsylvania's once vanishing wildlife to a point where it can compare favorably with any other state. The Commission now has over 978,000 acres of game lands. The Fish Commission established in 1949 began as a Board of Fish Commissioners and developed an extensive program of propagation and distribution of fish in Pennsylvania's streams, which has added greatly to the conservation of stream and recreational facilities. The greatest progress in conservation has been made within the last ten years as formerly scattered and uncoordinated programs and laws were brought into a central direction. A growing recognition of the relationship between forests and streams with their fish and game and the needs of an urban economy for pure water supplies for home and industry, along with the concern for greatly enlarged recreational facilities in the form of state parks, resulted in a unified Pennsylvania conservation program that tied together all these elements. Associated with it was the growing recognition that contamination of these waters by industry and by towns and cities must stop. Not all of the work in conservation has been done by government. Since 1931 the Western Pennsylvania Conservancy in Pittsburgh has acquired thousands of acres to protect the land's natural beauty and to develop it for public use and conservation. Several thousand acres have been presented to the commonwealth for use in state park developments in western Pennsylvania.

The land itself is so basic a resource that by 1930 Congress was impelled to authorize a nationwide study of the evils of soil erosion. As early as 1901 Pennsylvania State University, in cooperation with the United States Department of Agriculture, had started a study of soil conditions throughout Pennsylvania. As land was denuded of timber by unregulated lumbering the problem became more acute with every decade. Under the Federal legislation the university began a more active study of soil conservation, and demonstration projects were in operation in Indiana and Armstrong counties by 1934 to show how to control erosion. Two years later Federal benefits were authorized for farmers who would adopt soil conservation measures and in 1938 the Assembly authorized the creation, on a voluntary basis by vote of farmers themselves, of Soil Conservation Districts. Since at least 10 per cent of the state's farmland was by now submarginal, these measures were badly needed. Building dams on small streams to check flood waters, tree planting to control loose soil, strip and contour farming rather than plowing in the old-style straight furrow, which invited rain to wash soil away, and careful crop rotation were methods used to conserve the land. Soil conservation on a voluntary and democratic basis with help from both state and Federal sources, especially in terms of education in better farm methods, is now practiced in virtually every part of the state.

CONSERVATION OF HUMAN RESOURCES

In recent years conservation also has come to be understood as involving people, in relation to safeguarding public health, helping to solve problems of housing and slum control in cities, and giving better attention to care of the poor and the unfortunate, along with a concern to improve further the correctional institutions necessary for those who violate the laws. Few today any longer dispute the necessity for such measures or consider the problems as manufactured by social welfare workers. They are a product of urbanization and the growth of a mechanized and automated economy and challenge the best thinking of our modern social and political scientists in and out of government, as well as that of legislators who come from the rank and file of the people by election. As a result of these problems and their challenge, the operations of the state government at Harrisburg, as well as local government throughout the commonwealth, are today a far cry from those common at the turn of the century.

THE WELFARE CHALLENGE

The challenge of farm poverty is great, but poverty in the Pennsylvania city is more serious in terms of numbers and the consequences in delinquency and crime. A study in 1930 showed that more than a million dwellers in Pennsylvania cities lived in homes without modern sanitary facilities, a fact that alone was a danger to public health, but that also was a barometer of urban poverty. In 1959 the United States Department of Labor established a "modest but adequate" budget for a city worker's family of four as $5,898 in a city such as Philadelphia or Pittsburgh. Today this would be about $6,075. Out of 500,515 families in Philadelphia reporting on 1959 incomes there were 265,000 who reported incomes of less than $6,000; and when family and individual income figures were broken down it was estimated that 1,071,000 out of Philadelphia's population of 2,002,509, or 53.5 per cent of the total, had incomes below that needed to yield "modest but adequate standards of living."

Further breakdowns indicated that over 133,000 of Philadelphia's 500,000 families had incomes of less than $4,000 and over 98,000 of the city's 188,000 unattached individuals had incomes of under $2,000. This represented three out of every ten Philadelphians and was 6 per cent above national averages. The fact that Philadelphia has some 30 per cent Negro population, about fourth highest in the nation, helps explain the situation. It was further pointed out that this meant that 29 per cent of the city's population, or three out of every ten Philadelphians, were "living in poverty" in 1959. To these people there must of course be added the chronically unemployed. Philadelphia's 29 per cent, when contrasted with a 21 per cent average for the nation, points up the seriousness of the Pennsylvania situation. Especially disturbing as a social problem is the fact that while the city's Negro population is but 27 per cent of its total, 43 per cent of the poverty-stricken were non-white. A further disturbing social aspect of the situation is its relation to housing. In Philadelphia, the 29 per cent who are poor occupy only about 3 per cent of the city's streets, housing,

The Eastwich redevelopment in Philadelphia, before and after.

and total space, and are, as the *Pennsylvania Guardian* put it, "jammed into North Philadelphia's rundown rowhouses." Problems of housing, public assistance, public health and sanitation, along with juvenile delinquency and crime are wrapped up in such statistics, which could be repeated in large measure for Pittsburgh and other large Pennsylvania cities with many though minor variations. Issues that affected public health were first to receive attention for the simple reason that they became obvious through epidemics and disease, which threatened not only the poor but the well-to-do also. The State Department of Health has steadily increased its activities, as have cities and counties, and great progress has been made in curbing the problems of urban living associated with public health, though much remains to be done at local levels. The most noteworthy progress in this field in recent years has been in the field of public welfare, where problems resulting from urbanization and industrialization began in the last few decades to reach proportions that could not be ignored.

A NEW CONCEPT OF PUBLIC ASSISTANCE

The depression of the thirties brought problems of care of the needy to a head in the entire nation, and certainly in Pennsylvania, where Governor Pinchot faced for the first time mass unemployment of hundreds of thousands. Relief of poverty or unemployment from any cause earlier had been a local problem, and the poor and needy were taken care of in the "county home" or by private civic or religious charities. By 1961, in the words of an official state report: "New social problems have been created and old ones have been aggravated. Increasing numbers of those who find it difficult to compete in a complex and demanding society become the casualties of progress. Among them are those who have been denied an opportunity to make the most of their innate capacities because of lack of health care, discrimination, inadequate education and training, physical or mental handicap, family breakdown, or circumstances of birth." Just about every citizen now realized that the need for public assistance must be faced as a

312

permanent problem. Few voices at that time were raised to assert that those on "relief" actually were able to work and could find jobs if they had the proper initiative. Grudging grants to local poor boards by the state first made in the early 1930's were replaced with the Public Assistance Act of 1937, creating a statewide system of public assistance for the needy. It merged into a unified assistance program comprising emergency relief for the unemployed, mothers' assistance, aid to the blind and the aged, and "outdoor relief" (to those not living in public institutions). The care of dependent and neglected children and dependent adults, however, was left with a newly created County Institution District in each county, a holdover from the county home and classed as "indoor relief." In 1938 the state assumed care for all mental patients in county hospitals and all county mental institutions were closed or added to the system of state mental health institutions, which now had grown from one in 1851 to some eighteen.

Pennsylvania undertook two major surveys of organizational needs in the field of public welfare in the 1950's; in 1957 the merger of the state's Department of Public Assistance and the older Department of Welfare was ordered to be examined, and the study was completed in 1958, with the merger resulting. The commission that studied the merger situation defined public welfare as "the channel through which the responsible level of government assures to individuals and families the means of meeting those social and economic needs it recognizes as basic." Improvement in hospital medical care, and mental health programs, more attention to child welfare problems, the end of any discrimination in welfare programs as to race, color, or creed, and coordination and improvement of all public-assistance programs were a part of the new concept of public welfare adopted by Pennsylvania in 1961. State direction was implemented by county welfare departments and aided by the Pennsylvania Citizens Council as a planning and coordinating body of concerned private citizens. For the first time the full utilization of all the facilities of modern professional social workers was irrevocably established as a necessary part of the entire state and local welfare program. Training took the place of well-meaning charity and volunteer effort. Public welfare, which in 1900 was almost an unknown idea, was now fully adopted. A candid appraisal must admit that

Pennsylvania was far from being a leader in public welfare. Conservative political leadership in the Assembly and mainly from rural areas fought such measures bitterly, and it took the progressive Democrats and Republicans under the leadership of Governors Leader and Lawrence to push recent measures into legislation. Along with a new view of public assistance went expansion of state systems of unemployment compensation designed to provide relief for temporary unemployment problems.

Pennsylvania had a long-standing reputation for prison reform, and here it did exhibit some leadership. A new concept of "correctional institutions" was developed to replace the old "state prison" approach to treatment of those guilty of crime. Supervision was placed in the Department of Justice under a Bureau of Correction administering eight correctional institutions, each with specialized functions, and the entire system administered by trained penologists and other specialists. Arthur Prasse, an outstanding figure in correctional administration, headed the program. A Juvenile Court Judges Commission was also created under this department in 1959 as a step toward a more systematic approach to the treatment of juvenile delinquency at the court level. State aid was later made available to local governments to assist in the solution of problems of juvenile delinquency. By 1963 health and welfare programs were costing the state over $300,000,000 annually, nearly 30 per cent of the state's budget.

A State Housing Board was set up in 1937 to involve the state government in this acute urban problem, but state aid in this field has not been of any real importance. The money required to improve housing conditions and eliminate residential and industrial blighted areas in Pennsylvania cities runs into many millions of dollars, and the larger share of this money has come from Federal aid to urban renewal programs. Through the state's Department of Commerce, however, a community development division assisted materially in aiding urban planning and advanced some $10,000,000 in housing grants in thirty-four communities. The planning service of the department cooperated in developing local utilization

of the Urban Planning Assistance program of the Federal government, and by 1960 the Department of Commerce was aiding some 140 planning projects in ninety-two municipalities. Well over 1,200 Pennsylvania communities by 1961 were involved in urban planning programs concerned with zoning of urban areas for more effective future use and development, as well as urban renewal programs which involved additional park and recreational facilities, improved housing, and other basic improvements. Even in the areas in cities characterized by absolute poverty and slum conditions, progress was evident in housing though the problem was far from solved.

CONSERVATION OF CULTURAL RESOURCES

During World War II the Federal government recognized the existence of a problem of conservation of cultural resources, and state committees were created that concerned themselves with the problem, considering mainly measures to be taken to protect cultural resources against the hazards of war. In Pennsylvania the idea caught on and had permanent influence under the direction of Dr. William E. Lingelbach, noted University of Pennsylvania historian. The need to protect the great historical heritage of Philadelphia due to the gradual decay of the old and historic areas of the city was emphasized by the growing threat to Independence Hall and the complex of nationally important historic buildings in this immediate area. This led to agreements through which much of this area came under the administration of the National Park Service as Independence Hall National Park, and gradual restoration of these shrines was undertaken. A Philadelphia Historical Commission was created to supervise plans for proper protection and development of the historical resources of the city. Private enterprise more recently combined with city planning to preserve much of the old Society Hill section in lower Philadelphia, and some progress has been made in preserving surviving buildings in historic Germantown. Fortunately, many fine old historic houses once on the outskirts of old Philadelphia already had been saved in the Fairmount Park complex.

Independence Hall has been placed in a stately new setting by demolition of old loft buildings which hemmed it in. The spacious Mall, financed largely by state funds, will be flanked by a prestige business district and home offices of national corporations.

At the level of state government, a Pennsylvania Historical Commission was created by the Assembly in 1913, and a separate State Museum and State Archives developed about the same time. In 1945 these were merged into the Pennsylvania Historical and Museum Commission, and great advances in the museum, archival, and historical field have since resulted. The new William Penn Memorial Museum and Archives Building, completed in 1964, was the most notable monument to an improvement program launched by the commission in 1952, known as Operation Heritage. Major historical shrines such as Ephrata, Old Economy, Cornwall, Pennsbury, the flagship *Niagara,* and others were subjects of

restoration. A new museum was completed at Drake Well Park in 1964 and the new Pennsylvania Farm Museum at Landis Valley, near Lancaster, assumed importance as one of the finest agricultural museums in the nation. Progress in collection and conservation of historical manuscripts and state and local archives has been substantial in recent years. The commission developed cooperative relationships with county and local historical societies and associations that resulted in a statewide growth of interest and activity in the conservation of the state's once vanishing historical resources, many of which were threatened by modern changes.

Pennsylvania was a pioneer in making a state-

*Philadelphia City Hall framed by
modern Penn Center buildings.*

wide survey of historic sites and buildings by the Joint State Government Commission, and the Historical Commission under terms of a joint Assembly resolution introduced by Senator Israel Stiefel of Philadelphia. Pennsylvania by 1963 had become one of the leading states in moving ahead in the field of conservation of its historical resources and developing new, living historical museum projects.

LABOR IN THE NEW SOCIETY

One of the truly revolutionary developments of the twentieth century was the advance of labor in that it at last achieved organization as well as recognition of its concerns by government and the general public. The story of labor in Pennsylvania always had a significant bearing on the national labor pattern, because of the dominant industrial position of the state; this continued in the twentieth century. At the turn of the century

labor was in travail, as has been pointed out earlier, as the power of huge corporations literally broke the backs of such organized labor as had reared its head. Conditions were slow to improve, and as late as 1910 a twelve-hour day was common for about one-third of all western Pennsylvania steel workers, of whom nearly 60 per cent remained first-generation European stock. A steel strike in 1919, according to investigators, was provoked by "excessive hours" and the "boss system" of supervision in the mills that denied workers any individual rights.

The United Mine Workers, organized in 1890 in the coal fields, gradually increased its strength under the leadership of John Mitchell and his stalwart associate, William B. Wilson; both were schooled in the Knights of Labor. Wilson became secretary-treasurer of the United Mine Workers in 1900. Thomas Kennedy, native of Lansford, was another early mine union leader. Another Pennsylvanian leading in the growth of the miners' union was John Brophy, born in England, who came to Pennsylvania at the age of twelve and by fifteen was a mine worker near Philipsburg, in central Pennsylvania. Mitchell in 1900 called a strike for higher wages and recognition of the union in the anthracite fields, though he then had only some eight thousand members in his union. Wages averaged perhaps $300 a year and a ten-hour day in unsafe mines was common. The anthracite mines were owned for the most part by powerful railroad corporations, which in turn were allied with J. P. Morgan's banking empire. This was some challenge to be issued by a brash new union. Shrewd Mark Hanna, architect of the theory that what is good for McKinley is good for big business, saw the issue as politically explosive when some 100,000 miners responded to the strike call; he negotiated a quick settlement.

Two years later Mitchell forced the issue again with demands for union recognition, a nine-hour day, and a 20 per cent wage increase. George F. Baer, president of the Reading Company, took the lead in refusing to arbitrate or mediate with the miners. Baer made the statement, "The rights and interests of the laboring man will be protected and cared for, not by labor agitators but by the Christian gentlemen to whom God in his infinite wisdom has given control of the property interests of the country, and upon whose successful management of which so much depends." This was literally "divine right" capitalism. The *New York Times* called the words a close to "unconscious blasphemy." President Roosevelt in October called upon both sides to meet with him in Washington to consider the idea of an impartial arbitration commission. The miners accepted, but Baer and his associates refused. "T.R." then threatened the use of Federal troops to take over the mines unless the owners came into line. The settlement secured for the miners their nine-hour day and a 10 per cent wage increase but left unsolved union recognition.

Organized labor had won its first great battle, but it had not won the war. The National Association of Manufacturers, organized in 1895, began a program of active opposition to organized labor. In 1904, while saying that the association was not opposed to "organizations of labor as such," it did disapprove "absolutely of strikes and lockouts," along with the closed shop. The same leadership in 1900 had accused labor of "organized coercion" and attempting to force "socialistic or semi-socialistic" legislation that would deny "free competitive conditions in the labor market." Unions were further denounced as trusts and "a dangerous institution in a free country," which were preaching doctrines "not only of anarchy but also . . . based on woeful ignorance of economic laws of wages."

Labor organization continued to grow in strength as the American Federation of Labor, born in Pittsburgh, steadily increased its membership. The Pennsylvania Federation of Labor was organized in 1902. In 1919 new efforts to organize the steel industry were started. By this time there

John Mitchell, hero of the anthracite miners, visits an anthracite community.

317

was a Department of Labor in Washington; it was created by Congress in the Wilson administration in 1913 to "foster, promote, and develop the welfare of the wage earners of the United States; to improve their working conditions, and to advance their opportunities for profitable employment." The first head of this new department was Pennsylvania miner and labor leader William B. Wilson, who had written the legislation that created it, along with many other labor laws, while serving in Congress. His successor in the Harding administration was a laborer who had started work as a puddler in the steel mills of Sharon, "Puddler Jim," James J. Davis. Davis served as Secretary of Labor until 1930. Many looked upon Davis as a labor politician more or less kept by big business, and by no means the equal of Wilson.

Organization of the steel workers was a reality by 1918, but the steel strike in 1919 was broken in 1920. The large steel companies, led by the giant United States Steel, did make concessions in wages and improvements in working conditions and hours. By 1936 efforts at a stronger union produced the United Steel Workers of America. Among its major leaders have been Philip Murray and David J. McDonald. The United Mine Workers and the United Steel Workers formed the nucleus for the Congress of Industrial Organizations, the C.I.O., which was formally organized in Pittsburgh in 1938, continuing the Pennsylvania tradition as the birthplace of national labor unions. The New Deal in Washington gave American labor new encouragement and a new place in the nation's politics and government. Pennsylvania's "little New Deal" accomplished the same end with a series of labor reform laws which were a part of the progressive movement in politics. These involved strengthening many pioneer efforts at labor legislation that had either not been enforced or were mere palliatives rather than cures. Among the most important of these new measures was the creation of the Labor Relations Board and the Bureau of Employment Security in the Department of Labor and Industry. Conservatives screamed in outraged indignation, charging "socialism" and the "welfare state," but time failed to reverse any major progressive step

forward in legal recognition of the rights and problems of labor. In the meantime, no amount of new legislation could guarantee complete harmony between organized labor and organized management. Competitive bargaining, however, did achieve wonders and something of a miracle was wrought when in 1963 steel and labor came to terms without a steel strike. Labor by 1963 was not without grievances, but it had gained immeasurably in improved wages, hours, and working conditions, and in the strength of its organization.

EDUCATION IN THE TWENTIETH CENTURY

Every field of education and religion felt the impact of the twentieth-century revolution in the total economy, in transportation and communication, and the growth of urbanized society. The public schools naturally registered continuing increases in enrollment, until by 1961 it had reached in the elementary and secondary schools a total of 1,998,347 pupils, and was still on the increase. Another 614,023 were registered in nonpublic schools, mainly parochial, and numbering 23.5 per cent of the total school population. Public school enrollment had increased by about half a million since 1944–45. The total number of schools was decreasing as consolidation progressed, but the cost of education mounted steadily. In 1939–40, $136,544,000 in local tax funds and $36,769,000 in state funds were spent on the public schools, as compared with $476,-693,000 in local taxes and $356,963,000 in state monies in 1960–61. The expenditure per pupil increased in the same period from $20.56 to $185.58. Public education was taking about 50 per cent of all state funds in 1964. Better salaries for teachers, costs of transporting pupils to larger school units, more elaborate and expensive school building programs, and improved school curricula and programs were back of the mounting cost of public education, which by 1963 had reached a point where the state itself was hard pressed to meet the need. The total revenue from the state sales and use tax earmarked for education was not enough to cover the mandated expenditures on the part of the state government for public edu-

Aerial view of Pennsylvania State University campus, one of the largest state universities in the nation.

cation. This was a major factor in increasing this tax from 4 to 5 per cent in 1963 and spelling out the fact that this was a tax for education.

Needless to say, the Pennsylvania public school of 1963 was a far cry from that of 1900. Elaborate and highly modern buildings not only were erected in cities and larger towns, but began to dot the countryside as after 1940 the system of consolidation and school jointures moved ahead at a rapid pace, with the state contributing increased sums of money. A new School Building Authority to float bonds to aid school construction and improvements was set up in 1947. Between 1950 and 1961 over two thousand school buildings, alterations, and repair projects were approved by the Department of Public Instruction. The School Building Authority itself allocated $156,690,000 for financing or refinancing public school buildings in 1958–60.

The curriculum was enlarged and enriched to include many vocational subjects such as agriculture, home economics, industrial and shop training, and science. The dawn of the air and space ages led the Department of Public Instruction to ask for more attention to mathematics,

science, and world cultures. By 1963 the most modern city schools were approaching a level of education that would have been unthought of at the turn of the century and equaled in science, mathematics, and the practical arts the level of college and university training at the undergraduate level in 1960, especially that of small liberal arts colleges. Some educators were predicting that by 1970 the new and modern high school would replace the first two years of the orthodox college-level education. This could be true, but many were concerned by the sacrifice of the study of history and the humanities to science and mathematics.

The fact that change is not necessarily progress is well illustrated in Pennsylvania public school education. By 1960, if not earlier, it became evident that the increasing sums of money devoted to the public school system was not moving the state ahead in comparison with national education. During the period from 1940 to 1960, though it ranked thirteenth in 1960 in per capita income, Pennsylvania was thirty-seventh in state and local expenditures for education. The deficiencies in rural schools were especially evident.

319

The Heinz Memorial Chapel at the University of Pittsburgh.

As of 1940 half of the Pennsylvanians living in rural areas had not gone beyond 8.5 years of education; by 1960 it had increased to 8.9, which was still below the statewide average of 10.2. The best the state's school head could promise was that by 1970 Pennsylvania's average of education for farm children might reach that of Utah.

Increased attention to this problem was a product in large measure of a growing realization that the general economic decline of Pennsylvania was related to the failure of education to keep pace with demands of a modern technical economy. Governor Lawrence supported legislative Act 561 in 1961 as a product of recommendations of his Committee of One Hundred on Education that involved a sweeping reorganization of the state school system. As passed, this predicated a sweeping consolidation of schools that reduced the number of school districts from over two thousand to four hundred or fewer when fully implemented. This was based on the established view of educators that high-quality education for the state could be obtained only through larger consolidated districts. Act 561 became a red-hot issue in the 1962 election. Some leading Democrats who were connected with the schools and were legislative supporters of reorganization were defeated for reelection while newly-elected Governor Scranton called for a new look at the law. Several legislators demanded its outright repeal, and nearly won their battle in the 1963 Assembly. The compromise worked out limited consolidation and established at best a level of about five hundred districts. The new law also made changes in the State Council of Education, making it more responsive to lay interests and limiting the power of the Superintendent of Public Instruction. This was a major shift from the over two thousand districts, and recognized the soundness of the argument that consolidation was the major answer to a stronger school system. The resulting legislation was the most sweeping since the Edmonds Act of 1921, which had created the first State Council of Education and established the foundations for minimum salary and professional standards for all teachers.

Higher education was characterized also by sweeping changes, but likewise subject to criticism as to whether Pennsylvania had advanced as far as it should in this field as compared with other large industrial states. Pennsylvania continued to lead all the states in the number of colleges and universities. Pennsylvania State University grew from college to university status in 1954. The fourteen institutions formerly known as State Teachers Colleges were broadened in 1960 to State Colleges with more general education in academic and scientific fields made available to the students. Among the new institutions of higher learning created in the period were Carnegie Institute of Technology and Elizabethtown College, both in 1900. The increased support of higher education by the Roman Catholic Church was a major educational development. Catholic girls' colleges included Villa Maria College in 1925, Rosemont College in 1922, Marywood College in 1915, and Seton Hill College in 1918. Gannon College, founded in 1944 at Erie, developed as a growing Catholic college in the same era.

Wilkes College at Wilkes-Barre and Lycoming College at Williamsport emerged as more or less municipal college ventures. The state greatly increased its aid to higher education, making steadily larger appropriations to Penn State and the State Colleges, along with substantial grants to the University of Pittsburgh, the University of Pennsylvania, and later to Temple University and Drexel Institute. These private institutions aided by the state were after 1960 granted the right to finance capital improvements for building purposes from the state borrow-and-build General State Authority. The appropriation to Penn State grew from $619,000 in 1916 to over $25,000,000 in 1963. The total appropriations of the state to all institutions of higher education expanded from $1,731,000 in 1910 to $41,502,568 by 1963.

The enrollment in all these institutions, whether aided by the state or privately supported, has grown continuously and reached new levels every year. More important than numbers was the change in the type of education afforded. The demands of an age of mechanization and science were met by the expanding curricula of Pennsylvania's institutions of higher learning and especially by the larger universities such as Penn State, Pitt, Temple, and Penn, which developed distinguished departments of science and engineering and the faculties of which came to be known in more than an occasional instance as leaders in their respective fields. Penn State and Pitt, and more recently several of the State Colleges, have developed off-campus centers at key

cities and larger towns desirous of establishing educational centers in their localities, usually to meet the needs of those who could not afford to attend a more distant college and who wanted basic education in the humanities, science, and engineering.

While the Pennsylvania college and university has made great strides ahead since 1900, as have the public schools, there has remained a perplexing problem in the picture of higher education in the commonwealth. A series of studies of higher education in the sixties startled the complacency of many a Pennsylvanian by revealing that only 28.4 per cent of Pennsylvania high school graduates actually go to college. This compared most unfavorably with the national average of 50 per cent, and disastrously with California's 60 per cent and 55 per cent for Massachusetts. Pennsylvania ranked only ninth among the more populous states in the number of college-aged population actually attending college. This might be passed off as less than a crucial problem were it not for the fact that it was shown that 21 per cent of those in the highest intelligence level in Pennsylvania were among those who did not go to college.

This failure to train the best brains, as it were, of the state for future utilization was a most serious indictment of the commonwealth in terms not only of cultural but also of economic progress. The Committee of One Hundred on Education reported in 1961 that as a result of lack of state support, Penn State, the state's land-grant state university, charged the highest rate of tuition of any land-grant college in the nation, and that the total cost of a college education in Pennsylvania institutions with any form of state support was well above national averages. The lack of technical schools and junior or community colleges also was scored by the committee, which recommended that the state should accept "responsibility for providing up to four years of higher education for all qualified students who might otherwise not be able to attend a university or college." The 1963 legislature provided for the first time for state aid for community colleges and technical schools. As Pennsylvania entered the sixties it could point with some pride to the

A Russian Orthodox church in the anthracite region.

alive the cultural and scientific heritage of the commonwealth. The fact remained that Pennsylvania, despite the number of its colleges and universities and the quality of their faculties and curricula, was not providing enough financial support to maintain low-cost higher education, and was not able to educate anywhere nearly as many of the best brains of younger Pennsylvanians as were other large states.

RELIGIOUS CURRENTS IN THE NEW URBAN ERA

It is difficult to discern any marked differences in the pattern of Pennsylvania's religious life in the twentieth century from those common to the nation as a whole, other than that the state continued to be noted for the diversity of its religious life established from colonial days, and for the large number of its churches. Urbanization brought pressures to bear upon all religious faiths as churches in urban areas began to face up to certain social problems to which religion could or should be applied. Progressive religious leaders both spiritual and lay became concerned more and more with the social gospel and social education, which applied religion to everyday life and to its social rather than purely individual problems. Churches in urban communities found themselves engaged in social and educational endeavors within and without the church edifice that were not only unheard of in early days but continued to be frowned upon by many a conservative church member. Among these were supporting the Boy Scouts and Girl Scouts, cooperating and leading in developing recreational facilities for youth, and more recently helping to organize the golden agers or senior citizens. While city churches grew in size of congregations and magnificence of buildings and support, the typical rural church so common to early Pennsylvania suffered a continuing decline. The country church by 1960 had nearly breathed its last in the greater part of the state. The church scene, regardless of major denomination, was quite different by 1960 from that at the turn of the century. Only the Plain People of the Pennsylvania German country held to their old ways in the face of the revolution in transportation and modern ways of life, and even these

number of its institutions as well as the quality of its higher education. It offered great variety in terms of a large number of liberal arts colleges with rather small but steadily increasing enrollments, which were now offering some variety in science and engineering. Many were proving in the records of their distinguished alumni that the small liberal arts colleges, now often dismissed as a remnant of an earlier educational age, are capable of producing through their faculties, curricula, and facilities many leaders in very practical fields of business and industry. At the same time, the large universities were keeping ways, dating from colonial times, were shaken.

The religious faiths that had established themselves in early Pennsylvania remained a dominant feature of the state's religious life. Pittsburgh and western Pennsylvania still were very much a capital of Pennsylvania Presbyterianism despite the great growth of the Roman Catholic Church in urban mining and industrial centers. The areas settled by the early Germans were still the citadels of the Lutheran and Reformed churches. The Lutherans became in numbers the largest single Protestant denomination in the state by 1926. The Baptist Church was strong in Philadelphia, and in many parts of rural Pennsylvania. The Methodist Church emerged after 1900 as one of the leading Protestant denominations in the state, and Pennsylvania is second only to Texas as a Methodist stronghold. The United Brethren and Grace Evangelical churches, both founded in Pennsylvania, are now merged into a single organization with considerable strength.

The Quakers declined numerically in relation to other faiths, but Philadelphia and southeastern Pennsylvania remain something of the "capital" for the few thousand Quakers, who exercise an influence far greater than numbers might indicate through their fine private schools and colleges, such as Haverford and Swarthmore, and the American Friends Service organization based in Philadelphia. The same is true of the Moravians, who continue to maintain their center of learning and church government at Bethlehem. The German sects, the Mennonites and the Amish, are no longer limited to Pennsylvania, and indeed there are more in Ohio and Indiana. The rural Pennsylvania German countryside is still the center of influence for these two groups, which have held more closely to their old ways than any other religious group in America. The Roman Catholic Church has experienced a great growth since 1900, and by 1937 could claim about 40 per cent of the entire church membership in Pennsylvania. Pennsylvania and New York are the nation's major centers of Roman Catholicism. This

This Philadelphia synagogue, Rodeph Shalom, is typical of the many Jewish centers for worship throughout the commonwealth.

growth led to further breaking down of the administrative organization and increasing the number of dioceses, the latest of which were the Greensburg and Allentown dioceses, as well as creation of a growing number of colleges for Catholic men and women, and a marked expansion of parochial schools. The Episcopal Church is strongest in southeastern and western Pennsylvania among the more wealthy elements in the population. The German Reformed Church and the midwestern Evangelical Synod of North America took steps to merge completely in 1957 to form the United Church of Christ as an important Protestant group in the state. The Russian and Greek Catholic churches, and the Polish National Church, have a place in the mining and steel manufacturing areas. Such religious groups as the Church of Latter Day Saints and Jehovah's Witnesses have gained in membership in the state. Pennsylvania's Jewish population has grown steadily and reached some half a million by 1960, about one-tenth that of the nation. Nearly half the Jewish population is in Philadelphia, but other strong Jewish communities are in Pittsburgh and Harrisburg.

TWENTIETH CENTURY PENNSYLVANIA IN THE WORLD OF ART, LITERATURE, AND MUSIC

There is a tendency to dismiss the twentieth century as something of a dark age in the cultural and intellectual life of Pennsylvania and in defense to fall back on the glorious colonial and post-Federal years, when Philadelphia could claim to be the Athens of America. Such a point of view is hardly necessary, because Pennsylvania has not been especially backward in the realm of cultural and intellectual achievement. It would be hard to find any single region in the entire nation that has been more productive in terms of general cultural affairs than that which includes Philadelphia and its environs. It is outstanding not only in its creative individuals but also in the institutions such as museums, concert halls, theaters and orchestras that are the hallmarks of cultural accomplishment.

The Philadelphia Orchestra is one of the world's greatest, and the Academy of Music one of the fine and historic opera and concert halls of the country. The American String Orchestra, a chamber music group founded in 1957, scored a success in its European debut in 1963. The Philadelphia Museum of Art is one of the finer museums in the world. The Pennsylvania Academy of Fine Arts is both historic and productive as a center for teaching and displaying art. The Philadelphia Museum College of Art and the Philadelphia Art Alliance also have an important role in making Philadelphia an important art center. The Philadelphia Art Alliance is a center for exhibiting modern art. The University of Pennsylvania Museum, the Philadelphia Maritime Museum, the Franklin Institute and Memorial, the Library of the American Philosophical Society, the Rodin Museum, the Academy of Natural Science, The Historical Society of Pennsylvania, Fels Planetarium, Moore Institute of Art, the great University of Pennsylvania, the Library Company of Philadelphia—all these and many more are Philadelphia institutions that any American or indeed European city will find it hard to excel as centers of cultural and intellectual endeavor, and all of them are in a flourishing condition. Not least among the indications of a lively intellectual climate in Philadelphia has been its spirited renewal program, which combines preservation of fine old buildings rich in historical and architectural significance with modern structures in plans that a British visiting professor of architecture at the University of Pennsylvania recently described as the "most exciting in the United States." At the same time Philadelphia was said to be the best city in which to introduce a stranger to the United States because of its "deep roots" in the main American traditions of independence and puritanism, as well as its old historic churches, the Independence Hall area, Society Hill and other attractions which combine to make it one of the more distinctive in the world.

The Chadds Ford, Valley Forge, and New Hope regions are also one of the country's great havens for artists and creative writers, either natives of Pennsylvania or those who have taken up residence there because of the inviting countryside and its cultural climate. The names of Pearl Buck

Eugene Ormandy conducts the Philadelphia Orchestra.

and James Michener at once come to mind in literature, and Moss Hart, Oscar Hammerstein, and Claude Rains in the theater. And there are many others, not the least of whom is artist Andrew Wyeth. New Hope in particular has become one of the leading art colonies of the country. The entire area has been a birthplace and development area of the community theater, including the famous old Hedgerow Theatre of Jasper Deeter, and the more spectacular summer musical and community theater of recent years. There are also Valley Forge Park, and many houses now privately owned but rich in historical association and maintained and restored by the owners in the best traditions of historical preservation.

Though Philadelphia is by nature of its heritage the cultural capital of Pennsylvania, other cities experienced an encouraging growth of cultural life and institutions. Good though small museums may be found in Reading, Allentown, Scranton, and Greensburg, due in the main to

major private benefactions. There are considerably above-average historical-society museums and historical centers in Lancaster, York, Reading, Wilkes-Barre, and West Chester, which are under county historical-society management. The Bucks County Historical Society's Mercer Museum of early industry and crafts at Doylestown is outstanding. Historic Bethlehem is the leading example of a hinterland city that has turned attention to preservation and development of its finer historical treasures, which include the historic Moravian area and other portions of downtown Bethlehem. The Annie S. Kemerer Museum is a museum of general culture and a part of this development. Moravian College also gives Bethlehem a cultural association rooted in the past, while Lehigh University and Lafayette College, at nearby Easton, give a more modern trend to the cultural and intellectual life of the community. Lancaster has preserved Wheatland and Rockford as historic houses with the aid of private foundations created for the purpose. Nearby is the Pennsylvania Farm Museum at Landis Valley, an outstanding living agricultural museum operated by the state. Franklin and Marshall College has the small North Museum. York has given attention to a historic York development.

While none of the smaller cities can match the cultural resources of Philadelphia, there are good public libraries, art associations, community theater developments, and even small symphony and other musical organizations common in the typical smaller Pennsylvania city. Harrisburg, for example, has one of the finer small-city symphony orchestras, and a strong community theater organization. It has a good city library. It also has the new William Penn Memorial Museum, one of the nation's finest general museums, and the outstanding state museum of the country. Generally speaking, however, private fortunes have not found their way into the support of cultural institutions in Pennsylvania to the degree that might be expected, and the level of cultural achievement in the hinterland is lower than the size, wealth, and resources of Pennsylvania warrant.

Pittsburgh is certainly western Pennsylvania's cultural capital, though it is doubtful whether it can ever hope to equal historic Philadelphia, despite major advances in recent decades. Pittsburgh suffered from a failure of some of its great tycoons to follow the example set by Thaw, Buhl, and Carnegie in endowing cultural activity. Instead, the great Andrew Mellon art collection went to the National Gallery in Washington, and Henry Clay Frick's art went to New York City. This has been remedied since by liberal aid to Pittsburgh by Richard K. Mellon and the several Mellon foundations. Oakland is the heart of Pittsburgh's cultural life, and it was here that Carnegie placed his $5,000,000 Carnegie Museum and Library, which became even before 1900 one of the great museum and art centers of the country. The new University of Pittsburgh picked Oakland for its new location in 1908, and this led later to the spectacular Cathedral of Learning. The Stephen Foster Memorial was located on the Pitt campus in 1937. Heinz Chapel is a small but distinguished Gothic-style building nearby, endowed by the Heinz family. Oakland in 1937

became the home for the Mellon Institute, one of the country's major research centers. Carnegie Institute of Technology, founded and endowed by Carnegie in 1905, added to the cultural complex of this area. Chatham College, formerly the Pennsylvania College for Women, and Duquesne University are other Pittsburgh educational institutions. The Pittsburgh Playhouse in Oakland became a performing-arts school as well as a community theater of note. Pittsburgh's new and distinctive Civic Auditorium was built near Oakland.

The Pittsburgh Symphony Orchestra is acknowledged as one of the world's fine orchestras. Its recent conductor, William Steinberg, has enjoyed international renown, exceeded only by that of Leopold Stowkowski and Eugene Ormandy of the Philadelphia Orchestra. The Pittsburgh Opera Society, the Civic Light Opera, and the American Wind Symphony are other notable Pittsburgh musical associations. The architectural development associated with the great private homes and public buildings of the Oakland section, and more recently with the downtown Gateway Center, make Pittsburgh a city of considerably more than average interest for its examples of fine architecture. These range from the semi-Gothic common to some of the Oakland area to the skyscraper university building, and handsome, tall office buildings of Gateway Center. Point Park and the Fort Pitt Museum form a capstone, as it were, to the historic triangle in lower Pittsburgh where the Allegheny and Monongahela meet to form the Ohio. This attractive state park and museum development preserves for modern Pittsburgh a piece of its most historic ground, including the old Fort Pitt Blockhouse, saved for the city by the local D.A.R. The total development of all these resources of Pittsburgh took place after 1900, and the spurt forward in the last two decades has been most noticeable.

The total history of Pennsylvania's role in the world of twentieth-century art also is truly distinctive. The century opened with a productive group of artists already on the road to distinction and mainly centered around the great Thomas C. Eakins and the Pennsylvania Academy art school. George B. Luks. Robert Henri, Thomas Anshutz,

Interior of the world-renowned Rodin Museum in Philadelphia.

William J. Glackens, Everett Shinn, and John Sloan were all productive well after 1900. Arthur Carles before his death in 1952 won real leadership in the field of abstract art. Among more self-taught artists were Horace Pippin, Negro artist and World War I veteran notable for painting folk scenes of the Negro; Joseph Pickett, New Hope carpenter who projected realistic pictures of the local scene; and Pittsburgh's John Kane, who by 1927 was winning recognition for his work depicting the life of working people in the region and for his own *Self Portrait*.

Pittsburgh's Mary Cassatt, after studying at the Academy, spent most of her life abroad and became one of the most noted artists of her time. Lancaster's Charles Demuth was another product of the Academy, who after returning from abroad adopted somewhat cubist techniques and is looked upon by some as Pennsylvania's most distinctive artist between 1900 and 1950. Though

not distinguished art, the historical paintings by Violet Oakley in the new Capitol building at Harrisburg in the Governor's Reception Room, the Senate, and Supreme Court room are not to be ignored. Edwin A. Abbey's work on the interior of the Capitol dome and in the House of Representatives is notable, but symbolical in character. The new Capitol also provided a setting for presentation of the twin sculptures by George Grey Barnard, the "Burden of Life" and "Labor and Brotherhood." Barnard, Bellefonte native, came to be highly regarded as one of America's most noted sculptors of his time. More recently, the New York artist Vincent Maragliotti has done small ceiling paintings for the Education and Finance buildings, and the huge mural depicting a panorama of Pennsylvania's history for the Memorial Hall of the William Penn Memorial Museum. Janet de Coux, western Pennsylvania sculptor, did the large and vital statue of

William Penn that stands in the same Hall in front of the mural.

Pennsylvania artists of note in recent years are many, and only names can be given to suggest some idea of the scope of their talent. Edward W. Redfield emerged as a notable landscape artist of the century and was early elected to the National Academy of Design in New York. Pennsylvania artists among those elected to the Academy between 1907 and 1960 included Charles Morris Young, another dean of the landscape painters, Benton Spruance, Carroll Tyson, Alice Kent Stoddard, Catherine Morris Wright, Henry Pitz, Adolph Borie, Daniel Garber, Joseph Pearson, Jr., George Biddle, and illustrator Nathaniel Wyeth. Contemporaries of note, to mention but a few who have won attention in recent exhibitions, include Japanese-born Ben Kamihira, now living in Philadelphia, Franklin Watkins, Albert Gold, Betty Miller Bowes, and the incomparable Andrew Wyeth, termed "America's most successful artist." Samuel Yellin of Philadelphia was famous for his decorative work in metals, especially iron. George Harding was a prominent Pennsylvania muralist associated with the Academy. Sculptors of more than ordinary distinction in addition to Barnard include Charles Grafly, who died in 1929, Charles Rudy, J. Wallace Kelly, Edward F. Hoffman, Albin Polasek, now living in Florida, Ralph Sabatini, Victor Rin, Janet de Coux, and Robert T. McKenzie. The art exhibitions of Philadelphia and Pittsburgh, as well as other galleries, are filled with the work of Pennsylvania artists, and the number of lively art associations and extent of their work as revealed in local exhibitions promises well for not only the current state of the arts in Pennsylvania, but for their future.

A more affluent society also gave impetus to both extensive private and public building, and created new demands for the talent of the architect. While individual architects still stood out for their great personal contributions to the design of particular buildings, the trend of modern building has demanded the talents of various engineers along with architects organized as large firms. The talent of a single great architect such as a Latrobe no longer sufficed to design a great modern building. This does not mean that the talent of the individual was entirely swallowed up in the organization. Frank Miles Day and his brother, H. Kent Day, were outstanding Philadelphia architects of the turn of the century. Charles Z. Klauder was later associated with this firm and went on to become one of the more noted architects of the era. His work included the Heinz Memorial Chapel, the Cathedral of Learning in Pittsburgh, and several buildings at Penn State University, along with the Drexel & Company building in Philadelphia. Walter Cope and John Stewardson were a Philadelphia firm distinguished for twentieth-century college architecture at Bryn Mawr, Princeton, and the University of Pennsylvania. McKim, Mead & White of New York built the Girard Trust Company and Philadelphia National Bank as Philadelphia monuments of a neoclassic style of the period shortly after 1900. The talents of C. C. Zantzinger, Charles L. Borie, Jr., and Horace Trumbauer were combined on several monumental Philadelphia buildings; they did the primary supervising of building the majestic Philadelphia Art Museum, which heads Benjamin Franklin Parkway to provide one of the finest settings in any American city. Trumbauer was the architect for several of the fine residences of wealthy Philadelphians built soon after the turn of the century.

George Howe was another noted Philadelphia architect who after 1928 practiced modern architecture on his own until 1955. Paul Philippe Cret, who came to the University of Pennsylvania from his native France at the age of twenty-seven in 1903 to teach architecture and design, must be recognized as perhaps the greatest single architectural influence of his time to come from Pennsylvania. Associated with the firm of Cret, Harbison, Hough, Livingston, and Larson, he had as his co-workers such outstanding figures as John F. Harbison and Roy Larson. Larson recently became the architect for Penn State University. The Pan American Building in Washington, the Rodin Museum and the Federal Reserve Bank in Philadelphia are Cret monuments. He also exerted great influence on Pennsylvania architecture in its public buildings as a member of the State Art Commission over a long period. The Pennsylvania Savings Fund Society building at Twelfth and Market in Philadelphia has been termed as one of the one hundred finest buildings in America. It was the work of George Howe, William Lesaze, and Walter Behrman.

The firm of Eyre, Cop & Day represented another strong combination of architectural talents. Louis I. Kahn of the University of Pennsylvania has attracted attention for the new Richards Medical Research Building which demonstrates bold new theories in modern architecture. Charles M. Stotz of Pittsburgh emerged in the 1930's as something of a historian of early western Pennsylvania architecture and must be rated as one of the leading historical restoration architects of the nation, notable especially for his fine work on the restoration of Old Economy, near Pittsburgh, for the state. He and his brother, Edward Stotz, have designed several industrial research centers in the Pittsburgh area and several college buildings elsewhere. In the eastern area, G. Edwin Brumbaugh, son of a Pennsylvania governor, in the same period became the most notable authority on historical restoration, especially Pennsylvania German-type buildings, and did monumental work for the state at Ephrata Cloister. This work has been followed up successfully by Allentown architect John Heyl, another authority on Pennsylvania German architecture. Charles Peterson, formerly with the National Park Service in Region Five office in Philadelphia, and more recently engaged in private consulting work, is one of the more expert students of early American architecture and its restoration in the country. William Gehron of Williamsport had a major influence on the design of several buildings and the general plan for the state capital group of buildings in Harrisburg before about 1950. More modern high-rise office buildings have been the vogue in recent years. Lawrie and Green of Harrisburg, with Edwin Green as the architect, were responsible for the highly modern design of the new William Penn Memorial Museum and Archives Building.

The Pennsylvania literary tradition has been a proud one in recent decades. Owen Wister has helped make it with *The Virginian* and other works, as have essayist and biographer Agnes Repplier and Ida Tarbell, historian of Standard Oil and biographer of Lincoln. Christopher Morley, novelist and essayist, author of *Kitty Foyle,* and Joseph Hergesheimer with his historical novels such as *The Three Black Pennys* helped along, and were further abetted by Pittsburgh's Hervey Allen, who won fame with *Anthony Adverse* and then, before his untimely death, started his trilogy of the Pennsylvania frontier with *Bedford Village* and *The Forest and the Fort.* Mary Roberts Rinehart won a place among the nation's writers of the mystery novel. More recently Conrad Richter and John O'Hara have vied with each other as authors born in Schuylkill County who have entirely different approaches to the modern novel but are among the nation's most outstanding writers. Richter won the Pulitzer Prize in 1951 and the National Book Award in 1960. His first novel, *The Sea of Grass,* written in 1944, has been translated into some sixteen foreign languages and two of his novels have been made into movies, one of which is his *Light in the Forest,* which was one of a series based on life in early Pennsylvania. A New York critic has called Richter one of the nation's "finest and most honored writers." O'Hara represents a quite different approach, and has been termed the social historian among novelists for his brilliant and detailed portrayal of life in country club and suburban society circles, ranging back through some past decades. O'Hara's work is carefully researched. His novel *Pal Joey* was adapted for the stage and became a great musical comedy success.

Oddly enough, the same region has produced John Updike, who was born and grew up in Shillington and from his present Ipswich, Massachusetts, home at the ripe age of the early thirties is author of three novels, including *The Centaur,* which have won wide acclaim. Rachel Carson, writer in the field of nature and famous for the recent exposure of the menace of modern chemicals used as insecticides, *Silent Spring,* is a native of Springdale and attended the Pennsylvania College for Women. Pittsburgh's Gladys Schmitt gained her first recognition with *David the King.* Catherine Drinker Bowen of Bryn Mawr is a well-known writer who achieved special distinction with her popular biographies. Philadelphia novelist Albert Idell, Philip Van Doren Stern, novelist, historian, and anthropologist, and the poet Theodore Spencer, along with the journalist and commentator Louis Fischer are other Pennsylvania literary figures of contemporary note. Any list of notable American poets must include Stephen Vincent Benét.

In historical writing of a scholarly nature, there are names of importance that include John Bach McMaster of the University of Pennsylvania, with his pioneer and monumental *History of the People of the United States Since the Civil War,* a history that included social and economic aspects. Albert E. McKinley of the same university was not only a historian of stature, but a pioneer in the philosophy of the social studies. Ellis P. Oberholtzer's five-volume *History of the United States Since the Civil War* was the work of a nonuniversity historian who also wrote a *Literary History of Philadelphia* and some biography. Roy F. Nichols of the University of Pennsylvania emerged as an important biographer and historian in recent years, as did Lawrence Gipson of Lehigh with his Pulitzer-prize-winning *History of the British Empire Before the American Revolution.* Philip S. Klein, at Penn State has written, among other things, the definitive life of James Buchanan. Francis J. Tschan of the same university was a distinguished medievalist, while Wayland F. Dunaway also at Penn State, pioneered in writing the first comprehensive single-volume history of Pennsylvania, and in studies of the Scotch-Irish. John W. Oliver, at the University of Pittsburgh, was a pioneer in the field of the history of technology, inspired no doubt by Pittsburgh's mill environment. Fred Lewis Pattee at Penn State was the first to write a history of American literature. George Korson has done distinctive work in collecting and putting into book form Pennsylvania songs and legends. Frances Lichten's work on Pennsylvania folk art was equally distinctive in this field. All in all, the literary output of Pennsylvanians, only a small part of which has been touched upon, was not only distinguished but is rather significant in the upbuilding of American literature of the twentieth century.

Contributions in music are hard to pin down. Place of birth is important along with creative location in determining whether a notable is or is not a Pennsylvanian. The American supplement to Grove's well known *Dictionary of Music and Musicians* is a guide, and in 1950 it listed seventy Pennsylvania-born musicians ranging from composers and conductors to pianists and singers. The list has grown since that date. Stars of opera and concert stage included Paul Althouse, Louise Homer, Helen Jepson, John Charles Thomas, Henri Scott, Marian Anderson, David Bispham, and Jeanette MacDonald. Frank Black, Donald Voorhees, and Fred Waring are high on any list of conductors outside the symphony field, which has been dominated by such names as Victor Herbert, Fritz Reiner, and William Steinberg in Pittsburgh, and Leopold Stowkowski and Eugene Ormandy in Philadelphia. A list of musicians of national reputation must include the still-prominent name of Charles Wakefield Cadman, who ventured into writing opera, and in his later years was a major Hollywood composer for the movies. Oscar Levant, pianist, composer, and conductor, was born in Pittsburgh. Philadelphia's Josef Hofmann won a place in the musical world as a pianist and dean of the Curtis Institute of Music from 1926 to 1938. The institute itself, founded in 1924 by Mrs. Curtis Bok, has done much through free musical training to develop musicians. In the musical show field, Richard Myers and Manning Sherwin of Philadelphia have been composers of major musical productions for both the stage and screen. Ethel Waters from Chester has won fame as both an actress and singer.

With the growth of motion pictures, and more recently television, the stage and screen have become one in the world of the theater. In the days before the silver screen became the rival of the legitimate stage the names of Drew and Barrymore continued for many years after the turn of the century as leading names in the American theater. W. C. Fields, from Philadelphia, was a stage star of comedy before lending his art to the screen. Joey Bishop is Philadelphia's modern-day counterpart in the world of popular comedy. The great comic actor Ed Wynn is another Philadelphian. Writers of note for the American theater with a Pennsylvania connection include George

Kelly, author of the Pulitzer-prize *Craig's Wife;* Clifford Odets and his *Waiting for Lefty;* Maxwell Anderson, who won the Pulitzer award for *Valley Forge;* Marc Connelly with *The Green Pastures;* and Julius and Philip Epstein, Penn State graduates, famous for writing and adapting works for stage and screen, including *Chicken Every Sunday.*

In motion pictures and television, names are many, and among those that everyone would recognize are James Stewart, the former Grace Kelly, Gene Kelly, William Powell, Adolphe Menjou, Janet Blair, Janet Gaynor, Nick Adams, John and Lionel Barrymore, and Dick Powell. Oliver Smith has emerged as one of the principal artists in the design of stage settings for some of the most notable musical productions of the modern theater, such as *My Fair Lady, Camelot,* and many others. Donald Oenslager, of Harrisburg birth, is another of Broadway's leading stage designers. *Who's Who in the Theatre* lists some twenty persons born in Pennsylvania, and in many instances graduates of Pennsylvania colleges and universities, with their first theatrical training and experience gained within the commonwealth. Among them were Arthur Penn, stage and screen director; Vinton Freedley and Herman Levin, producers; Joseph Kramm, playwright and actor; George Kaufman, playwright and director; Cecil Holm, author and actor; Martin Gabel, writer and actor. Frances Carson, Florence Reed, Vivienne Segal, Nancy Walker, Charlotte Greenwood, Anne Jackson, Edith King, and Carmen Mathews are others listed.

Pennsylvania has enjoyed since colonial days a reputation for the extent and the quality of its newspapers and magazines. The world of the newspaper and the magazine changed greatly in the twentieth century. For one thing, economic pressures forced many a newspaper and magazine either into bankruptcy and failure or consolidation to provide more economic and efficient operation. Every Pennsylvania city witnessed this process of consolidation. Most Pennsylvania cities became "one newspaper" towns with at best a morning and evening edition under the same management. Even the larger cities of Philadelphia and Pittsburgh were reduced to two major

dailies. Philadelphia has the *Inquirer,* laying claim to the oldest daily in the country, and the *Evening Bulletin,* which "nearly everybody" is said by their ads to read. The two provide essentially a morning and evening daily combination. In Pittsburgh, the historic old *Post-Gazette* represents a merger but can claim to be the oldest newspaper west of the Alleghenies. The *Pittsburgh Press* is a unit in the Scripps chain as an evening paper. Interests from outside the state establishing newspaper chains have been increasingly active in acquiring larger Pennsylvania newspapers, as in Harrisburg, where two once independent newspapers were finally reduced to a single combination of the morning *Patriot* and the afternoon *Evening News,* controlled by an out-of-state owner. The country weekly has stayed alive in most rural counties, but is limited mainly to the county seat. An interesting journalistic development was a spectacular growth of suburban newspapers, meeting the desire of people in suburban communities for the type of "home news" not available in the region's metropolitan press. In a way these newspapers of suburbia have become the country weeklies of today with their fund of local news, editorials, and advertising. Because of the competitive nature of the advertising field, many newspapers acquired radio stations as an integral part of their informational and advertising services.

Philadelphia continued its reputation as a leading center of magazine publishing, but here again the pressure of changing times made differences. The city's purely literary magazines that were once the pride and glory of the magazine world came to an end. Consolidation was again the order of the day as the large Curtis organization brought together under one central business organization the famous old *Saturday Evening Post,* the *Ladies' Home Journal* and *Country Gentleman,* along with such newer ventures as *Holiday* and the children's *Jack and Jill* magazine. Efforts at state and regional magazines proved generally unfruitful. The *Bucks County Traveller* appeared for a time as a stylish regional magazine with some attempt at arousing statewide interest, but the venture failed despite the quality of the product. A magazine named *Commonwealth* flourished briefly, but also failed to achieve full orbit as a statewide magazine.

All in all, the era of change which came with the progress of the twentieth century left Pennsylvania a very different place, sharing with other industrial states the social changes and problems common to the modern era. At the same time, Pennsylvania could point with some pride to upholding some of the best traditions of the past in the course of its cultural and intellectual development, while admitting that all was not perfect.

The Allegheny Observatory in Pittsburgh. Here Samuel P. Langley made some of the pioneer studies of flight.

CHAPTER SEVENTEEN

THE END
OF A GOLDEN AGE -
PENNSYLVANIA'S
ECONOMY SINCE
1900

Few, if any, Pennsylvanians entered the twentieth century with any concern that the future might bring serious problems. It was a best of all worlds. The booming steel industry had progressed to a point where the United States Steel Corporation, based largely on Pennsylvania enterprise, had come into being as the nation's first billion-dollar corporation. Pennsylvania was by far the largest single producer of the nation's steel, having increased that production over 300 per cent since 1880, to a point where it was now about 60 per cent of the nation's steel total. About the same percentage of the coke used in making steel was made in Pennsylvania, and the commonwealth was by far the leader in producing such by-products of steel as tin and terneplate. The state had an entire monopoly of the production of anthracite coal and was far ahead of any other state in mining soft coal. Petroleum production was facing rivalry, but Pennsylvania as the birthplace of the oil industry in 1859 held onto a narrow leadership in production. The products of farm and forest were still leading manufactures, and farming itself was a major industry. While it had long since ceased to be first among the states in population and wealth, there appeared surely no threat to its position as second. State and local government were held to low levels of activity in terms of any interference with business or personal concerns, with resulting modest governmental expenditures making possible low taxes. It was a good world in Pennsylvania in 1900. But it was one subject to unforeseen changes.

THE HORSELESS CARRIAGE AND THE FLYING MACHINE

Perhaps the most powerful single influence changing America after 1900 was the continuing revolution in transportation and communication. It can be called continuing because the railroad, the telegraph, and telephone already were a revolution; it not only influenced Pennsylvania's economic life directly, but indirectly led to great new industrial developments centered outside the state, and helped eventually to undermine the industrial supremacy the commonwealth had once enjoyed. The country was ready for the automobile and the airplane by 1900. Mechanical know-how had already invented a horseless carriage. The petroleum industry had reached a point at which gasoline and lubricants were available, the former having been a waste product in the industry's earlier days. The birth of the aluminum industry had resulted in the new metal so badly needed to expedite heavier-than-air transportation. Improvements in making steel made it much more useful in building a satisfactory automobile.

The great age of railroading was nearing a peak about 1900 in terms of further expansion of mileage and improvements in the mechanics of railroading. In Pennsylvania, railroad mileage had just about doubled in the previous twenty-five years, but only about a hundred miles of additional track was laid in 1900. Pennsylvania railroads carried that year 478,684,683 tons of freight, of which more than half was listed as "products of mines." These were vastly improved railroads, thanks mainly to George Westinghouse, and railroads continued to improve; but by 1915 they had ceased to grow. It was not until 1934 that American railroads made any further improvement other than possibly larger and heavier freight cars, and this came about in the development of the modern "streamliner," the famous Zephyr for passenger service, first used on the Burlington out of Chicago. This pioneer venture in providing more modern passenger service used cars newly designed and built by the Budd Company in its shops near Philadelphia. The nearby Pennsylvania Railroad did not avail itself of this pioneer facility in developing a modern approach to passenger traffic. A gradual abandonment after World War I of short lines, as well as elimination of passenger trains on even main-line operations, gradually but surely reduced both passenger and freight service in Pennsylvania to a minimal level so far as many local communities were concerned.

Pennsylvania's connection with the development of the automobile is easily overlooked, but it could have been revolutionary in its conse-

quences had not a young mechanic named Henry Ford chanced to live in Michigan and made it the capital of the automobile industry. Some of the pioneer experiments in this country with an automotive vehicle were made by the Duryeas while living in Reading. A lot of people tinkered with the idea. Early automobiles were built by blacksmiths and machinists who improvised from just about anything and assembled the parts into a working machine. As late as 1912 Philadelphia, Pittsburgh, and Reading were leading cities for building or assembling automobiles, and now long-forgotten names such as the Chadwick, the Dragon, and the Pullman were well-known names for horseless carriages. The Autocar Company, a by-product of a Pittsburgh venture in automobile building, began building automotive commercial vehicles about 1908 and soon became a major manufacturer. The Mack Truck Company was launched at Allentown and went on to become a major designer and manufacturer of heavy truck equipment down through to the day of trucks powered by diesels. The Electric Storage Battery Company in Philadelphia was one of the pioneers in manufacture of automobile batteries and became a leader in the field. In Williamsport Lycoming Motors enjoyed a position as a well-known builder of both automobile and airplane motors. James W. Packard, Lehigh University graduate in mechanical engineering, was one of the half-dozen outstanding figures in the early evolution of automotive engineering in the country. Just how much the technological advances in making steel and aluminum in Pennsylvania mills contributed to the automobile as well as the airplane is usually forgotten, but the rapidity with which the nation took to the road on wheels and to the air in planes depended in no small degree upon these advances.

The art of forging and welding aluminum had been so advanced by 1930 that entire structures could be shaped from it. New ways of heat-treating steel and revolutionary advances in making alloys of steels, along with electric welding, equally revolutionized the use of steel in automotive transportation for frames, bodies, engines, and parts. These basic raw materials for both the automobile and the airplane continued to be produced to a larger extent in Pennsylvania than in any other state or region. But when a mechanic named Henry Ford made the simple, standardized, cheap Model-T Ford in 1908, the automobile industry was lost forever to Pennsylvania.

The same situation might have prevailed in the development of the airplane. Samuel P. Langley, after going to Washington's Smithsonian Institute from Pittsburgh's Allegheny Observatory, missed by about three years becoming the inventor of the airplane in 1903, but, as mentioned earlier, he did make many major contributions to the science of flight. As it was, Pennsylvania's leading role in aviation development was played by William Piper, Sr., in developing the small, light passenger aircraft that became famous in peace and war as the Piper Cub, or the "flying jeep." Piper's enterprise began at Bradford in 1930, and then moved to Lock Haven and soon became national in scope. Some seven thousand of these planes were built and used in World War II. The Piper Cub had come to stay. Lycoming-built motors were widely used in early planes. Last but by no means least, the heavier-than-air craft would not have been possible had it not been for the continuing revolution in the manufacture of aluminum and its adaptations to aircraft production, which by 1930 made possible the huge Douglas and Boeing aircraft. Pennsylvania geography was a determining factor in its failure to become a center for airplane manufacture, because its hills and mountains were hardly suited to the experimental development of aircraft. Indeed, in the early days of transcontinental air mail, started in 1924, and passenger service across the country, which began in 1930, Pennsylvania's rugged Alleghenies with their tricky air currents were feared by all as the most hazardous portion of their route.

By the 1930's air transportation was serving much of Pennsylvania, with five major airlines. There were over a hundred airports of varying degrees of worth, and over a thousand licensed pilots in the state. In fact, aviation had grown to such proportions that a totally new arm of state government had to be created to supervise it, an aeronautics commission. Pittsburgh and Philadelphia recently built two large, fine airports.

Well over two million persons were using Philadelphia's huge International Airport by 1961, an increase of 500 per cent since 1950. The new Greater Pittsburgh Airport saw an equal growth as both cities became a center of the growing pattern of air transportation in the jet age. By 1962 the state had over 150 commercial airports. Individual use of small planes was on the increase, and by 1960 Pennsylvania had a respectable number of "flying farmers." The number of passengers embarking on planes at Pennsylvania airports just about doubled between 1927 and 1963, and runs into millions of persons. The freight tonnage by air has shown an equal growth.

The automobile and the truck, however, did more by far than the airplane to revolutionize transportation for the average person and the average business. By 1961 the number of motor vehicles of all kinds registered in the state reached 4,842,400 of which 3,505,200 were passenger cars and 597,837 commercial vehicles. The number of operators' licenses issued amounted at that time to over five million. The total highway mileage of the state by 1963 reached well over 100,000 miles, of which over 42,000 were state highway. This was quite a jump from the time when a state highway department was first created in 1903 and when in 1905 the state first began to license those who owned automobiles.

NEW HIGHWAYS FOR A NEW AGE

The growth of pressure for better roads on which to operate the growing flood of cars and trucks was almost instantaneous, and in 1911 the Sproul Act really began the state highway system, with authorization to take over and maintain 8,835 miles of roads. This did not mean that all of these highways quickly became like those over which the motorist now speeds at fifty to sixty miles an hour. As late as 1931 the state highway system included only a little more than 13,000 miles of improved highway. Gradual improvement also took place in city and town streets to get the car and truck on firm paving. A real revolution took place after 1931 as Governor Pinchot fulfilled his promise to "take the farmer out of the mud," and by 1933 the state had im-

Boring a tunnel through the mountain barrier in constructing the Pennsylvania Turnpike.

railroad as a common carrier. Employment in the trucking industry increased 65 per cent between 1920 and 1960.

The end was not yet in sight, as the amount of improved state highways continued to increase. From 1911 to 1960 the state spent some $2,000,000,000 on highways. In 1940 the first link was completed in the famous pioneer Pennsylvania Turnpike, running from the Harrisburg area to within some twenty miles of Pittsburgh at Irwin. Built by a new type of highway authority set up by law in 1937 as the Pennsylvania Turnpike Commission, bonds were sold to finance the modern four-lane turnpike, and tolls were collected from its users as the means of paying off the debt. Started in 1938, the first link was opened October 1, 1940 as "the first long distance highway in America to be constructed without cross traffic at grade anywhere, and with all modern transportation necessities incorporated in its design." A Philadelphia extension of 100 miles was authorized in 1940 and completed ten years later. A further western extension authorized in 1941 for sixty-seven miles to the Ohio border was opened in December, 1951. The same year a thirty-two mile extension to the New Jersey border was provided for and opened in 1954. The new Delaware River Turnpike Bridge financed jointly by New Jersey and Pennsylvania to link the turnpike systems of the two states was opened in May, 1956, and Pennsylvania now had a modern toll road running the entire length of the state. A northeastern extension of the turnpike from Plymouth Meeting to Clark's Summit near Scranton was authorized in 1953 and completed four years later for 110 miles. The total cost of the system in bonds was $509,500,000, and this had been reduced by the end of 1961 to $382,410,000. By 1959 over twelve million passenger cars, and over four million commercial vehicles were using the main turnpike. Population, business, and industry grew at every turnpike interchange, illustrating its great economic value.

The turnpike was not the end of schemes for major highway improvement. In 1954 six men sat down in a Williamsport club to perfect a dream for a superhighway across the heart of central Pennsylvania from Ohio to New Jersey.

proved over 8,000 miles of rural road. These were the famous "Pinchot roads" which, while narrow and winding because they were built at the least possible cost, gave rural Pennsylvania what was without doubt the best country highway system in the nation. The average of improved highway in Pennsylvania by the 1930's was more than twice the national average per population, and as of 1934 over a million private passenger cars were registered, and some seven thousand certificates as public carriers were issued to operators of trucks and commercial vehicles. In short, by 1930 a genuine revolution in automotive transportation had been wrought. The impact upon the economy and the life of the people was real and growing. Farmers could now move their products to ready markets with greater facility and economy, and the motor truck was starting to compete with the

The dream became a reality under the leadership of Williamsport's Z. H. Confair and was authorized in 1955; construction was soon under way, with a target date of 1967 as its completion. In the meantime, the extension of Federal aid to the development of a great national interstate highway system brought more millions into Pennsylvania for advanced superhighway construction, with consequent promise of further contributions to the economic well being of the state. A total of 1,575 miles was included in Pennsylvania's portion of the interstate system, of which 720 were completed by 1963.

THE RISE AND FALL OF THE STREETCAR

While the state was being threaded with new and improved highways, a similar revolution took place in urban and interurban transportation, and one that had a close relationship to the growth of the city. The century opened with the electric trolley as the answer to transportation within cities and even between them. John G. Brill of Philadelphia was one of the leading figures in the constant improvement of the trolley from the days of the horse car, and his company was a leading builder of trolleys. The peak of trolley-car line building was reached by 1912, but as late as 1940 there remained over 1,700 miles of trolley line in the state. Trolley lines leaped out into the countryside as electric railways connected cities, and in 1912 it was possible to travel many miles by trolley in such regions as the Lebanon Valley, as lines were built connecting the small cities of the area all the way from Harrisburg.

As with the steam railroads, the trolley's downfall was a slow but sure result of the coming of the automobile. Autos made it even easier for people to get from countryside and suburb to city without depending on someone else to schedule

A modern highway interchange on the federal-state highway system.

An aerial view of Philadelphia today.

their ride. The internal-combustion motor was also applied very quickly to auto buses, and builders of trolleys turned attention to producing this new equipment. Electrically powered buses using the same current as trolleys were also developed. Trolley trackage decreased rapidly after 1940 as city after city abandoned the streetcar entirely. The use of the personal automobile and the bus put pressure at once on every city to improve its streets. Thousands of miles of improved city streets were built to meet the demands of motorized transportation. At the same time, the pressure of traffic going into cities as well as moving or parking within the city presented acute problems. Philadelphia and Pittsburgh for decades struggled with this growing bottleneck and it was evident by the 1950's that it demanded the attention of the state. The building of the Schuylkill Expressway helped Philadelphia, and a Delaware River and a Vine Street expressway

also were provided for by 1963. In Pittsburgh the Penn Lincoln Parkway with the Fort Pitt Bridge and Tunnel and extension of expressways to the west gave relief. Hundreds of millions of dollars are still necessary to solve the problems of access to the major cities of Pennsylvania, and to provide in many instances new bypass highways that will take major through traffic off the city streets. The auto and the bus proved both a boon and a headache to the city. Modern city growth would not have been possible without them, but in turn they produced major problems.

WATERWAYS AND PORTS

Waterways continued to provide a valuable service to Pennsylvania despite the development of other methods of transportation. The continued growth of Pittsburgh's economy even after 1900 was linked closely with the use of the western rivers that came to a junction at the Steel City to form the Ohio. The importance of the several hundred miles of navigable waterways feeding into and out of Pittsburgh was such as to produce constant improvement in terms of additional and improved locks. Probably the peak in river tonnage was reached in World War II, when in 1945 over 17,000,000 tons of river freight were moved out of Pittsburgh down the Ohio, and the Allegheny and Monongahela fed over 29,000,000 tons into the city. Pittsburgh reported in 1951 over 12,000,000 tons of shipping, making it a major port. By far the larger part of this tonnage was coal, followed by sand and gravel, oil and gasoline, limestone, and iron and steel products. The value of the waterways to the complex of steel and coal enterprises in the Pittsburgh district continues to be very real.

The Port of Erie until recently has been one of limited importance. In 1951 its nearly 8,000,000 short tons of freight compared with two to three times that amount for Buffalo and Toledo. The completion of the St. Lawrence Seaway was hailed as promising an era of greater importance for Erie as a lake port, now provided with an outlet to the Atlantic. The seaway thus far has not held up to expectations, though the number of foreign ships bringing goods into Erie in 1961 reached twenty-two, and fifty-one vessels moved exports from Erie.

Pennsylvania's most important port area continues to be Philadelphia and the other Delaware River ports, which make up what is usually termed the Delaware Port Area. This is the largest fresh-water port area in the world, and since 1960 has enjoyed the position of the nation's number one foreign-import trade center. In 1961 the port handled 43,882,000 short tons of foreign waterborne cargo, which amounted to 13.3 per cent of the foreign commerce of the entire United States, and 26.5 per cent of that of the North Atlantic region. The Delaware handled 7.6 per cent of the nation's import trade tonnage, due largely to heavy imports of iron ore from Canada and Venezuela for the furnaces at the great Fairless Steel works at Morrisville on the Delaware, and heavy imports of crude petroleum from South America and the Near East, feeding the huge oil refineries at Chester and Philadelphia. Export trade is in lesser volume, and in 1961 accounted for only 3,400,306 tons, made up mainly of iron and steel scrap, anthracite coal, and refined petroleum products. The total growth of the trade of the port has been spectacular when it is

The governors of New Jersey, Delaware, and Pennsylvania with other state officials join with President Kennedy in signing the federal-state compact on the conservation of the Delaware River basin. New York's governor was not present.

kept in mind that it amounted to only 19,000,000 tons in 1947. Beginning in 1954, Congress made liberal appropriations to improve the Delaware channel for shipping by dredging operations. In 1951 New Jersey joined Pennsylvania in creating a Delaware River Port Authority to facilitate development of the port area. The city has made the improvement of warehousing and docking facilities on the Philadelphia waterfront a prime consideration in its redevelopment program and has bid strenuously for even more foreign trade.

Foreign exports in recent years have become more important in the Pennsylvania economy and are on the increase. In 1961 they increased some $130,000,000 to a total of $877,000,000. Over two thousand manufacturers and fabricators in the state were indicated in 1961 as having an export business of over $500, and it went to 157 countries. Philadelphia is second only to New York as the port through which these products are put into export trade.

COMMUNICATION IN THE MODERN ECONOMY

Communication has become as important to the modern economy as transportation. It is easy to overlook the revolution in merchandising the products of today's industry that has come about in the last half century. Advertising of course was well known as a means of communicating to potential customers the availability of products long before the turn of the century, but what was not even foreseen in 1900 was the coming of such new advertising media as the radio and television. These two communications media not only created new industry through the manufacture of sets and their components, in which Pennsylvania shared richly, but also revolutionized the ability of industry to attract the consumer's attention with a message about a product. The growing development of mass distribution has been influenced more largely perhaps by mass-media advertising than even by advances in transportation, for the simple reason that it is mass desire for goods that makes possible their mass production and distribution. The story of the birth of radio in Pittsburgh in 1920 at station KDKA has been told. In a few years there were more than a

hundred local radio stations in the state filling the airways not only with music and lectures, but also with advertising messages. These were joined later by television, and every leading Pennsylvania city soon had one or more television stations. With the advent of television, radio devoted more attention to local interests and concentrated even more upon local advertising as a basis for support.

Other communications media played a part in revolutionizing business and the economy in the twentieth century. All of them were invented and in use before 1900, but their influence upon the economy had been slight. The telephone became increasingly valuable as a business aid, making it possible to conduct business over long distances by the simple expedient of placing a phone call. The role of the typewriter, and especially its adaptation to business machines of various types, has been material in the growth of mass production and distribution in the modern economy. It helped on the side to create a whole new world of employment for women, whose appearance in most business offices earlier than 1900 would have created consternation, if allowed at all. Even photography as further developed by George Eastman had its place in the changing economy because advertisers found out quickly the truth of the old adage that a "picture is worth a thousand words." Photography is so important to modern industry that the Bethlehem Steel Company, as one example, has an entire building at its Bethlehem headquarters to house a completely modern photographic production laboratory and plant, serving the needs of this large corporation. All of these new communications media were important to Pennsylvania because in many instances Pennsylvanians helped to create and develop them, and also because they helped to revolutionize the economy of the state through changing the nature of business, and even creating important new industrial developments as part of the state's economy to supply the needs of the new media. Atwater Kent, for example, was a pioneer in manufacturing radios. Atwater Kent radios were found in more homes than any other single make in the early days of radio. This enterprise in Philadelphia later formed the basis for the large Philco Corporation, a major manufacturer of

*Modern machinery replaces men in mining. Here, at the Maple Creek
Coal Preparation Plant of United States Steel, automatic coal
conveyor belts move coal rapidly and easily.*

radio and television, which in turn was absorbed
by the Ford Motor Company. The Westinghouse
complex of electrical manufacturing firms in
Pittsburgh played a large role in not only starting
commercial radio broadcasting, but also in experimenting with and improving the manufacture of
both radio and television products. The Sylvania
Company also developed largely through meeting
the needs of radio and television.

RESEARCH, AUTOMATION, AND
LEADERSHIP IN ATOMIC ENERGY

The turn of the century found Americans boast-
ing about the achievements of the past fifty years
in science and invention, and little realizing that
these would pale into insignificance in the light
of what was to come in the next half century.
The advance of science and research since 1900 has
been little short of phenomenal and, along with
the revolution in transportation and communication, transformed the life and the economy of
Pennsylvania and the entire nation. Entire new
fields of industrial enterprise were made possible
virtually overnight by new discoveries such as
radio, plastics, artificial fibers, and other wonders

of modern chemistry. At the same time, somewhat slower but equally important changes were
wrought in the perfecting of the automobile and
the airplane, and technological advances in making steel, aluminum, and petroleum products.
Pennsylvania was influenced directly or indirectly
by all of these changes and advances.

One of the most striking developments in
modern industry has been the increased use of
automatic machinery, and especially new devices
which through a machine direct and control industrial processes that once were dependent upon
the human hand and brain. A new word came into
use in industry after World War II—"automation." In its most simple terms automation
means the use of a mechanical device to run other
machines. The automatic device replaces not only
the worker's hands but his mind as well. Its justi-
fication rests upon the fact that automatic control
means more uniform products, greatly increased
production with consequent presumable lowering
of costs, and elimination of surplus labor. It is the
elimination of labor that has made automation a
subject of concern to the working man, especially
in such great industries as steel. A recently developed device can operate a battery of some 900

separate machine tools, selecting automatically the tool for the necessary task as well as recognizing defects in the resulting work, and even calling for an essential replacement. Machines of this type can eliminate easily half the skilled machine operators in a large mill.

It is this type of magic that made it possible for the United States to increase industrial production on an average of 3 per cent every year since 1957, and at the same time decrease employment in industry. The exact extent to which automation has been utilized in Pennsylvania industry, and its effect upon employment, has yet to be given specific study, but there is no reason to believe Pennsylvania does not follow the national pattern, because of the extent of large-scale industry in steel, aluminum, refining, and equipment manufactures. It is known that employment decreased by 86,951 workers between 1951 and 1956, and that even in the coal mines more coal was mined with fewer people. It is known also that in 1963 there were 340,000 unemployed Pennsylvanians. The consequences of automation have come to figure largely in negotiations between the United Steel Workers and the steel companies as labor seeks some protection from the danger of automation's job displacement.

Automation is new only in the extent to which automatic devices are now used to operate machinery. The period after 1900 witnessed a steady development of the use of improved machinery that inevitably displaced manpower. The steel industry, for example, made great strides forward in mechanizing steel mills to do away especially with the large mass of unskilled labor once employed. Mining was another industry where improved mining machinery slowly but surely replaced miners. Indeed, the beginnings and growth of scientific management and the birth of the so-called efficiency expert started with Carl Lange, who came from his native Norway to Philadelphia in 1881, and with Frederick Taylor began the first application of the idea of scientific management of an industry at the Bethlehem Steel plant in Bethlehem. University of Pennsylvania scientists have been credited with pioneering in the development of the modern electronic computer that is the basis of automation in modern business, industry, and government.

The importance of research as the basis for economic progress has been recognized in Pennsylvania but there was developed in recent years a keen realization that while much progress is evident, there has also been serious neglect of the potential of science and research in relation to the economy. In the field of agriculture, genuine progress has been evident, due largely to the concentration on this phase of research at Pennsylvania State University's College of Agriculture. Here, as early as 1887, the famous Agricultural Experiment Station began its long years of service under the leadership of the eminent scientist Henry P. Armsby. The station's world-famous respiration calorimeter for study of animal nutrition and energy produced results carried over into knowledge of human nutrition. It contributed to scientific knowledge of livestock feeding, fertilizers, and improvement of various crops, and the results of its research reached far and wide in American agriculture.

The Pennsylvania petroleum industry early saw the need for constant research to make most effective use of its dwindling supply of petroleum. In the words of the Pennzoil company, "It is not enough to pioneer once." Petroleum research by the Pennsylvania industry was concentrated mainly at Pennsylvania State University and supported by grants from leading companies. The coal industry, on the other hand, was lax in devoting serious attention to research other than study of technological improvements in mining. Some attention to coal was given by the College of Mineral Industries at Penn State and at the University of Pittsburgh. On the whole, until 1962, when a coal research laboratory was established at Monroeville near Pittsburgh, the industry neglected study of by-products and other uses of coal. The larger corporations were alive at an early date to the need for specialized study and research with a view to the constant improvement of their product and development of new uses for it. United States Steel, Gulf Oil, Aluminum Company of America, Westinghouse, Bethlehem Steel, H. J. Heinz, Pittsburgh Plate Glass, Allegheny-Ludlum Steel, and General Electric were among the corporations that set up their own research facilities to keep abreast of the most modern possibilities for use of their products.

Industrial research, however, answered mainly the problems of the particular industry and did not benefit the general public other than indirectly. The Mellon Institute, endowed by Andrew E. Mellon and dedicated in Pittsburgh in 1937, was the first major private research organization established in the state since the Franklin Institute more than a century earlier. The Mellon Institute quickly established a position as one of great research centers of the nation. The major universities are the other research centers open to general research, and the University of Pennsylvania, the University of Pittsburgh, and the Pennsylvania State University were first to meet this need. Lehigh University as a specialized engineering school became a nationally recognized institution for the quality of its training. Increasing amounts of money for specialized work, particularly for space and atomic energy research, have been allocated from Washington since World War II. Unfortunately, very small proportions came to Pennsylvania, for the simple reason that the only graduate research centers in the state were in Pittsburgh, Wilkes-Barre, State College and Philadelphia, and were limited to a small number of key institutions. A recent nationwide study showed that Pittsburgh and Philadelphia ranked very low among leading American cities in numbers of persons with advanced degrees in their total population, another indication that the state has not kept abreast of modern scientific training and advanced education. Pennsylvanians were made aware of some of these deficiencies in a recent report by the Committee of One Hundred on Education, which pointed to the lack of support of advanced education by the state as compared with other rival states with expanding economies. The picture is not entirely black, because petroleum, the glass industry, steel, the electrical industry, and aluminum in particular have greatly improved their position by continuous research. On the other hand, candid appraisal leads one to a conclusion that Pennsylvania has not kept entirely abreast of the growth of modern science and research.

The most significant indication of a new era in

The Mellon Institute, a modern scientific research center, at Pittsburgh. The building is noteworthy for its classic beauty and its monolithic column installation, the largest in the world.

science and technology dawning within the limits of Pennsylvania took place when on December 18, 1957, a switchboard operator named John Waugaman stepped in front of a panel of assorted lights and switches and pushed the buttons that put into operation a turbine generator. The place was Shippingport, a small western Pennsylvania town on the Ohio about twenty-five miles northwest of Pittsburgh. John Waugaman had activated the world's first full-scale atomic electric power plant used entirely for peaceful purposes. It was another Pennsylvania first. The project was a joint venture of the Atomic Energy Commission

The nuclear power station on the banks of the Ohio at Shippingport, the world's first large-scale completely commercial atomic power plant.

and the Duquesne Light and Power Company. The heat source was a pressurized water reactor, and the atomic fluid a combination of natural and enriched uranium. A second and similar plant was scheduled for completion by 1964 on the lower Susquehanna at Peach Bottom. In addition to an atomic reactor for research in atomic energy at Penn State, the resources of Quehanna, in central Pennsylvania near Clearfield, have been made available for similar use by the university. Pennsylvania has moved ahead in the pioneer work in peaceful use of atomic energy at an encouraging rate. Advanced space research is carried on at General Electric's research center at Valley Forge by over 4,000 scientists.

PENNSYLVANIA'S CONTINUING FARM AND FOREST ECONOMY

Throughout the golden age of large-scale industrial development in Pennsylvania, the forest and the farm continued to hold an important place in the state's economy and their continued stability helped to compensate for the decline of other industry. The peak of large-scale lumbering operations in Penn's Woods was not reached until well after 1900. Even as late as World War I tanning and woodworking industries were a key segment of the northern Pennsylvania industrial economy. Though forest industries showed effects of severe decline after 1920, a recent report from the School of Forestry at Penn State, one of the major centers

for forestry study and research in the eastern United States, points out that in 1962 forest-based industries in the state accounted for one-third of the total value of products from farm and forest sources—nearly $200,000,000. These industries provide employment for nearly sixty-eight thousand persons. The pulp and paper industry accounts for the larger percentage, with over fifty primary pulp and paper mills in the state providing the major employment for at least ten communities. Penn's Woods still cover 15,000,000 acres, or 52 per cent of Pennsylvania's total land area.

The plight of the forest industries can be laid at the door of the ruthless lumbering and tanning companies, which cut the virgin timber of the state without regard to conservation of this great natural resource. As late as 1900, trees were cut only to strip them of their hemlock bark for the tanning industry, leaving the bodies of giant trees to rot where they had fallen. Only when it was realized that the trees had value as lumber was this practice brought to an end, and the tanning company leaders themselves helped establish large-scale commercial lumbering. A half century of some attention to protection and recovery, especially within the last three decades, has resulted in major restoration of the forest resources of the commonwealth through expansion of both state forest lands and private conservation projects. Tree planting to cover the scars on the land made by strip mines has been started by more

344

progressive strip mine owners and will help in time to rebuild the forests. The potential of the forests to the future economy of the state is very great as not only a natural resource for timber, but also as attractions to the tourist using state forest and park lands for recreation.

The land resources of the state were not made the victim of the same ruthless exploitation as was its timber, but did become the unconscious victim of that persistent enemy of farm land through the centuries—soil erosion. Its results were sharp declines in the farm economy of large sections of once prosperous northern and central Pennsylvania, where erosion became most prevalent as covering forests were cut away. In many areas once-profitable forests were cut away, and once-profitable farmland was abandoned entirely. More than a million acres were standing idle by 1928 and in some rural regions the percentage was as high as 40 per cent. Average farm income in Pennsylvania in 1929 was hardly more than one-fourth that of California, and the state ranked twenty-fifth among all the states in farm income despite its still large farm acreage and population. Pennsylvania's agricultural economy had taken a bad dip since 1900. By 1910 12.8 per cent of those gainfully employed in the state worked on farms; by 1960 it was down to 2.7 per cent. In 1910, 3.2 per cent of the nation's workers on farms were in Pennsylvania, but by 1960 it had fallen to a meager 1.9 per cent. Farm employment fell from 362,000 in 1910 to 120,000 in the half century. Between 1900 and 1950 the number of farms declined from 225,000 to 146,887 and the acreage of crop land from 13,000 to 8,000. By 1962 the number of farms had fallen further to 67,000.

Lancaster remained the state's largest farm center, with 4,650 farms, when these figures were recorded. York County had 2,700, and the counties of Bradford and Crawford registered over two thousand farms. Other leading farm counties with over a thousand farms in 1962 were Adams, Armstrong, Berks, Butler, Chester, Cumberland, Fayette, Greene, Indiana, Lycoming, Mercer, Somerset, Susquehanna, Tioga, Washington, Wayne, and Westmoreland. The extent to which agriculture overlapped with mining and manufacturing as a part of the economy of many a Pennsylvania county is noticeable. The total of cash receipts from farm crops was reported as $812,145,000 for 1961, of which $8,798,000 were government-subsidy payments.

Livestock and livestock products now constitute the largest source of farm income in Pennsylvania, though subject to some decline in the last decade. Dairy products are next in line and have been increasing slowly in value. Poultry and eggs run a close third. Vegetable growing has been on the growth side as market gardening to supply city markets increased, and the canning and frozen-food industries added to the market for these products. The H. J. Heinz Company, based in Pittsburgh, is one of the world's largest processors of such products and has long since exceeded the list of its original "57 varieties." Grains have ceased to be a leading crop, a far cry from a century ago when Pennsylvania was still a breadbasket of America. Dairying took up the slack in northern Pennsylvania when general farming declined with depletion and erosion of the soil. Nearby cities, mainly in New York, and local evaporated- and condensed-milk plants absorbed the product. Adams, Erie, and Franklin counties long have been noted for their fruit growing. Erie grew grapes, and the largest grape processing plant in the country developed in this region. Adams and Franklin counties were centers for peach and apple production and processing. Bucks, Lancaster, and York counties have been leaders in vegetable crops, especially Bucks. Southeastern Pennsylvania became after World War II an area for grazing western cattle for the eastern market. It also became the center of cultivated-mushroom growing, especially Chester County. Lancaster County is by all odds the most diversified county in the state, if not in the entire country, in its farm economy and its prosperous farms lead or are close to leadership in almost every area of farm production. It is the first among all counties in the country in value of crops grown without irrigation. In general, Pennsylvania has ranked first or close to it in the nation through the last several years for chicken, eggs, dairy products, Christmas trees, leaf tobacco for cigars, mushrooms, graded apples, milk, fruits, maple sugar, and buckwheat.

The value of the farms, buildings, equipment,

Farming is now mechanized to the point where this equipment not only harvests but threshes the grain and puts it into bags.

and crops is such that agriculture still represents approximately a $4,000,000,000 industry. It has a larger capital investment than mining or the manufacture of primary metals. While Pennsylvania ranks but thirty-second in farm acreage it is fourteenth in value of farm products. The state's agriculture, however, has followed a steady pattern of a decreasing number of farms, and increased production has been made possible only by increased use of machinery and equipment, along with more scientific farming. The steadily decreasing number of farmers are more prosperous, though average farm income indicates a considerable degree of farm poverty or barely head-above-water existence for many Pennsylvania farmers. A study in Butler County in 1961 showed that 95 per cent of the county's farmers produced less than $10,000 in product value during the year, and when costs of production are

taken into account this is not an income indicating any farm prosperity. Farm youth have been fleeing the farms in large numbers and limiting the ability of a younger generation to recuperate the losses of the past. Expanded markets, better transportation, continued emphasis upon applications of science to better farming, and control of soil erosion are ways in which the farm economy has been assisted. Soil conservation districts by 1963 covered 95 per cent of the state and were an indication of how Pennsylvania struggled to preserve a healthy farm life and economy in the face of adverse conditions.

BLACK GOLD SLOWS ITS FLOW

Pennsylvania even by 1900 was far behind in petroleum production and became progressively more so with the fabulous discoveries in Texas, Oklahoma, Louisiana, South America, and the Near East. Hardly any other result could have been expected, because the region could never have hoped to supply the demand for petroleum once the age of automotive transport was born. The actual peak of Pennsylvania production was reached about 1891. A steady search for new and improved methods of getting oil from the ground developed after World War I on the part of the Pennsylvania producers, and this pioneering continued to forward the technology of petroleum as an industry. Production of Pennsylvania crude oil actually was higher in 1942 than in 1900, having expanded under wartime pressures to 17,779,000 barrels, the largest amount recorded since 1891. Production centers long since had shifted from the Titusville region to the McKean County area. Daily average production today is about 55,000 barrels, less than 1 per cent of the nation's total. Pennsylvania grade crude oil is turned into gasoline and other products, but its most important single use became motor oils, of which Pennsylvania production constitutes about 23 per cent of the nation's total. While constant research seeks for ways to reach what are known to be deep remaining reserves of the black gold, no one is optimistic enough to think Pennsylvania will ever again come close to producing any large part of the nation's petroleum.

Refining crude oil from other sources succeeded local production and refining as the state's most profitable connection with the petroleum industry. The Sun Oil Company and the Gulf Oil Company, two of the largest in the world, not only centered their refineries in Pennsylvania, but were founded by Pennsylvania pioneers of the oil industry. Sun Oil was created by Joseph N. Pew in 1886, and Gulf by William W. Mellon in 1907. Larger refineries center mainly along the Delaware River, and have a capacity of more than 416,000 barrels a day. The crude petroleum that supplies these giant modern refineries comes by pipeline across the continent from the fields in Louisiana, Texas, and Oklahoma, and by tanker from Venezuela and the Near East. The southeastern Pennsylvania refineries have become important not only for the basic products derived from petroleum, but also for highly developed petrochemical research leading to all kinds of remarkable new wonders in chemistry. Petroleum remained important in the state's economy despite the loss of leadership in production, to which northwestern Pennsylvania has long since adjusted. It was helped in this adjustment by the

continuing importance of refining petroleum and of the manufacture of tank cars and oil well equipment. The natural-gas industry was tied closely to the petroleum industry, because nature had placed the two resources close together. First discovered about 1874, gas was soon piped into Pittsburgh for both home and industrial use, and by 1900 Pennsylvania was the source of about one-half the nation's supply. The position of Pennsylvania later declined, but it is still seventh in natural-gas production and fifth in its use. New fields were discovered recently in northern and central Pennsylvania that promised much, and created speculative excitement, but proved short-lived. Northern Pennsylvania became, however, an important center for storage in abandoned wells of natural gas piped in from the southwest.

PALEOZOIC PAINS IN PENNSYLVANIA

In Paleozoic times some 285,000,000 years ago, more or less, nature laid down in over half the counties of Pennsylvania a rich store of coal—anthracite in the east and bituminous in the west. Pennsylvania was literally the nation's coalbin.

A farm scene about 1910, when little new machinery was in use. Note man sharpening scythe to cut grass.

347

It was a rich underlay of energy, which did more than possibly any other single thing to create the golden age of Pennsylvania industry after the Civil War. Earlier, anthracite had sparked a revolution in iron-making, and bituminous coal had lent itself to making coke for the steel industry. After the Civil War, steel became king in Pennsylvania, and bituminous was the king of coals. As late as 1937 the *Pennsylvania Manual* boasted, "Pennsylvania leads all other states in mineral production." But coal production was on the downward road, and thereby hangs a tale of how Pennsylvanians sank their heads in the sand and refused to view with realism the economic problems already upon them; the period of "Paleozoic pains" had already started. Anthracite had continued to thrive with just about continuous production increases until 1917, when it reached 99,711,811 net tons. Bituminous production also expanded to over 178,000,000 tons by 1918. World War I gave a last boost to Pennsylvania coal, and it was never the same afterwards. By 1927 the state lost first place in bituminous production to West Virginia. It regained it in 1929 and 1930, only to lose it then, forever, and to see West Virginia coal supply Pennsylvania mills.

All this took place despite remarkable improvements in the technology of mining bituminous coal that made the great Robena mine in western Pennsylvania the largest and most modern mine in the world. Anthracite had a similar story, and by 1941 production had fallen to 56,368,267 tons. The *Manual*'s boast in 1937 was an idle one but typical of Pennsylvania's refusal to read the handwriting on the wall. By 1960 anthracite production was down to 18,817,000 short tons and that of bituminous to 65,425,000. The net value of the coal produced also was declining. Equally serious was the fact that improved mining technology was enabling a steadily smaller number of men to mine the coal that was produced. Employment in the anthracite mines fell from the peak average of 174,307 in 1910–1914 to 19,051 for 1960. Mechanically loaded coal exceeded that of hand-loaded by 1960, and strip mining, which mined coal near the surface and used machines entirely, dumping the coal into trucks to be hauled away, now accounted for more than a third of all

anthracite mined. In the bituminous fields, strip-mined coal by 1960 was nearly half the amount of deep-mined, and mechanical improvements had decreased the number of workers needed even in the deep mines.

The question arises as to the causes for this situation. The most basic cause was the decline in the use of coal and consequently in demand for either anthracite or bituminous. The development of other sources of power, especially electricity, after 1900 worked a revolution in the use of power applied to industry equal to that of steam a century earlier. By 1900 the induction motor, the transformer, high voltages, and long-distance transmission of electricity were combined with the triumph of George Westinghouse's alternating current to make possible a power revolution. Electricity was applied to railroading and even used to power coal-mining machinery. The production of electric power increased about three times between 1920 and 1940, and another six billion kilowatt hours during World War II, and 70 per cent was used in industry. Pennsylvania utilities could not even keep up with the demand for electricity, since after 1920 the use of electrical power zoomed upward by some 600 per cent, while the use of coal actually declined.

Coal likewise fell behind in home heating as natural and manufactured gas and fuel oil steadily invaded the field after about 1940. The coal yard once so evident in towns and cities became virtually a relic of the past. Diesel locomotives ended the reign of coal-fired steam locomotives and with it a 130,000,000-ton customer. Even the steel industry found more effective ways to utilize coke, and demanded less bituminous coal for coke or direct firing of furnaces, which now used electricity. The tragic fact is that had the coal industry been alert to this situation, along with the state government, which had a stake in the situation in terms of unemployment in the coal regions and a generally adverse effect of the coal industry's decline on the total economy, much might have been done to ease the shock of the great Pennsylvania mining industry's literally falling apart. Coal could have been used to generate electricity much more widely than was done in Pennsylvania. New by-

Scars on the land resulting from unregulated strip mining, now placed under controls.

products from coal were not fully explored. Even the downfall of coal as a fuel in home heating might have been averted or lessened by development of new and better coal heating devices. The sad fact is that coal mining was allied with the railroads and the steel companies. The anthracite mines were looked upon as a source of revenue from freight. Steel companies looked to coal for use in the steel mills. Little attention was given by either the railroads or the steel companies to any other possible utilization of coal. The combination between the eastern railroads and anthracite mining was broken up by the Supreme Court in 1920, but it did not end entirely the reliance of one upon the other. The captive bituminous mines owned by the steel companies remained company property with little regard to the future of the mining industry as a whole. While the revolution in power has changed the position of coal throughout the world, it is evident that in Europe more progress was made in solving the problem of new and improved uses for coal. Hardly 1 per cent of the Pennsylvania coal industry's budget has gone into research on new uses for coal.

The decline of the coal industry quickly became Pennsylvania's most serious economic problem. It generated unemployment and stagnation in the coal regions, and it also hurt the railroads, which in turn hurt Altoona and other places. Decreased employment meant less wage income on the part of labor, as well as declining expenditures on the part of the mining industry. This hit all types of business in the coal regions. The anthracite region especially felt the shock after 1940. By 1954 the *New York Times* pointed to the unemployment of some 40,000 persons, mainly miners, in the anthracite region, creating an unemployment rate of 11 per cent. A Northeastern Pennsylvania Industrial Development Commission had been formed, headed by Victor C. Diehm and representing local government and business and industry, in an attempt to seek state and Federal aid as well as new industry for the coal region. Scranton already had turned to community self-help projects to bolster its declining economy.

Governor Leader was the first to direct specific and detailed attention to the problem of unemployment in the coal regions, as well as to analyze the causes, in his message to the Assembly on March 28, 1955. Leader pointed out that twelve areas in Pennsylvania were classified by the United States Department of Labor as having "very substantial labor surplus" and that of nine large areas in the nation with more than 12 per cent of the working force unemployed, four were in Pennsylvania. "Our worst error has been our failure to plan against this day; to understand and thus meet our potential troubles before they have us in their grasp," declared Leader. He proposed community development aid on the part of the commonwealth and "research in the technology and economics of Pennsylvania coal." An Industrial Development Authority Act was passed in 1956 and along with it a bureau of community development was created. While these measures were not designed solely for the benefit of the coal regions, in actual practice since 1956 a large part of the technical and financial aid from both state and Federal sources of necessity was poured into areas of distress that had accumulated as a result of the decline of the mining industry. Since over half the counties in the state were mining coal, it was inevitable that they should constitute most of the distressed areas. The redevelopment of these blighted areas to an extent to which permanent new industry can be attracted to them was the most serious problem of the administrations of Leader and Lawrence, and was inherited by Governor Scranton in 1963. Scranton, himself a resident of the anthracite region and active in the community effort to prop up the area economy, had firsthand experience with and knowledge of the problem. Industrial and community redevelopment were stepped up, and controls of anthracite and strip mining designed to end their largely uncontrolled devastation of the landscape were enacted into new and tougher legislation. Pennsylvania began at long last to realize that culm banks and strip-mine scars were deterrents to attracting any new industry to the coal regions. Efforts to develop programs through which workers in the mines or mills might be retrained for other jobs also formed a part of the effort under Governor Scranton to meet the crisis of unemployment in the once rich mining regions.

The coal industry itself at last began to put more money into coal research, as did the Federal and state governments, in an effort to find new uses for coal. This amounted up to 1962 to a meager $20,000,000 compared to $300,000,000 spent by the petroleum industry. Major utility companies moved in to find new uses for coal, with studies of the greater use of coal to produce electricity and atomic power. Construction at Atwood, in Armstrong County, of a $175,000,000 station for generating electricity and utilizing bituminous coal to fire the steam turbo-generator units was announced early in 1963 by two Pennsylvania utilities and a New Jersey and a New York utility company on a basis of joint construction, ownership and use. The plant when completed will use annually as much as 4,700,000 tons of bituminous coal. Another plant also located in the coal fields was announced in 1963; this is to be built near Morgantown, West Virginia, with West Penn Power Company participating and use made of Pennsylvania mined coal. It was evident by 1963 that strong measures to revitalize the coal industry were at long last in motion, but whether it would be a case of too little and too late could not be assured.

THE HEARTH OF A NATION

The economy of the twentieth century made extensive use of metals in constructing machinery, erecting buildings of all kinds, creating modern automobiles and aircraft, bridges for the marvelous new expressways and interstate throughways, and many other conveniences already developed but now vastly increased. The skills of metallurgists were put to the test to devise ways to fabricate the metals and sometimes to blend them with others to meet the constantly evolving, everchanging demand. World War II was a contest based on the use of metals, and spurred their use. Basic metals have been used in far greater quantities since 1900 than at any previous time in history. The story of steel since 1900 is by no means as heroic and spectacular as it was in the preceding thirty years, when Carnegie and his associates were not only learning how to make steel in ever-increasing quantities, but building a steel empire and their personal fortunes around it. That was the era of the "practical" steel man rather than the scientist studying metal structures and properties in his laboratory. It was during the era of the practical steel men that Pennsylvania reached the golden age of steel in terms of its dominance of the nation's steel-making. The very creation in 1901 of the giant United States Steel Corporation, though built it was on the foundation of the Carnegie enterprises, meant that making steel was now a part of the nation's industry rather than that of a single state. The steel industry continued to dominate large industrial enterprise in Pennsylvania, and the new corporation kept its headquarters quite properly in Pittsburgh, but making steel was something other states and other cities than Pittsburgh were increasingly concerned with after 1900. Names like Birmingham, Alabama; Gary, Indiana; and Sparrows Point, Maryland, began to appear as steel cities, and many had larger plants than any in Pennsylvania—even after the Fairless Works was built. Today there are over three hundred communities in thirty-five states that make iron and steel. Pittsburgh lost some of its luster even in Pennsylvania when Charles Schwab, once Carnegie's right arm, helped to build up the powerful Bethlehem Steel Company, with plants at Bethlehem, Steelton, and Johnstown, as well as outside Pennsylvania.

Pennsylvania steel had its finest hour in World War II when in 1945 production boomed to 29,679,000 tons—31 per cent of all the steel made in United States and 20 per cent of the known world's production. Despite the rally, Pennsylvania production has fallen about 20 per cent since 1900 and now amounts to from 25 to 30 per cent of the nation's total. Tonnage declined from 26,000,000 to 23,000,000 in the last decade, and the Pennsylvania share of the national market from 28 to 23 per cent. Pittsburgh's slice of the national production pie remains around 23 per cent.

"Though steel is going through a time of trouble, its leaders are not weeping at the wailing wall," commented a recent analyst of the industry. On the contrary, they are busily engaged in a continuous program of modernization. Most steel today is made in an open-hearth furnace, which is really a shallow-saucepan fireplace walled over with refractory brick. Its food is liquid pig iron, taken directly from the blast furnace, and cold scrap steel. After about eight hours of "cooking," some 200 tons of steel are poured. Bessemer steel can be made more rapidly, but it is not as good steel. At the Aliquippa plant of Jones & Laughlin, the new basic oxygen process may be seen in operation. A pear-shaped vessel somewhat like an old-style Bessemer converter is charged with about twenty-five tons of scrap steel, and about sixty-five tons of molten iron from the blast furnace, and finally the "soup" is spiced with smaller amounts of limestone and other ingredients. The furnace is then turned upright and a water-cooled oxygen "lance" is lowered above the bath and the flow of oxygen is started. When it strikes the molten iron, the first effect is like a giant Roman candle and in an unbelievable twenty minutes or so the furnace is ready to be tilted to a horizontal position to pour its liquid, molten contents into a large ladle and from it into ingot molds. By 1962 about five million of the country's 98,000,000 tons of steel were made in this fashion. More steel is being made by fewer and fewer people as a result of mechanization and research. Shiny new research centers for steel are everywhere.

A recent visitor to the steel mills at Bethlehem put it this way: "In sharp contrast to the magnitude and multiplicity of machinery is the paucity of people. It is not to be inferred that most of the machines are fully automatic, but it is amazing how so few workers operate so much machinery. For example, three shifts of men each run one of the world's largest blast furnaces that turns out 3,000 tons of pig iron a day."

Pennsylvania still makes more steel than any other state and has done so for almost a full century. In 1962 it poured 23,000,000 of the nation's 98,000,000 tons of ingots and steel for castings, which was comfortably ahead of Ohio.

Making steel is still a fabulous and awe-inspiring process that never ceases to arouse the excitement of those who view it. An observer of the mill at Bethlehem wrote of the "monolithic blast furnaces—giant structures of great girth that rise skyward with slowly constricting rotundity. . . .

Blast furnaces at the Bethlehem plant of the Bethlehem Steel Company.

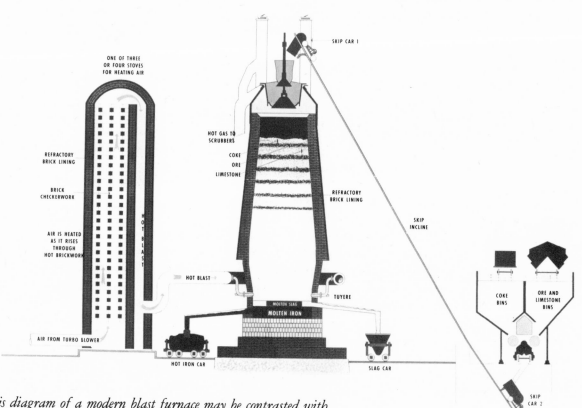

*This diagram of a modern blast furnace may be contrasted with
the charcoal iron furnaces of a hundred years earlier.*

Inside the shops . . . buckets big enough to hold 200 tons of liquid steel . . . heavily lined with firebrick to withstand the white-hot heat of the liquid metal. The soaking pits are livid infernos where chunky stumps of white-hot steel are kept in hot storage awaiting a mauling upon emergence. . . . Further on are mammoth hydraulic presses with great gaping jaws that squeeze a heavy angular ingot into a shape resembling a section of a tree trunk for subsequent machining into a polished propellor shaft or a rotor for a turbine. Such are the many mechanical monsters that carry, cut, hammer, squeeze, or bend great gobs of steel into innumerable useful products." And this was a small steel mill.

A major factor in bolstering the state's economy, especially in western Pennsylvania, was the steadiness of the business of using steel from the mills to make machinery, tubing, tin cans, beams for bridges and buildings, wire, alloy steels, oil well supplies, automobiles, transportation and electrical equipment and machinery, and a host of other products made from steel and demanded by the continuing industrial revolution in America. McKeesport, Donora, Monessen, Ambridge, Rochester, Sharon, Elwood City, Rankin, Aliquippa—all were mill towns whose prosperity rose or fell with steel and products from steel.

ALUMINUM BECOMES THE MAGIC NEW METAL

It is not without its irony that Pennsylvania should have been the birthplace of both steel and aluminum, because the two metals in recent decades have come into very real competition with each other. Before 1900 and for a decade or more thereafter aluminum was produced in small quantities, and its widest use was in making wares for the housewife's kitchen, where it came to displace heavy iron skillets and easily damaged enamel kitchenware. It was lighter, more durable, and quicker to heat. Production of the metal grew slowly and in 1907 the old original company was reorganized as the Aluminum Company of America, soon to be better known as ALCOA. The headquarters for the company and its newly built manufacturing center were at New Kensington, which remains essentially the aluminum capital. A new era opened for the use of aluminum when automobiles and airplanes, especially the airplane, began to be a factor in the nation's transportation system. It is a little hard to understand just how airplanes could have been built for extensive use and in steadily larger planes had it not been for aluminum. It became the basic metal in this great air age and grew with it from the early models right down to the latest transcontinental jet. Aluminum pistons, and even engines, along with other parts appeared in the automotive industry, though never displacing steel. By the time of World War II, ALCOA'S research center at New Kensington was busy studying new ways to develop aluminum as a usable product, and with great success. Sheet aluminum, aluminum foil, aluminum alloys, and even sizable forgings began to be commonplace. Aluminum even began to compete with steel in building construction. The demand became so great that ALCOA expanded its plants and other companies entered the picture as rival producers. The fact remained that the whole industry was born and developed in western Pennsylvania and centered at New Kensington. Steel fears aluminum today.

PENNSYLVANIA MAKES AND THE WORLD TAKES

Pennsylvania has already been noted for the variety of its manufactures. It has been said that Philadelphia makes more things than any other single city, and the same claim may be made for the state. There are over seventeen thousand manufacturing establishments in Pennsylvania, and they make more than three hundred different specific products. The variety of Pennsylvania industry was overlooked when steel and coal were booming, and even somewhat scorned as an antique handed down from earlier days. Pennsylvania industry has variety not only in products, but also in the number of small plants and factories that form a part of its industrial structure. There are, for example, more than two thousand single plants that are in the food and food-products business. Over two thousand separate plants make clothing and apparel. Metal fabrication and machinery along with lumber and wood products are other industries with over a thousand separate plants.

The variety of Pennsylvania manufactures proved a cushion when the bottom fell out from under coal, and steel began to falter. There were some bright spots in the economy also in terms of a marked growth of new industry. Thanks to George Westinghouse and his inventive genius, his company, centered in Pittsburgh, became a pioneer in the manufacture of both electrical and transportation equipment. Elihu Thomson of Philadelphia was another early leader in the electrical field, and his company eventually became a unit of General Electric. The work of these pioneers gave Pennsylvania an important role in these fields of manufacturing. The value of the product of electrical machinery, apparatus, and supplies zoomed up 376 per cent between 1914 and 1939, and employment by 279 per cent. Over 20 per cent of the nation's locomotive repair and maintenance shops are in Pennsylvania, and it kept its important role in building of locomotives and cars, and producing switch and signal equipment, and steel rails. The first applications of electricity to locomotives were in Pennsylvania, and one of the earliest railroad electrification projects was from Philadelphia to Paoli, and later to Harrisburg. In 1961 electrical equipment, machinery, and supplies continued to rank third in the state in total value of product. The primary metal industries—steel, iron, and aluminum—as of 1961 still held first place in value of product among Pennsylvania manufactures. Fabricated metal products and machinery ranked fourth and fifth, and represented the continued leadership of Pennsylvania in using the product of its steel mills to turn out a variety of metal products and machinery of all kinds. Transportation equipment was close on the heels of metal products and machinery.

A significant feature of Pennsylvania's industrial evolution after 1900 was the growth of the food-products industry. By 1961 this industry ranked second only to the primary metals in value of its product. It was not big business, because nearly three thousand plants were at work in production of food and kindred products as contrasted with less than six hundred in the primary-

metals field. Candy and confections are classified with foods, and the Horatio Alger-like rise of Milton S. Hershey is part of their story. After failure upon failure, at middle age Hershey at last achieved success in establishing in 1903 the now famous Hershey Company, and the "factory in a corn field" was built in the midst of what once had been Dauphin County farmland. The Heinz organization in Pittsburgh quickly outgrew the famous "57 varieties" and like Hershey became an international operation. Pennsylvania had a close association from earlier days with the nation's chemical industry, and this continued to have some importance, though its growth was not as substantial in later decades as the state's resources would appear to have justified. The use of coal to develop chemical by-products was limited largely to the coke industry. The Koppers Company, which had been founded originally to design and build modern coke-production equipment, turned attention to by-product chemical manufactures.

Philadelphia enjoyed some distinction as a manufacturing center for drugs and medicines and for other chemical products such as insecticides, pesticides, and chemicals for synthetics. The wood-chemical industry flourished in northern Pennsylvania in lumber days, and some of it remained after the lumbermen had departed. Older industries that continued to have a place in the state's economy were brewing, distilling, tanning, and milling. Glass-making remained a large and important industry, with the Pittsburgh Plate Glass firm leading the way in many advances in the nation's glass industry. Shipbuilding kept its place as a basic industry in the Delaware valley, while in Pittsburgh the Dravo engineering and construction organization entered into boatbuilding for use on western waters by industry and during World War II actually launched a seagoing ship. Thanks to the Armstrong organization, which began the manufacture of cork and linoleum products in Pittsburgh and moved to Lancaster in 1907, Pennsylvania assumed importance in this particular industry. A Philadelphia soap manufacturer named Fels made Fels Naphtha a household word. "Name it and Pennsylvania makes it" is still a sound slogan in the state.

NEW WAYS OF SELLING GOODS

The prosperity of the maker of goods in the modern economy depends upon the success with which those goods are distributed and sold. Mass production has been accompanied by the growth of mass distribution and a consequent revolution in the world of merchandizing or trade. John Wanamaker in Philadelphia began in the mid-seventies his experiment in the development of the department store that would sell under one roof a large variety of merchandise. Just about the same time a young man named Frank W. Woolworth, after some earlier failures, opened his first successful five-and-dime store in Lancaster. The five-and-dime was an application actually of the department store idea but selling a variety of low-priced articles under the same roof. Woolworth went on from Lancaster to build a nationwide chain of these stores. Department stores were a commonplace in cities at the turn of the century, but a majority of them continued to be locally owned and were associated most frequently with the name of some local merchant prince who founded them. Under pressure of competition from modern methods of selling, most department stores have been modernized and greatly expanded in their operations. In smaller towns a few still may be found that have stood still in a changing world and are in reality something of a living museum piece illustrating merchandising methods of half a century ago, even to the system of cable-operated metal containers in which a clerk deposits the customer's money and which whirs away through the darkened inner recesses of the store into some central-office cubicle where change is made . . . the transaction properly recorded with presumably equally old-style bookkeeping equipment, and the change and sales slip clanging their way back to the clerk's post to be turned over to the waiting customer.

This method of carrying on business disappeared rapidly with the appearance of modern equipment in the world of trade, such as cash registers, modern bookkeeping machines, trained sales personnel, and the complete revolutionizing of techniques of displaying and handling merchandise. The latest revolution in department stores has been the growth of the discount department store, found most commonly in suburbia's flossy new shopping centers. The history of these stores has yet to be written, but in the development of discount store chain merchandising, Town and Country Stores, started in Harrisburg, are certain to form a part of that story, along with the Food Fair organization centered in Philadelphia, which alone projected in 1963 ten new discount department stores. Woolworth's idea of the variety store handling lower priced goods was taken up by several Pennsylvanians. Among them were Samuel H. Kress, who in 1887 started a chain of variety stores at Nanticoke; Sebastian S. Kresge, millionaire Kresge Stores operator; G. C. Murphy with Murphy Stores at McKeesport in 1906, and John J. Newberry with the Newberry chain started at Stroudsburg. W. T. Grant was yet another.

In food stores the smaller grocery and meat market locally owned was largely unchallenged by other than the A&P stores until local chains began to develop with rapidity after World War I. The American Stores Company, known as ACME, an important eastern food-store chain, started in Philadelphia. The day of the modern supermarket was on the way. One of the more fabulous success stories in chain store merchandizing was written by Food Fair, founded in 1933 by Samuel Friedland, Louis Stein and Myer Marcus, who owned a small chain of grocery and meat markets in and around Harrisburg. The partners decided to open a supermarket operation, which they did in a converted garage. Twenty years later Food Fair had grown into 194 stores and by 1963 a billion-dollar business with 551 stores. By this time Food Fair had stores on the West Coast and was also engaged in the new discount department store business with nearly fifty such stores. The days of the small community grocery and the meat market or "butcher shop," as it was known in an earlier day, were numbered as mass merchandising of foods grew. In 1929 there were over 135,000 retail stores in Pennsylvania, but over 30 per cent did a business of less than $5,000 a year, which amounted to a mere 2.62 per cent of the retail business of the state.

Chain grocery stores sold more than half the groceries, though they made up about 18 per cent of the total stores. The role of small business declined steadily as that of the chain supermarket expanded, especially with the phenomenal growth of the modern shopping center. The trend toward mass distribution of goods of all types in chain stores has been a major feature of the growth of retail business in the state in recent years.

THOSE WHO STAND AND SERVE

Those individuals and businesses that render a service and are sometimes loosely termed the "service" industries grew rapidly in the era marked by greater wealth and mobility on the part of the population, modernization of business communications and practices, and the trend toward larger-scale promotion and distribution. The percentage of persons engaged in service, sales, and promotion grew in Pennsylvania nearly 60 per cent between 1910 and 1930, as contrasted with a 2 per cent increase in the number of those actually producing goods. Modern business offices, for example, employed larger and larger numbers of clerical people, mainly women. In the twenty years between 1910 and 1930 clerical employment increased by 3.5 per cent while that in manufacturing declined 1.9 per cent. The art of selling was greatly expanded, with consequent increases in the numbers of people in sales. Advertising became itself a major business demanding large numbers of people both in and out of offices. Mass marketing demanded larger sales forces. Trades people increased by nearly 3 per cent between 1910 and 1930. The automobile by 1920 was creating an entire new business of servicing and repairing these vehicles, with a consequent new field of employment as garage mechanics and filling station operators and workers. The motion picture up until 1954 led to increased employment, and need for those working in amusement enterprises generally continues to increase with more leisure on the part of more people. Mobility of people engaged in business or pleasure increased hotel and motel business by some 25 per cent in the four years from 1954 and

1958. The motel or highway motor hotel is itself a new and growing industry, and a continuing trend. Auto services increased about 60 per cent in the same period. Purely personal services such as those of the office worker continue to create the greatest demand for workers, and account for the largest percentage of income among all the so-called service industries, followed closely by business services in dispensing goods. The changing tide of the times was revealed by the fact that of the things Pennsylvanians were buying in 1929 on the eve of the great depression, gasoline and automotive supplies were second only to food.

Business connected with insurance and real estate also thrived in the new economy. No greater bonanza for the realtor and his salesmen could have been found than that provided by the growth of suburbia. Insurance, of course, was an old institution, but it took on new life as the appeal of life insurance became greater, especially among younger men in business with growing families. As hundreds of thousands of new homes were built and new automobiles were bought a demand for many types of insurance, some entirely new, was created. Over a thousand insurance companies were selling their policies in the state by 1960, and over four hundred were Pennsylvania companies. The amount of insurance of all types that was written was well over $2,000,000,000, of which nearly 50 per cent represented life insurance. Insurance provided service jobs for thousands of Pennsylvanians. Real estate experienced a similar growth.

MODERN BANKING AND CREDIT

New worlds of finance opened and old ones grew under the impact of the economy developing in the twentieth century. Following the economic trend toward larger-scale enterprise, one of the notable developments was the growing size of banking institutions, provided commonly by a trend toward the merging of once rival banks. Every Pennsylvania city saw the number of banks growing smaller, but their size in terms of capital and operations steadily on the increase. The number of banks decreased by over a hundred in just the three years between 1951 and 1954. Since that time the number of banks has decreased further from 866 to a total today of 670. About half the banks remaining are state banks. The persistence of banking in state banks serving communities is remarkable evidence of the strength of a local economy in Pennsylvania. The capitalization of state banks, perhaps surprisingly, is nearly one-half that of the state's national banks. The demand and time deposits of the state banks are very nearly as large as those of the national banks, with the result that the total value of all national bank operations in 1961 amounted to $10,168,810,000, as compared with $9,215,496,000 for the state-chartered banks. The strength of a few larger banks is indicated by the fact that eight banks in Allegheny County account for $3,860,144,000 of the national banking operations in the entire state. This in turn reflects the influence of the giant Mellon banking empire in Pittsburgh. Philadelphia, once the financial capital of the nation, is far behind with only $1,499,202,000 as the value of its banking operations, consolidated in three large banking institutions. Lancaster, in comparison, in 1961 had twenty-six national banks, but their operations amounted to only $305,560,000. Such was the growth of big banking.

The modern economy saw the expansion of savings and loan associations, along with the new development of the consumer loan and finance business. By 1961 there were nearly three hundred private sales—finance companies, nearly a thousand small-loan licensees, and over five hundred consumer discount licensees in the state, as well as over eight hundred savings and loan associations. The demands made upon those in smaller income brackets by purchases of automobiles, household appliances, and the like were a bonanza to the various types of small-loan concerns which provided individuals with needed capital for such purposes. By 1960 the resources and liabilities of the familiar building and loan association, which represented small savings and the investment of the growing number of owners of small and moderately priced homes in suburbia, amounted in the state to over $1,500,000,000. The resources and liabilities of the discount and loan companies

equaled $500,000,000 by 1961. The good old days when Pennsylvanians lived within their incomes for the most part were long gone by 1960. At the same time, these new institutions for financing the needs of the consumer meant more jobs in the category of those who were servants of the people in the modern economy.

THE CIVIL SERVANT

Not least among the growing numbers of persons whose task was serving the needs of the people were the steadily expanding numbers of those working as civil servants in public administration of government. A report issued in 1963 showed that 12.5 per cent of the nation's employed were on a government payroll. It also showed that state and local government accounted for nearly nine out of every ten new public service jobs. Contrary perhaps to public opinion, the rate of increase of persons on public payrolls in Pennsylvania has not been as great as that for the nation as a whole. The total in Federal, state, and local government employment in Pennsylvania increased, however, from 23,000 in 1900 to 92,000 by 1940; and from 146,000 in 1950 to 181,000 in 1960. These figures reflect the influences of two world wars, with the consequent growth of government, as well as the growing extent to which all government took a role in supervision of business and in administration of various types of public welfare and educational activities. Pennsylvania, however, had fewer persons on the state payroll than forty four of the other fifty states. The total number in 1962 was placed at 76,695. Total Federal civilian employment in the state in 1961 was 132,429, of which the Defense Department and the Post Office Department accounted for over 100,000. The number of salaried state employes in 1962 was just about three times that of 1937. As of 1962 about one-third of the total number of state workers were accounted for by the Department of Public Welfare. The number of workers in local government grew in the same ratio and here also the increase was due to demands made by streets, police, fire protection, and sanitation in the modern city. Those who work for state and local government are engaged for the most part in services demanded by a modern society and economy, and make a positive contribution along with those working in private enterprise as servants of the people.

THE PEOPLE AND THE ECONOMY

It is the people, themselves measured by basic characteristics of the population, who determine much of the nature and the future of the general economy. A recent critical study of the state's economy charges that Pennsylvania "is losing the fertile top soil of its working population." This compares what is happening to the people as a resource in the economy with the loss of topsoil from the land through erosion. There are several disturbing facts about Pennsylvania's recent population trends. One of the most serious in terms of the future of the state's economy is the shifting age pattern. The state in 1950 had a slightly larger percentage of people in the twenty-to-thirty-four age group than the nation's average, but by 1960 it had fallen slightly below the average. A 1970 projection estimated a further decline of over 4 per cent. Conversely, the percentage of Pennsylvanians over forty-five in 1950 was a little above the national average and has increased since that date. As of 1960 there were 2,452,000 Pennsylvanians between the ages of forty-five and sixty-four; 1,129,000 were over that limit. Pennsylvanians in the forty-five-to-sixty-four age bracket amounted in 1960 to 21.8 per cent of the population, while 9.9 per cent were sixty-five and over. Under conditions of modern employment, this represents a serious weakness in the status of prime productive labor forces. Another problem has been the increasing preponderance of women in the working force since 1940. Male employment in the state decreased by 43,000 between 1950 and 1960, while that of women increased 240,000. This reflected the declining employment of men in the mines and steel mills while apparel manufacturers moved in with factories employing women. The percentage of women over fourteen in the state's labor force grew from 25.4 per cent in 1940 to 33.3 per cent by 1960. In some regions it became a problem of "a man's place is in the home." Since the wages of women in these industries often were less than half that of male miners or steel workers, a consequent serious decrease in wage purchasing power was a clear-cut result.

Further, there must be taken into account the slowing down of general population growth on the part of Pennsylvania, which grew between 1940 and 1960 at the rate of only 14.6 per cent, as compared with 35.7 per cent for the United States. Only eleven states showed a worse rate of population growth, and these were mainly western farm state, and West Virginia and Kentucky, which suffered as did Pennsylvania a severe decline of the coal industry. Abundant evidence shows that along with this slowing down of population growth there has been a steady migration of Pennsylvania youth to other states. A recent survey, for example, showed that of recent college graduates who had prepared to teach by graduating from Pennsylvania colleges and universities the larger percentage were taking jobs in other states for better incomes.

The income of Pennsylvanians not only determines their standard of living, but in turn has its influence upon the total state economy, as measured by purchasing power of wages, salaries, and other income. It also has a relationship to the amount of monies state and local government can raise through taxes to support education and other desirable activities on the part of the government. Lowered income reduces the ability to develop needed educational advances, which in turn could help solve problems of the economy, creating a vicious cycle. State Planning Board studies showed that, excluding profits from the sale of property and durable goods, the income of Pennsylvania grew from $4,207,000,000 in 1916 to $7,531,000,000 in 1929, but that measured by 1913 dollars, this actually amounted to from $3,856,000,000 to $4,497,000,000. In these adjusted figures the per capita income grew from $462 per person in 1916 to $497 in 1929. The distribution of the income was such that in 1929 some 35 per cent of the people received 11 per cent of the total, while 46 per cent received some 34.5 per cent. A small 1.3 per cent received over 27 per cent and were in the $10,000.00-a-year bracket or above. In contrast, about 80 per cent of Pennsylvanians were in an income bracket of under $2,000.00 a year. Farmers received hardly more than half the average annual income of those in urban areas. Obviously, as of 1929, the purchasing power of a majority of Pennsylvanians was rather low. Between 1940 and 1960 the rate of income growth for Pennsylvanians was such that it placed the state, despite its size, forty-fourth among all the states. Since 1940 only Maine, Massachusetts, Rhode Island, and Vermont have had a lesser total-income growth rate.

A recent 1963 survey of Pennsylvania personal income between 1929 and 1961 provides an important measure of the economic status of the state. The study indicated that total personal income had grown from the $7,531,000,000 in 1929 to $25,933,000,000 in 1961. Wage and salary income since 1929 showed a growth from $4,710,-000 to $17,624,000,000. Mining income decreased from $435,000,000 to $272,000,000. Personal income from salaries and wages showed a decline between 1951 and 1960 of nearly 5 per cent, while other income areas showed slight increases. The decline of steel and coal largely explains the difference. Both property and proprietary income increased markedly in this period, the former from $2,000,000 plus to well over $3,000,000, and the latter from $1,884,000,000 to $2,161,000,000. A study completed in 1959 by the Joint State Government Commission sheds further light on Pennsylvania income, showing that per capita income in "constant dollars," that is, dollars adjusted to the consumer price-index average for the 1947–49 base, was $1,525 in 1946 and $1,744 in 1957, a 14.4 per cent increase. Total income on this basis was indicated as $15,061,000,000 in 1946 and $19,407,000,000 in 1957, a 26.7 per cent growth. The Pennsylvania per capita income measured thus was slightly above the national average, but was consistently lower from 1946 to 1957 than the average per capita income in New York, New Jersey, Massachusetts, and Ohio. Pennsylvania experienced a greater rate of growth, however, than New York or New Jersey. The growth, however, was not at a sufficient rate to create confidence in the future of the state's economy.

THE PENNSYLVANIA ECONOMY HAS PROBLEMS

Hardly anyone will dispute that the Pennsylvania economy today has its problems. A recent critical study refers to the "decades of neglect" which it feels characterize the economy since 1900. "The arrested progress of the state stands revealed in the Census volumes and other official reports," says a 1963 article in the *Business Review* of the Federal Reserve Bank of Philadelphia. Such criticism cannot be ignored as ill informed or prejudiced. The fact is clear that the once proud and prosperous commonwealth of Pennsylvania, which could claim properly to be a titan of American industrial might, has come upon hard times. A Pennsylvania Rip Van Winkle who had fallen asleep in 1900 would be pleasantly surprised when he awoke by the extent to which his state had changed and made progress on many fronts, but certainly he would also be shocked by the culm banks in the coal regions, the scars on the land made by strip-mine operations, and the run-down mill and coal towns, some of which were even now ghost towns or on the verge of becoming such. He would not like the reports on the failure of his state to keep abreast of modern progress in public education, or the place of Pennsylvania in higher education, as compared with other large states, and the failure of science and research to keep Pennsylvania in a position where it could compete with other states in the advanced research facilities demanded by industry and government. He would surely be upset by the persistent unemployment of close to 400,000 people; in some areas of the commonwealth this reaches as high as 13 per cent of the labor force.

Once he looked about and read a few accounts of what was going on, Rip certainly would start asking the big question: Why has this happened? Why has the golden age of Pennsylvania in industry fallen upon such evil days, even though great changes and apparent improvements in the life of the people have taken place in little more than half a century? Anyone who met these questions would be hard put to it to provide a satisfactory answer in a few short sentences. Certainly it was a combination of things. Obviously, changes in industry and living conditions led to a sharp decline in the nation's use of coal by mills, factories, railroads, and in homes. This produced a chain reaction of unemployment and declining income in the mining regions, with rough consequences for business and industry everywhere. It could be pointed out that other states began to make steel and that steel was faced with competition from other metals, with a consequent decline in Pennsylvania's place in the nation's steel industry. The fact that a mechanic named Henry Ford in Michigan got the jump on any Pennsylvanian in developing a cheap automobile and made the state miss a chance to continue its early leadership in assembling the new-fangled horseless carriages could be mentioned to Rip as a reason why Pennsylvania was not out front in this great industry. Reasons could even be furnished as to why the state was not a logical place for the later tremendous aviation industry. Its failure to get contracts for war and defense production could be blamed on "politics," though it is noticeable that Pennsylvania fared about the same regardless of the party in power in Washington or in Harrisburg.

These were questions that many Pennsylvanians began asking themselves, especially after World War II. Facing up to them, most of them agreed that one basic reason why Pennsylvania's economy faced problems was its own supreme self-confidence that it had the economic world by the horns, and it took some years of a downhill slide to awaken the leaders of industry and government to a realization that all was not well with the Pennsylvania economy. The exploitive and paternalistic nature of the spectacular economic growth when Pennsylvania was a titan of industry helped create a psychology of wealth and power that admitted no threats to its future. The barons of steel, coal, and railroads are subject to proper and severe criticism for the extent to which they exploited resources and even workers to build personal fortunes, with little regard to any concern for the public.

The degree to which this exploitation was carried out, including such evils as use of the infamous coal and iron police down into the 1930's, colored the coke and steel regions of Pennsylvania as if with a cloud, creating a psychology

that made Commodore Vanderbilt's "The public be damned" attitude of an earlier day mild indeed. Wages were held down, working conditions were bad, even basic safety standards in mines and mills were kept at the minimum, existing state laws were flouted or ignored, and unionization was fought tooth and claw. The semifeudalism of company towns and company stores was perpetuated in Pennsylvania longer than in perhaps any other industrial area in the nation. There were fantastic examples of the abuse of great wealth, such as the story of that otherwise well-meaning coal baron of western Pennsylvania, J. V. Thompson, whose second wife, appropriately named "Honey" Thompson, engaged in a carnival of wasting millions in a few years, which led to bankruptcy and ruin for not only the tycoon himself, but also for those who had trusted in his leadership in a major industry. Those who accumulated wealth and power in coal and steel all too frequently neglected to use it for any social benefits or to foresee that their wealth might itself be in danger from shifting patterns of economic growth. Coal and steel appeared to be kings forever and ever, and if any thought was given to the future it was an apparent philosophy of "After me the deluge."

By 1950 the abiding faith of most Pennsylvanians in the security of the state's economy began to be shaken, and very rightly so. The plight of anthracite was abundantly evident, and the citizens of Scranton, Wilkes-Barre, Hazleton, and other cities and towns sought remedies. But all the evils of inattention to deterioration of the state's economy were by no means limited to the coal regions. As has been pointed out elsewhere, Pennsylvania's great cities, including Pittsburgh and Philadelphia, were experiencing the problems of deterioration and the "blight of the city" that were afflicting so many of the older cities of the nation. Pittsburgh, by the way, offered an example of the way in which a new and more enlightened philosophy of the use of wealth and power by business tycoons had slowly dawned because the full power and influence of the Mellon dynasty, led by Richard King Mellon, was thrown behind plans and programs for the renaissance in Pittsburgh.

Governor Scranton inaugurates the "100,000 Pennsylvanians"
program to help sell Pennsylvania's economic advantages.
Frank Magee, chairman of the committee, is with the governor.

It is easier to answer Rip Van Winkle today than it would have been a decade or two ago. The spirit of planning and redevelopment is abroad in the land and community; state, and Federal government are united in tackling the grave problems of the present economy, as well as the general improvement of the urban society. Increased sums have been and are being poured into research and education. Governor Scranton in 1963 set up a statewide Council of Science and Technology to study ways and means to speed science-oriented industry, long neglected in the state. Conservation of natural and cultural resources, advances in public recreation through expansion of state and local park and recreational facilities—all these and many other things are going forward in today's Pennsylvania, and they give some promise that more life may be pumped back into a faltering economy. In any event, the therapy of shock has been working to produce the effective and serious attention being given to the economic ills and problems of the commonwealth.

APPENDIX

The Counties of Pennsylvania

Adams County was created on January 22, 1800, from part of York County, and was named in honor of President John Adams. *Gettysburg,* the county seat, was incorporated as a borough on March 10, 1806. It was named for James Gettys, who owned land there.

Allegheny County was created on September 24, 1788, from parts of Westmoreland and Washington counties, and named for the Allegheny River. *Pittsburgh,* the county seat, was named by General John Forbes in November, 1758, in honor of William Pitt, the great British statesman. It was incorporated as a borough on April 22, 1794, and as a city on March 18, 1816.

Armstrong County was created on March 12, 1800, from parts of Allegheny, Westmoreland, and Lycoming counties; and was named for General John Armstrong. It was attached to Westmoreland County until 1805. *Kittanning,* the county seat, was incorporated as a borough on April 2, 1821, and derived its name from a Delaware Indian village at the same place.

Beaver County was created on March 12, 1800, from parts of Allegheny and Washington counties, and named for the Beaver River. It was attached to Allegheny County until 1803. *Beaver,* the county seat, was incorporated as a borough on March 29, 1802.

Bedford County was created on March 9, 1771, from part of Cumberland County and named for Fort Bedford, which in turn had been named in 1759 for the Duke of Bedford. *Bedford,* the county seat, on the site of Fort Bedford, was incorporated as a borough on March 13, 1795.

Berks County was created on March 11, 1752, from parts of Philadelphia, Chester, and Lancaster counties; and was named for Berkshire in England. *Reading,* the county seat, was named for Berkshire's county town. It was incorporated as a borough on September 12, 1783, and as a city on March 16, 1847.

Blair County was created on February 26, 1846, from parts of Huntingdon and Bedford counties, and named for John Blair, a prominent citizen of the locality. *Hollidaysburg,* the county seat, was incorporated as a borough on August 10, 1836, and named for Adam and William Holliday, early settlers.

Bradford County was created on February 21, 1810, from parts of Luzerne and Lycoming counties, and named Ontario County for the lake of the same name. On March 24, 1812, it was renamed for William Bradford, second Attorney General of the United States, and formally organized. *Towanda,* the county seat, was incorporated as a borough on March 5, 1828, and named for Towanda Creek.

Bucks County was one of the three original counties created by William Penn in November, 1682. Bucks is a contraction of Buckinghamshire, an English shire where the Penns had lived for generations. *Doylestown* replaced Newtown as the county seat in 1812, and was incorporated as a borough on April 16, 1838. It was named for William Doyle, early innkeeper.

Butler County was created on March 12, 1800, from part of Allegheny County and named for General Richard Butler. It was attached to Allegheny County until 1803.

Butler, the county seat, was laid out in 1803, incorporated as a borough on February 26, 1817, and chartered as a city on January 7, 1918.

Cambria County was created on March 26, 1804, from parts of Huntingdon, Somerset, and Bedford counties; and named for Cambria Township of Somerset County. Cambria is an ancient name for Wales. It was attached to Somerset County until 1807. *Ebensburg,* the county seat, was incorporated as a borough on January 15, 1825, and named by Reverend Rees Lloyd for his eldest and deceased son Eben.

Cameron County was created on March 29, 1860, from parts of Clinton, McKean, Elk, and Potter counties; and named for U. S. Senator Simon Cameron. *Emporium,* the county seat, was incorporated as a borough on October 13, 1864; its name is Latin for "market or trade center."

Carbon County was created on March 13, 1843, from parts of Northampton and Monroe counties; its name alludes to its deposits of anthracite coal. *Jim Thorpe,* the county seat, was incorporated as the borough of Mauch Chunk on January 26, 1850. It was renamed in 1954 for the famous Indian athlete, who is buried there. Mauch Chunk is an Indian name meaning "bear mountain."

Centre County was created on February 13, 1800, from parts of Huntingdon, Lycoming, Mifflin, and Northumberland counties; its name refers to its geographical location at the center of the State. *Bellefonte,* the county seat, was incorporated as a borough on March 28, 1806; its name, French for "beautiful spring," alludes to a large spring there, and is said to have been suggested by the famous Talleyrand.

Chester County was one of the three original counties created by William Penn in November, 1682, and did not become an inland county until 1789, when Delaware County was created from a part of it. Its name derives from Cheshire (i.e., Chester-shire), England, from which many of its early settlers came. *West Chester,* the county seat since 1788, was incorporated as a borough on March 28, 1799. It was named for Chester, the original county seat (now in Delaware County), which in turn derived its name from the shire town of Cheshire.

Clarion County was created on March 11, 1839, from parts of Venango and Armstrong counties, and named for the Clarion River. *Clarion,* the county seat, was incorporated as a borough on April 6, 1841.

Clearfield County was created on March 26, 1804, from parts of Huntingdon and Lycoming counties, and named for Clearfield Creek. The creek's name alluded to openings or clear fields in its vicinity. For many years Clearfield County functioned as part of Centre County, not electing its own commissioners until 1812. It was organized for judicial purposes in 1822. *Clearfield,* the county seat, was incorporated as a borough on April 21, 1840.

Clinton County was created on June 21, 1839, from parts of Centre and Lycoming counties, and probably named for Governor De Witt Clinton of New York, promoter of the Erie Canal. Actually, the name seems to have been substituted as a political maneuver for the name "Eagle," first proposed. In this way the opponents of the new county were tricked. *Lock Haven,* the county seat, derived its name from its position on the West Branch Canal, which was completed to Lock Haven in 1834. It was incorporated as a borough on May 25, 1840, and as a city on March 28, 1870.

Columbia County was created on March 22, 1813, from part of Northumberland County; its name is a poetical allusion to America. *Bloomsburg,* the county seat after November 30, 1847, was incorporated as a town on March 4, 1870, becoming the only incorporated town in the state. Its name comes from Bloom Township, which was named for Samuel Bloom, a county commissioner of Northumberland County. Danville, the county seat from 1813 to 1846, is now the county seat of Montour County.

Crawford County was created on March 12, 1800, from parts of Allegheny County, and named for Colonel William Crawford, a frontier hero. *Meadville,* the county seat, named for its founder David Mead, was incorporated as a borough on March 29, 1823, and as a city on February 15, 1866.

Cumberland County was created on January 27, 1750, from part of Lancaster County, and named for Cumberland County in England. *Carlisle,* the county seat since 1752, was incorporated as a borough on April 13, 1782; it was named for the county town of the English county. Shippensburg was the county seat from 1750 to 1752.

Dauphin County was created on March 4, 1785, from part of Lancaster County, and named for the title of the eldest son of the French King. The little boy who was Dauphin at that time died in 1789. *Harrisburg,* the county seat, named for its founder John Harris, was incorporated as a borough on April 13, 1791, and chartered as a city on March 19, 1860.

Delaware County was created on September 26, 1789, from part of Chester County, and named for the Delaware River, which had been named for Lord de la Warr, an early governor of Virginia. *Media,* its county seat since 1850, was incorporated as a borough on March 11, 1850, and named for its central location in the county. Chester, its original county seat, was the county seat of Chester County before 1788 and the temporary capital of Pennsylvania, 1681–1682, before Philadelphia was laid out.

Elk County was created on April 18, 1843, from parts of Jefferson, Clearfield, and McKean counties; and probably named for Elk Creek. *Ridgway,* the county seat, was laid out in 1833 and named for Jacob Ridgway, who owned land there. It was incorporated as a borough on February 15, 1881.

Erie County was created on March 12, 1800, from part of Allegheny County, and named for Lake Erie, which in turn was named for an Indian tribe. It was attached to Crawford County until 1803. *Erie,* the county seat, so named because it was Pennsylvania's port on Lake Erie, was laid out in 1795. It was incorporated as a borough on March 29, 1805, and as a city on April 14, 1851.

Fayette County was created on September 26, 1783, from a part of Westmoreland County, and named in honor of the Marquis de la Fayette. *Uniontown,* the county seat, was laid out about 1776 as Beeson's-town and later renamed in allusion to the federal Union. It was incorporated as a borough on April 4, 1796, and as a city on December 19, 1913.

Forest County was created on April 11, 1848, from part of Jefferson County, and part of Venango County was added on October 31, 1866. It was named for its extensive forests. It was attached to Jefferson County until 1857, when Marienville became the county seat. *Tionesta,* the county seat after 1866, was incorporated as a borough on February 28, 1856, and was named for Tionesta Creek.

Franklin County was created on September 9, 1784, from part of Cumberland County, and named for Benjamin Franklin. *Chambersburg,* the county seat, was founded in 1764 by Benjamin Chambers, for whom it was named. It was incorporated as a borough on March 21, 1803.

Fulton County was created on April 19, 1851, from part of Bedford County, and named for Robert Fulton. *McConnellsburg,* the county seat, was laid out by Daniel McConnell in 1786 and incorporated as a borough on March 26, 1814.

Greene County was created on February 9, 1796, from part of Washington County, and named for General Nathanael Greene. *Waynesburg,* the county seat, named for Major General Anthony Wayne, was laid out in 1796 and incorporated as a borough on January 29, 1816.

Huntingdon County was created on September 20, 1787, from part of Bedford County, and named for its county seat *Huntingdon.* Dr. William Smith, provost of the University of Pennsylvania, owned the land where the town was laid out in 1767, and named it in honor of the Countess of Huntingdon, a benefactor of the University. Huntingdon was incorporated as a borough on March 29, 1796.

Indiana County was created on March 30, 1803, from parts of Westmoreland and Lycoming counties, and probably named for the territory of Indiana. It was attached to Westmoreland County until 1806. *Indiana,* the county seat, was laid out in 1805, and incorporated as a borough on March 11, 1816.

Jefferson County was created on March 26, 1804, from part of Lycoming County, and named for President Thomas Jefferson. It was attached to Westmoreland County until 1806, and then to Indiana County until 1830, when it was formally organized. *Brookville,* the county seat, was laid out in 1830 and incorporated as a borough on April 9, 1834. It is said to have been named for the numerous brooks and streams in the vicinity.

Juniata County was created on March 2, 1831, from part of Mifflin County, and named for the Juniata River. The Indian name Juniata is said to mean "people of the standing stone." *Mifflintown,* the county seat, was laid out in 1791 and incorporated as a borough on March 6, 1833. It was named for Governor Thomas Mifflin.

Lackawanna County was created on August 13, 1878, from part of Luzerne County, and was the last county to be created. It was named for the Lackawanna River, a name meaning "stream that forks." *Scranton,* the county seat, was laid out in 1841, incorporated as a borough in 1856, and became a city on April 23, 1866. It was named for the Scranton family, its founders.

Lancaster County was created on May 10, 1729, from part of Chester County, and named for Lancashire (i.e., Lancaster-shire), England. *Lancaster,* the county seat, named for its English counterpart, was laid out in 1730. It was chartered as a borough on May 1, 1742, and as a city on March 20, 1818.

Lawrence County was created on March 20, 1849, from parts of Beaver and Mercer counties, and named for Perry's flagship *Lawrence,* which had been named for the naval hero, Captain James Lawrence. *New Castle,* the county seat, was laid out in 1802, incorporated as a borough on March 25, 1825, and chartered as a city on February 25, 1869. It is not certain whether it was named for Newcastle, England, or New Castle, Delaware.

Lebanon County was created on February 16, 1813, from parts of Dauphin and Lancaster counties, and named for old Lebanon Township. Lebanon is a Biblical name meaning "white mountain." *Lebanon,* the county seat, was laid out in 1750. It was first incorporated as a borough on March 28, 1799, but the citizens did not accept incorporation. It was finally chartered as a borough on February 20, 1821, and as a city in 1885.

Lehigh County was created on March 6, 1812, from part of Northampton County, and named for the Lehigh River. The name Lehigh is derived from the German "Lecha," which comes from the Indian "Lechauwekink," meaning "where there are forks." *Allentown,* the county seat, was laid out about 1762 and named for Chief Justice William Allen of Pennsylvania, who owned land there. It was incorporated as the borough of Northampton on March 18, 1811, renamed Allentown in 1838, and chartered as a city on March 12, 1867.

Luzerne County was created on September 25, 1786, from part of Northumberland County, and named for the Chevalier de la Luzerne, French minister to the United States. *Wilkes-Barre,* the county seat, was laid out in 1772 and named for two members of Parliament, John Wilkes and Isaac Barre, both advocates of American rights. It was incorporated as a borough on March 17, 1806, and as a city on May 4, 1871.

Lycoming County was created on April 13, 1795, from part of Northumberland County, and named for Lycoming Creek. The name is derived from a Delaware Indian word meaning "sandy or gravelly creek." *Williamsport,* the county seat, was laid out in 1795, incorporated as a borough on March 1, 1806, and became a city on January 15, 1866. There are various theories about the origin of the city's name, that it was so called for Judge William Hepburn, that Michael Ross named it for his own son William, or that a boatman William Ross used it as a "port" years before the town was founded.

McKean County was created on March 26, 1804, from part of Lycoming County, and named for Governor Thomas McKean. It was attached to Centre County until 1814, when it was combined with Potter County to elect commissioners jointly, and also attached to Lycoming County for judicial and elective purposes. It was fully organized in 1826. *Smethport,* the county seat, was laid out in 1807, and named in honor of Raymond and Theodore de Smeth, Amsterdam bankers. It was incorporated as a borough on February 11, 1853.

Mercer County was created on March 12, 1800, from part of Allegheny County, and named for General Hugh Mercer. It was attached to Crawford County until February, 1804, when it was formally organized. *Mercer,* the county seat, was laid out in 1803 and incorporated as a borough on March 28, 1814.

Mifflin County was created on September 19, 1789, from parts of Cumberland and Northumberland counties, and named for Governor Thomas Mifflin. *Lewistown,* the county seat, was laid out in 1790 and incorporated as a borough on April 11, 1795, but this charter was apparently not accepted, for it was reincorporated on February 6, 1811. It was named for William Lewis, local ironmaster.

Monroe County was created on April 1, 1836, from parts of Northampton and Pike counties, and named for President James Monroe. *Stroudsburg,* the county seat, was incorporated as a borough on February 6, 1815, and named for Jacob Stroud, an early settler.

Montgomery County was created on September 10, 1784, from part of Philadelphia County, and named for General Richard Montgomery. *Norristown,* the county seat, was laid out in 1784, and incorporated as a borough on March 31, 1812. It was named for Isaac Norris, who owned land there.

Montour County was created on May 3, 1850, from part of Columbia County, and named for Madame Montour, famous French half-breed who figured prominently in Indian affairs. *Danville,* the county seat, was laid out in 1792, and incorporated as a borough on February 27, 1849. It was the county seat of Columbia County from 1813 to 1846.

Northampton County was created on March 11, 1752, from part of Bucks County, and named for Northamptonshire, England, where Thomas Penn's father-in-law, the Earl of Pomfret, lived. *Easton,* the county seat, was named for the Earl's estate. It was incorporated as a borough on September 23, 1789, and became a city on November 2, 1886.

Northumberland County was created on March 21, 1772, from parts of Lancaster, Cumberland, Berks, Bedford, and Northampton counties; and probably was named for the English county. *Sunbury,* the county seat, was laid out in 1772, incorporated as a borough on March 24, 1797, and became a city in 1921. It was named for an English village near London.

Perry County was created on March 22, 1820, from part of Cumberland County, and named in honor of Oliver Hazard Perry, victor in the Battle of Lake Erie. *Bloomfield,* the county seat after 1827, bears the name given to the tract of land in the original patent, but it is said that it was laid out in the month of June, 1822, when clover was in bloom. It was incorporated as a borough on March 14, 1831. The post-office name is New Bloomfield.

Philadelphia County was one of the three original counties created by William Penn in November, 1682, and its name to him signified "brotherly love," although the original Philadelphia in Asia Minor was actually "the city of Philadelphus." *Philadelphia* was laid out in 1682 as the county seat and the capital of the Province; it was chartered as a city on October 25, 1701, and rechartered on March 11, 1789. On February 2, 1854, all the municipalities within the county were consolidated with the city. The county offices were merged with the city government in 1952.

Pike County was created on March 26, 1814, from part of Wayne County, and named for General Zebulon Pike. *Milford,* the county seat, was incorporated as a borough on December 25, 1874, and probably named for Milford Haven in Wales.

Potter County was created on March 26, 1804, from part of Lycoming County, and named for General James Potter. It was attached to Lycoming County until 1814, when it was authorized to elect commissioners jointly with McKean County. McKean and Potter counties were separated in 1824, but Potter was still attached to McKean for judicial purposes. It was fully organized in 1835. *Coudersport,* the county seat, was laid out in 1807, and incorporated as a borough on February 7, 1848. It was named for Jean Samuel Couderc, an Amsterdam banker.

Schuylkill County was created on March 1, 1811, from parts of Berks and Northampton counties, and named for the Schuylkill River. Schuylkill is Dutch for "hidden stream." Parts of Columbia and Luzerne counties were added on March 3, 1818. *Pottsville,* the county seat after December 1, 1851, was incorporated as a borough on February 19, 1828, and became a city in 1910. It was named for the Pott family, early settlers. The original county seat was Orwigsburg.

Snyder County was created on March 2, 1855, from part of Union County, and named for Governor Simon Snyder. *Middleburg,* the county seat, was laid out in 1800, and incorporated as a borough in 1864. It was situated on Middle Creek near the middle of former Centre Township; hence the name, which became even more appropriate after the creation of the county.

Somerset County was created on April 17, 1795, from part of Bedford County, and named for Somersetshire, England. *Somerset,* the county seat, was laid out in 1795, and incorporated as a borough on March 5, 1804.

Sullivan County was created on March 15, 1847, from part of Lycoming County, and named for General John Sullivan. *Laporte,* the county seat, was laid out in 1850, and incorporated as a borough in 1853. It was named for John La Porte, a surveyor general of Pennsylvania.

Susquehanna County was created on February 21, 1810, from part of Luzerne County, and named for the Susquehanna River. It remained attached to Luzerne County until 1812. *Montrose,* the county seat, was laid out in 1812, and incorporated as a borough on March 29, 1824. Its name is a combination of "mont," French word for "mountain," and Rose, for Dr. R. H. Rose, a prominent citizen.

Tioga County was created on March 26, 1804, from part of Lycoming County, and named for the Tioga River. Tioga is derived from an Indian word meaning "the forks of a stream." *Wellsboro,* the county seat, was laid out in 1806, and incorporated as a borough on March 16, 1830. It was named for the Wells family, prominent in the locality.

Union County was created on March 22, 1813, from part of Northumberland County, and its name is an allusion to the federal Union. *Lewisburg,* the county seat after 1855, was laid out in 1785, and named for Ludwig (i.e., Lewis) Derr, its founder. It was incorporated as a borough on March 21, 1822. New Berlin was the county seat from 1815 to 1855.

Venango County was created on March 12, 1800, from parts of Allegheny and Lycoming counties, and its name comes from the Indian name for French Creek. It was attached to Crawford County until April 1, 1805. *Franklin,* the county seat, was laid out in 1795 at Fort Franklin, which had been built in 1787 by United States troops. Both were named for Benjamin Franklin. Franklin was incorporated as a borough on April 14, 1828, and as a city on April 4, 1868.

Warren County was created on March 12, 1800, from parts of Allegheny and Lycoming counties, and named for General Joseph Warren. It was attached to Crawford County until 1805, and then to Venango County until 1819, when it was formally organized. *Warren,* the county seat, was laid out in 1795, and incorporated as a borough on April 3, 1832.

Washington County was created on March 28, 1781, from part of Westmoreland County, and named in honor of George Washington. *Washington,* the county seat, was laid out in 1781, incorporated as a borough on February 12, 1810, and chartered as a city in 1924.

Wayne County was created on March 21, 1798, from part of Northhampton County, and named for General Anthony Wayne. *Honesdale,* the county seat after 1842, was laid out in 1827, and incorporated as a borough on January 28, 1831. It was named for Philip Hone, president of the Delaware and Hudson Canal Company. Earlier county seats included Wilsonville (1799–1802), Milford (1802–1805), and Bethany (1805–1841).

Westmoreland County was created on February 26, 1773, from part of Bedford County, and named for a county in England. *Greensburg,* the county seat after 1785, was incorporated as a borough on February 9, 1799, and as a city in 1928. It was named for General Nathanael Greene. Hannastown, the original county seat, was burned by the British and Indians on July 13, 1782.

Wyoming County was created on April 4, 1842, from part of Luzerne County, and named for the Wyoming Valley. Wyoming is derived from an Indian word meaning "extensive meadows." *Tunkhannock,* the county seat, was incorporated as a borough on August 8, 1841, and was named for Tunkhannock Creek. The creek's name means "small stream."

York County was created on August 19, 1749, from part of Lancaster County, and named either for the Duke of York, early patron of the Penn family, or for the city and shire of York in England. The name may have been suggested by the proximity to Lancaster County, as the names are linked in English history. *York,* the county seat, was laid out in 1741, and incorporated as a borough on September 24, 1787. It was chartered as a city on January 11, 1887.

The Chief Executives of Pennsylvania

GOVERNORS OF THE PROVINCE, 1681–1776

WILLIAM PENN, Proprietary and Governor	1681–1693
WILLIAM MARKHAM, Deputy Governor	June, 1681–Oct. 24, 1682
WILLIAM PENN, in Pennsylvania	Oct. 24, 1682–June, 1684
THOMAS LLOYD, President of the Council	Aug. 19, 1684–Feb. 9, 1688[1]
THOMAS LLOYD, ROBERT TURNER, ARTHUR COOK, JOHN SIMCOCK, JOHN ECKLEY, jointly Deputy Governor	Feb. 9, 1688–Dec. 18, 1688
CAPTAIN JOHN BLACKWELL, Deputy Governor	Dec. 18, 1688–Jan., 1690
THOMAS LLOYD, President of the Council	Jan. 2, 1690–Mar., 1691
THOMAS LLOYD, Deputy Governor	Mar., 1691–Apr. 26, 1693
Royal Province: BENJAMIN FLETCHER, Governor	Apr. 26, 1693–Mar., 1695
WILLIAM MARKHAM, Deputy Governor	Apr. 27, 1693–Mar. 26, 1695
WILLIAM PENN, Proprietary and Governor	1695–1718
WILLIAM MARKHAM, Deputy Governor	Mar. 26, 1695–Dec., 1699
WILLIAM PENN, in Pennsylvania	Dec., 1699–Nov., 1701
ANDREW HAMILTON, Lieutenant Governor	Nov. 14, 1701–Apr. 20, 1703[2]

---

[1] Exact dates given for the beginnings of terms refer to the days when incoming governors took office. They may not agree in all cases with other lists using dates of appointment, arrival, etc.

[2] Andrew Hamilton died on April 20, 1703, but the Council did not meet until May 4 to install Shippen as President.

PENNSYLVANIA

EDWARD SHIPPEN, President of the Council................. May 4, 1703–Feb. 3, 1704

JOHN EVANS, Lieutenant Governor......................... Feb. 3, 1704–Feb. 1, 1709

CHARLES GOOKIN, Lieutenant Governor.................... Feb. 1, 1709–May 31, 1717

SIR WILLIAM KEITH, Lieutenant Governor .... May 31, 1717–Nov. 3, 1718

JOHN (1700–1746), THOMAS (1702–1775), and RICHARD (1706–1771) PENN, Proprietaries................................... 1718–1746

SIR WILLIAM KEITH, Lieutenant Governor................. Nov. 3, 1718–June 22, 1726

PATRICK GORDON, Lieutenant Governor.................... June 22, 1726–Aug. 5, 1736[3]

JAMES LOGAN, President of the Council.................... Aug. 5, 1736–June 1, 1738

GEORGE THOMAS, Lieutenant Governor................... June 1, 1738–May, 1746

THOMAS (1702–1775) and RICHARD (1706–1771) PENN, Proprietaries 1746–1771

GEORGE THOMAS, Lieutenant Governor.................... May, 1746–1747[4]

ANTHONY PALMER, President of the Council................ June 6, 1747–Nov. 23, 1748

JAMES HAMILTON, Lieutenant Governor.................... Nov. 23, 1748–Oct. 3, 1754

ROBERT HUNTER MORRIS, Lieutenant Governor .... Oct. 3, 1754–Aug. 20, 1756

WILLIAM DENNY, Lieutenant Governor .... Aug. 20, 1756–Nov. 17, 1759

JAMES HAMILTON, Lieutenant Governor.................... Nov. 17, 1759–Oct. 31, 1763

JOHN PENN[5] (1729–1795), Lieutenant Governor.............. Oct. 31, 1763–May 4, 1771[6]

THOMAS (1702–1775) and JOHN (1729–1795) PENN, Proprietaries 1771–1775

JAMES HAMILTON, President of the Council .... May 6, 1771–Oct. 16, 1771

RICHARD (1735–1811) PENN,[7] Lieutenant Governor........... Oct. 16, 1771–Aug. 30, 1773

JOHN (1729–1795) PENN, Lieutenant Governor .... Aug. 30, 1773–July, 1776

JOHN PENN (1729–1795) and JOHN PENN (1760–1834),[8] Proprietaries... 1775–1776

PROVISIONAL GOVERNMENT

Committee of Safety

BENJAMIN FRANKLIN, President........................... July 3, 1775–July 22, 1776

Council of Safety

DAVID RITTENHOUSE, Chairman.......................... July 24–26, 29–31, Aug. 5, 6, 1776[9]

SAMUEL MORRIS, Chairman.............................. July 27, Aug. 1, 1776

THOMAS WHARTON, JR., Chairman......................... Aug. 2, 1776

THOMAS WHARTON, JR., President .... Aug. 6, 1776–Mar. 5, 1777[10]

---

[3] Patrick Gordon died in office.

[4] Governor Thomas sailed for Great Britain late in May or early in June, 1747.

[5] Son of Richard Penn and grandson of William Penn.

[6] John Penn sailed for Great Britain on hearing of his father's death.

[7] Son of Richard Penn and grandson of William Penn.

[8] Son of Thomas Penn and grandson of William Penn.

[9] The Council of Safety did not organize formally by electing a president until August 6, 1776. In the meantime, chairmen were elected, but only for the days of meeting.

[10] The Council of Safety did not cease to exist at this date, but from this time it was no longer the State executive.

July 4. Declaration of Independence adopted.

July 8. Election of first State constitutional convention; Declaration of Independence proclaimed.

July 15. Constitutional convention meets and assumes control of government.

September 26. Final adjournment of Provincial Assembly, ending the proprietary government.

September 28. First State Constitution adopted.

November 28. First meeting of the General Assembly under the Constitution of 1776.

First arsenal of the United States established at Carlisle.

1777 March 5. State government fully organized at Philadelphia.

June 14. National Flag adopted by Congress in Philadelphia.

September 11. Battle of Brandywine.

September 27. British under Howe enter Philadelphia.

September 27. Continental Congress at Lancaster.

September 30. Continental Congress at York.

October 4. Battle of Germantown.

December 18. Washington's army encamps at Valley Forge.

1778 June 16. The British evacuate Philadelphia.

June 27. Congress leaves York to return to Philadelphia.

July 2-4. The Wyoming Massacre.

1779 General John Sullivan leads expedition against the Iroquois.

Divesting Act ends Proprietary ownership.

1780 March 1. Final vote of the Assembly for the gradual emancipation of Negro slaves.

July 17. Bank of Pennsylvania formed to supply Continental Army by subscriptions of Philadelphia business men.

1781 February 20. Robert Morris appointed Superintendent of Finance by Congress.

December 31. Bank of North America chartered by Congress, the oldest bank in America.

1782 April 1. Bank of North America re-chartered by Pennsylvania Assembly.

July 13. Hannastown destroyed by the Indians.

December 30. Trenton Decree confirms Pennsylvania title to Wyoming Valley.

1784 September 21. First successful daily newspaper in the United States, *Pennsylvania Packet* and *Daily Advertiser,* begun in Philadelphia.

October 23. Purchase from the Six Nations at Fort Stanwix.

1785 Harrisburg, formerly Harris' Ferry, founded. January 21. Purchase from Delawares and Wyandots at Fort McIntosh.

1786 July 27. John Fitch navigates a steamboat on the Delaware.

1787 Charter granted for Pittsburgh Academy, the origin of the University of Pittsburgh.

September 17. United States Constitution completed by Convention at Philadelphia.

November 21. Meeting of Pennsylvania ratification convention.

December 12. Pennsylvania ratifies the United States Constitution.

1789 January 9. Purchase from the Six Nations at Fort Harmar.

November 4. Second State constitutional convention meets in Philadelphia.

1790 September 2. Adjournment of second State constitutional convention and proclamation of second Constitution.

Philadelphia the capital of the United States, until 1800.

1791 April 9. Act passed by General Assembly making a grant to the Penn family.

1792 Pennsylvania purchases the Erie Triangle from the United States.

February 1. Young Ladies' Academy of Philadelphia chartered, the first girls' school incorporated in Pennsylvania.

April 9. Philadelphia and Lancaster Turnpike incorporated.

1793 March 4. Washington's second inauguration as President, at Philadelphia.

1794 The Whiskey Rebellion in western Pennsylvania. General Wayne defeats the western Indians at the Battle of Fallen Timbers.

1798 Joseph Hopkinson of Philadelphia writes "Hail Columbia," the first national song of America.

1799 "Hot Water Rebellion," or Fries' Rebellion. November. State capital moved to Lancaster.

1800 Federal capital moved from Philadelphia to Washington, D. C.

1803 The Philadelphia Bank (Philadelphia National Bank), now the largest commercial bank in the Quaker City, opened its doors for business September 19, at 164 Chestnut Street.

1804 Philadelphia-Pittsburgh stagecoach line established.

1808 February 11. Judge Fell burns anthracite coal in a grate.

1811 October 29. First steamboat leaves Pittsburgh for New Orleans.

1812 Pennsylvania Company for Insurance on Lives and Granting Annuities chartered, the first trust company in the country.

April-May. State capital moved from Lancaster to Harrisburg.

1813 September 10. Oliver Hazard Perry wins the Battle

of Lake Erie.

1819 Philadelphia Savings Fund Society chartered, the first savings bank in America.

1823 March 31. First Railway Act in America passed by General Assembly.

1824 December 2. The Historical Society of Pennsylvania organized.

1826 February 25. Pennsylvania Canal authorized by General Assembly.

1829 August 8. First locomotive in the United States used on Carbondale and Honesdale road.

Delaware and Hudson Canal opened from Honesdale to Kingston, N. Y.

1830 Shipbuilding firm of William Cramp & Sons organized at Philadelphia.

1831 First building and loan association in the United States formed in Frankford, suburb of Philadelphia.

January 8. First successful American locomotive completed by Mathias Baldwin in Philadelphia.

1833 American Anti-Slavery Society formed in Philadelphia.

April 4. Philadelphia and Reading Railroad chartered.

1834 Railroad and canal communication opened to Pittsburgh.

April 1. Free Public School Act.

1835 Thaddeus Stevens delivers famous speech on Free Schools.

1837 May 2. Third State constitutional convention meets.

1838 February 22. Third State constitutional convention adjourns.

May 27. Burning of Pennsylvania Hall, Philadelphia, in abolition riots.

October 26. Third State Constitution adopted.

1841 Commercial manufacture of coke begun in Connellsville district.

1846 Lehigh Valley Railroad Company chartered.

April 13. Pennsylvania Railroad chartered.

1850 State Judiciary made elective.

March 11. Female Medical College of Pennsylvania incorporated, the first college for training women physicians.

1852 Pennsylvania State Teachers' Association organized at Pittsburgh.

1853 Pennsylvania Railroad opened to Pittsburgh.

1854 February 2. Law consolidating city of Philadelphia.

1855 February 22. Farmer's High School in Centre County chartered, the origin of Pennsylvania State University.

1856 February 22. Republican Party conference in Pittsburgh, to call the first national convention.

June 17. First national nominating convention of the Republican Party meets at Philadelphia.

1857 March 4. James Buchanan, of Pennsylvania inaugurated President of the United States.

1859 Philadelphia Clearing House System established.

August 29. Col. Drake drills the first oil well near Titusville.

1861 January 15. Governor Andrew Gregg Curtin, in his first inaugural, takes a firm stand for the Union.

January 24. Pennsylvania Assembly adopts resolution pledging "the faith and power of Pennsylvania" to the support of the Union.

April 18. Five Pennsylvania militia companies reach Washington, the "First Defenders" of the national capital; Camp Curtin established at Harrisburg as a training center.

1862 Bethlehem Iron Company (later Bethlehem Steel Company) erect ironworks.

September 22-24. Loyal War Governors' Conference at Altoona upholds President Lincoln.

October 10. Confederates raid Chambersburg.

1863 July 1-3. Battle of Gettysburg.

November 19. Dedication of cemetery at Gettysburg; Lincoln's Gettysburg Address.

1864 Andrew Carnegie enters the iron business.

July 30. Confederates burn Chambersburg.

1865 Pittsburgh Clearing House Association established.

1872 November 12. Fourth State constitutional convention meets.

1873 November 3. Convention completes work.

1876 Centennial International Exhibition at Philadelphia.

1877 Great railroad riots.

1888 Pittsburgh Reduction Company, now the Aluminum Company of America, founded at Pittsburgh.

1889 May 31. The great Johnstown flood.

1891 June 19. The State Banking Department created; Australian or secret ballot adopted.

1892 Duryea demonstrates first vehicle propelled by a gasoline motor.

1895 State Superior Court created by law.

State Department of Agriculture created.

May 16. Governor Hastings signs Compulsory Education Law.

1897 February 2. State Capitol burned.

1898 April 12. War with Spain. Pennsylvania National Guard mobilized at Mount Gretna.

1900 Philadelphia Symphony Orchestra organized.

1901 State Department of Forestry established.

1903 State Highway Department and Departments of Fisheries and Mines created.

1905 May 2. Pennsylvania State Police created.

July 19. First all motion picture theater in the world opened in Pittsburgh.

1906 October 4. New State Capitol dedicated.

1911 May 31. Sproul Highway Act approved.

1913 Public Service Commission organized.

1915 Workmen's Compensation Act passed.

1917 November. First detachment of Pennsylvania troops leaves for Europe in World War I.

1920 November 2. Radio station KDKA, Pittsburgh, begins daily broadcasting schedule, the first in the world.

1923 Administrative Code reorganizes State government.

1926 July 1. Delaware River Bridge at Philadelphia opened.

Celebration of Sesqui-Centennial at Philadelphia.

1929 Fiscal Code reorganizes State finances.

1931 Birthday of William Penn, October 24, designated as a day to be observed by schools and the public.

1936 March. Disastrous flood in central Pennsylvania.

1939 Department of Commerce created.

1940 September 16. Pennsylvania National Guard begins mobilizing for national emergency.

October 1. Pennsylvania Turnpike opened.

October 16. First registration for Selective Service.

1941 March 18. Army Reception Center opened at New Cumberland.

April 17. State Council of Defense established.

Pennsylvania Reserve Defense Corps (later the Pennsylvania Guard) created.

December 7. Japanese attack Pearl Harbor.

Chief Boatswain Edwin J. Hill, Philadelphia, was killed there, becoming Pennsylvania's first winner of the Congressional Medal of Honor in World War II.

1942 January 5. First rationing program set up by State Council of Defense.

June 23-25. First State-wide blackouts.

1943 July 1. Mechanicsburg Naval Supply Depot completed.

1945 June 6. Pennsylvania Historical and Museum Commission created.

August 14. Governor Martin proclaims two-day holiday, celebrating end of World War II.

November 1. State Council of Defense dissolved.

1946 General State Authority bonds amounting to $47,912,000 are retired by the Commonwealth, the largest single debt payment ever effected by any state in a single year.

A long-range program to conserve the State's physical resources and to clear its streams of pollution is begun.

1947 January 2-21. Within three weeks Pennsylvania has three governors, Edward Martin resigns on the second to enter the United States Senate and is succeeded by Lieutenant-Governor John C. Bell, who serves until the inauguration of Governor-elect James H. Duff on the twenty-first.

September 17. Carrying the Nation's most significant historic documents, the Freedom Train is appropriately dedicated in Philadelphia prior to its tour of the country.

1948 Pennsylvania and seven neighboring states enter into an agreement to act cooperatively in purifying the waterways of the Ohio River Valley area.

Postwar industrial development and expansion in Pennsylvania reaches two billion dollars.

1949 Pennsylvania manufacturers and dealers supply goods worth $164,549,480 to the Federal government during the fiscal year 1948-1949.

The first complete natural resources map showing the known sources of plants, animals and minerals in the State, is issued by the Pennsylvania Department of Internal Affairs. Production of anthracite coal drops to 38,967,000 tons, the lowest output in 47 years.

On August 17 the oil industry commemorates the 90th anniversary of the drilling of the world's first oil well by Colonel Edwin L. Drake at Titusville, Pennsylvania.

1950 January 21. Milton S. Eisenhower is chosen president of Pennsylvania State University.

June 4. Gloria Dei (Old Swedes') Church celebrates its 250th anniversary at its present location, the oldest church in the State.

November 2. The Census count gives Pennsylvania a population of 10,498,012, third in rank after New York and California.

November 7. James H. Duff is elected U. S. Senator, and John S. Fine, Governor of the State.

1951 January 2. Independence Hall and other historic buildings in Independence Square placed under the jurisdiction of the National Park Service.

March 1. Ground broken for erection of the multi-million-dollar Fairless steel plant of the U. S. Steel Corporation at Morrisville.

May 23. Bill introduced in General Assembly to create Metropolitan Study Committee of Allegheny County.

November 6. For the first time in 67 years Democrats win control of Philadelphia city government.

1952 January 7. Joseph Clark inaugurated as Mayor of Philadelphia, and new City Charter placed in operation.

March 12. The Philadelphia Bar Association observes the 150th anniversary of its founding.

April 27. The last train leaves the old Broad Street Station, Philadelphia.

April 28. Demolition of the Broad Street Station and

the "Chinese Wall" begun.

1953 Philadelphia ranks fourth in current gifts and second in bequests for philanthropic purposes in the U. S.

January 7. The Commonwealth acquires the Landis Valley Museum, near Lancaster, as the first step toward the establishment of the Pennsylvania Farm Museum.

February 11. The State Government Survey Committee (Chesterman Committee) submits its report recommending numerous far-reaching changes in the State's government.

1954 Pennsylvania farm income reported double national average.

Port of Philadelphia reports greatest tonnage in history with 18,972 ships, topping New York in tonnage.

February 8. Hazleton meeting of Northeastern Pennsylvania Industrial Development Commission considers plight of anthracite region.

September 6. President Eisenhower in Denver generates the electrical impulses starting machinery to break ground for America's first atomic power plant for peaceful uses at Shippingport in Western Pennsylvania.

November 2. George M. Leader, Democrat, elected Governor of the Commonwealth.

November 4. Survey shows that 4 out of every 10 Keystone farm homes have television sets.

1955 Alexander Calder, third generation of noted Philadelphia sculptors, commissioned to do five pieces for Penn Center.

February 27. Death of Tom Howard, one-time Philadelphia grocery boy, and star of radio and motion pictures.

March 28. Governor Leader reviews the State economy for the General Assembly, and recommends a program for economic recovery to expand industry and create new jobs for Pennsylvanians.

April 19. Governor Leader submits record General Fund budget of $1,273,164,930 for the 1955–57 biennium with accompanying tax program.

May 9. Rural Electrification Administration celebrates 20th anniversary, and reports that Pennsylvania tops the national average with 94 per cent of farms electrified.

1956 January 17. The 250th anniversary of Benjamin Franklin's birth is celebrated with ceremonies at his grave, Fifth and Arch Streets, Franklin Institute and Independence Hall in Philadelphia.

March 7. Pennsylvania's 3 per cent sales tax becomes effective.

May 22. Legislature adjourns, ending the longest session in state history.

May 25. Governor Leader and Governor Meyner of New Jersey officiate at ceremonies opening $14,000,000

bridge across Delaware River, linking Pennsylvania and New Jersey Turnpikes.

November 6. In a most unusual display of split ticket voting, Pennsylvanians give U. S. senatorial candidate Joseph S. Clark (D) a 17,000 majority over James H. Duff (R) while at the same time they give U. S. presidential candidate D. D. Eisenhower (R) 600,000 more votes than Adlai E. Stevenson (D).

March 20. First transmission of television images over ordinary telephone wires at Franklin Institute, Philadelphia.

March 25. Pennsylvania Supreme Court rules Korean Conflict an "act of war" rather than the military expedition given in a 1953 opinion.

1957 May. Walt Whitman Bridge, linking South Philadelphia and New Jersey and costing an estimated $85,000,000, dedicated and opened to public.

1958 June 1. Merger of the State Departments of Public Assistance and Welfare into the Department of Public Welfare as provided by an Act of Legislature.

September 16. Federal Court rules reading of Bible and recitation of Lord's Prayer unconstitutional in Pennsylvania public schools. Appeal pending.

1959 January 3. Alaska admitted as 49th state of the union.

January 20. David Leo Lawrence sworn in as 102nd Governor of the Commonwealth at Farm Show Arena due to snowstorm which cancelled the inaugural parade and outdoor ceremonies.

August 21. Hawaii officially admitted as 50th state of the union.

September 24. Russian Premier Nikita Khrushchev visits Pittsburgh, his only stop in Pennsylvania during his tour of the United States. Governor Lawrence tells him people stand solidly behind the President on foreign affairs.

November 7. Longest steel strike in industry's history (116-day nationwide stoppage) ended by Taft-Hartley injunction. Thousands of Pennsylvania steelworkers return to jobs.

1960 January 5. Pennsylvania's General Assembly convenes at noon in its first annual session.

January 14. John L. Lewis retires after 40 years as president of the United Mine Workers. Thomas Kennedy of Hazelton replaces him.

May 2. State Supreme Court meets in Independence Hall, Philadelphia, for the first time since 1802 in observance of Law Day.

July 4. New 50-star American Flag officially unfurled at Independence Hall.

July 30. Commonwealth Court (Dauphin County Court) rules that state motion picture censorship code is illegal; decision appealed.

1961 March 18. Barnes' Foundation's famous art collection at Merion opened to public after successful suit by the state Department of Justice.

April 5. First harness racing license issued in Pennsylvania for a track to be built in Philadelphia.

May 16. First Sunday sales of liquor in hotels approved by voters at primary elections in Pittsburgh and Philadelphia.

July 26. Governor David L. Lawrence appoints first woman to State Supreme Court, Anne X. Alpern.

July 26. State Supreme Court rules 4–3 that state censorship code is illegal.

September 1. First radar control to curb speeding put into operation by State Police.

October 9. U. S. Supreme Court refuses rehearing on its decision upholding Pennsylvania's Sunday closing, or "blue," laws.

November 6. U. S. Supreme Court declines to hear appeal from State Supreme Court's ruling that state censorship code was illegal.

1962 Farming reported to be a billion-dollar industry in terms of value of crops and livestock, highest on record.

Nine scheduled air lines reported serving Philadelphia's International Airport with direct jet service to Europe available.

Philadelphia Fellowship Commission Award presented to State Senator Charles R. Weiner for his support of fair housing and education.

Philadelphia Award established by Edward Bok in 1921 to recognize service to the "best and larger interests of Philadelphia" presented to Judge Edwin O. Lewis in recognition of his work in forwarding the preservation and restoration of Independence Hall.

The Philadelphia Grand Opera Company schedules six performances and the Philadelphia Lyric Opera Company twelve operas for the 1962–63 season.

The Philadelphia Orchestra announces seventy performances for the season.

January 3. Constitution Year opened to commemorate the 175th anniversary of the framing of the Constitution at Independence Hall with the raising of the flag of Delaware, first state to ratify the new Constitution.

January 23. Groundbreaking ceremonies held at Harrisburg for the new nine-million-dollar William Penn Memorial Museum and Archives with Governor David L. Lawrence turning the first spadeful of earth.

February 12. Richardson Dilworth resigns as Mayor of Philadelphia, a post he has held for six years and after twelve years in the city government, to run for the Democratic nomination for governor.

February 20. John H. Glenn, Jr., orbits the earth three times and on October 17 receives the Elisha Kent Kane gold medal of the Geographic Society of Philadelphia for his feat.

March 2. Richardson Dilworth wins the endorsement of the Democratic State Committee as candidate for governor despite the opposition of Philadelphia Democratic boss, Congressman William Green.

May 8. Stockholders of the Pennsylvania Railroad and the New York Central Railroad vote approval of the proposed merger of the two railroads.

May 26. New $8,000,000 American Baptists Convention headquarters dedicated at Valley Forge.

June 13. Dauphin County Court in Harrisburg ordered the General Assembly to reapportion the legislative districts in the state during its 1963 session or face legal action.

July 10. Telestar communication satellite placed in orbit and the next day Pennsylvanians see the first live pictures on TV from France and Great Britain.

July 11. Special grand jury investigation of charges made by the Republican Alliance of corruption in Philadelphia city government ordered by Judge Eugene V. Allesandroni.

August 2. Congress Hall reopened to the public following completion of restoration undertaken by the National Park Service in 1960.

September 17. Former President Harry Truman delivers the address at ceremonies at Independence Hall commemorating the 175th anniversary of the drafting of the Constitution in 1787.

September 24. Centennial of the Loyal War Governors Conference at Altoona commemorated with Governor Lawrence as the principal speaker.

October 9. Japanese firm announces its intention to build a new and large plant for production of plastics at Hazelton.

October 26. State Supreme Court by a 6–1 vote throws out the special grand jury investigation of Philadelphia city government authorized by Judge Allesandroni.

November 6. Republican William W. Scranton, 45, serving his first term as a member of Congress, elected to the governorship, swamping Richardson Dilworth though Democrat incumbent Joseph S. Clark is returned to the Senate by the voters along with Genevieve Blatt as State Secretary of Internal Affairs.

1963 January 3. Governor Lawrence receives the report of his special study committee on the proposed merger of the Pennsylvania and New York Central railroads: that the merger is opposed to the best interests of the state's economy.

January 15. William Warren Scranton inaugurated as 103rd Governor of Pennsylvania at the State Farm

Show arena on a clear cold day.

January 28. Governor Scranton announces appointment of a Council of Business and Industry to study the state-economic problems.

January 29. Governor Scranton intervenes to settle the Philadelphia transit strike.

March 20. Initial steps taken by Governor Scranton to establish a Council of Science and Technology to report on ways in which the state may advance these interests.

May 1. Governor Scranton makes his first TV report to the people on state finances titled "The Hidden Giant."

May 14. Merck, Sharp and Dohme's new John S. Zinsser Pharmaceutical Laboratory at West Point, Pennsylvania, one of the largest in the world, dedicated.

May 29. Governor Scranton signs into law legislation increasing the sales and use tax to 5 per cent with the proceeds devoted to education.

Executive order by Governor Scranton creates a Council for Human Services to combat "the social ills of our time."

July 1, 2 and 3. Centennial of the Battle of Gettysburg celebrated under the leadership of the Pennsylvania Gettysburg Commission headed by General Milton Baker.

August 27. David Fellin and Henry Throne rescued after a fourteen-day entombment in an anthracite coal mine near Hazelton over three hundred feet below ground level.

November 5. Voters approve Project 70 to acquire land for park, recreation, and historical preservation purposes but reject by some 40,000 votes the proposal to amend the Constitution of 1873 by calling a convention for the purpose.

James H. J. Tate elected mayor of Philadelphia, having filled out the term of Richardson Dilworth, but by the lowest majority polled by the Democrats in the city since 1948.

November 22. News of the assassination of President John F. Kennedy at Dallas, Texas, strikes a blow at the hearts of all Pennsylvanians. One of the first to react is Governor Scranton with a strong eulogy of the late President.

December. General Assembly enacts reapportionment law, but it is challenged at once in the courts.

1964 January 7. Governor Scranton presents to the legislature his $1,168,000,000 budget for 1964–65, highest in the state's history, but without imposing new taxes.

Governor Scranton mentioned increasingly as potential Republican nominee for the presidency despite his continued emphasis upon his unwillingness to run other than as a result of a definite draft.

January 16. Pennsylvania Historical and Museum Commission holds its 50th anniversary meeting in the Union League in Philadelphia, where it held its initial organization meeting in January, 1914.

January 23. Representative Norman Wood of Lancaster County announces his retirement from the General Assembly at the end of the 1964 term after 42 years of service, longest in the history of the legislature.

January 24. Increased valuation of Philadelphia real estate reaches a record high of $5,537,106,000.

January 26. Announcement made that Harrisburg is the first place in the nation to be used to test the automobile-installed radio telephone. Greensburg and Carnegie in Western Pennsylvania are announced also as the first in the nation to be offered push-button telephone service.

March 21. Governor Scranton wins bitter fight to reform unemployment compensation law.

April 28. Primary election upsets M. Harvey Taylor, longtime Republican leader. Genevieve Blatt wins Democratic nomination to U. S. Senate, first woman in Pennsylvania to run for this office. Governor Scranton receives largest write-in vote for President in state's history.

June–July, 1964. Governor William W. Scranton becomes active candidate for Republican Presidential nomination, opposing what he termed "Goldwaterism" in the Republican Party.

October 24. William Penn Memorial and Archives Building completed.

What to Read about Pennsylvania

Rather than burden the text with footnotes or chapter bibliographies, which must be referred to laboriously, if indeed at all, by the average reader, it has been my thought that those who use this volume might wish to read beyond its pages into some of the riches of Pennsylvania history that I have found most useful and rewarding in my writing. These references are designed to encourage further reading. Many of the older and heavier tomes have been omitted in favor of more recent and more readable books that are at the same time representative of sound scholarship and writing on Pennsylvania history. Most of these books contain further specialized bibliographies, and who knows but that many a reader may be led to explore in some detail many phases of the story of Pennsylvania revealed in these pages. After all, it is impossible to list all of the books and articles of importance on Pennsylvania's rich history. It is hardly necessary any longer to do so because the voluminous *Bibliography of Pennsylvania History* (Pennsylvania Historical and Museum Commission, 1957) which will be brought up to date from time to time, is a full-scale bibliography.

My own earlier books, *Pennsylvania, Titan of Industry* (Lewis Historical Publishing Co., New York, 1948), in three volumes, may be found useful for economic history, and *Pennsylvania, the Keystone State* (American Historical Publishing Co., New York, 1956), has more detail on most aspects of the state's history, and one volume of original source materials. *The Pennsylvania Magazine of History and Biography,* distinguished publication of The Historical Society of Pennsylvania, in Philadelphia; *Pennsylvania History,* the quarterly of the Pennsylvania Historical Association, with offices at Pennsylvania State University, University Park; and the *Western Pennsylvania Historical Magazine,* of the Historical Society of Western Pennsylvania, Pittsburgh, are indispensable sources for fine articles and frequent published

journals, letters, or diaries. It is my earnest hope that the selections made here will not only be useful as references, but will also encourage further reading. For better or for worse, these are my suggestions. In order to avoid frequent repetition, I have grouped the suggested readings into larger, rather than single-chapter subjects.

THE EARLY YEARS AND THROUGH
THE REVOLUTION

For the geographical story of Pennsylvania, the volume by Raymond E. and Marion Murphy, *Pennsylvania, a Regional Geography* (Penns Valley Publishers, State College, 1937) continues to be a standby. The Bureau of Topographic and Geologic Survey of the Department of Internal Affairs, Harrisburg, has published specialized studies through the years, and recently started a series of popular educational bulletins, among which are *Pennsylvania Geology Summarized; Common Fossils of Pennsylvania;* and *Common Rocks and Minerals of Pennsylvania.* The earlier special bulletins of the Geographical Society of Philadelphia are worth while where available. Recent work of note on Pennsylvania Indian life and culture includes *Susquehannock Miscellany* (Pennsylvania Historical and Museum Commission, hereafter given as PHMC, 1959); *Indians in Pennsylvania,* by Paul A. W. Wallace (PHMC, 1961); *Prehistory of the Upper Ohio Valley,* by William J. Mayer-Oakes (Carnegie Museum, 1955); *Conrad Weiser, Friend of Colonist and Mohawk,* by Paul A. W. Wallace (Oxford University Press, 1945); and Anthony W. Wallace's *Teedyuscung, King of the Delawares* (University of Pennsylvania Press, 1949). The *Pennsylvania Archaeologist,* quarterly of the Society for Pennsylvania Archaeology, is indispensable for specialized articles, and the special studies of the Carnegie Museum in Pittsburgh should be watched for excellent material resulting from field researches. Almost all earlier books and articles on the Pennsylvania Indian are very unreliable. The work of Amandus Johnson in his two-volume *Swedish Settlements on the Delaware* (Appleton-Century, 1911) has been hard to surpass. Christopher Ward's *The Dutch and Swedes on the Delaware, 1609–1664* (University of Pennsylvania Press, 1930) and *New Sweden on the Delaware* (University of Pennsylvania Press, 1938) are readable and reliable. C. A. Weslager has made contributions to both the archaeology and the early Swedish history of the Delaware Valley in *Dutch Explorers, Traders and Settlers in the Delaware Valley, 1609–1664* (University of Pennsylvania Press, 1961).

Material on William Penn and the story of the early Quaker beginnings is voluminous, and some worthy additions have been made in recent years. Samuel Janney's *The Life of William Penn,* published back in 1852, is still worth reading. The work of Sidney G. Fisher, *The True William Penn* (Lippincott, 1900; reprinted 1932), and his discussion of settlement in *The Quaker Colonies* (Chronicles of America, Yale University Press, 1919), are very worthy of attention. More recent important works include Edward C. O. Beatty, *William Penn as a Social Philosopher* (Columbia University Press, 1939). Frederick B. Tolles, distinguished Quaker historian, with *The Witness of William Penn* (Macmillan, 1957) and *Quakers and the Atlantic Culture* (Macmillan, 1960), has done brilliant work on both Penn and the basic Quaker influence and contribution. The tercentenary of Penn's birth produced *Remember William Penn* (PHMC, 1945) as a series of essays on Penn's life and work, along with the reprinting of Penn's *Some Fruits of Solitude, More Fruits of Solitude* and a detailed chronology. *Tributes to William Penn,* published at the same time, contains several important tributes. William C. Comfort's *William Penn, 1644–1718* (University of Pennsylvania Press, 1944) is a part of the parade of Penn materials. Hildegarde Dolson's *William Penn, Quaker Hero* (Landmark—Random House, 1961) is a recent, popular biography of Penn, very readable and presenting Penn as a human being, which has not very often been the case. Critical evaluation of the Holy Experiment and accompanying treatment of Pennsylvania political history

through the colonial era is provided in some really new studies. *David Lloyd, Colonial Lawmaker* (University of Washington Press, 1959), by Roy N. Lokker, is good on the anti-Penn political leadership. Theodore Thayer's *Pennsylvania Politics and the Growth of Democracy, 1740–1776* (PHMC, 1953) surveys the entire political scene for this key period. *William Penn's Holy Experiment, the Founding of Pennsylvania, 1681–1701* (Temple University Publications, 1962) is the product of research by Edwin B. Bronner into this significant era of the problems of Penn as a liberal proprietor. The *Pennsylvania Archives* (*Colonial Records* series) contains printed sources.

The peopling of Pennsylvania by major and minor ethnic groups has been the victim of much glorification by the societies organized to perpetuate the memory of each group, and the publications of these societies need to be read with several grains of salt. The Pennsylvania Historical Association launched in 1948 a series of three scholarly booklets, which include Guy S. Klett, *The Scotch-Irish in Pennsylvania;* William S. Comfort, *The Quakers;* and Russell W. Gilbert, *A Picture of the Pennsylvania Germans,* and all are available through the association's office at University Park. The various works by Frederick Tolles, eminent Quaker historian cited elsewhere, are very fine studies of Quakerism. Wayland F. Dunaway, *The Scotch-Irish of Colonial Pennsylvania* (University of North Carolina Press, 1944); Ralph Wood, *The Pennsylvania Germans* (Princeton University Press, 1942); James G. Leyburn, *The Scotch-Irish, a Social History* (University of North Carolina Press, 1962); Frederic Klees, *The Pennsylvania Dutch* (Macmillan, 1950); Jesse L. Rosenberger, *The Pennsylvania Germans* (University of Chicago Press, 1923); John Hostettler, *Amish Society* (John Hopkins Press, 1963); William I. Schreiber, *Our Amish Neighbors* (University of Chicago Press, 1962) are all modern scholarly studies. John Hostettler also did a booklet on *The Amish* and one on *The Mennonites,* published and widely distributed by the Herald Press, Scottdale, Pennsylvania.

The boundary disputes of Pennsylvania receive treatment in several places. Hubertis Cummings prepared a fine booklet on *The Mason and Dixon*

Line (Department of Internal Affairs, Harrisburg, 1963). The Connecticut story is best reviewed in the essay and documents contained in the four volume *The Susquehanna Company Papers* (Cornell University Press, 1962f) edited by Julian Boyd for the Wyoming Historical and Geological Society at Wilkes-Barre. Solon and Elizabeth Buck's *The Planting of Civilization in Western Pennsylvania* (University of Pittsburgh Press, 1939) has a very readable history of the Virginia controversy, and Thomas Abernethy's *Western Lands and the American Revolution* (Appleton-Century, 1937) is also helpful. Charles Miner's *History of Wyoming* (1845) and O. J. Harvey's *History of Wilkes-Barre and the Wyoming Valley* (1909) are important local sources on the Connecticut claims and settlements. *Pennsylvania's Boundaries,* by William A. Russ, Jr. (Pennsylvania Historical Association, 1964) is a recent and comprehensive review of the subject. Readable source material of interest on Virginia's claims and activity are found in the *George Mercer Papers Relating to the Ohio Company of Virginia* (University of Pittsburgh Press, 1954) edited by Lois Mulkearn, and the *Western Journals of John May, Ohio Company Agent* (Historical and Philosophical Society of Ohio, 1961) edited by Dwight L. Smith.

Much new material has been brought to light in recent years on the French and Indian War era, mainly through efforts of the Pennsylvania Historical and Museum Commission. The commission has been able thus far to publish only one volume in *The Papers of Colonel Henry Bouquet,* titled *The Forbes Expedition* (PHMC, 1951), but it covers the climax of the war. *Wilderness Chronicles of Northwestern Pennsylvania* (PHMC 1941), *The French Invasion of Western Pennsylvania, 1753* (PHMC, 1954), by Donald H. Kent, and *Forts on the Pennsylvania Frontier, 1753–1758* (PHMC, 1960), by William A. Hunter, embody this new material. The monumental work of Lawrence Gipson, *The British Empire Before the American Revolution* (Knopf, 1939) is important. Thayer's *Pennsylvania Politics and the Growth of Democracy, 1740–1776,* cited earlier, is important to understanding the politics of the entire era down to the Revolution. *The Papers of Benjamin Franklin* (Yale University Press) is rich in sources. Hubertis

Cummings' *Richard Peters* (University of Pennsylvania Press, 1944) is a fine biography of an important figure. Books cited later on the Indian trade help in understanding the resulting war. *George Washington in the Ohio Valley* (University of Pittsburgh Press, 1955) is sound reading. Lee McCardell, *Ill-Starred General Braddock* (University of Pittsburgh Press, 1958) is an interesting study of this expedition. Theodore Thayer's *Israel Pemberton, King of the Quakers* (Historical Society of Pennsylvania, 1943) shows trade in relation to the frontier and its problems. *James Burd, Frontier Defender* (University of Pennsylvania Press, 1941), by Lily Lee Nixon, is a biography of one of the worthies of the era. Paul A. W. Wallace, *Thirty Thousand Miles with John Heckewelder* (University of Pittsburgh Press, 1958) presents the story of the Moravian missions in the Ohio country. *Council Fires on the Upper Ohio* (University of Pittsburgh Press, 1940), by Randolph C. Downes, is a comprehensive account of Indian affairs. *Drums in the Forest* (Historical Society of Western Pennsylvania, Pittsburgh, 1958), by Alfred P. James and Charles Stotz, is the story of Forts Duquesne and Pitt. Alfred P. James, *Writings of General John Forbes* (Collegiate Press, 1938) is excellent source material in a small package. Buck and Buck, *The Planting of Civilization in Western Pennsylvania,* cited earlier, is good reading. This book can be cited for the entire early period of western Pennsylvania history, and includes its politics, economic growth, and early cultural life.

The total colonial economy of Pennsylvania has not been well treated. The agricultural aspect, which is naturally of basic importance, has been given a fine general treatment and interpretation in Stevenson W. Fletcher's *Pennsylvania Agriculture and Farm Life, 1640–1840* (PHMC, 1950); as the title indicates, it serves later periods also. Arthur C. Bining's *Pennsylvania Iron Manufacture in the Eighteenth Century* (PHMC, 1938) is the comprehensive work on this industry. Frederick Tolles in *Meeting House and Counting House* (University of North Carolina Press, 1948) provides an incisive analysis of Quaker mercantile affairs, as well as important commentary upon Quaker society and culture. *Pelts and Palisades, the Story of Fur* (Dietz Press, 1959) has a popular story of the value of the fur trade. *Diplomacy and Indian Gifts* (Stanford University Press, 1950), by Wilbur R. Jack; *George Croghan, Wilderness Diplomat* (University of North Carolina Press, 1959), by Nicholas B. Wainwright and *William Trent and the West* (Archives Publishing Co., Harrisburg, 1947), by Sewell E. Slick, deal with persons prominent in the Indian trade and its relationships to diplomacy and the French and Indian War. Paul A. W. Wallace in his *Conrad Weiser* (University of Pennsylvania Press, 1945) is in the same vein. *George Croghan and the Westward Movement, 1741–1782* (Arthur H. Clark, Cleveland, 1926), by Albert Volwiler, is an older study. *The Rise of an Iron Community, an Economic History of Lebanon County, 1740–1865* (Lebanon County Historical Society, 1950–52), by Frederic K. Miller, is a very detailed study for the colonial and later charcoal-iron industry. Older works such as Percy H. Bidwell and John I. Falconer, *History of Agriculture in the Northern United States, 1620–1860* (Washington, 1925); Victor S. Clark, *History of Manufactures in the United States, 1607–1860* (Washington, 1916); J. L. Bishop, *History of American Manufactures from 1608–1860* (Philadelphia, 1860); B. H. Meyer and C. MacGill, *History of Transportation in the United States Before 1860* (Washington, 1917) contain many references to the Pennsylvania economy.

County and local histories are worth consulting, and the numerous general articles and source accounts in the *Pennsylvania Magazine of History,* such as those by Marion V. Brewington, "Maritime Philadelphia, 1609–1837" (April, 1939) and "The Working People of Philadelphia from Colonial Times . . ." (July, 1950), along with many others are worth reading. Arthur L. Jensen's *The Maritime Commerce of Colonial Philadelphia* (University of Wisconsin Press, 1963) is a fine study. Charles A. Hanna's two volume *The Wilderness Trail* (Putnam, 1911) and Arthur B. Hulbert's *Historic Highways of America* series (1902–05) though old are also not to be neglected for early Indian trade and paths. Wallace's *Indians in Pennsylvania,* already mentioned, is a reference on the Indian trade.

Similar neglect of Pennsylvania cultural history

in the colonial era is evident, though more has been written on this subject. Carl Bridenbaugh's *Rebels and Gentlemen* (Reynal & Hitchcock, 1942) *The Colonial Craftsman* (New York University Press, 1950) and *Cities in the Wilderness* (Ronald Press, 1938) provided penetrating studies of the colonial life and culture of Philadelphia and of the total colonial culture. Harold D. Eberlein and Cortlandt Hubbard in their *Portrait of a Colonial City, Philadelphia* (Lippincott, 1939) did an admirable study of colonial and later Philadelphia. *Penn's Great Town, 250 Years of Philadelphia Architecture* (University of Pennsylvania Press, 1961), by George Tatum, is superb, and not limited to the colonial era. *American Science and Invention, a Pictorial History* (Simon and Schuster, 1954), by Mitchell Wilson, is broader than colonial times. *The Pursuit of Science in Revolutionary America* (University of North Carolina, 1956), by Brooke Hindle, has Philadelphia material. Lewis B. Wright, *The Cultural Life of the American Colonies, 1607–1763* (Harper, 1957) has Pennsylvania material. Fletcher, cited before, is important for rural life. Frances Lichten's *Folk Art of Rural Pennsylvania* (Scribner's, 1946) was followed by John Joseph Stoudt's *Pennsylvania Folk-Art* (Schlecters, Allentown, 1948), *The Muhlenbergs of Pennsylvania,* by Dr. Paul A. W. Wallace (University of Pennsylvania Press, 1950) covers more than the colonial era. *James B. Logan and the Culture of Provincial America* (Little, Brown, 1957), by Frederick Tolles, is a delayed recognition of the importance of this figure. Almost anything written about Benjamin Franklin is worth reading. *The Papers of Benjamin Franklin,* mentioned before, are fascinating. *Two Hundred Years in Cumberland County* (Hamilton Library and Historical Association, Carlisle, 1951) is a worthwhile volume not only for this subject and period, but for other periods. T. J. Wertenbaker, *The Founding of American Civilization; the Middle Colonies* (Scribner's, 1938) is useful. *James Wilson* (University of North Carolina Press, 1956), by Charles P. Smith, is a sound biography of a long-neglected figure in political and other affairs. Again the local histories should be consulted, with caution, and in particular the *Pennsyl-*

vania Magazine of History and Biography for scattered but significant contributions in articles and sources. It is not possible to mention this invaluable publication at every step, and any interested person should consult its *Index* as well as the *Guide to the Manuscript Collections of The Historical Society of Pennsylvania*. The contributions of the society to the history of Pennsylvania are, in Hollywood terms, "simply colossal." Scharf and Wescott's *History of Philadelphia* and Watson's *Annals of Philadelphia* are on our list of "oldies" but still are worth a reading.

Among biographies of importance for colonial cultural development not already listed are *David Rittenhouse, Astronomer—Patriot, 1732-1796* (University of Pennsylvania Press, 1946), by Edward Ford; *The Autobiography of Benjamin Rush* (Princeton University Press, 1951, 2 volumes), edited by Lyman Butterfield; *William Smith, Educator and Churchman, 1727-1803* (University of Pennsylvania Press, 1943), by Albert Gegenheimer; *John and William Bartram* (University of Pennsylvania Press, 1940), by Ernest Earnest; *Johann Conrad Beissel* (University of Pennsylvania Press, 1942), by Walter C. Klein; *Friend Anthony Benezet,* by George S. Brooks (University of Pennsylvania Press, 1937). Education is treated most fully in Saul Sack's *History of Higher Education in Pennsylvania* (PHMC, 1963). It covers in two volumes the story from colonial times to the present. Fletcher T. Woody tells the story of *Early Quaker Education in Pennsylvania* (Columbia University Press, 1920), and C. L. Maurer does the same for *Early Lutheran Education in Pennsylvania* (Dorrance, Philadelphia, 1932). *Dwellings of Colonial America* (University of North Carolina Press, 1950), by Thomas T. Waterman, has a chapter on the Delaware Valley. *Andrew Bradford, Colonial Journalist* (University of Delaware Press, 1949), by A. J. De Armond, and various biographies of Franklin, along with his *Autobiography,* are good for early journalism. Douglas McMurtrie's *A History of Printing in the United States* (Bowker, 1936) has Pennsylvania sidelights. Luella Wright's *The Literary Life of the Early Friends, 1650-1725* (Columbia University Press, 1932) is useful. Studies of various religious de-

nominations and special articles on their development need to be read for religious history, which has not been covered in any comprehensive way. Studies on the Scotch-Irish, the Pennsylvania Germans, and the Quakers contain material on the religious life and culture of these groups. Buck and Buck has material on early missionary efforts in western Pennsylvania. The Beissel biography tells the story of this powerful leader of the Seventh Day Baptists at Ephrata. Delber W. Clark's *The World of Justus Falckner* (Muhlenberg Press, 1946) is an excellent story of the work of an early Lutheran pastor. Wallace's book on the *The Muhlenbergs of Pennsylvania* cited earlier is good for the Lutheran story. William W. Sweet, *Religion in Colonial America* (Scribner's, 1942) has material on Pennsylvania religious life in the first volume. C. H. Maxon, *The Great Awakening in the Middle Colonies* (University of Chicago Press, 1920) treats the religious revival movement both during and after the colonial era. *Journals of Charles Beatty, 1762-1769* (Pennsylvania State University Press, 1961), edited by Guy Klett, are most interesting. These, along with local histories, are a valuable source. *Philip Vickers Fithian: Journal, 1775-1776* (Princeton University Press, 1934), edited by Albion and Dodson, is another interesting journal of a mission worker.

The Revolutionary era has had the benefit of much new study since Charles H. Lincoln explored it in 1901. J. Paul Selsam, *The Pennsylvania Constitution of 1776, a Study in Revolutionary Democracy* (University of Pennsylvania Press, 1936) added new and important material and interpretations. Robert L. Brunhouse in his *Counter-Revolution in Pennsylvania, 1776-1790* (PHMC, 1942) gave an equally detailed study of the politics of the Revolutionary period. Thayer, cited earlier, brought the story down to 1776 in terms of colonial politics which had to do with the Pennsylvania reaction. Kenneth R. Rossman, *Thomas Mifflin and the Politics of the American Revolution* (University of North Carolina Press, 1952) and Richard C. Knopf's *Anthony Wayne* (University of Pittsburgh Press, 1960) are important biographies, and of course anything on George Washington, of which Douglas Freeman is best, is worth reading for the portions bearing on Pennsylvania. Van Wyck Mason's *Valley Forge* (Doubleday, 1950) and Harry Emerson Wildes's *Valley Forge* (Macmillan, 1938) have been added to by a more scholarly account by Arthur H. Bills, *Valley Forge, the Making of an Army* (Harper, 1952). Julian Boyd, *Anglo-American Union* (University of Pennsylvania Press, 1941), has information on Tory Joseph Galloway's ideas. Clarence L. Ver Steeg, *Robert Morris, Revolutionary Financier* (University of Pennsylvania Press, 1954) is the best and latest Morris biography.

Russell J. Ferguson, *Early Western Pennsylvania Politics* (University of Pittsburgh Press, 1938) begins with the year 1773 and from then until 1820 is the best interpretation of western affairs in the period. The James Wilson biography and many other works cited earlier are applicable. John B. McMaster and Frederick D. Stone, *Pennsylvania and the Federal Constitution, 1787–1788* (Historical Society of Pennsylvania, 1888) is an older book but ever valuable. Louis Hartz, *Economic Policy and Democratic Thought: Pennsylvania, 1776–1860* (Harvard University Press, 1948) shows a Beardian interpretation of economic influence on politics from the early days of the Revolution to the Civil War. Biographies of worthies cited earlier are useful through the Revolution. The campaigns of the Revolution on Pennsylvania soil are reviewed, naturally, in all the standard and most recent histories of the Revolutionary War. J. C. Miller's *Triumph of Freedom, 1775–1783* (Little Brown, 1948) is one of the most interesting. John R. Alden *The American Revolution, 1775–1783* (Harper, 1954) in the New American Nation series is also a recent treatment. Edmund C. Burnett's *The Continental Congress* (Macmillan, 1941) is the standard book on this subject. Allan Nevins in *The American States During and After the Revolution, 1775–1789* (Macmillan, 1941) has good Pennsylvania history. Wilbur H. Siebert's *The Loyalists of Pennsylvania* (Ohio State University, Columbus, 1920) is the standard book on the Tory influence, and Julian Boyd's *Anglo-American Unity: Joseph Galloway's Plan to Preserve the British Empire* (University of Pennsylvania Press, 1941) has a valuable essay on Loyalist viewpoints.

THROUGH THE CIVIL WAR

The political history of this era has had the benefit of several fine studies, which began with Philip S. Klein's *Pennsylvania Politics, 1817–1832: a Game Without Rules* (Historical Society of Pennsylvania, 1940) and continued the story of *The Whig Party in Pennsylvania* (Columbia University Press, 1922), by Henry R. Mueller. Harry M. Tinkcom, *Republicans and Federalists. 1790–1801* (PHMC, 1950) covered this period, and S. W. Higginbotham's *The Keystone in the Democratic Arch: Pennsylvania Politics, 1801–1816* (PHMC, 1952) adds information. Leland Baldwin's *Whiskey Rebels* (University of Pittsburgh Press, 1939) has details on this story. Russell Ferguson, *Early Western Pennsylvania Politics* (University of Pittsburgh Press, 1958), and Buck and Buck on the political affairs of western Pennsylvania should not be neglected. The recent definitive biography, *President James Buchanan* (Pennsylvania State University Press, 1962), by Philip S. Klein, covers in detail not only a man but a key figure in Pennsylvania politics with inevitable sidelights. Sister Geary's *A History of Third Parties in Pennsylvania, 1840–1860* (Catholic University Press, 1938), and Roy A. Billington's *The Protestant* Crusade (Macmillan, 1938) help with the fringe-party anti-Catholic story. Eugene P. Link's *Democratic-Republican Societies, 1790–1800* (Columbia University Press, 1942) is a meritorious and detailed work setting a stage for later developments.

William Brigance, *Jeremiah Sullivan Black* (University of Pennsylvania Press, 1934) is a fine biography of a neglected figure. Charles B. Going, *David Wilmot, Free Soiler* (Appleton-Century, 1924) is in the same category. Richard N. Current, *Old Thad Stevens* (University of Wisconsin Press, 1942) is a more recent book of merit, though James A. Woodburn (Bobbs-Merrill, 1913) and Thomas T. Woodley (Stackpole, Harrisburg, 1937) wrote worthwhile biographies of Stevens. Dwight L. Drummond *Anti-Slavery Origins of the Civil War* (University of Michigan Press, 1939) is valuable for this background. Arthur M. Schlesinger, Jr., *The Age of Jackson* (Little Brown, 1945), and Roy F. Nichols, *The Disruption of American*

Democracy (Macmillan, 1948) are general studies.

Allan Nevins, *The Ordeal of the Union, 1847–1857; The Emergence of Lincoln, 1857–1861; The War for the Union: the Improvised War, 1861–1862;* and *The War for the Union: War Become Revolution, 1862–1863* (Scribner's, 1960) form a four-volume history of which the first two deal with the historical background of the Civil War and which are hard to surpass for detail and insight into the history of the era. Bruce Catton's *Glory Road* has the Gettysburg story. *Gettysburg* (Rutgers University Press, 1948), edited by Earl S. Miers and Richard A. Brown, is a very readable source book. *Northern Railroads in the Civil War* (Columbia University Press, 1952), by T. Weber, is useful for Pennsylvania railroading. Janet Book's *Northern Rendezvous* (Telegraph Press, Harrisburg, 1951) is a very readable account of Camp Curtin at Harrisburg. Edward Nichols, *Toward Gettysburg, a Biography of General John F. Reynolds* (Pennsylvania State University Press, 1958) is excellent. The works of Samuel P. Bates in his five-volume *History of the Pennsylvania Volunteers, 1861–65* (1869–71), *Martial Deeds of Pennsylvanians* (1876), and *Battle of Gettysburg* (1875) prove the worth of older works on the role of the state in the Civil War. Alexander K. McClure's two-volume *Old Time Notes of Pennsylvania* (1905) is useful, and actually source material.

The social and cultural history of Pennsylvania from 1790 through the Civil War deserves more attention in terms of research and special study. Fletcher's story of Pennsylvania farm life, which ended in 1840, is picked up in the following volume published by the Pennsylvania Historical and Museum Commission, titled *Pennsylvania Agriculture and Country Life, 1840–1940* (1955) and is invaluable for life in rural Pennsylvania. *Charles Willson Peale, 1741–1827* (American Philosophical Society, 1947), by Charles C. Sellers in two volumes contains much of interest. Harold Dickson's *One Hundred Pennsylvania Buildings* (Bald Eagle Press, State College, 1954) and *Pennsylvania Painters* (Pennsylvania State University, 1955) are fine sketches in architecture and art for this period as well as later years. *Historic Philadelphia* (American Philosophical Society, 1953) is a delightful book on the queen city of the state. Elizabeth Pennell's *Our Philadelphia* (Lippincott, 1914) is illustrated by Joseph Pennell. Charles M. Stotz did *The Early Architecture of Western Pennsylvania* (William Helburn, Pittsburgh, 1936) for the Buhl Foundation. Talbot Hamlin's *Greek Revival Architecture in America* (Oxford University Press, 1944) has a good Philadelphia chapter, and Tatum's study cited earlier is excellent on the city's architecture and architects.

The Benjamin Rush works already cited also are good for this period. Earl D. Bond's *Doctor Kirkbride and His Mental Hospital* (Lippincott, 1947) is a good biography. Howard K. Petry edited *A Century of Medicine, 1848–1948* for the Medical Society of Pennsylvania in 1952. Articles by Richard Shryock on the history of medicine should be checked in historical journals. His *The Development of Modern Medicine* (University of Pennsylvania Press, 1947) is excellent, also *Medicine and Society in America* (New York University Press, 1960). Books on the history of science, medicine, and technology that have more or less Pennsylvania interest include John W. Oliver, *History of American Technology* (Ronald Press, 1956); Bernard Jaffe, *Men of Science in America* (Simon & Schuster, 1944); Henry B. Shafer *The American Medical Profession, 1783–1850* (Columbia University Press, 1936); Edgar Fahs Smith, *Chemistry in America,* (Appleton, 1914); *Joseph Priestley, Selections from His Writings* (Pennsylvania State University Press, 1962), edited by Ira V. Brown, is excellent. Dwight R. Guthrie, *John McMillan, Apostle of Presbyterianism in the West* (University of Pittsburgh Press, 1952) is basic for religious history.

Material on rural education is found in Fletcher. Louise Walsh, *History and Organization of Education in Pennsylvania* (Grosse, Indiana, Pa., 1930) brings the story down to this date with many source quotations. James P. Wickersham's *A History of Education in Pennsylvania* (Lancaster, 1886) is still an old standby. The volume on higher education by Sacks already cited is indispensable. Those interested in a particular college or university will want to look for its history and many have been written recently for centennials or older anniversaries have appeared. Robert

Mohr's *Thomas Henry Burrowes, (1805-1871)* (University of Pennsylvania Press, 1946) is a study in ideas and trends. Local histories are important for the story at this level.

General works that can be cited as having better than average references to Pennsylvania affairs are Ray Billington, *The Prostestant Crusade, 1800-1860* (Rinehart, 1952) for religion; Alice Tyler, *Freedom's Ferment* (University of Minnesota Press, 1944) for religious and reform upheavals; Edward D. Branch, *The Sentimental Years, 1836-1860* (Appleton, 1934); George R. Steward, *American Ways of Life* (Doubleday, 1954); J. T. Howard, *Our American Music, Three Hundred Years of It* (Crowell, 1955); Arthur H. Quinn, *A History of the American Drama* (F. S. Crofts, New York, 1943); W. G. Bleyer *Main Currents in the History of American Journalism* (Houghton, Mifflin, 1927). Biographical studies of particular note include Claude M. Newlin, *The Life and Writings of Hugh Henry Brackenridge* (Princeton University Press, 1932); Harry R. Warfel, *Charles Brockden Brown* (University of Florida Press, 1949); Kenneth W. Rowe, *Matthew Carey* (Johns Hopkins Press, 1933); Merle M. Odgers, *Alexander Dallas Bache, Scientist and Inventor, 1806-1867,* (University of Pennsylvania Press, 1947); Burton A. Konkle, *Joseph Hopkinson, 1770-1842* (University of Pennsylvania Press, 1931); Agnes A. Gilchrist, *William Strickland, Architect and Engineer* (University of Pennsylvania Press, 1950); Richmond C. Beatty, *Bayard Taylor, Laureate of the Gilded Age* (University of Oklahoma Press, 1936.)

The economic history of the era is found for the most part in books already cited. Fletcher's story of agriculture and farm life, Bidwell and Falconer on agriculture, Clark's study of manufacturing, and MacGill on transportation shed light on Pennsylvania before 1860; James W. Livingood in his *Philadelphia-Baltimore Trade Rivalry, 1780-1860* (PHMC, 1947), and Catherine L. Reiser, *Pittsburgh's Commercial Development, 1800-1850* (PHMC, 1951) are detailed accounts. A. W. Bishop, *The State Works of Pennsylvania* (1907) remains best. William Sullivan, *The Industrial Worker in Pennsylvania, 1800-1840* (PHMC, 1955) has the labor story and sheds light on labor's influence on politics as well as its organization and activity. Howard Eavenson, *The First Century and a Quarter of the American Coal Industry* (Pittsburgh, 1942) is the best treatment of coal. James M. Swank's *History of the Manufacture of Iron . . . and Particularly in the United States from Colonial Times to 1891* (Philadelphia, 1892) and *Introduction to a History of Iron Making and Coal Mining in Pennsylvania* (Philadelphia, 1878) are old but essential. See also Stevens, *Pennsylvania, Titan of Industry,* previously cited. Arthur Bining's *Pennsylvania's Iron and Steel Industry* (Pennsylvania Historical Association, 1954) is a brief general bulletin. The birth of the oil industry has a considerable literature; within it Paul Giddens's *Birth of the Petroleum Industry* (Macmillan, 1938) and *Pennsylvania Petroleum, 1750-1872, a Documentary History* (PHMC, 1947) stand out. Ernest Miller's *Pennsylvania Oil Industry* (1954) is another Pennsylvania Historical Association booklet, along with R. D. Billinger's *Pennsylvania's Coal Industry* (Pennsylvania Historical Association, 1954).

Early days in the oil fields are treated in the first volume of Allan Nevins, *John D. Rockefeller* (Scribner's, 1940). Hildegarde Dolson's *The Great Oildorada* (Random House, 1959); Harry Botsford, *The Valley of Oil* (Hastings House, 1946); Herbert Asbury, *The Golden Flood* (Knopf, 1942) are popular and colorful treatments of the oil boom. J. H. Newton (editor), *History of Venango County and Incidentally of Petroleum, Etc.* (1879) is worth attention for early local color. Ida Tarbell's famous *The History of the Standard Oil Company* (McClure, Phillips & Co., New York, 1904) came from the pen of a woman born in the oil regions. S. J. M. Eaton's *Petroleum: A History of the Oil Regions of Venango County,* published in Philadelphia in 1866, is one of the best of the early contemporary accounts. Andrew Cone and Walter R. Johns published a book called *Petrolia* (Appleton-Century, 1870) which is another fine contemporary story. The monthly *Bulletin* of the Department of Internal Affairs in Harrisburg contains a wealth of articles on mineral industry in the state, and are worth hunting out. Thomas P. Cowan, *Nicholas Biddle, 1786-1844* (University of Chicago Press, 1959); Henrietta M. Larson,

Jay Cooke, Private Banker (Harvard University Press, 1936); Ellis P. Oberholtzer, *Jay Cooke, Financier of the Civil War* (G. H. Jacobs, Philadelphia, 1907); John B. McMaster, *The Life and Times of Stephen Girard* (Lippincott, 1918); Harry E. Wilde's *Lonely Midas* (Farrar and Rinehart, 1943) are fine biographies shedding light on trade and finance.

The history of railroading in the state in the era remains to be written as a whole. New material is contained in my *Pennsylvania, the Keystone State.* W. Van Metre, *Transportation in the United States* (Brooklyn Foundation Press, 1950) is a general reference. Thomas C. Cochran's *Railroad Leaders, 1845–1890* (Harvard University Press, 1953) is helpful. Louis C. Hunter's *Steamboats on the Western Rivers* (Harvard University Press, 1949) has Pennsylvania material, as does Philip D. Jordan's *The National Road* (Bobbs-Merrill, 1948). Emory R. Johnson, and others, *History of Domestic and Foreign Commerce of the United States,* (Washington, 2 volumes, 1922) is a notable reference work with Pennsylvania materials.

SINCE THE CIVIL WAR

The writings on this period considerably overlap the turn of the century and an effort to break them down as to the period from the Civil War to 1900 or since 1900 would be repetitious. For this reason I have considered this entire era as a unit. It should be kept in mind also that books on recent history are notable for their absence, and especially since 1900. I must thus refer readers to my own works, such as *Pennsylvania, Titan of Industry* and *Pennsylvania, the Keystone State,* cited earlier, as containing more detail on the period since 1865, though lacking certain new materials even more recently available. The materials on more recent Pennsylvania history, though on the increase, remain deficient. The references that can be cited and are readily available to the reader are few and far between, or simply do not exist. The bibliography for this period, therefore, is necessarily rather sparse.

There are several books of special interest for the political history of the period, though much of it must be researched from newspapers and other contemporary sources. The source material on Pennsylvania governors down to 1902 is continued in the *Pennsylvania Archives,* Fourth Series, and is of course of value for the years before as well as after 1865. McClure's *Oldtime Notes* is actually source material. Mathew S. Quay's *Pennsylvania Politics; the Campaign of 1900* (Philadelphia, 1901) is a sample of Quay's political oratory and ideas. Frank A. Burr's *Life and Achievements of James Adams Beaver* (Philadelphia, 1882) is good as a sample of campaign biography of the times. James T. Du Bois and Gertrude S. Mathews wrote *Galusha Grow* (Houghton Mifflin, 1917), which is good on Grow's leadership as an independent in politics after the Civil War. Harry W. Tinkcom, *John White Geary, Soldier-Statesman, 1819–1873* (University of Pennsylvania Press, 1940); Nelson McGeary, *Gifford Pinchot, Forester-Politician* (Princeton University Press, 1960), is invaluable for politics of the Pinchot days; Martin Faushold, *Gifford Pinchot, Bull Moose Progressive* (Syracuse University Press, 1961); Ann Hawkes Hutton, *The Pennsylvanian—Joseph R. Grundy* (Dorrance, Philadelphia, 1962) are significant biographies. Autobiographical accounts of value include *William S. Vare, My Forty Years in Politics* (Ronald Swain, Philadelphia, 1933); Joseph F. Guffey, *Seventy Years on the Red Fire Wagon* (privately printed, 1952); George Wharton Pepper, *Philadelphia Lawyer, An Autobiography* (Lippincott, 1944); Gifford Pinchot, *Breaking New Ground* (Harcourt, Brace, 1947); Samuel Pennypacker, *The Autobiography of a Pennsylvanian* (Winston, 1918). Lincoln Steffens' *Autobiography of Lincoln Steffens* (Harcourt, Brace, 1931) and *Shame of the Cities* (McClure, New York, 1904) are famous as *the* exposé of graft and corruption in Philadelphia and Pittsburgh. Frank Evans in his forthcoming *Pennsylvania Politics, 1872–1877* will add an excellent study for the Pennsylvania Historical and Museum Commission series. Walter Davenport's *Power and Glory, the Life of Boise Penrose* (Putnam, 1931) is a good journalistic treatment of this powerful figure.

Unfortunately, nothing of worth has been done on the Camerons or Quay, and Pennsylvania politics has been generally ignored in books dealing with national affairs. The evolution of state government has not received much attention in terms of a history of its more recent growth. *The Pennsylvania Manual* is informative on the organization of and change in state government if used over a period of years. *County Government and Archives in Pennsylvania* (PHMC, 1947) edited by S. K. Stevens and Donald H. Kent is good for the evolution of county government from early times to the present. *The Pennsylvania Citizen,* by Elinor S. Deatrick (Rutgers University Press, 1958) is a very useful and readable book on contemporary state and local government, but lacking in any references. *Pennsylvania at War, 1941-1945* (PHMC, 1946), by S. K. Stevens and Marvin Schegel, provides a full history of the Pennsylvania war effort; *Pennsylvania, 1947: a Survey* and *Pennsylvania, 1948: a Survey* (PHMC, 1948 and 1949), by S. K. Stevens and Norman Wilkinson, were an effort to keep up with contemporary history with an annual survey, but this fell by the wayside because of the burden of writing and cost of printing. The volumes for these years are useful, and their content is broader than politics. Pennsylvania governors customarily have issued a *Final Message to the General Assembly* consisting of a review of their four years in office. While they naturally are somewhat personal and laudatory they are nevertheless a valuable source of information of the operations of the state government in recent years. Publications of departments, of state government, bulletins and news reports of the Pennsylvania State Chamber of Commerce, and the monthly *Bulletin* of the Department of Internal Affairs are sources of information on the progress of governmental affairs in Harrisburg. *The Organization and Administration of Pennsylvania State Government, A Report to the General Assembly* (1941) is excellent, though never actually put into printed form.

The social and cultural history of the commonwealth since the Civil War have been sadly neglected, and the decline of the once common county history after about 1890 leaves local cultural and social history a complete void. Lacking local material on which to rely, the more recent general works on the history of the United States,

such as the *History of American Life* series and special histories of literature, the arts, and the theater are equally barren as to Pennsylvania. Saul Sack's volume on the history of higher education, already listed, is very useful for this important story. Fletcher's second volume on Pennsylvania agriculture and farm life is priceless as a source from which to view aspects of the evolution of farm life and culture. Philip Klein, *A Social Study of Pittsburgh* (Columbia University Press, 1938) continues where the Sage Foundation study of Pittsburgh and its environs left off in 1900. The general works on architecture and science continue to be useful, especially Tatum's work on architects and architecture of Philadelphia. Harold Dickson's work, already mentioned, is basic. Clyde F. Lytle, *Pennsylvania Song and Story* (Burgess, Minneapolis, 1932); Anna M. Archambault, editor, *A Guide Book of Art, Architecture, and Historic Interests in Pennsylvania* (Winston, 1924); Frances A. Wistar, *Twenty-five Years of the Philadelphia Orchestra* (Philadelphia Orchestra, 1925) are useful. Harriet A. Gaul and Ruby Eiseman, *John A. Brashear, Scientist and Humanitarian, 1840-1920* (University of Pennsylvania Press, 1940); Agnes R. Burr, *Russell H. Conwell and His Work* (Winston, 1926); David Hinshaw, *Rufus Jones, Master Quaker* (Putnam, 1951); Eric F. Goldman, *John Bach McMaster, American Historian* (University of Pennsylvania Press, 1942); Connie Mack, *My 66 Years in the Big Leagues* (Winston, 1950); Ernest Earnest, *S. Weir Mitchell: Novelist and Physician, 1829-1914* (University of Pennsylvania Press, 1950); Elizabeth Moorhead, *These Two Are Here: Louise Homer and Willa Cather* (University of Pittsburgh Press, 1950); Elizabeth Pennell, *The Life and Letters of Joseph Pennell* (Little, Brown, 1930); Henry Pleasants, Jr., *A Doctor in the House* (Lippincott, 1947); George S. Stokes, *Agnes Repplier* (University of Pennsylvania Press, 1949); Charles D. Koch, *Nathan C. Schaeffer, Educational Philosopher* (Telegraph Press, Harrisburg, 1952); Ida M. Tarbell, *All in a Day's Work: An Autobiography* (Macmillan, 1939); Edith Finch, *Carey Thomas of Bryn Mawr* (Harper, 1947); David Woodbury, *Beloved Scientist: Elihu Thomson* (Whittlesey House, 1944); Cornelius Weygandt,

WHAT TO READ ABOUT PENNSYLVANIA

On the Edge of Evening (Putnam, 1946) are all biographical studies of worth.

Marvin W. Schegel, *Ruler of the Reading: The Life of Franklin B. Gowen* (Archives Publishing Company, 1947) tells the story of this iron-handed tycoon and with it the story of labor, coal, and the railroad monopoly after the Civil War. Milton C. Stuart's *Asa Packer, 1805–1879* (Princeton University Press, 1938) is a study of this key railroad tycoon and the Lehigh. Henry O. Evans, *Iron Pioneer, Henry W. Oliver, 1840–1904* (Dutton, 1942) is well written and worth while for the story of steel and iron, as well as Peter Roberts, *The Anthracite Coal Industry* (Macmillan, 1901). Hal Bridges in *Iron Millionaire: Life of Charlemagne Tower* (University of Pennsylvania Press, 1952) is excellent for this obscure Philadelphia coal and iron ore baron. Richard Bissell in his *The Monongahela* (Rinehart, 1952) emphasizes the use of the river as a coal carrier. Richard E. Banta's *The Ohio* (Rinehart, 1949) and Frederick Way, *The Allegheny* (Rinehart, 1942) continue the story of the western rivers and their value to trade and industry. All are *Rivers of America* series volumes. J. P. Shallo, *Private Police* (American Academy of Political and Social Sciences, 1933) along with Muriel Sheppard, cited earlier, tell the coal- and iron-police story. Burton Hendrick's *Life of Andrew Carnegie* (Doubleday, Doran, 1932, two volumes) is the best Carnegie biography. George Harvey's *Henry Clay Frick, the Man* (Scribner, 1928) is a sound biography of the coke and steel king. *Industries of Western Pennsylvania* (Pittsburgh Chamber of Commerce, 1885) is very valuable, though a scarce item. John Fitch, *The Steel Workers,* a volume in the Sage Foundation's all-important Pittsburgh Survey is indispensable to understanding the problem of steel and labor at the turn of the century and sociological conditions in Pittsburgh and other towns related to steel. George H. Thurston, *Pittsburgh's Progress, Industries, and Resources* (1886) is overly patriotic as to Pittsburgh, but a highly useful (and scarce) book. Leland Baldwin, *Pittsburgh, The Story of a City* (University of Pittsburgh Press, 1937) is very readable but lacks much depth. Labor's story is told indirectly in many books already cited, but more particularly in *The Path I Trod: The Auto-*

biography of Terence V. Powderly, edited by Harry J. Carman and others (Columbia University Press, 1940). Jonathan Grossman, *William Sylvis, Pioneer of American Labor* (Columbia University Press, 1945); J. R. Commons and others, *History of Labour in the United States* (Macmillan, 1935) are useful; Joseph Rayback, *History of American Labor* (Macmillan, 1956) is a good general history. The railroad strike, the Homestead strike, and the great anthracite strike are treated rather thoroughly in a variety of standard volumes on American history. J. Walter Coleman has the best book on the controversial *Molly Maguires* (Garrett and Massie, 1936), though much of value is in Schlegel's *Ruler of the Reading.*

There are several special reports from various sources dealing with the Pennsylvania economy that hardly make good reading, but are highly valuable for reference purposes. Among them are *New Growth, New Jobs, for Pennsylvania* (Shapp Foundation Report, Philadelphia, 1962); *Structure and Growth of Pennsylvania's Economy, an Outline of Trends, 1946–1956* (Joint State Government Commission Report, Harrisburg, 1959); *Preliminary Report of the State Planning Board to Governor Pinchot, 1934* (State Planning Board, Harrisburg, 1934).

The history of the economic development of Pennsylvania since the Civil War has excited more attention than any other major phase, an interesting indicator of how economics has overshadowed in the general story other aspects of the state's heritage in more recent decades. For general background, Victor S. Clark's volumes on the history of manufactures already cited, the last two of which relate to this era, are sound general history with much Pennsylvania material. Thomas C. Cochran and William Miller, *The Age of Enterprise, a Social History of Industrial America* (Macmillan, 1942) is good. Harold Berger and Samuel Shurr's *The Mining Industries, 1899–1939* (National Bureau of Economic Research, N. Y., 1944) and Pearce Davis, *The Development of the American Glass Industry* (Harvard University Press, 1949), are good for the general history of these industries. Harold Berger's *Distribution's Place in the American Economy* (National Bureau of Economic Research, 1955) and Godfrey M.

389

Lebhar, *Chain Stores in America, 1859–1950* (Chain Store Publishing Corporation, 1952) are background for new methods of merchandising. John Wanamaker's part in new ideas in department store merchandising is told, along with much else, in the two-volume *John Wanamaker* (Harpers, 1926), by Herbert A. Gibbons. *The Magic Powder* (Putnam's 1945), by Earl Hadley, is a history of the cement industry and of Universal Atlas Cement Company, while Charles E. Carr in *ALCOA, An American Enterprise* (Rinehart, 1952) has another industry-sponsored history. *Steel Serves the Nation* (United States Steel Corporation, 1951) is not attributed to an author but is a colorful and useful publication. Fletcher's *Pennsylvania Agriculture and Country Life,* cited before, is indispensable. Paul Gidden's books on the oil industry remain valuable, as do the Pennsylvania Historical Association pamphlets on oil, coal, and steel. Stewart Holbrook's *Iron Brew: A Century of American Ore and Steel* (Macmillan, 1939) is a popular history, very readable and informative. *Pennsylvania's Mineral Heritage* (Department of Internal Affairs, Harrisburg, 1944) is an indispensable summary of the history of the mineral industries. Eavanson and Swank continue useful for the coal and steel story. *Cloud by Day, a Story of Coal, Coke and People* (University of North Carolina Press, 1947), by Muriel E. Shephard, is a brilliantly written story of the coal and coke baronage in western Pennsylvania, the union troubles, and life of the workers in company towns. Jules I. Bogen, *The Anthracite Railroad: A Study in American Enterprise* (Ronald Press, 1927) examines anthracite railway development. Robert Casey and W. A. S. Douglas in *The Lackawanna Story* (McGraw-Hill, 1951) cover a century of the history of this railroad. The Pennsylvania Railroad has sponsored three histories of the company, starting in 1875 and concluding with its centennial in 1946.

Further economic informational material is in Carl Hasek and George Leffler, *Industrial Trends in Pennsylvania Since 1914* (Pennsylvania State University, 1942); *Pennsylvania's Industrial Economy, An Outline of Trends and Strategic Factors, 1929–1944* (Joint State Government Commission Report, Harrisburg, 1949); *Trends in the Bituminous Coal Industry in Pennsylvania* (State Planning Board, 1940); *Coal in Pennsylvania* (Joint State Government Commission Report, Harrisburg, 1963), *Report of Findings and Recommendations on the Pennsylvania Tax System by the Tax Study Committee* (Harrisburg, 1949) *The Cost of a Good Educational Program for Pennsylvania* (Department of Public Instruction, Harrisburg, 1955); *Pennsylvania, Keystone of the Interstate Highway System* (Greater Philadelphia Chamber of Commerce, 1958); *Pennsylvania's Personal Income, 1929–1960* (Department of Internal Affairs, Harrisburg, 1963); *Report of the Governor's Committee on Education* (Harrisburg, 1961). Statistical and other reports and studies made by the business research bureaus at the major universities, the State Planning Board, the Pennsylvania State Chamber of Commerce, the Greater Philadelphia Chamber of Commerce, the Pittsburgh Chamber of Commerce, the Allegheny Community Development Conference, and the Federal Reserve Bank of Philadelphia are of great value and should be searched carefully by anyone desiring detailed material on the Pennsylvania economy in recent years. The fruits of such material will be found in some detail in my own *Pennsylvania, the Keystone State* for the period down to 1956.

The story of conservation in Pennsylvania has not been well developed. Fletcher's volume on Pennsylvania agriculture since 1840 has good material on the organization of conservation on the farm, and some references to the development of forest conservation, but stops in 1940; much has been done since that date. *Man Is the Steward* is a brief but colorful booklet on soil conservation (Pennsylvania Department of Agriculture). The College of Agriculture at Penn State is constantly researching economic and sociological aspects of Pennsylvania farming, and its list of published bulletins is always worth consulting for special studies. McGeary's Pinchot biography, cited earlier, is vastly important for the development of the forest-conservation movement. Publications of such state agencies as the Department of Forest and Waters, the Fish Commission, the Game Commission, and the Soil Conservation Service are valuable though sporadic resources.

INDEX

Illustration Credits

ALLEGHENY CONFERENCE ON COMMUNITY DEVELOPMENT, Photo by A. Church: p. 308.

AMERICAN HERITAGE LIBRARY: pp. 78, 123, 137, 153 (top—photograph from U.S. National Museum), 162 (Courtesy of The New York Historical Society, New York City).

AMERICAN SWEDISH HISTORICAL MUSEUM: pp. 24, 25.

Courtesy of AMERICAN TELEPHONE AND TELEGRAPH COMPANY: p. 248.

Courtesy of BASILICA OF THE SACRED HEART OF JESUS OF CONEWAGO: p. 94.

Courtesy of BETHLEHEM STEEL COMPANY: p. 352.

THE BROOKLYN MUSEUM: p. 141.

Photo by Chappel Studio: p. 139.

CHARLES SCRIBNER'S SONS, Revised from *Atlas of American History:* p. 53.

Courtesy of the DUQUESNE LIGHT COMPANY: p. 344 (Photo by Samuel A. Musgrave).

Courtesy of the EAST BROAD TOP RAILROAD AND COAL COMPANY, (Photo by Gordon R. Roth): p. 206 (top).

From *Exploring Pennsylvania* by Stevens, Cordier and Benjamin, copyright, 1953, by Harcourt, Brace & World, Inc. and reproduced with their permission: p. 73.

THE HISTORICAL SOCIETY OF PENNSYLVANIA: pp. 41, 48, 58, 62, 81, 119, 157, 161, 168, 174, 180, 183, 191, 255.

Reproduced from the Collections of the LIBRARY OF CONGRESS: pp. 6 (Photo by Marion Cost Wolcott), 197, 276, 317.

Courtesy of the MELLON INSTITUTE: p. 343.

THE MUSEUM OF MODERN ART, Photo by Soichi Sunami: p. 140.

NATIONAL ARCHIVES: p. 257.

Courtesy of the OFFICE OF GOVERNOR SCRANTON: p. 297.

THE PENNSYLVANIA ACADEMY OF FINE ARTS: p. 117.

PENNSYLVANIA DEPARTMENT OF AGRICULTURE: p. 303.

PENNSYLVANIA DEPARTMENT OF INTERNAL AFFAIRS, from *Pennsylvania Geology Summarized:* p. 4.

PENNSYLVANIA HISTORICAL AND MUSEUM COMMISSION: pp. 5, 7, 9, 10, 11, 26, 31, 32, 35, 39 (Photo by Karl Rath), 44, 47, 52, 55 (original painting in possession of Mrs. George A. Robbins), 56, 64, 65, 66, 67 (Photos by Robert H. Thompson), 68, 76, 77, 85, 90, 92 (Photo by Karl Rath), 93 (top photo by Barnum), 95, 97, 98, 100 (Photo by Karl Rath), 101, 102, 107, 108, 110, 111, 112, 115, 121, 125, 126, 127, 128, 129, 131, 133 (Photo by Karl Rath), 134, 142, 145 (Photo by Karl Rath), 149, 151, 152, 153 (bottom), 154, 155, 156, 163, 169, 170, 171, 173, 177, 181, 188, 192, 194, 195, 198, 199, 202, 206 (bottom—Courtesy of Bethlehem Steel Co.), 207, 208–209, 210, 211, 213, 214, 215–16 (Mather Collection, Drake Well Museum, Titusville), 219, 223, 224, 225, 227, 229, 232, 233, 234, 235, 239, 240, 241, 242, 245, 246, 251–252 (Photos by George F. Johnson), 259, 260, 264, 265, 266, 269, 271, 273 (Photo by Allied Picture Service, Inc.), 274, 277, 281, 283, 284, 286, 287 (Philadelphia *Inquirer* Photo), 288, 291, 294, 298, 305, 322, 323, 327, 332, 339, 347, 349, 361 (Photo by Allied Picture Service, Inc.).

PENNSYLVANIA STATE PLANNING BOARD: p. 337.

PENNSYLVANIA STATE UNIVERSITY, Agricultural Extension Service: p. 301, p. 319 (HRB Singer, Inc. Photo Department), p. 346.

PENNSYLVANIA TURNPIKE COMMISSION: p. 336.

Courtesy of the PENNZOIL COMPANY: p. 217.

PHILADELPHIA CITY PLANNING COMMISSION: pp. 315, 316 (Photo by Claire Kofsky), 338 (Photo by Skyphotos)

Courtesy of the PHILADELPHIA SYMPHONY, Photo by Adrian Siegel: p. 325.

REDEVELOPMENT AUTHORITY OF THE CITY OF PHILADELPHIA: pp. 312, 313.

Courtesy of U.S. STEEL CORPORATION: p. 341 (Associated Photographers).

UNIVERSITY OF PITTSBURGH: p. 320.

UNIVERSITY OF PITTSBURGH PRESS, from *The Planting of Civilization in Western Pennsylvania:* pp. 83, 84, 150.

WESTERN PENNSYLVANIA CONSERVANCY, Photo by Michael Fedison: p. 310.

WIDE WORLD PHOTOS: pp. 221, 293.

ABOUT THE AUTHOR

SYLVESTER K. STEVENS received his B.A. and M.A. from Pennsylvania State University, where he was Assistant Professor of History before receiving his Ph.D. from Columbia University. Dr. Stevens was State Historian of Pennsylvania from 1937 to 1956, President of the American Association for State and Local History from 1946 to 1950, President of the Pennsylvania Historical Association from 1948 to 1951, and since 1937 he has been Executive Secretary of the Pennsylvania Federation of Historical Societies. Since 1956 the author has been Executive Director of the Pennsylvania Historical and Museum Commission. He has written or co-authored seven books, some of them multi-volume studies, on various aspects of Pennsylvania history. Dr. Stevens and his wife live near Harrisburg in Camp Hill.

A NOTE ON THE TYPE

THE TEXT of this book was set in GARAMOND, a modern rendering of the type first cut in the sixteenth century by *Claude Garamond* (1510–1561).

Composed by Graphic Services, Inc., York, Pennsylvania.
Printed by Edward Stern & Company, Inc., Philadelphia, Pennsylvania.
Bound by The Haddon Craftsmen, Inc., Scranton, Pennsylvania
Typography and binding design by
HERMANN STROHBACH